AF379181

THE SKATE BOARD LIFE

THE SKATE BOARD LIFE

MOVERS SHAKERS & RULE MAKERS BREAKERS

THE QUINTESSENTIAL STORY OF SKATEBOARD CULTURE

NEFTALIE WILLIAMS, PhD

Director of the SDSU Center for Skateboarding, Action Sports, and Social Change

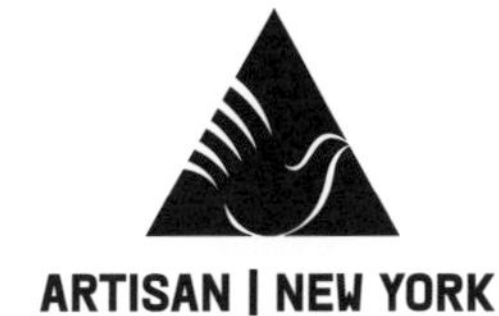

ARTISAN | NEW YORK

Library of Congress Cataloging-in-Publication Data is on file.

ISBN 978-1-64829-151-7

Cover Design by karlssonwilker
Interior Design by Heitman-Ford + Co.

Artisan books may be purchased in bulk for business, educational, or promotional use. For information, please contact your local bookseller or the Hachette Book Group Special Markets Department at special.markets@hbgusa.com.

The publisher is not responsible for websites (or their content) that are not owned by the publisher.

The Hachette Speakers Bureau provides a wide range of authors for speaking events. To find out more, go to hachettespeakersbureau.com or email HachetteSpeakers@hbgusa.com.

Published by Artisan,
an imprint of Workman Publishing,
a division of Hachette Book Group, Inc.
1290 Avenue of the Americas
New York, NY 10104
artisanbooks.com

The Artisan name and logo are registered trademarks of Hachette Book Group, Inc.

Printed in China (APO) on responsibly sourced paper

First printing, September 2025

10 9 8 7 6 5 4 3 2 1

This book is dedicated to the two lights of my life,
Rachele Williams and our baby girl, Wren Williams.
Holding you both in my arms is when I feel the
most complete and truly whole. Thank you for the
blessing of your love.

CONTENTS

INTRODUCTION

Welcome, and I'm glad you are here. I'm excited to help you ride through a journey about skateboarding culture in a way that gives you a sense of who, where, why, and how we roll together.

To give you background on who you are cruising with: I'm Neftalie Williams. Scholar. Diplomat. Activist. Artist. Skateboarder. The most important title is that last one—skateboarder. I'm a lifer, and every aspect of my self has revolved around what fun and family can be built on four wheels. Some of those orbits include my time as a writer, photographer, and team manager, learning the nuts and bolts of the industry. Skateboarding has been my love for decades now, so much so that my PhD is on the subject. For realz? Yep, Real Talk. You can come study and work with me at San Diego State University (SDSU) and be part of our Center for Skateboarding, Action Sports, and Social Change.

Since the beginning, people outside the skate sphere have asked, *Why skateboarding?* It's simple— skateboarding is utilitarian. It's for you, it's for me, it's for everyone. Plus, it's a *whole hell of a lot of fun*. Skateboarding—the unlikely merger of form and function. Skateboarding—the noun, the verb, the activity, and the culture.

Whether as the vehicle and mode for transportation of body or thought, skateboarding is about movement. It's a versatile tool toward better days. It's been used to inject life into a humdrum excursion to the local bodega, to free minds from oppression, to get in a workout, to move hearts past a workload, and to build coalitions and turn strangers to friends and family across the globe. Skateboarding has been my passport: I've seen its power, from my earliest days.

I grew up skateboarding in Springfield, Massachusetts, a far cry from the sun-soaked shores of my current home in California. Back East you have to care about skateboarding to stick with it because it's not the go-to athletic or career path for most of the populace. However, the community that chose to identify as skateboarders—even though there was hazing, hassling, or downright harassment when I began—are the ones who helped me arrive. In my formative years I saw what galvanized support can occur through skating, and that left an indelible impression on me.

One day in my mid-teens, when returning home from the corner store, I found one of the newest members of our 18-story apartment building outside, utterly inconsolable and surrounded by 30 "building kids," as we were known. Now normally that might be from the teasing that could happen, and more than once I had been at the center of a haranguing, but I could sense that this time was different. Our building was made up of multiple racial and ethnic communities, and on most occasions "nary the two would meet." Kids were raised to look out only for their own. The Latinx and Hispanic kids did their own thing. The Black and African American community watched out for their own. The African community and Asian and Asian American community—same vibe. You really didn't parley often, and since the parents kept apart, the kids absorbed that, too.

Yet here they all were. Everyone impatiently crowded around Lil' Markus. Sure, some people were pointing and jeering, but most of the kids looked concerned and upset.

"Yo, why is this kid crying and being a baby?" someone said. "Why are we even over here with him? He ain't Puerto Rican, it's not our business," said another. "Yo, *shut up*!" said one of the older kids. "He got-got at the Civic Center! He got his skateboard stolen!"

Silence. I still feel that moment now. We had all started skateboarding over the past year and were all getting more and more bit by the bug.

For the first time in my five years of living at the building, there was a community response to a "crisis" that crossed racial, socioeconomic, and gender lines (thanks to our friend Ellen) and preteen and full teen position. I left the groceries at the front desk—throwing caution and trouble with mom to the wind.

We decided collectively to contribute parts to build a new board for Markus. And we did.

Just like that we had gone from disparate kids living in the building with nothing but proximity in common into something else—we were skateboarders. We were protecting our own and making community decisions. This did not go unnoticed.

We heard from our parents, "What are you doing with those kids?" Meaning, "What on earth are you doing with that multiracial menagerie?" We were something our parents couldn't see—a new family unit. We skated together for years, and those experiences only grew with time.

From driving in snowstorms to Vermont in search of a small wooden skatepark to searching for empty parking garages and empty pools and discovering everything that the city and later New England had to offer, we were all in. Exploring allowed us to discover something else—togetherness. We rolled together no matter what. It's something we still need more examples of, and I have tried to embed this in the book and incorporate it into my work.

I know this isn't everyone's experience. It's not even the experience of everyone in this book. Many have dealt with multiple instances of discrimination and obstacles on various levels, some we know about and some we don't, but that's just it. The people in this book chose to be skateboarders regardless of the adversity they faced getting started or soldiering on. They found something unique and inspiring in skateboarding and in themselves, the same way we did.

Once that happens, well, there is nothing left to do but try to lead by example. The people on these pages do, and I'm in turn doing my part to continue the legacy of my old neighborhood and all the skaters before me. Harness what's special, help others identify it, and spread it around. When you do that, that love is catching.

Skateboarding has given me the ability to help people break a smile and to help people not break their legs when they are starting out so they know that skateboarding can be for them. Skateboarding's secret sauce is the organic way it allows unlikely partners to share experiences. Despite any differences in backgrounds, the space between it all is that anyone can love or learn to love skateboarding.

With all that skateboarding has accomplished—and all the media attention, the movies and the video games, and the popularity of X Games and even our inclusion in the Olympics—you would think that skateboarding might become more accepted. Yet that's not the case. Skateboarding is still banned in most areas. Skaters are still heavily policed and stereotyped, and somehow there remains this disconnect between who skateboarders are, what skateboarders can accomplish, and what those positive outcomes can mean to everyone.

This book hopes to bridge that divide.

The book is broken by section—the Uberists, the Artists, the Documentarians, the Activists, the Olympists . . . you get the picture. *The best of the best.* And each one gives you insight into the innovators, influencers, developers, and advocates who helped build skateboarding culture.

They are all icons and stars in the night sky of skateboarding. Together they form clusters and shine bright, trust me. Some just appear brighter than others at times depending on where you are situated. That's also what makes skateboarding special: you can be inspired by people through liking the cuff of their jeans. If that moves you, then so be it. It is never solely the physical activity of skateboarding that inspires, it's always how things appear in contrast to the other celestial bodies. You find your own stars.

This book features a small swath of the people who have made skateboarding appealing and continue to push it forward. I can't begin to tell you about them all, but I have attempted to give you a great map toward meeting your extended family.

Building this book took the lifting of the skate community to accomplish. I am lucky enough to have earned a place in the culture the same way as people before me and after will. By being present and loving it, defending it, and fighting for and against it when necessary.

The Skateboard Life represents the very individual yet collective way skateboarding operates—we do it by ourselves together, alone but for each other. The volume you hold is the same. It's work I've done by myself with the family.

The members of that collective are the roots, the trunk, the branches, and the blossoms and buds that always move outward, taking up space. They connect to the breeze that brings the seeds forth to begin the process over again. It is that tree that skateboarding literally comes from—the merger of wood, wheels, and wonder—that pushes us all forward.

I'm lucky to be moving forward with this family, and I'm excited you are along for the ride.

THE UBER ISTS

In the air, in the streets, on the mic, and on the move, the Uberists bring out the best in skateboarding by living, breathing, airing, and sharing the stoke. They take a cue from the old High German word for "over" and "beyond" by dishing out excellence in everything they do. An alchemical mixture of wild energy, selfless abandon, and cerebral fantasy percolates within their bones and reverberates into a vibe we all feel.

The Uberists don't try to be icons; they simply are, and it comes from countless hours of manifesting motions and wrangling emotions as they teeter on the edge of doing the impossible.

Motivated by the fire within, they do not let this expression of themselves be denied. They skate when the lights are out and forever dream of tomorrow's next turn, revolution, and revelation. Their pursuit of excellence lights a fire under us all and provides the spark to warm a million nights as we pursue our own version of the dream.

THE GLASS BREAKER

CARA-BETH BURNSIDE

Skateboarding Hall of Famer

Member of the first U.S. Olympic Snowboard Team

First female skater with a pro model shoe

First woman on the cover of *Thrasher*

Cofounder of Hoopla Skateboards

Quiet, please. Let us praise CB, from whom all vert things flow.

Begin the hymns . . . Ahhh, the first woman on the cover of *Thrasher* magazine . . . Mmm, the first woman in skateboarding to have a signature shoe . . . Ohhh, the first skater since Shaun White to medal in Winter and Summer X Games. Cofounder of the woman-led brand Hoopla Skateboards . . . Ohhh, member of the first Olympic women's snowboarding team . . . Yesss . . . The one who slayed every day, the skater in me recognizes the skater in you . . . Bring your hands in together above your heart . . . Exhale . . . Ahhh—maaannnnggg.

Before women graced the pages of *Vogue* for skateboarding's impact on fashion, freedom, and flyness, one woman aired through the glass ceiling to create room for that conversation: Cara-Beth Burnside. She pushed the envelope for women's skateboarding when men had forgotten they even had a better half. Let me refresh the feed.

"CB," as she is affectionately known, began her career on roller skates at the rink across the street from the legendary Big O skatepark in Orange, California. Launching a now decades-long love affair with skateboarding, CB took to Big O fantastically when skating called her in in 1978.

Turning it into a second home before reaching her early teens, she cascaded across the concrete landscape with that special approach acquired by those raised in the '70s and early '80s—skating like their lives depended on it. One of the first to notice her was a godmother of skateboarding, Gale Webb. Gale took CB under her wing and placed her on the mixed-gender skateboard team Powerflex that toured extensively in the U.S. with the goal of showing the broader public that skateboarding belonged to everyone.

Looking back at the black-and-white pics of CB skating during the late '70s and into the '80s on early tours and amateur contests at Big O, Upland, Whittier Skatepark, and legendary now-demolished skateparks like Skatopia in Buena Park, California, it's easy to recognize that those floating, steezy fakie ollies were delivered with a side of badass. Crushing it in contests, Cara-Beth competed in the amateur girls' divisions and dominated in her early teens. Her track record during '79 and '80 alone reads out like a blistering rash of pain for the other competitors. Blessing every contest she entered, CB earned top honors in women's divisions and in mixed pro/am contests, gracing the pages of skateboarding magazines along the way. However,

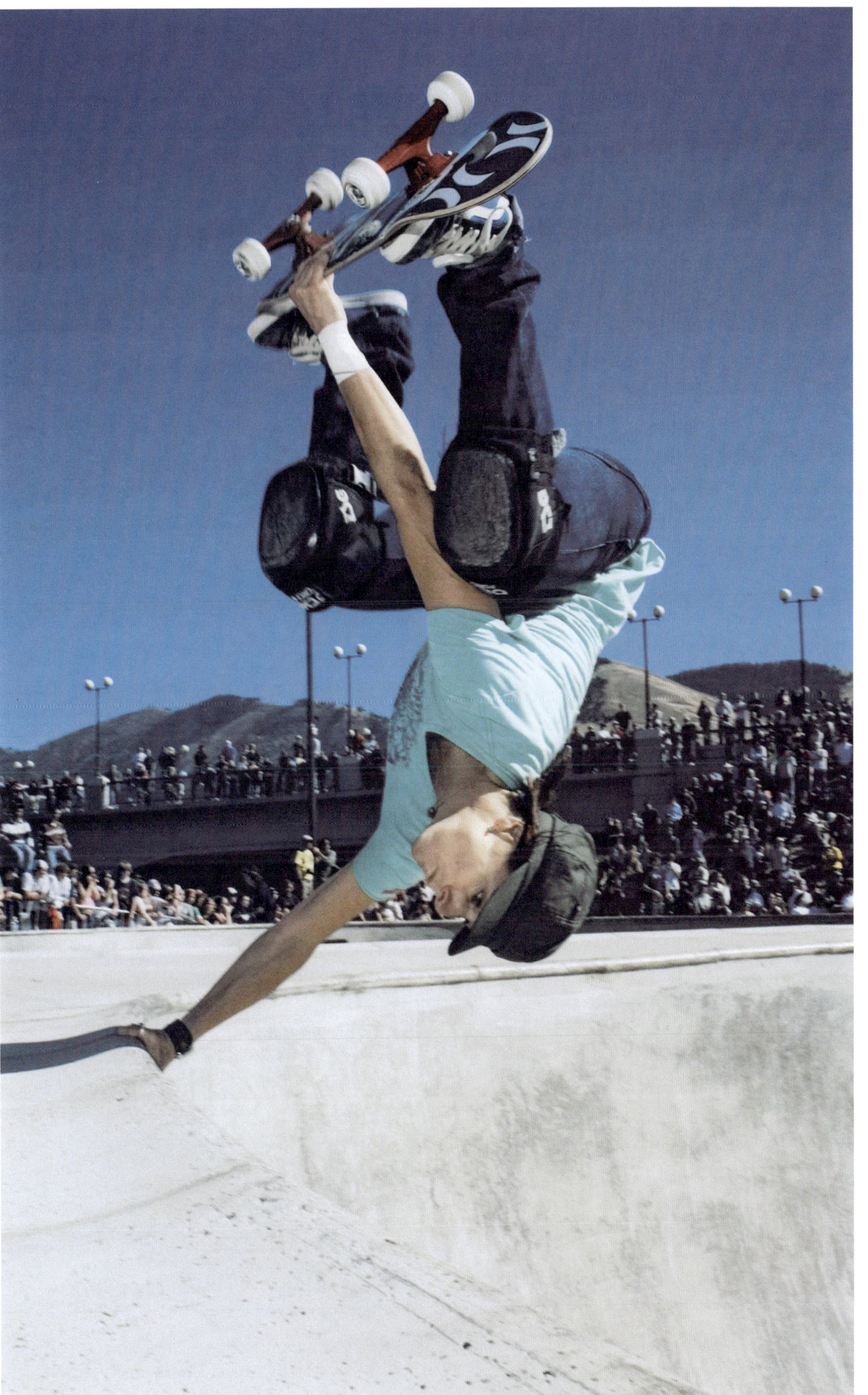

unlike in the early '70s when more women were highlighted across disciplines, by the end of the decade men's presence far outweighed women's in terms of media exposure. Despite this lack of representation, CB always remained optimistic and dedicated to skateboarding. She simply wanted to skate and made it known. So known, in fact, that she quickly earned her place among world-class skateboarders across the board, including the infamous Duane "The Master of Disaster" Peters, the ferocious and fear-inducing antihero of the early skatepark generation. Duane was a hard-charging pro from the 1970s who made a habit of precarious tricks like the disaster and the acid drop—tricks so dangerous you could lose your front teeth or even die. Scary stuff.

More outrageous than his skating was Duane's punk persona, which is why his pairing with and soft spot for Cara-Beth blew minds. He helped her get sponsored by Santa Cruz Skateboards, one of the most prominent skateboard companies then and now. The unlikely duo spent hours connecting at the skatepark. CB even credits him for coaching her on how to defeat the great Pattie Hoffman, who had consistently kept her in second place—a feat CB accomplished while riding a custom Duane Peters board cut down to match her mini-powerhouse frame.

Alas, though she dominated the ranks in women's and mixed competitions, by the early '80s the costs of insurance at skateparks headed skyward, leading to the closing of many parks. Between a lack of resources and many skate companies closing shop, it was difficult for skaters to pursue their future—especially female skaters. CB persevered during those lean years, until the wheels finally fell off. There were no more women's contests. And while men were able to move forward, there was no way for a young woman to pursue a career. CB tapped into her expertise in other sports and in academia. She attended UC Davis as a psychology major and focused on school until things began to change for the better.

Cara-Beth Burnside, feeble grind in the pool

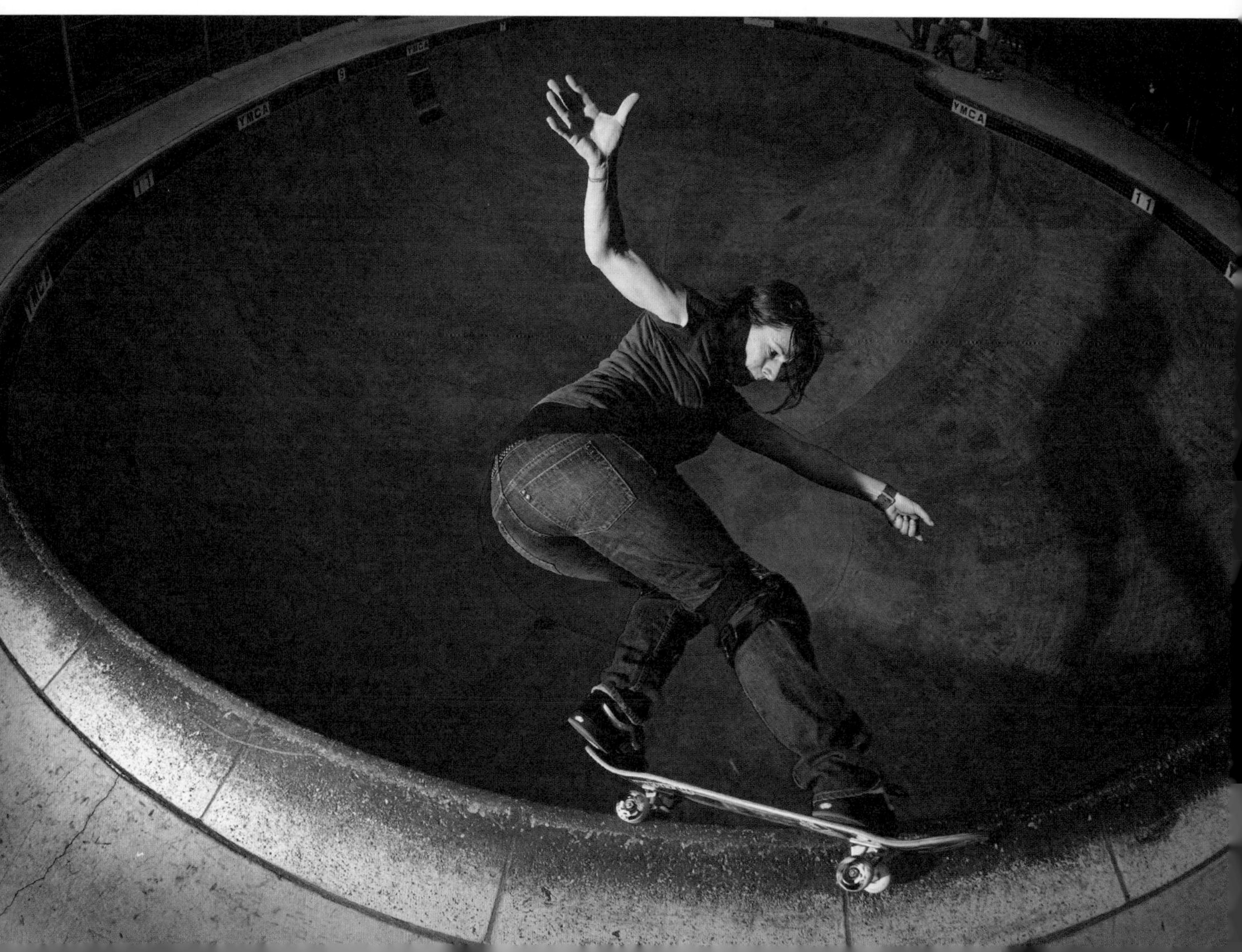

She's been featured in Lynn Kramer's women's skate magazine *Equal Time* and in the beloved but now defunct magazine *PowerEdge,* questioning the lack of women's representation and pushing the notion that skateboarding belongs to anyone who participates. *PowerEdge* offered more fun interpretations of skateboarding and prominently featured the then-emerging form of street skating along with vert. It recognized a changing movement in skateboarding styles and terrain. The magazine and CB's article made an impression on me early on because they told stories that were missing from the mainstream West Coast representations of skateboarding. For my crew, made up of skaters of color and a young woman, it was refreshing to see not only skaters of color but on occasion female skaters. Then in 1989, CB scored the cover of *Thrasher,* and her words and images lit a fire in all my friends and anyone hungry to imagine a more inclusive skateboarding future.

Cara-Beth would go on to ride for Vision and Swatch in their heydays as well. The Pop Swatch was the ish then. It was a clockface you could wear anywhere on your body by locking the back onto your clothes. There is no way CB wasn't wearing at least three of them, making everyone jealous. I know I would have been. And Vision skateboards, they were one of the most elite teams in the game: Marty "Jinx" Jimenez, Mark "Gator" Rogowski (before the fall), Ken Park, Johnee Kop, and the greatest of all time, Mark Gonzales. (One of the best things I ever owned was a baby blue Vision "I skate therefore I am" sweatshirt. I worked paper routes to buy that and still needed ma dukes to help pony up the cash. CB could get them for free-ninety-nine.

Cara-Beth was also *the* solo woman in the Santa Cruz Skateboards *Risk It* video. She was unstoppable. She found the fortitude to ride out the next wave of skateboarding and be present when its resurgence came to life with the X Games. Cara-Beth got busy racking up multiple medals from 2003 to 2007, inspiring a new generation of women, including Vanessa Torres, Amy Caron, and the girls of Villa Villa Cola, a landmark female-led skateboarding collective. Striking back hard when skateboarding returned to the mainstream, Cara-Beth was still an absolute ruler, cutting down the competition with tricks like the Miller flip. Only the best skaters attempted this kick-ass trick, and at the time it was performed by few women.

Cara-Beth also knew what it was like to be in the field alone, and how to grow the field. She was a Vans team member, and part of that expansion included her persuading the company to invest in the women's market by putting out a skate shoe. (She skated vert, so she knew how much support you needed when coming in from those big airs and Millers.) CB became the first woman to receive a pro model shoe for Vans—a version of which is now housed in the Smithsonian.

The accolades rack up. CB not only competed against the men and kept skateboarding alive; she went on to become an Olympic snowboarder, too. She was one of the early pioneers in snowboarding, riding experimental boards. She's also won as many Winter X Games medals as Summer X Games ones. Shaun White is the only other person who's done that.

Beyond medals and accolades, it's what she's done for others that makes her rise above the competition. Her cofounded brand, Hoopla, in partnership with Mimi Knoop, unabashedly set goals "to encourage girls' participation and progression in skateboarding." Launched in 2008, Hoopla became the first board for countless upstarts and the professional home for many of skateboarding's best, including Alana Smith and Samarria Brevard.

Cara-Beth built a home in Hoopla so that other women could participate in her first love, skateboarding. She also cofounded the Women's Skateboarding Alliance with Mimi Knoop and Drew Mearns.

Cara-Beth Burnside was always more than just a superstar athlete. CB understood the landscape and pushed through the difficulty of skating against not only top women but top men when there was a lack of female competitors. Despite the dark times in skateboarding for women, CB's tenacity and efforts shined throughout the years as she fought to create balance in the forces of the male-dominated skateboarding industry. Her impact as an action sports role model to generations of women and icon to men is still being fully discovered and appreciated. Her newest collaborations with H-Street Skateboards (which briefly sponsored her in the early days) stand as recognition of her contribution to skateboarding and a marker of what might have transpired had she been supported more thoroughly and competed on a level playing field. Call it a resurgence, call it admission of fact, but whatever you do, don't call it a comeback: she's been an icon for years and clearly ain't going nowhere.

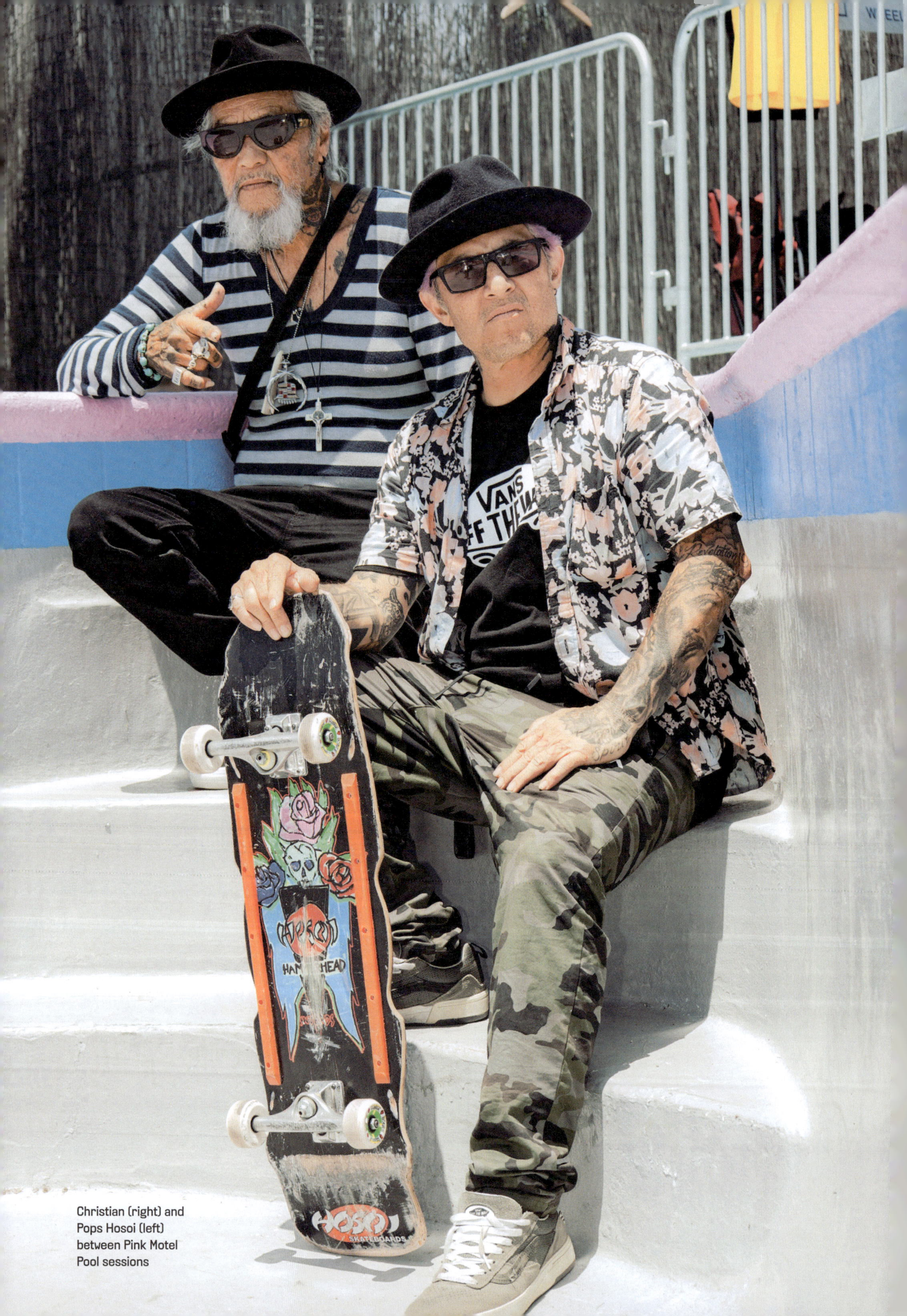

Christian (right) and
Pops Hosoi (left)
between Pink Motel
Pool sessions

CHRISTIAN "HOLMES" HOSOI

Hall of Fame inventor of the Christ air and rocket air

Tony Hawk's *only* rival during the 1980s

Few skaters defined the revolution from 1970s grassroots skateboarding into the explosion of the 1980s and its time of excess more clearly than Christian "Holmes" Hosoi, skateboarding's high-flying Icarus who fell to earth, then rose again like a phoenix. "Christ," as he was also affectionately known, delivered on the promise of the period through excessive style, excessive speed, and excessive *air*! He rocketed through the stratosphere and inspired generations of skaters by merging the foundational style and expression of surf-spawned skating with unstoppable power and ferocity seldom seen before or after. Raw as Hendrix, Christian kissed the sky, then punched through it, rocking harder, better, and stronger than any competitor. From the mid- to late '80s, Christ reigned supreme and delivered an unstoppable show.

Born in 1967 in L.A. and raised in Hawai'i by a Japanese American father, Ivan "Pops" Hosoi, and a Scots-Dane and native Hawai'ian mother, Bonnie Puamana Mitchell, Christian was a child of the island, small in stature but big in heart and unafraid to stand up to bullies. Christian's altruism, good looks, and innate aptitude for surfing made the "Little Protector" the people's champ, the first of a laundry list of nicknames.

While all was good in the streets, life at home was less than ideal. Citing irreconcilable differences, Christian's parents split up, and he relocated to Los Angeles with his father, where Pops found work as an art professor with an activist streak. Formal education was important to Pops, but so was real-world experience, and Pops quietly guided his son's early career. Pops even managed the short-lived but historic Marina Del Rey Skatepark, exposing Christian to this and other spots visited by the best skaters of the era, including the Dogtown crew.

Christian thrived among the beers, BBQs, and brouhahas that accompanied the backyard pools that made up the outlaw skateboarding scene of the '70s and early '80s, frequented by exalted elder and Z-Boys powerhouses such as Stacy Peralta and Tony Alva (see page 43). Christian quickly made a name for himself, and received tutelage under the great Asian American skater Shogo Kubo (RIP) of Z-Boys fame. Everyone knew the child prodigy's skateboarding skill was beyond his years. The Hosois thought their 14-year-old was slated for a spot on Stacy's team but that didn't happen. That free spot on the team allowed Stacy to pick up another skater—Tony Hawk.

Christian wound up with SIMS Skateboards, then with the other legendary Z-Boy, Tony Alva, but each time the family felt promises were delayed or reneged on. "There's no ethics in business," Pops told me.

At the time, Pops believed that skate companies operated similarly to shady record producers—no one wanted his son to be a star without them. "When they see someone like Jimi Hendrix or Miles Davis, they say 'wow' and want to control the talent rather than letting them shine," said Pops. "That mentality hurts everyone." Finger-pointing aside, there was no denying that this high schooler was the future of skateboarding.

Christian became a vertical ruler—competing well as an amateur for years, then fully arriving with a first-place win in 1985, as a 17-year-old. From that point on, Christian built a portfolio of victories and influence. He contributed two signature tricks to the vernacular, each still a staple in vertical skateboarding (the aerial side of the sport, performed on half-pipes and in pools, also referred to as transition skateboarding). First is the rocket air, a blasted backside air (back turned toward the facing wall) where the body soars, then turns horizontal, staying in a reversed coffin position at the peak of its skyward arc. To do this trick right is to be fearless: stalling, falling, and motionless against the blue, waiting until the last possible second, then finally shifting your weight to meet the plywood landing.

The Christ air was even more dramatic. Christian blasted as high as possible, then held his skateboard in one hand, arms outstretched and legs locked, akin to the image and shape of historical accounts of bodies on the cross. Need I say more?

This, combined with the massive quantities of Swatch watches on his wrist, spandex biker shorts, and innumerable bandanas, set the crowd afire.

Christian was born ready-made for the MTV generation. His wave crested in line with all things youthful and antiestablishment that could only debut during the timeline that produced once-in-a-lifetime icons like Prince, Madonna, and Michael Jackson—and skateboarding's Hosoi.

Scan YouTube if you need to update yourself on the prowess of the high-flying Hosoi. Mike McGill invented the 540, but Christian made it a thing of beauty, ripping through the rotation as effortlessly as a baby catches a cold. Thousands of skaters might have done backside airs, but only Christian did them 10 feet high. The smith grind's been done countless times, but only he composed like Michelangelo, sculpting his signature across the ramp.

For a time, Hosoi soared unequaled above the competition. Yet on the horizon was a quiet young upstart from Carlsbad whose ability to develop unimaginable combinations of tricks led to the most historic rivalry in skateboarding—a battle for supremacy of the skies with Tony Hawk.

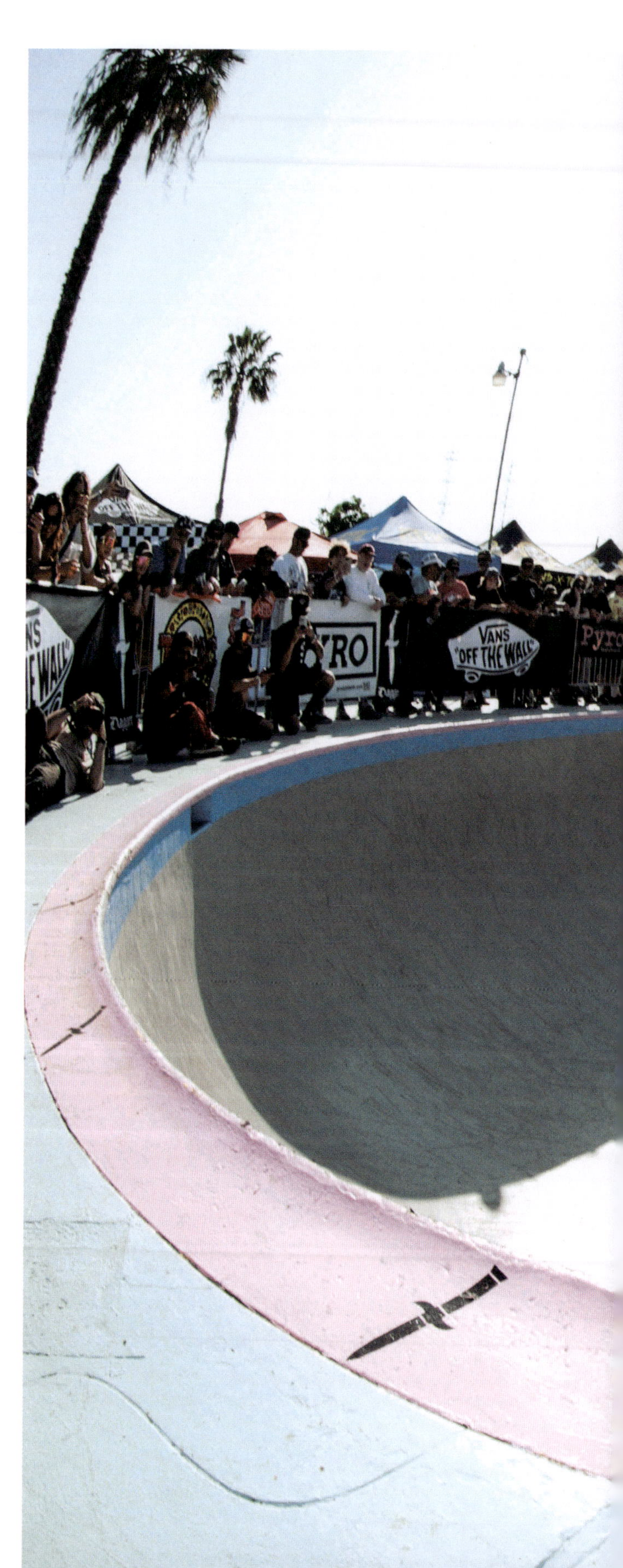

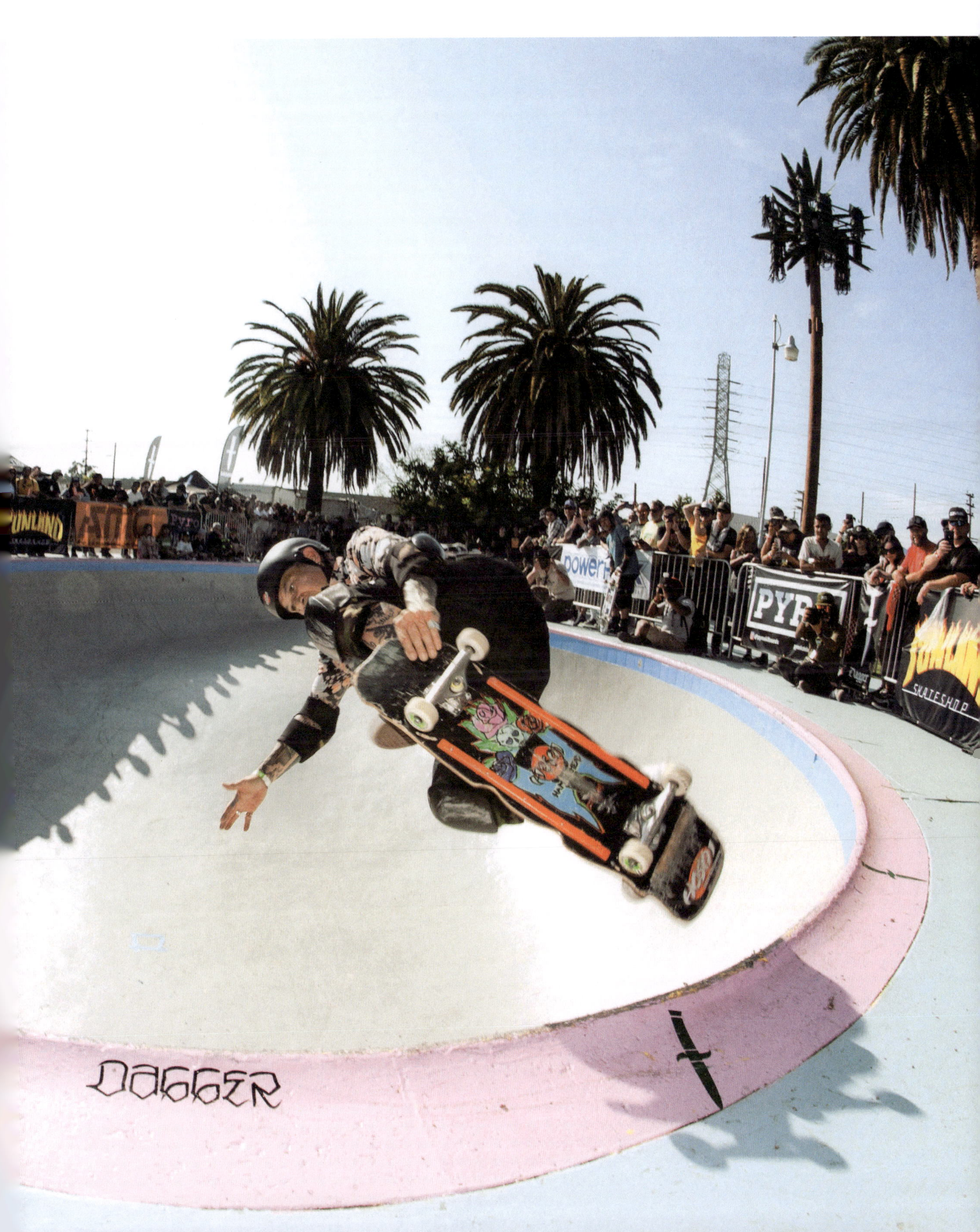
DAGGER

Fighting head-to-head, contest after contest, Tony offered technicality and imagination, and Hosoi countered it by embodying each trick with every fiber of his being. One example of their legendary tilts: Christian—just barely—edging out Tony through sheer ferocity during the 1988 Vision Pro Escape. Winning that contest and flashing his new Rising Sun graphic (though now admittedly problematic for its ties to past Japanese war crimes), Christian used the platform to insert his Japanese cultural heritage into the skateboarding canon; his graphic became a symbol of his indomitable spirit in skateboarding.

With that same spirit and respect for his lineage, Christian incorporated the image throughout his brand, the bestselling Hosoi Skateboards. His was one of the few skateboarding companies at the time created *by* a skateboarder *for* skateboarders, and it became a hub for Asian Americans and Pacific Islanders with teammates such as Bo Ikeda and Johnee Kop, and for overall excellence with Scott Oster, Aaron "Fingers" Murray, and Cesario "Block" Montano.

The Hosoi moniker also became home to one of the most unique skateboard shapes, the Hosoi Hammerhead. The skateboard shape featured several cutaways at the nose, which made it easier to manage and lock your hands on to the board while airborne. It was an ingenious design that sold incredibly well. Unfortunately, the path to that innovation was also paved with pain.

The early iterations of that design were the reason for the rift between Christian and his hero, Dogtown Z-Boy Tony Alva, in the early days. One of the greatest skaters of the mid-'70s, Alva helped define pool skateboarding. According to Pops, the initial design and production of the skateboard began while Christian was under contract with Alva Skates: "Christian wanted a better way to hold on to his board, and I was doing his graphics and shapes at the time. Together we designed the original Hammerhead style for his signature model."

According to Pops, instead of crediting and making the design his signature model, Alva coveted the design and used it in his own models, crushing sales and Christian's heart. This resulted in a decades-deep malaise. Disillusioned, Christian and Pops created their own brand, trademarking Hosoi Skateboards and Hosoi's Rockets wheels, and the Hammerhead's avant-garde design.

Hosoi's Hammerhead iterations and Rising Sun graphic proved so popular that Christian's board would eventually become one of the most pirated decks in history. "Our first trip to Brazil, everyone rode Hosoi—but they were all bootlegs," Pops told me, laughing.

Still, Hosoi kept rolling. He won vertical and emerging street skateboarding contests like the Lotte Cup in Japan. He claimed first or second in every contest he entered, starting with the National Skateboarding Association event in 1985. Thus began the Christian Hosoi reign in skateboarding.

Christian became an A-list celebrity, rolling with crew in tow to any club in Hollywood, renting the former home of early twentieth-century actor and comedian W. C. Fields to house his parties and increasingly rowdy lifestyle. Unfortunately, that love affair with the late night would eventually move him toward dark times: Christian's focus on the party and not the *patina* began to hurt him. Simultaneously, the popularity of vertical skateboarding shrank. This affected his budgets, delivering a one-two punch that brought him back to terra firma.

His version of street skating was still largely based on transition skateboarding, and it began to show its age. Eventually there were no more jump ramps and quarter-pipes at contests where Christian could meld his years of experience into an impressive amalgam of styles. Skateboarding outlets like *Thrasher* and *TransWorld SKATEboarding* largely declared vertical skateboarding dead.

Street skating took over, and a new crop of skaters invented a host of tricks that moved away from Christian's original high-flying, aggressive style and toward the technical wizardry of Rodney Mullen (see page 54). While the style wasn't always pretty, it *was* progressive. Christian recognized the change and brought in a host of young street skaters to push his new brand, Milk Skateboard Goods, known as MSG. MSG's collapse coincided with Christian's partying and drug use, which led him to lose his connection to contemporary skating and gain a spot in the penitentiary.

He earned early release for good behavior and returned to his longtime sponsor, Vans, with a renewed spirit and love for skateboarding, witnessing for Christ, and mentoring a new generation of skaters. Always with an eye toward those from the AAPI community, Christian offered advice to other prodigies such as Olympian Sky Brown (see page 263) and her brother, Ocean. Christian also relaunched Hosoi Skateboards, adding young members such as his own offspring, sons Classic and Endless Hosoi.

Christian Hosoi continues to inspire the next generation, imparting his newfound knowledge of how to fly high without losing your wings—a lesson that he learned the hardest of ways and now spreads freely to the masses, like sunshine on a California summer day.

THE GNARHUNTER EXTRAORDINAIRE
ELISSA STEAMER

Greatest female street skater from the mid-'90s to the early '00s

First female street skater featured in *Tony Hawk's Pro Skater*

X Games multiyear winner

While the 1970s saw a greater number of women skateboarding than in the past, there were considerably fewer from the '80s through the early '90s. With the start of the 1990s, partially as backlash to the bro-brahs in charge of the mini ramp and the privilege needed to gain access to vert ramps, skateboarding headed back outside and that return to the streets delivered the opportunity for a brilliant gem to emerge from the Sunshine State: Elissa Steamer. She reset the status quo, effortlessly inspired female skaters, and proved to a generation of haters that women belong in skateboarding.

Unpretentious yet stately, Elissa grew up in Fort Myers, Florida, a stone's throw from Tampa and the incomparable Skatepark of Tampa. She was known as the silent ripper from Florida who slowly moved onto the radar.

In the early days she was the only woman in her Fort Myers crew, and they were a unit that made sure to protect her as much as they could from those who sought to exclude her based on her gender. While it wasn't always rosy being the only girl, she felt safe with her clique. She recalled an incident that took place at a friend's mini ramp. Someone had snuck in at night and painted a four-letter derogatory word on the ramp aimed at dissuading Elissa from returning. However, she was so young, she didn't know what the word meant. When she asked, her friends wouldn't answer, trying to shield her from anything that might affect her enjoyment of skateboarding.

While Elissa began her journey skating for fun, multiple companies soon showed interest in sponsoring the rising talent. The first team to vie for her attention was led by skateboarding icon Lance Mountain and his company, The Firm Skateboards, a huge accolade for any skateboarder. Joining The Firm as an amateur (receiving product without signing a contract) provided the initial support Elissa needed to start her professional career. At that time, in the early- to mid-'90s, the number of sponsored women in skateboarding could be counted on one hand. Both the sponsorship support and the local Florida scene gave her the space to improve.

From here, Elissa exploded onto the national and, eventually, global scene with clean, inspiring street skateboarding. Part of her rise to fame came from leaving The Firm and instead compiling skate footage with a skater who would become a legend in his own right, Jamie Thomas. That footage helped Elissa earn a place on Toy Machine's new team, helmed by celebrated artist and skater Ed Templeton. Elissa skated alongside the new members of the Toy Machine team in their debut, *Welcome to Hell*, one of the most beloved skate videos of all time. The film proved a launchpad for other East Coast skaters who became household names, including Kerry Getz, Brian Anderson, Donny Barley, Bam Margera, and Jamie Thomas.

With a clean bag of tricks including the kickflip melon (a hefty kickflip caught with both feet and adding in a backside grab), the mid-'90s monarch began her reign. Her exceptional skateboarding from 1996 onward reminded skateboarders that women had always had a place in elite skateboarding. It might seem like a no-brainer now, with so many women, LGBTQ+, and nonbinary skaters crushing it, but this was the first break in the levee of the drought years.

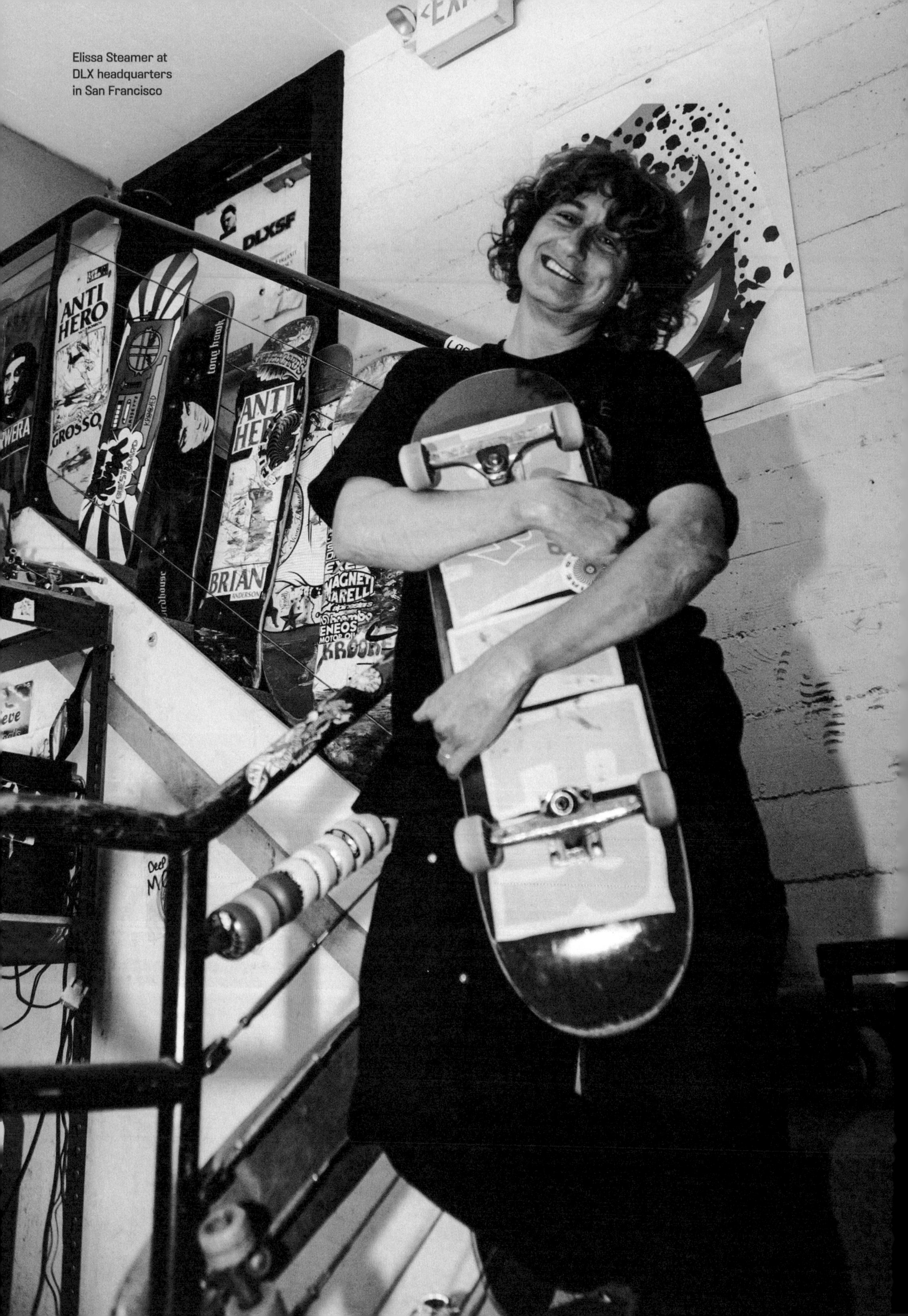

Elissa Steamer at
DLX headquarters
in San Francisco

Filmmaking and skateboarding are practically synonymous, and certainly symbiotic. Sometimes their titles and vibes are a lit-crit glimpse at a sociocultural moment. *Welcome to Hell*, Toy Machine's full-length video showcasing the team, is a great example. For skaters, the title implies the shared experience of chasing a trick, falling and flailing. That is all par for the course, but the last ingredient in the mix is ultimately *succeeding*. That success is for the camera, the team, and yourself. Skate videos are an integral component of demonstrating your skate identity and style as you join the professional ranks.

For Elissa, the video and the subsequent fame it brought her were often a double-edged sword. While she gained exposure, her identity as a female pro skater was awe-inspiring for some but a reason to challenge her authenticity for others. Skateboarding was supposed to be all love, but it was clearly a hostile environment at the time, with adherence to patriarchy at an all-time high and teen boys jealous of her spot on the team. I saw skaters trying to one-up her at a demo circa 1996, when, after she did a kickflip over the pyramid box, another hometown hero decided that he also needed to kickflip the pyramid right after her—the ultimate sign of disrespect at a demo. She remained a class act, ignored him, and proceeded with the demo. She was in fact on the team and didn't need to push back at every pissant looking for the spotlight.

Unfortunately, that disrespect also happened within some forms of the skateboarding industry and media, who chose to remind her that she was an anomaly rather than embrace her as one in a lineage of women from Patti McGee (RIP) to Peggy Oki (page 98) and beyond. Yet, despite the slander from the media, Elissa continually skated hard and proved the haters wrong.

Take her run at multiple skate contests, including the X Games. She won the Slam City Jam women's contest in '98–'99, and dipped down under to the Women's World Cup in Australia in 2003. After that, she went on a tear at the X Games, with gold medal wins for four years from 2004 to 2008. She was unstoppable. Steamer has the ability to simply show up with little practice and blast across the course like she's been there all weekend practicing. On top of those wins, she also became a playable character in the Tony Hawk video game franchise, instantly transforming her into a female skateboarding icon for skaters and non-skaters alike.

All of that talent and visibility earned her a signature model shoe with one of the longest-running skateboarding footwear brands, Etnies. On the outside it would seem she had all the trappings of superstardom. However, some crucial changes in her life would lead to less-than-desirable outcomes behind the scenes.

First, she left Toy Machine, the brand that had brought her into the business, partially because the skaters she grew up with on the team during the filming of *Welcome to Hell* and *Jump Off a Building* all felt they had outgrown the brand. Her formidable skills quickly earned her a home among the Andrew "The Boss" Reynolds's–led Baker and Bootleg skateboards crew, and a spot in the classic skate video *Baker 2G* and subsequent releases. Those videos kept Elissa in the limelight and earned her an official spot on Bootleg Skateboards from roughly 1998 to 2003. That was a highly popular crew, with a subset of the team members forming an inner circle notoriously known as the Piss Drunx. Luminary members included Reynolds, Jim "Hammers" Greco, and Dustin "Spawn" Dollin, and Elissa, all of whom who lived on a razor's edge—drinking, doing drugs, and partying in the prime of their skateboarding careers. Team members ran out of control, with many entering rehab and one phenomenal skater, Shane Cross, passing away in an alcohol-related death.

In 2004, when she was beginning her X Games run, she would become part of the Zero and Fallen Footwear team, founded by her original Fort Myers filmer, Jamie Thomas. Jamie was an old friend who had turned into a skateboarding mogul. However, those old habits died very hard. While she was winning contests, she didn't make the time to film full parts for the Zero video yet found time for partying. As I said before, your video proves you deserve to maintain your pro model. If you don't, it is curtains for your career. Elissa began to earn a reputation for being unable to deliver and connect with the skateboarding audience and the people who wanted to support her. She came to understand that fame is fast and fickle.

Elissa would leave Zero in 2011. Upon the departure, she found a way to make her own path without the pressure of being a pro skater. She surfed, found a life partner, got clean, and returned to the community. With vastly more women and LGBTQ+ skaters today, she also reaps the benefits of the work she started by being a pioneer.

Today, Elissa Steamer is back in the limelight, with a return to Baker, a place with Nike, and her own brand, Gnarhunters. This is a welcome encore for the greatest female skater of her generation, and for everyone she inspires.

A GODFATHER OF STREET SKATING
NATAS KAUPAS

Signature electrifying "Ollies" and Wall–Rides

Designed first sport-specific pro model skate shoe

Created the iconic 101 Skateboards brand

"Captain / there are doubts / regarding / your ability."

For anyone who spent time on asphalt and concrete during the late '80s and early '90s—golden eras of street skateboarding—that line from fIREHOSE's 1989 song "Brave Captain" just made their heads explode in five-alarm-fire fashion. That's because those words signal two things. First, the sound of Mike Watt, the funkiest white bass player this side of Flea. Second, the delivery of the full-frontal assault on our skateboarding senses in the *Streets on Fire* (1989) video by the holy trinity of influential street skaters: Mark "Gonz" Gonzales, Mike Vallely, and, of course, Natas Kaupas. They skated the handrails of the city together and made Rodney Mullen's (see page 54) freestyle tricks street, akin to taking samples and breaks and turning them into hip-hop. Natas, Mike, and Gonz were pushing skateboarding and making music where before there had only been noise.

Before we get to Natas's impact, let me run down just a lil' bit of the original tale. Born in 1969, by his early teens this first-generation Lithuanian American had been skating around Venice and Santa Monica, making a bit of a stink. He soon showed up at the back-alley surf woodshop that housed skateboard company Santa Monica Airlines (SMA) and a symbiosis formed. Skip Engblom—the proprietor, a god of surf- and skateboard making and shaping—gained a lifeline that day, and Natas earned a new sponsor.

In '83, Natas won the first contest he skated in. By the next year, he was already influencing the skateboarding world, perfecting a version of the no-handed wall ride (fellow L.A. street pioneer Jesse

Martinez was mastering the other), and earning the cover of *Thrasher* before he knew the magazine existed. Even the editors questioned if the boy was legitimate. But every image of Natas caused a commotion. Stills of full-speed, rugged smith grinds, frozen in motion, exemplified the strength of the newcomer. Beyond his street genius, even in his teens, Natas had a mind for business. Skip Engblom's artisanal ways couldn't keep up with the demand for Natas's decks, so Natas secured a manufacturing and distribution deal for SMA from NHS/Santa Cruz Skateboards, one of the largest skateboarding manufacturers in the world.

Natas was already changing the landscape. His part in the original Santa Cruz Skateboards promotional video, *Wheels of Fire* (1987), pointed the world to where the future of skateboarding was headed: the streets. There *were* rumblings of street skating happening. Skaters like John Lucero were inventing slappies (grinding across curbs); Tommy Guerrero (see page 109) was also on the scene as the first street skating pro, inspiring skaters around the world through his mind-blowing use of the hilly San Francisco landscape. They, along with others, were thinking of street skateboarding as an emulation of vert skating, which in turn was an emulation of pool skating, and in that lay a replication of surfing. Natas broke with that by making street skateboarding a genre of its own, not simply the by-product of getting kicked out of the park or an afterthought for those getting ready to skate a pool or a vert ramp, the choice terrain of the 1980s. Form as function: Natas is an original interpreter of the city's architecture as *the* thing to skate. The streets offered a wealth of possibilities much deeper than

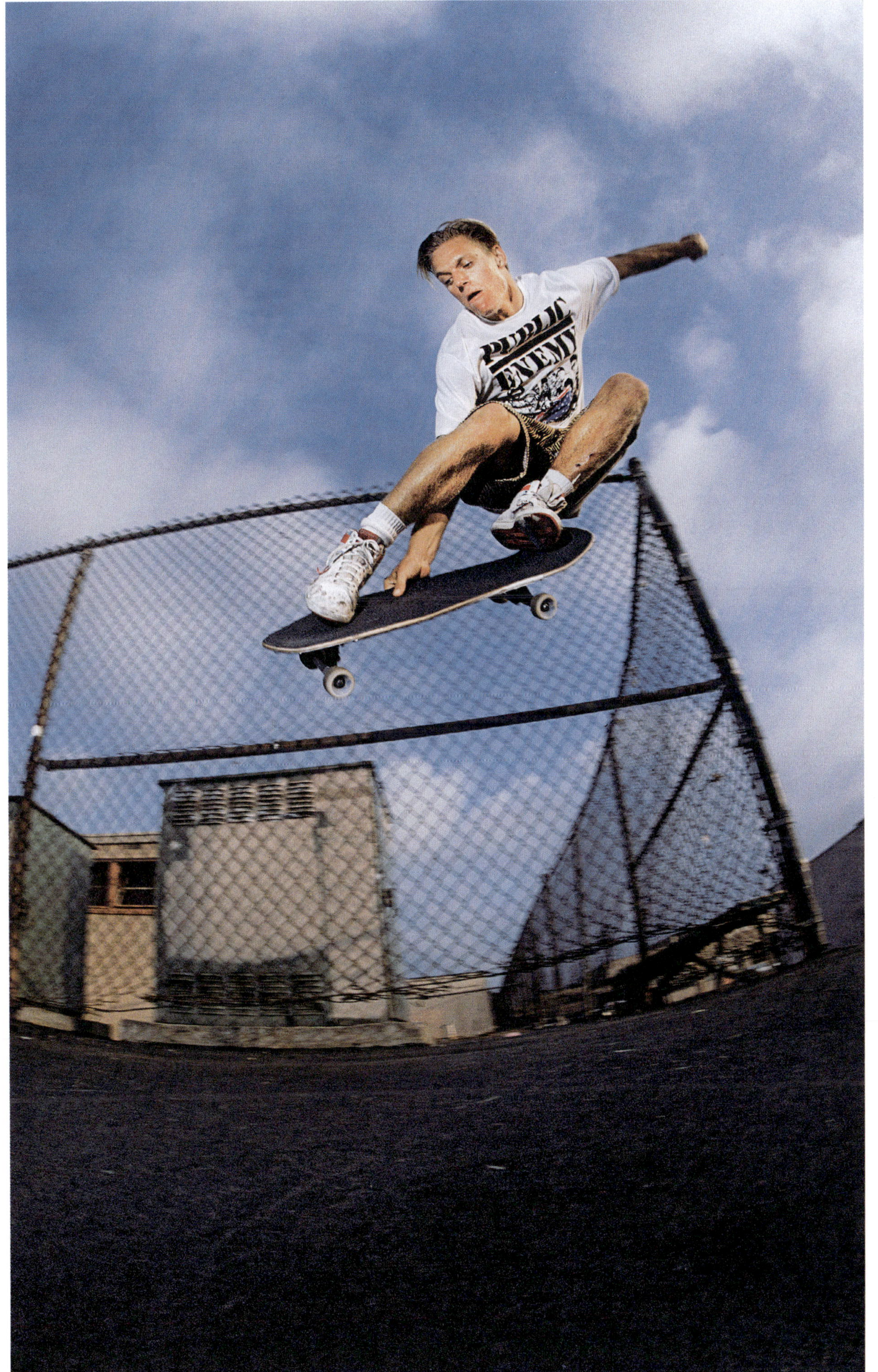

rolling back and forth in a ramp or a pool. Where the world saw a fire hydrant and a curb cut, Natas saw an obstacle course. He decided that ollieing onto a fire hydrant, landing on the topmost nut, and spinning around 540 degrees in a pirouette was something that could be and should be done.

Natas ollied from a launch ramp to rail-slide across a four-wheel pickup truck roll bar. He annihilated every set of stairs, rails, benches, and curbs in Santa Monica. The kid with bleach-blond hair did kickflips and ollie street plants, ollie 180s, one-footed ollies, and every grind imaginable. In 1989! Not only were these ollie tricks major feats, but this all happened at a time when pro skaters were on the fence about the viability of the ollie. Yes, there was a time when skaters did not ollie or jump up a curb, let alone a fire hydrant. Instead, they used the "boneless" to traverse obstacles. A boneless one (also known as footplant variation) consists of popping your board up into your grabbing hand while keeping one foot on it and jumping back on

the board. While this did get you up a curb or bench, it was a slow way to get through the city, always stopping your flow. Few skaters besides Rodney Mullen had incorporated ollies into their repertoire.

Enter Natas. Not only were ollies in his arsenal but he did every variation of them. He expanded the vocabulary for all of us, but also inspired a change in our approach. Skaters, pro and enthusiast alike, might have figured out how to ollie to 50-50 (a front and back truck grind) on a curb. Natas? He ollied from halfway across *the road* to 50-50. He made us rethink our relationship with the streets. Natas also paid homage to the legacy of the Z-Boys squad, shooting his video parts in *Wheels of Fire* in historic Venice and Santa Monica and incorporating the group's flowing and surfing style. Then he went up to San Francisco. He ollied onto and off picnic tables that were already *on top of* the little concrete skateparks. He provided an absolutely unimaginable display of power skating, fast as dreams and loose as shoelaces. His movement entered skateboarding's lexicon. We would imagine "Natas could" handle any obstacle, no matter how outrageous. Which inevitably led to every skater calling out all the things that "Natas did."

Natas Kaupus, frontside boardslide

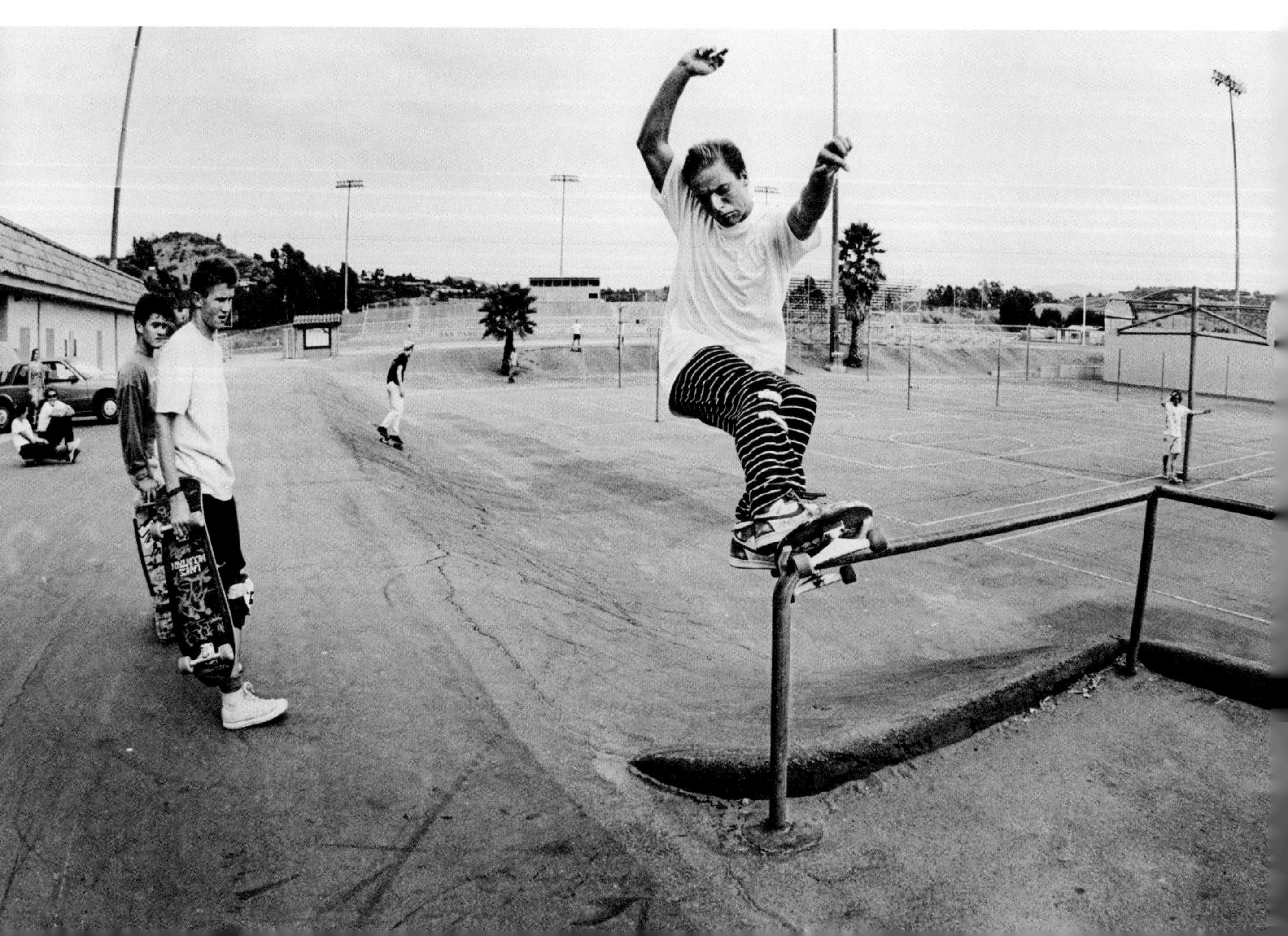

Natas also gave us style to emulate. When he wore a Public Enemy T-shirt, it became skate fashion. He single-handedly put hip-hop on display in his 1986 *TransWorld SKATEboarding* interview. If it was cool enough for Natas, it was cool enough for everyone. His influence (and Gonz's and Mike's) helped propel the notion that skaters were artists, and decades later that's still an element of the skateboarding lifestyle.

Then there is the first skateboarding-specific shoe of the modern era: the Natas-designed high-top manufactured by French skater Pierre André Senizergues for then-upstart brand Etnies (originally called "Etnics" in France) was *the* pro model shoe. It was made to Natas's high standards as the leading skateboarder of the time, and it dropped in 1988. Spearheaded by Senizergues, the Etnies brand would later be known as Sole Tech footwear, with multiple divisions, including Etnies, Emerica, and éS. Sole Tech would start the skateboarding footwear revolution and allow us to control one more important component of our skateboarding lifestyle. Having the power to shape our own narrative is integral to skateboarding culture today, and also happens to be uniquely tied to Natas's experiences during his professional journey.

Natas's rise in the mid-'80s to early '90s coincided with a fervor for "protecting" kids from exposure to potential harm (thank Tipper Gore and Prince's "Darling Nikki" for the U.S. introduction of the Parental Advisory sticker). Parents of that era were happy to ban or "cancel" anything that could be remotely construed as non-Christian. As you know, skateboarding hasn't been every parent's favorite activity since . . . its inception. Unfortunately, Natas couldn't have picked a worse moment to become the world's leading street skater. Why? Oh, because his first name spelled backward—well, it happens to spell *Satan*, which is rich ore if you happen to be in the mining-for-drama club. Talk about looking for messages everywhere! Natas Kaupas was his real name, and as he told the media countless times, his parents thought he was going to be a girl and simply shortened his name from Natasha to Natas. A name like Natas is different, but it never caused controversy until he joined the upper echelon of skateboarding. Just like

that, his products were banned in several parts of the country, including his own, L.A. County.

Despite this obstacle and the heights he could have reached if his board sales were not hindered by controversy, Natas's prowess and reputation continued to grow and over time he and his collaborators amassed an army of foot soldiers who became innovators of their own.

Natas's team at SMA included Jim Thiebaud, Sean Sheffey, Julien Stranger, and Alan Petersen, all of whom would go on to become legends under his tutelage. The same would hold true when he began his own endeavor away from SMA—101 Skateboards. The brand was home to Gino Iannucci, Jason Dill, Clyde Singleton, Marcus McBride, Kris Markovich, Andy Stone, Eric Koston, Adam McNatt, and Gabriel Rodriguez (RIP), and every 101 skater is forever etched into skateboarding history. In scant time their collective efforts showcased a trick list too long to write here—I would need to create a separate glossary just for the combinations.

Beyond the team was the artistry in 101's videos: the stop-motion ads, the eclectic soundtracks, and Natas's cavalcade of creative ideas. His artistry wasn't contained by the proverbial concrete canvas. His hand guided some of the greatest skate art of the '90s at renowned skateboard and apparel company World Industries, and eventually his talent was recognized by those outside of skateboarding. After he parted ways with 101, his career in design was his next marquee as he created his own (sadly short-lived) sneaker company, Vita Shoes, with partner Mark Oblow. Natas would even obtain a new pro model for Element Skateboards for a time, as well as multiple reissues celebrating his impact on skateboarding. Recently involved in a design collab with New Balance Numeric, the skateboarding division of the brand, he gave the shoe an '80s color treatment and featured a solid throwback to his original Etnies design. Setting up his own firm, Designarium Skateboards, one of the greatest to ever step on a board continues to show us the value of being an artist in any medium and how the skateboard can remain the canvas of ideas for years to come.

"Natas did."

> **NATAS IS AN ORIGINAL INTERPRETER OF THE CITY'S ARCHITECTURE AS *THE* THING TO SKATE.**

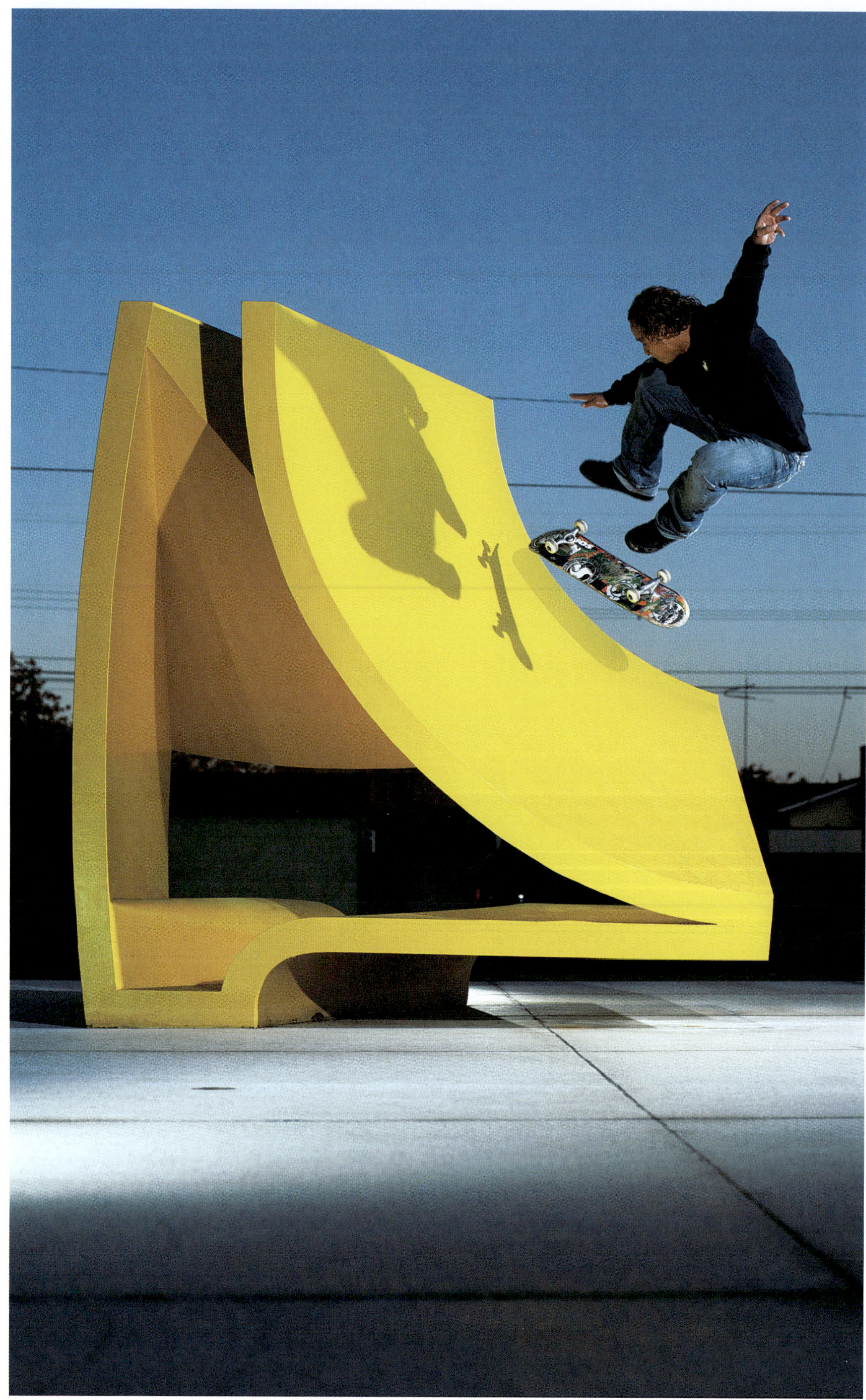

THE SOULFUL MASTER TECHNICIAN
DAEWON SONG

Skateboarding Hall of Famer

***Thrasher*'s 2006 Skater of the Year**

Created an entire category known as Daewon tricks and Daewon spots

One half of the pseudo-rivalry Rodney vs. Daewon

Ashes to ashes, dust to dust. What does the cosmic life cycle have to do with introducing a skateboarder? It is the only way to prepare you for the mythical level of Daewon Song's skateboarding moves.

More so than any other skater in our lifetime, Daewon foresees the potential energy in obstacles (tables, benches, water, rocks, trees) and shapes them into possibilities. He unlocks each object's dynamism, extracting and enacting its power through a dance of kinetic wizardry. Daewon wields the magic that stays intact and activated until the moment the man, the matter, and the mastership are captured for posterity. Then the objects are returned to their initial inert state.

Okay, truthfully, *mostly* returned to their original state. I am sure many baffled janitors and maintenance staff left a tidy schoolyard on a Friday afternoon, only to find on Monday morning chairs, dumpsters, and swing sets corralled and placed in an unexplainable manner. *C'est la vie.* Under the Tao of Daewon, objects are birthed, created, given life, and skated. I can attest that we are all the better for it.

The tale of 1970s-born Korean American Daewon begins in Gardena, California. The child of an immigrant family, Daewon spent his grade school years as a bright young kid with an affinity for art and was rewarded with early honors. His natural creativity and imagination began with the pen, brush, and easel, but to the joy of skateboarding and the chagrin of his parental units, morphed into the mobile palette and concrete canvas that is the skateboard and the city. Regardless of the medium, Daewon's artistry is undeniable.

Daewon's early relationship to "skate life" followed an argument between his parents and his mother's attempt to create a temporary respite from the tension. Her singular gift of a new skateboard seeded a lifelong obsession with an artifact that would be both creative and time-consuming for Daewon. This duality served as an important and stabilizing function within the sometimes-turbulent life of the youngster for whom siblings and elder family members did most of the child-rearing.

At 14, he befriended Daniel Castillo, a Filipino American skateboarder, sparking a 30-year friendship. Their camaraderie and inseparability—trading licks, jokes, and tours—are part of the annals of skateboarding history, as captured by Mexican American videographer Socrates Leal (see page 167), who was crucial to the duo's visibility. Socrates would come to film or contribute to Daewon and Castillo's countless videos across the decades, including Daewon's debut video section of the World Industries–produced film *Love Child* (1992).

The video captured two remarkable things: the first hardflip caught on cam, by Daewon, which added a new trick to the arsenal of skateboarding, and the joy and innovation and solidarity behind the scenes. From dancing to claps to hallelujah screams, Castillo rolls ride or die with Daewon. Theirs remains one of the most visibly enduring and inspirational friendships in all of skateboarding.

It demonstrated to all of us groms coming up that we did not need to compete against each other—we needed to *be there* for each other.

This early crew also included another complementary element, the famed Rodney Mullen (see page 54). At that time, Rodney recruited for the upstart, influential skateboarding company World Industries. The then-15-year-old Daewon and his cohorts, Castillo and Kareem Campbell, were introduced to the skateboarding world via a tongue-in-cheek ad prominently featuring the words "White Power," yet spotlighting the three skaters of color. They would become part of the new wave of multiracial World corps who would soon besiege and dominate all of skateboarding. Eventually Rodney began spending considerable time with Daewon, first as a team manager, then as a friend and skate mentor.

Daewon was cut from the same cloth of experimentation as Rodney, but instead of having years of freestyle skating behind him, Daewon came of age loving high-flying Christian "Holmes" Hosoi (see page 17), the rough-and-tumble explosiveness of Dogtown, and all things Z-Boys. That background interacting with Rodney's expertise would produce a different type of skater, one who had the power of the past but also the technical prowess driving modern innovation. Together, Daewon and Rodney moved tricks once reserved *only* for Rodney into the realm of the everyman. Or, realistically speaking in Daewon's case, the *extra*ordinary man.

It's hard to imagine that we *lost* Daewon for a moment in skateboarding. Yet he is still The One. It sounds crazy now, but Daewon once told me that despite a promising career, he decided that hanging out with a girl and lifting and tuning cars might be his future.

Luckily for us, the itch for skating came back following two runs of historic departures from World and its affiliates—prompting Rodney to reach out to his former mentee and ask him to come back into the fold. The two built a shorthand, moving at lighting speed, skating L.A. schoolyards, eventually able to finish each other's skateboarding sentences in Lennon and McCartney fashion.

Daewon and Rodney practiced, bonded, and performed mind-blowing combinations of styles. Skating never looked hard—even when they pushed the conventional limits of technical skating. There was always one more variation or element to add to the trick. They might both do a 360 flip to nose wheelie (balancing on the front two wheels only), to nollie 360 flip-out on a manual pad (any smooth concrete "island" that can be reached from either

side), but they would push each other to move beyond the nose wheelie (centered in freestyle) and make it street by doing it to nosegrind. Then they'd transition it from the island to a bench. Then to a picnic table. Next, they'd stack those picnic tables down a flight of stairs. Then . . . well, you get the point. They progressed skateboarding and we all *felt* that transition. Rodney was science, and Daewon the flow, and together they equaled fun.

The culmination of these efforts appeared in the incomparable skateboarding film *Rodney vs. Daewon Round 1*. Skaters chose sides: either Rodney, creator of every trick, for his technique; or Daewon, with his next-level ability to take *any* trick into difficult and unlikely terrain. Tree stumps, vertical concrete slabs, rugged transitions are all fodder for Daewon. Where a skater might be lucky to add a soulful smith grind to a difficult spot, Dae can bring his entire repertoire to that place of soul and reimagine what's possible. Furthermore, with the exception of Rodney, there are few current skaters who are more comfortable than Daewon rolling on two wheels rather than four. Dae's even been experimenting with losing one wheel mid-trick . . . then putting it back on and rolling away. For fun.

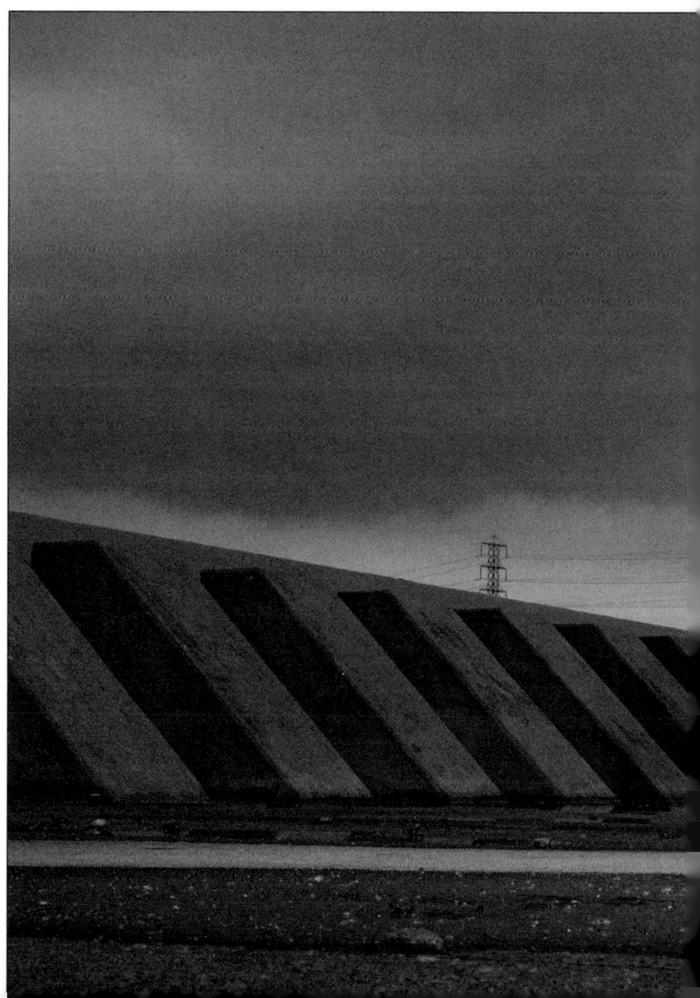

Daewon was obsessed with skating everything. Skating the gaps between 18-wheeler trucks by placing a rail between them. Skating rooftop gaps between buildings. Some skaters lost interest because these daring escapades felt too far out of reach.

But that changed when Daewon found his kindred spirit in Chris Haslam, and the pair created a small slice of absurdity, a video called *Cheese & Crackers*. With a modest budget from World, the pair constructed a makeshift mini ramp in a decrepit, secret Long Beach, California, warehouse. Sections of the ramp exploded, fell, were inundated with tires, refrigerator parts, and even an operable, skateable door—makeshift contraptions that became home to the most outrageous mini-ramp skating of all time.

Like freestyle, mini ramps had fallen out of vogue due the lack of backyards and space in L.A. and many other big cities. Mini-ramp skating was left to those who could afford the square footage and had the cash for a ramp. By that time, it was thought not to be the terrain of true street skaters. Daewon and Chris brought it back in spades.

I've traveled a lot thanks to skateboarding. Out on the road, I witnessed the impact of *Cheese & Crackers* on the skateboarding zeitgeist. In my 20s, I worked for Dwindle, the home of Daewon and Rodney's Almost Skateboards.

I came with free copies of the video and an order form for more. Truthfully, these cowboys didn't know what hit 'em. *Cheese & Crackers* demonstrated a level of control and partnership so in sync, Daewon and Chris could do tricks onto and through each other's boards. Nothing, including the kitchen sink, was off-limits.

In the early aughts, as his star rose, Daewon's schedule became hectic. He was unable to say no to tours, videos, and maintaining his highly visible status, which triggered a separation from his then-wife. As for his parents, he didn't want them to know he had full-sleeve tattoos, and managed to keep it from them, and by extension, most of the skate world, too. These little bits about Daewon were not out in the public because—well, who cares? So many of us took seriously what this man, 2006 *Thrasher* Skater of the Year, did. For regular people, what became known as a "Daewon spot" was a place where conditions were impossible for other skaters.

Then, like clockwork Daewon would shoot a cover photo of *TransWorld SKATEboarding* demolishing that same spot.

Adidas's skateboarding event "Daewon Did It" serves as testament to his ability to skate anything. The contest drew over 2,500 fans dedicated to re-creating "Daewon tricks," forever putting respect on his name and adding real legs to his legacy.

After 30 years under Dwindle with Rodney, in 2018, Daewon founded Thank You Skateboards, working alongside *his* former mentee now turned partner, pro skater Torey Pudwill. Even that effort is the most Daewon of Daewon tricks, to use a brand to give back and to shine a light on others.

THE GAME CHANGER
NYJAH HUSTON

Generational talent who turned pro at age 10

Biggest bag of tricks and most NBDs (never-been-dones) in the game

2024 Olympic bronze medalist in street skateboarding

A defining, and dividing, force

No matter from what angle, the story of Nyjah Huston is one of the most compelling in skateboarding: Nyjah, the home-schooled child prodigy who became one of the winningest skaters of the modern era.

The Huston trophy room screams DJ Khaled vibes; he shows up to the contest and it's "another one." For a good portion of time, contests were a wrap for Nyjah with first place nearly guaranteed, leaving other skaters chasing second. Street League, Dew Tour, X Games. He came to win and to make people put some respect on his name.

Nyjah is a phenomenon. No other skater is working on so many NBDs (never-been-dones) *all* the time. IIe is one of few skaters to work on tricks in private at his own indoor facilities before debuting them at contests. It is not a stretch to say that he is the reason people believed the U.S. would win the gold medal in street skateboarding during its Olympics sports debut in Tokyo, Japan. Heavy expectations, but heavily favored to win. Alas, the best-laid plans . . . Enter the pandemic, delaying the Olympics a year, then causing the games to take place without a crowd. Nyjah, a skater who thrives on the roaring fans and tense conditions, found himself in the strange, muted tones we all did, experiencing the games as something else. Which in turn was exactly what he delivered at the games. Nyjah did not provide the divine experience we expected. However, he laid bare what it is to be a true skateboarder: he battled a single trick—a gapped-out Caballerial kickflip (fakie 360 ollie kickflip) to backside lipslide down the flat golden handrail. It's as challenging to say as it is to accomplish. These types of tricks are tough enough to do practicing alone and even more ridiculous to try to set down during a contest. Yet chasing the great white whale—the bucket-list trick that makes you feel the most fulfilled and accomplished—is a fundamental element of skateboarding. Nyjah put everything on the line during the Olympics. Rather than digging into his deep bag of tricks for one he could deliver on command, he fought for NBD contest perfection. My phone blew up across time zones, the way I'm sure it did for others. "What's happening? Why doesn't he do something else?" Millions of skateboarders and viewers witnessed Nyjah seeking to best the beast until it was simply too late. *Bzzzz* . . . the buzzer rang, and we heard the announcers declare, "That, my friends, is time." No one could believe it. Nyjah, a generational talent, did not podium at skateboarding's Tokyo debut (though in true Nyjah fashion, he would redeem himself with a bronze at the 2024 Paris Olympics).

It could be argued that this was not the time or place for his blind dedication. On the other hand, his performance clearly demonstrated his dedication to true skateboarding. Nyjah skated his way, just like he always did. This time it didn't pan out. That's skateboarding. Some days you work to tame it, and some days it tames you.

Nyjah started on this path as a youngling, becoming the avatar of his father's own skateboarding dreams. Understandably, parents have wishes for their children and there is no denying that his father hoped he would become the greatest in skateboarding. His father skated with his kids and tried his best to develop for them the most conducive lifestyle to skateboarding. This included living on a sustainable small family farm with a skatepark. However, it is well documented that this pressure was a lot for the youngster and his family. It would eventually lead to Nyjah's parents separating over how to raise their children. While the correct path forward was debatable, the young skater had undeniable talent, so much so that he turned professional at age 10.

Nyjah the young superstar conquered handrails two to three times his height, floating down them effortlessly, long dreadlocks flowing behind him, skating exceptionally and with a skill well beyond his years. He was a game changer. He set a new standard for man-size skateboarding done with boyish ease and disregard for failure. He was heralded like an incoming king, and we all knew that 'Jah brought something new. Something to inspire young skaters and an older generation.

And yet he kept coming in second. In retrospect, looking at Nyjah's early days as a skate protégé, you can see the difficulty that led to turbulent times in the family and internally. What could have been a celebration of a young man developing into his body and skills was not. Within skateboarding, the difference between first and second place is often subjective, and this was especially true in the early to mid-aughts. At the time, judging still lacked a clear rubric for skaters to use to strategize what tricks to do and when, the way they do now. You just went out and skated and hoped for the best. For Nyjah, competing was often a tense and tearful time. When I filmed those contests, it was easy to see that there was no space for a lighthearted moment of self-acknowledgment of a job well done. It hurt my heart to see. Here was a quiet, soulful, dreadlocked youth whose skating should have been grounded in love, fun, and irie vibes; instead, he radiated disappointment. There was nothing anyone could do to make him feel that he was accomplishing greatness in those days. Coming close to the top of the podium was not enough. Few

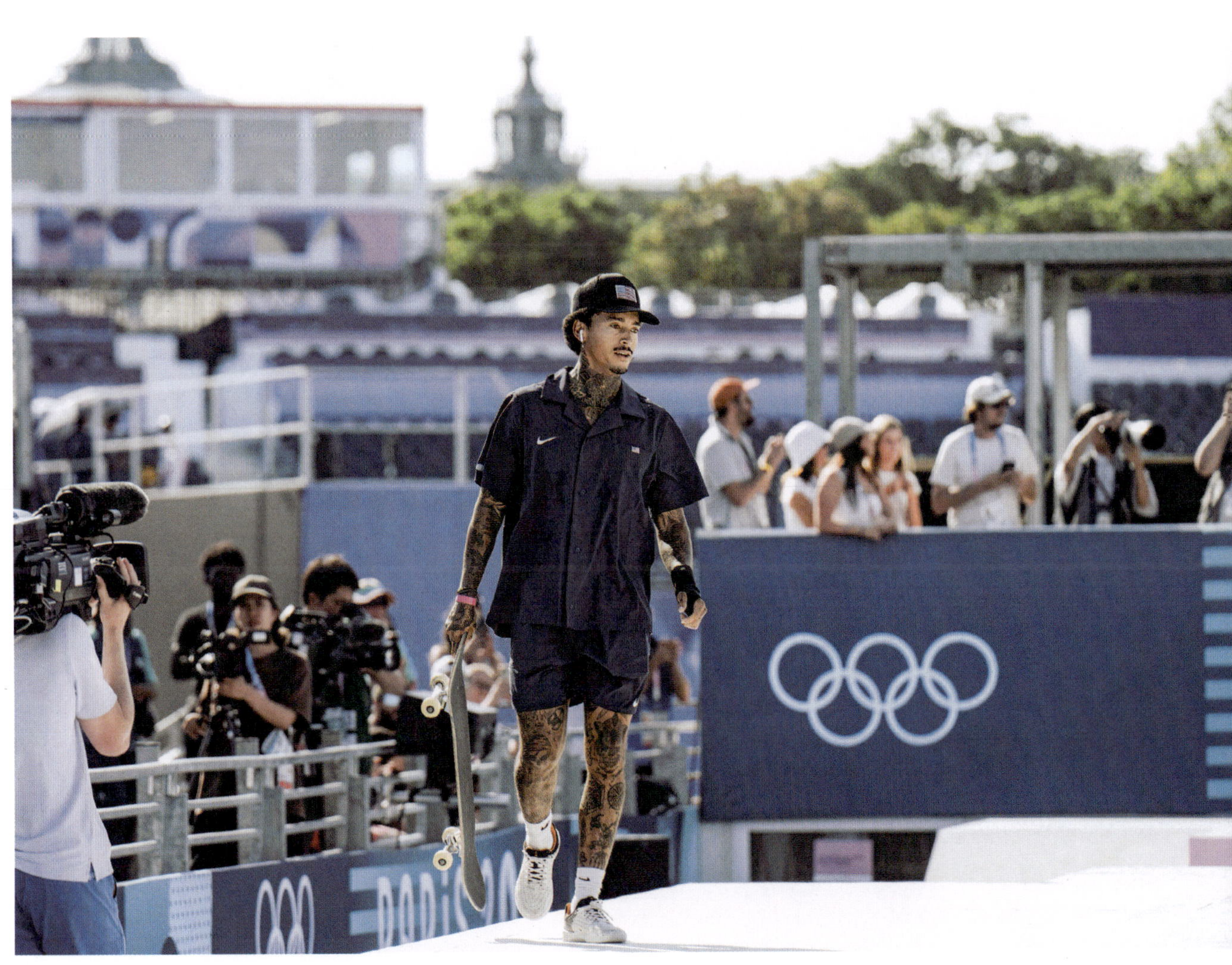

skaters have felt the kind of pressure Nyjah did, and it began from the jump.

Things shifted in his family in 2011, when Nyjah, his mother, and his siblings escaped from under the patriarchal thumb and moved into a home without their father. This created a path out of their father's shadow, and the pressure that went with it. That's when Nyjah went on a tear—more NBDs, more consistency, more joy in his skateboarding—and he became what he always wanted to be, an undeniable champion. Nyjah belongs in any GOAT conversation.

He skates hard and parties hard. And, sure, some of us have parties at the house, but Nyjah's are thrown in an architectural dream house overlooking Laguna Beach, California, with a Lamborghini Aventador in the garage and rocking decibel levels that earn airtime on TMZ. Then, just like that, he is out skating in the streets, in the park, filming boundless video parts, pushing skateboarding's limits.

His lifestyle choices also make him not everyone's cup of tea. There are lots of reasons to throw shade—maybe you don't like his style or his trick selection, or the pants-shorts combination he's been rocking for the past few years. Either way, he deals with it in the same way he handles a 17-stair slam. He rolls away from it, and shakes it off. It shows in his skating and his mindset—he is out there to send it, crush it, then move on. Winning and riding, wildin' and vibin'. He was the game changer then and is now. Skateboarding hasn't been hit this hard by someone capable of every marketer's dream since Christian "Holmes" Hosoi (see page 17) brought out the cheat code—skateboarding prowess + magnetic attraction = rock-star status.

Now the rock star Nyjah, popping one-wheelers on his motorcycle in Hollywood, differs from the young skater with long dreadlocks living under his father's purview. This Nyjah—the tattoos, the short hair, the wholly engaged athlete with his own style—is someone Nyjah has grown into.

That time of discovery, however, means the rise is going meteoric, the falls historic, and the mistakes will be doubly confounding with time and the public eye. In fact, he has faced multiple moments of darkness on the way to becoming the man he is now. Those bigger battles are for Nyjah to discuss with you, and his God. However, what we can all agree on is that he is out there trying to win and has the power and brilliant trick selection to do just that.

Make no mistake, Nyjah is a controversial character, maybe one of the most contentious in skateboarding. There are people who believe he is

God's gift to skateboarding and others who believe he has taken his gift and the power that comes with it too far. As one of the greatest skaters of his generation, he is a defining and dividing force in skateboarding culture and a dynamo of athleticism exploding with arguably too much talent for some, but just enough to match his lifelong ambition to make every moment of skateboarding monumental.

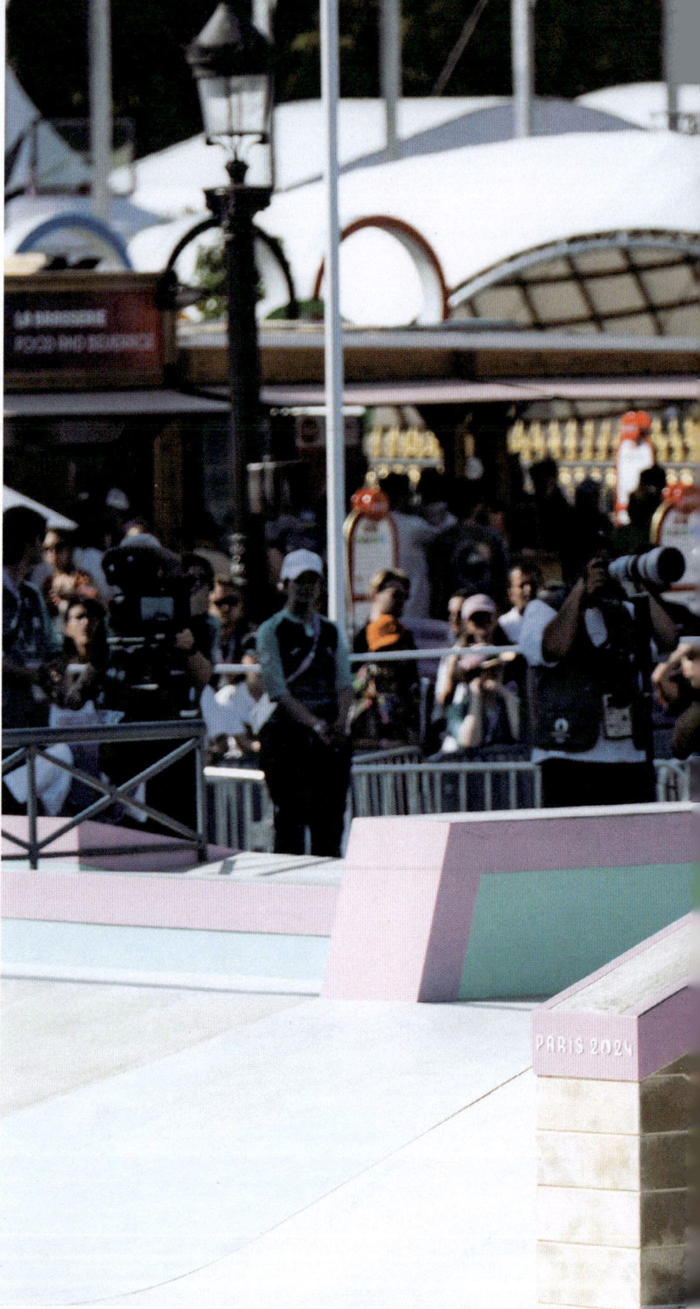

Top: Nyjah Huston, switch heelflip to frontside tailslide down the Hubba, 2024 Paris Olympics

Right: Forever clean, backside smith grind, 2023, X-Games, Ventura, CA

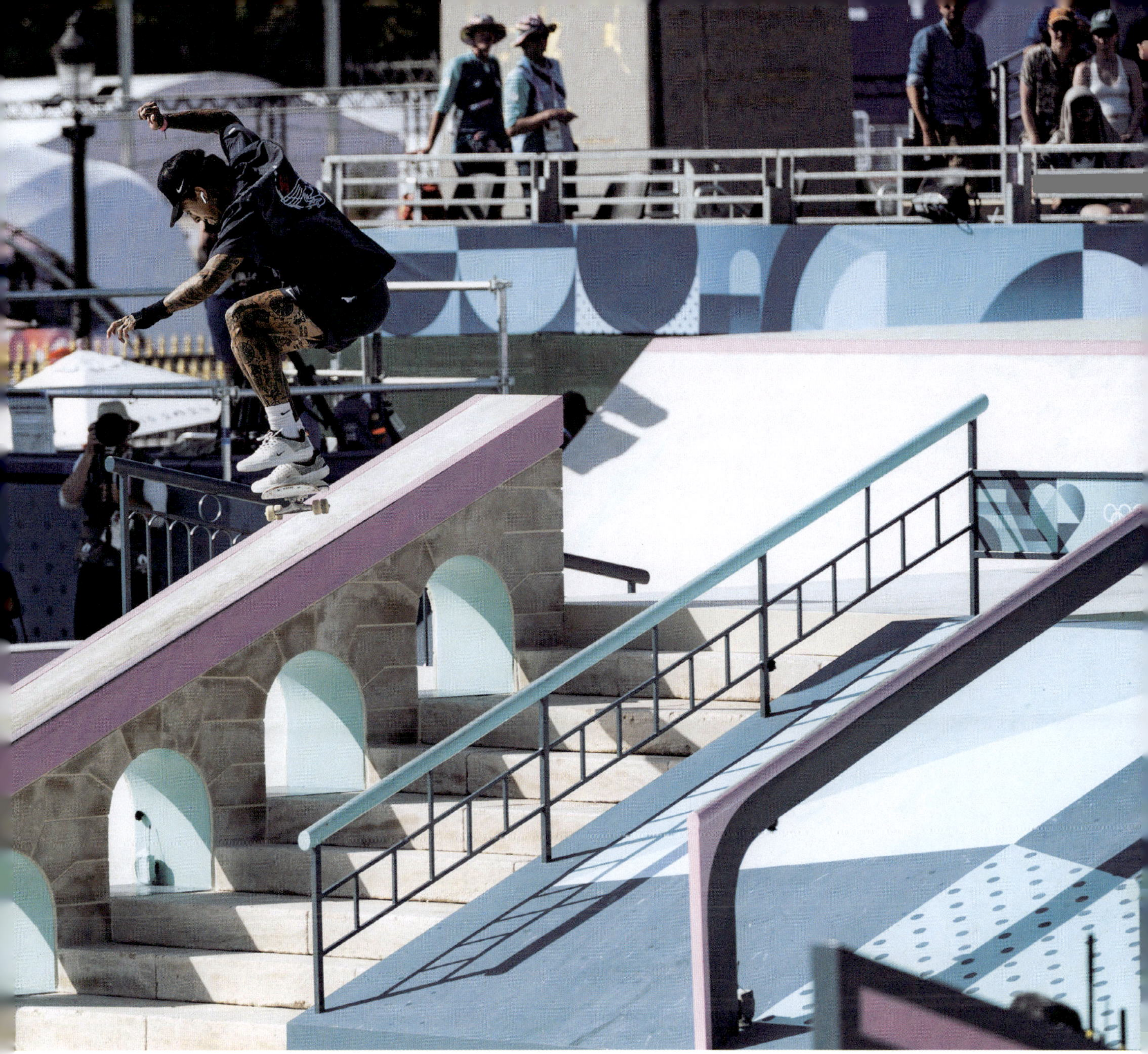

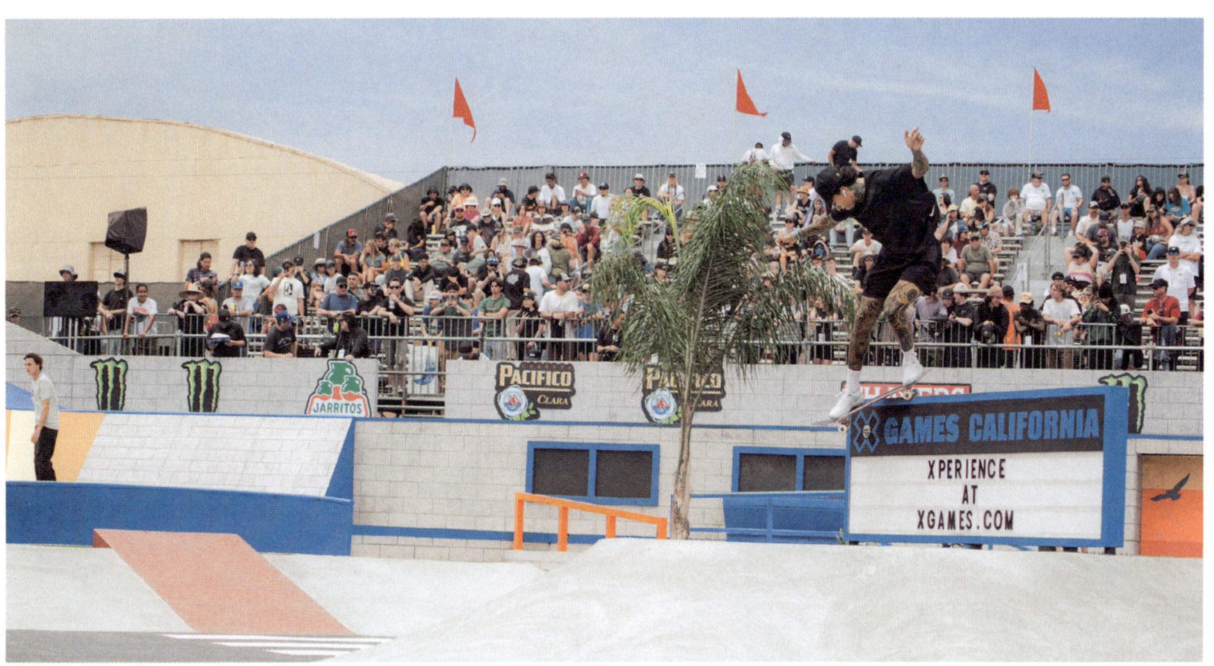

PACIFICO
CLARA
JARRITOS
X GAMES CALIFORNIA
XPERIENCE
AT
XGAMES.COM

THE TRUTH

PAUL "P-ROD" RODRIGUEZ

Child prodigy

X Games and Street League champion

Founder of Primitive Skateboarding

Paul Rodriguez aka P-Rod is the only skater with a nickname that pays direct homage to another sporting great. Though now retired from competition, he was the cornerstone of the Nike skateboarding team, the winner of countless X Games medals, Dew Tour accolades, Maloof Money Cups, and made years' worth of "day in the life" appearances for MTV, ESPN, and global outlets.

P-Rod had countless endorsements to his name. There was a P-Rod product for every category. Out skating and the sundial not cutting it? Paul'll hit you with rose gold Nixon watch joints. Thirsty? Paul designed water for you, *and* a Saint Archer craft-brewed adult beverage. Some skaters have a pro model shoe, but few have been sponsored by the actual Target corporation or have banners of them skating hanging regally outside of prominent buildings, including the former Staples Center. That's P-Rod, the skater to drop a host of firsts, the skater who brought up a new generation in the aughts and who continues to drop gems. Only in his 40s, he has already lived a remarkable life by impressing upon an entire generation that skateboarders are about skateboarding again. Oh, and about gettin' that *paper*. Not partying, and watching their career disappear, but making dollars appear and leaving a legacy for their family.

Sports history is littered with those who worked just hard enough to earn a little fame and an appearance fee—then nothing. Fame can eat you alive, especially in L.A. However, for most of his life P-Rod lived on the "other side" of life in the Valley. Maybe that plus a heavy dose of religious faith is what made Paul immune to the trappings.

P-Rod is from the San Fernando Valley and grew up in a family of mostly working-class Mexican American backgrounds and with friends across multiple middle-class backgrounds. His father, the comedian Paul Rodriguez, paved the way for many Latinx entertainers to gain cultural acceptance in the entertainment industry, both in the U.S. and abroad. But it's P-Rod who pushed that envelope for skaters of color in the mid-aughts.

P-Rod had the right mix of athleticism and "street aesthetic" to inspire a generation. He also came up in the skateboarding ranks at a time when a growing market of young people came up watching Jordan and Kobe *and* X Games, and later Bam Margera's TV antics on MTV's *Jackass* and *Viva La Bam*. Paul's fresh face and preternatural ability to hit streets, screens, and shelves was a potent combo at a time when non-endemic brands were trying to find their footing in skateboarding culture beyond their reach in legacy spaces.

Anyone looking back at his footage and his work ethic from the early days would see that the kid was destined for greatness. The seeds of that greatness, however, took root in the Valley. Andy Netkin, the team manager for 118 Boardshop, discovered the 13-year-old Paul and helped him and later his friends gain greater exposure by utilizing his skate shop network to get eyes on their skateboarding "sponsor me" tapes.

Earning his first spot on DNA Skateboards, Paul and his Simi Valley crew were the next in a long line of Valley skate rats. Later, under the auspices of Kareem Campbell (see page 46), this group of teens would blossom at CityStars Skateboards.

Paul took his skating seriously. Being raised in a conservative religious family, he could even be found praying before the day's skate session, and before some tricks. Around that time, in the early aughts, Paul Sr. had a conversation with Kareem. "'You want to do what with my kid? You want to give him free stuff—*suuure*,'" Kareem recounted to me. Paul Sr. had no idea about the legacy of skaters of color at the time and jokes about it in his stand-up to this day. It took an exorbitant level of verbal gymnastics and contortions for the senior Rodriguez to let Jr. out for "work release" with a bunch of "sketchy" skaters. However, after handshakes and the assignment of watchful caretakers—Kareem, plus pro skaters like Joey Suriel, Fabian Alomar, and DJ Speed (former N.W.A. master of the ones and twos)—the rest is history.

The skateboarding world was ill-prepared for what was unleashed upon them in a short time. Under the tutelage of Kareem, a group of virtual unknowns would become skateboarding A-listers known as the terror squad. The title stood for two things: First, their ability to strike fear in the hearts of current pros and the competition. Second, that they were more than a handful for their team managers, DJ Speed and Suriel, who were forced to deal with the boatload of shenanigans involved with monitoring a team of skaters under 18. Those future superstars included Mikey Taylor, Justin Case (RIP), Kevin "Spanky" Long, Ryan Denman, and Devine Calloway—and heaviest among them, Paul Rodriguez.

Paul's debut video part for the CityStars promotional video *Street Cinema* included two milestones: earning the coveted last spot (curtains usually belong to the most seasoned), and skating to another skater's song, the Jackson 5's "I Want You Back." This song is forever associated with Guy Mariano's debut as a wunderkind for the famed Spike Jonze–directed Blind Skateboards' *Video Daze* (1991). To choose another skater's song was unheard of, especially one used by an icon like Guy. Paul masterfully employed the controversial strategy to put the skateboarding world on notice.

What made Paul special? His skills were the perfect merger of street wizardry and contest consistency. True athleticism. Some skaters might work weeks to link difficult combinations of tricks together or face months of failure tossing their body and their board down a set of stairs or a gap to complete a NBD (never been done).

These are tricks with magic in the moment captured for posterity; they act as cultural milestones. Some skaters prefer this type of skating but shy away from the challenge of the nerve-wracking "do your best trick in 60 seconds" demand of contest skating. Other skaters thrive in that environment and shine when the pressure hits.

P-Rod did both.

That boy was truth in any circumstance. Never-been-dones in the streets like kickflip back tail to backside heelflip out. Done. You want tre flip-out instead? Choose your own adventure. Regardless, Paul had you covered. NBD at the contest, nollie noseslide to nollie flip-out on a handrail. The streets, the contests. Same, same. All day, every damn day.

Nothing operated beyond his grasp. Paul could not find a gap too big or a rail too far to grind or a tech trick out of his reach. 'Reem told me Paul's hunger was insatiable. He described those days: "He would bring in

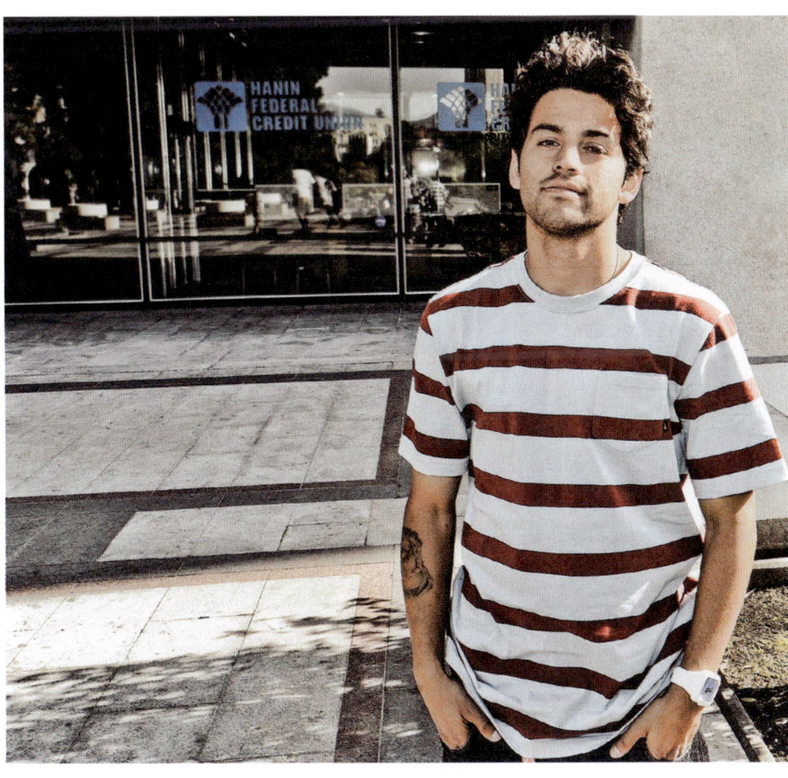

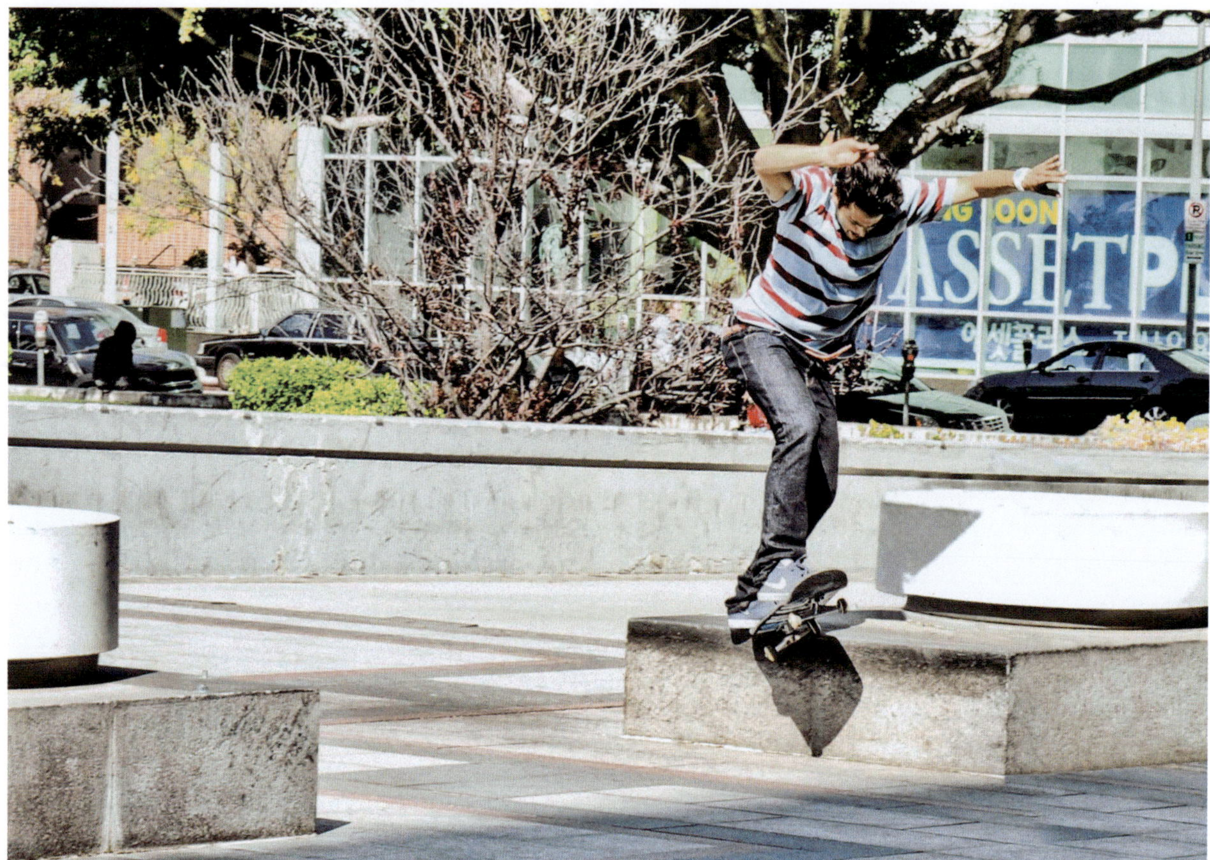

P. Rod, backside 180 to switch front crooked grind

footage skating a 10-stair, then a 12-stair. I'd say it was amazing, and he'd ask, 'What's next?' " Kareem laughed. "'Okay, take it to the 16-stair.' Bam, he's bringing me the footage the next day. There was nothing he couldn't do, and he was am [amateur]. There were no more goals for me to set for him. It was madness." Understanding it was time to turn Paul and Mikey pro, Kareem ran a CityStars ad in *Thrasher* and *TransWorld SKATEboarding* asking the fans to vote by phone and mail: Who did they believe was ready to turn pro, Mikey or Paul? It was a tie, and they both were scheduled to turn pro.

Enter a change of plans.

What happened to Paul is what happens to someone when they realize they have no boundaries, no discernible limits—they try to fly free. Paul did just that. On the eve of his pro debut, in 2003, with his signature City Stars pro model about to be released, he decided to tempt fate and branch out on his own. After a signature part in *TransWorld SKATEboarding*'s phenomenal skateboarding video *In Bloom* (2002), the kid with the golden boot and the hottest hands was on the market and in demand. While he was in limbo, he still skated Girl boards and was approached by everyone, from Baker Skateboards to the now defunct Seek Skateboards. When icon Eric Koston

asked him to officially join Girl Skateboards while on a photo mission with Atiba Jefferson (see page 143), the clouds parted and Paul said yes.

At Girl, Paul would bring new power and energy to the team delivering excellence in the streets and in contests. Crailtap, owned by Spike Jonze, Mike Carroll, Megan Baltimore, and Rick Howard, and home to both the Girl and Chocolate camps, was one of the most storied and elite brands in skateboarding (see page 240). Brought into the fold by Koston, a decorated legend in skateboarding, Paul was now in Olympus with the gods.

After delivering phenomenal video parts for Girl Skateboards over the next few years, Paul would eventually take flight from Girl and join the stellar team at the resurrected Plan B Skateboards. Rekindling the feeling of the small elite team of his CityStars debut, Paul would be part of the lauded halls of another of skateboarding's most celebrated teams.

Back then, people knew Paul would have an impact on skateboarding, but few imagined he would unlock another milestone that lifted all boats: signing with Nike. Here is where Paul set the tone for a game-changing era of business. After several notable failed attempts at branching into the skateboarding market, Nike had created a separate division, Nike SB, and enlisted P-Rod as brand ambassador. The combination of Paul and an already star-studded team that included pro skater Stefan Janoski would deliver the best-selling shoes in the market and help Nike become a leader in skateboarding footwear.

But Paul's transition to Nike wasn't smooth. Skaters everywhere ballyhooed—okay, I'll say it right—skaters *hated* on his move. The question on the streets was: Why would he want to sell out to Nike, a brand that had been a literal failure in skateboarding? Why support them and the other non-endemic brands creeping into the culture over the independent skate brands that better matched the skater ethos? All true, yet here is the flip. Nike was the brand that skaters wore in their off-time. Everyone wore Nikes as "chillers." Factor in that Nike was also the home of Michael Jordan and later Kobe Bryant, and it's hard not to want to be associated with that type of greatness. Beyond this, Paul's father is a celebrity who built his name through hard work. He knew nothing about skateboarding but he *damn* sure understood Nike.

Arriving at the Nike junction took real work on the part of Paul and his manager, Circe Wallace (see page 236). In my conversation with Paul, he told me he admired two non-skateboarders in his life, Michael Jordan and Bruce Lee, for their determination and work ethic, and how each set the standard for others to aspire to. Paul wanted to accomplish a similar feat.

Twenty years into the partnership, it's clear that P-Rod's decision to take a chance on Nike SB benefited all of skateboarding. It triggered other skaters to join the team but also forced Nike to make skater-friendly marketing and commit to real engagement in efforts to elevate skateboarding's profile both IRL and in the media.

While there are numerous Nike videos that show P-Rod and other members of the team, my favorite is the 2009 *Today Was a Good Day*, a reinterpretation of the Ice Cube song. On that day, he had an amazingly good day in L.A., making every trick he attempted without having to run from security or the police after a session, finding perfect spots while meeting up with the crew of Eric Koston and Theotis Beasley, then getting dapped by the man himself, Kobe Bryant. Every aspect of the day is perfect up until Ice Cube appears and runs over P-Rod's board in his '64 Impala.

I happened to be there the day they were filming, at Loyola Marymount University. Watching Eric and P-Rod shredding across campus, it looked like gathering footage on any random day. In L.A., it's not uncommon to see pro skaters "stacking skate clips" for their next video part across the city. But turns out they were shooting the commercial with Kobe, making it extraordinary.

That video placed P-Rod and skateboarding on the level with the other Nike superstars. In exchange, P-Rod added a level of newness and flair to Nike, and Nike got a dose of the street that it can't get in the same way from basketball, football, or other organized sports. The simple nod and fist bump with Kobe equated to mutual respect. If there was anyone who might move regular sports fans over into the skateboarding column, Kobe could.

Turns out joining Nike wouldn't be the only arena where P-Rod would be the rising tide that lifted all boats. This time to fully become his own man, more than to make a name for himself, he sought to own the things he built. P-Rod launched Primitive Skateboarding with Andy Netkin. Although Andy would eventually move on, Primitive remains a highly influential and successful skateboarding company. Remember the "terror squad"? Paul would offer a home to Devine Calloway, and bring in Heath Brinkley as team manager. Heath himself had been the filmer for CityStars. Additionally, Paul would employ 'Reem's tactic of bringing in unknown skaters and unleashing them on the world: Brian Peacock, Carlos Ribeiro, Robert Neal, Marek Zaprazny, and Franky Villani. Throw in a mix of the other Brazilians, like Giovanni Vianna and Skater of the Year nominee Tiago Lemos, the million-dollar man. The bench is *deeeep*, and Primitive is crushing it. With several other companies under his belt, Paul Rodriguez—the golden child and a once-in-a-decade talent—politicked his way into the C-suite with signature finesse.

Now, after 10 years at his own board company, with medals in numerous Street League Skateboarding events, P-Rod the executive retired from contests, but clearly ain't retired from skateboarding. Every day the 'gram is putting up new clips getting tricks back-to-back with new talent in his state-of-the-art indoor skatepark that leaves your grandma shakin' her head.

The man. The shoes. The medals. The vids. The accolades. The brands. The team. One of *TransWorld SKATEboarding*'s most influential skaters of all time—and I'm calling it.

P-Rod. The Truth. The End.

MACBA, the Museum of Contemporary Art of Barcelona, or the Museo de Arte Contemporáneo de Barcelona, to call it by its government name, is a famed part of skateboarding's history. Located in the historic El Raval neighborhood in Barcelona, MACBA and its sister spots Parallel, Bibliotec, and Black Marble have become a second home to pro skaters around the world and a meetup spot for countless others from Spain and across the globe.

The actual museum opened in 1995, right at the time when U.S. pro skaters, with their photographers and videographers in tow, were really learning to spread their wings and look for locales that might add a new visual story to skateboarding's panorama. It also coincided with the absolute ticketing craziness and outlawing of skateboarding around the U.S. Skaters were not only burned out on skating the same urban street spots, but getting tired of being hassled by "the man" when they were simply trying to do their job.

Enter Macba, and Plaça dels Àngels (the 1000m² of public space outside the museum), and the skater who really kicked it all off, luminary Enrique Lorenzo. The Spanish national earned his spot on the famed World Industries team by sending in a "sponsor me" videotape. Lacking English skills but fluent in skateboarding prowess, he is one of the only skaters to earn a pass and join the ranks of L.A.'s finest, including Daewon Song (see page 28) and Rodney Mullen (see page 54). As Enrique told me, he'd admired the beauty of Barcelona's architecture for years. It was simply built for skating, from dusk till dawn. "People would say, 'Whatever, man.' If it was that good, why hadn't they seen any of it in the magazines before?" he told me, laughing. As hard as it is to believe now, few outside of the skaters in Spain had borne witness to the majesty that is MACBA and Barcelona as a whole. Enrique himself was a second-generation street skater from the city and has been unabashed in saying that as much of a legend as he is to all of us in skateboarding, he wasn't even as good as the ones who came before him or grew up around him—he was simply the one who got out.

Enrique described "magical, mystical MACBA" as the K'un-Lun of skateboarding, a place where skaters could film and train endlessly. He enticed skaters with tales of marble stairs, ledges that go on forever, out ledges, and the like. It also had a spot for manuals, short stairs, wide stairs all on just one side of the building! MACBA, where the streets were paved with gold—or at least smooth, endless marble and granite. What skaters need more than anything is space, and MACBA has the space and the ground and the obstacles.

Hearing Enrique tell it, there isn't anywhere better designed for skateboarding. That's without even going to the other side of the museum. Back then there was a giant roughly story and a half high, set of four stairs (now reduced to three due to construction). All with smooth ground on the runup and landing. Oh, and did he forget to mention that around the corner of that there's a *biblioteca* with a set of descending ledges along with another set of banks to skate? Oh, and there is also . . . yep, the list went on as Enrique propagated the legend of MACBA.

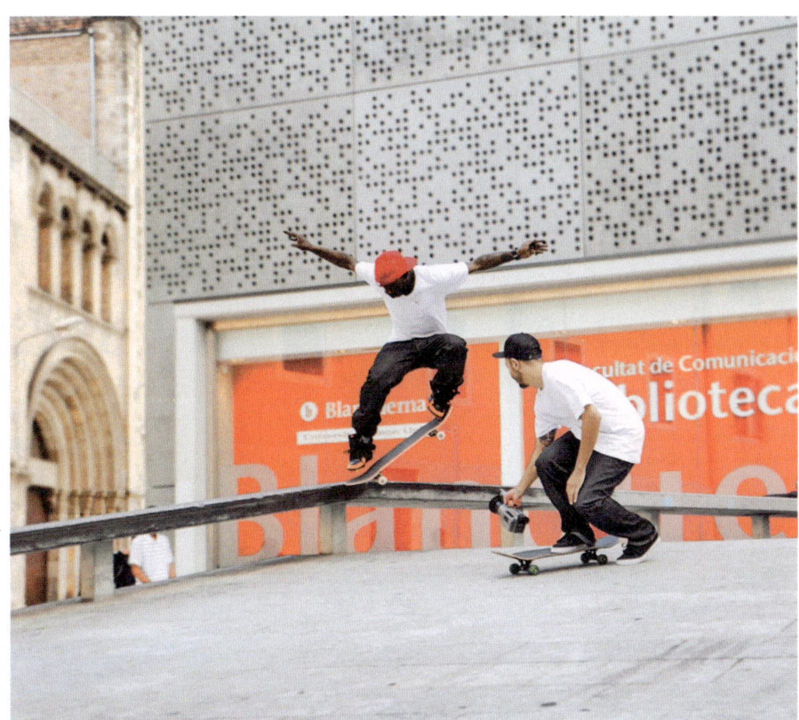

Top: Stevie Williams, nollie–
crooked grind at Biblioteca,
Facultat Comunicació, Barcelona

Bottom: Local skater at Paral·lel
in Barcelona

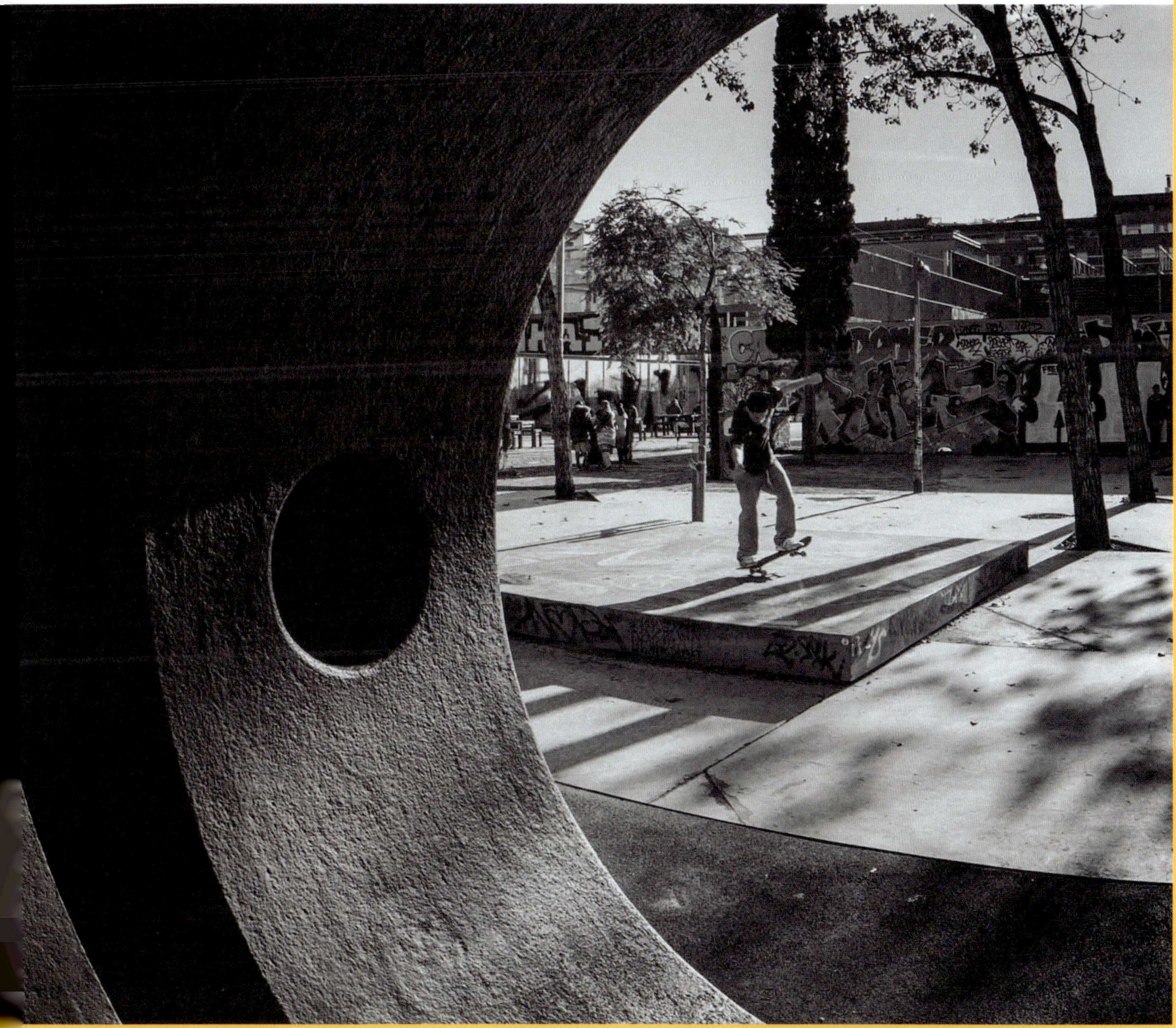

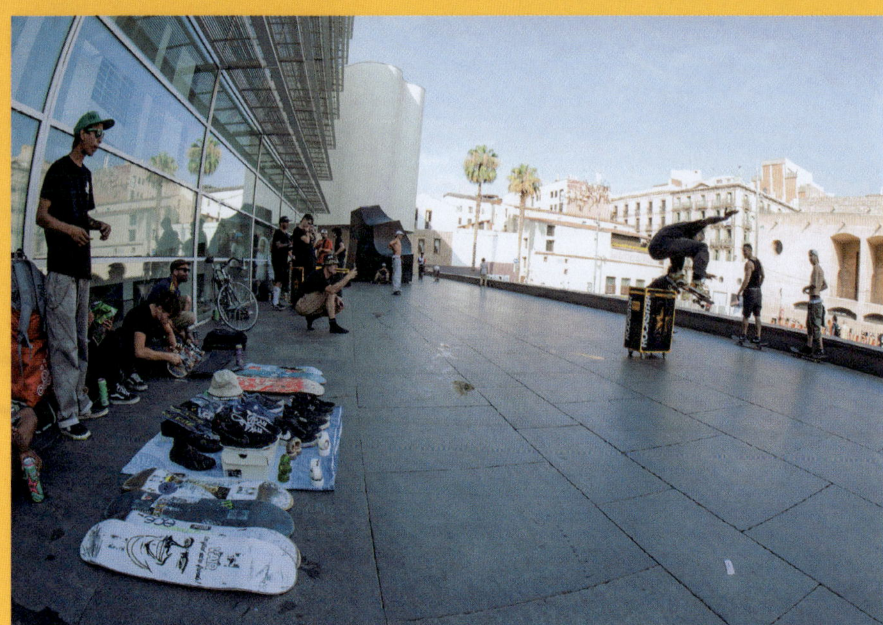

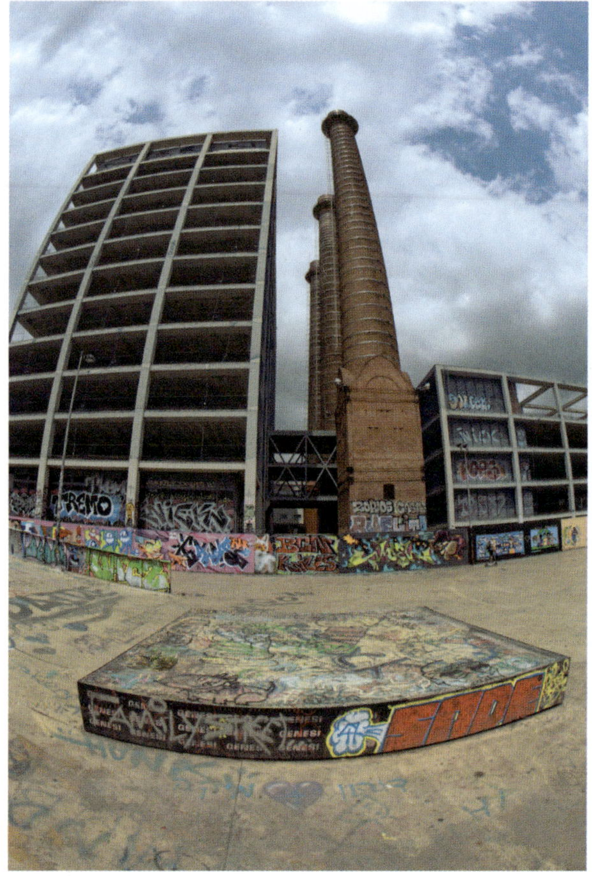

Then one day the dam broke. Too many pro skaters were getting tickets skating in the U.S., one too many security guards was tackling skaters to the ground. Everyone had simply had enough. You couldn't film your video part or get photos without being harassed. Give me a ticket for an air-o-plane. Skaters needed more freedom and novel places to skate undisturbed and get their mojo back again. They also wanted two-euro beers, siestas, and a lovely nightlife and population—they just didn't know it yet.

Enter MACBA. When the World team finally arrived in the mid-'90s, they realized, Enrique—he ain't no lie. MACBA was paradise lost and now reclaimed. Quickly word spread and every U.S. skateboarding team headed to BCN. Not only did they come to film their video parts but with the exchange rate at that time, whole teams would post up in BCN for months. It became *the* place to get work done away from the stress, pressure, and visibility of the U.S. Skaters would enjoy the day, then at dusk move onward into the nightlife and all the spoils of the war from battling it out skating through the day.

Of course, you're wondering if tourists visiting the museum were catching strays from the ungodly number of skaters practicing in front of the museum. Well, as luck would have it, over time, with so many skaters coming, a deal was struck. Skaters were allowed use of the space out front as long as they weren't interfering with museum visitors' ingress and egress. The tentative truce famously forged between one head security guard and the skateboarding world breathed life into a scene of epic proportions.

MACBA remains a proving ground and *the* meetup spot. Skaters moved, loved, skated, and, most important, filmed a lifetime of skateboarding there and eventually at all of the spots throughout Barcelona.

You can even follow MACBA's Instagram account (@macbalife) to see the latest men and women ripping and slaying the concrete dream of the city. While there are modern changes to the dynamics of the scene, some things remain the same. Every summer skaters still show up to live the good life and experience a change of pace that reminds us the best things in life are skateable.

TONY ALVA

The most heralded skater of his generation

Z-Boy who jump-started a movement

First pro skater to launch his own brand, Alva Skates

TA. The initials say it all. Tony Alva. Totally awesome. In some eras, mhm, totally arrogant. Today? Totally awe-inspiring.

Few skaters have been the defining persona of their era, and during the '70s, it was the often imitated but never duplicated original bad boy, Tony Alva. As Glen E. Friedman told me, "Tony Alva is the best natural skateboarder I've seen in my life and the talent of his generation."

TA set the tone for all of skateboarding. It's not only that he was a part of coastal Venice, California's—and then the whole damn world's—celebrated Zephyr competition team; it's that he was the gnarliest of them all. The first to pull airs in pools, the first to win every category there was. He was child of the '70s, and the wildness that sparked his career might not have fit in with traditional sports of the time, but it fit perfectly in this new iteration of skateboarding.

The '70s era of skateboarding, when TA and the Z-Boys burst on the scene, is fabled, but it was so powerful because skateboards were still considered toys by the general public. Many early enthusiasts were just learning how to stand on or work *with* a skateboard. What TA and the Z-Boys (and later Z-Flex) team did was show us that skateboarding could be an extension of the self. Driven by the surfers running low-low in the waves like Buttons Kaluhiokalani, who put the swag in surfing in Hawai'i, the Z-Family took that style and turned it on its ear by bringing it to the streets and exploring the city. TA and the Zephyr team cut their teeth surfing the boneyard, the derelict Pacific Ocean Park near the Santa Monica Pier, a wasteland of debris. Cutting through that space day after day bred a surfer who could navigate the seas and a skater who could shoot for the stars.

While the entire team burst on the scene in 1975 and turned skateboarding on its head with their radical interpretation of flow, style, and aggression, it was TA who became the face of the team. Known as "Mad Dog," he feared nothing and would accept any challenge. When his crew barged backyard pools and revolutionized skating, TA was often the first one to drop in and prove his mettle, and the last one to leave. As their style of pool skating moved to new heights, with skaters carving the pool walls higher and higher, it was TA who tamed the tiger by blasting an air out of the pool, piercing the sky and bringing it home to terra firma. Radical!

If that was all Tony Alva did, it would have been enough. He jump-started an entire style of skateboarding and reset the status quo for the sport.

That wasn't all that happened, however. He went on to set the tone for what it meant to be a pro skateboarder. How? By striking out on his own and leaving Zephyr to start his own brand, Alva Skates.

With that, the first pro skater–owned company was born and Mad Dog blew down doors. He was radical in the pools and radical in the ads, and with his racially ambiguous look, wild curly hair, and caramel skin, he was the "other" and he was not scared of that shit. From the first images of him holding a stuffed cheetah head to his lure as the ultimate Z-Boy as written by C. R. Stecyk in the original pages of *Skateboarder* magazine, the mythos was there and the apple set to be plucked from the tree.

Pluck he did. Truthfully, why not? Only so many stars could stay in one place at the time.

While his leaving the Z-Family would eventually cause the breakup of the gang, it also sparked a skater-owned revolution, and TA got the money and notoriety he felt he deserved. He was the greatest skater on the planet: to the victor go the spoils. However, beneath the bravado and the need to dominate in competitions was a tension: his home life. Growing up in a rocky family situation with his mother and various difficult father figures, he rebelled against the world. That rebellion put him in an insecure place that could be fed only by adulation and, eventually, substance abuse.

Part of it, of course, was the era itself, the '70s and early '80s. TA was a rock star. He was in the Hollywood scene, skating the backyard pools of stars, getting the girls, the money, and the fame. It was a time of easy access and excess. What was entirely on him, however, was his infamous attitude—the other interpretation of the TA name, Total Asshole. Unfortunately that moniker came from those who loved him, too. It was them against the world in the Z-Boys and Dogtown days but also TA against everybody else. With his eventual departure and signature brand, he clearly signaled no need to claim the "Z" moniker. However, it was also made clear when it was Jay Adams, not Alva, who kept the Zephyr name alive under the name Z-Flex and brought over original Zephyr team members—Japanese American Shogo Kubo; Canadian American Paul Constantineau; and the first African American pro skateboarder, Marty Grimes, to the roster.

But back now to TA: Alva Skates, on the surface, was a showstopper. Tony continued to rack up wins and sell boards and eventually bought himself the true markers of the American Dream: a house and a Cadillac in the driveway.

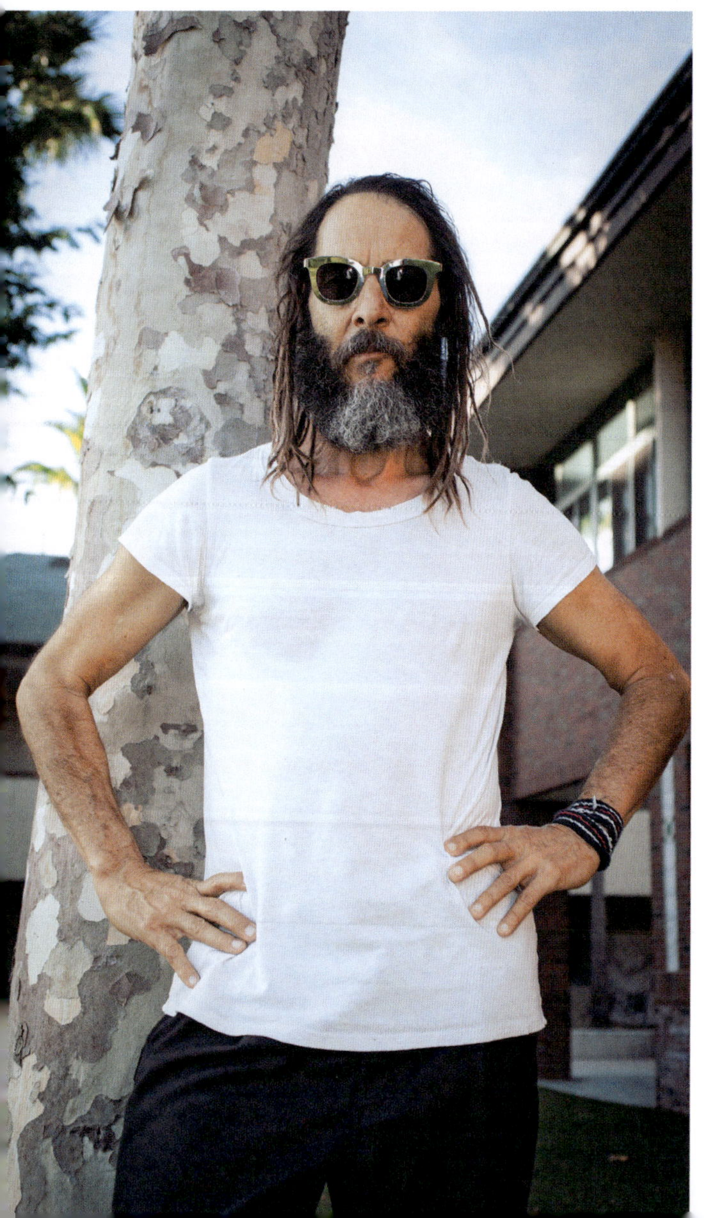

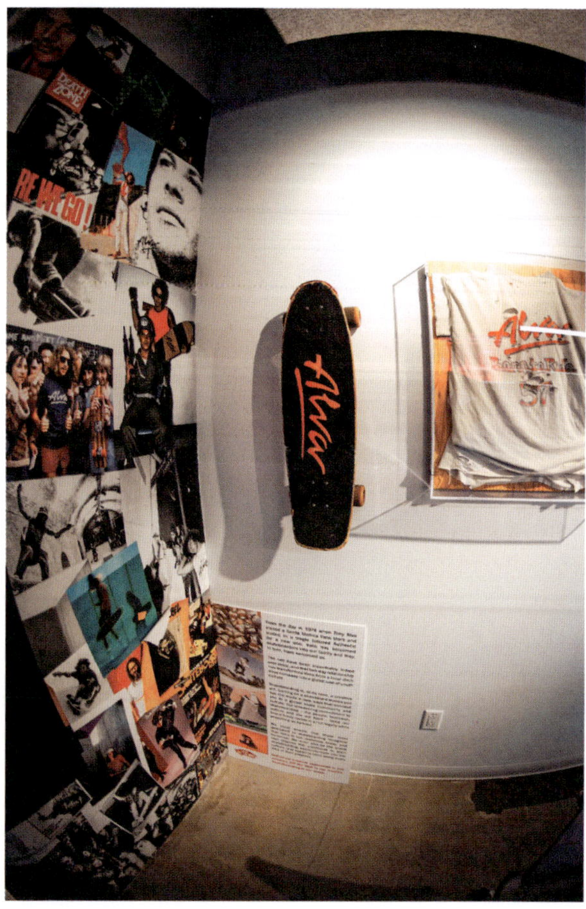

Besides the ripping skating and the competitive spirit, Tony had another highly sought-after skill: the ability to spot talent. He not only created his own brand but acquired what is now a who's who of athletic prowess for his teams. A short list includes names you may recognize: Christian "Holmes" Hosoi, Tony Hawk, and Mark "Gonz" Gonzales. What was difficult during that time was TA's ego. The brand was Alva Skates, and all things remained Tony's intellectual property. You could not outshine him; coming up with ideas yourself was off-limits. Plus, those legendary skaters were all in their teens at the time. When Tony did something that upset them, of which there were multiple incidents, they became crestfallen and it would ultimately cause some of those relationships to sour.

Despite all that, in the mid-'80s his company would sponsor a huge tear of amazing skaters. These were adults like Eddie Reategui, Stevie Dread, Bill Danforth, and others. This crew of black-leather-clad skaters (some of whose key members would eventually form their own subgroup known as the Daggers) took the skate world by storm in their own way. They skated in backyard pools but also ruled the sky in the vert skating that was popular then. The famed Alva posse, which ran nearly 20 pro skaters deep, was a terror and force to be reckoned with. Their bad-ass rocker vibe (with behavior to match at times) would be immortalized on film during a Chicago team photo shoot. That image would become a defining moment of '80s skateboarding cool.

During their heyday, the Alva name was good in the streets with amazing skaters in Texas, California, and on the East Coast. A new generation of skaters knew Alva and the brand name. This all came crashing down again as vert and pool declined and street skating became skateboarding's ultimate form. In the late '80s and early '90s, the Alva brand fell out of favor with the newest upstarts. TA himself would have problems with the locals in the Venice and Santa Monica territory he once ruled like a king.

This did not stop him from figuring out a new plan, and Alva Skates was rebranded as New School Skateboards. With Tony in the first ad, standing behind the newest skaters on the roster, names like Mario Rubalcaba and Noah Salasnek came to the fore. The brand had moderate success with those great skaters and held its own in the market, with few aware that TA was truly behind it all.

Flash forward from the 1990s to the aughts and the Alva name comes back into the fold. TA has undergone rehab and fully embraced sobriety since 2006. He found religion and repaired his reputation

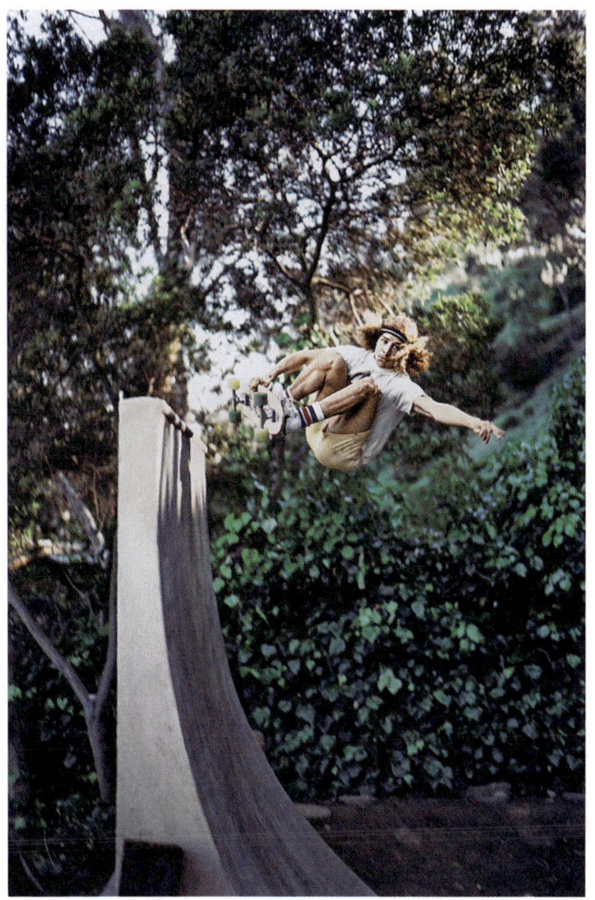

Opposite left: Tony Alva

Opposite right: the Tony Alva Room at Van's HQ

Above: Tony Alva, textbook frontside air

with a brand that he helped integrate into the minds of the global skate consciousness, Vans.

TA was an early adopter of Vans sneakers, and they became the defining shoes for skateboarding for generations due in part to TA's original endorsement. Newly clean and ready to do the work, TA set out to be a better person and let his demons rest. This all happily coincided with the release of *Dogtown and Z-Boys*, the 2001 documentary by Stacy Peralta and Glen E. Friedman. The film would be turned into the 2005 major motion picture *Lords of Dogtown*, which propelled all of the Z-Family back into the spotlight.

Since then, it has been a nonstop ride of touring globally with Vans and still delivering unforgettable skateboarding even now that TA's in his late 60s. Tony's bravado is gone but not his spark. He remains a founder of the culture and has recently become a grandfather, ready to impart the lessons from a hard-won battle with life.

THE MICHAEL JORDAN OF SKATEBOARDING

KAREEM CAMPBELL

Hall of Fame inventor of the ghetto bird

Put the hood in the high-rise, the projects in the penthouse

Millionaire mogul who launched, nurtured, and sold multiple brands

Pioneering POC in *Tony Hawk's Pro Skater*

"Don't talk about it—be about it." This mantra characterizes the exploits and accomplishments of Kareem Campbell, the man Tony Hawk dubbed the Michael Jordan of Skateboarding. Campbell's maxim produced an unprecedented run of athleticism, business, and influence, and introduces a tale of Black ingenuity par excellence. An endorsement from 'Reem is an angel investment. His lifetime achievements pass any fact-check.

Dominant in contests? Affirmative: beast mode since day one. Sneakerhead turned footwear and apparel mogul? Confirmed. Cinderella'd startups from inception to institution? Unquestionably. Mentor to the greatest in skateboarding? Two words: Paul Rodriguez. Ambassador for skateboarding worldwide? One title: *Tony Hawk's Pro Skater*. Congratulations, Mr. Campbell, GOAT level achieved!

But before the games, fames, and vids with Lil Wayne, Harlem-born and Los Angeles–raised Kareem Campbell's enviable career took shape unpretentiously in the mid- to late 1980s. A disciple of two OG Venice pros—Latinx Jesse Martinez and Asian American Jef Hartsel—Campbell proved right at home amid L.A. street politics and occasional gang warfare. Sunup to sundown, 'Reem—or

'Reemo, as he's affectionately known—could be found cutting his teeth on the ramp owned by Cesario "Block" Montano, a godfather of Latinx skate and celebrity photography.

Once Campbell's grit, bravado, and athleticism aligned, Hartsel ushered him into World Industries' fledgling skateboarding team. In the early days, this scrappy upstart with crudely crafted decks somehow held its own against the behemoth brands of the day. (Aptly known as the "big five," these brands and their subsidiaries were Powell Peralta, NHS / Santa Cruz, Tracker Trucks / *Transworld SKATEboarding*, Vision [Schmtt Stix and Sims], and Independent Trucks / *Thrasher*. Gordon and Smith also held a storied history in both surf and skateboarding.)

Cunningly, World embraced its low budgets, lo-fi production, and even lower-brow humor, all of which enchanted skateboarders. This David and Goliath approach transformed the rules of engagement, turning brawn into bloat and poking a finger in the eye of companies that had more money than a mint but were disconnected from the skaters they claimed to serve. Their neglect left skateboarding open to a changing of the guard. Enter 'Reemo.

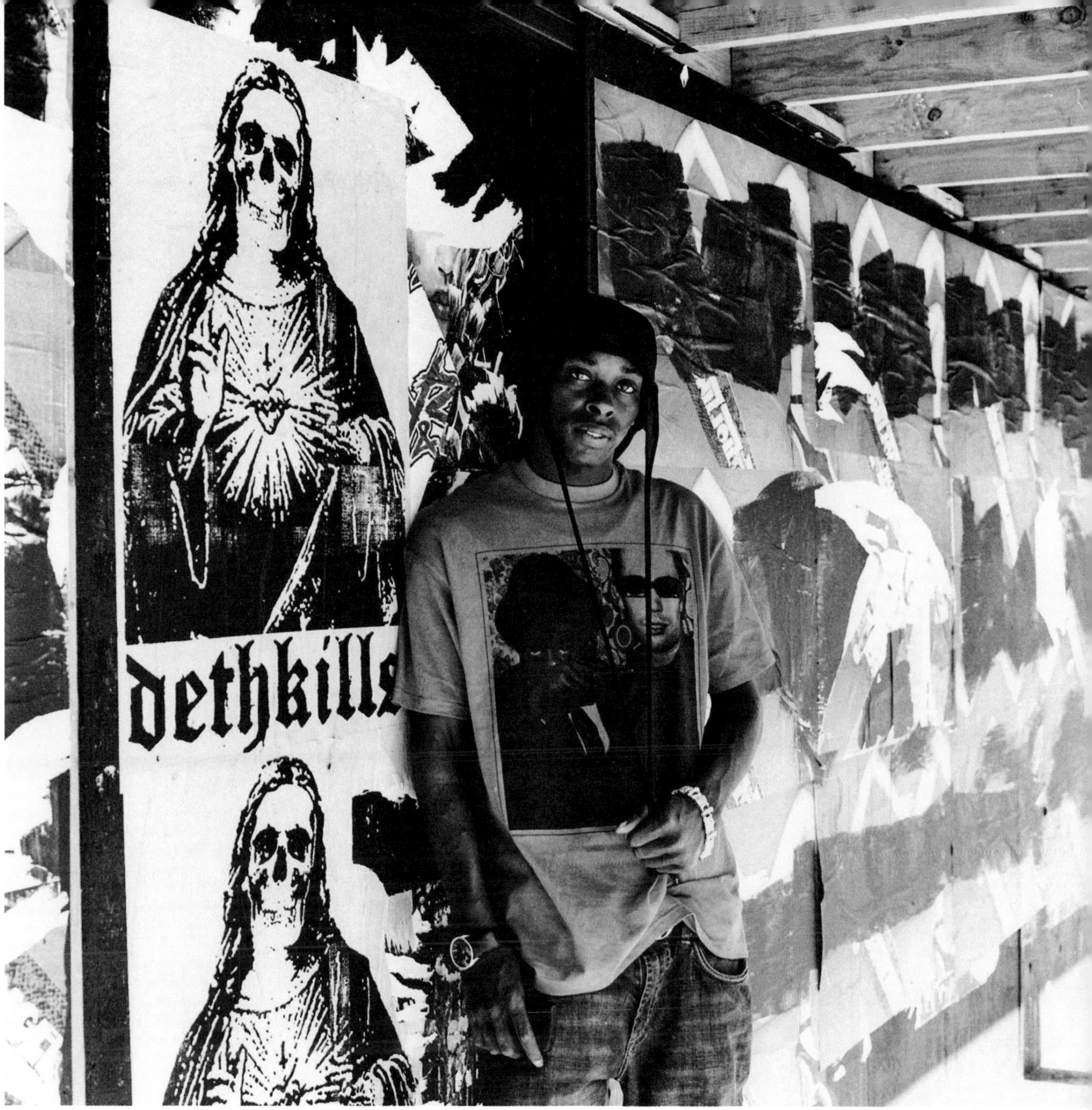

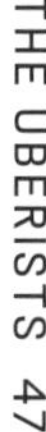

Blossoming under the storied tutelage of World's owners—the mad scientist Rodney Mullen (see page 54) and Steve "Take No Prisoners" Rocco—Campbell's precocious personality, Harlem hustle, and pro-Black agenda made him a natural leader among the team's cadre of fearless BIPOC skaters. Campbell became part of a new generation of street skaters who utilized their cities' stairs, handrails, and walls as urban laboratories. This new wave of skaters tested security guards, property owners, and the limits of their imagination and physical prowess, all at breakneck speed.

Those responsible for capturing 1990s zeitgeist on tape and celluloid found a gold mine in Kareem's grace and agility. Few skaters looked more natural and at ease in front of the lens. Even a failed attempt by 'Reem appeared more breathtaking than the successes of many of his contemporaries. This alchemical presentation made him one of the most in-demand professionals of the era—a master of existing tricks and an innovator who added a blast of wildfire to every session.

A quintessential expression of that daring came in 1991 during the most famous of the European contests, Germany's Münster Monster Mastership. Against his team manager's wishes for him to skate conservatively, Campbell unveiled what quickly became a signature trick: the ghetto bird, a whirlwind of muscled contortion. (Or, more technically: a nollie hardflip to late-backside 180.) Flashing his million-dollar smile, Campbell launched his NBD (never-been-done) trick into a decisive podium-earning finish.

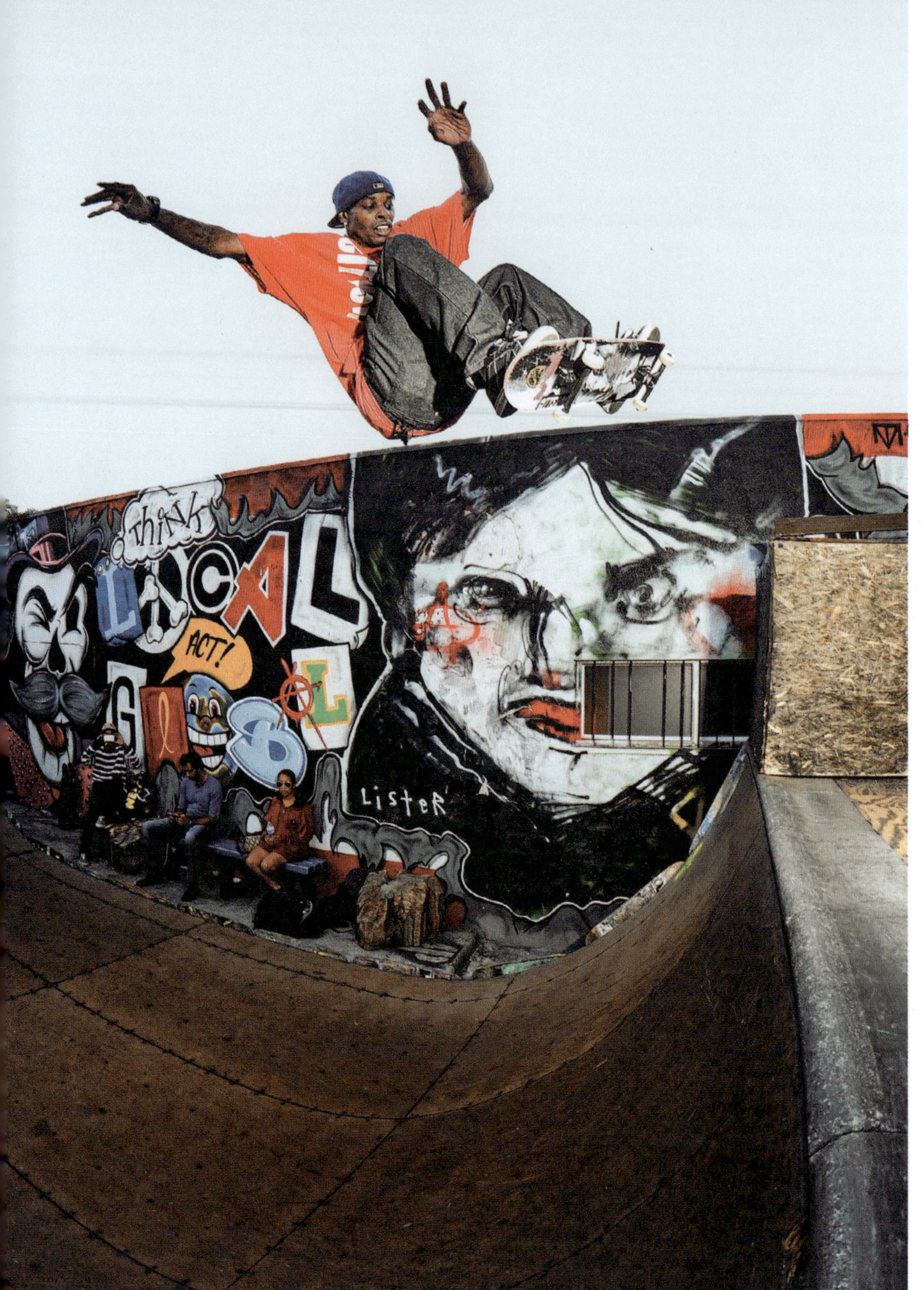

Kareem Campbell, 360–flip to fakie at Brooklyn Projects in L.A.

burgeoning skate superstars via friendly competitions and pseudo rivalries between the brands he owned or co-owned under his appropriately named Mastermind Distribution.

By the aughts, Menace would mature into the global brand CityStars. Campbell's kicks company, Axion Footwear, would become home to a pride of influential young skaters, including one of the world's all-time most wholesome and decorated skateboarders, the then–child prodigy Paul "P-Rod" Rodriguez (see page 36).

Campbell's avant-garde attitude set ablaze norms that had placed player/owner status beyond the reach of BIPOC athletes. That's why 'Reem's story is highly personal for me. Across the globe, for skaters of color like myself, 'Reem embodied the Black hammer smashing through every sports norm that evaluates Black bodies for our brawn rather than our brilliance. 'Reem recognized that glass ceilings were designed for shattering and freed himself from limitations. Even more profoundly, he released the rest of us—the greatest of gifts.

Campbell's boss-like movements extended to every aspect of his life. He effortlessly navigated skating the city's underbelly at dawn. Middays were spent meeting with Fortune 500 CEOs. Then on weekends, he'd apply his no-holds-barred approach from creative to competitions.

Plus, those glorious nights. Always a master of ceremonies, 'Reemo was never one to miss out on a happening. There was that time in Amsterdam, that chaos in Paris, and even that time in Houston when we were at . . . actually, I probably can't talk about that. Suffice to say, there were *times*—and 'Reemo was at the center of them all. Jamming with Travis Barker. Photo shoots with Mario Testino. Music

That effort alone would have secured his place in skate history. The open frontier of skateboarding, however, allowed Campbell to apply his trailblazing approach beyond the physical. Here, Campbell's greatest trick emerged—the ability to visualize trends, identify talent, develop multiple competing brands, and capitalize on them all.

Akin to Shawn "Jay-Z" Carter's development of a unique sound, an undeniable appeal, and a squad that influenced the game, Campbell ushered in early urban trends—first by himself and later through protégés. Debuting with Ghetto Wear clothing and then Menace skateboards (both decidedly influenced by '90s gritty hardcore hip-hop), Campbell brought street swag and "urban" culture into the action sports lexicon. Xeroxing the Roc-A-Fella playbook, he cultivated videos with Pharrell, Lil Wayne, and the Game. Kareem Campbell stood shoulder to shoulder with A-listers across fields, always carrying the realness of a 100 percent skateboarder into every interaction.

In the greatest testament to Campbell's influence connecting the boulevard to the boardroom, Tony Hawk presented Kareem with the ultimate level-up—a playable character in the *Tony Hawk's Pro Skater* (*THPS*) video game franchise. While not the only POC in the iconic game, Campbell was the first African American pro skater featured back when *THPS* debuted.

"DON'T TALK ABOUT IT— BE ABOUT IT."

Campbell's inclusion showed that Black people were originators in the sport and deserving of a place in the imagination of countless would-be skaters' first forays into e-sports. His presence as a giant in skateboarding, draped in attire relatable to BIPOC communities, signaled to African American players that skateboarding existed for them even if they didn't look or dress like Hawk or fit a stereotypical Southern California image. Across the globe, everyday gamers and famous fans like Denzel Washington utilized Campbell's avatar to connect to a critical thread of Afrofuturism—the idea that Black people might exist not only in the physical world but the virtual one, too.

Kareem's ability to break barriers and develop community helped drive the immense popularity of his brands. This widespread appeal was partially responsible for private equity firm SPC's acquisition of World Industries in 1998 for $29 million (roughly $48 million in today's dollars). The sale and financial windfall eventually allowed him to bring his brands CityStars and Axion under his own distribution, where they live today.

Kareem Campbell's success stemmed from using skateboarding to transform what could easily have been a life as "state property" into a state of imagined possibilities. CityStars' motto, "Every city has a star," and Axion's, "Don't talk about it—be about it," continue to resonate from the flatlands to the favelas, sustaining and inspiring skaters across the globe. I've seen MLB and NFL Hall of Famers chase him with paparazzi in tow just to take selfies "for their kids." In Brazil, in Cuba, and in points beyond, any young skater with a little bit of street swagger and skills on board eventually becomes dubbed the little 'Reem or 'Reemo of the barrio. The man is a force of nature—locally known and internationally respected.

Proof of the importance of 'Reem's place as the progenitor of street style finally came full circle in 2020. Influential white pro skater Chad Muska politely declined his induction into the Skateboarding Hall of Fame in a show of solidarity and requested that Campbell be inducted in his place, an acknowledgment of Campbell as the most significant influence on the urban aesthetic that had allowed Muska to flourish. With this gauntlet thrown, and the racial reckoning ignited by the murder of George Floyd and by the Black Lives Matter movement, in 2021 the Skateboarding Hall of Fame addressed a glaring omission and at long last inducted one of the greatest of all time, the legendary Kareem Campbell.

SELEMA MASEKELA

Authentic voice for action sports

VP of culture for the X Games

Built a new kingdom for BIPOC action sports enthusiasts

Musician, producer, actor, singer, and director

Skateboarding and action sports culture can move blindingly fast, with some elite athletes and wunderkinds sprouting from the brow like Minerva. They explode onto the scene and impact skateboarding culture through their presence, charisma, and soul. Selema Masekela is one of those individuals.

Disruption is in the Masekela bloodline: Selema is the son of Hugh Masekela, the legendary jazz trumpeter and political activist (an ally and friend to Nelson Mandela) who spent three decades exiled from apartheid-ridden South Africa. During his expatriation, Hugh added his jazz and rhythm and blues to the U.S. and global musical conversations. Unable to be seen as a first-class citizen at home, he used his music to spit fire at the formalized segregation and discrimination imposed within his home country, and caught the ear of the world.

Hugh was a fighter since the beginning; jazz great Dizzy Gillespie sent him a trumpet in support of his talent and leadership of an all-Black ensemble he helped organize in his youth. Hugh's non-political music even became a part of the U.S. Black experience. I first heard of him through my mother, who continually played his remake of "Grazing in the Grass," a number-one hit on Black radio.

Despite humble and oppressed beginnings, the Masekela name grew in prominence through the exploits of family members such as Selema's aunt Barbara, an activist and poet and a seminal figure in the African National Congress.

Operating beyond his father's footsteps (and at times his wishes), Selema created his own waves and riddims. He earned one of the most visible roles in the history of action sports media, hosting the X Games in the late '90s, when it was still in its infancy. On some early telecasts, Selema stood shoulder to shoulder with the ESPN-dubbed "Birdman," Tony Hawk. Beamed into millions of household television sets worldwide, the visages of both men grew synonymous with action sports.

While the cool and collected Selema always looked at home onscreen, few know of his original reluctance to take the mic. In fact, it required a substantial leap of faith to even apply for the gig. Besides working as an intern at the *TransWorld SKATEboarding* magazine office, where he announced a few local contests, he also worked part-time at a local Southern California skate and surf shop. Despite Selema's excellence on the sales floor and dynamic rapport with repeat customers, the white owner relieved him of his position due to a misguided belief that a Black man who surfed

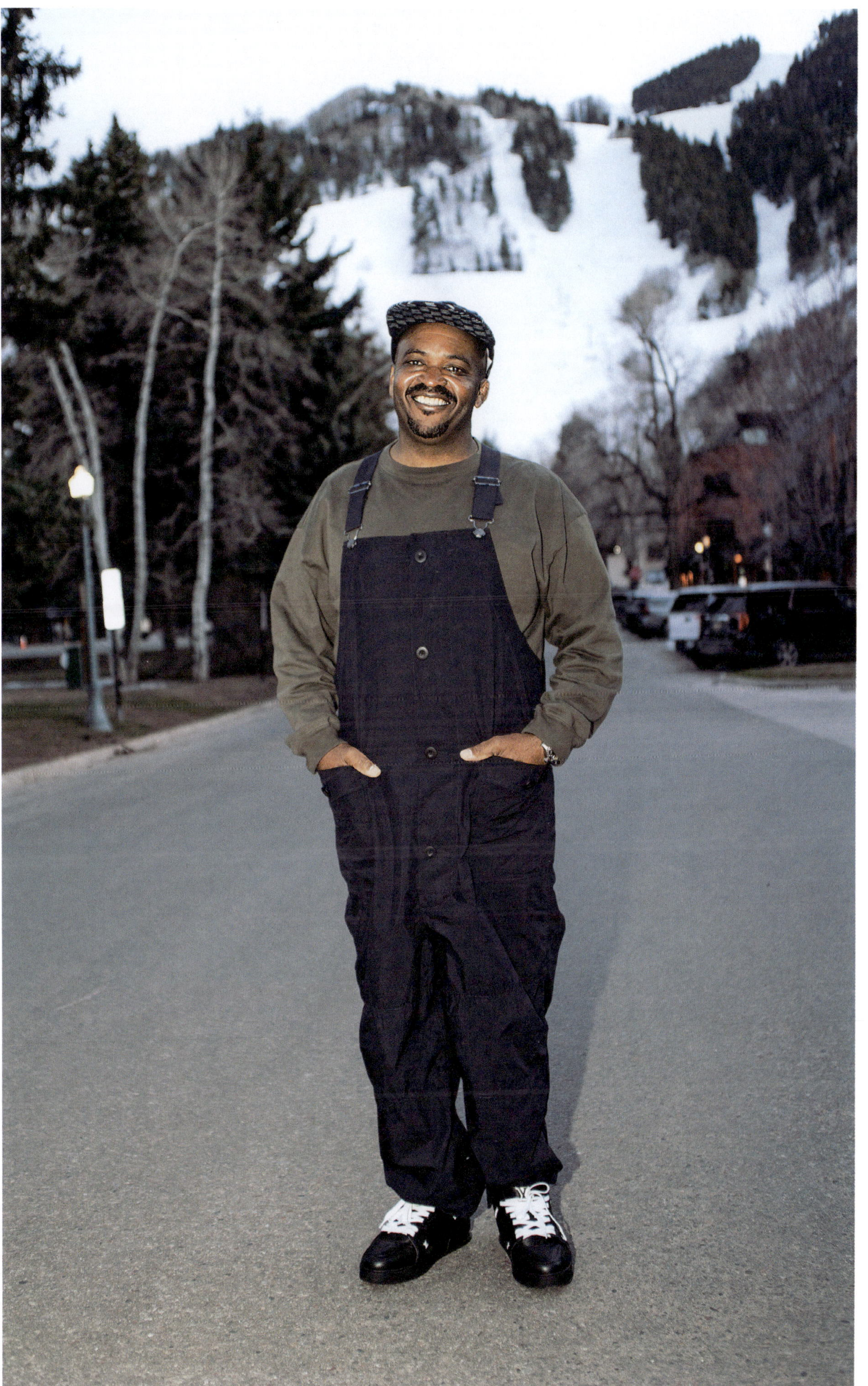

and sold surfboards was too progressive and bad for business.

This trauma stayed with Selema, igniting a fire to improve the representation of Black people in action sports. His career as an announcer began slowly with Board Aid at Snow Summit, a nascent snow and music festival focused on AIDS awareness. Gaining confidence at the mic, he made an impression on those in the action sports space, even landing an audition with the MTV Sports & Music Festival. Though he didn't get that gig, he remained undeterred and in the game, looking for any

ONCE HE WAS BITTEN BY THE BUG, HOWEVER, NOTHING COULD CHANGE YOUNG SELEMA'S LOVE OF THE HOLY TRINITY: SKATEBOARDING, SURFING, AND SNOWBOARDING.

opportunity to flex his knowledge. It was a moment of X Games rebranding in 1999 that would lead him to become an undeniable force in the history of action sports media.

Selema's presence painted the X Games as hip, even when its owner, Bristol, Connecticut–based ESPN, was a traditionalist sports enterprise light-years away from anything innovative. Action sports lacked a natural voice of legitimacy within the walls of ESPN. No one really knew the histories and nuances until Selema. This made him the perfect choice for an X Games announcer when the games were still under ESPN.

Originally from New York and raised in northern San Diego, the transplanted Selema found himself amid the literal dreamscape of action sports. Big Bear was a short drive away for the powder days, surfing for the soul was just off the shoreline and, of course, skateboarding is for #everydamnday.

His father understood that Selema was an avid enthusiast of all these activities, but what could you do with action sports (or alternative sports, as it was called then)? After being exiled from South Africa, fleeing apartheid, and becoming one of the most famous jazz musicians in the world, the elder Masekela lived a life with incredible stakes. When envisioning a future for the young Selema, living in the U.S.—a land of opportunity (albeit a problematic one)—and earning a living were real priorities, as in so many immigrant families. As many families in that situation feel, "Sure, you could fall in love with these American leisure activities, but they were not gonna pay the bills."

It all might sound quaint now that we have the Olympics as a reference, and Nyjah Huston (see page 32) and Jagger Eaton (see page 277) walking the Tom Ford catwalk and earning medals, but this was not the case during those early days. Action sports and their potential were new terrain for communities of color trying to get by in America, especially for a recent immigrant family. That's asking for trouble no matter how you slice it. Once he was bitten by the bug, however, nothing could change young Selema's love of the holy trinity: skateboarding, surfing, and snowboarding.

Though he never became a professional athlete, the time spent in the SoCal scene plus his globally informed upbringing manifested in a unique, authentic perspective. Selema offered audiences a comprehensive outlook that engaged with the nuances of international competition. To the benefit of the X Games and all involved, the son of music royalty became the everyman capable of balancing reverence and relationships with the guests and other commentators.

Regardless of position, he played his part exceptionally well. Selema would dole out X Games gold, then turn around and catch choruses with everyone from Rage Against the Machine to Radiohead, No Doubt to Nas. Leave it to Selema to show up and show out, rolling with a Wu-Tang visit, only later revealing that he shared history with celebrity guests like Method Man and others, derived from an early stint in New York City. If it happened in the culture, Selema was there, putting Black people on the action sports map daily. The combination of preternatural calm when dealing with stars and technical calamities, a smile for the ages, and those signature dreadlocks created a complete win and saluted to and for BIPOC culture. He showed the world that BIPOC folks were present and deserving of a visible role in every aspect of action sports culture. We were Selema and Selema was We.

No good deed goes unpunished, however. As Selema stepped up for us, he took the heat for his prominence. He always heard rumblings and voices of detractors when working to earn his place as a host. Many people outside of action sports questioned the convention of allowing a young Black man to share the stage with the GOATs. Here comes our man, sharing the ramp with Hawk, chasing waves with Kelly Slater, and hitting the pow-pow with Shaun White, operating at dream level and without breaking a sweat. That invites hate.

Selema continued to level up, eventually landing a regular spot hosting on E!, the 2010 FIFA World Cup, and even the 2014 Winter Olympics. He transitioned beyond action sports to bona fide media personality and tastemaker. His easygoing personality even added levity to the animation world when he played a big-bodied walrus in the kids' movie *Surf's Up*.

Over time he would glean what anyone in the limelight learns, that being in front of the camera earns only a fraction of the money, power, and respect that being behind the camera, producing the content, earns. Armed with a more profound and hard-won understanding of the politics affecting his upward trajectory and the value he brought to any franchise, Selema took his undiminished love of action sports into new territories.

Approaching from that vantage point, he moved via a position of strength, a new player who understood the Hollywood chessboard. Exercising new creative control, he moved deeper into the media sphere with his *Red Bull Signature Series* collaboration and then his award-winning *Vice World of Sports* series. These elevated Selema beyond the level of TV host into titles he had always deserved: editor, producer, and leader as the winner of the Producers Guild of America's Outstanding Sports Program award, beating out competition including the fabled Bryant Gumbel. The series evidenced the power of sports to address social change in new ways. Many would not know until later that the win also silently addressed the unwritten, often never-ending, struggle of operating as a Black creative within industry confines.

Oh, and in case the brother's plate wasn't full enough: we all should have predicted that he would eventually add to his family's aural legacy through his new musical endeavor, the R&B and jazzy band Alekesam (Masekela spelled backward).

As influential as his media and musical portfolios are, more transformative is his work with his friend the businessman and community activist Steve Larosiliere to codevelop their nonprofit, Stoked Mentoring. Stoked was a new way to guide young people through the high school experience and keep BIPOC on the mountains, in the surf, and skating in the streets. The endeavor continues to this day, in new hands.

In time with the Black Lives Matter movement and his Paddle Out for George Floyd event and cries for racial and social justice, Selema's latest metamorphosis is one that the world felt. He put all of us on notice when he transformed from Sal to Selema, reclaiming his South African birthright. Part of this change involved a vow to never shrink himself before those who might have a problem with the number of syllables in Selema. This personal act of resistance speaks to his solidarity with everyone working to make BIPOC voices seen and heard.

Furthering this agenda is his newest endeavor, penning the foreword to and developing the *Afrosurf* book and launching Mami Wata surfboards and apparel. These attempts at increasing BIPOC representation in action sports have been sorely needed. Now we witness the son carrying on the work of the father, a true Masekela, placing Africa at the heart of global conversations. It is only fitting that the royal everyman would take his passions and introduce a truly African and American experience into our action sports holy trinity. And his new role as VP of culture for the X Games signals to everyone that BIPOC experiences and histories now have a new platform where they will be included alongside other traditional narratives of action sports. As he launches into these endeavors, wearing a new hat as director of a film by Burton Snowboards and with a leading role at Red Bull supporting BIPOC communities through action sports, Selema continues to aim his heart and energy toward the heavens and an inclusive future. Thankfully, he's bringing us all along for the ride.

THE SAVANT OF SKATEBOARDING AND THE FATHER OF MODERN STREET SKATING AND DECK DESIGN

RODNEY MULLEN

Graduated from "The Mutt" to "The Maestro"

Genius inventor of the flat ground ollie and a host of "Rodney tricks"

Design and engineering marvel whose boards changed the game

Freestyle showman who guided generations to the street

"Neftalie, Rodney Mullen is the most underrated skater of all time." Tony Hawk's statement stunned my USC class on skateboarding and action sports culture. The students had gathered 'round, expecting to hear an obscure name that they might have to google, trekking diligently past the first results page, ultimately turning some forgotten figure into an extra-credit project. Or even worse— that would force them to ask their prof for access to his library of vintage issues of actual physical magazines.

But *Rodney Mullen*? *Our* Rodney Mullen?! The safety of their extra-credit lifeboat may have been deflated, but damn were my students' interests piqued. What did they not know about *Rodney Mullen*?

Is this TED Talk Rodney Mullen with a million-plus views? Rodney Mullen, cofounder of World Industries and later the multiple brands under Dwindle Distribution's umbrella? Rodney Mullen, the chemical engineering dropout with patents under his belt, plus an MIT fellowship? Or just regular ol' mentor Rodney Mullen, responsible for launching hundreds of professional skateboarders' careers across generations, from Chris "Dune" Pastras (see page 79) to Chris Haslam? Dumbfounded, I thought, "Well, I guess it is?" Tony made me think about Rodney Mullen the *person*.

The person who made all these movements quietly, sans fanfare—he just did them because they needed to be done.

Therein lies his genius. Rodney sees things where others do not. Even more so, he institutes change so smoothly that there is no wake, it just becomes part of the fabric of skateboarding, soft as a whisper.

John "Rodney" Mullen was born in 1966 in Gainesville, Florida, hardly the epicenter of skate culture. Growing up within a strict family, the son of a military father turned dentist and a concert pianist mother, Rodney began skating in 1977 when his dad unexpectedly agreed to buy him a board for New Year's Day. For this 11-year-old who previously felt out of place, this prize became a tool for expression. The youngster's creative energy earned rapid reward through a sponsorship by local brand Walker Skateboards.

Under today's rubric, an early sponsorship might lead a path to the Olympics. Back then, the concept of skateboarding as career was sketchy—or a stretch at *best*. The elder Mullen gave Rodney a stern warning: his first major injury would mean the end of his skating career. Though skateboarding did cause Rodney to lose one of his eyeteeth, he evaded his father's capture, learning his routines forward and backward with enough planning and precision to account for every possibility of chance, injury, or imperfection. With maddening dedication, Rodney turned pro at age 14, joining the illustrious Bones Brigade team under the tutelage of former Z-Boy Stacy Peralta. Rodney quickly stood as the undisputed champion of freestyle and remained so for over a decade, eventually winning 36 out of the 37 freestyle contests that he entered. During the 1980s, everyone else was in a battle for second place, because there was no stopping Rodney Mullen. He was the king of freestyle.

But what is it to be king of a land that bears no fruit? In subsequent decades, Rodney would talk about the hollowness of those victories. He lived for creating tricks and exploring the possibilities of skateboarding, not performing for a crowd. He thought about what skateboarding could be, and how it could evolve. Luckily for us, that process of evolution included inventing the flat ground ollie, the kickflip, the heelflip, the 360 flip, the impossible, and so many more. Innovation was exciting; contests and spectacle took away from creative endeavors.

At the height of his freestyle career, in the 1980s, Rodney was the in-demand, one-man showman. Freestyle demonstrations were much less arduous than the vert skateboarding of Christian Hosoi or Tony Hawk. You didn't need jump ramps either, which street skaters like his teammates on the Bones Brigade, Lance Mountain or Tommy Guerrero, used during the mid- to late '80s. Freestyle required only an empty bit of flat ground.

While always grateful to be sponsored, Rodney found that the satisfaction and fun diminished considerably. In retrospect, I only now realize how lonely he must have felt and how mentally taxing the weight of the crown must have been on the introverted Rodney throughout his life. He's always preferred to skate by himself when the world is still and quiet. That remains the case; the best time to reach him is always after midnight, when he can be alone. Art often imitates life, and one of Rodney's most memorable board graphics for Powell Peralta skateboards featured a skull and bones figure performing a Casper stall (standing with one foot on the truck, and one behind the deck in reverse) while twirling its crown. Looking at the image now, it conveys a double meaning. He was overworked, bored in his own world, and without a peer. Luckily, this would change.

Rodney the late-teen phenom rode for Powell Peralta from 1980 to 1988. However, Rodney Mullen, the father figure to a new generation of skaters, emerged only upon finding the yin to his yang in ex–pro freestyler Steve Rocco, who had retired after being bested by Rodney during a contest. When you can't beat 'em, join 'em. With Rocco's coaxing, Rodney would depart Powell. The two would form a symbiotic partnership in late 1988 to early 1989 that would create the company World Industries. Joined by luminary street pro Mike Vallely, who also defected from Powell, the seed of World Industries would grow into a multigenerational, multiracial family tree that became home to generations of phenomenal skateboarders, with Rodney as team manager and fount of invention and design.

The new influx of family within that original World Industries team in the late '80s to early '90s would be pushed by, and in turn challenge, Rodney. The House of Mullen and Rocco included a roll call of skateboarding icons such as Chris "Dune" Pastras, Jason Lee, Jef Hartsel, Jesse "The Mess" Martinez, Randy Colvin, Mike Vallely, Kareem Campbell, Daniel Castillo, Daewon Song, and the team sprite, Chris Branagh. World would eventually house multiple skaters and skater-owned brands like Blind, 101, Enjoi, Darkstar, and Axion Footwear. Ever the satirist, Rocco renamed the company Dwindle Distribution in the mid-aughts.

In 1989, however, they were far from becoming Dwindle Distribution. In those days they were still tuning the company and that required adjustments. Rodney was a world-class skateboarding superstar, and the stronger personalities, independence, and multiracial backgrounds of other World Industries skaters would take him out of his comfort zone. The silence of the Florida farmhouse where he began his career was replaced by a cacophony of musical styles blasted at World headquarters and in the tour van. Team member Jef Hartsel may have been Japanese Korean American, but he was also a Rastafarian, and his roots reggae and Mike Vallely's punk rock battled for aural supremacy against the hip-hop played by then-teens Daniel Castillo, Kareem Campbell, and Daewon Song. You can guess where Rodney's Mozart playlist ended up—dead last.

Beyond new sounds, the team also exposed Rodney to the wonders of navigating the L.A. penal system, via posting bond for Martinez or paying for skating citations for the teen titans, Daniel, Kareem, and Daewon. He also learned the ins and outs of loan shark repayment in those early days of financing with Steve. The country skater nicknamed "The Mutt" for his scraggly hair was now getting lots of exercises in city life. Through it all, Rodney grew a bit more "street" from encountering such a diverse group under the World banner. Some of that street and the interplay between Rodney and the team members would begin to show up in his actual skateboarding.

While he remained the king of freestyle, we all witnessed the beginning of Rodney's transformation into a new sovereign of street at the end of the first World Industries video, *Rubbish Heap*. In that promotional video, then-amateurs Ron Chatman and Jeremy Klein (skateboarding's Lilo and Stitch) destroyed Rodney's freestyle board

RODNEY HANDLED SKATEBOARDING LIKE IT WAS AN EQUATION THAT NEEDED TO BE SOLVED.

with a stomp during his attempt to film for the video. Reading a handwritten note from Rocco that announced that this was Rodney's new board, they tried to force him to ride what was then a regular-size street board. Crushing his board released his imagination, and in that moment Rodney released himself from freestyle's largely stationary style of skating. Heckled by Chatman and Klein, he took the regular-size board and proceeded to unleash a flurry of double kickflips, ollie-impossibles, and 360 flips while pushing through the schoolyard. This was unheard of in '89—only the best pro street skaters could do a 360 flip. In those moments Rodney Mullen embedded himself into street skating and our consciousness forever.

Over the next two decades, Rodney moved the dance and technicality of freestyle into the realm of the street and put us all on notice. While we were riding bigger boards with fishtail shapes and beyond, he quietly changed the design of the boards to better suit his style of technical skating, only in the street. By shaving down our wild fish shapes over time, he moved us toward the modern popsicle shape, which could really be said to be an expanded freestyle board. Touché, Rodney, touché.

From the early '90s onward, Rodney's transition to street skateboarding was marked by a mix between street and freestyle. There were some tricks that were specifically Rodney tricks, like the darkslide—a half-flip of the board to the dark grip tape side, sliding across a surface and then flipping the board back over to the wheels. We watched in awe as he would do a triple heelflip or quadruple kickflips and underflips. It was well beyond our grasp. For us, it was magic. For him, mathematics.

Rodney handled skateboarding like it was an equation that needed to be solved. Then, in '97, he dropped the seminal skateboarding video series *Rodney Mullen vs. Daewon Song*. Though it was a promotional series for World Industries and its multiple subsidiaries, the main focus was the "battle" between Rodney and Daewon. Rodney proceeded to skate benches, handrails, picnic tables, and the urban environment like he was born there, delivering skating 10 times better than ever imagined. Rodney was *really* out there, hopping fences, getting chased by cops, living the "trife life" of a street skater, hat backward, jeans big, taking his lumps like the rest of us.

Now that he was really "in them streets," skateboarding's "thinker" addressed problems for street skaters. Take broken boards, for example. Rodney's freestyle boards would wear out but didn't break because they weren't subjected to the forces of a skater launching onto or over a 10-stair handrail. While Rodney wasn't launching that far, he was table-stacking and skating down stairs with new technical tricks that could result in a broken board if you were off by a nanometer. Rodney tired of that *real* quick and introduced carbon fiber into skateboarding manufacturing, which made World and Dwindle brand boards four times as strong. He and Steve would eventually offer a 90-day guarantee against breakage of Dwindle boards—a skateboarding first.

Boards warping in humid climates? Rodney introduced epoxy glue instead of water-based glue. When he got super nerdy, he even made the Über deck, his personal model, a carbon-fiber board somehow laid within seven plies of hard rock maple. He told me once, "It's the only center-weighted balanced board, meaning it will always rotate symmetrically."

The truth is, Rodney invented 90 percent of all the skateboarding that exists today. He moved us from the high-flying space to the streets (alongside other greats like Mark Gonzales, Mike Vallely, Natas Kaupas, and Tommy Guerrero).

But Rodney never stops—even when the scar tissue that built up after years of skating fused the ball-and-socket joint of his hip together. Most of us would have quietly bowed out at that point, but not him. He simply analyzed the problem and solved it. *Hmm, scar tissue holding me back from skating? What is the force necessary to rectify this situation?* It turns out the answer lies somewhere between the square root of lodging your leg inside of the wheel well of a Hummer and the sum of adding your body weight to forcibly rip apart the scar tissue, divided by the time it takes for your neighbors to call in your agonizing nightly screams to the authorities. This is that "new math" and it ain't for the fainthearted, folks—it's for Rodney.

In regaining the ability to skate, he retaught himself to have unity with body and mind and not to favor any particular side. The body has natural affinities. We write with the left hand or the right. We plant one leg and push with the other. Skaters overcome this by learning to skate switch, or with the "wrong" or non-dominant foot. It makes tricks doubly hard. Learn it one way and then the other. For Rodney, this meant something was wrong with the way the brain and body connected, so he set out to fix it and become stance-less.

That's probably why Silicon Valley has latched on to him lately, and why he's been featured in *Wired* and other tech outlets. In TED Talks, he has discussed the similarity between the way hackers repurpose tech and the way skaters repurpose city spaces and obstacles, which is why he was drawn to both.

Looking back, Tony Hawk was right. Rodney Mullen is the most underrated skater in the world, but I'm fairly sure he wouldn't want it any other way.

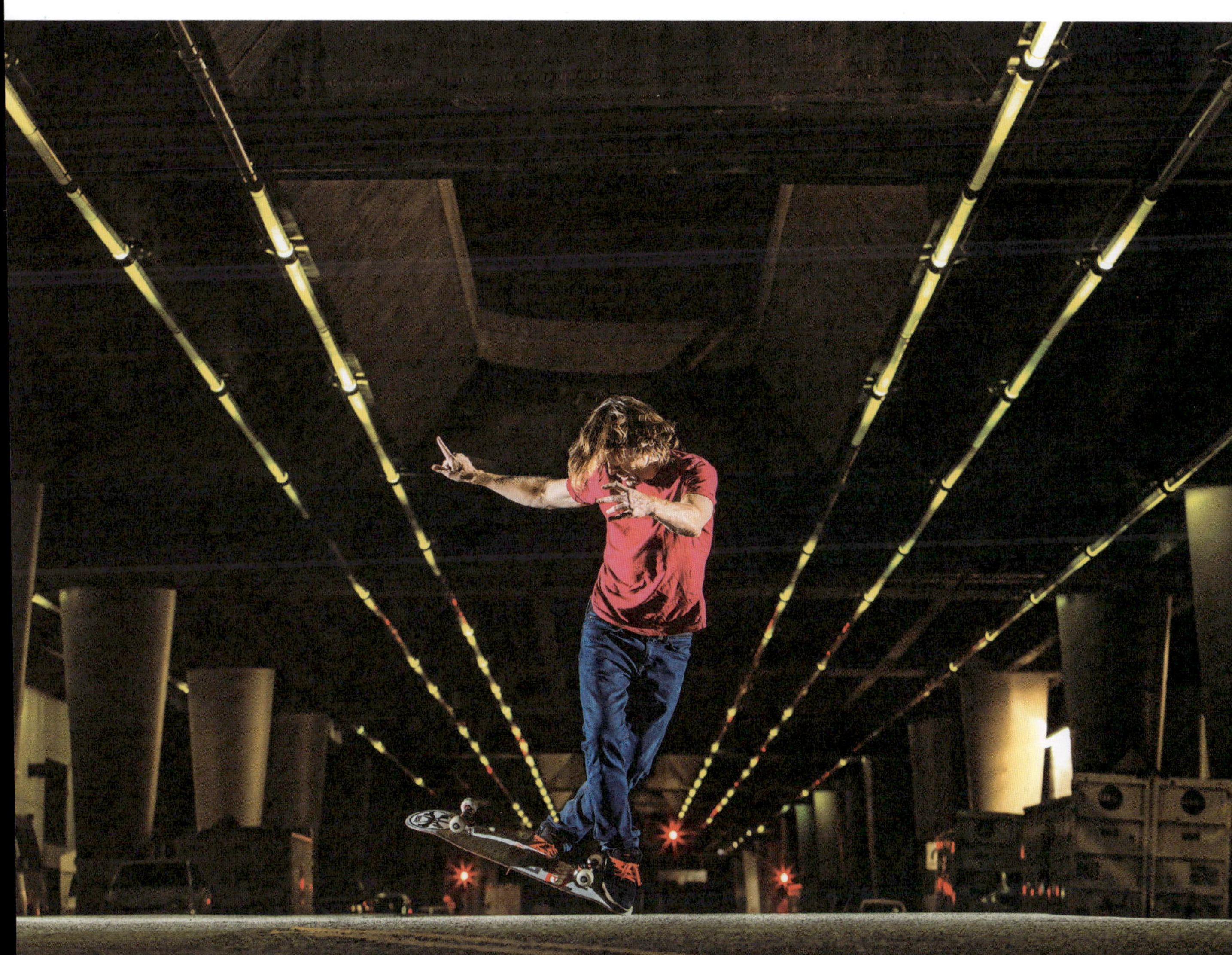

SKATEBOARDING HALL OF FAME INDUCTION CEREMONIES

There is a Skateboarding Hall of Fame? When did that happen? I'm often asked this when it comes to skateboarding's growth among the masses. Well, in the immortal words of Pusha T, "If you know, you know . . ."

For the uninitiated, the Skateboarding Hall of Fame Induction Ceremony is the place where once a year we honor our greatest for their contributions. Conceived by Todd Huber and Steve Van Doren (of Vans), it is the Grammys, Emmys, and ESPYs of skating rolled into one.

It's a place where regular skaters like myself can brush up against skateboarding royalty and also be reminded that even at the height of their career they are just people who love skateboarding and are pushing it to the edge—whether that came through shredding on their boards, like John Lucero and Jeff Grosso; designing the graphics, like artist Jim Phillips; or capturing the moments that set all of our imaginations aflame, like Glen E. Friedman or J. Grant Brittain. The Skateboarding Hall of Fame tries to honor everyone.

The original 2009 inductees to the Skateboarding Hall of Fame (SHoF) were a small but mighty influential crew: Tony Hawk, Tony Alva, Danny Way, and Bruce Logan. Within the next year, the group grew larger and more diverse, with women like godmother of skateboarding and *Life* magazine skate cover model Patti McGee (RIP); skaters of color Steve Caballero, Eric Koston, and Stacy Peralta; design innovator Larry Stevenson; style king Torger Johnson; and artist C. R. Stecyk.

Interestingly, the SHoF inducts artists and brands into the annals as well as skaters. This is a great way to accurately reflect a culture made up of mavericks who all weave a bit of life into skateboarding. The SHoF gives space to recognize that the most impactful maneuver from skaters like Steve Rocco (an elite pro skater) was developing World Industries and the skater-owned company movement in the '90s.

It's a framework that allows for the nuance and richness of skateboarding to receive recognition and why you see brands like Tracker Trucks and bands like Black Flag sharing accolades for their contributions to the culture.

The induction voting process is managed through a secret ballot. Current inductees are sent a list of previously vetted nominees and each person has an equal vote. Once those votes are tallied, it's on to the main stage, and what a stage it is.

Vans recently hosted a SHoF event in Orange County, and a who's who of skateboarding culture attended. Very few places allow such a generational centering of skate history. You could see *Thrasher* Skater of the Year Mike Carroll and Rick Howard and the entire Girl team in the same room as one of skateboarding's earliest pros, Cindy Whitehead. And since it's sponsored by Vans, well, that also means you got to see Steve Van Doren and other legends, like *Thrasher* editor Michael Burnett roaming around with a Leica camera, taking photos of all the highlights, like Jesse Martinez's hard-earned SHoF induction.

The way the SHoF operates now is rather simple. You are voted in by your peers and judged by them too. Once you are inducted, you then become a voting member and can nominate and advocate for people you believe should also be inducted. There have been controversies,

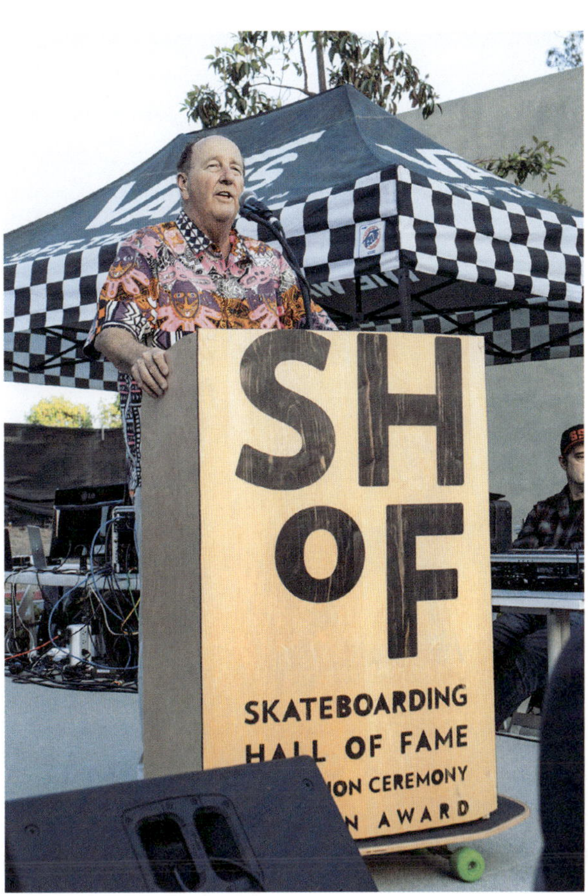

Left: Steve Van Doren at the Skateboarding Hall of Fame Induction Ceremony at Vans HQ

Bottom: Skateboarding Hall of Fame inductee murals

as one might expect. Sometimes problems arise when debating the impact of a nominated skater. Their contributions may not have resonated with every skater in the same way or every generation of skaters. This can be further complicated when the skater represents a traditionally marginalized group. In those rare instances, it can take the nominating committee or those nominated themselves to advocate on behalf of others.

Take the induction of Chad Muska into the class of 2020. Muska is one of the greatest skaters of all time. He burst on the scene riding for Toy Machine skateboards and attacked the biggest rails and stair sets. His ads let skaters know that a new movement was quite literally underfoot. However, right before the premiere of his video part, in classic skate fashion, there was a falling-out and his part was pulled from the video. He would leave Toy Machine

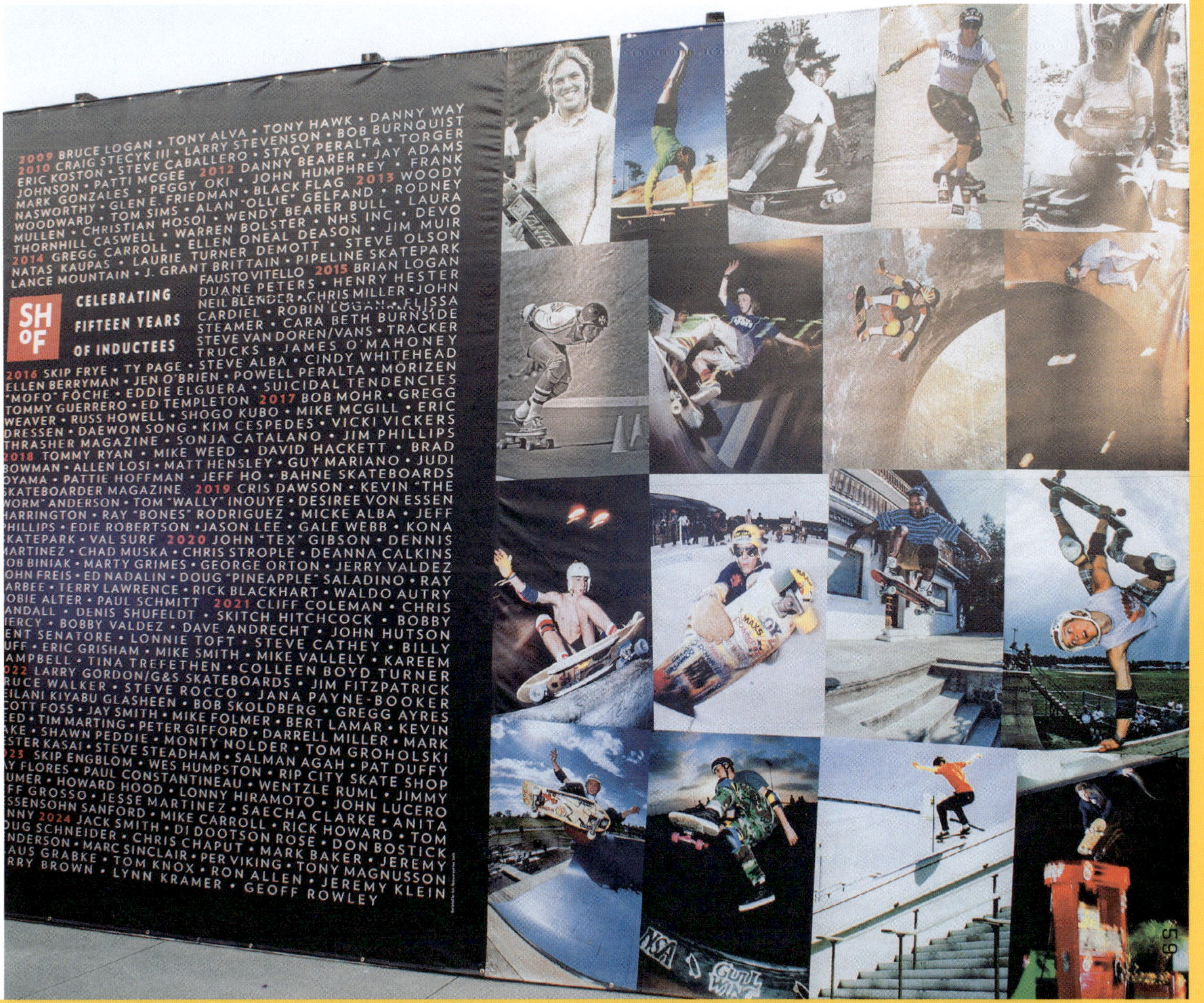

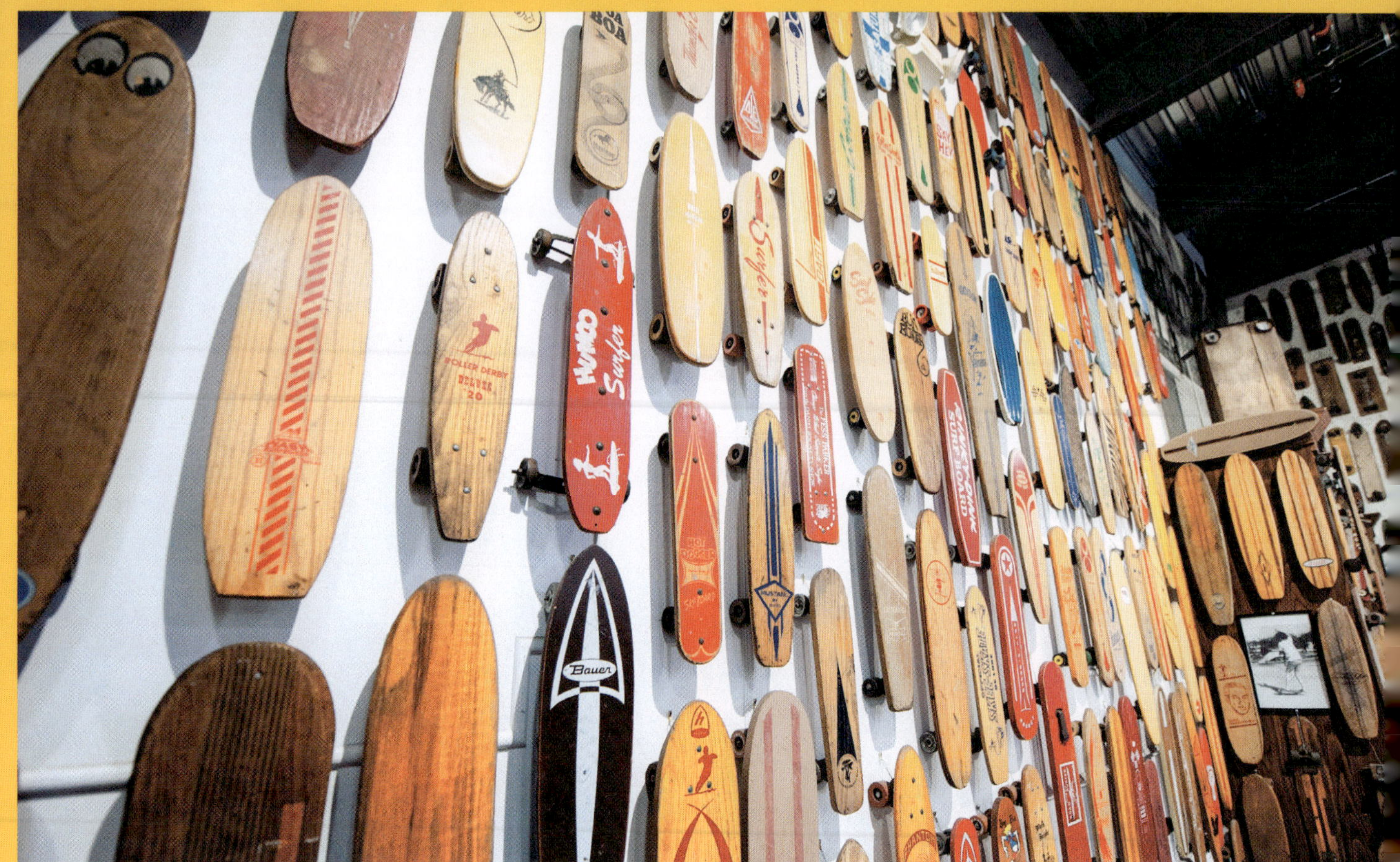

Vintage skateboards at the Skateboarding Hall of Fame Museum

to start his own brand, Shorty's; launch once of the bestselling skate shoes of all time, éS's "Muska"; and develop his own sneaker brand, C1RCA Footwear. He would even create a wheel company called Ghetto Child with other famed skaters like Tom Penny—now a Hall of Famer as well—and would leave an indelible mark with his signature style, boom box in arm, making mind-blowing moves in a fly mesh tank top and "swishy" athletic pants. Muska helped explode "street"- or "urban"-style attire into the skate mainstream. The fact that he blasted hip-hop and eventually created his own album, *MuskaBeatz*, with hip-hop legends from Raekwon to KRS-One to Biz Markie and Prodigy (RIP) didn't hurt either. Muska was "for the streets" and that certainly solidified his place in skate history.

However, when it came time to accept his induction, he respectfully declined. In the midst of Black Lives Matter protests following the murder of George Floyd, he told the committee he could not in good conscience be inducted before his mentor, Kareem Campbell (see page 46) was. Kareem was an originator in skateboarding, and one who proudly put his Black and street identity at the core of all of his brands. Muska felt that being inducted for his love of hip-hop and street and urban aesthetic would truly ring hollow if it happened before the acknowledgment of the one who put it out there for all of us.

This historic twist took the skate world by storm and made everyone rethink what representation really means and who else might have been overlooked who was crucial to skateboarding's development. What is great about the skateboarding community is our ability to critique ourselves in the moment, then move forward with a new intention of inclusivity.

After much discussion prompted by Muska's refusal of the honor, the next year the SHoF inducted both Kareem and Muska. In a show of brotherhood, Muska's award was accepted by Kareem Campbell, while Muska delivered colorful commentary on Kareem's speakerphone for all to hear.

That is the joy of skateboarding, to not take yourself too seriously unless the situation calls for it.

SKATEBOARDING HALL OF FAME AND MUSEUM

The Skateboarding Hall of Fame and Museum was germinated in 1997 by Todd Huber, who owned Skatelab, a skatepark in Simi Valley, California.

What began as a personal collection morphed into the largest assemblage of professional and folk skateboards (made by the user) in the world. A privately owned, funded, and curated collection, it dwarfs most public institutions' holdings for the sheer volume of artifacts on hand and the amount consistently donated yearly. As Todd told me back in the Skatelab days, once he started displaying his own boards from the walls and rafters, the story spread about the impressiveness of his collection. Skaters told skaters, visitors told non-skaters, and as luck would have it effort begat more efforts and the mecca of skateboarding artifacts became the go-to place to deposit any skateboards in your family's lineage to hopefully become included in the history on display. That word of mouth continued to grow until finally the number of boards rivalled the actual space of the skatepark, and a transition into a newer facility began.

Now located in a large suburban mall in Simi Valley, since 2018 the collection has been easily accessible and home to not only artifacts but also an indoor mini ramp, lest you forgot why you came. Donated by the family of pro skater Alex Midler, who came up through the Skatelab program in the Valley, the ramp is a testament to perseverance in skateboarding leading to greater fruits in the future.

To enter through the doors is to step back in time and honor the forefamily. The section dedicated to the origins of skateboarding reminds us that we're intrinsically linked not just to the DIY aesthetic of punk rock and hip-hop but to that of a good ol'-fashioned woodshop. Through images and pieces in the collection, we return to the milk-crate-nailed-to-plank OG days of the scooter, roller skates, and the ingenuity of the go-cart—folk skateboards, as Huber calls them. The ones built by hand, all before the fateful day when, without a handle or a bid adieu, skateboarding broke away from the taming of the frame it was assigned to and distilled down to its essence—four wheels and a board—then headed for the hills.

Within the museum we also experience the transition of skateboarding from those initial hills and the clay and metal wheels of the earliest days of the sport, to the revolution of the urethane wheel. Huber's got every variety on display, from the early Cadillac wheels to the UFOs or Kryptonics, on period-accurate boards that line the walls and hang from the ceilings, showing the moment of change building to the explosion of skateboarding onto the scene.

The museum really heats up when we get to the boards of the late '70s and early '80s, when skateboarding moves from fad to rad to outcast. The boards are every shape and design and present in living color—gems, warts, and all the in-betweens.

Sure, there are the classics you would expect—a Tony Hawk, a Rodney Mullen, along with boards belonging to other members of the Bones Brigade—but it's also Laura Thornhill's space and houses Ian Logan and Cindy Whitehead's Girl Is Not a 4 Letter Word board as well. (That's also the name of the social impact skate org Cindy runs.) There's the Nightmare by Lake Skateboards, with its strange twin, double-edged nose and tail. Metallica and the art of Pushead and Zorlac? Sure, it's there, next to the Walker and Sims. If it was made, the museum has it.

Along with the boards from the '80s, '90s, and onward, which mark the progression from backyard pools to the vert and street skating we know now, there are the installations that were presented at all of the Skateboarding Hall of Fame events, starting from the organization's first year. There are also giant 48-by-60-inch painted canvases by Ben Jay of SHoF legends like skaters like Christian Hosoi and Lance Mountain hanging from the ceiling. Gonz's pencil and line drawings, or Elissa Steamer's screen prints, or Chris Miller and Neil Blender's signature boards? Present and accounted for. Beyond that, there are a host of elements from every induction ceremony giving you an eyeful of history from any vantage point in the museum. There is nothing more inspiring than seeing the legacy of the skaters that have come before you wherever you look.

THE *LONDON CALLING* EXHIBITION

The Skateboarding Hall of Fame is also home to events that impact global skateboarding culture. It makes sense that *London Calling*, an exhibition highlighting the original '70s skaters who inspired the U.K. '80s scene, held the U.S. version of the show in the Skateboarding Hall of Fame and Museum in May 2024. Led by '80s pro skaters turned entrepreneurs and industry heavies, the show was envisioned by Steve Douglas and Bod Boyle to bring the U.K. history into focus and mark how current prominent skate brands like Palace and others can trace their history back to the '70s.

The exhibition featured the work of James Cassimus, whose first photos of the U.K. scene graced the pages of *Skateboarder* magazine and showed the skaters who would become '80s superstars that California wasn't the only place for skate culture. The U.K. and European spirit have been imbued in skateboarding culture since the '70s and a direct lineage can be traced to those first images that greeted skaters on both sides of the pond—and as we know in skateboarding, once the fire was lit, it was inextinguishable.

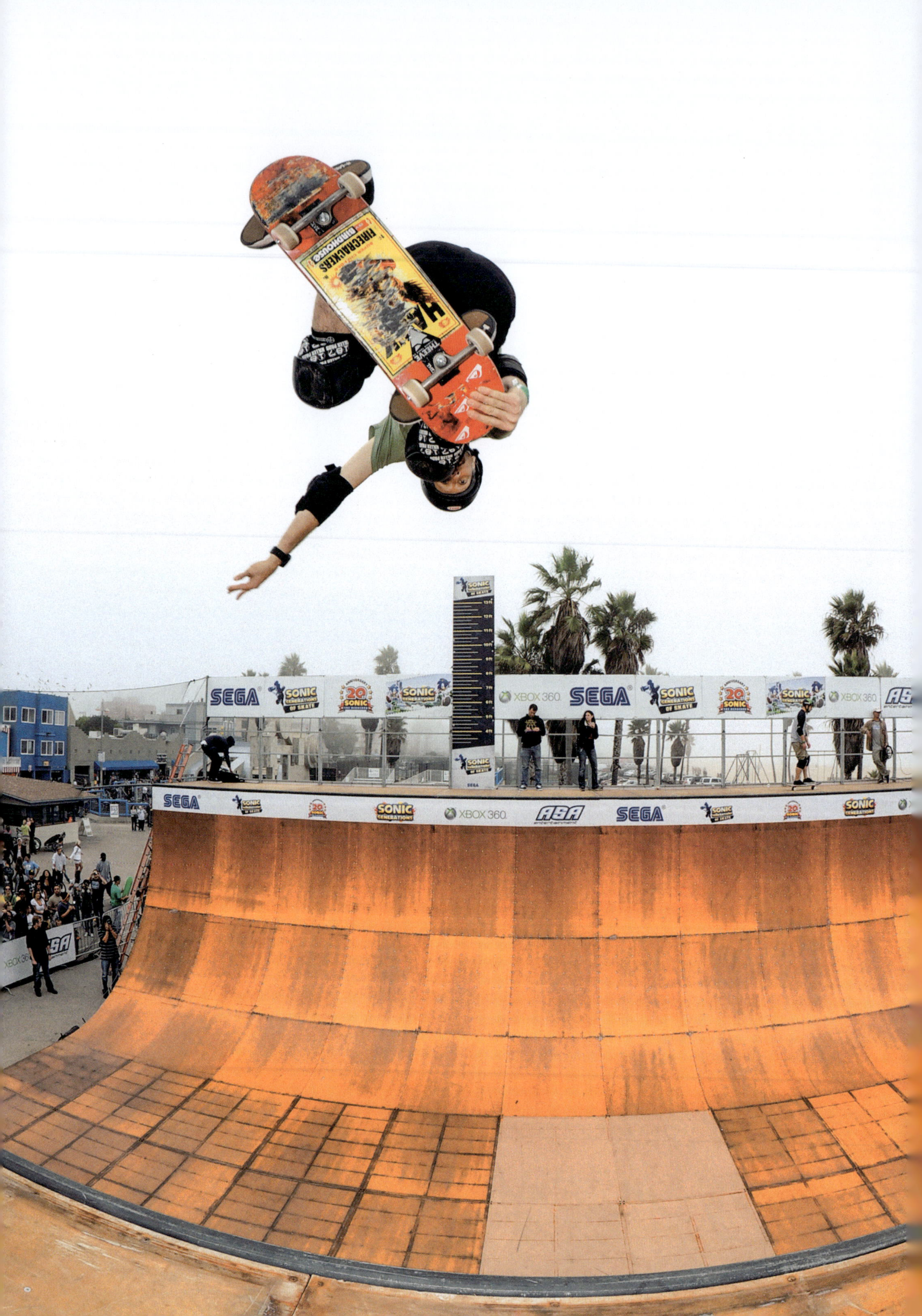

THE GOAT

TONY HAWK

Brought skateboarding into the mainstream and the global imagination

Wrangler of the 900

Founder of the Skatepark Project; owner of Birdhouse

Signature video game series: *Tony Hawk's Pro Skater*

Lives and breathes inclusion, holding countless doors open

There is no name in skateboarding as recognizable as that of the GOAT (Greatest of All Time), Tony Hawk. His accolades and accomplishments and coolness under pressure are the pride and aspiration for most every past, present, and future skateboarder. Tony's an author, entrepreneur, skater, philanthropist, restaurateur, husband, father, grandfather, and friend.

A true local, Tony was born in San Diego, California, to Frank and Nancy Hawk. He still resides in neighboring Encinitas with his wife, Catherine Goodman, and their family.

Tony is the youngest of the Hawks' four children; the nuclear family consists of Tony, his sisters Lenore Hawk Dale and Pat Hawk, and his brother, Steve Hawk. Tony is a decade younger than any of his siblings. While we know that he is the greatest in all things skateboarding, I want to shout out to his stellar siblings for each growing their passions and respective communities.

Lenore Hawk contributed to the education system in San Diego schools for more than two decades with a particular focus on bilingual education and providing opportunities for everyone and influencing generations. Pat Hawk's passion for singing landed her on stage and in studio with all the people that would make your parents, grandparents, and your aunties go mad. She sang with Michael Bolton, the Righteous Brothers, Pet Shop Boys, and

Merry Clayton and Peabo Bryson to throw in that extra side of soul.

Steve Hawk also hit boss-level status within his interests. He not only cut his teeth to fully claim his status as a card-carrying California surfer (who fulfilled a life goal of surfing in Antarctica), but as the Hawk family tends to do, he turned that passion into a vocation when he earned the position of editor of *Surfer Magazine* from 1990 to 1998, and heavy contributor in the aughts. He also contributed to skateboarding by giving eight-year-old Tony his first board in the late '70s.

Frank Hawk himself contributed to skateboarding in ways that aren't discussed much these days. When Frank found out that Tony was going to give up Little League Baseball because of his infatuation with skateboarding, the elder Hawk decided to put his time and military training into organizing the activity and making it more palatable to laypersons. Frank founded what became the National Skateboarding Association when times got lean in the '80s, just to support skateboarding and his youngest son's love of the sport. The Hawk family *gets it done*.

That first board of Tony's, a Bahne skateboard outfitted with red Stoker wheels, has benefited everyone in skateboarding, and provided Tony the ability to raise a family and change the perception of skateboarding. He's built the Ride Channel with YouTube, produced a bestselling video game franchise, created the Vert Alert contest series, gone on the road with *Tony Hawk's Boom Boom HuckJam* tour, launched tech start-ups, and offered support to Black and Brown chefs and restaurateurs and to sustainable enterprises like Hawai'i's Holey Grail Donuts. He even went from being a skater in the X Games to part owner, giving it the heaviest of cosigns. Next time you are in D.C., feel free to stop at the Smithsonian to pay homage to that tattered board with wooden blocks under the trucks (to better emulate his heroes like Tony Alva and the Dogtown crew with their slashing and fluid skate style).

Tony took to that battered board and, instead of becoming a surfer like his brother, became the Tony we know now. Taking that 144 IQ that was pushing him to leave the team-based experience of baseball and allow him to fully flourish and learn to push his boundaries, which would later become a benchmark for all of vertical skateboarding.

Soon, Tony was good enough to be sponsored by the skateboard brand of his dreams, the legendary Dogtown Skateboards. It would eventually go defunct without officially sending notice. Luckily, he made the decision to skate for the esteemed Powell Peralta. Stacy Peralta vied for Hawk against the lure of a hometown favorite, the San Diego–based Gordon & Smith (G&S).

Recognizing Tony's early talent and determination, Stacy thought he would be the perfect addition to his Bones Brigade—a team of young upstart skaters first assembled in 1979 and updated with some of the best amateurs in the land. The elite team of 11-to-15-year-old skaters included the inventor of the ollie on vert, Alan Ollie Gelfand, and though it would come later, the inventor of the 540 arial or McTwist (a 540-degree turn), Mike McGill. The Bones Brigade members also included teen phenoms Steve Caballero, Lance Mountain, and Tommy Guerrero, all amateur upstarts who became a powerful dominating competitive group in the '80s. Mixing with those skaters, Tony could develop with a pool of the best underage skaters around.

Seeing Tony skating and winning contests with skaters taller and stronger than himself, Stacy knew he had a fighter on his hands willing to think and dream bigger and more technically than any other

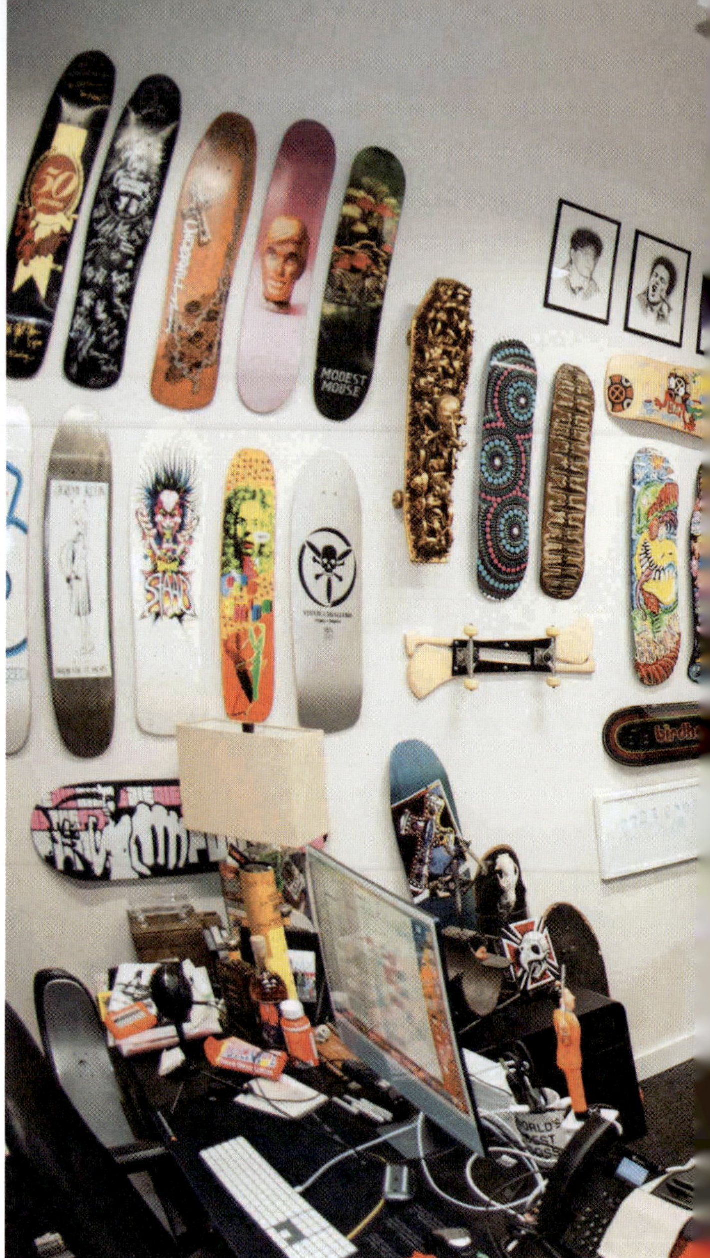

skater. Stacy was correct, and after winning amateur championships at age 12, Tony became a driving force in professional vert skating within the next few years, inventing tricks and beating skaters much his senior. The skater who began in 1977 would have the wind at his back as he sailed into the mid-'80s. From that perch, Tony would go forth and conquer vertical skateboarding.

Winning contests? Tony earned standings and trophies as tall as a mountain. Though he kept very few (usually giving them away at contests), they did help fuel the fire that showed the world that he had arrived and he meant business. Inventing tricks? That list is as deep as the sea, including pushing teammate McGill's trick, the McTwist, even further with a 720 arial, aptly named the McHawk at the time.

In fact, in vertical skateboarding (first in parks like the legendary Del Mar Skate Ranch, Tony's home away from home where he would practice for hours,

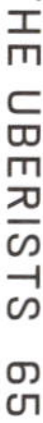

hone his craft, and connect with other skaters, and then later on vertical wooden half-pipes), no one other than the legendary street and freestyle skater Rodney Mullen has invented more, and in a different discipline. Fittingly, it's Rodney, the other GOAT, who helped keep Tony inspired.

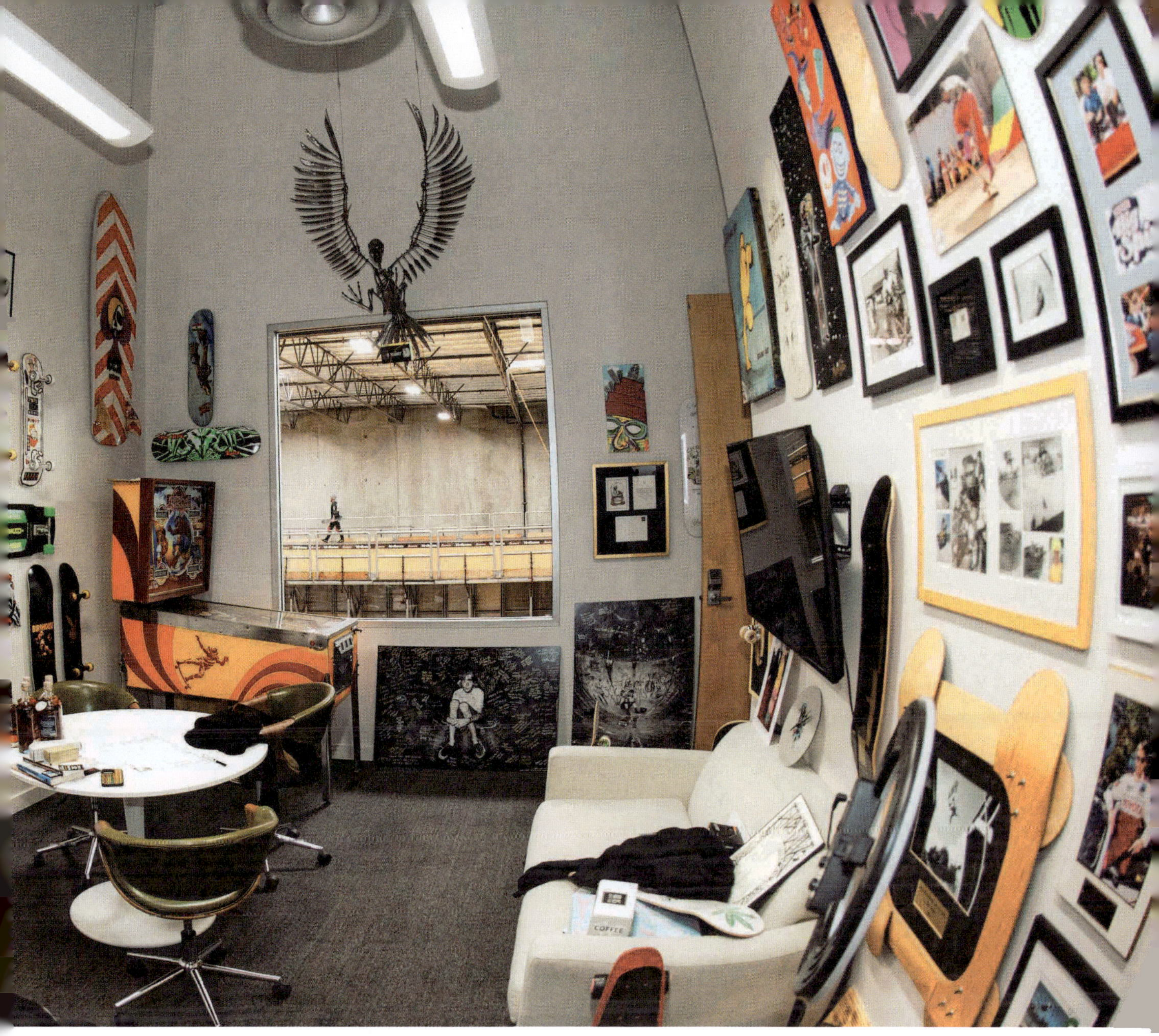

The fact that Rodney could do a zillion tricks with only seconds to reengage terra firma kept Tony thinking about how much wizardry he could accomplish with so much hang time in the air. As teammates on the Powell team (as it's more commonly called), they could watch each other soar in their respective idioms and push the level of everyone around them.

For both Rodney and Tony, past a certain point of quieting the naysayers, it was never about the competition. Both won almost every contest they entered by the late '80s. They were so far ahead of the curve. Progression became about possibilities and how much one could stretch one's imagination and the relationship between board, rider, and gravity. However, that does not mean Tony did not have competition: the two names synonymous with mid- to late '80s skateboarding are Hawk and Hosoi, and they generated a Bird vs. Magic type of rivalry in skateboarding. As always, the "best" skateboarding is subjective because some people like style, flair, and a bit of showmanship in their skating, and plenty of others want to see progression and technicality.

In the earliest days, Tony was known for the technicality, and Christian "High-Flying Holmes" Hosoi (see page 17) was known for the biggest airs. Over time, with Tony growing in height, weight, and maturity, he could deliver it all, pushing those big airs into unmatched technicality and prowess.

Although Tony is retired now, progressing skateboarding is still on his mind. The grandfather,

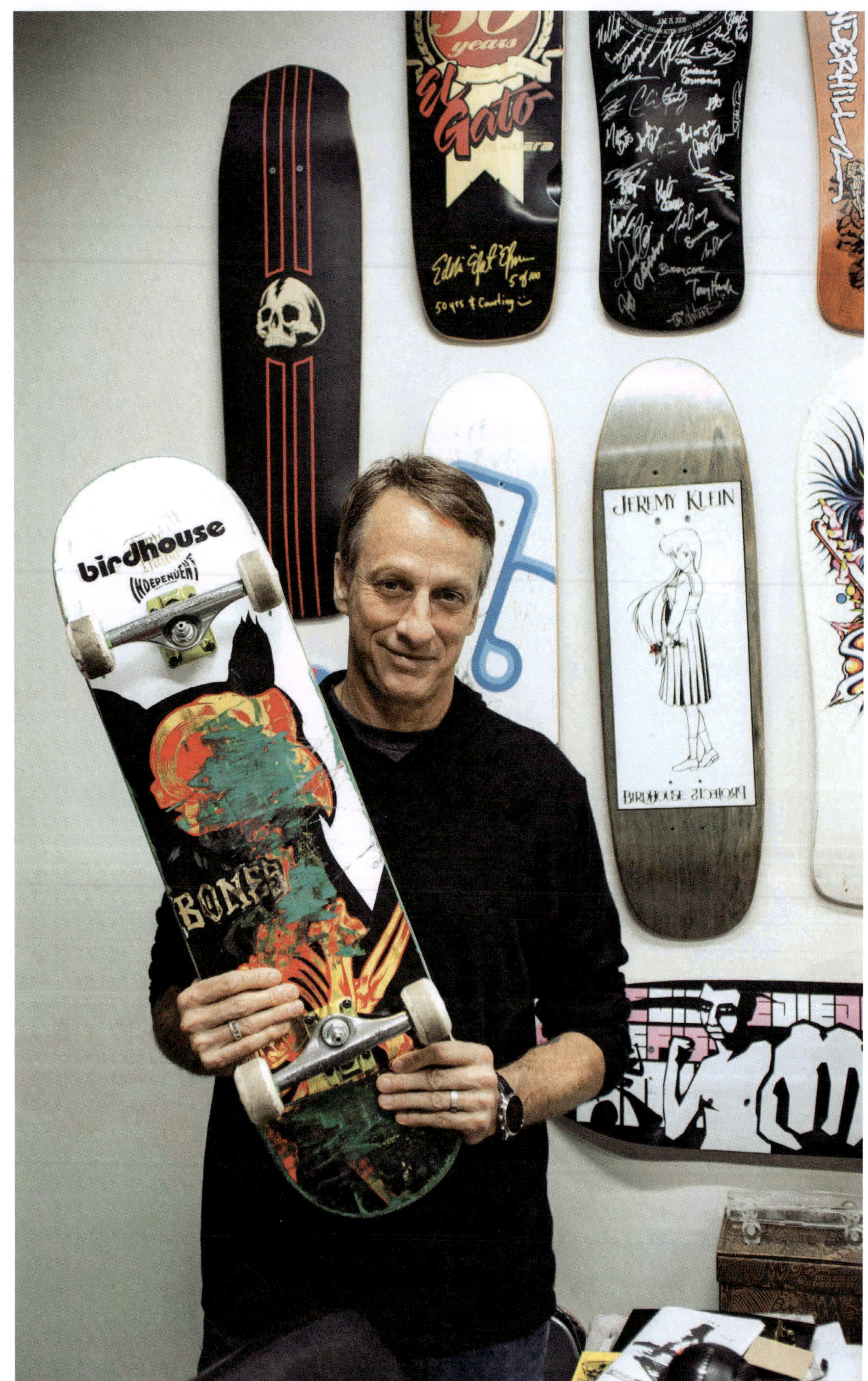

birdhouse
(INDEPENDENT)
BONES
JEREMY KLEIN
BIRDHOUSE PROJECTS
El Gato
50 years

author of two books, and first skater to be invited to the White House (and sneak in a cheeky skate) just invented a new trick at the X Games. If his daily Instagram feeds show anything, it's that he doesn't plan on stopping. Who else still operates on that level? Even Tom Brady had to bow out.

As an elder stateman in skateboarding, it is expected that at some point he will stop adding to skating's repertoire. But rather than rest, Tony offers another *planche à roulettes* maneuver to the people. Even after breaking his femur. He came back, skated, hurt it, then recalibrated again. Most of us would be out of commission, but the GOAT found another way to pay the price to play and kept moving forward.

That tenacity is what has helped make him skateboarding's leader. There are moments that have made Tony famous in the public eye. Take his landing the 900, a two-and-a-half-revolution rotation that had never been done on a vert ramp. *Plus*, he landed it during a moment of majesty— the 1999 X Games. Under the full pressure of the cameras, Tony's brain figured out the adjustments necessary to bring a trick to life that no other skater had been capable of. That level of expertise permeated the air and the screen, so much so that even the producers knew that something special was happening on the vert ramp.

While the X Games have always been secondary to ESPN's main focus on traditional sports, on this day action sports ruled the night. ESPN delayed its feed into an NFL game in order to show the unbridled athleticism of Tony Hawk chasing the dream. An unstoppable force propelled toward the immovable object, the 900—the trick—and he would not be denied. Undoubtedly the best in skateboarding to ever do it. The man who pushed himself harder than any other person could have glimpsed the mountaintop, conquered it, and sent every demon of defeat he'd experienced galloping off while he entered the annals of history.

That's not even counting the Loop. Tony did a full 360 loop—full-circle, riding upside down—on film, and I saw it in person. *Tony Hawk's Boom Boom HuckJam*, yep. Tony and all his friends making a Beatles-esque magical mystery tour that

included skateboarding, BMX, and motocross. The pyrotechnics, the giant ramps, and the spectacle were unlike anything ever seen before or since.

So many firsts, so little time. There is not enough ink for the proper acknowledgment of each of Tony's accomplishments on board. Don't take my word for it, even the Smithsonian had to make choices on how best to honor him. The documentary on his life, *Tony Hawk: Until the Wheels Fall Off*, rightfully paints the portrait of Tony as one of the greatest athletes of all time.

However, what Tony should be *most* remembered for in every historical archive is using his skateboarding to open doors for others. He did what others didn't and couldn't do—he paid it forward. Selema Masekela (see page 50) said it best: "Tony could have just been out for himself. Instead, he held the door open so that all of skateboarding could skate through on his back and on his momentum."

He singlehandedly has done more for skateboarding than any other skater in history on multiple fronts, starting with his choice of teammates and continuing with the creation of the *Tony Hawk's Pro Skater* billion-dollar video game franchise and the establishment of his Tony Hawk Foundation. (Full disclosure: Since 2020, I have been lucky enough to serve as a member of the board.)

There are other aspects of Tony's life that never receive the light they deserve.

Let's start with the diverse team Tony built with his brand, Birdhouse. First, Tony chose Willy Santos, a Filipino American skater and the shining light of San Diego. Not only did Willy win the National Skateboarding Association contests in the 1990s, but he competed in every category. He skated mini ramps, street, vert, walls, pools, whatever, wherever, just one of the best all-around skaters at that time. Tony also had Dan Rogers, a Southeast Asian skater from S.D., who demolished handrails and whose aggressive style filled a great position in a well-rounded team. Those days were far from the arguments about doing things for PC reasons; these were major skaters who earned their place and resonated with other skaters of color. While these moves may seem insignificant, for many skaters of color, particularly Asian American skaters, their presence was a source of pride. Tony helped show everyone how to put a team together with those skaters alongside legends like Jeremy Klein, Ocean Howell, Steve Berra (and later Andrew "The Boss" Reynolds) and how to nurture them, even though Tony himself was only in his early 20s.

That was the future of skateboarding, even though Tony was still inventing tricks on transition and ramps, some believed the discipline would eventually be put out to pasture. You would have never known it from Tony, though. He took it all on with dignity, and did not miss a beat, with classic clips at Webb Park with noseblunt slides, 360 ollies, flip tricks, and always spinning the odd-540s on tour to remind us that he hadn't lost a step, he had just changed the dance form.

What most people don't realize is that Tony started that roost of the Birdhouse with not much money, and just a little support from another former pro freestyle rider leaving Powell, Per Welinder. While Tony bought his first house when he was still in high school, and made bank riding for Powell Peralta, when the bottom fell out of vert, he funded the team and the upstart Birdhouse (then called Birdhouse Projects) and took that responsibility seriously. He built the team, edited the video, made the ads, drove the van, and did everything in his power to do the thing he loved with the people who mattered to him. During that mid-'90s era, with its battles between Powell and World Industries and full-page ads throwing midnight levels of shade, Tony bowed out. Birdhouse was a refuge from that and dedicated to fun and friends. Even if you didn't think Tony was cool, the team was awesome.

What Tony wanted was for skateboarding to be a place for everyone. This aspect still guides his actions today, where the current iteration of the team still holds something for everyone. Lizzie Armanto is a force in women's vert skating and the first woman on the cover of *TransWorld SKATEboarding*, and powerhouse Candy Jacobs is known for her tasty trick selection in the streets. Tony has made greatness the center of any Birdhouse project since day one. That day exploded with the introduction in 1999 of *Tony Hawk's Pro Skater* (*THPS*) and, a year later, *Pro Skater 2* (*THPS2*).

The best way to describe this time is before *THPS* and after *THPS2*. *THPS* offered a representation of skateboarders in ways that no one outside of skateboarding discussed or was aware of previously. Tony's foray into the digital realm meant that a new generation of skateboarding reflected the culture in the public eye, and that crew was diverse. Players could choose to skate as Steve Caballero, Daewon Song, Kareem Campbell, Elissa Steamer, Cara-Beth Burnside, Bob Burnquist, Stevie Williams, and more recently, Leo Baker, the first trans skater to be featured in the game. The names have changed since the first game, but the cast has never been short of amazing. Each version of the game has offered visibility to the characters who made up the fabric of professional skateboarding culture at the time.

What the Tony Hawk video game set in motion in a deeper way was a landscape where skaters determined their images within the game. If you wanted to shave your head or wear gold chains, warm-ups, or skinny jeans, it didn't matter. The skateboarding that propelled you through your pro career wasn't watered down or sanitized. If you were in *THPS*, you could do *you*.

Tony had seen the boom-and-bust period of skateboarding in the 1970s. With a new group of skaters pushing the sport, there was reason to celebrate, not least of all because vert was back in the public eye with the advent of the X Games and other contests. Brazilian skaters Bob Burnquist, Pedro Barros, and Lincoln Ueda were eating vert and enthralling the masses. Kareem was ruling in the streets, and Elissa gave us all someone to respect when women faced a darker time in skate history. As Kareem has stated, Denzel Washington told him that he knew who we were because he had played him in the Tony Hawk video game.

THPS and the franchise introduced millions of players around the world to the full breadth of what skating had to offer in a way that wasn't patronizing or tokenizing—it was simply real skateboarding for real skateboarders.

When Tony became the mouthpiece for skateboarding, everyone ate a little better and everyone moved a little easier. Everyday skaters faced slightly less persecution and skaters further up the food chain in the industry had a greater level of respect put on their name. Especially those skaters whose likenesses appeared in the video game.

But Tony didn't stop there. For his next trick, he attempted to reach the ultimate level-up: giving skaters a home in our own hoods.

Enter the Tony Hawk Foundation, now renamed the Skatepark Project (TSP). Tony decided to dedicate not only a percentage of his wealth but the actual resources necessary to help other skaters create skateparks in their neighborhoods. TSP was founded by Tony and his family and initially led by his best friend Miki Vuckovich (storied photographer, former editor at *TRANSWorld Skateboarding*, and so dedicated to structure in his life he put himself in military school), himself one of the skateboarding greats. Generating money through auctions and donations, TSP has delivered and funded more than 600 skateparks and tens of million dollars dedicated to the creation of skateparks.

Beyond this, TSP is also a resource to help anyone learn how to advocate for themselves and their skate community. It offers a lifeline and toolkit for a skater to move from being in the city looking for places to skate, to taking the first step toward designing and creating the skate space they imagine. Following the guidelines in PDF form, skaters can connect with TSP, learn what is in the area, and move from petitioning city hall to creating their own Hall of Justice—the skatepark.

The Skatepark Project is also the first skateboarding institution to truly invest in skateboarding's future with a sizable donation toward research on the sport. It stems from TSP's and Tony's goal to move beyond anecdotes about how skateboarding saves lives. Their goal is to understand how skaters from a variety of backgrounds interpret their own lives and employment and educational career trajectories through the lens of skate culture. Their first endeavor was the USC × TSP skateboarding study, which explored how young people interpret the opportunities and obstacles that arise in their lives due to skateboarding, the stereotypes they face, and how the skateboarder identity can help skaters of color navigate a world that can be hard and outright dangerous for people of color. It also pointed to the work needed to create greater gender equity within skateboarding and at the skatepark. Keeping with the theme of empowerment, TSP has now helped build skateparks on Indigenous lands in the U.S.

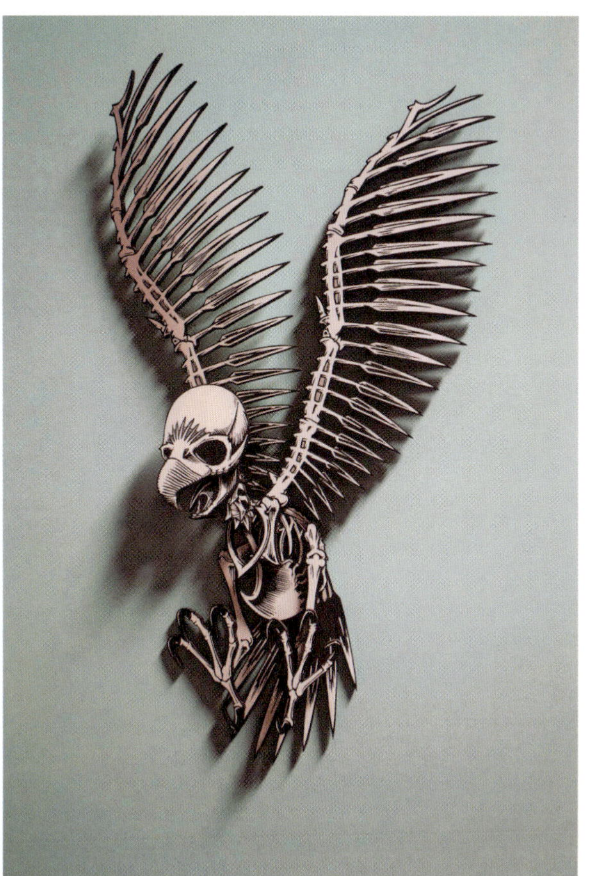

The vintage Tony Hawk "skull and bones" graphic on display at Tony Hawk Inc.

Also recognizing the need to preserve historic skateparks, TSP, in partnership with Vans, helped renovate the historic NYC Brooklyn Banks. They have even extended the reach of Ivy league graduate, architect, and Olympian Alexis Sablone (see page 254) by helping fund her Candy Courts skateable architecture in New Jersey and supported the work of Skateistan (see page 196) around the world.

In support of the future of skaters from marginalized communities, TSP created the BIPOC Fellowship Program to provide resources for members of those communities as the stewards of skateboarding civic engagement.

Tony opened the door, then gave us all the keys to the kingdom and wanted us to build it for ourselves. Think of how many superstars you can say that about. They are few and far between, which is why Tony Hawk is in a league of his own.

Tony has become the spokesperson and built the institutions for skateboarding to roll onward into the future, bringing in as many people as possible, in a way that's fun, engaging, and inclusive.

THE CULTURALISTS

The culturalists. The avant-garde.
The ones who make skateboarding live
beyond sport, not as a lifestyle but as
a life of style. The skaters who add the
spark that keeps skateboarding moving
through the decades. These skaters
set the standard by embodying the
spirit of skateboarding. They spread
the stoke and inspire others by doing
what feels right to them no matter the
time or place. Their timeless aesthetic,
spreads outward and helps create the
next generation of icons. These are
the culturalists. The ones who drive
skateboarding culture and leave us all
thinking about the future—or just in
awe of the wonderful skateboarding
world we live in.

FOR THOSE WHO COME FROM NOTHING
STEVIE WILLIAMS

Founder of DGK skateboards

First skateboarder to have a Reebok pro model shoe

First African American to have a pro model with DC Shoes

Playable character in *Tony Hawk's Pro Skater* video game

There was a lil' kid from Philly in the early 1990s doing what most kids did then—they looked for fun. This was way before the kid would become *TransWorld SKATEboarding*'s 27th most influential skater of all time. And way before the chartered planes and corporate deals. Stevie Williams was just a kid with all the prospects that North Philly had to offer—which, at that time, meant anything but going to school. His mother worked days at the bank, so that left plenty of hours for a kid to abscond through the city. In his own words, Stevie (known then as Lil' Stevie) hopped around the city looking for shenanigans. Part of a BMX "biker" gang comprised of seven- to eight-year-olds, they would roll up on whoever they could, steal bike parts, dance in the street for tourists, and run quick hustles for money. Like all kids do at some point, Stevie tried to figure out where the line was. A product of their environment, Stevie and the kids on the block owned toy skateboards, but there was no indication that he would have a future in the culture—especially on those subpar Kmart boards. That all changed in 1991, when the Williams family moved from North Philly to West Philly. Stevie could now witness Black skateboarders, including Philly great Roger Brown. Stevie was transfixed the moment he witnessed and heard actual tricks: ollies and kickflips by Terence and Razul, two OGs of the West Philly scene. As he asked me jokingly, what was this magic and why was he the last to hear about it?

While Stevie absorbed the magic instantly and wanted to roll with, he wasn't immediately brought into the fold. The first-degree burn happened when the West Philly crew relayed that his "budget-ass board" with its plastic wheels and janky bearings "wasn't gonna roll anywhere." Plus, Stevie was a troublemaker—terrorizing everyone in the city with bits of theft and panhandling for money, which he was the first to admit. And he liked attention, the antithesis of what you need when skating, which is to avoid security and slip into the shadows. With time, his dedication to learning the craft (and promises not to be a nuisance) softened the reservations of the OGs and his peers began to understand that this was no hustle. Stevie was trying to skate. He also happened to live adjacent to a legendary skate spot, Love Park. Philly, the City of Brotherly Love, and its suburbs have birthed a plethora of skaters: Sergei Trudnowski, Ricky Oyola, Roger and Matt Reason, to name a select few from the '90s to early aughts era. The cement wonderland had benches, ledges, and stairs that were the envy of skaters globally. It looked like a playground, albeit a heavily policed one, where cops often appeared in the same video footage tackling and harassing skaters—you know, just a reminder that Philly never was, and still is not, a joke.

Within a few years, the barely 12-year-old Stevie earned his place on the Underworld Element team with a skateboarding video part filled with highly advanced technical skills that blew minds. Stevie's rise from knucklehead to notoriety deserved all the flowers he earned. When other Philly skaters returned skateboarding back to its flowy basics,

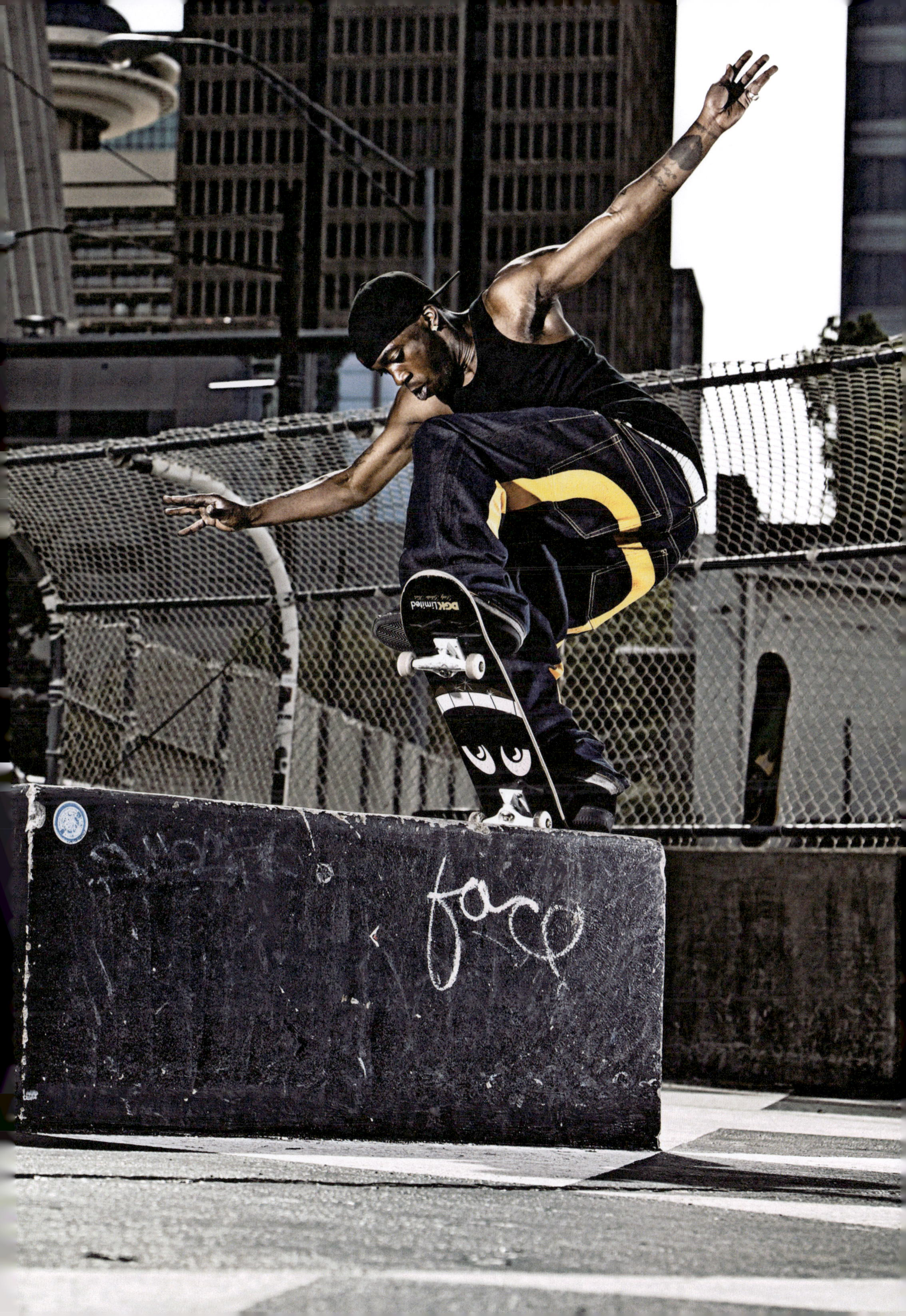

face
DGK Unlimited

Stevie was crushing it, sponsored by a West Coast company (a demarcation of talent at the time) and proving that he could match and surpass anyone's skating out there. In the City of Brotherly Love, however, the cracks began to show. Some older skaters eagerly told visiting media not to shoot pics of Stevie and his crew because they were just "dirty ghetto kids"—the ones who come from nothing. Whether this was racially motivated, with the reigning champs being mostly white, we will never know. What was apparent, however, was the centrality of class, an issue forever burned into Stevie's psyche. Never underestimate the way that Black excellence exists at every level and might roll up and pop out on you. Feeling the indignity, 15-year-old Stevie opted to migrate to San Francisco via a hitchhiking thumb—without telling his mother. With no clear plans, Stevie rolled into S.F. and cut his teeth at its famous spots, like Pier 7 on the Embarcadero, a mecca of skateboarding.

What he found in San Francisco was a difference in the culture: Stevie wasn't the only young skater, and many were his age or just a few years older. Most importantly, he wasn't the only skater of color. In fact, the S.F. scene was and remains one of the most culturally diverse hubs. Confirming his whereabouts to his mother but not his sponsor, he would lose their support. Later, joining forces with young skate phenom Henry Sanchez, the pair would turn pro

for the short-lived, Profile Skateboards. Devastated, and surfing between couches and teams, something had to give. Stevie focused on filming an undeniable video part. Something to force teams to recognize his talents and jolt them into taking a chance on him. The illest brand with a street aesthetic at the time was Menace/CityStars, founded by mastermind Kareem Campbell (see page 46) and a natural fit. An equally respected name in skateboarding culture, Girl/Chocolate was making changes to the brand and adding to the roster. Eventually joining Chocolate, the "sponsor me" tape he created ended up as his section of the Chocolate video, with little to no editing, and that footage is still fire. Stevie is hungry, skating hard, and super tech, putting the world on notice and showcasing a repertoire of tricks that only he could manifest. Switch pop shove-it nosegrinds? Those became his signature. Switch heelflips into manuals with fakie hardflips out of them? Dream sequence. Others might have done that trick, but not with Stevie's style. His part ignited a passion for Stevie from fans across the globe. The skills and the swagger had always been there, but the question in all minds was: Would Stevie Williams be an accident or an asset? He proved all the haters wrong in 2000 by crushing his time with Chocolate, then penning a deal with DC Shoes, then a powerhouse in skateboarding. Similarly to Chocolate, DC wanted to tap into a new vein of raw street skating, and Stevie gave them the rush they needed, first by joining the team and then by delivering his first pro model shoe.

Paying homage to the Jordan 2 shoe, it spoke to skaters and non-skaters by mixing skate needs with urban aesthetics. Beyond the personal accomplishments, he wanted to show skaters, who lived a similarly complicated life, what was possible. Those who were more likely to choose Kareem's avatar (and later Stevie)—in the *Tony Hawk's Pro Skater* video game—than Mr. Hawk himself. People who came from 'hoods where "hand to hand" meant something else. To do this, it was time to make moves, and according to Stevie, this created tension. Stevie wanted to show that skateboarding was for everyone, including those left on the margins. By focusing on those folks, any brand would gain the growth and movement it craved. Feeling unheard, even with a bestselling shoe, Stevie signed a deal with Reebok, which was controversial at the time. "Sellout" rather than "selling" became an oft-used phrase in some circles when discussing Stevie.

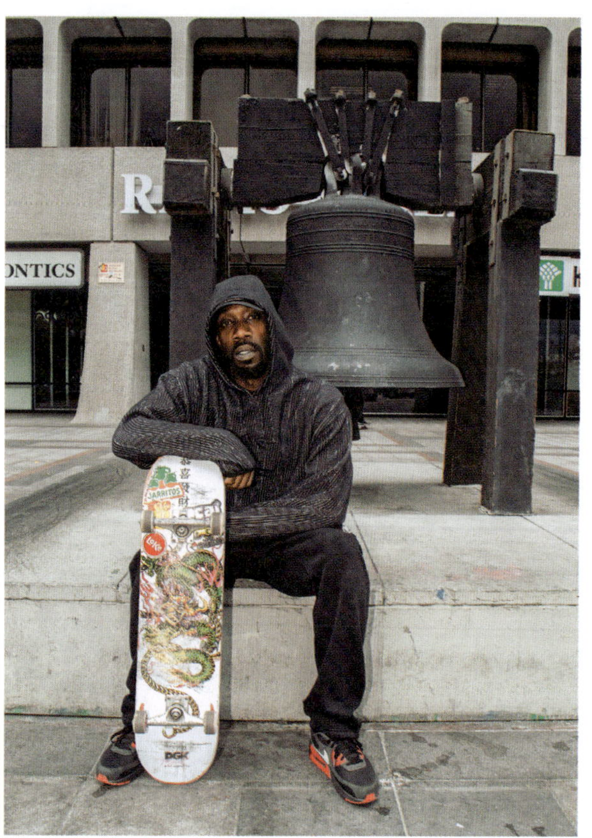

Stevie Williams in between sessions at J-Kwon, in L.A.

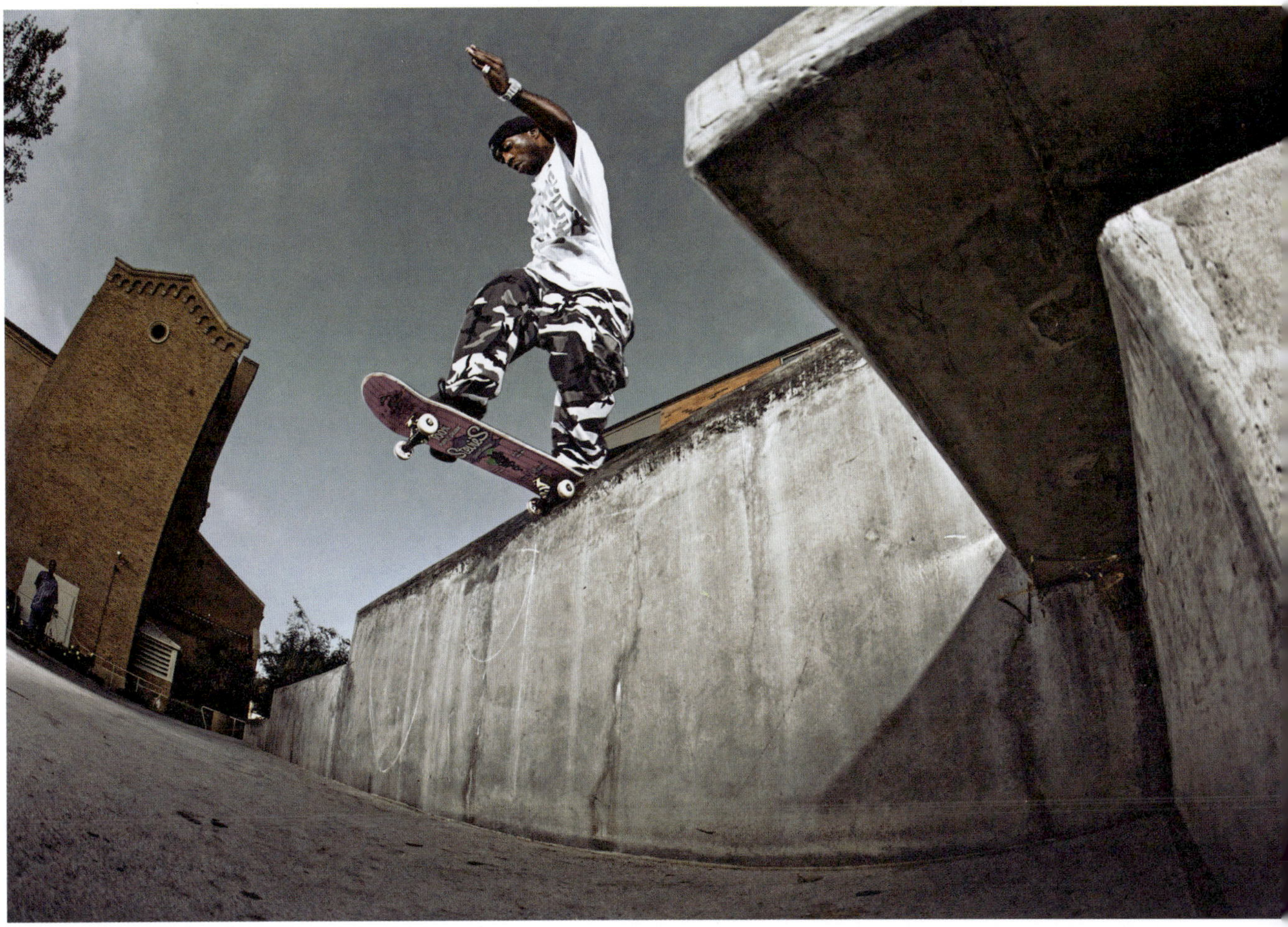

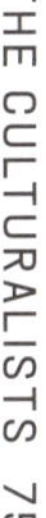

Stevie Williams, backside tailslide

However, Stevie's experience was uniquely his own, and many of his detractors probably never viewed life through his lens—one with a mother who was a former Black Panther, or one who thought that the punk rock music in early skateboard videos was devil's music. They might not have had family crashing in their room, trying to exorcise skateboarding from his soul. I know for certain that they didn't have the kind of heat where not only were people embarrassed that you skateboarded, but that skateboarding meant you routinely hung out with white people. This sense of shame was on his mother to explain to the community even when she didn't understand *why* he would choose to skateboard. Those scars drove Stevie and motivated him when he signed with Reebok. To do big things and inform those who didn't know that skateboarding was something of value. It was right there in the ads, magazines, videos, and billboards that showed Stevie's neighborhood and how this street kid had created a lane for himself—a product of their lives, their strife, and success on the billboards with the words "I'm eating." Sentiment cut through the noise and let his community know that skateboarding was for a new generation of

Black people—a place for makin' paper and making oneself whole. Amen. What moves beyond all of this is what became legend, the flip. First, Stevie paired skateboarding and hip-hop by launching his Stevie Williams DGK (Dirty Ghetto Kids) shoe with Reebok and his capsule collection concurrently with Jay-Z and his own Reebok shoe and billboards. Second, he did the ultimate flip, by turning the money from Reebok into the seed investment to make DGK Skateboards its own full-fledged brand. The "Dirty Ghetto Kids" now had a home. One that spoke to them and was built by them. You couldn't ask for more, except Stevie gave an encore. With program director Coach Don Cooley, Stevie set up DGK's social impact arm, Saved by Skateboarding, supported Cooley's Pushin' Forward and a collab with Virgil Abloh (RIP). DGK stands as a testament to Stevie's ingenuity and perseverance. DGK's hottest T-shirt reads, "I heart haters," the kiss of death to Stevie's detractors, and chef's kiss from the wildest rose to grow from Philly's concrete.

THE BOSS

ANDREW REYNOLDS

Transformed the frontside flip into a pièce de résistance

Voted tenth most influential skater of all time

Founder of skate, clothing, and distribution companies

The pride of Lakeland, Florida

Good ol' southern boy Andrew "The Boss" Reynolds put Florida back on the map by obsessively working hard to deliver part after video part equally loaded with power and precision that continue to fuel his mystique and persona. Most pro skaters have a frontside flip in their repertoire. Drew transformed this skateboarding staple into his signature brushstroke. His powerful approach bodied the trick so hard he elevated it to MC Rakim Allah status— meaning he flipped it—and "now it's a daily word" for skaters around the world. After Drew added his flair to the trick, popped high, caught clean midway no matter if it was across a huge gap, down stairs, or over handrails, everyone wanted to frontside flip like him. His way became *the way*, influencing skateboarding style from the mid-'90s onward. Everyone wanted to be like him and be near him.

A little evidence: He had 12 signature shoes with Emerica, all smashes (the Reynolds 1, the slip-on, the high-top, the Vulc, etc.). He cofounded a clothing brand in 2006, Altamont, which embraced a throwback Easy Rider–aesthetic and skateboarding's counterculture roots. Despite the menacing subtext and frenetic artwork created by Heroin Skateboards founder and artist Mark "Fos" Foster, Altamont generated lines of skaters hungry to own a piece of Drew's apparel, often selling out before the clothes had even hit the skate shop floor.

Drew "influenced" long before we had the term. He helped pull skateboarding out of the big, clownish baggy pants era of the late '90s to early 2000s into the (sometimes equally comical) skinny jeans. That ability to drive culture helped earn him the title of "The Boss," and led him to be voted the tenth most influential skater by *TransWorld Skateboarding* magazine. You also are clearly "The Boss" when you can steal Tony Hawk's son, Riley, from his perch at Birdhouse and have him join your brand. (It's all good: Drew's daughter, Stella, has an open invitation to ride for Hawk at Birdhouse.)

Reynolds started out as a too-skinny kid from suburban Lakeland, Florida, near Tampa. At nine years old, he played other sports until he caught a glimpse of a legendary skate video, *Psycho Skate* (1988), on MTV. That, coupled with the inclusion of skateboarding videos in his local video store, aligned the stars, and the ship of organized sports sank into the night. His mother went above and beyond by transporting him to contests in the late '80s and early '90s without any expectation it could become a meal ticket. The Reynoldses had a history of adult vices that had affected the family negatively, and Drew's love of skateboarding seemed an easy proposition to support, which included building a mini ramp at their home just to keep him close and out of trouble.

Florida has one of the greatest skate scenes in the world. It is loose, it is loud, and it is laid-back and fun. The state has of the oldest operating skateparks in the country, Kona in Jacksonville, along with the Skatepark of Tampa, already in its twentieth-year run; the Boardr trio of businesses (see page 246); a slew of backyard ramps; the sunshine; and all of the beauty. In between the sun and fun came lessons from a man with an eagle eye for talent, who became an early mentor: Florida skateboarding legend John Montesi. I'm sure John's eyes will roll at the thought of being anyone's mentor, but it is true. John pushed the G&S skateboards team manager to recognize the skills of 14-year-old Drew. This set a chain of events in motion that landed his homemade "sponsor me" tape inside Tony Hawk's (see page 63) VCR and got him a place on Hawk's amateur team.

Here was a young skater, just like Hawk himself at that age, a scrawny kid—a kid a bit too big for his britches trying to launch tricks across grown-ass-person-sized stairs and handrails with such a tiny frame. Yet somehow, Drew feasted on the slams and stayed determined. Thirty, forty, sixty tries later he emerged victorious, just like a young Tony Hawk back when he too was the kid too small but too determined not to earn a place on Stacy Peralta's fabled Bones Brigade.

That relentlessness is what prompted the call from Tony telling Drew he'd earned a place alongside one of the greatest in skateboarding. Drew would internalize that as a subtle reminder that "dedication to skateboarding brought you here—dedication to skateboarding keeps you here."

Tony wanted a team of skate rats and that's just what he got with Drew and the crew from Birdhouse Projects (the earlier iteration of Birdhouse). During that time, Birdhouse transitioned from an upstart company built on Tony's maxed-out credit cards and penny-pinching to an enterprise. From '94 to '98, Drew's bowl-cut mane and lanky figure would be immortalized in skateboarding history as the inspiration for pro skater/artist Ed Templeton's iconic cartoon character Turtle Boy.

After his initial video game success, Tony would reimagine the skateboarding video with his magnum opus, 1998's *The End*. The legend of Drew Reynolds would begin here. His part had a huge impact on the video by adding a cool factor based on his technical skateboarding (performing tricks where the board often flips or rotates) and nonchalant ability to hurl said trickery down huge stair sets. The 16-millimeter film by Jamie Mosberg was then the most expensively produced skate video of all time.

Hurricane Drew, as they called him at Tampa's SPoT Skate Shop, mixed old school and new school in his skating for the video, best epitomized by the kickflip melon out of the snake run at the Bro Bowl, a skatepark built in the 1970s and one of the first in the U.S. These are boss moves—slapping your hometown on your back and bringing the thunder as part of one of the greatest teams and videos of all time. However, the video's title foreshadowed exactly what would happen—the end.

After appearing in the video, Drew transplanted himself to Surf City: Huntington Beach, California. Falling into the beach life and the home of the skate industry, The Boss would meet the skaters he idolized, Tom Penny and Chad Muska, who were etched into the skate pantheon and partied with ferocity, as well as Jim Greco, Brian Sumner, and later Elissa Steamer and others seeded from what would be called the Warner Mob, a group of exceptional skaters fast becoming a crew of powerhouse pirates. They filmed constantly with few off days. Their vernacular, like "hammers"—meaning throwing down the hardest tricks—and "after-black hammers" entered the lexicon. (The

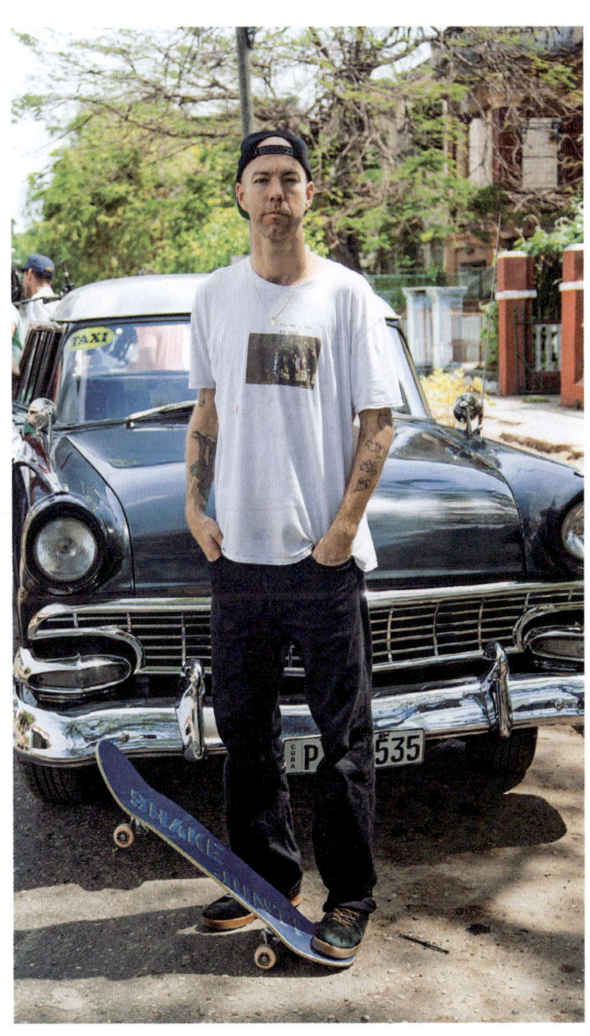

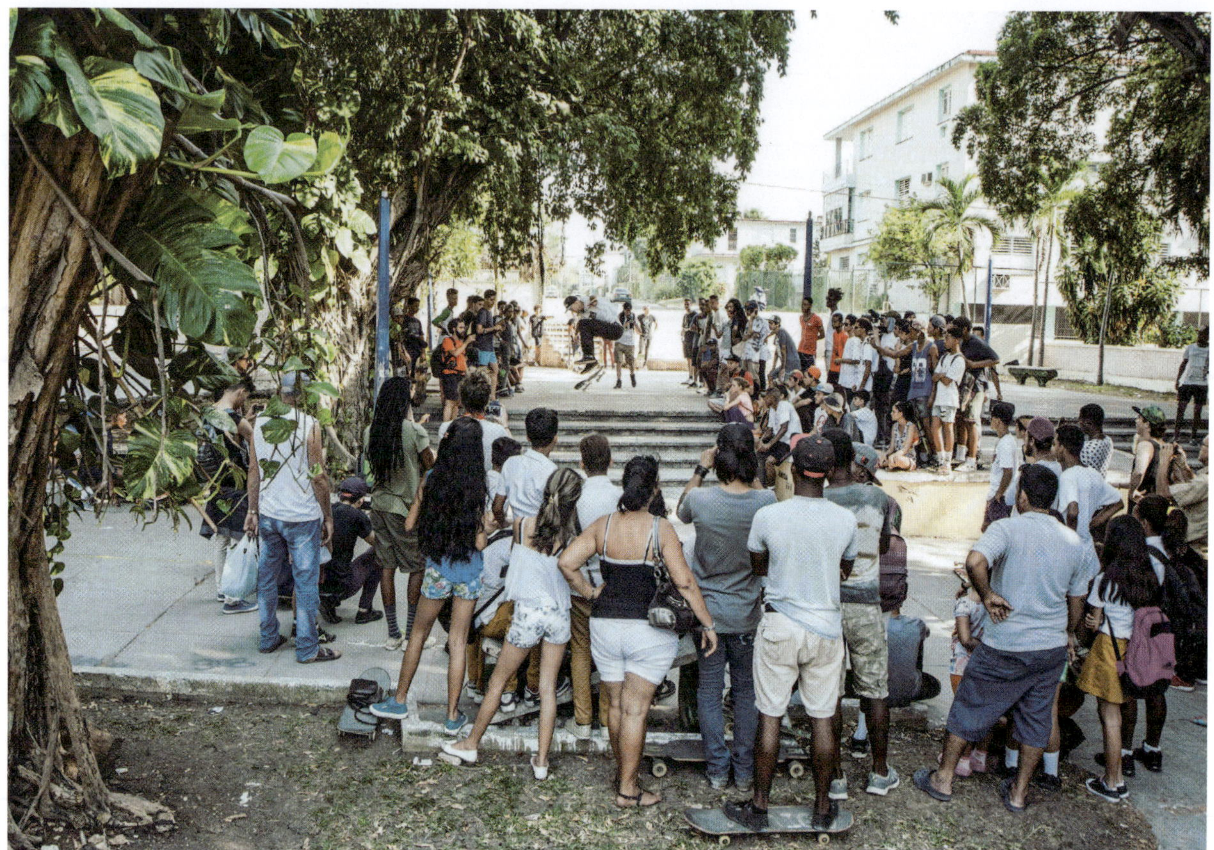

Andrew Reynolds, varial-heelflip for the crowd in Havana, Cuba

latter term was given to tricks that popped up, surprise style, after a video had ended and the screen had gone black.)

Drew found kindred spirits in the Warner Mob and forged a deep relationship with those closer to his own age and skating style. He soon went to Birdhouse with a proposition: Let me go or help me stay and create my own brand. That brand would become Baker, a nickname for a skater who woke up, smoked weed, and skated day and night. Baker introduced a new visual style under videographer Ryan "Beagle" Ewing. Unlike the high-end production of Birdhouse, Beagle's approach unflinchingly showed all the falls, fools, and fallibility of skaters. Sometimes you needed Bondo (the hardware store putty fix-all) to patch up cracks, and other times you navigated crack vials while skating spots and narrowly avoiding police. That unapologetic truth propelled the brand to the top. With that growth, Drew stepped into a new space and was bestowed the proper title for the head of a crew. The Boss brokered the deals and led the crew; a wave of his hands could cause trends to change overnight, and he could shut down any skate spot with his patented frontside flip. To the victor go the spoils.

While these skaters were some of the best in the world, they also developed world-class addictions.

The crew transformed from the Warner Mob to a posse with a more appropriate title, the Piss Drunx. Each hammer meant first a celebratory beer, then a sniff, and gradually, a bender. All on camera— and in full-page color ads. Eyes barely open but skating fully locked. Expertly marketed, the chaos and the crack-up simply appeared as the best in skateboarding having the best of times. They led the skate world like mad Pied Pipers, throwing flames and feeling they could roam unsinged, even after they lost one of their closest friends in a motorcycle accident fueled in part by the perils of excess.

Luckily for all of skateboarding, as Drew himself has said, once he moved into illicit substances. he found his cap. He channeled his energy into building up his mind and his body and perfecting his skate techniques so he could skate bigger things with fewer tries. He leveled up in a huge way, delivering standout parts in the Emerica videos *Stay Gold* (2010) and *This Is Skateboarding* (2003), inspiring others with his sobriety, earning magazine covers, and showing everyone that The Boss was back.

Respect.

THE SOULFUL SOUNDS OF STEREO SKATEBOARDING

CHRIS "DUNE" PASTRAS

Founding member of World Industries skateboards

Reinforced jazz and blues music's place in skateboarding culture

Inspired countless skaters to pursue photography

Cofounder of Stereo Skateboards

Announcer for global TV skateboarding contests

African American artist, pro skater, company owner, and TV announcer Chris "Dune" Pastras's efforts as one half of the early 1990s dynamic duo Stereo Skateboards solidified the integration of jazz, blues, and Americana into skateboarding iconography. Born to a Greek professor and jazz musician father and an African American elementary school teacher mother, the native of Metuchen, New Jersey, was indoctrinated into skateboarding through his godbrother Rodney Smith, who gave him his "Dune" nickname and promised to watch over him during their early searches for skateable terrain in the tristate area. Pastras eventually earned his place as part of Smith's team, the legendary East Coast powerhouse SHUT Skateboards. Those excursions placed the young teen in the company of one of the most innovative street skaters of all time, New Jersey–born pro skater Mike Vallely.

Maturing and eager, at 17 years old Pastras migrated west under the wing—and shaved head—of Mike V. The passage across the country included a front-row bench seat in Vallely's '81 Buick Regal and resulted in an *Iliad*'s worth of stories, many of them involving instances of racism and reverse racism in specific locales where people tried to comprehend which offense offered the greatest sin: A white skinhead-looking 21-year-old driving around a young Black man? A young Black man bringing a strange-looking young white man into Black neighborhoods? Or the crème de la crème for Not In My Backyard types—"dirty, raucous multiracial" skateboarders invading any town on the drive westward. Pastras summarized the trip as equal time spent on hillbilly hijinks, hormonal teen angst, and learning to court while on the road.

Deposited in Los Angeles, Pastras joined the now-infamous skateboarding brand World Industries, run by the uber-talented Rodney Mullen (see page 54) and the infamously committed Steve Rocco. However, during the early 1990s, World was little more than a fledgling startup with the slightly sinister aspiration of reshaping the industry. The dramatic change they proposed? Giving pro skateboarders more power and control over their signature products and public personas. Pastras solidified his place within that legacy by codeveloping the artwork for his then-controversial board graphic, the Dune "Baby."

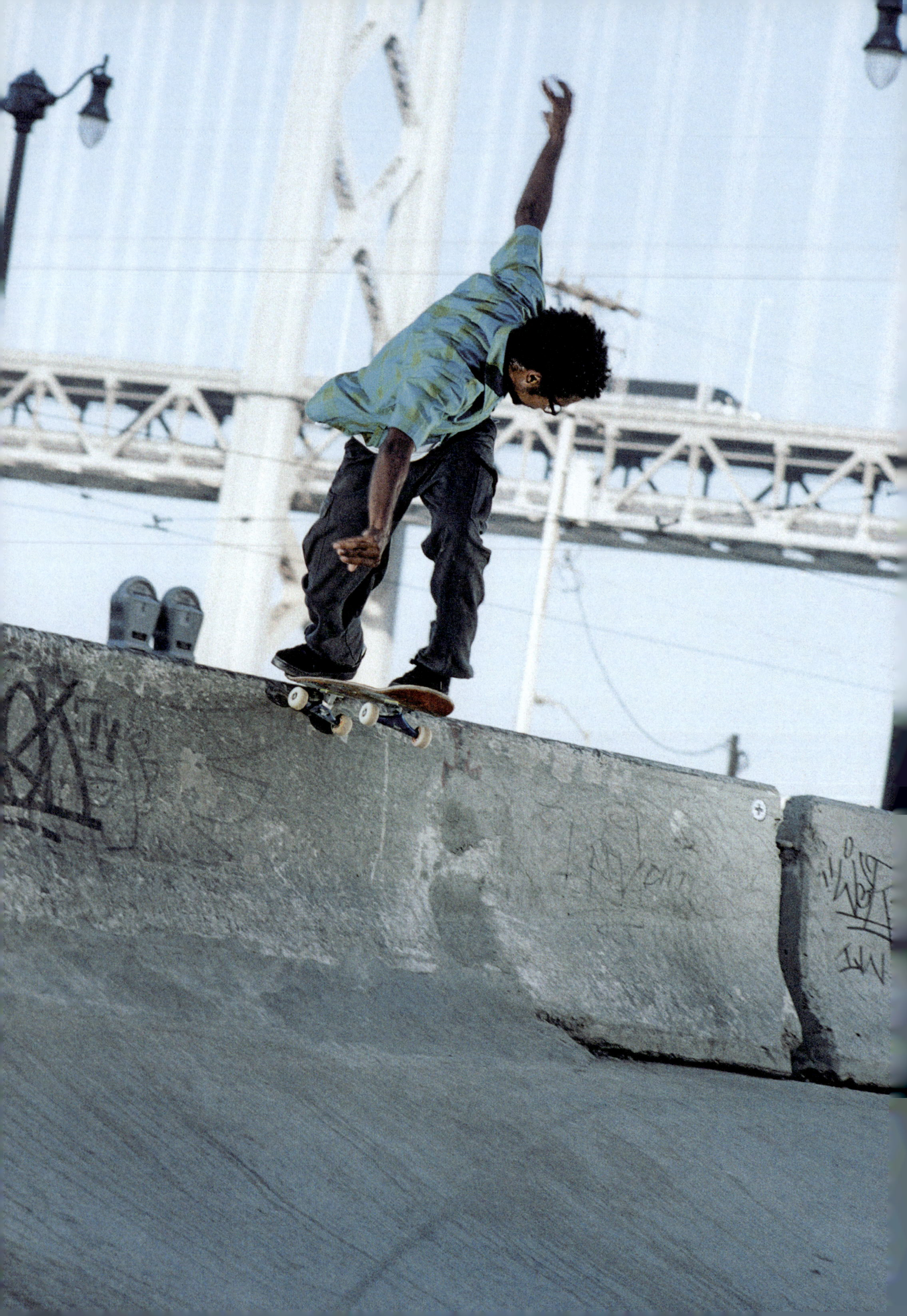

The Dune "Baby" would be the first to feature an easily discernable image of an African American figure—instantaneously intertwining racial politics, skateboarding culture, and commercialism. According to Pastras, it was really simple: he was an African American skater, and he wanted an African American image to represent him.

While that graphic came into the zeitgeist as one of the first intentionally pro-Black graphics and as a predecessor to skateboarding graphics in the activist arena (see The Activists, page 174), skateboarding careers operated differently then. Back in '91, while on tour with pro skater and future partner Jason Lee, both Pastras and Lee felt the writing was on the wall at World Industries. Things were moving fast and new talent was coming in droves. At the ripe old legal age to imbibe, Rocco believed Pastras and Lee were too old to remain on the World team. Feeling the pressure on tour, the two commiserated while shopping at thrift stores and music shops and discovered they had similar interests beyond skateboarding. Lee picked up wax Stax and the same jazz record labels that had been critical at points in Pastras's life—the sound of Pastras's father's music and that of his family. While Pastras had been chasing Kiss more than Coltrane at the time, their common pursuits sparked conversations around the quintessential sights and sounds of the American experience.

Departing World in 1992, Pastras and Lee—who later became a successful Hollywood actor—sought to present skateboarding through what they defined as "timeless, classic" imagery. It took a second for them to home in on the right mix—the first attempt being the short-lived Blue Skateboards, which also involved legendary African American pro skater Kareem Campbell (see page 46) and was backed by Vision Skateboards. The second attempt brought about the perfect formula sans Campbell and Vision but in a partnership formulated during a meeting in San Francisco with pro skaters Jim Thiebaud and Tommy Guerrero (see page 109) from Deluxe Distribution, owners of REAL Skateboards, and artist Jeff Klindt (RIP). This group of skater-musician-artists built a vibe that manifested as Stereo Skateboards. Their enduring brand pays visual and aural homage to early 20th-century Black, Brown, and roots musical styles. Pastras and Lee's brainchild also built upon the notion that there should be power, command of the instrument, and fluidity *within* the expression *of* skateboarding—the quintessential elements of jazz and blues.

Furthermore, inspired by the spontaneity of, and the beauty in, imperfections, Pastras and Lee embraced the analog mediums of 35mm photography, painting, illustration, and 8mm and 16mm film to document their exploits. Their

mid-'90s opuses, the films *A Visual Sound* and *Tincan Folklore*, presented skateboarding as a physical and visual manifestation of the spirit of full self-expression. Set to a 4-track soundtrack of improvisational music, Pastras and the team developed their own retro-themed, reflective style while their contemporaries utilized video and hip-hop. Their films weren't about popping off a million tricks as fast as they could. Stereo came from their collective vision to show how incredible skateboarding could be—the power of documenting someone flowing down the street, looking comfortable in their skin.

Pastras told me that countless people come up to Lee, and write letters, saying they would never have listened to jazz and blues if it weren't for Stereo. Others have told the pair that they went to film school and studied photography because they were inspired by Stereo's singular use of 8mm and 16mm film when everyone else was using video.

Pastras's contribution through Stereo provided an alternative outlet for thinking about the possibilities of skateboarding not as a verb but as an *aesthetic* or a way of being—in tune with oneself, one's board, and the city. Before the lure of the "vintage" filters, the "TBT" and return of the artisanal, Pastras and Lee were 'bout that life.

Skateboarding's most visible model of allyship and shared responsibility, Stereo remains their love letter to skateboarding and as impervious to change as your parents' love of the Stones and your auntie's love of "Uncle L" (LL Cool J) and to this day is a home for creative skateboarding.

THE GIFT THAT KEEPS ON GIVING
ISHOD WAIR

One of the greatest skaters of the modern era

Sickest with the tricks

A skate rat's skate rat

Thrasher **2013 Skater of the Year**

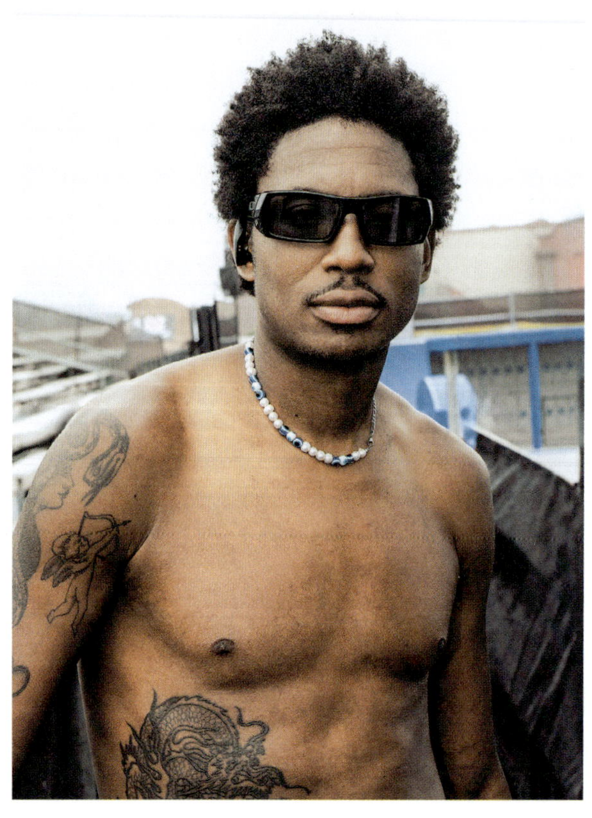

The Young OG. That's the perfect description of African American pro skater Ishod Wair. The man with "the gift." Easily in everyone's top five skaters of modern times. Video parts? The heaters he puts out on the 'gram are, for him, throwaway clips that are better than some people's actual footage for their sponsors' full-length promo videos. No shade to others, but no one throws up wetter kickflip frontside noseslides—then frontside flips or switch tre's in a line—better. There are people who do all of those tricks in amazing fashion, but what distinguishes Ishod is that there's no end to the tricks he calmly holds under his belt. Not since Lavar McBride in the '90s, the king of forever lines, have we seen talent like that. Ishod can go on trick after trick until the person filming (commonly referred to as a filmer) runs out of battery, and all skaters know that when they see it. He's not trying to figure out what tricks to get for his video part; he's figuring out how the hell he's gonna make an edit with the overabundance. Few skaters get to have that problem.

I hear it from anyone who has been on tour with Ishod: He shows up at the spot, gets tricks and more tricks while you're working on your fundamentals—hella casual. He's not flaming you at all, he just has so much gift, it's hard to stop him from giving.

What's more, Ishod has earned a special place in the heart of modern street skaters because he is serving *e'rythang*. He can skate street, he can skate contests, the elusive mini ramp, backyard pools, and jarring concrete transitions anywhere in the world. Through it all, his skating offers an easy finesse and precision that makes it seem like every aspect of skating is simply in his vocabulary. As if he were born to do this.

The thing is, he was, but that doesn't mean he's not trying. Ishod Wair is a thinker—or in skateboarding, a 100 percent skate rat. It is that

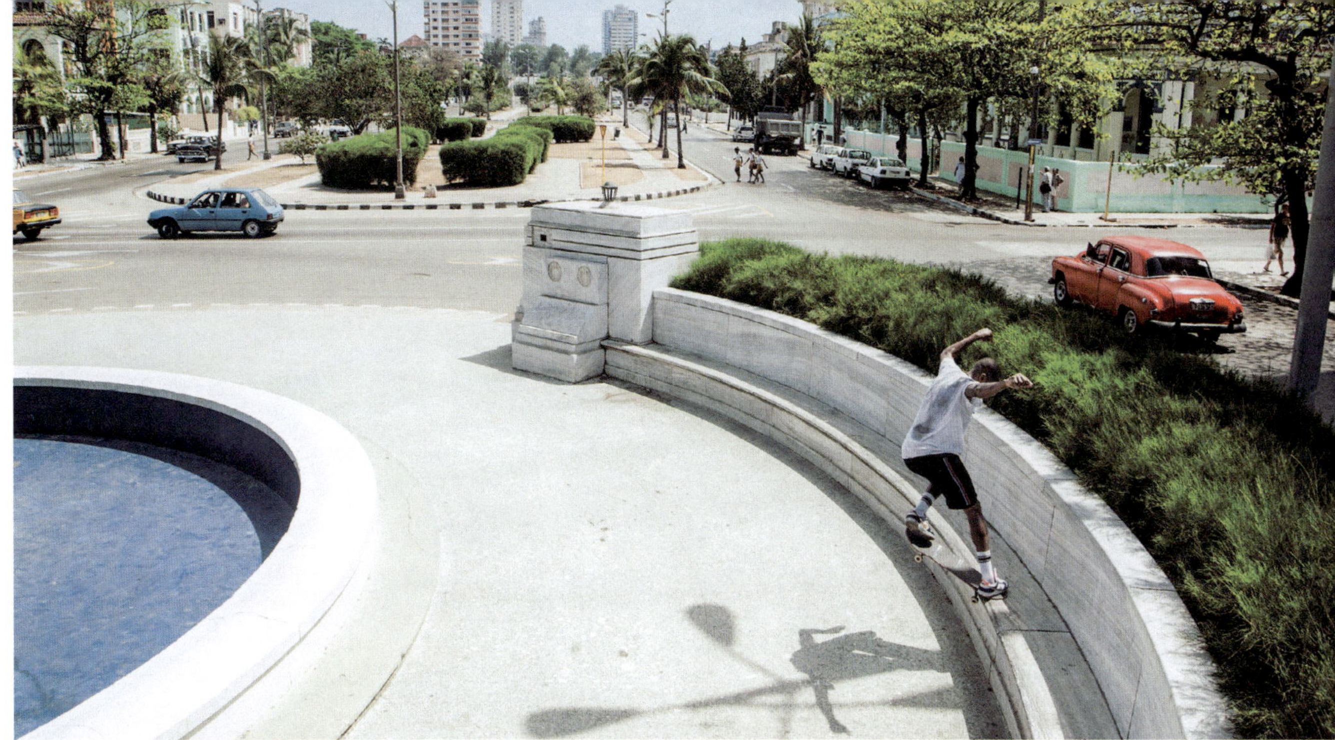

Ishod Wair, frontside crooked-grind in Havana, Cuba

part that surprises people. Ishod is living and breathing and processing the thought and feel of skateboarding constantly. He examines videos of others' and his own skateboarding with a laser focus and precision for how things work. While his execution looks flawless, he earned his place in the current echelon and truthfully, if you knew him in his old days in Philly, it would have been easy to overlook him. Even he didn't know if his skating was gonna get a spark.

In retrospect, he thinks he was probably too young at 13 or 14 to be taking the train into Philly to skate with the heavyweights at Love Park. But his love of skating and his time with a crew that ate up every second of skate content they could just made it too appealing to not try to do *every* trick and visit *every* place they saw in skate videos, magazines, or *Tony Hawk's Pro Skater*. He just wanted to be in the mix, even if he wasn't ripping.

"I was always a little shrimp," Ishod told me. "I didn't have power, even though I was skating all the time. I had tricks but they just weren't anything special because I was so small. Once I grew into it, though, that's when it really changed."

During his transformation from Lil' Ishod, he became a staple at Woodward skate camps in Pennsylvania and won contests that helped him travel to other competitions and get noticed. As his power emerged, he started placing top-three in amateurs around the U.S. That makes him different from other skaters of his era; though he is an aughts skater, his approach is like those of the late '80s who turned pro by not being camera-shy and giving their all even when the camera was on.

With heart, power, experience, and trick selection combined—bam! Ishod shot a bullet into the heart of skateboarding, and we have loved him ever since. His 2013 *Thrasher* Skater of the Year win is testament to that love affair. He is HIM, as they say.

Yet despite the accolades, he is still the same skate rat, rolling as if he has things to prove and skills to be sharpened. I watched him compare angles of approach for tricks and the perfect hand placement for grabbing stalefish (an ollie-grab variation) on transition for hours with Andrew Reynolds (see page 76) on our *Vice* magazine/Stance Socks tour supporting the Cuba Skate NGO in Havana. Dinner consisted of arroz con pollo with a side of skateboarding trick–based what-ifs.

Ishod brings a sense of lightness and authenticity that keeps skateboarding pure. It's a thing we do, and love, and that the absolute best of us, like Ishod, still work on. Even with huge endorsements, and global traveling, Ishod keeps it 100. He's even modeling in Paris for Pharell and Louis Vuitton, but still talks skateboarding between fit changes. Two decades into his career, what more could he give to the culture than what he does every day, rolling around serving looks and serving up the goods at skate spots across the globe?

ROOKIE SKATEBOARDS
THE RISE OF THE SUPER FRIENDS
AND THE SUPER HOMIES

JUNG KWAN, ELSKA SANDOR & CATHARINE LYONS

Rebel trio who built a more inclusive culture

First East Coast women–led skateboarding company

Led a team of phenomenal multiracial multiethnic female (and later male) skaters

First "for us, by us" lauded women's skateboarding brand, boards, and apparel

In 1996, lightning struck when the trio of Jung Kwan, Elska Sandor, and Catharine Lyons banded together to create the first female-led, East Coast–based skateboarding company, Rookie. That thunderclap reverberated around the world and provided inspiration—directly and indirectly—for a new era of skaters. Skateboarding culture owes a debt to these ladies.

Rookie entered the market at the perfect time. There was an infatuation in the '90s with the type of gritty East Coast skating popularized by brands like Zoo York and their subsidiaries, and a broader boost in skateboarding visibility through the X Games (1994) and later the bestselling *Tony Hawk's Pro Skater* video game franchise (launched in 1999). That meant that not only was there a scene but there were enough contests for Rookie team members like Hall of Famer Jaime Reyes and Jessie Van Roechoudt to earn money from the events, remain authentically hip skating in the streets,

and earn extra coverage in non-skate media outlets because of the buzz around skateboarding. Armed with some of the best female skaters in the world, Rookie took the action sports media's scantily clad, sun-kissed representations of passive female skateboarders watching the boys and spun them on their head. They presented women with real skateboarding skills, like Van Roechoudt, Reyes, and Lauren Mollica.

Reyes, for instance, could skate anything in her path—mini ramps, parks, contests. One of the few women and people of color to grace the cover of *Thrasher* (a copy of her issue lives in the Smithsonian), she delivered photos and video parts that are a clinic in smooth, flowing skateboarding with power and technical precision. She could throw her specialty 360 flips and nollie 360 flips at a moment's notice and bust down the handrails at the Brooklyn Banks, or any spot for that matter, that men wished they could step up to. Boardslides,

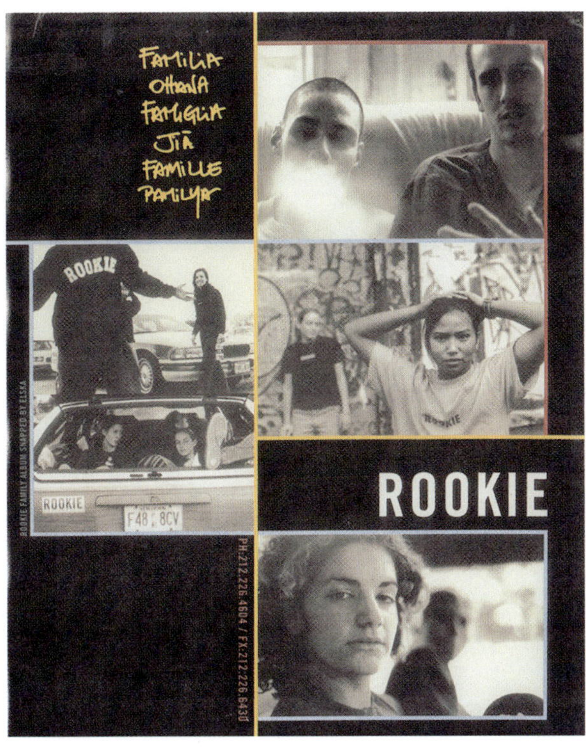

backlips, flip-ins, flip-outs—she was a skater's skater and remains a hero to this day.

What also made Rookie unique was that Kwan, Sandor, and Lyons envisioned a more inclusive skateboarding culture. They put that dream into practice by having a multigendered, multiracial, and multiethnic roster. In the melting pot of New York City, where cultures, histories, and political action all share confined common space, the result is an explosion of community. Of course, the team would represent everyone willing to ride night and day regardless of identity—it was a product of the city. Rookie was a love letter to NYC and to women in charge of their lives in skateboarding.

Every Rookie ad made you want to skate cutty (hidden) spots with them into the wee hours of the morning and to join them at Max Fish, the quintessential skate bar stickered from floor to ceiling with skate brand logos, local bands, and street art. That vibe permeated the brand and the city, and they were the people to roll with and to crash with when the night ended.

Kwan, Sandor, and Lyons, as active female skaters amid the sweaty skate days and faded nights, took their ownership and brands seriously and rebelled against the ill-fitting men's clothing often passed off as women's clothing, misogynistic board graphics, and the dominant ideology of men creating a woman's skate endeavor, to "shrink it and pink it." Rookie was on the front lines of change, designing clothing and skateboards that women and men wanted to skate in and on. Any Rookie paraphernalia was highly coveted and those brandishing the six-letter word epitomized cool.

Rookie was also uber street-certified because it was synonymous with the local scene, and just as "True East" as Zoo York. It was also part of a broader collective that shared pride in being underdogs. New York brands like 5boro, Brooklyn Boards, and street phenom Supreme were all in the same boat with Rookie, new brands pushing to make themselves and their East Coast perspectives heard. The chips on everyone's shoulders lent themselves to the sharing of information regarding production artwork and design.

Rookie team riders contributed to the art and design, which meant they all had agency and a voice and place within the brand. One of Rookie's most impactful graphics was a quiet celebration of Reyes's dedication to, and representation of, her AAPI heritage. Her signature model featured the lyrics from a native Hawai'ian lullaby and drawings of foliage from the island. While that

Classic Rookie Skateboard "ads," top and bottom, late '90s.

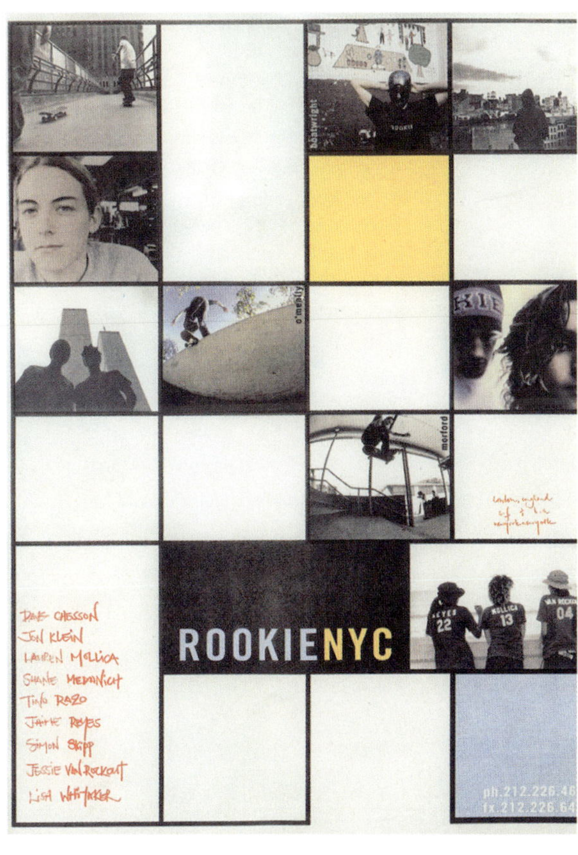

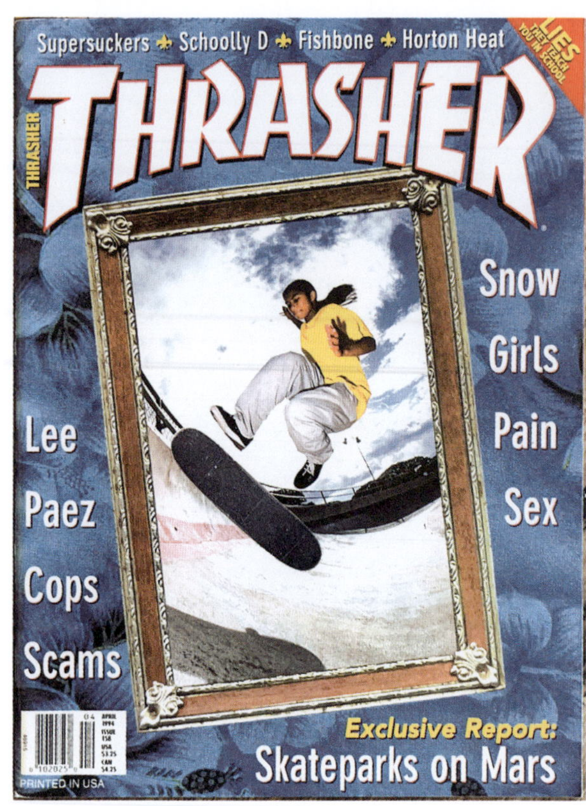

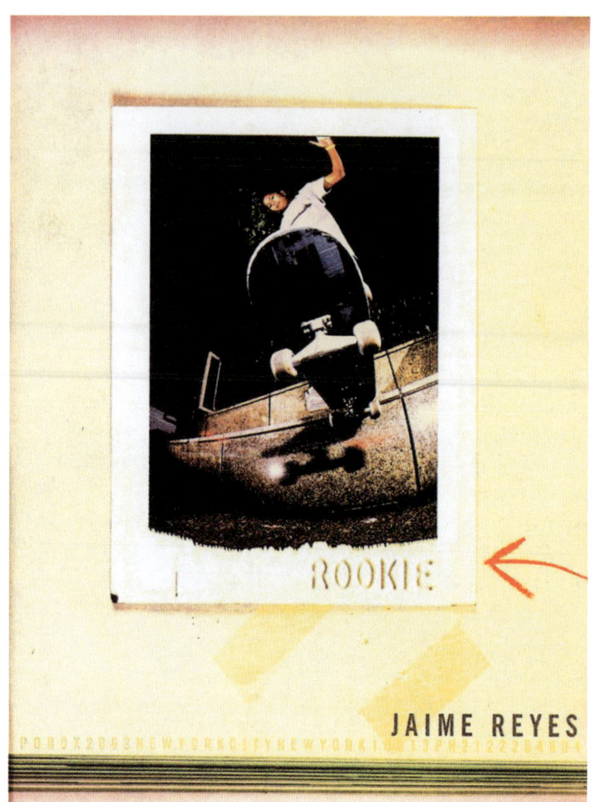

Jaime Reyes on the cover of *Thrasher* and in Rookie ad.

board represented a quieter, gentler Reyes, another equally important Rookie-created signature model graphic illustrated her less contemplative side. No less authentic, this Reyes graphic depicted her on the top of a pile of people fighting below her, with a sly smile, quietly indicating her place as conqueror and catalyst of the melee. Though Reyes presently lives as peacefully as a monk, back then—well, those who knew her joked that she might be at the center of a storm on any given Sunday. When I asked her to elaborate on that graphic, she noted that she could neither confirm nor deny that the image is an accurate rendering of a particular night of debauchery at Max Fish.

Rookie's place in skateboarding is a significant one, marking a moment when the skate DIY ethos stretched across gender barriers—and naming a pioneering trio who turned the idea of equal positioning for women and men into action. While Rookie would eventually go under during the U.S. financial crisis of the early aughts, each member of the crew's U.S. and international team (Reyes, Mollica, Van Roechoudt, Monica Shaw, Jon Klein, Sean Kelling, Kyla Duffy, Stefanie Thomas, Shane Medanich, Amy Caron, Tino Razo, Lisa Whitaker, Dave Chesson, Simon Skipp) contributed to the majesty that made Rookie the low-key phenomenon that proved women as equals in skateboarding. Guided by the hands of the super friends Kwan, Sandor, and Lyons, they were the first to show that we are all stronger together.

THE LOUISIANA SWAMP RAT WHO WAS "SUUUPER" GOOD

SALVADOR "SAL" LUCAS BARBIER

Skateboarding Hall of Famer & inventor of the Sal flip

First African American to design a pro model shoe

First African American to have his shoe design in the Smithsonian

Founder of iconic brand 23 Skateboard Co.

It is 1995 and shit is just hitting. Your headphones, locked and loaded. You just finished an *epic* skate mix. A lil' ODB, *"Shimmy shimmy ya, shimmy yam shimmy yea . . . For you to even touch my skill, you gotta go through one killer bee and he aim for the kill."* You go the Roots, Tupac, and that Mobb Deep for the East, E-40 for the Bay, and that southern slang with the Goodie Mob. Cracking. The sun is high in the sky and your pants are BIG. Clearly a size 40 waist, as mine were, wrapped tight with an excessively long, graying shoestring.

"Put a real belt on!" parents yelled, but what do they know about dat skate life? Leather belts broke down under long-term exposure to salt and skate sweat. Scout and web belts? Almost worse. They held the scent of all-day skating like dollar-store tube socks—it leached out after skating, lying in a cold knotted mess atop your dresser. Blah. You got it right, shoestring belt, 40s pants, and the most important kicks in the game from Etnies: the Salvador Lucas Barbier pro model (SLB).

Ahhh, that new-new. The Sal 23. You can almost still smell the black suede from the unboxing. Those joints with the little 23 sewn on the outside changed everything. The number 23 is an homage to the greatest team-sport athlete, Michael Jordan.

The nod created a shared history between African Americans impacting mainstream U.S. sports and the newcomers taking the show on the road through skateboarding.

This iconic shoe resonated so deeply with the culture that 20 years and several reissues later, it almost seems like it never left. And the hits don't stop—the original SLB sample resides in the permanent collection of the Smithsonian Museum. (The photo I took of this cultural icon is in the mix there, too.)

For most of us, creating a shoe that became synonymous with skateboarding would be plenty. But this is only one aspect of a lifetime of achievement for the African American designer, company owner, and entrepreneur, the incomparable Salvador "Sal" Lucas Barbier.

Raised in Baton Rouge, Louisiana, in the 1970s, Barbier spent his earliest days among a middle- and upper-class, predominantly Black community, many of whose members worked for a major oil and gas manufacturer. Barbier knew engineers, designers, and a spectrum of blue-collar and white-collar affluence and influence. His family's proximity to historically Black colleges and universities (like Southern University and A&M

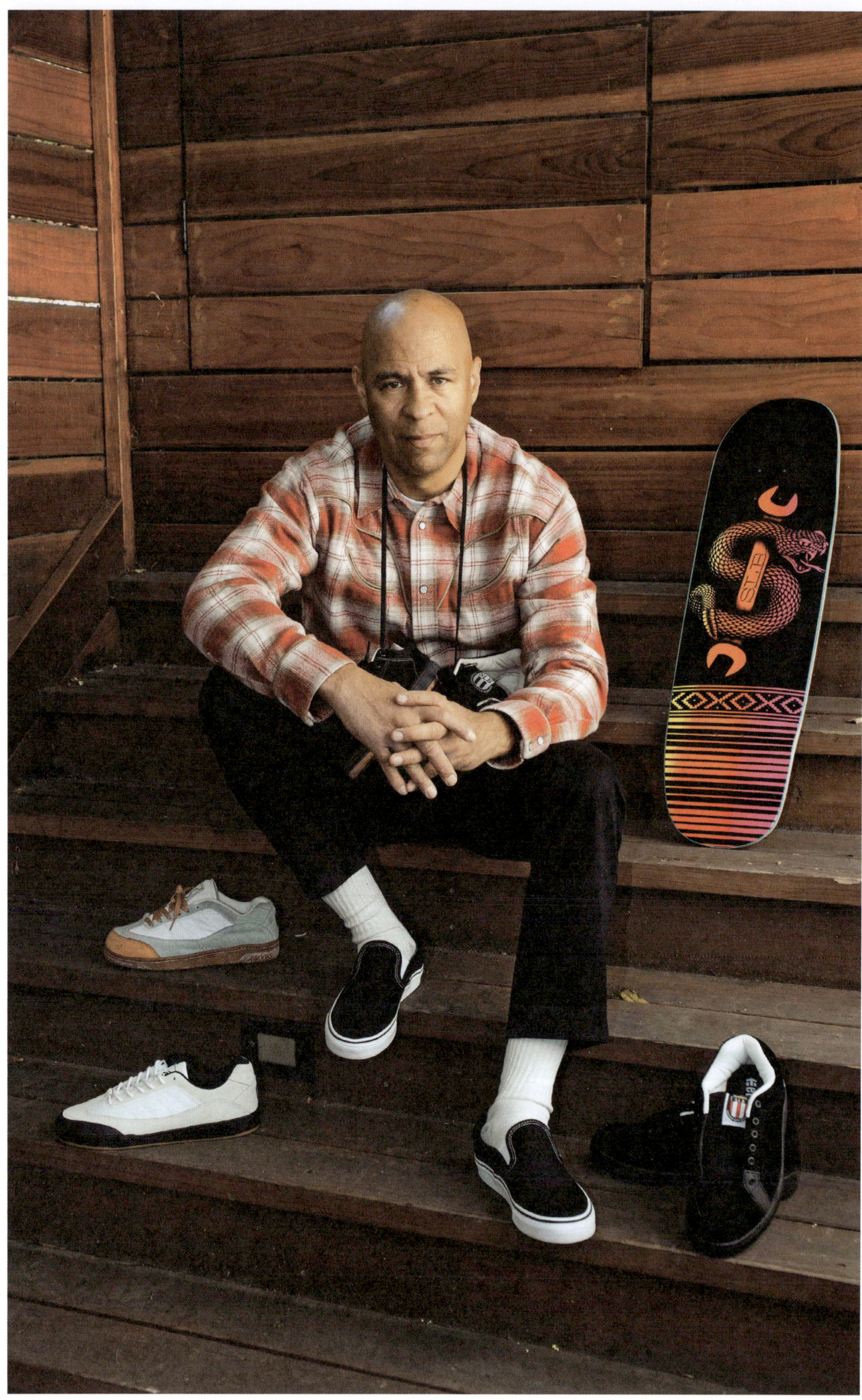

College) and Black success also offered Barbier the chance to envision his Blackness and ingenuity as a badge of pride rather than an anomaly. Among the populace, Black greatness was the standard—and the kids of this world knew they were more than capable in any situation. The positive affirmation imparted two sets of formative questions to young Barbier: Why not me? And, if not me, then whom? That thinking would lead him to always put himself and his ideas first, not because of ego, but out of a sense of fairness and equity that would propel him during several pivotal moments in his career.

While his early days were joyous, the separation of his parents during his preadolescence jolted him. He moved to a less affluent part of town, where the realities of the disparity made themselves plain. Black and white less-affluent folks lived together, but unlike the synergy of the previous community, they interacted differently. Here, Sal witnessed the way race, class proximity, and contempt manifest in the worst ways, even among similarly oppressed people. Barbier recalled how a darker-skinned Latinx truck-driving neighbor would hurl racial slurs (too rough to be printed here) at Black youth. "It let me see that ignorance can also be geographical," Sal told me. "He was the *only* Latinx guy in the neighborhood. Here he was acting like this toward other minorities. It made no sense to us. He didn't understand that he could also be public enemy number one."

Barbier's awareness of race would continue to grow throughout these pre-skateboarding days. Although Sal was well-liked and reveled with neighborhood kids across the racial spectrum, he realized that he was one of only a few capable of that feat. There was no unifying force amid racial tensions, and no daylight between the unwritten norms. Luckily, Sal found solace under the cover of the blurred lines of skateboarding's anarchy. In all its newness, Sal became aware of its ability to roll into, and eventually over, boundaries.

Early 1980s skateboarding's place as an outsider activity was clear. Skaters still wandered in packs searching for empty pools and cobbling together backyard ramps. Some of the edgiest migrated deeper into the streets hoping to quench their ravenous hunger for skateable space. The innovations that occurred during those wanderings showed up in *Thrasher* but rarely made mainstream headlines. Unless of course it was to declare these groups a "menace" or to portray them as marijuana-addled, antiestablishment youth. The plea "Skateboarding is not a crime" emerged from that heavy crackdown. From marginalization, though, came unity. Outlaw times build an outlaw tribe and that is exactly where Barbier thrived. Sal told me: "Back then it was living the lifestyle of an outcast, and with that culture comes the music, and the fashion, and you end up very relatable to someone else sharing the same passion."

Not everyone got the message—especially the adults. Multiple times Sal heard the hushed (or sometimes loudly broadcast) comment, "No Black people are allowed at this house," and the crushing outcome of friends struggling to make excuses for their racist parents. I've felt that whiplash myself. Skaters rolling ahead of the curve and parents kicking and screaming to pull them back. It was the minefield of 1980s backyard ramps. "Racism just came with the territory, when only a select few even had a backyard to build in," Sal said. "Not everyone had access to wood, tools, and space. But we always found a way around the obstacles."

Despite the parental environment, Barbier spent his teens building bridges with other desperados, making a name for himself as a great skater and getting sponsored by several skate shops. During that time, he invented a trick still popular today, dubbed the Sal flip (a 360 varial flipping and moving the board by hand). If you don't know, imagine the nose of the board as your morning coffee spoon. You pop the board into your hand then swirl it once around like a spoon in your cup, while turning the spoon upside down and back again at the same time.

Sal was skating upward of 35 contests a year, but still not defining himself as an athlete. Instead, he identified as a tastemaker with a confident sense of culture, style, and business, helping guide local shops in their decisions about what products to carry and what pros to bring in. After placing top-three in a National Skateboarding Association contest—the premier contest of its day—Sal decided to call in a previously lobbed, "if you're ever in SoCal" offer. Still only half-heartedly believing in "professional skateboarding," Sal dove headfirst into an equally challenging action sport, California couch surfing.

Intending to just sniff around the beach and savor the breeze, Sal found a startling change in perspective around race relations and social mobility. Though not perfect, it certainly was not Louisiana, where the hard, fast, and unwritten rules quietly governed and policed Black bodies and their relationships to their white counterparts. "You just knew where you could be, and where you couldn't be," said Sal. This was different. California presented a gold mine of new ideas and perspectives. People were living as pro skaters! Okay, truthfully, "living" might be a stretch—it was probably closer to subsisting—but they were having *fun*. Sal started to let loose, too. Now he wasn't just a fire skater, but a personable human. You need the right mix of sick skating and sense of humor to make it, and Barbier delivered.

Sal became part of a relatively new outfit out of Carlsbad, H-Street Skateboards, home to vert icon Tony Magnusson and co-owner and team manager Mike Ternasky (RIP). There, Sal took his place beside the first African American professional street skateboarder, Ron Allen. During the mid- to late '80s, turning pro for street skating was novel. Vert still ruled, and street was something to do between sessions. However, H-Street and other newcomers saw the potential in street skating and its relatability to the everyday skater lacking the acreage and carpentry skills for a backyard ramp. Still, H-Street was largely unknown until the premiere of its homemade video, 1988's *Shackle Me Not*, turned the industry on its head. *Shackle*'s raw homemade feel and straight-to-VHS format took a no-frills approach to skateboarding. All killer, no filler.

Showcasing vert and emerging street skaters, including Sal, Ron Allen, and Matt Hensley, among others, the video launched our minds into a frothing sea of skateboarding possibilities. Instantly relatable on first viewing, these kids showed that the urban landscape was a ready-made playground begging for exploration. It also relayed the underground nature of skateboarding culture and the ever-watchful eyes of the security apparatus, and how it would forever play out in all our lives.

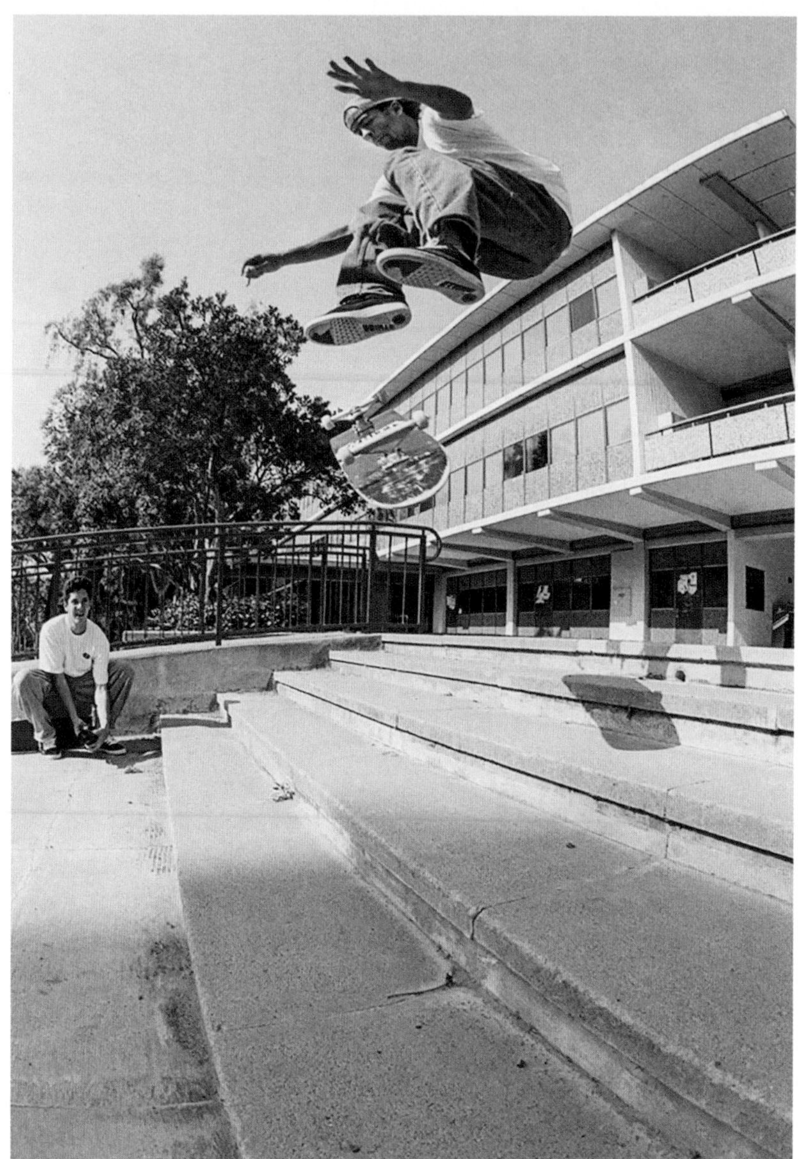

A simple video exchange and overdub between Barbier and a female police officer summed up our collective experience: "Name?" "Sal Barbier." "Age?" "Nineteen." "Do you have a job or anything?" "No, ma'am, just a vagrant." There it was—skateboarding in a nutshell.

Sal brought a southern flair, hospitality, and the slightest drawl, which on the mic was pure comedy. And the only thing stronger than Sal and his cohorts' runs in *Shackle Me Not* was the nuclear fallout from the *next* H-Street release, 1989's *Hokus Pokus*. There we found Sal among an even deeper roster of talent. A seven-word introduction forever stomped a Godzilla level of understatement into the skateboarding pantheon: "Sal Barbier, Louisiana swamp rat. Suuuper good." No ish. Barbier's part is still fire.

When Sal left H-Street, he joined Plan B Skateboards, with H-Street's departed team manager, Mike Ternasky (RIP). Under the Steve

Rocco and World Industries header, Plan B delivered the most technically innovative and inspiring videos: 1992's *Questionable* and 1993's *Virtual Reality*. These were harbingers of many shifts and surprises that would typify 1990s skateboarding culture. The latter also signaled the retirement of Sal Barbier as a pro skater, and the jump-start of the next phase of his career.

Sal began designing shoes for éS Footwear and started his first skateboarding company, 23 Skateboard Co. A short-lived affair, it let Sal's humor loose—23's logo was a skateboard adorned with classic Hot Wheels lettering. 23 gave a home to skaters' skaters such as Drake Jones and Jason Dill, now the owner of seminal skate company Fucking Awesome, and all-terrain fireball Anthony Van Engelen. Sal's hands-on approach affected every aspect of his skate life. I watched him take a screwdriver to the innards of a cupsole just to make the shoe more skateable.

Sal's other big success can be found in the magic of his brand Aesthetics Skateboards, "the Stüssy of skateboarding," Sal stated. The look was super clean and stretched far beyond the early inside jokes of 23. Aesthetics presented a more mature graphic and brand identity, more collegiate than comical, and offered another side of the Barbier genius.

He also expanded into apparel design with Elwood Clothing, which offered a more refined kit for skaters by injecting button-downs and wovens into skate attire. Elwood struck a chord, expertly drawing from some of Aesthetics's collegiate styling, Western wanted posters, and Japanese car culture without missing a beat. Endorsed by superstars Sean Sheffey, Shiloh Greathouse, Daewon Song, and Gino Iannucci, how could it not be a smash? It skewed heavily POC, apart from Iannucci, who gets a forever pass for nearly always skating to Wu-Tang. The addition of Keith Hufnagel (RIP), founder of the clothing brand HUF, and the ever-stylish Kenny Anderson produced the dreamiest of teams.

In an almost ironic turnaround, the final team that Sal assembled for Elwood—a veritable who's who of clean styles and perfectly executed skateboarding—would be stolen by the Stüssy clothing brand.

In the most hat trick of hat tricks, when his partner in Aesthetics chose to act funny with the money, Sal simply Cinderella'd his entire Aesthetics team to the seminal brand Zoo York. Under Barbier, Zoo York obtained an influx of skateboarding credibility, while Sal and the team gained significant financial footing. Together, they grew exponentially, until a change in direction came from investors more focused on the Zoo York IP than its skateboarding roots.

Never one to rest, Sal departed and launched his signature brands, SLB and Skateboard Veteran. A smash with older skaters, the limited-edition products continue to sell out immediately. Fortunately for us non-hypebeast types, samples from the small runs now reside within the Smithsonian's permanent collection. The artifacts serve as testaments to the ingenuity of one of the greatest to ever do it, with another rerelease of the indelible Sal Barbier pro model, this time dubbed the Sal 20 (turns out the 23 might carry a trademark these days). Thirty-plus years in and Sal Barbier continues to define the game.

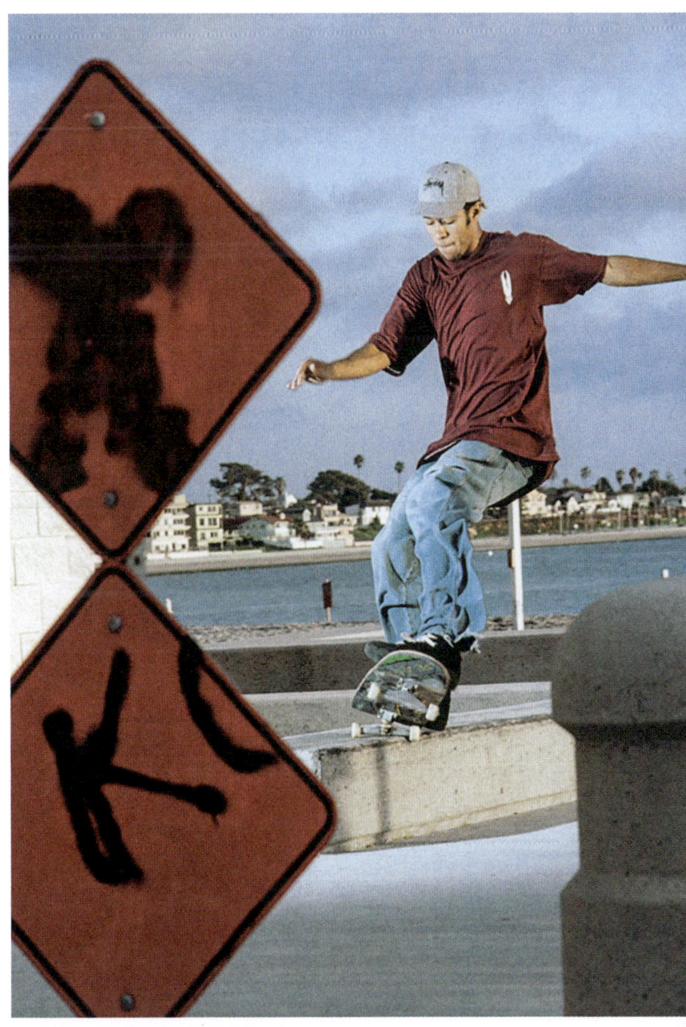

MARK "GONZ" GONZALES

The standard in street skating

Artist who brought playfulness and wonder to skateboarding

Switch skateboarding innovator

Co-creator of Blind Skateboards' *Video Days* with Spike Jonze

A 1985 Vision skateboards ad with the Salvador Dalí quote "I cannot guarantee that this fragment of a dream will be well received" introduced us to the person who would become *TransWorld SKATEboarding*'s and Tony Hawk's choice for the most influential skateboarder of all time, Mark "Gonz"—or, more often, "*the* Gonz"—Gonzales.

Unlike in a typical ad photo of a vert skater in the air with throngs of fans below, which was customary for the mid-1980s, Gonz is on the street performing a hyper-tweaked Japan air over a park bench within an '80s stylized three-tone ad. A simple introduction to the world, but upon review you see something that for years would be indicative of Gonz. It shows him delivering an amazing trick when people least expect it. The crowd appears to be almost looking away from him in the shot, as if there could *possibly* be something more important.

That reverence no longer escapes him. The Gonz lives in that space of the inconceivable and the imperceivable. He brings inspiration to skateboarding—not by exacting technical precision, but by letting miracles and mishaps flow through him. That is part of his practice. "If you can not be afraid to be laughed at," Gonz has said, "you could do so many things."

Gonz injected a sense of playfulness and wonder into skateboarding that emphasized the relationship between experimentation and innovation. His shameless pursuit of that practice has left skateboarding better than he found it.

Mark Gonzales was born in 1968 in Huntington Park, a small, mainly Latinx city in Los Angeles County. Skateboarding arrived early: his grandfather handcrafted lacquered boards for his older brother before Gonz even began skating. However, once the siblings received proper store-manufactured boards, the lifelong obsession began that created skateboarding's engineer of innovation.

Not long after he entered his teen years, Gonz's skating caught the eye of the legendary Christian Hosoi (see page 17), and later, Tony Alva's brand, Alva Skateboards.

As Christian's dad, Pops Hosoi, tells it, he and Christian were Gonzales's first sponsors, giving him boards from their personal collections before Tony formally enlisted Gonz as a member of the Alva team. They recognized the young skater of color's ability to place mind over matter and to will inventive new tricks into existence. That extra ingredient is what would eventually lead Gonz to do the first board slides on handrails (with Natas

Kaupas, see page 74), the first 50-50s, and the first 180 nosegrinds. Nearly the first to do everything on street. It's more a question of what Gonz *didn't do* rather than vice versa.

In 1985, Gonz won the National Skateboard Association's street style contest. At that time, these contests were not the Olympic events they are now. They were usually held in a parking lot with random obstacles, like a car with some jump ramps, a few parking blocks, and a picnic table. During that contest, Gonz blasted over every obstacle and ollied across, atop, and beyond anything put in his path. People hadn't learned how to fully ollie yet, and Gonz was already doing far more advanced tricks throughout the competition than anyone had seen, a blur that hadn't even been named. This would continue throughout his career. He was the standard in street skating, teaching people how to ollie, 180, and boardslide.

What was unique is that Gonz didn't suppress his ingenuity. He put it on display, whether we understood it or not. For example, light-years ahead of everyone else, Gonz skated switch stance, meaning he performed tricks with the "wrong" foot forward, not just on his own time but during contests. He demonstrated how to skate switch stance when we were barely learning how to push with speed. He would 180 up to switch 50-50 grind down the rail. Switch ollies, switch boardslides, switch everything. Now we recognize that skating with the nondominant foot adds another level of difficulty to a maneuver. In fact, it is skating switch that helps some skaters eke out wins over their peers and earn medals at the Olympics and other events. But when Gonz was inventing those tricks, the judges didn't know what to make of them or how to score them. They were just Gonz tricks—too fantastical and incomparable to be from anyone but the prince of progression, Mark Gonzales.

Gonz taught us to look at skateboarding as art in motion. Not only did he show us how to flow, he established that "this is the way." He delivered that art in both figurative and literal terms, demonstrating that skateboarding could be not only movement but the actual canvas. His quiver of boards resembled the best zines loaded to the brim with hand-drawn images and photos, all strung together with homemade grip-tape frames. The crème de la crème? Gonz's paint pen game hiittin' like barbs, with captions like, "Yes, I try to act weird." Within all of his art, from boards to notepads, from napkins to kitchen cabinets and

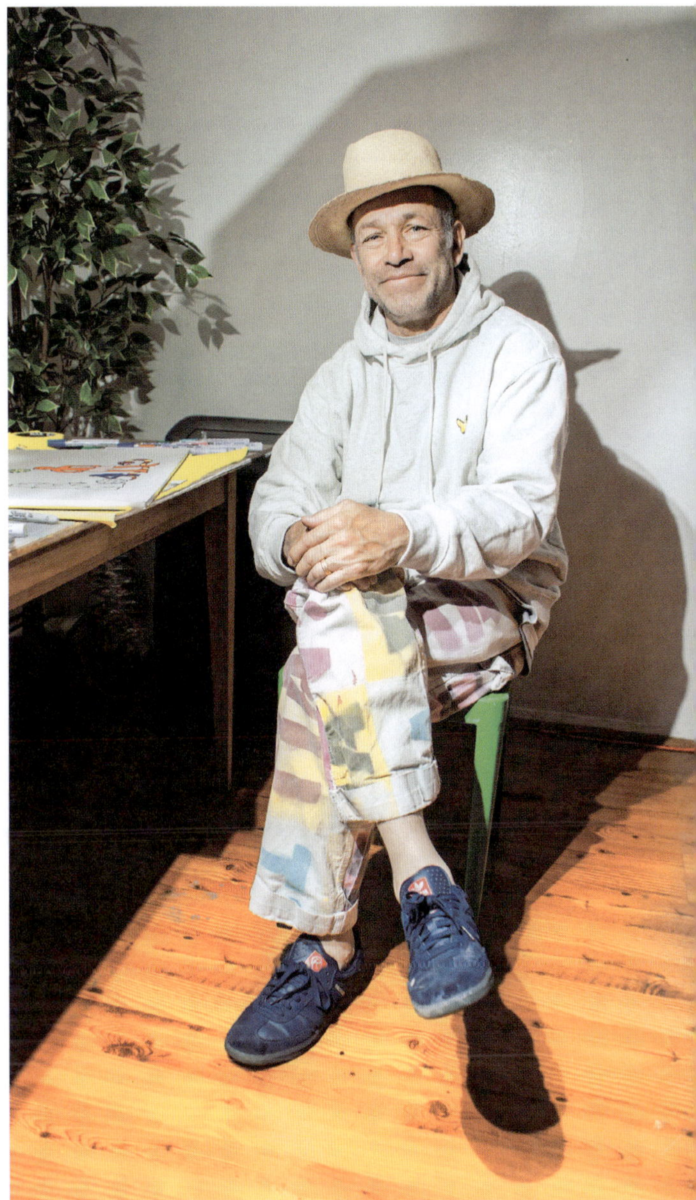

chairs, Gonz created small diatribes on society, from street drugs and sex to the *Mona Lisa*.

His kit, his art, and his skating always look invented in the moment. Part of that ingenuity came from Gonz learning Rodney Mullen's (see page 54) freestyle tricks, but instead of doing them in an exacting way like Rodney, Gonz reveled in dipping those tricks in a bucket of impromptu and mopping them nonchalantly all over the earth. He normalized skating the empty pools underneath the Eiffel Tower just as easily as dropping into a coffin (riding your skateboard on your back with your hands across your chest) while skating down a San Francisco hill.

Gonz's fearlessness extended into his commercial products as well. His original board with Vision featuring an '80s Technicolor abstract mockup of his face is one of the most recognizable and bestselling boards of all time. He created each subsequent model with his own art and set the precedent that an *entire* skateboard should be viewed as a canvas. This was virtually unheard of at a time when skateboarding was dominated by the three biggest board companies: Vision, Powell, and Santa Cruz / NHS skateboards. Eventually his relationship with Vision soured and he went on to develop a partnership with oft-maligned robber baron Steve Rocco from World Industries, which launched Blind, Gonz's own brand.

This change of address was also a change in direction announced to the world in an ad written in poison pen: "I've lost my Vision and gone Blind." The old era was over. Rocco's once fledgling brand now had all three kings of street skateboarding under its roof: Mike Vallely at World Industries proper; Natas with his own brand, 101 Skateboards, in partnership with Rocco; and Gonz with Blind. A stacked house, and an indication of the new direction of the skateboarding industry— the skater-owned company. For now, Gonz was in the driver's seat.

Gonz's house also featured skater-turned-actor Jason Lee, one of the best skaters of the time, and would include riders stolen from Stacy Peralta, the crown jewels of a new generation of skateboarders: Guy Mariano and Rudy Johnson. Gonz was the greatest street skater of the era and with his laid-back and fun-centered approach to skateboarding, something special was on the horizon.

Gonz and the Blind team, along with filmmaker Spike Jonze, making his directorial debut, would create one of the greatest skateboarding videos of all time. *Video Days* (1991) placed self-expression and fun at the core of what would become a heralded skit of skateboarding cinema, in which a rented blue Oldsmobile 98 Regency was driven off the side of the road in Mexico and came complete with an obituary for the skaters. It featured a flawless soundtrack—the Jackson 5; Dinosaur Jr. covering the Cure. Gonz's part began with a clip of Gene Wilder as Willy Wonka delivering the classic line "We are the music makers, and we are the dreamers

of dreams." And in the same manner that the sweets visionary changed the perception of candy in the film, Gonz proceeded to destroy everyone's notion of skateboarding. He skated rickety contraptions and shaky obstacles. The frontside 360 ollie off the loading dock. The lightning bolt rail. Linking tricks together in a way that had never been done before. At every minute within the 7:11 run time, Gonz delivered skating that spoke to the freedom and the movement and the spontaneity that gets us up on our boards in the first place.

Gonz also made legendary spots out of every location he skated. He noseslid the 10-stair Wilshire rail. Memorialized the long powder-blue rail along the wheelchair-access ramp in Santa Monica, California. Also, the double-kinked 20 stair rail just behind Main Street in town. And hurled his body down the monstrous giant 4-stair set of the Wallenberg school in San Francisco. He double-kickflipped off the ARCO bump in L.A. Now skaters pay homage to all of those spots and prepare to add their own NBDs (never-been-dones). All because of Gonz.

It didn't stop there. While studying ballet in Germany (yep—only Gonz), he created a performance art piece with director Cheryl Dunn that is one of the field's hallmarks. Gonz skates in a fencing outfit with "aloha" embroidered on the back in homage to skating's historical ties to surfing and its Indigenous and Asian Pacific Islander heritage. For the piece, he set up tunnels, pathways, and quarter pipes within the Städtisches Museum Abteiberg; he also filmed street footage on an elongated 46-inch beast of a board, his reminder that when skaters ride hard in unforgiving cityscapes, it feels like a duel between them and the setting. Who will win always depends on the moment.

Mark Gonzales remains our inspiration, constantly reminding us of what we might do if we weren't afraid of ridicule. Take his *Thrasher* cover in the mid-'90s. Only Gonz would ride a wooden vintage two-by-four board with clay wheels from the late '60s–early '70s, and frontside ollie on a mini ramp. Most people couldn't roll in a straight

"I DO THE TRICKS— NOT YOU."

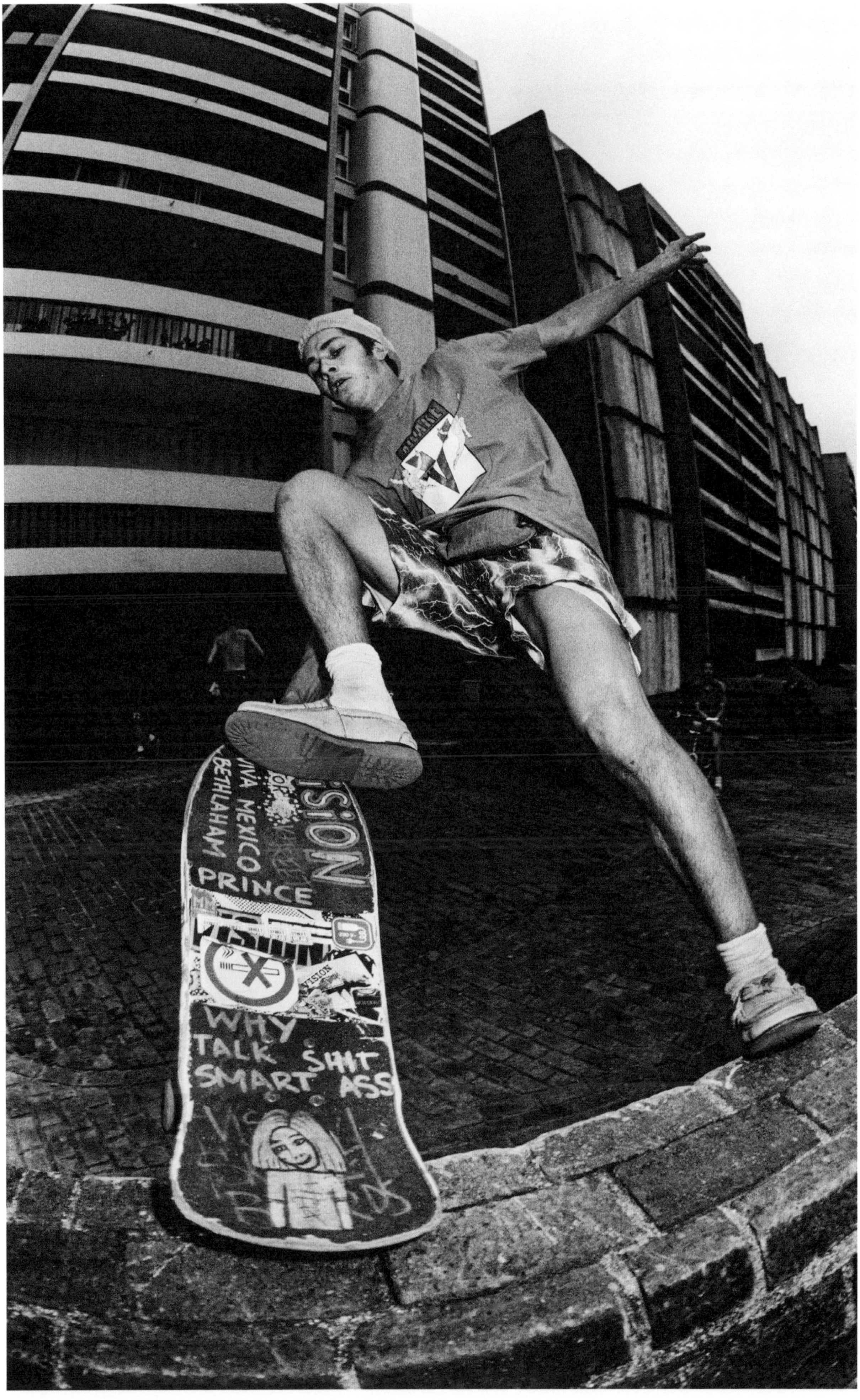
BETHLAHAM
PRINCE
WHY
TALK SHIT
SMART ASS

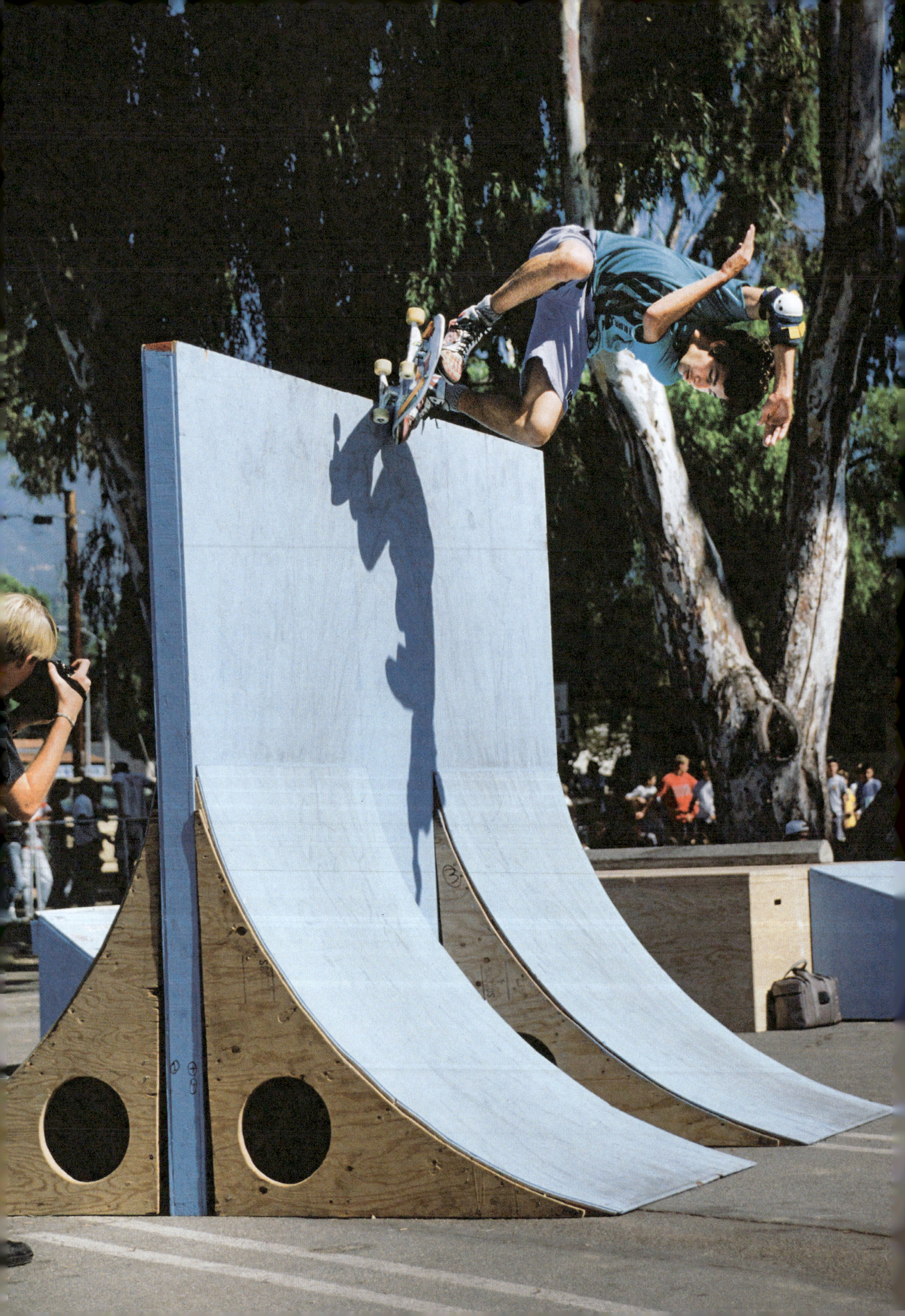

line on clay wheels. On the opposite end of the spectrum, there is his creation of Circle Board, nine skateboards connected like a human-size hamster wheel, with Gonz as the hamster. This wonderwheel was most recently re-created and shot below a luxurious sunrise in front of the Eiffel Tower.

Gonz built something intertwined and inseparable as an art piece that connects to the way we feel about skateboarding—we ride it and it rides us. It's why Gonz is often portrayed laughing at and talking to his board with comments like "I do the tricks—not you" when a trick has gone awry. It is the price we pay for being connected to this fountain of youth: temporary insanity in pursuit of tricks and a feeling. We are lucky to have this connection to the city, to each other, and to Gonz.

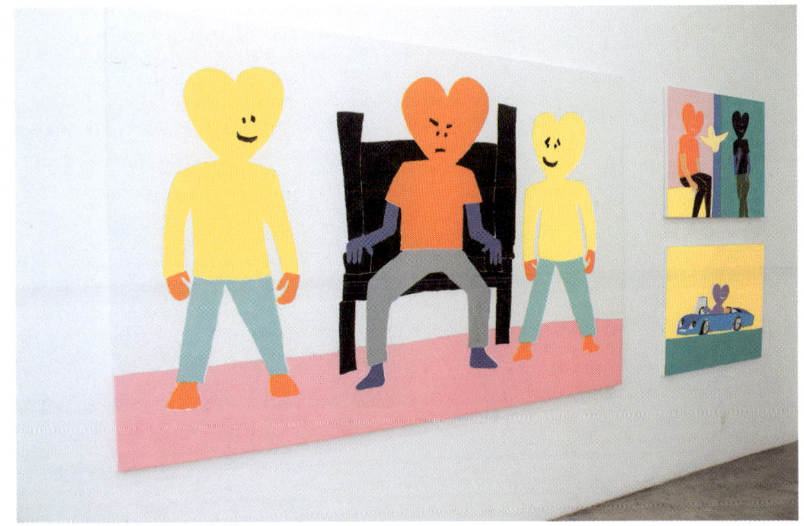

Opposite: Mark Gonzales, alley–oop grind in Santa Barbara, 1988

Top: Gonz's artwork on display at the HVW8 Gallery in L.A.

Bottom: Gonz working in his studio in NYC

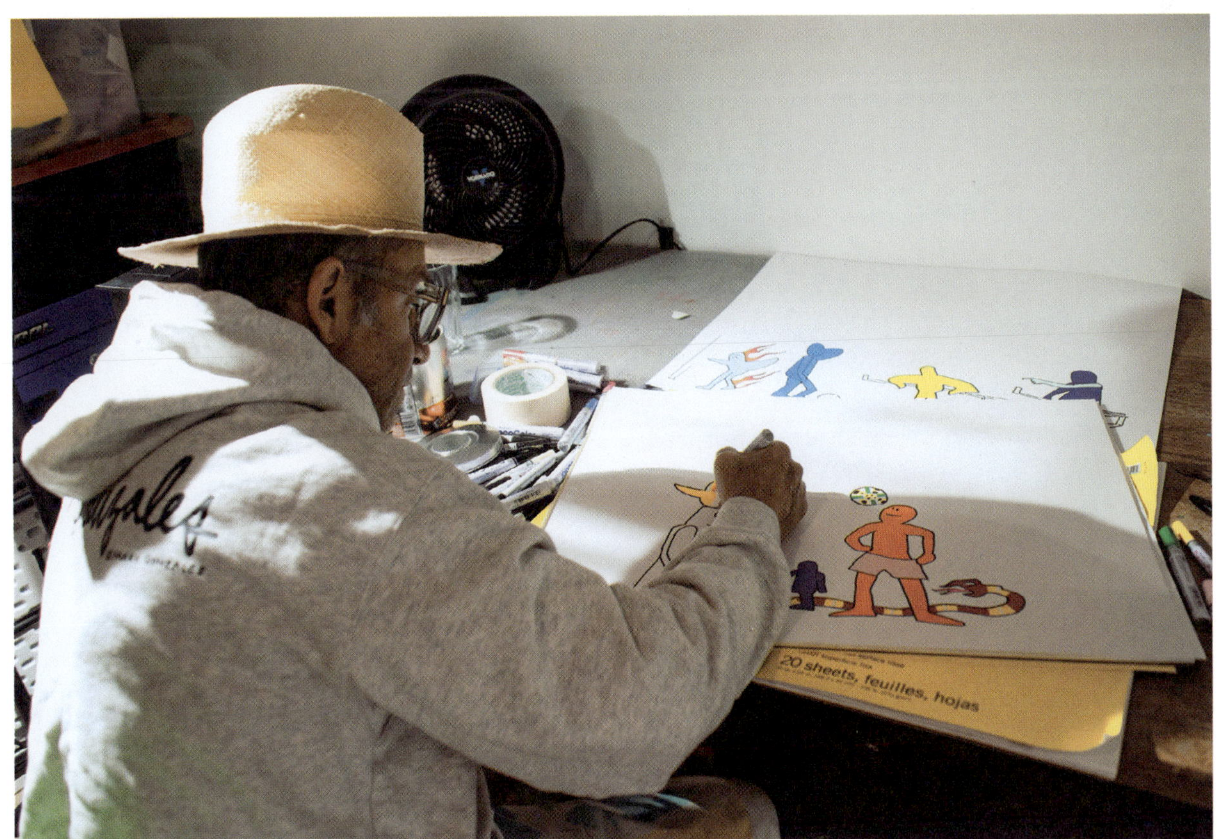

QUEEN OF THE QUIET RIOT
PEGGY OKI

First Lady of surf-style skateboarding

Monarch of the Z-Boys

Skateboarding Hall of Famer

Marine environmentalist

The tale of the globally famous Zephyr competition team, known as the Z-Boys, is one that includes the kaleidoscopic athletic and cultural maelstrom at modern skateboarding's birth. The 1970s were a riotous time for skateboarding, and the constant at the heart of all those stories is the centering soul of the First Lady of the Zephyr family, Peggy Oki.

Born to Ben and Sadako Oki, with family ties to Hiroshima, Japan, Peggy quietly set out on the path that would lead her into skate history at age 10, while living in a predominantly Asian American enclave within West Los Angeles. Peggy's father gifted her and her sibling a pair of the now-infamous mid-1960s Black Knight skateboards. While the gift was surely applause worthy, the department-store skateboard was not the epitome of skate technology. Yes, it was four wheels and a board, but this board had clay wheels and loose ball bearings, a deadly combination. Loose ball bearings could be counted on to pop open or suffer damage, and clay wheels produce one of the roughest and most dangerous rides in skateboarding's history. If the wheel touched a rock at any point, it was curtains for the rider. However, despite this, or perhaps because of it, Peggy still found love in skateboarding.

To quench her thirst for skating, her sibling made her a board during shop class and outfitted it with Bennett trucks, some of the best of the era, and the greatest gift to skateboarding: a set of urethane wheels. Having skated such rough equipment made Peggy shine once the right tools were underfoot.

She would explore the neighborhood hills in Santa Monica and Venice and the banks at schools like Kenter Canyon Elementary that would all become known as Dogtown territory. Eventually word got around about this female marvel and she met famed Z-Boy Jay Adams. He introduced her to the rest of the Zephyr team in Santa Monica, founded by Asian American surfer Jeff Ho and Skip Engblom, with support from C. R. Stecyk. From that moment on, Peggy embarked on the ride that would become one of the most revolutionary teams and new movements in skateboarding: the Zephyr competition team. The Z-Boys (and later the Z-Family of companies, EZ-Ryder and then Z-Flex) would inspire generations of skaters across the globe.

Photos of Peggy Oki in the '70s nearly always depict her flowing and in the zone. Skating low, aggressive and limber, she moves with ferocity across the image and into the viewer's soul. Those there for her debut alongside her fellow Z-Boys still talk about how her freestyle routine transformed the flat land into a new realm by infusing her skating style with her Venice surfing techniques.

Throughout her Skateboarding Hall of Fame career, Peggy delivered glowing, signature sweeping lines across the parking lot, contorting so deeply that her hair touched the ground along with her hands, as if she were placing her hand into the foam of a wave to create a dramatic pause—to quiet. She drew the world into her centrifugal force, figuratively and literally, since her spinning 360s

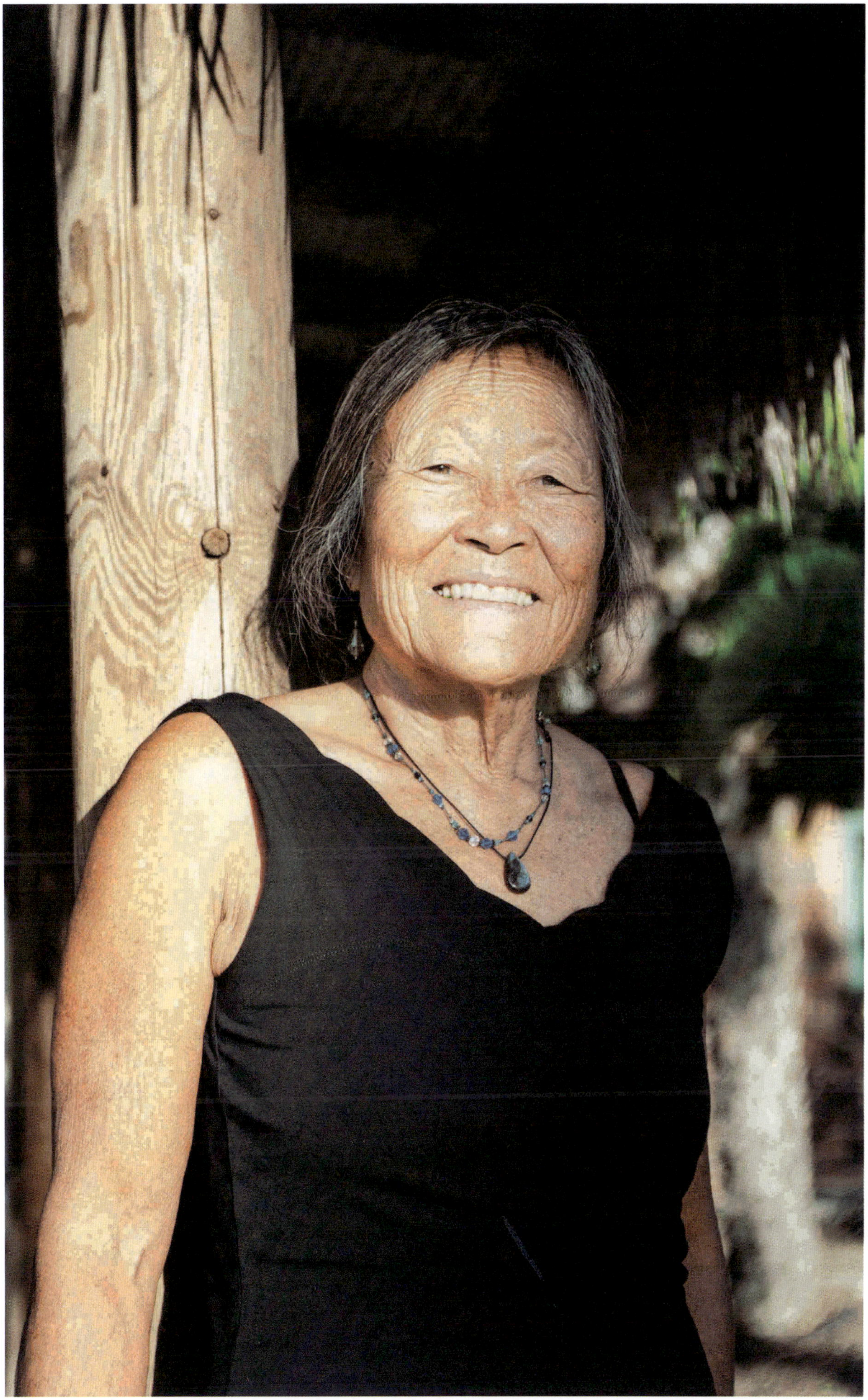

were a centerpiece of her magnetic skateboarding. By talent, by style, and by gender, she was truly in a league of her own.

Peggy was a winner in several contests in those early days, and featured prominently in the first ads for Zephyr right alongside the boys in a 1975 issue of *Skateboarder* magazine and in other publications, with photos of team members Jay Adams, Stacy Peralta, and Paul Constantineau all pushing the limits of modern skateboarding. "Peggy Oki 1st Girls' Freestyle (Del Mar–Ocean Festival Contest)," "1st Girls' Slalom (Santa Barbara Contest)," "4th Girls' Free Form (Santa Barbara Contest)." Those wins and her style propelled her to notoriety and made her an icon for generations.

One image of Peggy that stands out is the 1975 photo of her in the Bahne/Cadillac National Skateboard Championships contest winners' lineup with OG skaters like Russ Howell and Chris Yandall. Everyone is looking one way, and there's Peggy standing next to skater Michele Brunot—smiling and looking the other way. It could have been

Peggy Oki, Kenter Canyon Schoolyard, 1976

anything at the time, but what is emanating from her is an excitement that differentiates her from everyone else. She looks like someone who loves skateboarding and who keeps an eye out for the horizon and the future.

And that's exactly what made her the best of that time. Peggy and the Z-Boys ushered in a new era that transformed skateboarding for all skaters.

That motley crew of Z-Boys included a wide range of culturally diverse individuals inspired and drawn together by skateboarding, such as Zephyr cofounder Jeff Ho, who is Chinese American; Shogo Kubo (RIP), who was Japanese American; and Tony Alva and Stacy Peralta, who are mixed-race Latinx skaters. Peggy was the only woman in the crew, but she was never lesser than the boys. In fact, she ran her division, winning the prestigious Del Mar Nationals in 1975, delivering her sweeping surfing-informed lines—low and tight, cutting backside and frontside across the concrete, reminding everyone of the integral connection between surfing and skating at that historic time. She set the tone for a generation.

As Peggy told me, skating was fun, but those were also "wild times." While they were part of the

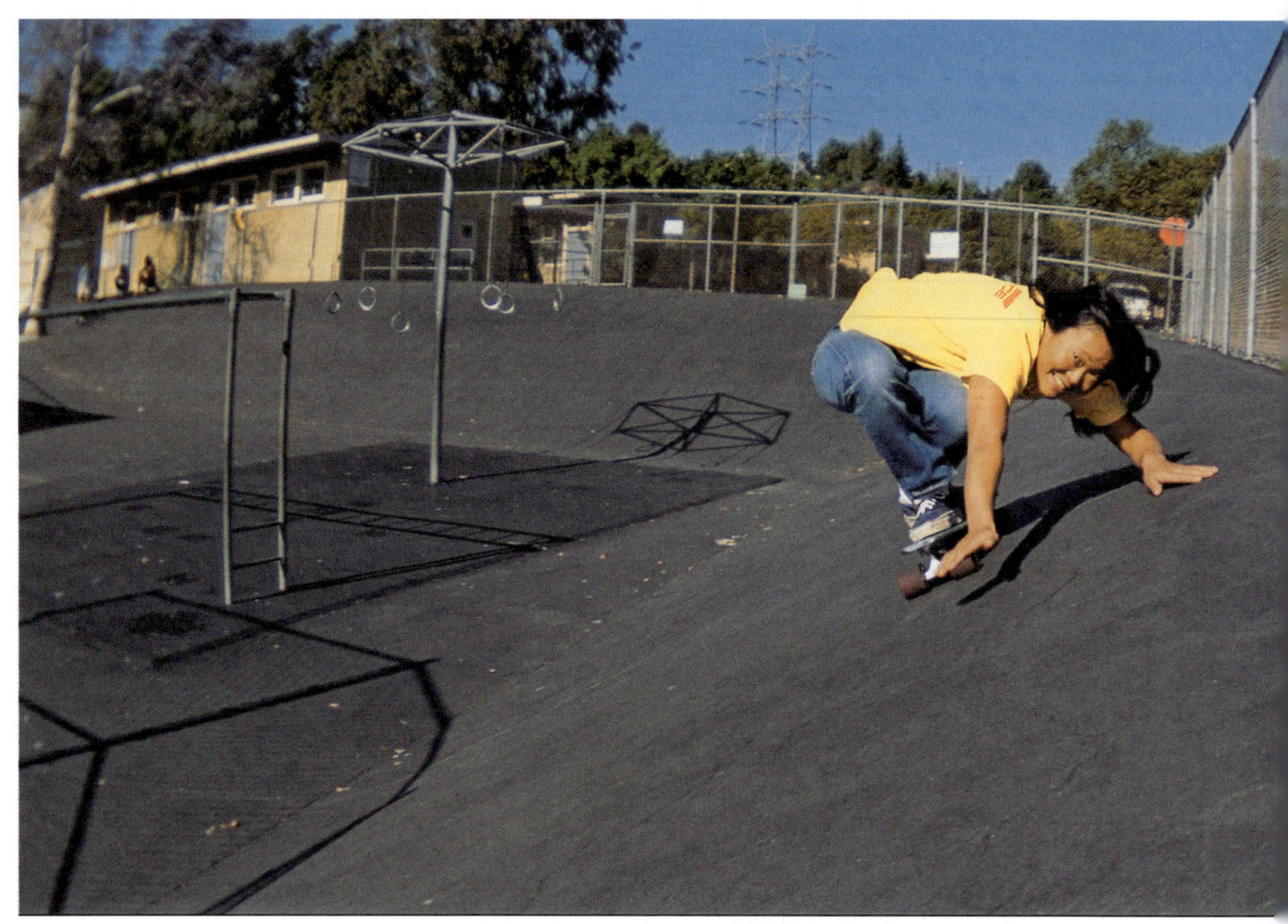

superstar team of the moment and had a meteoric rise, the Z-Boys were short-lived. The westside of L.A. during the mid-1970s was an environment with more than enough paraphernalia of sin for you to get lost in. Compounding this was the crew's youth. They were crushing it as the best skateboarders in the world but they were also just teens—and the era was not necessarily a great one.

Race wars were an everyday occurrence at schools in L.A. during that period. The oil crisis loomed large and so did the California drought, putting a damper on the California Dream of keeping a full swimming pool, which signified wealth. Venice and Santa Monica were often dangerous spaces where gang activity and rampant "localism" or territorialism flourished.

With all of that in the background, Peggy found kindred spirits in the Zephyr family. In our discussions, she talked about how every member of the family had their own level of shine that came out when they were together. Tony Alva (see page 43) was the mad dog of the group. He could fly off the handle as easily as he flew out of the pool. He loved the limelight and stepped into it.

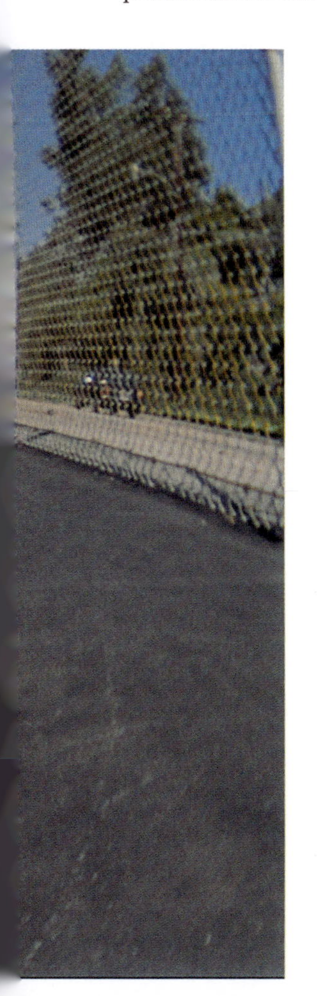

Stacy Peralta, the quiet one, was contemplative and kind but just as tenacious as Tony when it came to competition. In quiet moments, Peggy's relationship with Shogo Kubo moved beyond skateboarding; as first-generation Asian Americans they both experienced racism outside of their tight clique and Shogo would be the first to offer a knowing look or right hook when the shit hit the fan.

While Peggy's success shone brightly at contests, the confining format of skateboarding competitions was too repressive for her expressive skateboarding, and caging the spirit was never in the cards for Peggy. She loved skateboarding, but the politics and favoritism in contests, often influenced by event sponsors, soured her on that aspect of skateboarding culture. Her professional career ended with her last contest in 1977.

But what she closed down in skateboarding opened the door for moments of magnetism in the surf and in the schools. She eventually earned an associate in arts degree in biology at Santa Monica City College and a BFA at Santa Barbara City College. Making a name outside of skateboarding

PEGGY AND THE Z-BOYS USHERED IN A NEW ERA THAT TRANSFORMED SKATEBOARDING FOR ALL SKATERS.

did not quell her connection to the ocean. On two instances she had encounters with dolphins and whales, where they were watching her, playing with her, and, in her opinion, communicating with her in a way that had never occurred before—she felt it in her soul.

This was the catalyst for beginning her career as a marine conservationist, where she focuses on protecting our water-bound neighbors through art and activism. She's made it her goal to travel around the world lecturing on the importance of patience and being one with the world, waiting for it to tell you what's next. When I was living in New Zealand/ Aotearoa, where Peggy spends her winters, I was lucky enough to bear witness to her outpouring of love across both chapters of her life—speaking regularly to young people about animal activism and blessing the next generation by leading an All Girl Skate Jam in Raglan/Whāingaroa in the summer. On those days, the former monarch of the Z-Boys spends time with anywhere between 40 and 50 young girls, encouraging the next generation of female skaters. Peggy imparts words of wisdom to them about saving the planet and saving their own lives through meditation, exercise, skateboarding, and surfing, which she sees as helpful ways to cope and improve their mental health.

While Peggy Oki is no longer a competitive professional skateboarder, she forever remains a teacher and inspiration to generations—an original architect of modern skateboarding culture.

The scenic and wildly popular city-owned and -operated 16,000-square-foot Venice Beach Skate Park is located steps away from the Pacific Ocean, and, more crucially, in the same Los Angeles neighborhood (Venice/Venice Beach) where skateboarding was born and raised back in the 1970s.

For those lucky enough to have come up in the area, the park has been a place to live, learn, train, and continue the legend of Dogtown and the Santa Monica and Venice crews that came before. It's in the DNA there, and everyone who's in the know gets a moment to revel in the legacy of our skate forebears like Tony Alva, Peggy Oki, Stacy Peralta, Shogo Kubo, Skip Engblom, Marty Grimes, Pep Williams, Eric Britton, and Jesse Martinez. Then there are the new locals at the park like Sky Brown, Fabiana Delfino, and Briana King, and in truth, every skater venturing into this L.A. gem may find a home.

You don't have to be an old-school Z-Boy or a modern Olympian, though, to drop into this cement paradise for the people, with 10-plus-foot bowls, pool tile, and pool coping in homage to the legendary backyard pool skating that occurred in Venice and Santa Monica and set the world on fire. The park also features a relic of early skateboarding with a "snake run," poured cement in a winding shape that gives skaters—especially new ones—a place to learn how to carve back and forth with speed without having to face the deep end of a 10-foot pool.

For those so inclined, laid against the snake run is a cement mini ramp with bowled ends. It's an ideal place to learn mini-ramp and transition skills because it's not as deep. The capsuled end can be skated back and forth and around the corner as well—the perfect way to cue up learning to skate the big pool later.

Venice hasn't forgotten about its street roots, either: There are stairs, handrails, and banked walls to ride. There is an entire outer perimeter with metal laid along the ledges for skaters to shred.

What's more, this lil' pearl by the sea is the most heavily visited and used skatepark in the United States. A mural of the skatepark even graces the walls of the international arrivals terminal of LAX. Every day, tourists take pics of this park and the skaters in it. Its proximity to the filming capital of the world also allows plenty of local skaters the chance to be in commercials and movies. When casting agents need skaters, they pull up and skaters pull out their SAG-AFTRA cards.

Though the Venice park is idyllic now, it wasn't always this way. A noted Venice spot nicknamed "The Pit" featured abundant skateable architecture near the previous beach restroom. Sadly, that site was a haven for drug trafficking, ultimalty leading its burial in the sand by the authorities after a drug-related death.

Barring that, there has been a skatepark present since the late 1990s, but the previous park design did not live up to the legacy of Venice skateboarding. A knee-high quarter pipe does not a kingdom make. Don't get it twisted though; skaters made due. What were fully functional were the manual pad and half-moon ledge, which remain a proving ground. Just a stone's throw away from the new park, those elements survive and remain worthy of any skaters efforts.

Top left: The last relics of "The Pit" that now serve as a public mural for graffiti

Top right: The next generation of Venice Park locs, Kanon Jones-Shearer.

Bottom: Cocoa Beach–born ripper, Grace Marhoefer

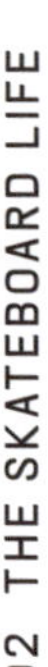

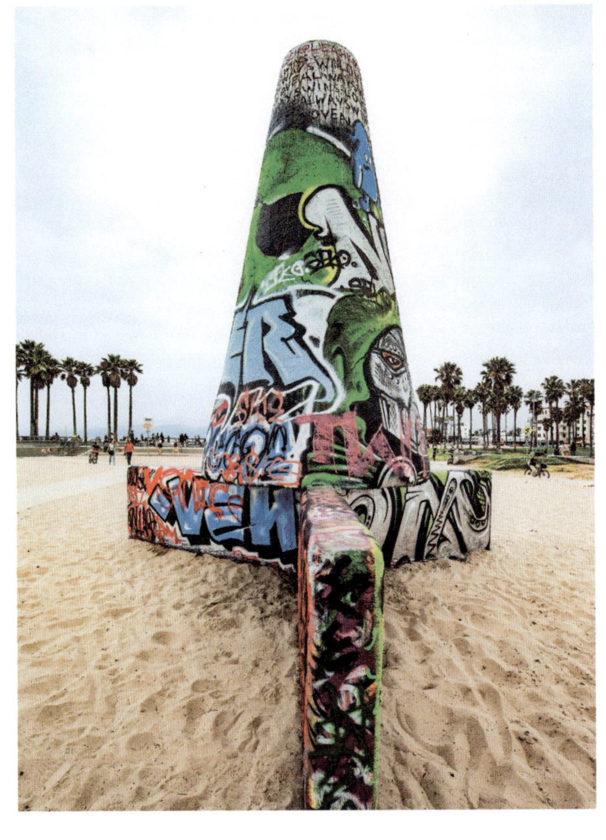

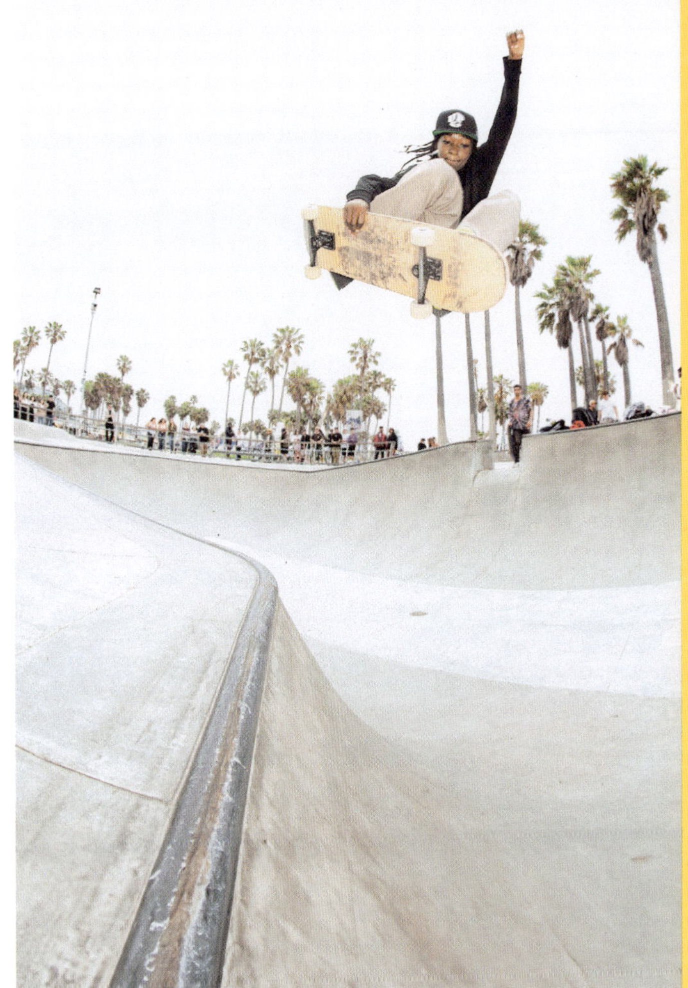

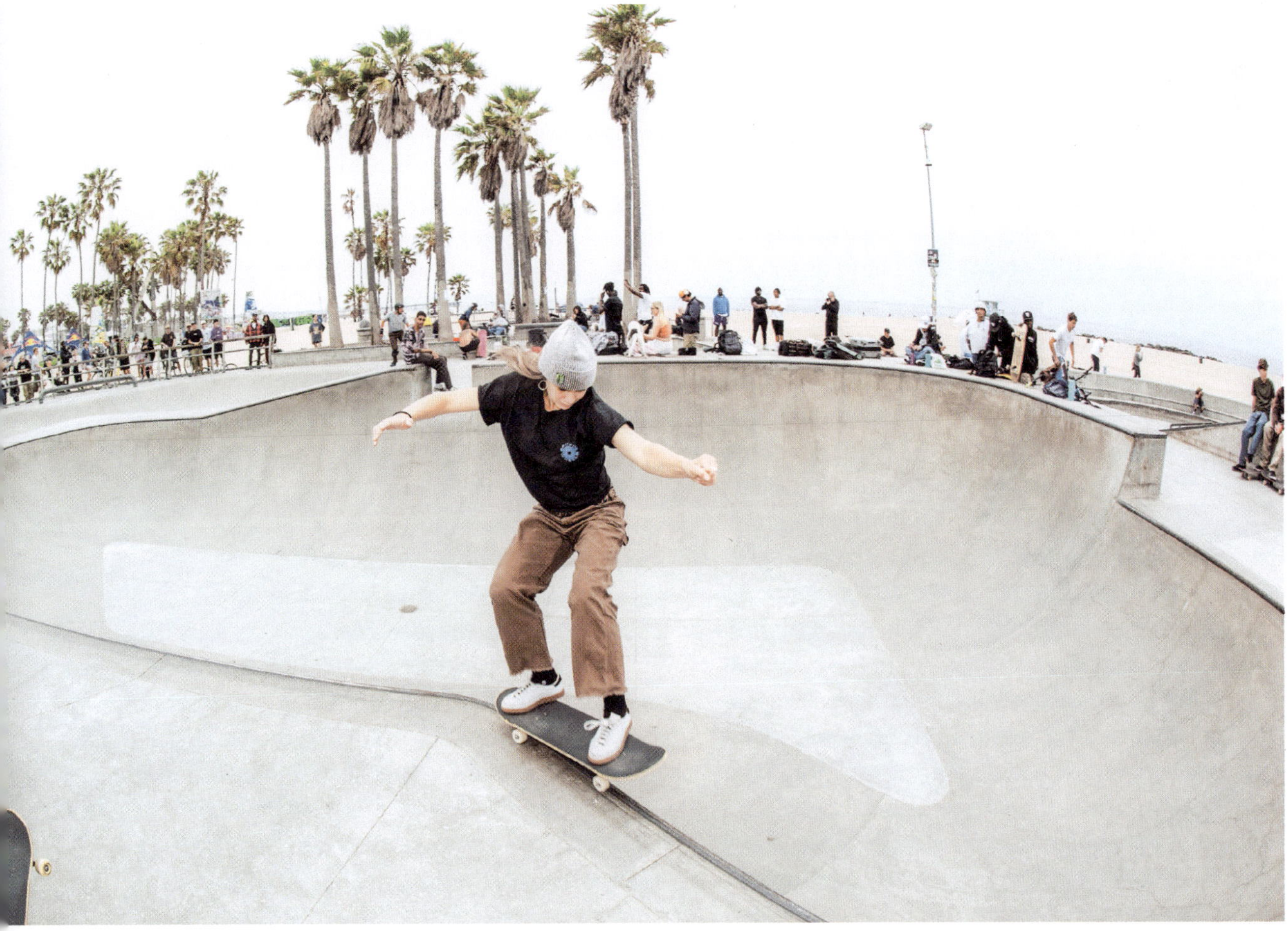

FROM MISFIT TO *MS. IT*

STEPHANIE PERSON

The first female African American professional vert skateboarder

The first Black woman sponsored by Santa Cruz Skateboards

Trailblazing woman in action sports event organizing

The first Black woman to appear in *Thrasher*

The first Black woman to appear skating vert in *TransWorld SKATEboarding*

Close your eyes, and you are on the vert ramp with the Skate Gods—Christian Hosoi, Rob Roskopp, Tony Magnusson—skating at Candlestick Park for the NFL's San Francisco 49ers 1984 halftime show.

You hit the first wall on the vert ramp, you're climbing to the top. Wait for the click of your tail against the coping. Bam! It's go time! You blast a huge frontside Indy air. Front leg boned out and hyperextended. Back leg tucked tight. *Daaaaamn.* The crowd goes wild. Caballerial on the next wall. You got this. Layback to tail. You unleash what you got across the coping. Layback smith. Mixing up equal parts airs and lip tricks. And then it begins. *Steph-a-nie, Steph-a-nie, Steph-a-nie.* Christian is calling your name, Magnusson is clapping, Roskopp is screaming—the high council of vert skateboarding losing their minds over you. As they should.

You are Stephanie Person, the first African American female pro vert skater, lighting the world on fire on the biggest stage at the time. You are an ambassador for skateboarding, introducing people to the airs of a lifetime, and displaying Black womanhood as capable of standing toe to toe with the greatest men in vert skating, who are all congratulating you and shouting your name, too.

The five-foot, four-inch unlikely powerhouse was an all-star woman pushing airs and the men around atop the vert ramp. Largely alone as a woman and definitely alone as a Black woman during that time, in her own words she was a unicorn: situated with power and grace on board and always slightly removed from the mainstream stereotype of skateboarders as white and male.

Stephanie started out skating street, ditches, and whatever was in front of her in her early teens. She was a quintessential California girl, born in the '70s, when skateboarding was everywhere in Southern California and it seemed like every kid had a banana board to play with.

The concept of racial politics entered the family early on, with her Creole father and strong, pro-Black African American mother. Her father left her mother and the family, and when Stephanie was seven years old, her mother and the family's white male neighbor were married. They moved from Los Angeles to the Bay Area for her stepfather's new job, which meant the family no longer resided in a mixed-race community. Gone were the diverse backgrounds and working-class folks; instead came classic Victorian houses and the largely white families within them. The new move would require of Stephanie a very tough skin and a system of acquiescence in order for her to persevere. While racial backgrounds never mattered in her household, it didn't stop the gawkers once they left the safety of the home. On their biweekly Friday movie outings, she remembered walking at least 10 steps ahead of her mother and stepfather to lessen the blows from the stares and comments. Her mother raised her to embrace her Blackness, but after being told she was ugly and called the N-word so often during primary school, by the time she entered her teens, she knew survival involved a display of deference to white classmates. No way around it, lest her teens years be spent in solitude. She worked hard enough to enter the establishment, earning a coveted space in the upper echelon of "coolness"—her high school cheerleading squad. She would later become a skateboarding cheerleader, noting with laughter in our conversations that at that time—the early '80s— it was clearly an oxymoron.

It was a moment within the circle of "cool" people that exposed her to skateboarding, something that had been missing since her L.A. days. Seeing an extra beat-up board at a sleepover, she quietly inquired into the ownership, masking her excitement. No one knew whose it was and as they told her, "Who would want to ride it?" In that circle, not one. They said it was ragged and old and unfit for anyone. Stephane took that as her cue to quietly dislodge that board from its original owner.

The borrowed board became a lifeline for Stephanie, and was never to be returned. Being free to push and move at the pace she desired was just what the doctor ordered. It gave her a sense of control over her life where previously she'd had none. Falling in with a few boys who skated at school, she instantly became a lifer, which became most evident on her 16th birthday. To her mother, this meant a new epoch for her daughter— the evolution from being a girl who got bumps and bruises from skating to becoming a more sophisticated and feminine version of herself, and with that, getting a fancy new dress for her birthday. Instead, Stephanie asked for a new skateboard.

That board under her feet was a blast of energy and renewal. She would skate every section of the Bay and the suburbs after school, making progress in the banks and ditches, and keeping up with the boys and their tricks. She learned boardslides, berts (lying

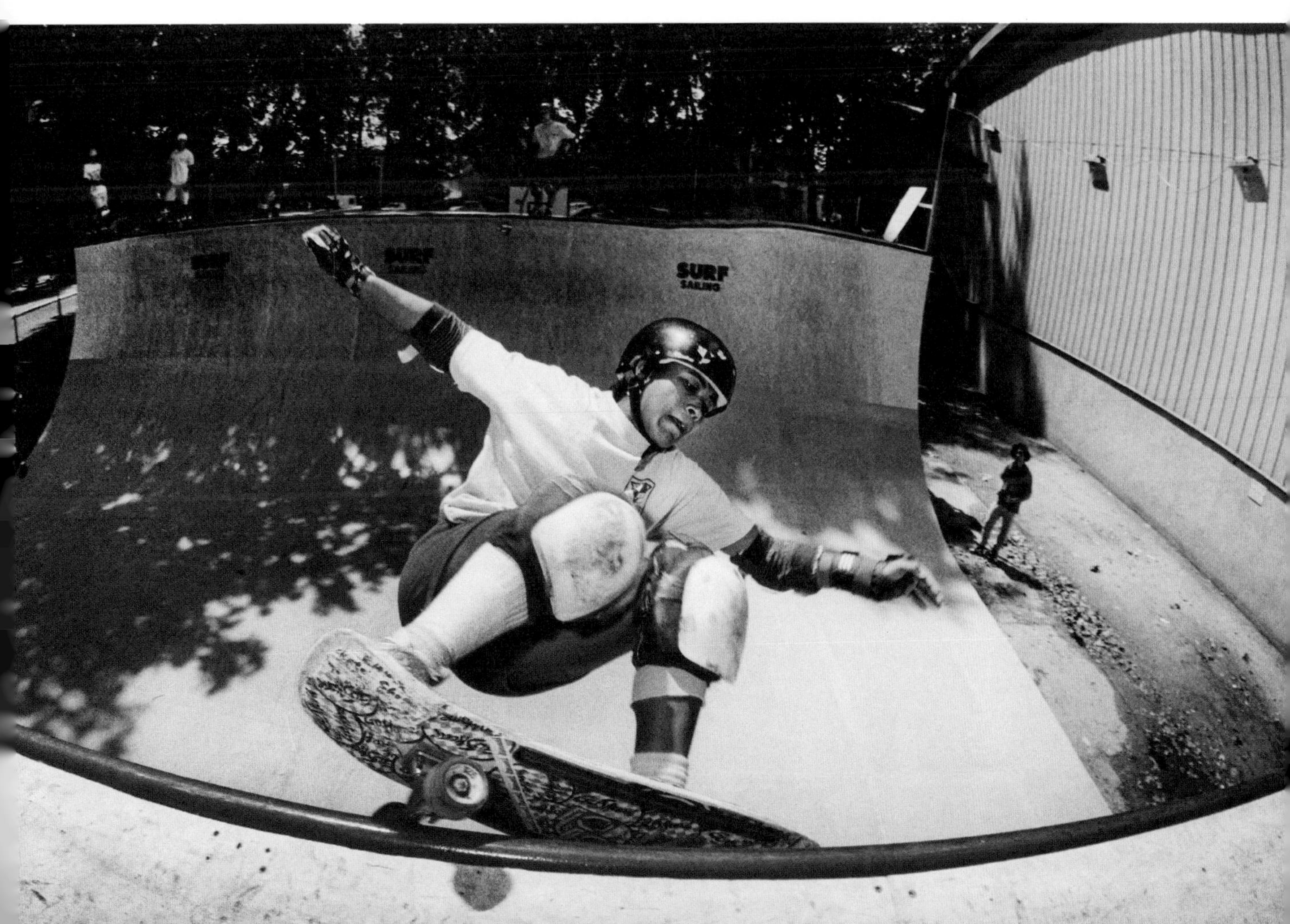

low in surfboard style and power sliding with all four wheels horizontally), and boneless ones (grabbing your board with your back hand and planting your front foot to propel you into the air) in record time. It wouldn't take her long to impress the local skaters and the owner of the local skate shop, Gremic, with her skills. She became shop-sponsored as a teen, rocking the Gremic team logo. On a dare she held an amateur skateboarding contest in town, taking the reins from a male partner too afraid to call skateboarding companies to ask for their support. Shaky-voiced, she contacted every brand in the back of *Thrasher* magazine and went 30 for 30 wrangling them in.

Soon she went from skating the curbs behind the skate shop to running contests that every legendary skater, including Steve Caballero, showed up to as if it were the X Games. She understood how to market skateboarding to skaters, obtain temporary permits for the event, talk to the local press, and reach out to skate companies to get free product— the building blocks of any great skate event. Beyond the promotion and planning, her skateboarding was also exploding. She progressed so quickly from all of the competitions at her events and through her own tenacity that she earned a spot on the famous Santa Cruz Skateboards team. Unlike in the 1970s, there were few "women-only" amateur contests in this era, so she skated against the men. She was on a roll, one of the only women with ads in *Thrasher*.

She skated all the legendary contests: Montezuma, the Capitola Streetstyle Classic in '83–'85. She was taking the world by storm and poised to be the next big thing from Santa Cruz. But the more fame she gained, the tougher her outward shell had to become. Jealousy reigned supreme during that transition from sponsored to elite. She needed to skate twice as well and to never be a woman in the minds of her compatriots. She always had to be a skater and one of the boys. Caught between extremes, she never had room to let down her hair.

Those she beat would try to berate her, so her guard needed to be up. Held to an impossible standard, she was labeled a no-nonsense firebrand who would punch you in the face if you got out of line. If they didn't want to beat her, they wanted to date her—or worse. That type of sexual harassment caused a deep rift in her psyche. In school, she had never been thought of as attractive compared to her white counterparts and her life was always lived in the shadow of a white standard of beauty. Now

on the road, she had cultural cachet from being a fantastic athlete and fierce competitor but was also being recognized as a beautiful Black woman. Tense times for a person of color coming into their own during the mid-'80s. While it was overtly hostile at times, meaning all the time, she also noted that there were great skaters who had her back, like Christian Hosoi and Pops Hosoi, Natas Kaupas, Tommy Guerrero, Mike McGill, and Tony Hawk. Among elite skaters, she was seen as a skateboarder and a peer.

The dichotomy of her position as an attractive woman and a great skater came to a head during a battle she never asked to be in. The owner of Santa Cruz Skateboards, Richard Novak, had asked for team-rider response on Santa Cruz's first skate video, *Streets of Fire* (1989). Only Stephanie responded, with honest feedback, and she earned Novak's ear from that day forward. Later, on a short tour for her and the other amateurs, those jealous of her relationship with their boss spread lies about her values, dedication to the company, and supposed promiscuity. When she returned from the trip, she no longer had a position on Santa Cruz, even though the team member knew there was no truth to the rumors. Sorry to have her go but afraid that the climate was against her, Santa Cruz removed her from the team. Devastated, she was reminded how cruel the world could be to a young woman when her word is ignored in a male-dominated space. This

wouldn't be the last time this would happen to her in the skate industry.

Each time she gained a foothold in the U.S., something would backfire and pull her away from a bright future as a professional skater. Even when she'd obtained new sponsors, she still had to deal with other pro skaters calling her the N-word during her contest runs. I won't use their names here, but they know who they are. Although people claimed to support her and her skating, when racial epithets were tossed at her, no one defended her. When Black vert skaters led by Black skater Don Hillsman did attempt to band together to combat the racism occurring, it still did not quite hit the mark for Stephanie. Using an intersectional lens, she faced multiple oppressions that couldn't be easily solved by creating a Black league or a separate coalition.

She needed equality on multiple fronts, and it was simply hard to achieve.

While on tour in Europe in the early '90s for a skateboarding demonstration, Stephanie found some respite. She appreciated being away from the racism and sexism in the U.S. and that in Europe she garnered respect as a woman of color and a skilled athlete, so at the end of the tour she stayed and turned pro. Europe offered a win-win scenario for her: better conditions for her mental well-being and a reverence for the type of skating she enjoyed, so she could make a living. Vert remained her preferred format and it was still the rage in the E.U. and U.K., while it was falling out of favor to street skating in the U.S. In Europe, she was more valued and gained sponsors from big brands in skateboarding like Deathbox (before it became Flip) and Etnies as well as stints with Swatch, Converse, and Jean Paul Gaultier.

Some of these times were good, but too many were not. The unfair burdens on her took a toll. She left the professional skateboarding industry in the late '90s, moved to Sweden, and began working on her own mental heath and repairing her body, which had been badly damaged by so much aggressive vert skating. There she healed herself from the inside out and now is a fitness and workout guru who is finally able to talk about her role as a pioneering figure in skateboarding history. She went from being the misfit to being *Ms. It*. The secret to that? Believing in herself since the beginning.

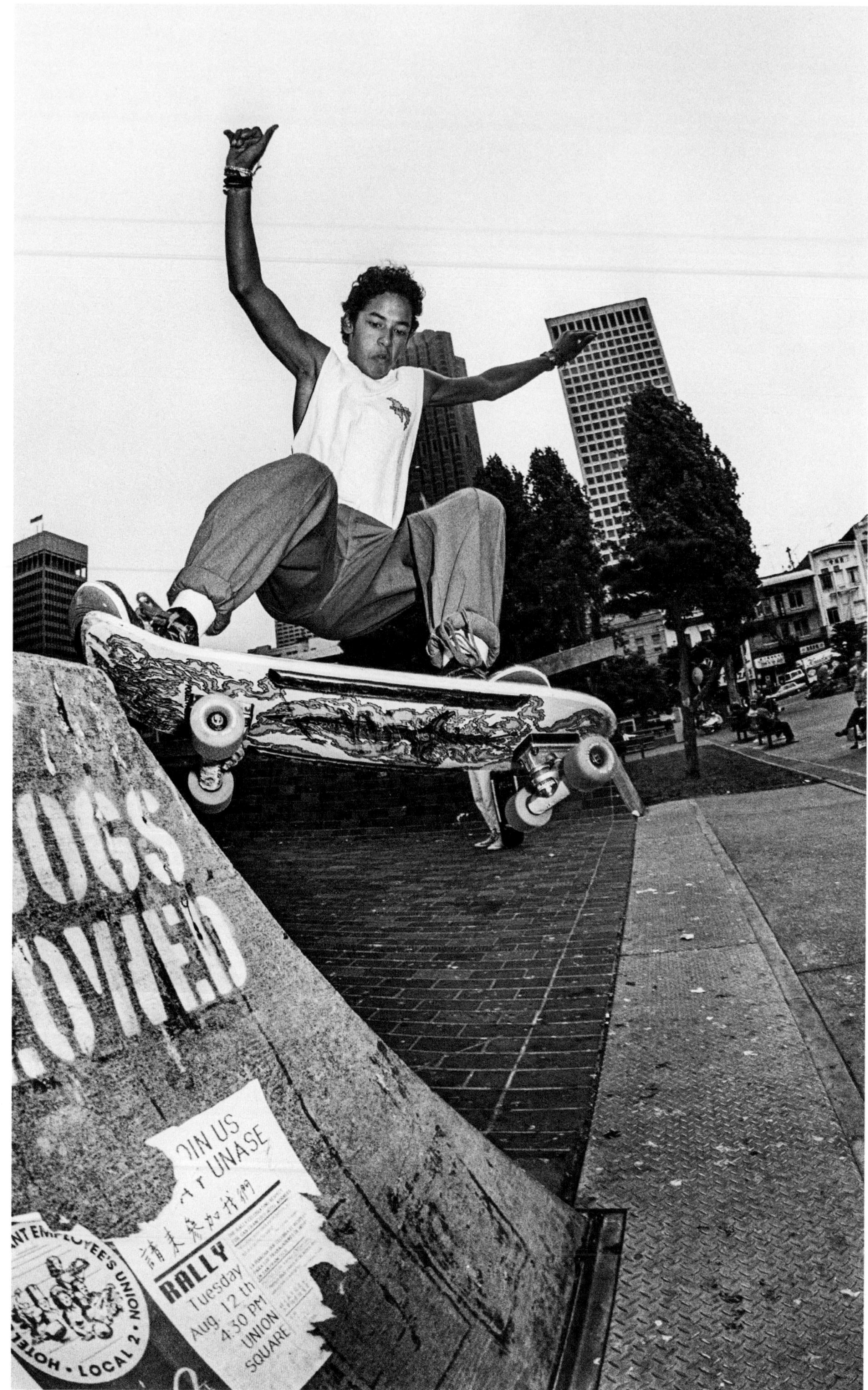
OGS
OWED
OIN US
r UNASE
請支援我們
NT EMPLOYEE'S UNION
RALLY
Tuesday
Aug 12th
4:30 PM
UNION
SQUARE
HOTEL · LOCAL 2 ·

TOMMY GUERRERO

Original member of the Bones Brigade

Skateboarding Hall of Famer who repped San Francisco to the core

Co-owner of REAL Skateboards with business partner Jim Thiebaud

Wrote "End Racism" on his board to create solidarity

Bzzzz, hey, you in the white T-shirt and you in the red hat! Please get off the course and meet security at the edge of the roller rink. Ahh, man. Busted.

There I was, trying to quietly skate unnoticed after having snuck into a local skateboarding camp in Wilbraham, Massachusetts. Since the money to attend said skateboarding camp was not in the family budget, me and my boy Dave got the bright idea to sneak onto the grounds. However, there we were, caught by security hired by this skate camp as it was in the middle of a demo and clinic offered by two seminal figures in professional skateboarding: Jim Thiebaud and Tommy Guerrero.

I thought this was the end of skateboarding for me—forever. Security arrived and just before they put hands on me and Dave, I heard the voice of the titans. "Yo, we're going to have a private session for the team after 5 p.m. We both agreed that you guys can come skate with us all then. If you're down."

That was the first real encounter I had with Tommy Guerrero, or Tommy G., and his compadre Jim Thiebaud—and an early example of pro skateboarding as a communal practice. Those gentlemen affected my life and illustrated what the true role of a professional skater was: to transform people's opinion and experience of skateboarding into a positive one.

Combined, Tommy G., Jim T., and their company, REAL Skateboards, are the soul of San Francisco skateboarding. Tommy G. is the celestial figure who made skaters see the city as a place where new skate royalty could and later would be created.

Tommy G. is the youngest of the Guerrero brothers, and his family lineage includes musicians on both sides of their Indigenous, Native American, Chilean, and Filipino ancestry. Skating and music went hand in hand for both Tommy and his older brother Tony as soon as they discovered skating in the mid-'70s. In fact, they both played in punk bands and later funk explorations, separately and together, from age 12 onward, with skating always providing the motivation and inspiration for those musical flights.

Running through Tommy G.'s kudos comes easy: The first street skater on the legendary Bones Brigade Powell Peralta team. Skateboarding Hall of Famer. Co-owner of Deluxe Distribution with Thiebaud. Together the duo helped launch the careers of generations of skaters starting in 1992. We all owe a debt to them, especially Tommy G. Founding REAL skateboards required a leap of faith and a hit to his wallet. At Powell, Guerrero's annual salary ranged from $60,000 to $80,000 (in '89–'91 dollars). His paycheck dropped by nearly one-third in '92, when he opened his own company. He changed his lifestyle in order to deliver the type of skateboarding that he and Jim thought the world deserved. Their efforts were a blessing to the SF scene. Through REAL, Tommy G. and Jim helped launch the careers of Jovontae Turner, James Kelch, Lavar McBride, Jeron Wilson, 1993 *Thrasher* Skater of the Year and Hall of Famer Salman Agah, and 2013 *Thrasher* Skater of the Year Ishod Wair, just to name a few.

Originally recruited by Hall of Famer Stacy Peralta in the early 1980s, Tommy G. offered a change from the vert-heavy skateboarding that dominated the era. His focus on street became the future. When he turned pro in 1985, his part in the Powell video, *Future Primitive*, paid homage to the style and stunts of the '70s generation and to C. R. Stecyk's sentiment that America created a concrete playground best appreciated by the youth of today. Skaters owned the streets and Tommy Guerrero wasn't afraid to show it.

As he carved at full speed, doing barking four-wheel slides (sliding horizontally on your skateboard until the friction forces you to go straight), loud and infectious, we could feel the rough concrete

Tommy Guerrero street–style, late 1980s

under his wheels, those sounds traveling deep into our bones. He was operating in unison with the hills of San Francisco. Push here, slide there, when to give and when to jump off before you lose it all and earn a full-size helping of road rash. He would pilot the streets, exploring every driveway curb cut, and interjecting ollies across the steps and grass gaps. Stacy Peralta documented Tommy G.'s first steps in claiming the streets of the City by the Bay, and we were all mesmerized.

Tommy G. injected a new relatability into Powell-Peralta's Bones Brigade team and into skateboarding, with his focus on street skating. This young Latinx and Native American skater grabbed our imagination as stealthily as Prometheus stole fire and brought it to the people. If you could imagine the city the way he did, you could make its warmth your own. Of course, big vert ramps and the vert skaters who

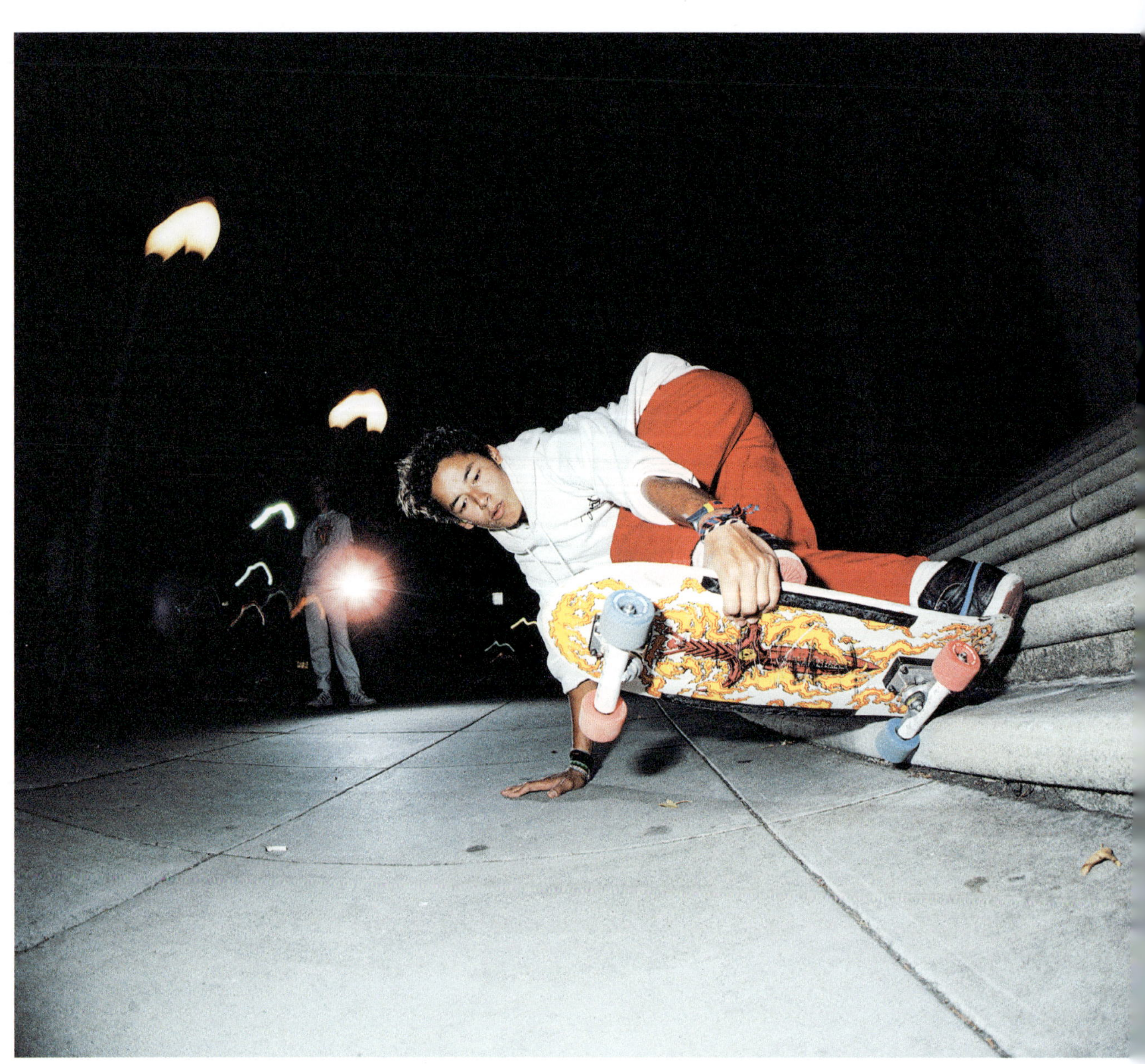

tamed them, like most of the Bones Brigade team, were something to aspire to; we all loved Caballero, McGill, Lance Mountain, and the others. So were the mavens who found and thrashed empty backyard pools, but Tommy G. was someone you could *be*.

His status was only further cemented when his next part came out in Powell's *Public Domain* (1988) video. It was a blistering, dizzying push through downtown S.F. Without harassing a single pedestrian, he dropped into the city's arms and whipped around like he was piloting a "chariot turning tight ones" (shout-out to the other Yay-Area icon, MC E-40).

Tommy G. offered an extra element—supreme speed—to the trinity of Mark "Gonz" Gonzales, Natas Kaupas, and Mike Vallely's radical innovations in street skating. Tommy G. would do no trick if it didn't involve skating fast. Sometimes skaters forget that Tommy helped hone that element in skating, and then Julien Stranger and John Cardiel pushed it further—do no trick before its time. Then blast it fast and to the nines. Tommy laid the foundation for so many. It's apparent to anyone watching current shredders launch beautiful ollies over obstacles at S.F.'s China Banks that they are doing a new interpretation of Tommy's moves.

In his Powell *Ban This* video part, Tommy G. spoke directly to racial tensions in America in simple ways. He had been handwriting "End Racism" on his board throughout '88–'89, and when it was time for the cameras to capture him for the new video, he made them zoom in deep to his deck. To some people, that might seem minor, but for thousands of skaters of color facing everyday racism, that image of Tommy holding his board let us know that we were not alone. It was a clear marker that skateboarding was a place to make these types of statements and to try to create change.

Propelling the notion of the skater-musician-activist, he even inserted his basses and guitars into the fight, overlaid

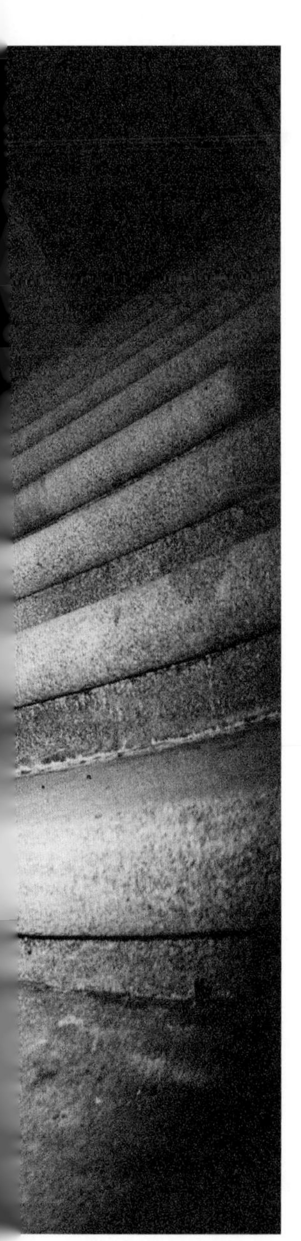

with his anti-racist skateboard graphic, signaling that either weapon of choice—the skateboard or the sonics—could bring about change. He would move from punk rock to groovy, spaced-out music and hyper-expressive Bojangled blues. These "bastard blues," as he would label the style, would become the soundtracks to his videos when he eventually left Powell to start his own endeavor with Jim, REAL Skateboards, in 1992. In later years, Tommy, supported by a host of skater-musician-activists, would also create the voicing and themes for other brands under their new umbrella organization, Deluxe Distribution (DLX).

For REAL Skateboards, Tommy G. and Jim T. created more imagery associated with anti-racism, including the "Hanging Klansman" graphic that adorned Jim's first pro model. They also focused on images of MLK and quotes from other leaders, aligning the brand and their skateboarding with progressive politics. Tommy G., Jim T., and their partners at Deluxe would create the space for Stereo Skateboards, spearheaded by Chris Pastras and Jason Lee (see page 79). Stereo would push the musical aspect of REAL, focusing on jazz and blues and establishing a true home for Black music and Americana in skateboarding culture.

When Tommy's music began to take on a life of its own, Jim T. became the face of REAL and Deluxe. The two had been inseparable since their days at Powell and remain "Jim and Tommy" in our minds, like "John and Paul." It's Jim who has been a mentor to me for most of my career, always open to any question or opportunity to support skateboarding on the grassroots, local, or international level. He is on the board for Skateistan (see page 196) and the Skatepark Project (formerly the Tony Hawk Foundation), and he supports and shows up for local skate shop events around the world. In Tommy's stead, Jim will pour concrete, send out free boards for fundraisers, or promote your event on the DLX website.

That remains the special sauce of REAL. Tommy G.'s ability to lead from behind and Jim's humility and omnipresence allow everyone around them to flourish. The newest addition to Deluxe has been the queer-skater-led There skateboards. Building brands with friends is Tommy and Jim's mantra at REAL and continues to this day. This became clear during Tommy G.'s induction into the Skateboarding Hall of Fame. Instead of simply thanking everyone, he noted that he was never alone in his accomplishments and invited *any* skaters in the audience to come up onstage and stand next to him. As with any request by Tommy G., the crowd obliged.

THE HARBINGER OF WOMEN'S SKATEBOARDING
VANESSA TORRES

Champion for women and LGBTQ+ skateboarders

X Games gold medalist

First female professional for Element Skateboards

Founding member of Meow Skateboards

There are few skaters who have had a bigger impact on women's skateboarding than the greatest to grace the grip tape, Vanessa Torres. Winning her first X Games Park at 17 years old, Vanessa consistently racked up victories in every contest of champions and held the torch high for women and diversity across every aspect of skateboarding.

One of the first women to earn true ATV (all-terrain vehicle) status, Vanessa could claim it all: street-style contests, park contests, and then bangers in the streets. Her cover of *SG Magazine* (the *SG* stands for Surf, Skate, and Snow Girl) is still one of my favorite examples of her proving she had the juice to make it all look easy, with a lovely kickflip to fakie on the bank that I know she had in the can after just one or two takes. Vanessa inspired women and young girls and made the men want to skate just as smoothly and tastefully. That's not hyperbole—when you spend any time watching her demolish a skatepark course, you get a sense of what it must be like to skate as easily and as naturally as drawing a fresh breath in New Hampshire. Her backside disasters and backside lipslides are the envy of anyone who has ever spent more than seven minutes on a skateboard. Vanessa offers anyone within view a eureka moment—an acknowledgment that what they are seeing is what skateboarding should look like. Throw in her textbook front boardslides locked in and flexed down any handrail, at any length, in front of anyone—fire AF. She is that girl.

Seeing Vanessa skate firsthand for years, those images are burned into my mind and forever seared into the collective consciousness of skateboarding history. What's more, all that power and effortless flow reside in a lithe athletic frame that punches well above its weight—whether tooling around the skatepark, acing a contest, or acting as a catalyst for change. While there are names within the women's game that followed Vanessa—for example, Nora Vasconcellos, Nicole Hause, and Lizzie Armanto—Vanessa's name symbolizes the game.

Growing up with her grandmother in Anaheim, California, as an active child, Vanessa found a place for herself in many traditional sports such as basketball, soccer, and anything that got her out of the house—she told me she always enjoyed mixing it up and found joy competing in sport. While on her grandmother's block, she discovered BMX and then skateboarding with a crew of neighborhood boys, but unlike those who saw skateboarding as the flavor of the day, Vanessa found her calling.

Vanessa helped revitalize a women's skateboarding scene that had been largely out of view for decades. She and a host of her contemporaries, including Amy Caron and Leo Baker (see page 185), were a force in making skateboarding appealing to everyone. Through Vanessa's standout parts for Element Skateboards and other women-led videos, she was introduced to the world as a preeminent professional skater.

As she told me, riding for Element was an important part of her life and the dream of any skater. She was a professional and traveling the globe as an integral part of one of the best and most popular teams in skateboarding history. Vanessa's original board featured a flower and her first name in bold letters. I sold her boards in the skate shop I managed, Traders Boards in Framingham, Massachusetts. Vanessa's board was a great offering for parents of new skaters looking for a role model for the next generation, and Vanessa was an exemplary young woman in skateboarding.

Looking back, while this was one of the most important parts of Vanessa's career, she was operating under the utmost pressure. Element's 1999 decision to turn her pro at 16 was a rarity in professional skateboarding. That type of heat is usually reserved for child prodigies who have been groomed for skateboarding since before they could walk. Vanessa came up more humbly, yet her skating prowess was no less undeniable, and the more she was placed in front of people, the more she moved the needle on normalizing women in every aspect of skateboarding.

One of the veterans in women's street skating, legend Jaime Reyes, remembered young girls like Vanessa exploding onto the scene with a new, infectious, slightly rambunctious energy. They brought a different vibe and a different level of fun. Vanessa at 16 was living the life. Endeavors like Globe footwear's *AKA: Girl Skater* (2003) provided documentary footage of the lives of young skaters Vanessa Torres and Leo Baker. Villa Villa Cola's *Getting Nowhere Faster* (2004) and other homegrown videos produced by Lisa Whitaker (see page 158) kept the fire alive for women's skateboarding in media. Furthermore, Lisa and a trio of other women developed the Action Sports Alliance and would later cofound Meow Skateboards and recruit Vanessa as one of the first professionals on the team.

Monumental as turning pro at 16 was, it still created difficulties. While Vanessa was one of the greatest of the time, ripping parks everywhere and leaving top-placing podiums in her wake, both she and Johnny Schillereff (see page 231), founder of Element, now recognize that it was a bit early to bring her into the full spotlight. Admittedly there

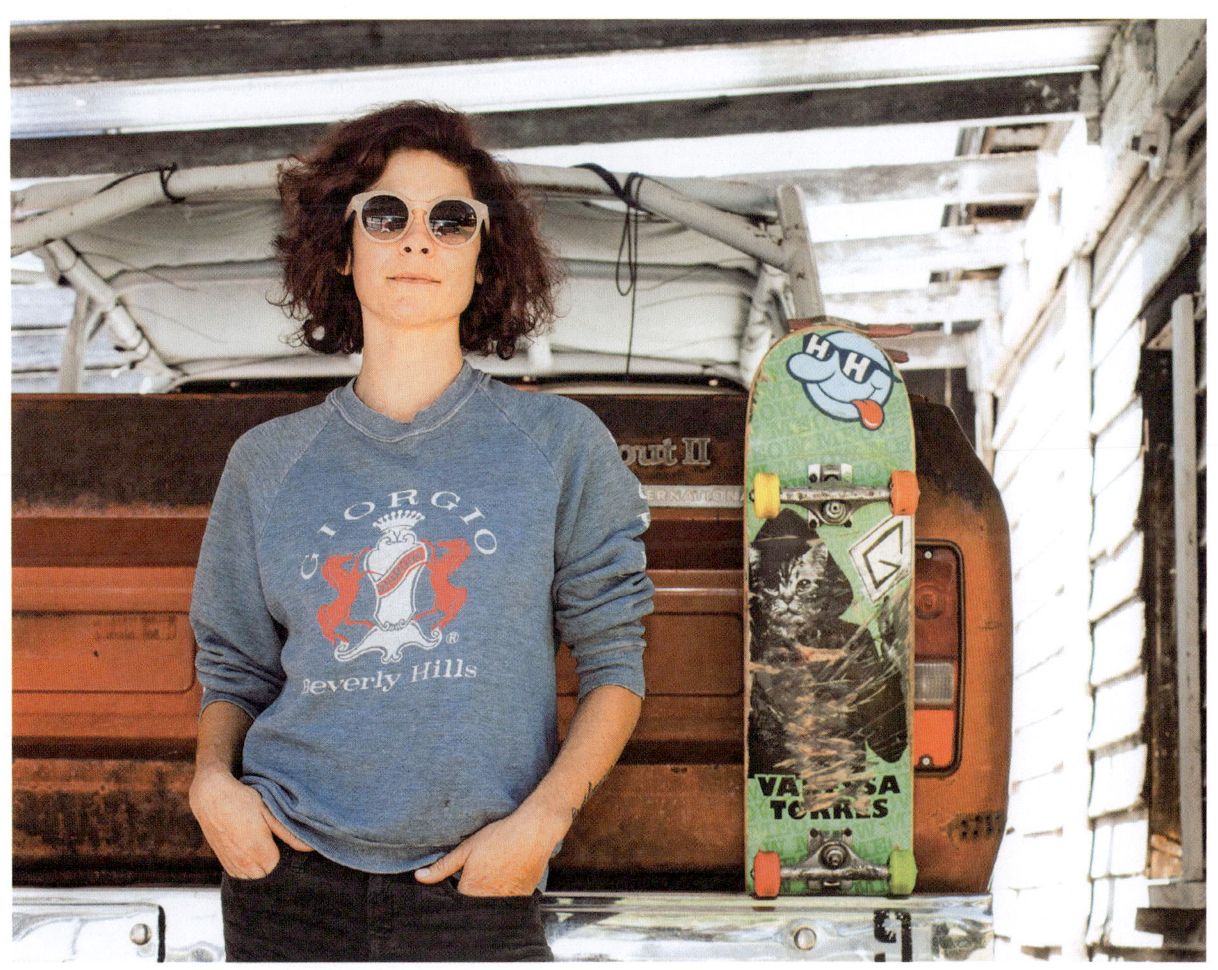

are more young pros now than in the Y2K days, but while we are making an earnest effort to bring back the clothes from the '90s, the '90s attitude to women's skateboarding is some ish we are trying to leave in the rearview.

Skateboarding was less kind to women at that time, and the whupping she put on the park didn't mean there weren't detractors looking for any excuse to ignore or denigrate women skateboarders. Sometimes they'd treat Vanessa as though she were the exception to the rule: I was there when male skaters said they liked her because she didn't have "girl style." But that was a backhanded compliment, to say the least. This was ill-conceived shorthand to say there was power to her skating—as opposed to other women's skating. In that era, men's compliments about women's skateboarding consisted of inadvertently putting down other women. We are still trying to get beyond that.

Luckily, even with the backhands lobbed, Vanessa always found a way to spring forward by rolling with women who believed in her and in women's skating. Though the fame and the visibility arrived, it was never the reason she entered the game. In her own words, skateboarding brought a sense of peace, creativity, and exploration that she would indulge at every opportunity.

One of those ways evolved through her clothing. Vanessa belonged to the "upcycle" set long before that became a buzzword. Her crush on vintage clothing and its aesthetic inspired female skaters as she followed the larks of her independent spirit. Unfortunately, that spirit also placed her in constant breach of contract. Most skaters are sponsored by several brands that they identify with and that fit their needs in boards, wheels, apparel, and whatever else their heart might desire. Vanessa was sponsored by Element, head to toe. As you might guess, this could prove undesirable for a young girl finding her own path. Element didn't truly make clothes for a girl at that stage of her life. While they were the biggest clothing and skateboarding company in the world, their ears were not attuned to her needs. And although the boatloads of gear available to her might have sated any young man, for her they were simply ill-fitting traditional men's and boys' clothes, which stifled her persona. Even more devastatingly, when men expressed themselves through a similar aesthetic, it created new market trends. Companies worked feverishly to cater to the changing needs of male skaters. Women? Not so much. Not a good look.

The same could be said for her first board graphic, meant to celebrate her turning

Vanessa Torres, lofty ollie at the Skate Like a Girl's YMCA Skate Camp in Sequoia National Park, USA

professional, the culmination of all her hard work. Vanessa lacked any input on the image. It wasn't that she was ungrateful for the blessing of the best company and the best team, nor was it Element's intention to alienate their key rider. However, looking back, riding graphics that aren't your own, swamped in clothes that don't fit, with lawyers ready to sue you into submission all breeds an environment of hostility and stifles growth.

With that on her mind, tensions began to silently compound. During a dark time that began with a skating trip to Australia, there came a moment when she decided to spend more time drinking than skating—it started to get messy, to put it lightly. On top of this, as many people do from their late teens through adulthood, Vanessa began to explore and then wrestle with her sexuality. The combination of exploration, self-realization, and alcohol took time to sort out. Which was the vice and what was true life? Vanessa needed time to feel her way through the darkness. Supported by then–Element team manager Ryan Dewitt (RIP), Vanessa began to pull herself out of the depths of the struggle.

Meanwhile, some of the seeds Vanessa had planted began to blossom. While fighting for women to have a clearly defined space within Element, Vanessa collaborated with Element women's cofounder Kori Schillereff to design an entire line that would go on to help the company grow exponentially. Furthermore, in a twist of fate, Vanessa was directly responsible for creating the men's skinny jeans trend in the mid-aughts. Popularized by Element teammate Bam Margera during his appearances on MTV, those "skinny stretch jeans" belonged to the women's denim line that Vanessa spearheaded.

Pulling through it all, Vanessa returned to skateboarding's limelight and in 2015 earned a silver medal at the first women's Street League Skateboarding contest. Vanessa would build a home with Lisa Whitaker and join her new women- and nonbinary-led skateboarding company, Meow Skateboards, where she would continue to develop a partnership and fellowship with the team. A mentor to the women's skateboarding movement, an exceptional skater, and now an announcer for televised contests, Vanessa Torres is finally experiencing the myriad types of success and visibility she deserves.

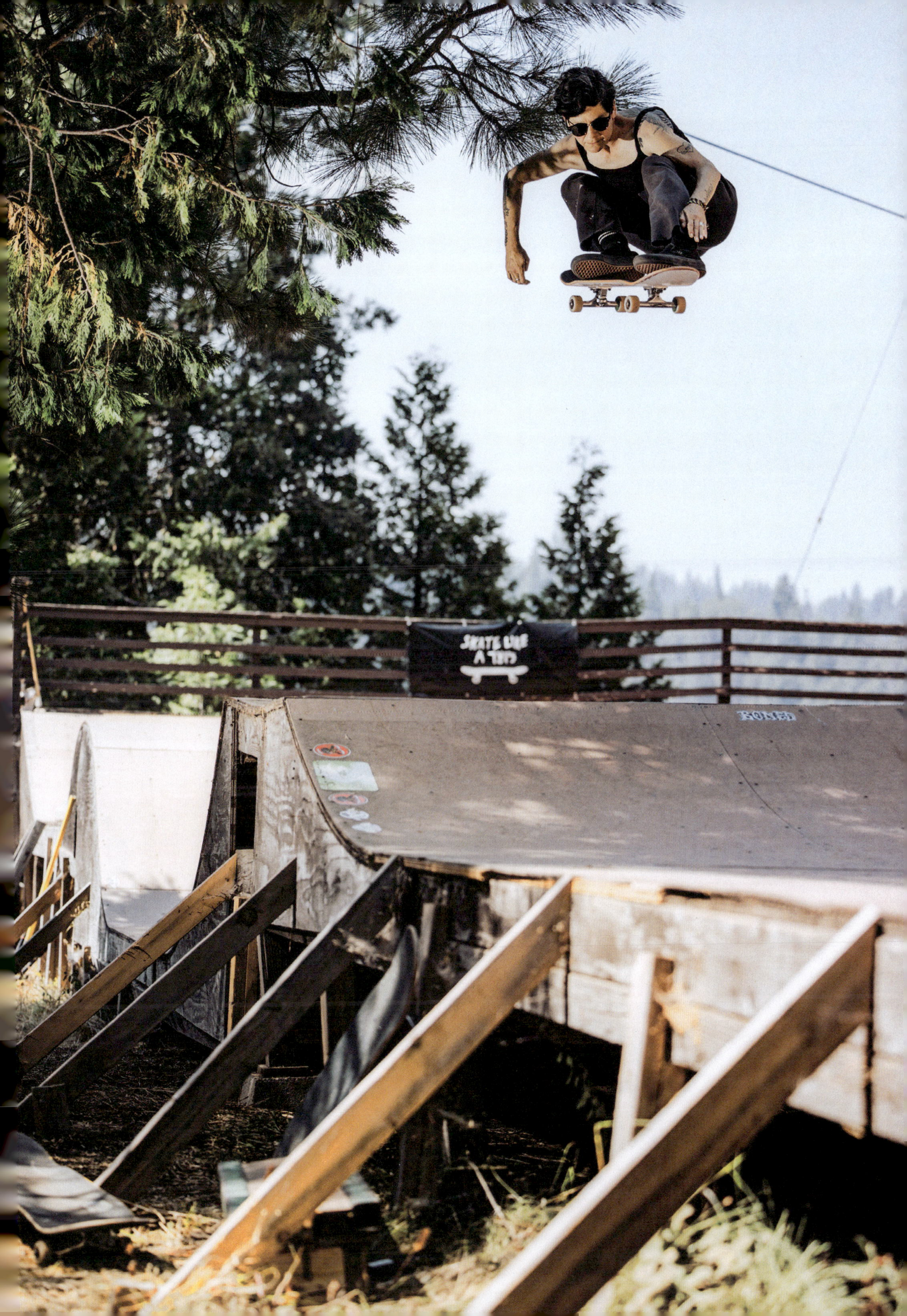
SKATE LIKE
A TURD

THE
ART
ISTS

Get the lines right and get the mind right. Or at least get them moving in the right direction.

That philosophy is evident when analyzing the key components running through the pens, pencils, markers, paints, plumes, and styluses of the Artists. These actors add flavor to skateboarding and infuse the culture with something well beyond a brand name or "brand identity," as they say— they infuse skateboarding with heart.

Art in skate culture (and the artists who deliver it) is the fourth estate— reporting, chronicling, and distributing skate culture. The artists entice, disgust, inform, and inspire. Their work places a cacophony of free expression, politics, humor, heartache, and figurative hand grenades on the skate shop wall and outside in the streets. These artists and generations of others stomp out the blandness and inject the radness, proving there is more than one way to make your mark in skateboarding.

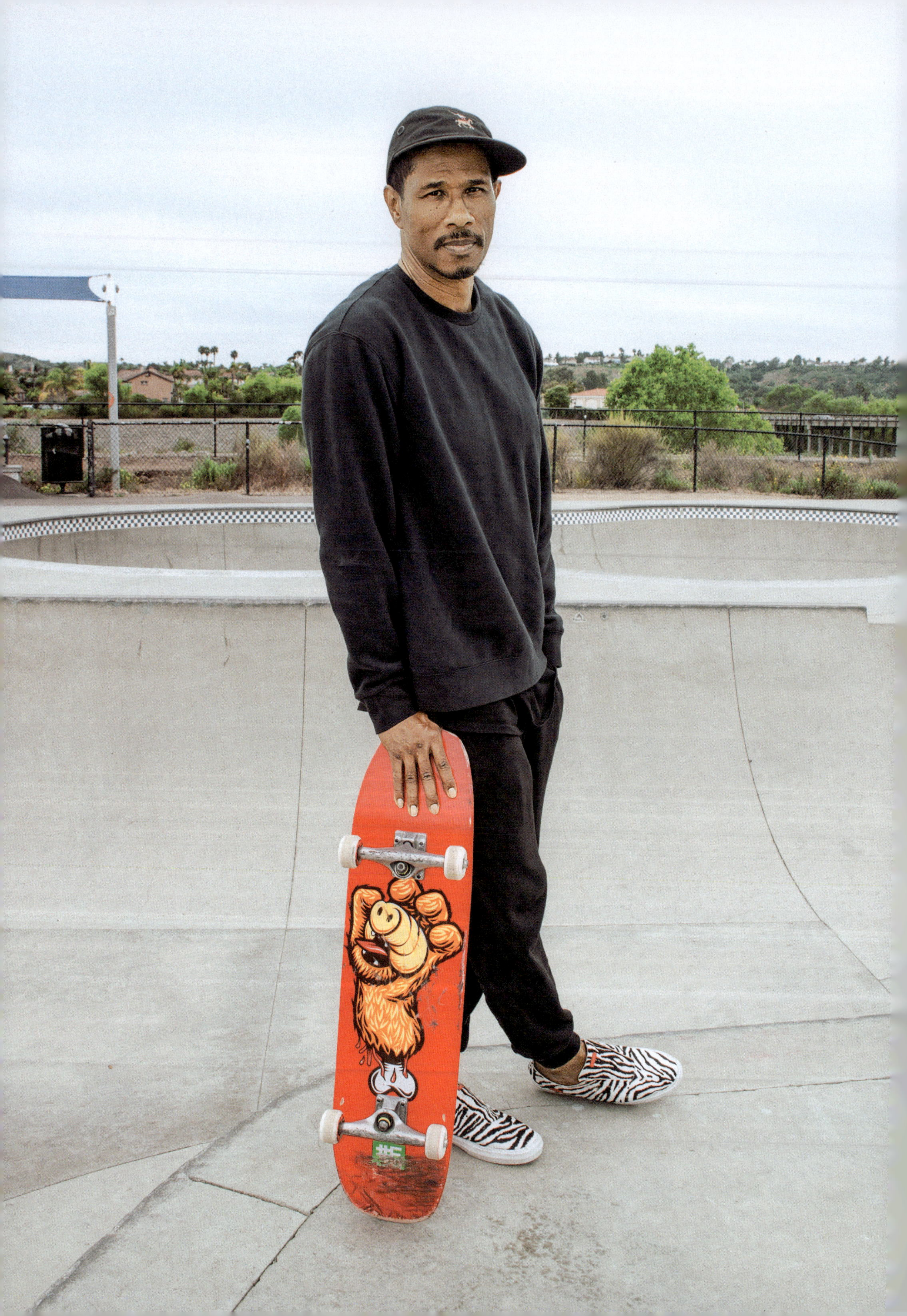

ALPHONZO "ALF" RAWLS

Pioneering Black skater who excelled at street, vert, and mini ramp

H-Street Skateboards star

Founded Savalé Footwear

Created #Everybodyskates, inspired by movies and pop culture

Developed the #Thankyou skateboard

An all-terrain vehicle spinning 540 airs. A *TransWorld SKATEboarding* and *Thrasher* cover star. A skateboarding footwear designer. A legendary African American pro skater, OG founder, graphic designer, and developer of some of the first and finest color-coordinated fits in skateboarding. This is one of the most heralded names in skateboarding: Alphonzo Rawls.

To some readers, Alphonzo—aka Alf—is the guy selling the most intricately designed footwear via his brand Savalé. To others, he is the designer of some of the hottest new graphics for legendary team Plan B Skateboards. Still others know him from his place on the H-Street Skateboards team, where skaters were handpicked by the great Mike Ternasky (RIP).

Like A Tribe Called Quest's Phife Dawg sang, "Back in '89, [he] simply slid into place." Alf was simply skating, ripping, shredding all up in ya face. On the H-Street team in '87, and one of skateboarding's first all-terrain skaters, Alf introduced all of us to the potential to bust in any idiom: vert, street, park, or mini ramp. He personified progressive transition, or ramp skating,

in the early '90s. Put him in the street, no problem, he hit gaps, handrails, and stairs like he was walking down them. Mini ramp? Crushing it, no smoother style, skating to MC 900 Ft. Jesus's remake of Sly Stone's "Don't Call Me N—, Whitey." Alf destroyed the mini ramp, with more lip tricks and combos then nearly any skater at that time. Alf flew across, behind, and could have skated *under* those ramps.

Alf's main competitor in terms of bringing the fire was Danny Way. You know, the guy who jumped the Great Wall of China on his board? The first to do 360 flips on vert ramps, switch kickflips, you name it, he was right there. That's who Alf grew up skating with, neck-in-neck and brother-in-arms on H-Street. That blood runs so deep that it only seems a match made in heaven for Alf to now operate as brand director and designer for Plan B Skateboards, co-owned by Danny.

As if that weren't enough, when it came to vert skating, Danny was one of Alf's main training buddies. The other was none other than San Diego's biggest name, Tony Hawk (see page 63). The trio of Alf, Danny, and Tony was the most progressive in transition skating and couldn't be touched. Alf was also regularly featured in Tony's *TransWorld SKATEboarding* column, Beyond, demonstrating the newest tricks in vert skating.

With all that talent, Alf became well-known for regularly spinning 540s at vert contests and pulling off tricks way beyond the pale, like late foot flips, switch flips, kickflip grabs, and more. More important, it wasn't just that he could skate vert—in fact, when he joined H-Street, vert was falling out of vogue. What he brought to the mix was skating giant vert ramps like those you find at a bank or a schoolyard. For example, he would perform a Caballerial backfoot flip—a trick that at the time was already next to impossible on street— and here goes Alf doing it on vert, putting heat on the ledger in ways that slowly drove many of the older vert skaters to retire. Between Alf and Danny, skateboarding felt limitless.

Now, for those of us on the ground, street skating, Alf was the great Black hope. He was unstoppable in any field. Plus, Black vert skaters were few and far between in the late '80s and early '90s. Access to the resources and time to get good at vert were unavailable to most skaters. Alf became part of the historic Black rippers capable of skating it all: from Marty Grimes and his brother Clyde, the first African American pros to rip in pools and street, to Steve Steadham, a member of the first Bones Brigade, skating pools and vert (later with his own Steadham brand). Later on there was Darin "Cookie Head" Jenkins and Ned "Peanut" Brown. I'm naming them because they are important and Alf carried on their legacy. Alf ushered in the next gen of Black skaters, proving we had a place in any skateable space.

Even now, when we watch him in his retirement, Alf is still blowing up the 'gram as one of the greatest to ever skate transition, making it all look so good and effortless yet remaining as tech as the skaters in the streets.

At H-Street, he had seminal parts in *Not the new H-Street video* (1991), *H-Street Next Generation* (1992), and *Lick* (1993), before moving on to another top San Diego brand, Expedition One, where he not only crushed with the tricks but also slayed with the fits. The only pro skater to shoot his cover photo in full cream-colored sweats, Alf hit 'em with that head-to-toe drip—which no other skater would have attempted at the time. Most skaters were still rocking an old-school quintessential punk style and Alf—well, Alf put his stamp on everything. He was oozing style on and off his board, making a name for himself that easily translated when it came time to enter the world of design.

He would take his artistic flair and his experience understanding how to make board graphics and design for himself, team members, and eventually brands.

The crème de le crème was his work as a shoe designer, beginning with Evol skateboards—the next iteration of H-Street after it closed—then moving into designing Evol footwear in the mid-'90s. With a heavy-hitting pro team that included African American San Diego legends Tyrone Olson and Marcelle Johnson and others in front of the camera, he crafted a new career behind it in design. He would eventually move beyond footwear into T-shirts and apparel and then take that knowledge and use it to build a consulting firm, quietly delivering for some of the best skate brands in the business.

For Alf's third act, he launched his own footwear brand, Savalé. Purposefully curated and created with the highest quality and bespoke craftmanship at price points that are a reminder that you get what you pay for, his footwear continues to buck conventional thinking.

Alf has also been unafraid to put the bounce back in bidness too, through his irreverent creations under his apparel brand #Everybodyskates, launched in 2015, where he features celebrities and characters in pop culture skateboarding, like LeBron James and Beyoncé. #Everybodyskates has also operated with a more serious tone when Alf created his #Thankyou skateboard graphic. It celebrates Black skaters and skaters of the African diaspora by listing all of their names in black and white text as a board graphic. When first released in 2020, the board saluted the skaters best known to Alf, but the list became an interactive crowdsourced project, with the heralded list growing with each subsequent release.

The all-around ATV (all-terrain vehicle) has proven for decades that there isn't a thing he can't perform at the highest level. When he sets his mind to it, it's done, and skateboarding is all the better for it.

KEEPING THIS THING FUN
ANDY JENKINS

Celebrated artist for Girl Skateboards

Designed the RED-branded Girl board

Started his career as a BMX rider

Founder of the Art Dump design co-op

Andy Jenkins holds a vaunted place in the skateboarding art and graphic design world. Creator of the famed Girl Skateboards logo, art director for Girl Skateboards, and head of the Crailtap Art Dump, he is one of few skaters and artists to earn the opportunity to originate iconography that's so widely recognized.

You may think the Girl Skateboards logo looks like the universal image for the women's bathroom. Excellent assumption—*you are correct*. The simplicity of the logo builds directly upon the widely used illustration. As is often the case in skateboarding and life, the simplest responses endure the longest. That is where the inspiration for the skate company founded by Mike Carroll, Megan Baltimore, Spike Jonze, and Rick Howard came from. Only skateboarders in the '90s would hurl an insult at pro skater Howard for "skating like a girl" while in the same era another group of skaters defanged the insult and transmogrified it into gold. Innovator Andy turned that frown upside down by developing Girl's portfolio into countless designs that formed the basis for a lifetime of illustrations, mixed media, and craftsmanship. With more than 30 years under its belt, the Girl logo and brand have been through skateboarding's boom and bust cycles since the company's founding, with Andy steering the ship for nearly all that time.

Andy was part of an elite crew of skateboarding artists in the '90s who produced seminal work for World Industries. His work is aligned directly with that of the other artistic greats of the times, such as Sean Cliver and Marc McKee (see page 134). A sponsored BMXer and a transplant from art school in Denver, Andy landed a job at *Freestylin'*, a BMX magazine. Alongside skaters Spike Jonze (see page 154) and Mark Lewman, he founded *Homeboy* magazine and *Dirt*, a first-of-its-kind publication that featured music, BMX, and skating within the same pages. Those magazines were located within the offices of R. L. Osborn, a famed BMX rider, where Megan Baltimore (see page 240), the future CEO of Girl Skateboards and Crailtap Distribution, worked in business administration. Tie in the fact that R. L. also sublet office space to pro freestyle skateboarder and empresario Steve Rocco, the eventual founder of World Industries skateboards, and the magic that resided under that roof is still astonishing.

Andy told me that although they all felt a strong affinity to riding, the BMX business world was feeling a bit too straitlaced at the time. BMX had a longer history as a "serious" sport than skateboarding, and it had begun to lose allure for many within the outfit. With a little prodding, the aforementioned group succumbed to the temptation of the start-up business model and jumped ship to support Rocco's fledgling skateboard company.

While most of his compatriots went to World Industries directly to seek their fortune, Andy quietly planted a foot in skateboarding as well. He never officially joined World, but he became a pen for hire, designing board graphics for them from 1989 to 1993. While McKee and Cliver are two

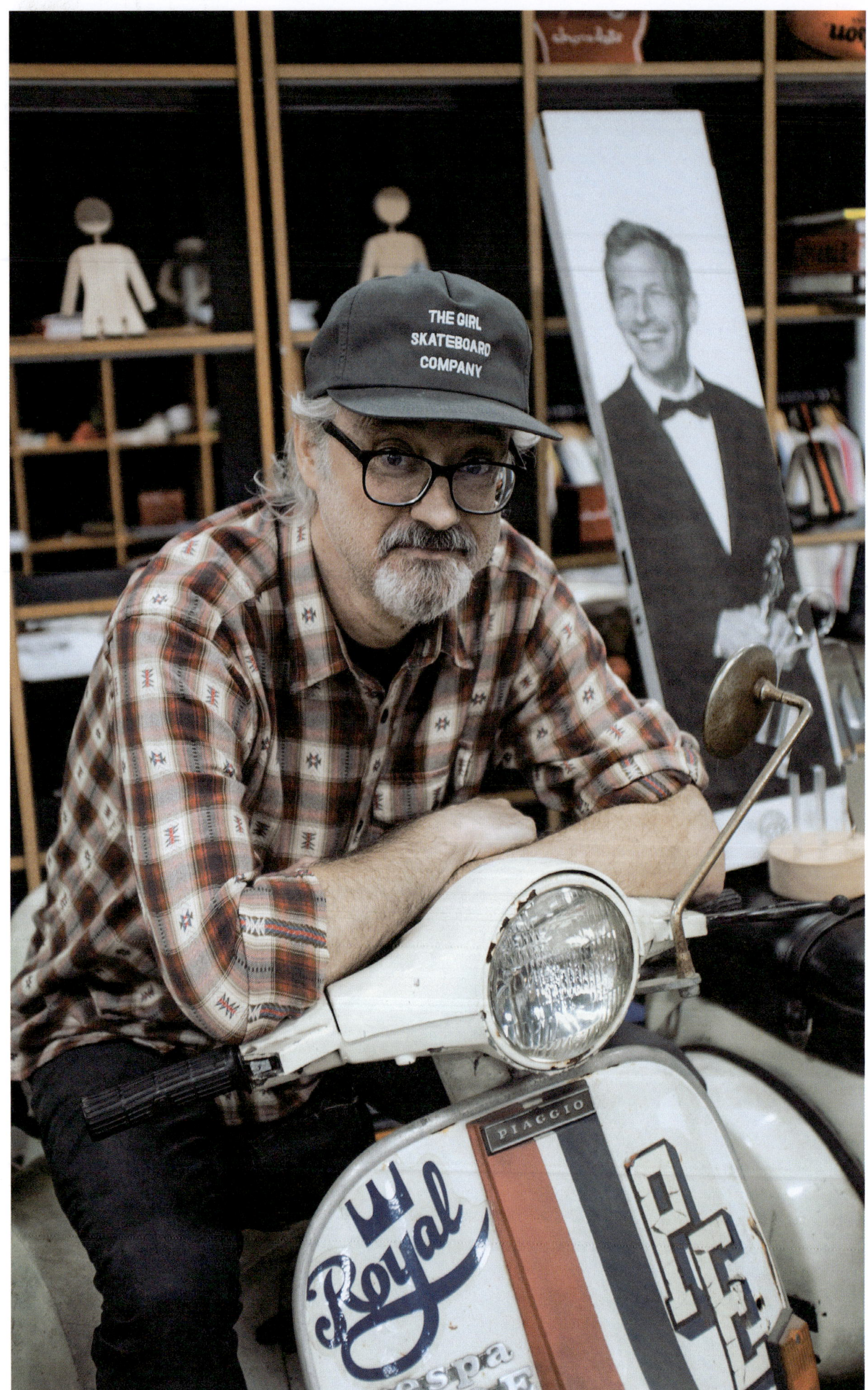
THE GIRL
SKATEBOARD
COMPANY
PIAGGIO
Royal
espa

skateboarding art luminaries who loved to roll a hard *R* in their humor, when given the chance, Andy was more apt to poke fun in a less serious manner, without burning down the house. That lighter touch is exemplified in his beloved original Jason Lee Cat in the Hat skateboard graphic for Blind. Complete with a lick of rhyming poetry, the image features a hatted and gloved figure with his hands over his face, closely resembling the star of Theodor Geisel's famed story of the same name—if only he were drawn to resemble the celebrated pro skater and actor Jason Lee. Andy's take on the Grinch is another early example where the Grinch hasn't just stolen Christmas; he revels in quietly roasting the citizens of Whoville on a spit above an open fire. Andy continued to create board graphics ad hoc for World Industries and its subsidiary brands like Natas Kaupas's (see page 24) 101 Skateboards for years before an opportunity to finally make a significant change arrived. That break was the aftermath of one of the most infamous mutinies in skateboarding history: pro skaters Rick Howard, Mike Carrol, Megan Baltimore, and Spike Jonze left World Industries under the cover of night to form Girl Skateboards and, one year later, Chocolate Skateboards.

When Girl began, Andy was tapped to become creative director for the brand. Rather than creating one-offs, he was in charge of establishing all the imagery for the rough-and-tumble venture.

Andy's team operates out of one room, with him as Girl's art director and across from him Carlos Gutierrez, art director for Chocolate, and Paul Chan, art director. The Art Dump, as Andy named it, is the design co-op he founded right there at Girl HQ in Torrance, California, where he and fellow art luminaries work together in the office on commercial and noncommercial projects and keep each other inspired.

Andy found a way to consistently develop new combinations that retool the brand from the windows to the wall to steadily deliver a product that resonates across the decades. That's from the boards to the videos to the ads to the collaboration with the AIDS foundation Project RED.

Andy's illustration style also begat a legion of followers beyond board graphics. What originally might have gone on to be part of *Thrasher Comix* instead landed at *TransWorld SKATEboarding*, where, under the pen name Mel Bend, he created the character Lettus Bee, a capricious skater rendered in black and white. Lettus embodied all of skateboarding . . . magical imagery of a skater delusional and in love with skateboarding, just as

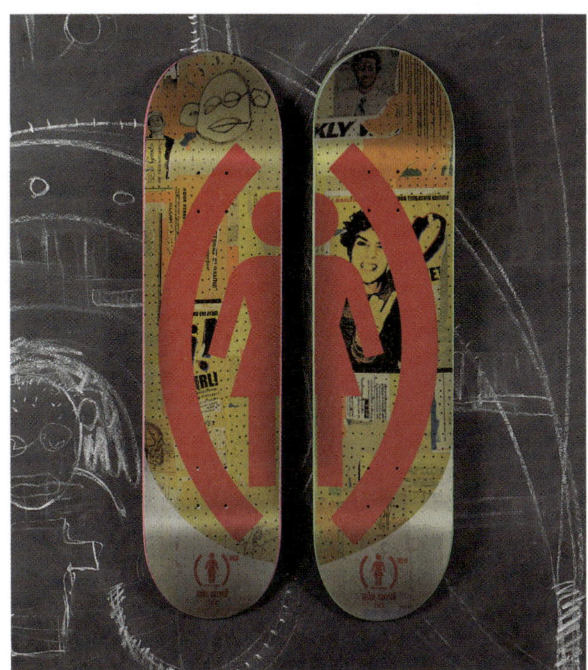

Girl Skateboards x (RED) collaboration designed by Andy Jenkins on Mike Carrol decks

likely to skate in a pool as to skate coffee cups and sinks. The character struck a chord in every skater, whether he was being chased by the cops, heading to school, or, as in one amazing escapade that ran in *TWS*, stopped by a rock. We all knew. We all felt. We all loved.

Andy also began to work in mixed media, creating images, overlaying them, painting, using papier-mâché—you name it. He added layer upon layer of texture in order to support his vision and tell a new story with more depth, often ending up with 40-by-30-inch works that he then photographed and turned into board graphics.

One of his most potent pieces arrived in the form of a graphic for World's offshoot, 101 Skateboards. It involved a painting, a dried human bone, reworked metal sheeting, and an abandoned World War II grenade—all corralled together then expertly captured by Spike Jonze.

When it was time for the mass exodus from World to form Girl, it was only natural for Andy to be part of that early collective. He's proven himself as an artist and as someone down for skateboarding, and someone who delivers a fresh and beautiful perspective on the familiar or everyday encounters with a wink.

It's those inside jokes that continue to drive Andy and the Art Dump. Now, after 30 years at Girl, Andy still lives by the mantra "If it gots to get done, it better be fun."

MAKING SPACE FOR SKATEBOARDING'S ART CULTURE
TYLER GIBNEY

Gallerist and curator at the center of skate culture, the HVW8 Gallery

Created the POLITICAL MINDED anti–gun violence graphics for Popwar Skateboards

Tyler is an artist? I always thought he was just the money behind the HVW8 Gallery. I didn't know he swung a brush or threw up a tag anywhere.

These and similar phrases came out of the mouths of several famous artists who have exhibited their work at the quintessentially badass and often skateboard-centric HVW8 Art + Design Gallery in Los Angeles. HVW8 is *the* L.A. place for the best in show and those in the know.

As a muralist and more, Tyler Gibney had been delivering hits for more than a decade before he manifested the little gallery spot right off Melrose Avenue. HVW8 is where you might see a Mark "Gonz" Gonzales (see page 92) installation filled with skaters, or Ric Clayton's artworks associated with the punk band Suicidal Tendencies, or Donald Glover's art incarnations, or Estevan Oriol's photographs. HVW8 is tapped in, too, as one of the premiere locations for skateboarding films.

It takes patience and a true love for the life, along with taste and conviction, to remain a curator of street and skate culture because for so very long there was no money in it. Why provide a space for would-be artists and musicians? Because the streets are where life and love intersect, and that mattered to Tyler long before street art became marketable. If there is a venue that can claim OG status, it is HVW8.

Tyler himself has been in the art and skateboarding life since the late '90s, throwing up art in unique spaces as part of the early HVW8 crew. Then known as the Heavyweight Art Installation, the camp consisted of Tyler, Gene Pendon, and Dan Buller, and made their debut art at the most celebrated of spaces, the 1999 Montreal International Jazz Festival. From then on they toured around the world working the room and developing their mashup of graffiti around classic images of monsters in music and politics. They were a fire in any city, working with DJs and building the room to a boil while they created live art as the room got turnt. Imagine you are at the party getting your flirt on and hitting the floor when you see Tyler and his lanky six-foot-plus frame working a 15-by-15-foot canvas. Working in time with the music and a three-man crew, they would spray-paint and use oil paint to adorn the canvas with giant images that paid homage to the musical styles you were shaking your thang to.

Those sessions often occurred in the midst of hip-hop, deep soul, and house. During a three to four art set the image might be Ella Fitzgerald, at another, Sam Cooke. I've seen it range from Stevie Wonder to Chaka Khan to Fela Kuti to Mos Def to Miles Davis to J Dilla. Watching the HVW8 crew create lifelike magic out of thin air inspired the DJ, the dancers, and anyone in proximity.

That level of talent operated domestically and internationally, spreading the vibes, leaving people's mouths agape as they created in front of

IF THERE IS A VENUE THAT CAN CLAIM OG STATUS, IT IS HVW8.

your eyes, pulling from the sounds and energy of the room to develop one-of-a-kind pieces.

"Gun America" portrayed several parts of the U.S. as guns, including the Florida panhandle, and other works depicted crime or controversies facing the U.S. These later became board graphics that sold out immediately and helped solidify Tyler's and the HVW8 crew's reputation. They were all deeply connected to hip-hop, jazz, skateboarding, and street culture. While Tyler and his crew no longer operate as the underground, they are not new to this "thing of ours." This thing of *ours* that lives on in the halls and walls of the HVW8 gallery. It proves the spot for new artists and old alike to throw up their thoughts on the state of the state or the power of the part and anything in between whenever the need arises.

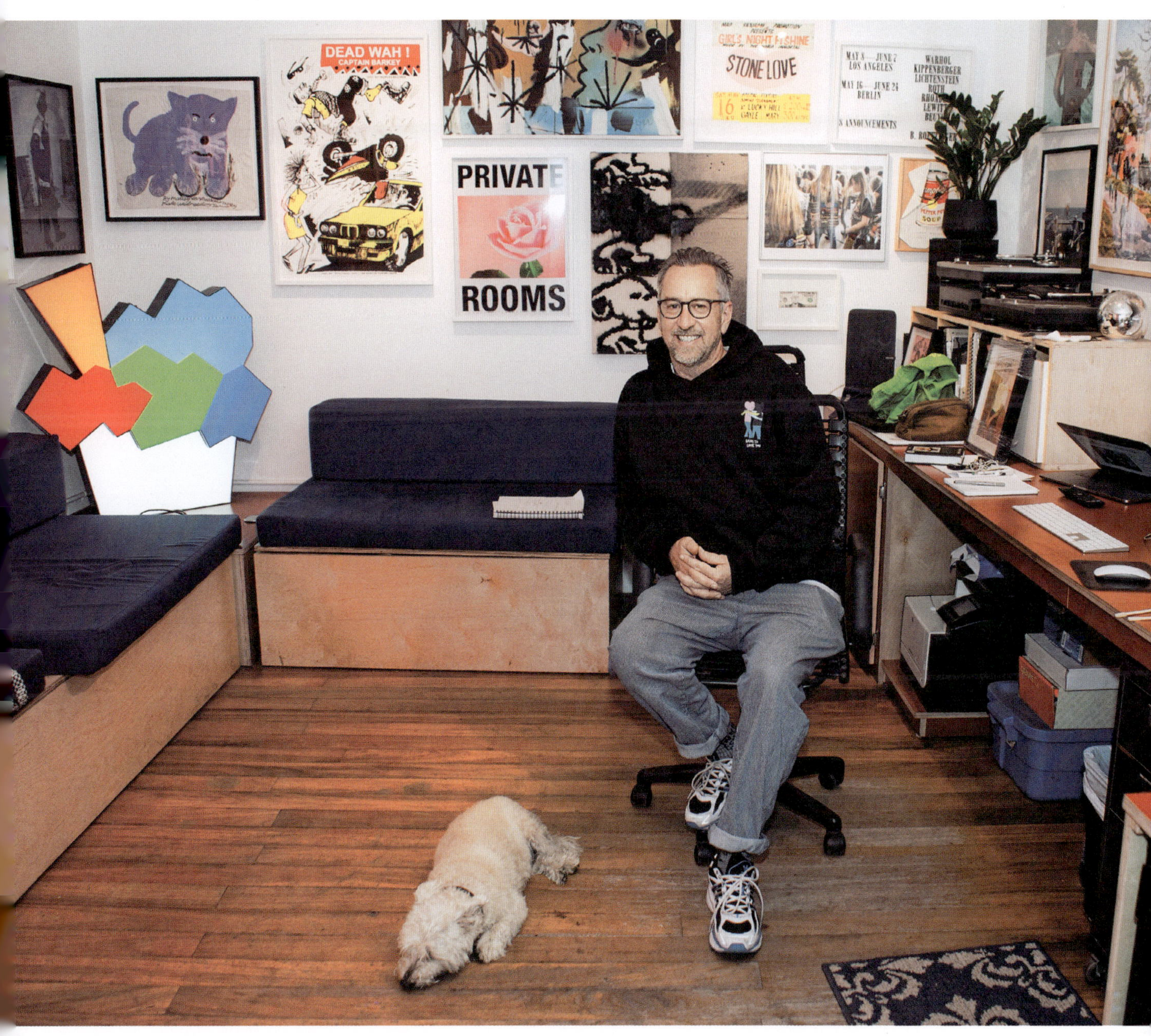

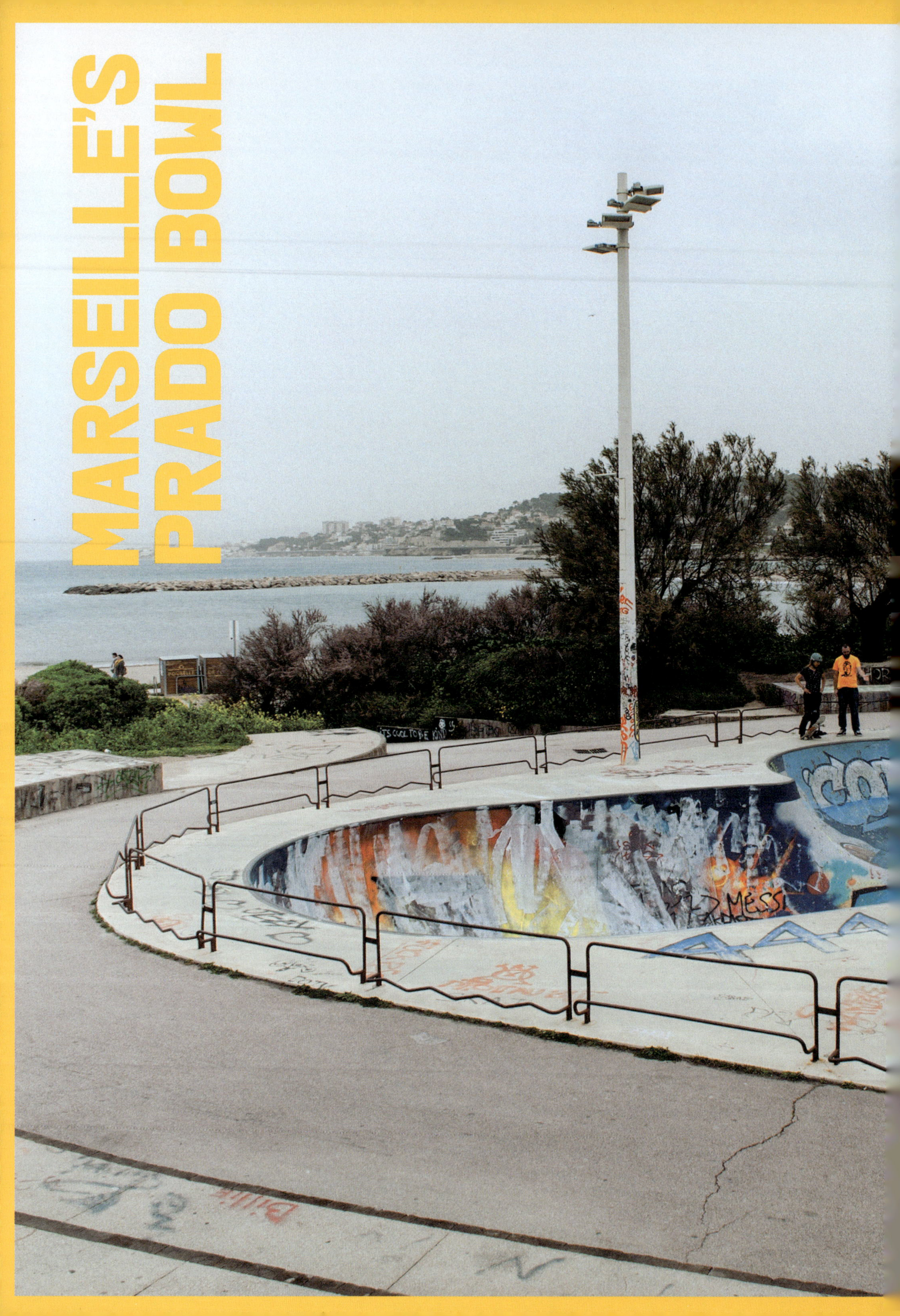
MARSEILLE'S
PRADO BOWL

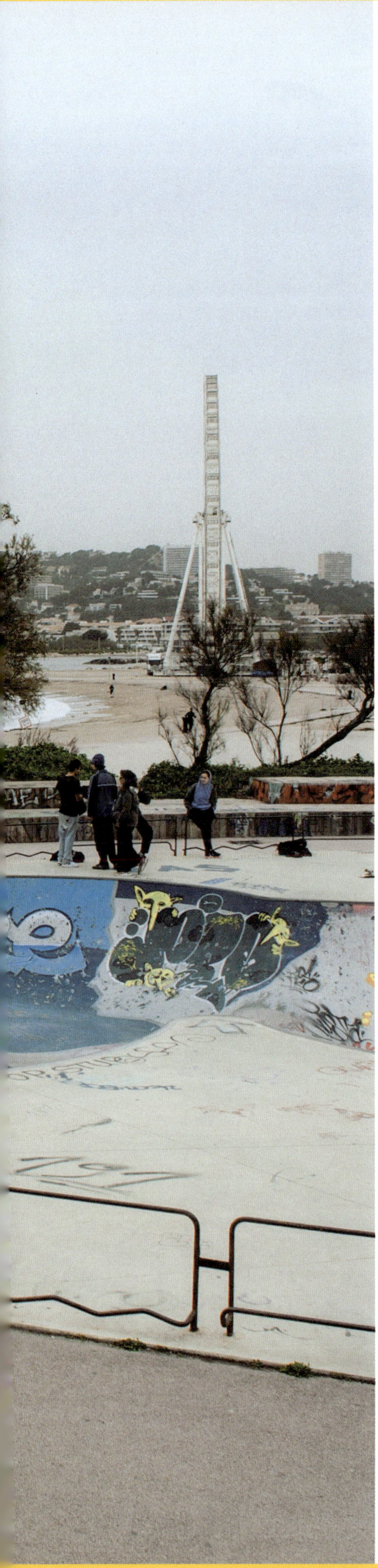

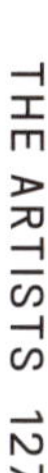

The legendary Prado Bowl. A coveted feather in the cap of any skater since 1991. Very few places have everything a skater could ask for: a bowl by a beach, beautiful sunsets, and a luscious sea to dive into after a session. There is even an amazing sculpture, *The Seven Gates of Jerusalem*, created by David Soussana to celebrate the Jewish community and their contributions to Marseille, in the south of France. All of it can be observed by taking a seat along the cement steps cut into the hill above the bowl.

Now about the bowl. Unlike many skateparks that are focused on street skating based on the feel of the city—ledges, handrails, and stairs, and the harsh obstructions of the built environment—the Prado Bowl is all curves. It is a pool built for you to have never-ending lines and for your flow to blossom. You can start in the shallow end, learning how to lock in smith grinds frontside, then how to steeze them out backside, adding your own flair and style.

Pretty soon though, you will be doing two things: learning transfers over the spine (the point where two transitions laid back-to-back come together), then how to do airs over the hip (the outside corners where transitions meet roughly perpendicularly).

Learning those two things prepares you to not only skate the rest of the bowl, but also for skating transition anywhere. Lucky dogs. Most street skaters don't get to skate these types of transitions, so Marseille's fortunate locals gain the ultimate lessons and expertise in transition or mini-ramp and pool skating.

For those of us whose experience is in skating mini ramps, used to the ease of skating back-to-back or just hitting one wall, turning around, then hitting the other, with the same amount of energy on each trick, the Prado Bowl ain't that. You have to use your brain to skate the labyrinthine series of hips and bowled ends in the shallow, the midsize hips, and the deep end, and that doesn't come easy—you need speed.

If you don't have that and the proper flow, rather than working the curves and transitions, you will miss the cues under your feet and hit all of those face walls and decelerate instead of using them to propel you forward. *Pas bon.*

If you lock into the flow, you will blast airs across the park, linking one transition to the next full speed, feeling like Tony Alva (see page 43) on his best days; if not, you will do what the uninitiated have done: hit the corner, land in the flat, and not have the speed and strength to get up the next wall. At that point you are out of steam and have to climb unceremoniously out of the bowl, 'cause your run is over. To succeed in the Prado Bowl, you need to learn to pump every inch around the perimeter and the interior, and to link all your tricks together. If and when you do, the treasure will be plentiful.

When skating the bowl, you know you are a part of history. Not just France's skate history but global skate history. You feel it in your bones and know that original rippers put their marks on this place. The first accolades and love go to the Marseille OG local skaters. They were the ones who first showed the rest of the skate world this most magical place. And how can it not be magical? Nestled on the shores of the

Mediterranean Sea, Marseille is a slice of heaven on earth. As a friend told me, the city is the heart of bohemian life in France. It is where the most laid-back, SoCal vibe exists. Paris is a personal favorite—it is the New York or L.A. of France—with the movement, the hustle and bustle, and all the beauty that cascades from that energy. But Marseille? Marseille will have you questioning if the Beach Boys might have got it wrong singing about California Girls instead of *filles françaises* (or *garçons français* or anyone in between depending on your tastes).

It's that vibe that keeps the Prado Bowl discussed in whispers and exclamations. What would you do there, how could you add to the mystique? A true holy grail of skate spots.

The legendary locale was designed by Jean-Pierre Collinet. Born and raised in Nantes, France, he took to skateboarding early and received his first real skateboard, a Banzai, in 1977, after designing one of his own as many did during that early era. Building his love of skateboarding from the late '70s into the '80s and beyond, he skated every inch of the city during his teens and frequented the few skateparks available to him. That enduring search for the thrill of skateboarding is what helped drive him to get his degree in architecture in Marseille, even though school was not his first love. Skateboarding gave light to his life and in return he delivered one of the most joyful love letters back to the skateboarding community.

Collinet's connection to skateboarding the old full pipes in Marseille (brought in for drainage), combined with his design prowess, created what he categorized as the quintessential California skateboarding dream—a pool to skate all your own—placed lovingly at the water's edge in Marseille. It supplements the actual experience he and his friends had skating a duck pool in Marseille, when they were barely in their teens. An overgrown and steeply banked actual mallard oasis, that pool served as the first place for skaters to test their skills and attempt to rip. It offered them the chance to imitate the skaters they saw in the fleeting skate media that arrived in France, everyone from the Z-Boys to Powell Peralta's Bones Brigade, while carving French architecture. It was a place to reflect on their skating and see it in the light of American media. Those OGs bombed the streets and added their grit and determination to the fabric of the skate scene and became the original advocates for the creation of the Prado Bowl years later.

What Collinet would take from those years in the duck-laden piece of hallowed architecture intertwined with his notions of creating an "endless wave," a bowl that could be skated with lines forever—meaning the only limit to how far and how long you can ride is the amount of energy and imagination you have to offer. If you provide the amps, the bowl will give you back the charge and let you go forever.

Debuting in 1991, when street skating was really taking over as the dominant form of skateboarding, the bowl itself was almost a throwback to a different era. It was skated by the locals at first and helped them all arrive at a proper surf-skate flowy style of skateboarding. The major trend toward street didn't keep all skaters away, however, and once word got out, skaters worldwide made the pilgrimage to see the possibilities of the limitless lines on the shores of the Mediterranean.

The Prado Bowl had its major moment during the 1999 Quiksilver Bowl Riders contest. That contest connected the European and U.S. park and bowl scenes like never before. One of the most famous skaters to add their stroke to the canvas of the Prado Bowl during that contest was the powerhouse John "Cards" Cardiel. An all-terrain vehicle (ATV), John can skate anything, street, pools, vert, and, of course, bowls.

Amid a flurry of skating from the likes of Tony Trujillo, Omar Hassan, and Wade Speyer, themselves all ATVs, it is Cards who blasted a backside 360 ollie from one section of the bowl over the lip blindly into the deep end and tight transition of the connecting pool. That is truly trusting in the power invested in you by the skate gods—to know that when you land, you will be in the right place and to absorb the shock of the landing and roll right into the next wall of the pool. Bonkers.

That is the spirit embedded in the bowl—absolute abandon. Make it or break it. It's the same energy that connected the Z-Boys searching for pools and the Marseille locals pursuing the same. It's that same energy that connects the Prado Bowl with the Venice Skate Park now. Carving and finding a line and blasting airs as hard as you can. When I'm at the edge of the Venice bowls or the Prado Bowl, the lines connect. Skaters speaking a universal language.

While there was a lull at the place for a time as trends shifted, the Prado Bowl once again took the spotlight with a new generation of skaters in 2016, when Red Bull launched a new contest there. Hopefully everyone will get to make the pilgrimage to a skater's Valhalla to enjoy the Prado Bowl amid the endless lines and summer sun in Marseille.

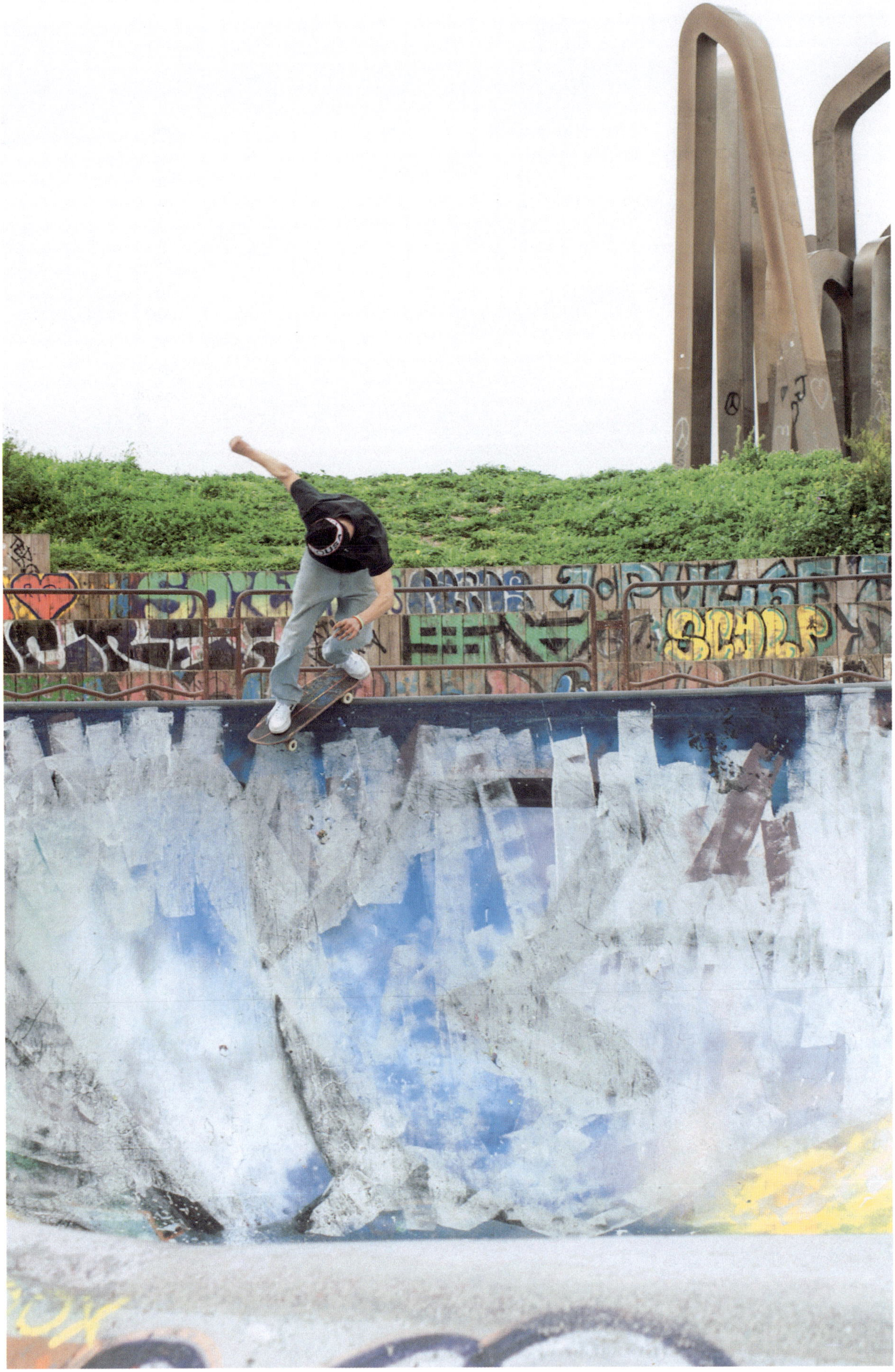

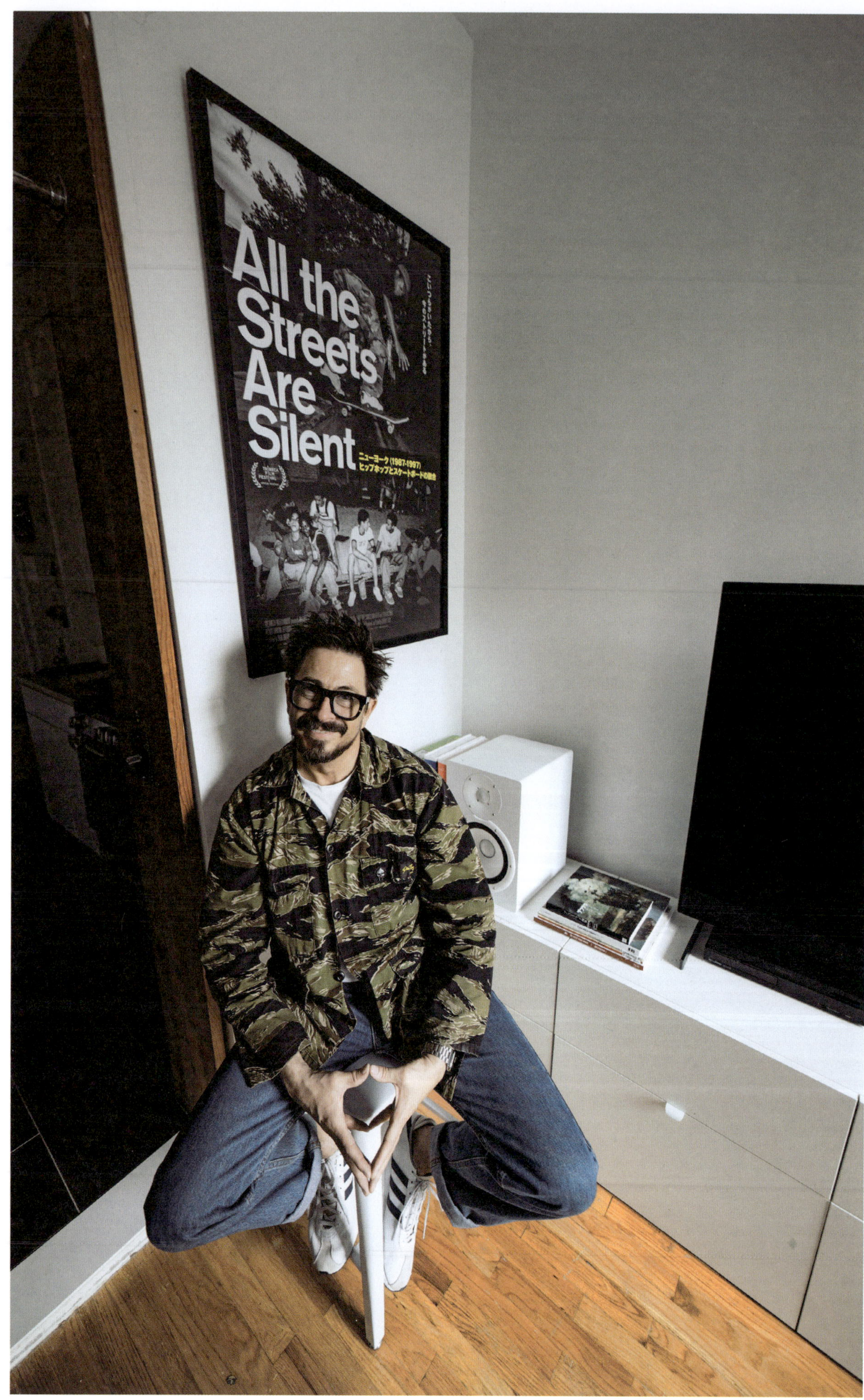

All the
Streets
Are
Silent

PRACTICE TRUTH, FEAR NOTHING

ELI MORGAN GESNER

Centered hip-hop in New York skateboarding culture

Designer for Phat Farm clothing and SHUT Skateboards

Zoo York art director

There are people in life who are nexus beings. You know the type? Always at the right place, at the right time, doing *their* thing. And by the time you really understand *their* thing, it's become *the* thing for everyone. That is Eli Morgan Gesner, a New Yorker in the classic sense of the words. Fast-talking. Connected. Moving. Thinking. A master of the convo and chronology, and deputized under SHUT Skateboards, New York City's first skateboarding company, this skateboarder, graffiti artist, and early hip-hop head was also part of a dynamic duo with close friend and African American artist Alyasha Owerka-Moore.

Together they designed for SHUT and then landed a gig as designers for Russell Simmons's highly successful '90s clothing brand Phat Farm. The sum of all those experiences came to a head when Eli began to turn subterfuge, street couture, and cultural conspiracies into bona fide art as director extraordinaire for Zoo York skateboards.

Eli's training in art direction began in the mid-'80s at SHUT, founded by the godfathers of the New York scene, African American and Native American Rodney Smith and French and Italian American Bruno Musso. It was the original East Coast powerhouse with deep credentials. The boards, first handcrafted by Rodney and Bruno in 1986, are the stuff of legend and part of the Smithsonian's permanent collection. There's the SHUT Street Posse board, the first to depict hip-hop and graffiti culture *as* skateboarding. It featured a B-Boy in a

classic B-Boy stance—'80s warm-ups, hoodie pulled tight, sporting a SHUT four-fingered ring. It even had the NYC skyline etched into the posse lettering. The SHUT Shark reminded competitors they'd be "sleeping with the fishes" and still never get a rest. Then the SHUT Assault Vehicle, damn—jus' the name let you know this was gritty NYC. Last but not least, there was the image of the rat sniper with the smoking gun shooting from behind bars with Zoo York written in graf letters by a young Eli. Lifted from some the OG graffiti writers of New York City (the Soul Artists of Zoo York), it demonstrated how street life influenced the skaters of the city. The beasts of the east took flight on these SHUT vehicles, spreading the gospel of the ferocity of New York skateboarding.

While SHUT closed down in 1993, Eli, Rodney, and partner Adam Schatz, with the blessing of the original Soul Artists of Zoo York, launched what became the iconic East Coast brand Zoo York skateboards. Eli was installed as the art director, working under the pseudonym and tag Ocularge, a riff on his grand vision for the brand and his trademark glasses.

Eli is a conversationalist—actually he would call himself a talker. Someone with lots of ideas and concepts to explore at a moment's notice. That conversationalist spirit was evident even when it came to the Zoo York ads. Eli would create a conversation in the minuscule text written sideways in the margins of the Zoo York ads in places such as *Thrasher*, especially when that magazine moved from black-and-white to color circa '96. Through that text, Eli brought you into the secret society of Zoo York and that naturally had tentacles that stretched around every aspect of New York culture. The illuminati in skateboarding? Yep, Eli put it in. Crazy gangsta and mafia references? *Si, prego.* Wheels with Gucci links and gold rope chains printed on 'em? Say less. When you forgot that the Zoo was the connector to all things, they dropped the Master series, bringing the classic Shaolin flicks that inspired countless Saturday-morning mock kung fu sibling battles, and Wu-Tang Clan. It was all there, every time.

Like Posdnuos of De La Soul, Eli had been "stylin' abstract since loose leafs was the shit." All of his experiences in graffiti culture, hip-hop, and punk rock manifested in those Zoo ads and signified a handcrafted, hardcore, East Coast hustle.

When Zoo York hit, the stars aligned and the streets fell out. It wasn't just that they had a style that was definitively New York or that the iconography was of the greatest city on earth, it was the fashion, the parties, the food, the parties, the culture, the parties. Did I mention the parties? It was true then and still true now. Skaters, snowboarders, artists, musicians, DJs, celebrities, all existing together—that's a New York City thang and Eli has been at the center of it all. Connecting and introducing and reintroducing and contextualizing—everything in its right place.

The same applied to their first team video, *Zoo York Mixtape* (1997). Ever the underdogs, Eli and R. B. Umali, the filmer, figured out a way to create a cinematic masterpiece that errrybody was part of. And it delivered.

It begins with the New York City skyline coming into focus and then the cutaway—to the lab of the legendary Roc Raida of the X-Ecutioners. *Boom!* "Big shout-out to the East Coast," he cuts into the mix, and the intro begins. WTF, the frenetic pace of East Coast skateboarding is unleashed, and Roc Raida beat-juggling with his hands behind his back, and with his nose! No other skate video ever had that caliber of technique. (Don't think I forgot about *411 Video Magazine* issue #1 with MC Erick Sermon of EPMD in the MF'n booth—that comes in as a close second.)

As if that wasn't enough to solidify the connection, the video didn't just show a skate section playing over a music track, as most do. Instead, this video was blessed by a young Busta Rhymes, Method Man, Diamond D, and a host of the most celebrated names in hip-hop, courtesy of WKCR-FM's *The Stretch Armstrong and Bobbito Show*, through Eli's close friend Robert "Bobbito" Garcia. Eli converted these gems of hip-hop into the soundtrack and aesthetic of the team, the tour, and the brand and parlayed their underdog status into the most authentic skateboarding video of the era.

With the success of the *Zoo York Mixtape* video, Zoo then granted one of their most prominent riders, Philly's own Ricky Oyola, his own brand, Illuminati, with art direction led by Eli. For that brand, Eli leaned fully into conspiracy theories and Philadelphia history to produce imagery for the ads and board graphics. That is, until the name was forced to be changed to Silverstar due to claims

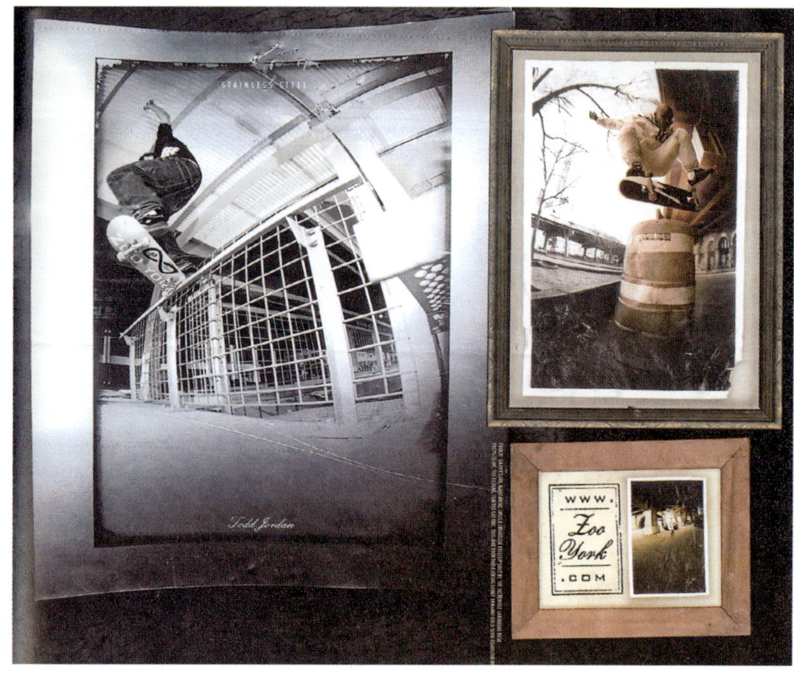

Left: Original Zoo York ads from the '90s–2000s, created by Eli Gessner, featuring pro skaters (left) Todd Jordan, (right) Danny "Supa" Supasiriratana

Opposite: Original '90s Zoo York ad featuring NYC's Harold Hunter (RIP), created by Eli Gessner

of copyright infringement. Ricky and Zoo and Eli then launched First Division Wheels, the first contemporary East Coast wheel company. Zoo and its subsidiaries were the hot ticket items at every skate shop.

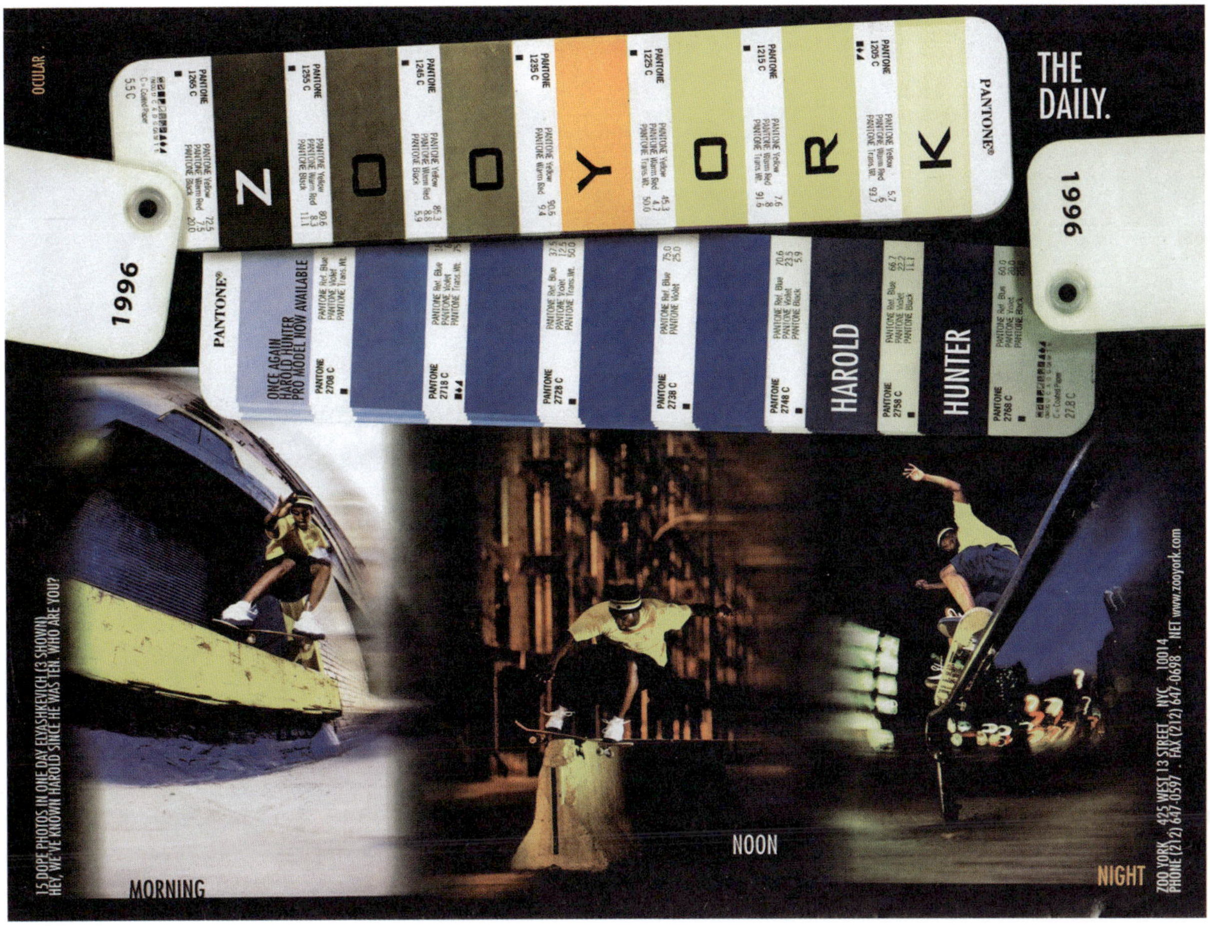

To quote the *Zoo York Mixtape* and artist Blahzay Blahzay, "When the East is in the house, OMG— danger!" Zoo took over. They were soon in every fashion magazine, were lauded in Europe, and as Biggie said, "laid their game down quite flat" in Japan. All this glow-up would not go unnoticed. The explosive growth also brought them into full contention with the West Coast skateboarding industry. Zoo York was wildly outselling other brands in many skate shops on the East and West Coasts. Demand was high, and this contributed to manufacturing and production sustainability issues. Like many companies, Zoo would get so big that it couldn't possibly exist without the guiding hand of a holding company or a large investor who might want to swoop in and grab one of the realest brands to every come out of New York.

Enter Marc Ecko, who is always adjacent to skateboarding. His brand, Iconix, took over as Zoo's management company in 2005. Marc even brought Iconix skate superstar Sal Barbier (see page 87) into the fold. Barbier rebuilt the Zoo skate team, which had largely disbanded, with former team riders from his brand, Aesthetics. This worked for a time, as those skaters were well-respected names and several had East Coast roots. But times changed and the spark was gone. Eventually all the king's horses couldn't put Zoo back together again. Eli and company departed.

New York City's greatest brand, now selling yoga pants. A sad state of affairs. All good things must come to an end, and all tragic things must eventually be burned to the ground. Amid all of this, Rodney restarted SHUT for a time and launched his own brand, All One Universe, which he runs to this day. Eli continued creating art, film, music, and photography across a number of outlets.

But in 2019, rising from the ashes of the Zoo-tastrophe, the original crew came back to revive the golden child and free the city from the malfeasance of uncaring corporate overlords. Rodney, Adam, and Eli Morgan Gesner returned to reclaim their legacy and restore the beast in the east.

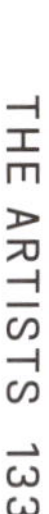

THE MICHELANGELO OF ILLUSTRATED MAYHEM

MARC McKEE

Pushed skateboarding graphics into the realm of the sublime, subversive, and controversial

Created iconography rooted in pop culture

Created legendary skateboard brand characters Flame Boy, Wet Willy, and the Devil Man

Designed an iconic board trolling zealots who saw Satan in a skater

If you want a company's vision of skateboarding plastered on the bottom of a skateboard, by all means hire a good graphic designer. If you want iconic artwork that reverberates for generations and doubles as edgy skateboarding graphics? You gotta call the original *provocateur du pinceau*, Marc McKee.

Since the late '80s, he has been the go-to artist when it comes to creating skateboarding art. Marc is even called in to bail out brands when they've forgotten how to connect to the fire.

Marc's interest in art began during his elementary school days, as did his love affair with skateboarding. Originally from Marin County, California, Marc made his way to L.A. to work for BMX legend R. L. Osborn and his Bully Bikes company. R.L.'s office was also home to other skaters/artists/entrepreneurs and auteurs who would set modern skateboarding ablaze, like filmmaker Spike Jonze, artist Andy Jenkins, and CEO of Girl Skateboards Megan Baltimore. Along with Marc, the team would leave the BMX world in the late '80s to create or contribute to the legacy of World Industries, which would become one of the most influential skateboarding brands of all time.

An Asian American artist surrounded by World's multiracial team, Marc found that the brand was built upon a menagerie of urban experiences that were new to skateboarding at the time. He would be given free reign to incorporate those elements into his skateboarding art.

In those early days, Marc and the entire team worked for peanuts on shoestring budgets. Marc would earn a few hundred dollars per board graphic at the time. That contrasted with the artists working at some of their competitors, known in skateboarding as the big 5—Powell Peralta, NHS/Santa Cruz, Vision, Independent Trucks/*Thrasher*, and Tracker/*TransWorld SKATEboarding*—whose graphic artists were often more serious and receiving substantially more serious salaries. Moving thousands of skateboards a month, at giant factories, they had skin in the game and were already leading the industry—no need to rock the boat with controversy. World, on the other hand, created its first boards in a furniture shop with no idea how to make quality product and a need to make a name for themselves.

While the other brands had more money, they did not have more heart or humor, nor did they have an owner willing to give his artists carte blanche. Nor did they have Marc, who was unafraid to deliver a joke. Take his initial images of World founder Steve Rocco as the beloved children's book character Winnie-the-Pooh, but with a set of devil horns, a goatee, and shades, standing in an unemployment line with Arnold Schwarzenegger and Ronald

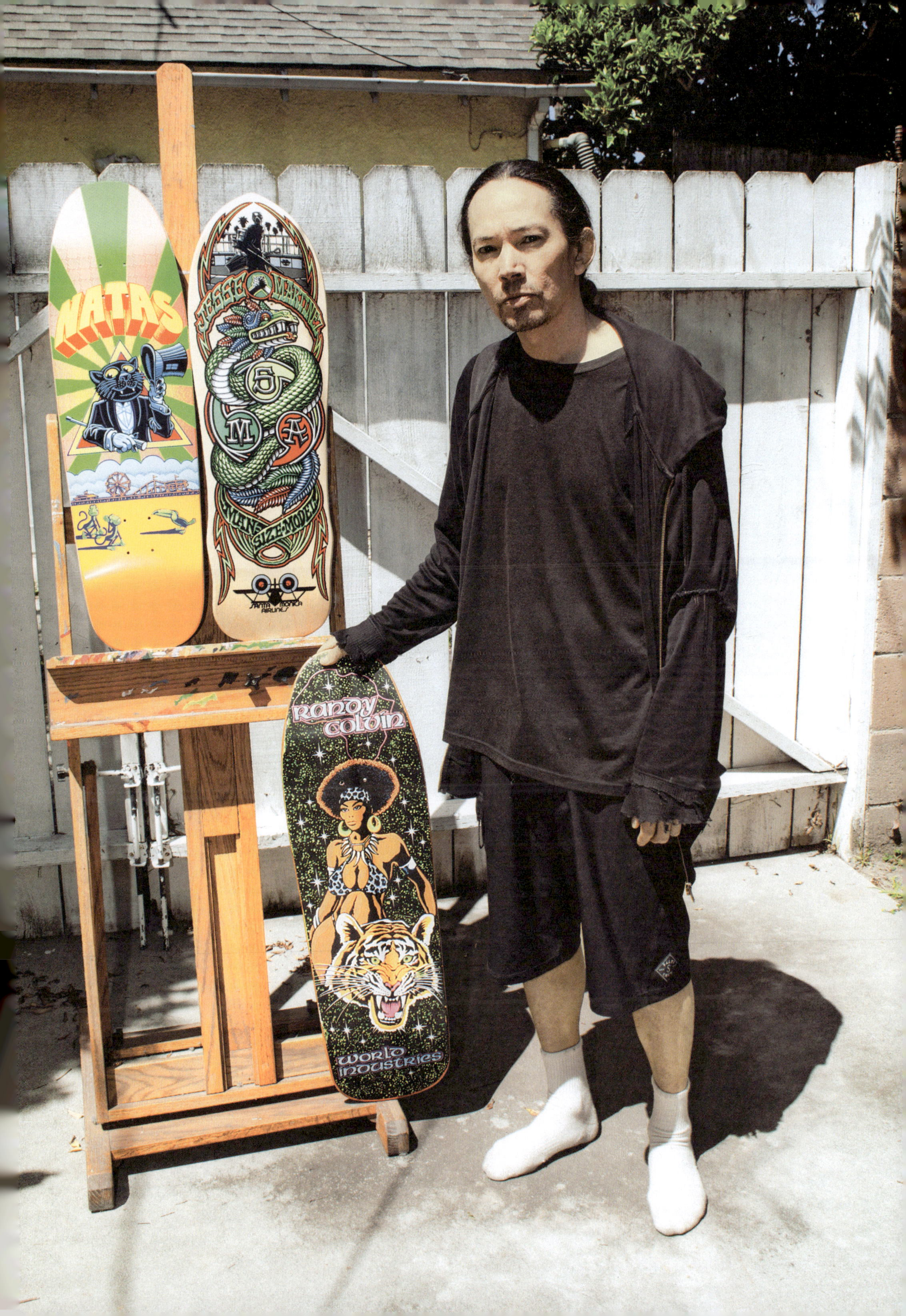
NATAS
JESSE MARTINEZ
SJ
M
SA
VLADE-SIZE-MODEL
SANTA MONICA AIRLINES
RANDY COLVIN
WORLD INDUSTRIES

Reagan, accompanied by a top graphic with the quote, "I used to be doing okay before Rocco ruined my reputation." Marc's witty illustration encapsulated Steve's growing infamy, which was partially based on his ability to lure major skate professionals away from their former teams, often singeing their reputation in the process. That became part of the World Industries aesthetic and a key to its eventual reign over skateboarding culture decades later.

Marc steadily delivered a full range of emotions in his artwork for World—from the humorous to the sublime to scathing commentary, the best of which would become iconic graphics. Take "The Ron Chatman Experience" graphic, a direct parody of the Jimi Hendrix Experience's album cover for *Axis: Bold as Love* but with Jimi's face replaced with pro skater Ron's. Already controversial for its depiction of Jimi and the band as Hindu deities, the joke here was that the imagery was the antithesis of the Ron Chatman "experience" of city life growing up as a young African American skateboarder in Long Beach, California.

Marc's work on the 1991 Jeremy Klein pro board, another parody, featured a Norman Rockwell–style illustration of a boy with a black eye, sitting on a stool with a magazine draped over his lap as if placed in time-out for his actions. The board was an instant success, partially thanks to the inside joke that Klein was well known for being a prankster who could surely use a time-out.

Marc's ability to pull from pop culture and hit the right notes, as in his spin on the late '80s Chris "Dune" Pastras board graphic the Dune "Baby" (see page 81). Dune portrayed a young child race-swapped from white to African American, adding a touch of inclusion to the canon of skateboarding graphics, which had never featured a Black figure previously. While this was a simple swap, Marc's work in the mid-'90s would dive into the discussion of race much more satirically and controversially. Among the standouts that incorporated both those elements were the "Napping Negro" graphic, based on a racist illustrated book the World team picked up while on tour in the South. Releasing it as a board graphic to remind America of its racist history was incredibly controversial and often misunderstood.

Pushing it even further, Marc brought race and racism to the fore by creating a "Runaway Slave" graphic that depicted a young Black man smiling, essentially breaking the fourth wall with the viewer while hiding in the treetops and thwarting the dogs and soldiers looking for him.

This was a subtly scathing commentary—simply re-creating the "Napping Negro" image was more than enough to point to America's racist past and the need for an inclusive society.

Speaking to this series of graphics, Marc put them in context, telling me that "Napping Negro" is the only graphic he probably wouldn't have created now, but he and other artists in the era were in their 20s, feeling insular and speaking to a like-minded audience. "We couldn't believe that a whole book existed with these crazy racist images," Marc said. "We found it so outrageous and wrong that we worked it into a board graphic just so people could see that is how people in America thought, and it wasn't that long ago." The mirror to U.S. history held true for the "Runaway Slave" graphic screened for African American skater Jovontae Turner, which remains a tense topic of discussion to this day. While startling and disturbing, it stands as testament to an artist using the skateboard graphic to comment on society.

That was not the end of controversial graphics and isn't meant to imply everything was a hit—there were some that stretched the limits of good taste. Take the Roy Lichtenstein Pop Art style that Marc parodies to depict the Space Shuttle *Challenger* explosion with a board graphic simply called "OOPS." Marc was unafraid to pull from the good and bad of the era and attempt to propel it with a Deadpool level of zing.

Sometimes people forget the context—that these graphics were products of their time, created in the '90s by twentysomethings to serve a 10- to 20-year-old demographic. The work reflects the love, lusts, ills, and aspirations of the era, and often evolved from a feeling of marginalization. More often than not it involved poking a thumb in the eye of perceived power or flipping the bird to the status quo. The movement was grounded in a simple sentiment: everything should be available for skaters. There would be no sacred cows—for anyone.

Take the Mike Vallely "Barnyard" graphic. It has the distinction of being one of the first double kick boards in skateboarding, which marked a change in technology and a hard right toward street skating. It features a cartoon depiction of barnyard characters in neon colors with a thought balloon bubble reading, "Please don't eat my friends." In one swift blow Marc introduced Mike's now famous veganism while simultaneously undercutting the seriousness of an element crucial to young Mike's identity.

A Marc McKee piece might offer a reflection of societal problems like the Shiloh Greathouse board graphic, in which racist police officers attempt to accost Shiloh's Black body in L.A. Another iconic image was the "Accidental Gun Death," in which parents arrive home to the horror of their young children's antics with water pistols and unlocked pistols resulting in sad consequences.

Each take by Marc was set to grab you by the nethers and either make you laugh or turn your world upside down. Take the tired old crack about pro skater Natas Kaupas's first name spelled backward: yes, it spelled *Satan*; no, it did not mean he was a satanist. Marc got tired of the endless Christian right tirades against Natas (see page 24) and went full-blown apeshit, creating a Beelzebubian graphic loaded with decapitated babies' heads and bodies for Natas's company, 101 Skateboards. Putting out fires with gasoline, the ad put the fear of God in everyone (but also included a note that these were just jokes). It is a seminal piece of skateboarding history, regularly cited as one of the most phenomenal graphics of all time.

Marc's ability to add rizz to even the most plaintive imagery came full circle in the mid- to late '90s, when the World Industries team suffered a shattering blow. First, Megan Baltimore, Spike Jonze, and a host of the best skaters left World to form Girl in '93, then returned to the camp to take another entourage for Chocolate in 1994. Rather than utilize their tried-and-true scorched-earth strategy of attack, World called on Marc to create something that would make the company bigger than any individual pro skater: an icon. In 1996, Mark gave them three: Flame Boy, Wet Willy, and the Devil Man.

The smiling cartoon characters of a water drop and a flame ember immediately captured the attention of the new demographic of elementary

school skaters who joined the fold after the X Games boom in skateboarding popularity.

Flame Boy and Wet Willy engaged in high-level PG- to R-rated spy vs. spy shenanigans and were boards for an entire generation of skaters. Building upon that success, Marc then created the Devil Man, a satirical take on Uncle Sam as the "devil on the shoulder" artwork of Flame Boy and Wet Willy, prompting them to terrorize each other and the world. Moving onward to the other World subsidiaries, Marc created the Blind Reaper, whose antics moved deeper into R-rated territory.

Despite having made such a huge contribution to skateboarding and to World, and earning a seven-figure payment from the company when Flame Boy and Wet Willy were sold off as their own subsidiary, Marc McKee has stayed the same humble individual. Hell, he drove a junker for years after the acquisition, running his Honda into the ground.

Marc still lives in Venice, California, chilling, taking one day and assignment at a time. The man remains one of the mellowest, most humble individuals I have met in my life, and my students treasure his class visits. As I write this, I'm sure he would be embarrassed that I am giving him all his flowers, but I say he's the greatest. Everyone in skateboarding art knows it. Marc works across every medium: pencil, pen, crayon, marker, plume, canvas, brush, digital. You name it, he can handle it. The question always is, looking at his work: Can you?

SHEPARD FAIREY

Developed the iconic Obama "Hope" poster

Creator of the Obey brand

Birthed the global "Andre the Giant Has a Posse" movement

South Carolinian turned New England fam turned L.A. transplant

Shepard Fairey was and remains one of the most important figures in skateboarding and a nexus point for skate and art, community and culture. Shepard hails from South Carolina, a place that has always had conflicting stories and shifting alliances on race, progress, and civil disobedience but that despite the odds produces deep loving hearts. Shepard pushed back on the negative elements in S.C. and found art as a way to express himself. Once he made the move to Providence to attend the Rhode Island School of Design, his love of freedom in skateboarding, punk music activism, and the joy of the sticker and the stencil found a real home.

And, man, was that home mobile. Everywhere you went in the late '80s and early '90s, you'd come across a street art sticker that featured a familiar figure of the era and the words "Andre the Giant Has a Posse." The black-and-white (later also in color) image of the seven-foot, four-inch 420-pound sleepy-eyed pro wrestler and *The Princess Bride* co-star is forever burned in my mind, and probably yours as well. A staple in the punk rock, hardcore, and early skate days, these stickers signified the beginnings of an art movement. You would see the slaps at skateparks in Massachusetts, on streetlights in Connecticut, in bathrooms at CBGB's in New York. I've seen them in New Hampshire, in Florida, in L.A. to this day. Andre really did have a posse and that posse was repping him hard. Unbeknownst to us all, the image was the brainchild of one Shepard

Fairey. He was a punk rock skater and artist and also a student of the game.

For many, that's hard to believe now because he *is* the game. The person who created Barack Obama's "Hope" poster and Kamala Harris's "Forward" definitely brought the heat. Not to take anything away from any candidates, but you can't really get that kind of on-the-ground street endorsement anywhere anymore. However, he began low-key and simply worked to improve his craft over time.

Like many an auteur, Shepard pivoted to the next level—a simplification of form. "Andre the Giant Has a Posse" became "Obey Giant" with an image of Andre above the word "obey." That would prove the perfect combination. The art would move from stickers to stencils with some images part of a limited run, which drove demand. So much so that imitation became the sincerest form of flattery on multiple fronts with the "Obey Giant" moniker. There was Giant skateboard distribution—the home for brands like Element and New Deal; other brands straight up appropriated, saying *they* had a posse, and multiple companies co-opted Shepard's work and words. Rolling with the Giant cast a long shadow.

All the original work and the copycat work collided into exceptional PR for Shepard, and in the early aughts he exploded on the art scene, particularly in New York. His work lived somewhere between street art vandalism and the new art world, which was looking to embrace or embarrass (depending on whom you asked) the next generation of artists.

Soon enough, he made his way westward, aligning with the skate art movement. It was fitting that he set up shop in downtown L.A., the heart of the skate art scene at the time, and that his warehouse became both an impromptu space to house a mini ramp for the highly artistic Stereo Skateboards and for the other tenant in the space to be famed pro skater Clint Peterson.

Skateboarding influenced Shepard's art and now his art was influencing skateboarding. The proximity to pro skating created a synergy that I know personally influenced members of the Stereo team and vice versa. Many a party was thrown in that warehouse where artists, skaters, and musicians collided and talked about their work, and the Obey brand became well known for being the impetus of it all.

All of this artistic energy in L.A. coalesced just before the Obama campaign that propelled him to new heights and made him *the* Shepard Fairey. The thing is, if you were there at the time, on all those nights you would have seen him still doing his regular thing—spinning records, printing posters, screening prints—all with a love of creating art and space for the masses. Between it all he still found time to take runs on the mini ramp and enjoy the skate-rat life. That's why Shepard will always be a part of the skate community.

The massive Obey enterprise is now in its third decade, rolling on and contributing to skate and art culture with limited releases like the Shepard Fairey × Greyson Fletcher × "Juice Mag" Dan Levy collab. The resulting prints are testament to Shepard's roots in supporting venerable skate outlets like *Juice* and making sure the art gives back to the community where he began. Shepard, his team, and his fans started a movement of the people, by the people. Those original stickers were even used for true billboard vandalism, pushing back against a politician running for mayor of Providence, Rhode Island. Now he is called up to paint building-size murals to display his views on activism and advocacy—which remains for the people and by the people. That's why the cost of his prints is so low. His need to democratize movements and make the conversation available to anyone stems from his OG skateboarding roots, blurring the line between highbrow and lowbrow, whether in the streets, the subways, or the skyscrapers.

His work is irreverent and he has the earned the ability and clout to paint murals around the world that support change and independence—a far cry from a call to simply Obey.

Shepard remains part of the origin story of skateboarding, operating on a higher plane of art, community, skateboarding, and social change. It's that combination that reminds me that skate DNA remains in everyone touched by skateboarding, no matter how big they become in the eyes of the world. People have asked, is Obey even really in the skate game? That's when I remind them that the skate game is propelled by every one of us and one day someone might question their own authenticity. I give those flowers to him here.

Today, regardless of the room, he is still the same student of skateboarding, art, love, and innovation. I've heard much talk about him selling out or growing too big, but the thing is, he and his work have always been just right and on time.

Shepard's been just big enough, just bold enough, and just humble enough to dedicate himself to a vision of a world that can be unified through sight, sound, and skateboarding—that's just what we always needed.

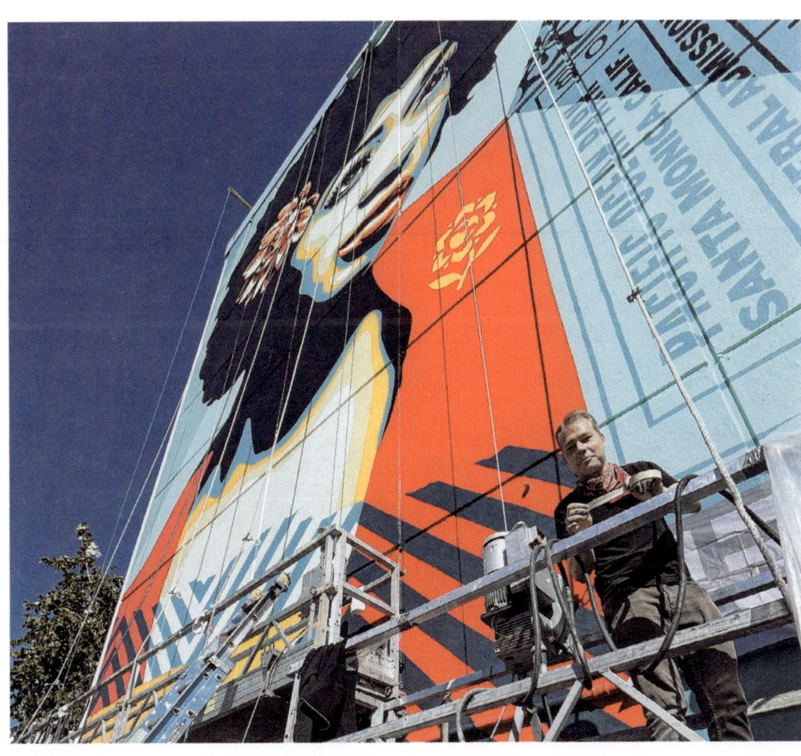

THE DOCUMENTARISTS

If you kickflip in the woods when no one is around, does it make a sound?

The trinity within skateboarding—the skater, the photographer, and the videographer (or filmer, as we like to call them in the streets)—unite like the Wu to form a unified force and deliver the goods, by ensuring a trick is never missed.

The alliance has propelled skateboarding, and astonished skaters, across the decades. The Documentarists are responsible for sending out the message that hard work, grit, and determination pay off. They log and edit the hours of footage and photos to create video parts and editorial spotlights that move the culture. They stand in the blazing sun or freezing cold to capture skaters in their moment of glory, even if they have to keep coming back for three weeks to get one trick. Together they create a singular vision and place it in the zeitgeist.

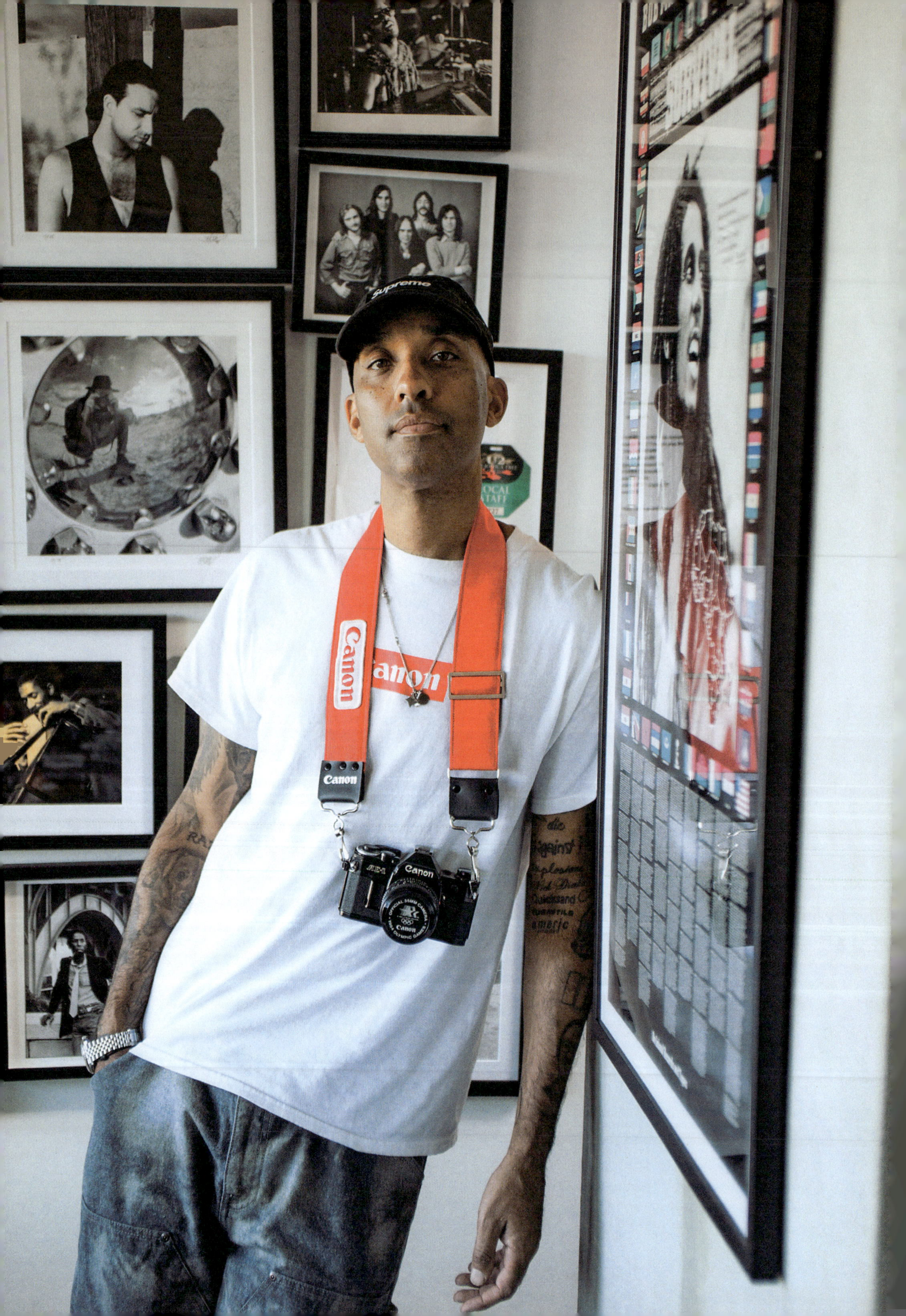

THE LEBRON JAMES OF SKATEBOARD PHOTOGRAPHY
ATIBA JEFFERSON

TransWorld SKATEboarding alum and *Thrasher*'s greatest hired photo gun

First skate photographer to adopt the Hasselblad camera and start the medium-format film trend

First skate-photog to abandon film and initiate the digital camera revolution

First skater to shoot for the NBA full-time

Emmy nominee and Silver Clio winner for the documentary *Monochrome* on Black skateboarders

"Atiba shot your photos? Damn. He's the best skate photographer in the game," said every pro skater in the world. Facts.

It's hard to argue against that statement, and why would you? Jefferson's name is hallowed in skate media. There can be only one—actually, that's not quite right. There are two Jeffersons: Atiba and his minutes-younger twin brother, Ako, a seminal figure in skateboarding videography in his own right.

The duo, born of an interracial union in Colorado, were raised by their white mother, who worked hard to make sure that they identified with their heritage as Black men. Atiba jokes that the white side likes alt-rock, Thin Lizzy, and Bad Brains, and the Black side likes jazz and Coltrane. Luckily for us, the sides combined and have produced the most influential skateboarding photographer ever to clench a rubberized grip.

Atiba, who began skating in his early teens, would become recognized worldwide for his genre-bending work in sports, music, Hollywood, and all points between. As easy to find shooting courtside at the Lakers with LeBron as nailing portraits of Flea or Tiger Woods or shooting jazz's avant-garde

Shabaka Hutchings. Images of A$AP Rocky, Kylie Jenner, Steph Curry, and Tyler, the Creator, all explode from his lens, offering a storied list that continues to evolve in style, perspective, and output. His movie poster work sits on billboards in L.A. that loom over the iconic skate spots he's photographed for *TransWorld SKATEboarding* and *Thrasher*. Atiba has done it all, surpassed the early founders of the skateboarding photo game and made them proud of his ability to bring the culture to a new level. His path to the mountaintop is one of the greatest stories in skateboarding.

Pre-internet, the only way to have your work seen as a burgeoning skate photographer was to mail your negatives or slides to a magazine editor. Then pray they arrived undamaged and that someone might actually take a peek at them without hurling them into the trash. Like everyone from the late '80s and early '90s, Atiba sent his early shots to *TWS*. As luck would have it, Atiba got the attention of J. Grant Brittain (see page 150), the godfather of skate photography. Grant had a reputation for being not only the most technically proficient photographer but also one of the most upstanding and respectable people in the skateboarding industry. That combination of elements worked to Atiba's benefit. Not many lenspeople would have responded to a fledgling photographer's inquiries, but Grant Brittain is one. Over time, their correspondence increased, and Atiba continued to improve his photos off a salvo of questions with each new submission. "Grant, where should my flash be set? Five feet, six feet? How close do I need to be?" Grant would respond—"A lot closer"—and make recommendations: "This photo is flat. You have to wrap the subject in light. You need two bigger, stronger flashes, like the Sunpak 656s." Little did Grant know, Atiba and Ako would be packing up and moving from Denver to Southern California to pursue their dream of working in the skate media world. Were there any openings at *TWS*?

Just as Atiba was about to take a job at a local convenience store, Grant came through: *TWS* found enough in the budget for him to hire an assistant. The rest is history. Grant took Atiba under his wing, and Ako worked for other big names like photographer and videographer Dave Swift and now-legendary video and filmmaker Ty Evans.

Working at *TWS* gave Atiba access to some of the biggest names in skateboarding and tutelage extraordinaire. Under the *TWS* banner, dues were paid. That meant hauling gear, watching and not shooting, documenting the photos, logging the images, and scanning the slides, all for just a bit over minimum wage.

Atiba used the *TWS* position to satisfy his hunger for information. He roamed the halls working long hours with every photographer in the building, studying their techniques, mantras, and philosophies and observing and learning from the best. He even looked beyond skateboarding for inspiration, particularly to the work of legendary portrait takers such as Herb Ritts, Gordon Parks, and Annie Leibovitz.

Atiba also had a sense of pacing and composition and a discipline that many young skate photogs don't have. Rather than running and gunning, as many are apt to do, especially when first shooting skate superstars, Atiba was producing magical moments. Under his direction, each image would truly be one of a kind. Atiba would do things like chase the golden hour and make skaters get up

at the crack of dawn to bring his vision to life. If you wanted to work with him, you operated on his schedule, no matter how famous you might be. While skaters were progressing at a breakneck speed, Atiba found a way to make their efforts look distinct and thoughtful and to set trends. He learned how to print photos and took master classes from well-known photographers to learn new techniques employed in other fields, like cross-processing for heavily arty and saturated effects, then shifting from the skateboarding industry standard 35mm film to the famed medium-format Hasselblad camera. This switch-up set the skate photography world aflame. Each medium-format image he delivered was filled with experimentation and a distinct point of view. His photos and tenor became the standard, and every other photographer ran out to purchase a Hasselblad.

Atiba's run didn't stop there—he even earned the holy grail of skate goals from the *TWS* offices when he interviewed and photographed legendary Kareem Campbell (see page 46), who was notorious for "ghosting" and missing photo shoots, but was one of the most in-demand skaters of all time. When you did get a photo of Kareem it was always needed by no fewer than five companies at a time. It seemed impossible to hold on to enough pics to create a multipage interview. Yet, painstakingly and one photo at time, Atiba crafted that interview over the course of nearly two years. His tenacity earned him the well-deserved cover of the June 1998 issue of *TransWorld SKATEboarding*, now an inspirational part of skateboarding photography lore.

Atiba's energy and understanding of the city and urban life were also the right fit for a moment when skateboarding was growing nationally and internationally. Atiba went anywhere—he wasn't afraid to get ticketed by the cops as long as he got the shot. He didn't worry about his gear getting stolen in the sheistiest neighborhoods in Barcelona or about getting shivved at the hottest skate spots in L.A.

Atiba was close in age to the best skaters during the mid-'90s and early aughts. Skating became more Black and diverse, and Atiba was the right man for the job. He was at home scaling walls or ducking strays in tough neighborhoods to get the shots. After surviving the skate session, he could also talk

Tyshawn Jones's NBD Kickflip on the cover of *Thrasher*, photographed by Atiba Jefferson in NYC

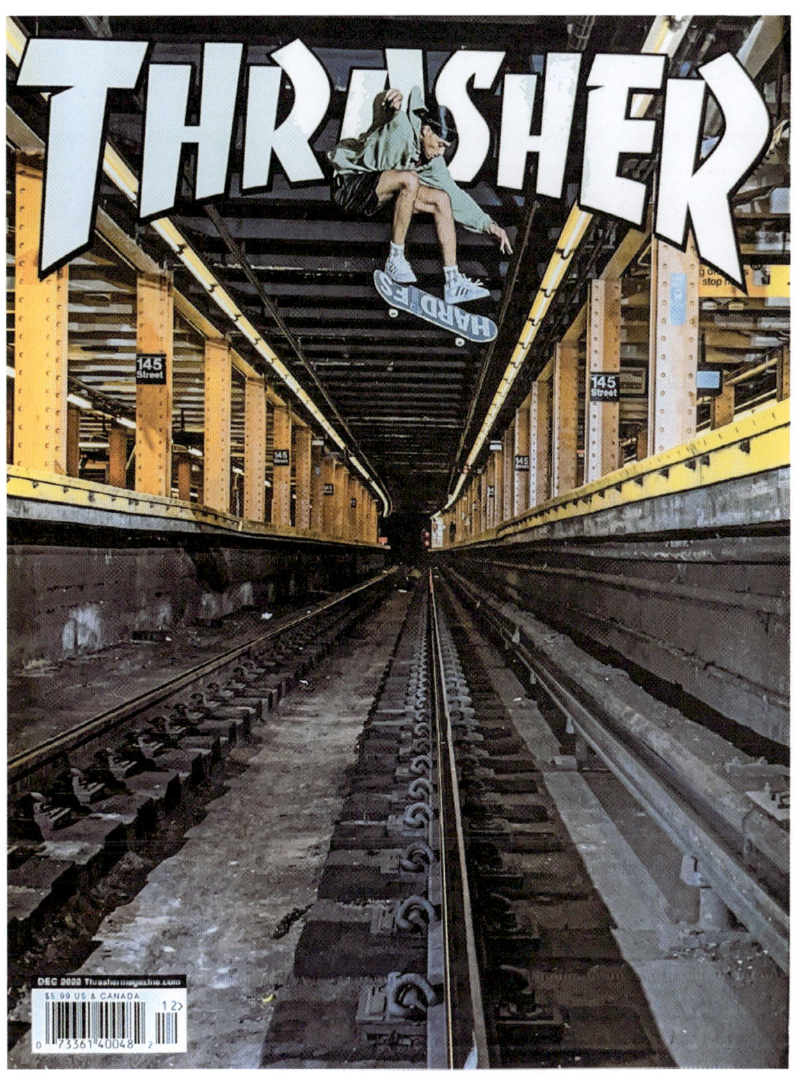

with skaters about everything from his love of the Los Angeles Lakers to new films and fashion or whatever was poppin' off at the time. He knew the pulse of street culture and it made him relatable when most of his mentors had either slowed down or aged out. Instead, Atiba was also taking time to try to shoot photos of new bands, new sounds, and new movements in youth culture. Eventually, he gained the coveted assignment of L.A.-based photographer for San Diego–based *TWS*. He set up shop with a studio in Hollywood. Atiba's move to L.A. was a perfect storm. He would have access to some of the greatest skaters in the industry and be able to mix in his love of the nightlife and street couture.

Beyond this, Atiba was always looking for greener pastures and sought out new technologies and approaches that could improve his craft. He was an early adopter of digital cameras, while others were still shooting film and living in his old medium. His new approaches made his work stand out from that of his peers and caught the eye of many of the era's top pros.

Once embedded in L.A. culture, he went on to become the head photographer for Kareem Campbell's City Stars Skateboards team, and Kareem introduced him to the who's who of L.A. skating. In no time the young star was shooting Eric Koston, Keenan Milton, and the Girl and Chocolate crew. He also shot Andrew Reynolds (page 76) and the entire Baker team, allowing him to reach every aspect of skateboarding culture, from fresh to hesh—meaning street and transition and all points between. Atiba was the man in demand.

The last rung on the ladder of his success came from his love of basketball. He took an assistant stringer position shooting pics for the Lakers and built on his stunning skate repertoire, and the same magic happened. He was one of the only young Black photographers and quickly became the go-to for all the players of color—from Kobe to Iverson to LeBron—nabbing a spot at the basketball and hip-hop magazine *Slam*.

Atiba has a host of ventures. He even turned his expertise into ownership and went on to found *The Skateboard Mag* with Grant Brittain and all his original mentors at *TWS*. While the mag is defunct, Atiba is far from it. He is now a staff photographer for *Thrasher*. And he started skate-related businesses, from Bravo bags to Open Beer. He also shot pics with and of the late Virgil Abloh (RIP), whom he honored with a photo show in Miami, and gives back to L.A.'s Leimert Park neighborhood.

With full sponsorship as a Canon ambassador and the success of his Emmy-nominated *Monochrome* (2021)—an ESPN documentary about the experiences of legendary Black skateboarders—what more needs to be said? Atiba Jefferson: the Undisputed.

GLEN E. FRIEDMAN

First creator at the epicenter of multiple youth culture movements from the '70s onward: skateboarding, punk rock, and hip-hop

Author of *Fuck You Heroes*

Photographed iconic images of Tony Alva and the Dogtown crew

Placed the first Black skater on the cover of *Thrasher*

Created classic album covers for Fugazi, Slick Rick, LL Cool J, Ice-T, and Public Enemy

Only the luckiest among us live a life where our identity, community, and work converge. Even fewer can craft a world for themselves and their communities to inhabit. Glen E. Friedman, a child of the '60s, is one of those unique personas simultaneously inhabiting multiple scenes—skateboarding, punk rock, hip-hop—and providing a critical role and platform for many who became legends within their respective cultures.

Glen has lived and created images on the edge. He knew he wasn't there to just document life, he was there to direct it and make images with impact. While other photographers gazed at those cultures from the outside, any conversation with Glen will remind you of the difference between capturing and *producing* an image. Capturing is shooting what's there; producing images requires creating something larger than life. The image is not *of* the thing; It *becomes* the thing. It is no longer an illustration. It is an exemplar. Such is the work of Glen E. Friedman. He is a diviner, transforming ordinary people into heroes for their communities, and oftentimes changing the way these underground agents and outcasts see themselves—all with a twist of the aperture ring on his favorite 20mm lens.

His early, mid-'70s iconic skate photos showcasing the lawlessness and energy of skateboarding became prototypes for the zeitgeist. Some of those shots are found in books and photo exhibitions worldwide—London, Paris, L.A., and beyond, still drawing in generations today. For example, he's famous for pics of the Z-Boys and Z-Flex team, such as the iconic image of Tony Alva flipping the bird while skating the Dog Bowl in Santa Monica, Peggy Oki ripping the berm in the asphalt jungle, and Marty Grimes straight rocking through backyard pools, inches away from smashing Glen's lens into oblivion in sessions at Kenter Canyon Elementary School, in Brentwood, California.

The New York transplant whose family headed west for brighter prospects found himself in California at 14 years old, skating among the legendary Zephyr (or Z-Boys) team, one of the first to see and reveal to the world that a new guard had emerged in skateboarding—backyard carnality with trucks and wheels leaving the pool to reach for the sky. A stint in a cast prevented him from skating for a time. His friends were ripping, and he had the burning desire to let the world know.

Glen witnessed it all and pushed this relentless band of outsiders to go harder and give their total

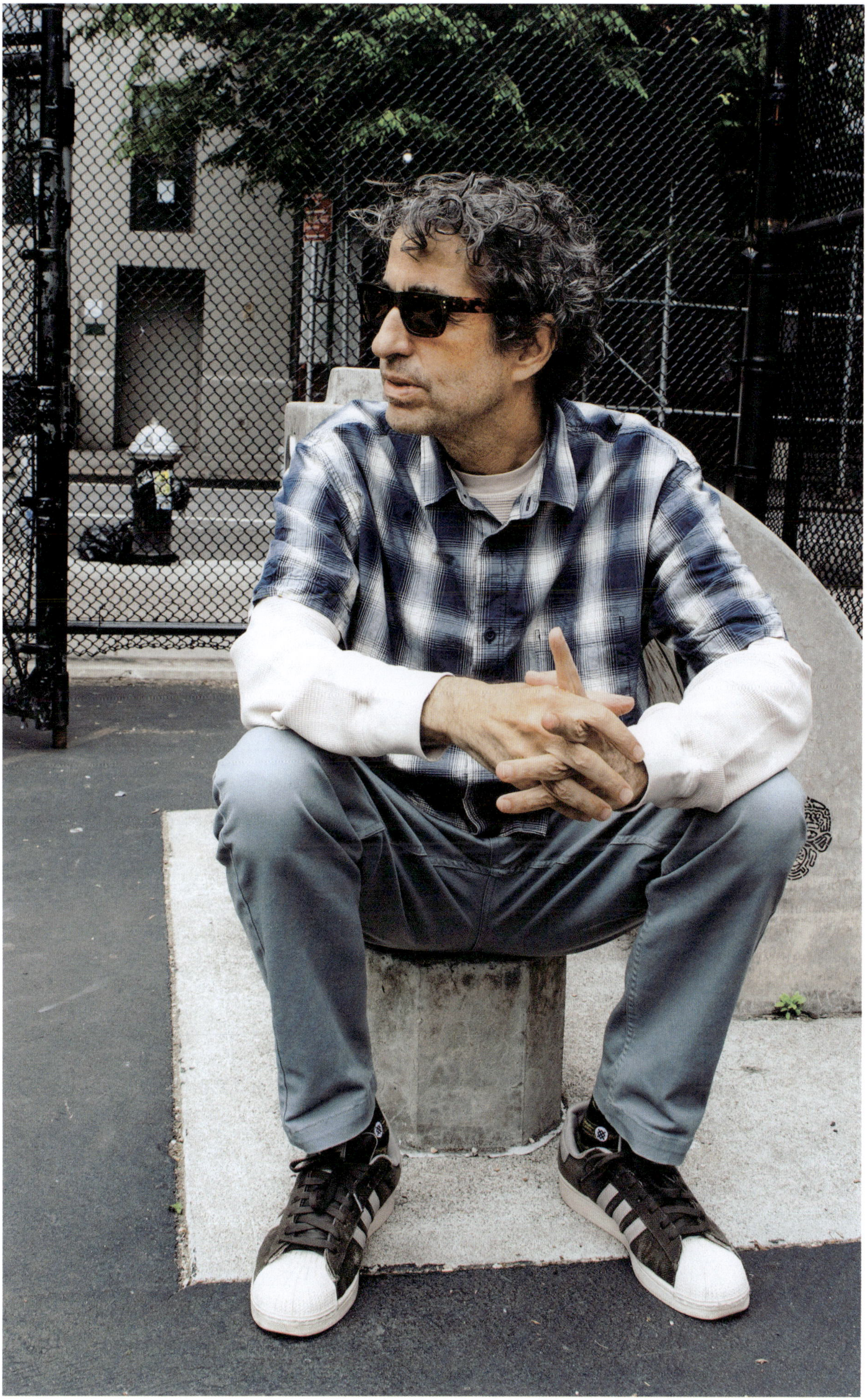

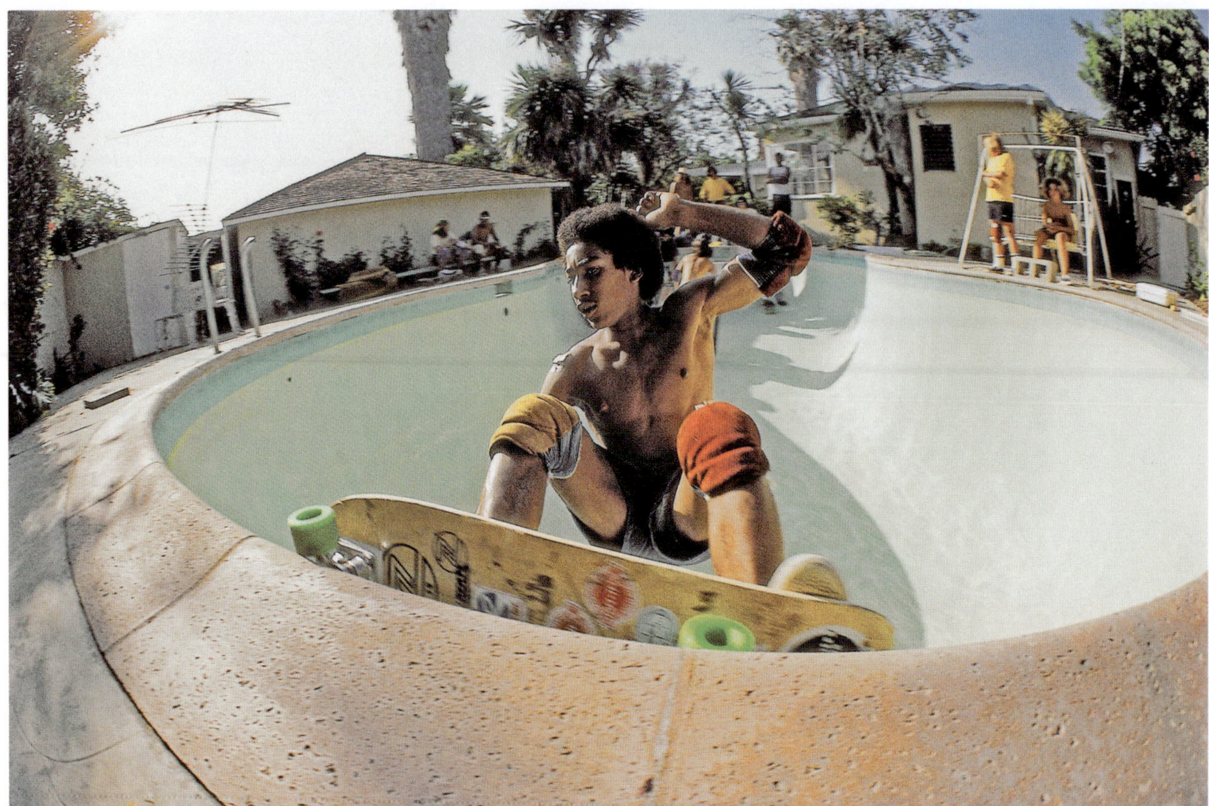

The inspiration for generations of skateboarders of color and the first African American male pro skater, L.A.'s own Marty Grimes, photographed by Glen E. Friedman

commitment to the camera so he could release the shutter and capture the spirit within each of them. Glen's images helped define skateboarding's unbridled ferocity and displayed how these often misunderstood teens in Venice were "monsters" of the culture, presenting to the world how radical things could be. Those early images didn't just document the shredding; Glen communicated dreams to the public and to the skaters themselves that the shred must be magnifique. He turned ordinary people into super soldiers and heroines or, as he likes to call them, "Fuck You Heroes," which he also titled his blockbuster book of photos from 1976 to 1991. These underdogs showed the normies that you should live life on the edge and out loud.

The same could be said of his photos of punk rock bands and the punk rock scene, which showcase the outcasts who wanted to make a difference and stand against a wave of politics they felt did not reflect their ideals. When it came to photographing hip-hop, the most disenfranchised party in all of these groups, Glen's reputation as a chronicler of outsiders and youth culture helped give voice to the voiceless and propel those people into the stratosphere.

From hopping fences to trespassing in empty pools to heat-packing hip-hop shows or punk rock sets where anything goes, Glen has been at ground zero of nearly every early youth movement worth

discussing and, unlike most, left it better than he found it. Sometimes those giants led by pushing the levels up on the fader, and sometimes Glen pushed those agents to grind farther, slide faster, or stand and deliver vocals and vibrations. As per his part in the equation, Glen delivered the lines, the tricks, the fire, and the fury to readers and listeners of bibles such as *SkateBoarder* magazine and record labels Dischord and Def Jam.

Take the Minor Threat, Fugazi, and Bad Brains concert photos—all so powerful. From steely glaze to crouching tigers, these pics gave light to the passion of the Washington, D.C., punk music scene in the '80s. Glen's pics also offered an in-your-face forced perspective when he orchestrated band album covers that dragged you into the center of the mosh pit with lead singer Ian MacKaye and the crowd. Part of Glen's connection to these bands came from many of the members being former skaters. This meant that there was a shared language between them; Glen brought his experience developing the best in skateboarding to his work with the bands. The black-and-white images reverberate with the rejection of a spoon-fed diet of mediocrity developed under Reaganomics. F the fascists, as Glen would say. Instead, take up arms against the tyranny by draping yourself in a guitar and screaming your soul into the mic until the house comes down. Glen placed you in that show, on that stage, amid a typhoon of sound, and delivered it in stark black and white that felt like a sledgehammer. Those sounds and slides fundamentally altered the way a generation felt about music. The thing is, that was just his second act. Loving the revolution but departing when it began to repeat itself, Glen would put that same energy into the new revolutionary sound: hip-hop.

Glen produced the album cover of *The Great Adventures of Slick Rick*. He put out the iconic book *Together Forever: The Run-DMC and Beastie Boys Photographs*. His pics for LL Cool J's *BAD* and Ice-T's *Power* showcased the pride, strength, and attitude of these artists: LL glowering into the frame daring anyone to compete with him, Ice-T with a sawed-off shotgun behind his back, hidden from the front cover but apparent on the reverse of the sleeve. These are all burned into the historical landscape of hip-hop. Public Enemy's album cover for *It Takes a Nation of Millions to Hold Us Back*, shot with Chuck D. and Flavor Flav behind bars—these are the definitive sights and sounds of the era. Glen created the conditions for these now hip-hop icons to deliver the new sound of the underground. Black and Brown lives transforming into giants, with the weight of each gold chain, the clang of cold black steel, the fuzz of a Kangol, or the glint of a gold-toothed smile.

Hip-hop is all about authenticity, a throughline from Glen's work in skateboarding and punk rock, too. That's one reason why he was always welcome, and always unapologetically himself. It's also the reason that he stopped shooting skateboarding in

HE CHASES THE REALNESS AND ACCEPTS NO SUBSTITUTIONS.

the mid-'80s; he was looking for more passion, and he found it first in punk and then later in hip-hop. He chases the realness and accepts no substitutions.

Glen is a firebrand because he has an opinion and a point of view. That's why you hire him. He will roll up on you with his unpretentious 20mm lens, no big lighting rig, and no entourage, and somehow make you show your best self. That makes him unique, and his photography is a collector and observer's dream. Glen E. Friedman brings good things to life. No fluff. All killer—no filler.

THE GODFATHER OF MODERN SKATEBOARDING PHOTOGRAPHY

J. GRANT BRITTAIN

Skateboarding Hall of Fame member

Cofounder of *TransWorld SKATEboarding* magazine

Mentor to the greatest skate photogs of all time

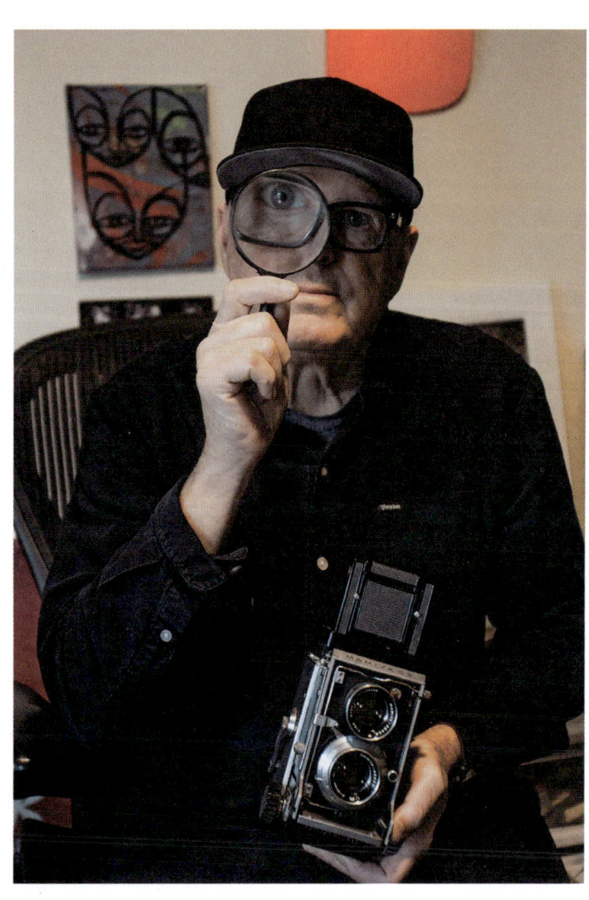

J. Grant Brittain is a bridge to a bygone era of skateboarding photography. Grant was influenced by photogs like James Cassimus, C. R. Stecyk, Warren Bolster, and Jim Goodrich, and those who shot surfing as well, early shutterbugs who laid the foundation for modern skateboarding photography. Their iconic images filled the pages of *Skateboarder* magazine and beyond in the 1960s and '70s and became part of the skateboarding zeitgeist in the U.S. and abroad for decades. In retrospect, they created the hallmarks of skateboarding's visual language. The components were captured, contained by the camera, then released upon the viewer. This was the beginning of skaters establishing the visual and physical language of skateboarding both in front of and behind the lens. You can still feel the connection to that era in Grant's early photos.

Grant didn't merely create replicas of those images or simply document moments, he understood the joy of experimentation, and eventually innovation, which would become the signature of a G. Brittain photo. His singular shots happened through trial and error and from being in the right place, at the right time, with the right frame in mind.

Grant started his skate photography career unpretentiously, as a shy skater working at the famed skateboarding mecca Del Mar Skate Ranch. This venerated California skatepark was active for roughly a decade, from August 1978 to July 1987. It was *the* proving ground for vertical skaters at the time. Using a borrowed camera, Grant began shooting photos of his friends at the park and occasionally stole away to snap pics of the visiting pros. Sunrise to sunset, he could be found posted up in the clubhouse building, where he worked his way from custodian to concessions to landing in the catbird seat as manager of the skatepark and pro shop. The six years he spent there helped him build a rapport with the hordes of talented skaters who came through, especially those who visited the shop. Any pro alive will tell you how important it is to have a good relationship with the person behind the counter. You might need a new board, wheels, bearings, or a clean shirt when your money is low or you're between product coming in from your sponsor. Grant was incredibly quiet, but having a camera to stand behind helped him push to build a better connection with the skaters. Those young skaters and largely secret snapshots would be the nuggets that started Grant's career.

It's all fun and games until reality calls. That call came in the form of a request from one of the most notoriously gifted gabbers of colorful language, *Thrasher* magazine photo editor Mörizen Föche, also known as Mofo or Richard Knoll. Housed in the San Francisco Bay Area, *Thrasher* had NorCal covered, but the hassle of heading south to San Diego to consistently cover SoCal proved too much for the start-up publication. For those finding the idea of *Thrasher* as penny-pinchers unimaginable, just know this was during the "hater daze," long before everyone from Rihanna to Justin Bieber sported a T-shirt or hoodie from the brand. Early *Thrasher* rolled FUBU (for us, by us) and existed as a newsprint labor of love created by Argentinian immigrant, skater and genius entrepreneur Fausto Vitello. Back then, he and a small core group of skaters organized together to keep the fire burning and the community in touch after insurance companies refused to cover skateparks, which caused them to close and contributed to the crash of skateboarding's popularity in the last gasps of the late '70s.

Necessity breeds invention and called for an emerging new role, the SoCal *Thrasher* contributor, which gave Grant his first photo credits, the OG currency that sustains every emerging photographer—at least until the bills come due.

While seeming a dream career, making a living as a full-time skateboarding photographer was not really possible back then. So Grant continued to work at Del Mar as well. Seeing his photos in the magazine, and further inspired by the alchemy of the darkroom process, Grant decided to study his craft further at Palomar College.

Delivering the goods to *Thrasher* kept him moving along for a few years, but the real change in Grant's life began on a fateful day in 1983, when his photo contributions to a new "newsletter" (as its founders called it) out of the San Diego suburbs became a different affair once a veil of secrecy was removed. Stay with me here for a moment. Creating newsletters or zines was normal for the time, and sending photos to zines across the U.S. was an OG version of posting on the internet and Instagram. You would shoot some pics of your friends, caption that ish and use a Xerox or copy machine to slice and dice it into a newsletter or zine and send it out to friends in the mail. Low-key, lo-fi, and the basis for skate communiqués. Grant had been using zines as a way to document other skaters and report on his scene like many skaters during the early '80s.

At that time, Larry Balma and partner (now wife) Louise Balma of Tracker Trucks, and later a handful of other companies, were the direct competition to NorCal's Independent Truck Company, with subsidiaries that included *Thrasher*, and they decided it might be time to put out a "newsletter" with a little more heft. Across the country, skaters like graphic design luminary Garry Scott Davis (known as GSD); Bryan Ridgeway, an iconic African American skater; and others each developed little zines chronicling the skate scenes in their respective regions with local knowledge that could be gained only from spending time in the streets. Larry Balma and Peggy Cozens (an employee at Tracker) recognized the potential of a singular outlet that might speak to everyone, and they crafted a strategy to tap into the new creative energy bustling on the periphery. Believing he was being called in to Tracker to check out the newsletter, Grant instead found a full-fledged magazine being born in secret: *TransWorld SKATEboarding*. Birthed in August 1983, *TWS*'s inaugural issue delivered a fully developed magazine (not a zine) blessed with a full-color cover photo of heavily influential pro skater of color Steve Caballero. In the image taken by Grant, Caballero is beautifully caught midway through an air out at Del Mar Skate Ranch during his contest-winning run.

Aside from legendary Caballero, the magazine differentiated itself instantly by expressly offering an alternative to *Thrasher*'s "skate and destroy" mantra with its own motto, "skate and create" developed by their publisher, Peggy Cozens, one of the first woman action sports leaders of the era. While not directly a shot to the jaw, it certainly had the trappings of a back-alley beatdown.

By the third issue, the epoch of *TransWorld* vs. *Thrasher* beef began. Skaters took sides. However, few knew that that while Vitello and Balma were creating brands that exist to this day, locked in combat as mortal enemies, obscured within the melee lived an astounding truth: the two would regularly meet secretly in San Diego and San Francisco to plot out the direction they felt skateboarding could go and should go under both their umbrellas.

Before *TWS* became a household name, with 400-page regular runs during the aughts, Palomar College acted as its default darkroom. Mind you, it wasn't legal to run a for-profit business on the campus of a nonprofit college. Its success stands as a testament to skateboarding, the original DIY ethos, and the essence of *TWS*'s philosophy of "skate and create"—albeit in this case on someone else's dime. Grant ran the hustle as long as he could until eventually *TWS* had its own darkroom in Oceanside, California. That's when Grant Brittain hit the accelerator.

Grant came to power by treating each photograph as a distinct object, a venerable artifact of skateboarding culture. It took a decade for him to hone his craft, but then he was on the path toward greatness.

Importantly, this takes nothing away from Mofo and others at *Thrasher* who were delivering spellbinding issues in photos and text; it's that they were birthed under different aesthetics. *Thrasher* kept it fast and loose, and *TWS* moved solid and stable. You read *Thrasher* for the articles and *TransWorld* for the photos.

TransWorld offered a new way to look at skateboarding, cleaner and a bit more refined, but in reality, what it offered was master lensman Grant Brittain, who filled the magazine with beautiful, indelible shots.

The images he created helped entrance a generation of skateboarders. In the '80s, Grant lay in the bottom of the pool, or on the deck of the ramp, collecting some of the greatest pics of the decade's aerialists. An entire generation knows the Bones Brigade and Tony Hawk (see page 63) through Grant's lens. His key contribution is that he didn't simply press the shutter—he created compositions.

Each incremental step in tech allowed him to focus on bringing life to the page. The quiet Grant became more verbose and learned to direct skaters in ways that made their skating more epic and allowed readers a sense of scale and drama. Take Grant's still of Christian "Holmes" Hosoi (see page 17) slashing a layback smith grind, beginning at the left and extending right to the edge of the frame. You felt how powerful and fluid Christian was and that he barged the lip of the ramp. You can imagine the deck shaking under your feet when he slashed by—all through that photo.

Just as quickly, Grant could offer a sense of reflection when it counted, as he did with a pic of Rodney Mullen (see page 54) doing his signature Casper slide, a literal meditation for him. The image is instantly made sweeping by Grant's choice to offer Rodney's silhouette to the world. It proves just as compelling as his pic of Rodney in an ollie airwalk, sweaty and bare-chested, or Mark "Gonz" Gonzales's (see page 92) boneless one trick boosted with height and abandon at Gemco Bank. Each skater is focused on the outcome with zero sense of the camera. Yet there it is, plain for all to see— burning ambition embedded inside each processed roll of Grant's 35mm film.

One of his most memorable *TWS* cover pics is a still of his assistant, Tod Swank, pushing down the sidewalk. Paying attention to the way light and shadows fell on a particular wall in San Diego, Grant snapped the image from across the street, an overpass causing a harsh shadow to cut perfectly against the white wall while Swank (now owner of the renowned skateboard distribution company Tum Yeto) skated across the frame. The resulting image emerged as Grant's attempt to create a universal "skateboarder" photo—to capture the essence of the unnamed soldier out in the streets. While it was hated by many at the time for its simplicity, it became one of his most iconic images.

Through it all, Grant provided decades of inspiration and wonder, enrapturing everyone from the Bones Brigade to Mark Gonzales and beyond. His pictures earned a spot on the bedroom walls of skaters around the world. It's why he is still called upon to remake some of those iconic photos of yesteryear for new and nostalgic audiences.

His invisible hand touched everyone in skateboarding—names like Daniel Sturt and Skin Phillips all cut their teeth at *TWS*. They all brought

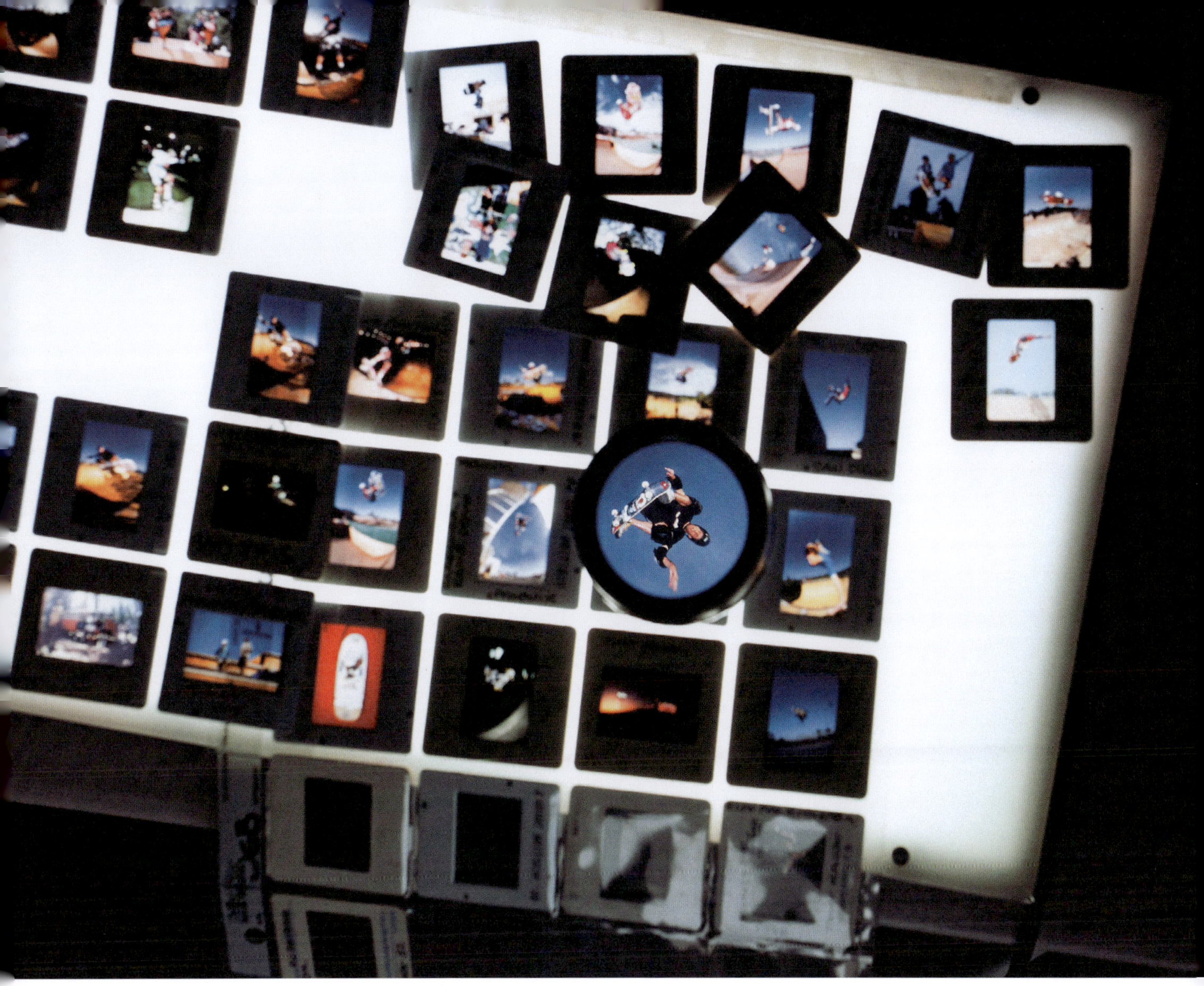

A collection of Grant's archival photos of the GOAT, Tony Hawk

their perspectives and beauty through celluloid and Grant kept the line moving.

When he couldn't jump the fences anymore, he opted to send the next generation of photographers into the streets. That's how names like Atiba Jefferson (page 143), Seu Trinh (page 163), Mike O'Meally, and others earned their stripes. Their slides came under the loupe of Grant Brittain, and his thumbs-up gave them a great push forward.

During the late aughts, when *TWS* came under a new non-skateboarding ownership, a mutiny occurred. Key staffers including Grant, Atiba, Dave Swift, and Miki Vuckovich went on to found a new skate publication, the self-published *The Skateboard Mag*.

A return to its essence, the self-published mag would offer 100 percent skateboarding. However, it launched at a time when media consumption moved online and the magazine faced a crowded field of competitors from other action sports publications along with the venerable *Thrasher*. Despite this, Grant and friends still gained a foothold in readership due to *The Skateboard Mag*'s unwavering focus on skateboarding culture and rule on endemic-only advertisers.

Skateboard Mag had a fantastic run of 100 print issues over roughly 10 years, but would eventually be sold to The Berrics, an online skateboarding platform, and later closed up shop entirely. While missing from the newsstands, Grant's presence remains in book form and in his lectures, reminding us why skateboarding should look epic and ephemeral. It is a link between extremes. In the mind of skateboarding's longest-running master lensman, it should always be visualized as such.

WHERE THE WILDEST ONE RESIDES

SPIKE JONZE

The biggest crossover artist of the action sports era

Created iconic skateboarding videos

Auteur filmmaker and Academy Award winner

Cofounder of Girl Skateboards and Chocolate Skateboards

"Okay. Whatever you do, don't stop and don't look back. Everyone, quiet on the set . . . Action!" Those were roughly the directions given to pro skater Mike Mo Capaldi by the man born Adam Spiegel but best known by his pseudonym, Spike Jonze. With one smooth flick, Mike Mo tossed a switch flip down a 10-deep stair set in an abandoned lot in L.A. Unbeknownst to the viewers and barely understood by Mike Mo at the time, within seconds said stair set would be eviscerated by a three-story fireball. The slo-mo capturing Mike Mo's face revealed the tension of an inexplicable moment. Mike Mo may never have seen how close that fireball came to him, but as we watched it happen, the look of fear and then relief on his face is one we all felt. And the singe heard around the world that brought in the L.A. police and fire department helicopters wasn't the only technological breakthrough in the film.

Amid the crystal-clear 60-frames-per-second slo-mo, legendary skater Eric Koston kickflipped perfectly what we all felt was a perfectly benign small stair set—nothing especially difficult for a *Thrasher* Skater of the Year. However, what was odd was that Koston immediately careened straight toward a brick wall after landing. Watching in slow motion, we could see he was headed face-first into the brick wall. WTF is up? Ten feet . . . seven feet . . . five feet . . . three feet. While we viewers waited patiently for him to jump off his board to avert disaster, something miraculous happened— he smashed through that brick wall. The slo-mo of a righteously defiant Koston with fists down,

shouting into the sky as he broke through the wall— that broke our brains.

What was a milestone for skateboarding cinema, however, was in fact just another magnificent day for Spike Jonze to blow off steam, drop in some pyrotechnics, and spend a wholesome day bonding over fear of life and limb while creating an awe-inspiring, technological marvel and instant classic, Lakai Limited Footwear's *Fully Flared* (2007) skateboarding video.

The video was already of the highest caliber, featuring outstanding skateboarding videography by best-in-class Ty Evans and skating from the some of the greatest from the Lakai team, including Mike Carroll, Guy Mariano, Marc Johnson, and Rick Howard. But when sprinkled with the fairy dust of skateboarder, creative director of *Vice*, co-creator of *Jackass*, and auteur filmmaker extraordinaire Spike Jonze . . . that's when every skater knows this isn't just *any* skate video. This was a Spike Jonze production, the chef's kiss where the imagination runs free, and each facet of his work is deeper than it seems at first glance.

The crux of Spike's strength both inside and outside of skateboarding is capturing our imagination and never letting go. Take his 2009 film adaptation of *Where the Wild Things Are*. The film, based on the bestselling and beloved children's book by Maurice Sendak, still stuns for its boldness and beauty and the visceral manner in which it makes us connect to the characters, brought to life though full-scale furry beastly marionettes more fantastical than we ever imagined. On the other side of the spectrum, Spike's stories captured the electricity involved in the affairs of the heart. Remember 2013's *Her*, a film that whisked us all into the enchanted land of a future Los Angeles where useful AI operating systems might deliver both a compass and companionship? *Being John Malkovich* (1999), *Adaptation* (2002), *Three Kings* (1999)—all of these reached critical acclaim.

Spike is simply a master of the indie film and of pushing the boundaries of storytelling. His singular vision has impacted all of skateboarding media and beyond. He has made us all understand that there is unlimited potential in film and video, and that with enough know-how and ingenuity it can be shaped to our whims.

The thing is, Spike has been setting fire to the kindling of our skate imagination long since day one and he has been in the habit of showcasing spellbinding examples of limitless creation. In films, his work is often described as absurdist, but when viewed from a skater's perspective what we see is that he simply applies skateboarding's DIY aesthetic to everything he touches. Mixing that with his tenacity and intuitive vision, he kicks aside any preconceived notions of limitations. Spike marches on. If he doesn't know how to do it, he will learn on the fly and will it into existence and, well, you should hang on and go for the ride. With a glint in his eye, he shows us that our only limit is our imagination.

Trust me, it is that glint and spark that make skaters get up for a 5 a.m. call time, like when he made the skateboarding film *Las Nueve Vidas de Paco* (1995) for the Chocolate skateboarding team. Pro skaters don't wake up that early for anyone . . . but they got up for Spike, though many were confused about why they were dressing up as cowfolk and filming with 10-gallon hats and mock six-shooters. When the curtain came up and that video was screened in the mid-'90s, it became an instant classic, and everyone knew why . . . because it was fucking fantastic, witty, and no one else in the world could have envisioned how a diverse group of skaters could tell the tale of the Wild, Wild West via subtitles, subterfuge,

gunslinging, and skateboarding. From that point on, no one skateboarding ever doubted Spike again. When he calls, everyone runs. They don't need to understand it—whatever he creates will be a gem.

It's that artistry that led him to create some of the most impactful videos with his friends outside of skateboarding: Björk's "It's Oh So Quiet," the Beastie Boys' "Sabotage," Fatboy Slim's "Praise You," the Pharcyde's "Drop," the Breeders' "Cannonball" . . . the list goes on and on. Whether behind the lens, or in front of it, Spike has done it all—without even using his real name.

However, long before he was a darling of the film medium, he was a photographer and jack-of-all-trades at World Industries, where he found his place in skateboarding and his beginnings as a maverick. That would kick into high gear once he departed World Industries to co-found Girl Skateboards and later Chocolate Skateboards. Those brands, along with later created subsidiaries, would become known collectively as the products of Crailtap Distribution.

Sure, it was a risky move but that's what drives a bit of his creative process. It flourishes when he does, and we have been all the more enriched. Well, sometimes we're just entertained, like with *Jackass*, but you get the drift. Spike has no limits, my friend, and he's bred that same ethos into skateboarding and its vocabulary. That means that, yes, you can make a movie about AI. Yes, you can art-direct a skateboarding company, which he did until things soured with Steve Rocco at World Industries. Yes, you can leave one of the most successful and infamous skateboarding companies of all time, and strike out on your own to make a new skateboarding company. Sure, Spike. While you're at it, you can set up your warehouse in the famed X-Large shop in the early '90s. Yeah, that will work, and so will taking a call from Francis Ford Coppola, whose daughter you will eventually wed (and later divorce), while packing the first boxes for your and your cohorts' newly launched Girl Skateboards. So will teaming with MTV and Vice Media to create *Jackass* and a host of other shows and films. Spike has the Midas touch—it's undeniable. They don't give out Oscars just for showing up.

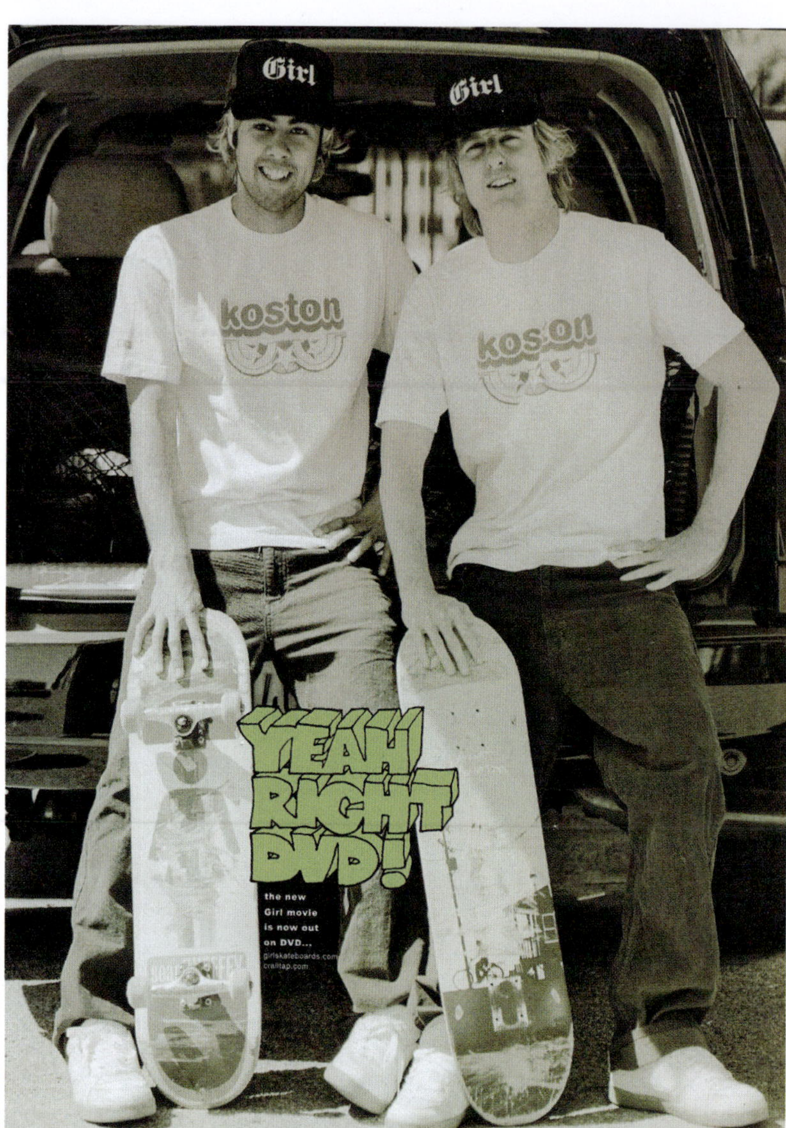

Cover of the *Yeah Right DVD!*, featuring Eric Koston (left) and Owen Wilson

Opposite: Spike Jonze at the 30 Years of Chocolate Skateboards premiere

in service of a good joke, creating the conditions for magic to happen across every medium.

A Spike photo from that era is always recognizable. In most pictures, you're looking for consistent lighting, the subject lined up to textbook perfection. You know, clean shit. Spike's pics? They were always moving. Instead of just using the shutter to stop the actions, any of Spike's images look like the action is heading beyond the confines of the image.

Take his image from the early '90s of Jeremy Klein performing a kickflip backside grab of a curb in Huntington Beach, California. Shot at night, the end result was a mind-boggling multiple exposure across a single two-page magazine spread. There is light, darkness, and the birth of a trick that has been done by skaters since but never captured with the same level of ephemerality. It is one of one, and it will never look as engrossing as it does in that sequence. That's why a copy hangs on the wall of famed skate photographer Atiba Jefferson (see page 143). Even a GOAT needs to stay motivated.

The hits keep coming. Spike's shots of pro skater, now actor, Jason Lee? Everyone had those on their wall. Jason looking as if he were a crazed man in a straitjacket. The backside tailslide on the mini ramp out of the darkness and caught at a height that makes you feel the satisfying *brrapp!!!* that came when that tail touched down on coping . . . I can feel it now as I type. Every Spike photo featured the most unsung element of photography: a sense of drama.

Spike's palate would truly open up even more when he created *Video Days* (1991), a film for Blind Skateboards featuring Mark "Gonz" Gonzales (see page 92). It is that video that set the first stages of Spike's liftoff and put him on a trajectory to influence the world. Remember the word *limitless*?

Prior to holding that bite-size version of Marvel's Adam Warlock, an Oscar, and delivering his acceptance speech, Spike had an early stint during his late teens at *BMX Plus!* magazine. He would later defect with his partner in crime, art director Andy Jenkins (see page 121). As Andy tells it, Spike had been his main partner at the publication, with Andy creating custom cartoons and illustrations and Spike shooting photos. A young Megan Baltimore (see page 240) would take a position there as well and eventually become Spike's roommate. Though it's difficult to believe now, the BMX world was simply too straitlaced and corporate for this trio. Needing space to spread their artistic wings, they flew the coop and landed at one of the most storied homes in all of skateboarding, World Industries, then called Santa Monica Airlines.

While Steve Rocco might have been the man-child running the organization, and Rodney Mullen (see page 54) the mother hen, Spike was the provocateur, always willing to push things further

Well, here is where it begins. In a skateboarding video that featured the greatest skaters of their era such as Gonz, Jason Lee, Rudy Johnson, Jordan Richter, and a young Guy Mariano, Spike showed that he was unafraid to off our heroes for the sake of cinema and a good joke. The video didn't just feature amazing skating—what it showed was limitless imagination. The young skaters were filmed in a classic fully-chromed-out blue Oldsmobile 98 Regency, simulating drinking behind the wheel, set to the good vibes and tunes of War's "Low Rider." That is until said vehicle goes careening off the road and into the distance, sending all of the greatest skaters of a generation to a fiery death in a Mexican ravine. The cojones it took to create that in real time and capture it on celluloid!

No permits, no permissions, just locking a steering wheel to a gas pedal and *go*! Send that car to meet its maker. There is a real blue Oldsmobile somewhere out there still—rusting in the Mexican sun.

It's that film that made Nissan search Spike out and put him at the helm of a commercial for a Nissan Frontier that featured Gonz in a recliner, puppy in tow, asleep and rolling downhill through the streets of L.A. into traffic, only to wake up to a new car purchase. Sound cray? Just another flicker of light in Spike's imagination—and there are so many more in there.

While many skate companies create skateboarding videos that look phenomenal, Spike injects the fantastical. From the solo rolling board that catches on fire in the *Hot Chocolate* (2004) film to Mike Carroll on a Vespa with Rick Howard in a giant mouse suit to a micro-sized Keenan Milton skating the city and taking refuge from a mouse in a rat hole on a curb in Crenshaw, limitless. Whatever can be dreamed, can be gleaned. From the green screen and magic board in *Yeah Right!* (2003) to Owen Wilson cameos to Jack Black, VR, drones, or just plain practical effects, whatever the future has shown, you can guarantee it will play a part in the latest Spike Jonze production.

Spike's work offers a love letter to skateboarding and filmmaking with every frame, and reminds us not to take ourselves too seriously even when creating extraordinary art, on our own terms.

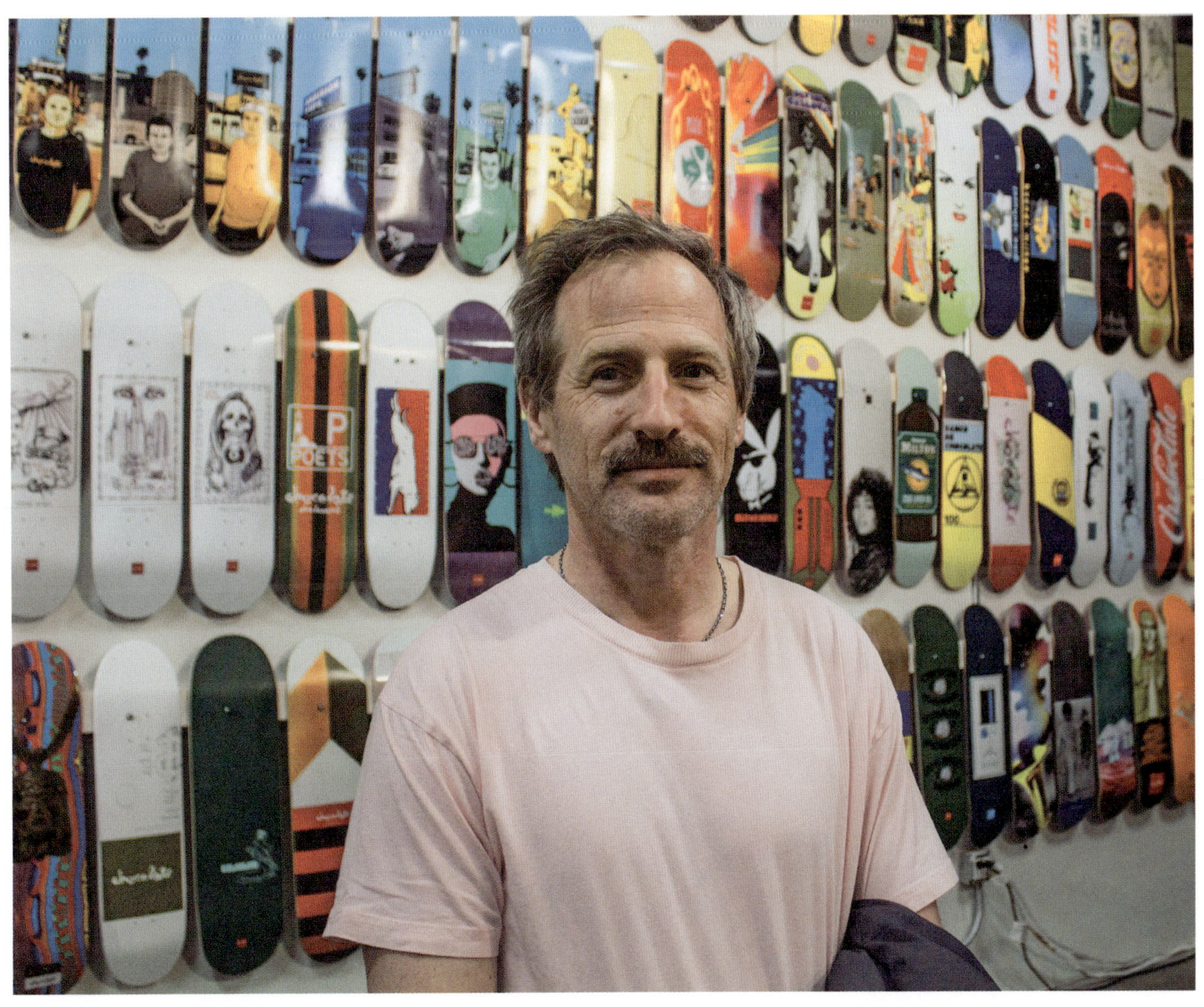

SKATEBOARDING'S MAVEN OF MOVEMENT
LISA WHITAKER

Skater, entrepreneur, video maker

Founder of Meow Skateboards

Started the Girls Skate Network

The glue of the scene since the mid-'90s

Quiet. Quiet. Envelope, please. "The award for the most valuable contribution to skateboarding culture goes to the queen of all queens—Lisa Whitaker." *And the crowd goes wild!* Skaters aged 5 to 50 swarm the stage to honor the one above all, Lisa.

While Lisa has yet to *receive* that honor, the campaign begins here. She has provided the blood, sweat, and tears that have kept women's skateboarding vibrant and documented from the '90s until now. It is not hyperbole to state that the evolution of women's skateboarding would not have been possible without Lisa and her cohorts, notably the Women's Skateboarding Alliance and later Poseiden and Skate Like a Girl, which functioned for decades as the lifeblood and unyielding heart of women's skating.

Since her introduction to the skate life, Lisa has operated behind the camera—but she's done much more than that. She skated in local contests and eventually earned a spot on one of the most celebrated teams in skateboarding, Rookie Skateboards. While sponsored, she added California sunshine to the New York City scene. As she made her mark in front of the camera, she continued to keep the red light shining on her crew, building up the legacy of the team. When it came time to make room for the next generation of ladies, she gladly kept the camera focused on the future.

The punkest of punk, she often ran on fumes to ensure that generations of women and girls would have their place in the sun. Long before the opportunities of the present, Lisa and the collective power of her court saved a spot in the van for every young woman, girl, or female-identifying figure of that era. That we now see young girls on the covers and in the pages of both skateboarding and non-skateboarding magazines is a testament to those efforts. While it may look like a tidal wave of change, it can be traced back to Lisa, who promised to never stop until parity between women's and men's skateboarding was achieved.

Now of course there are many queens in the movement, but the responsibility to bring the royal family forward fell squarely on Lisa's shoulders. She literally created the videos and archives that have moved three decades of women's skateboarding in the right direction, from early days with the Element Skateboards team filming for The Side Project (which morphed into the Girls Skate Network) to her Villa Villa Cola–produced video, *Getting Nowhere Faster* (2004), starring a who's who of women skaters.

Lisa started the Girls Skate Network in 2003 as a platform for all the footage she had captured as well as all the footage sent to her of phenomenal skateboarding occurring across the U.S. and worldwide. From Vans to Element to Globe, from the X Games to the Dew Tour and now the Olympics . . . you name it, she captured it. There is no storied organization within skateboarding that doesn't bear her stamp. She is right there along with Vanessa Torres, Mimi Knoop, and Cara-Beth Burnside. She put her Jane Hancock down on every bit of equipment to keep the scene alive. Through broken cameras, shattered lenses, and atmospheric rivers' worth of "one more try," her dedication ensured that women's skateboarding survived long enough for us all to take notice of the talent around us.

In 2012, Lisa founded Meow Skateboards, which has been home to every amazing skater from Vanessa Torres to Amy Caron, Leo Baker, Samarria Brevard, Mariah Duran, and Nora Vasconcellos.

On a personal level, Lisa did it all without ever raising a fist or her voice. I've been there when she listened to the myriad supposed reasons a woman's program doesn't work. The shrinking budgets, notions of what people "want" to see, and negative comments about influence. Lisa never complained; she simply did the damn thang. I've seen her loading gas in the van, maxing the credit cards, and keeping it moving all the while doing what's right. Lisa provided the labor, and never asked for all the glory. And she did it while working at the same companies where she had watched male pro skaters gain superstar status with our sisters left behind.

Luckily for us, she persevered. There is no way we would have arrived where we are with women's skateboarding had she taken a break. The surrogate mother to every skater across the decades, she did it then and continues to do it now. Even after she became an actual wife and mother and, of course, guardian of the world's cutest corgi.

When discussing her contributions, she remains as humble as ever. To hear her tell it, all her efforts are part of a reciprocal process, an act of appreciation for skateboarding inspiring her, an inspiration she in turn wants to instill in others. Take her discussion of the skateboarding videos by Powell Peralta, *Public Domain* (1988) and *Ban This* (1989). These videos gave Lisa life. It was the first Powell video, centering teens street skating, that brought out a new generation of multicultural, multigendered skaters, and when these hit, they hit hard.

The lone girl among a group of boys, Lisa recalled how she was aware that there were few girls in skateboarding other than herself, but skateboarding at that time was also underground. Anyone who loved skateboarding was an outcast anyway, and her group gladly bonded over their shared love, consuming every bit of media they could digest.

Lisa would be forever inspired by the first women she saw on video, namely Lori Rigsbee, Sophie Bourgeois, Leaf Treinen, and Anita Tessensohn. Anita and Leaf were featured in ads for Powell Peralta's campaign "Some Girls Play with Dolls. Real Women Skate." Though the slogan might be slightly problematic, it didn't make it any less impactful on every skater who saw the ads and accompanying video footage— including Lisa. "When I saw Anita—that's what did it," Lisa told me. "She was skating banks, kickflip to rock and rolls! It made me see that if she could do it . . . I was also a girl street skating and I can do it, too."

IT AIN'T NO FUN IF THE PHOTOS AIN'T SHOWIN' NONE

MICHAEL BURNETT

Longtime editor of *Thrasher*

Manages the largest global audience of any skate magazine

Master of the candid photo

Started in DIY skate zines that foreshadowed his career

Shepherd of "the stoke"

Michael Burnett cares about skateboarding in a way that few get to witness and hold on to. Not in the "I get to go on cool trips with the Old Gods of the Board and New Thunder Bringers" kind of way, but more like, "I gotta get up, nurture, and shepherd this thing that gives me life." As the longtime editor of *Thrasher* magazine, Burnett aims to make every page of this skate bible give life to readers around the world. A heavy task, but one that he gladly accepts each and every day.

Burnett operates under the mantra that skateboarding is the sum of its parts and that each skater helps make up the fabric of skateboarding culture. He thinks about what's missing from your skate life and makes the hard choices to fill the pages of *Thrasher* with what you don't even know you need. Burnett wants *Thrasher* to continue to be the place where skaters lay their heads and hold on to sweet dreams of skateboarding. That's what I did when I was a kid, hiding a rolled-up *Thrasher* under my pillow, then reading it long after Mom declared lights out.

Like me, Burnett came of age outside Southern California. His upbringing in Texas and college experience in Colorado, all far away from the skate industry, helped him retain a reverence for the magazine and his own independent perspective. With the largest distribution of any skateboarding magazine worldwide, *Thrasher* has all the hopes and aspirations of skaters everywhere embedded in its pages. He first contributed to *Thrasher* in 1994, while a college student in Boulder, before becoming the editor-in-chief in 1998. He's remained ever since.

Creating zines was a tradition in '80s skate culture. It was the first experience you got laying out photos, writing captions, and ultimately finding your voice—and, most important, putting it out there for your like-minded friends and for yourself. Those little DIY publications were the way that most of us got our first taste of the sport, and the same held true for Burnett. His early zine, *Feedbag*, did just that, with pics of events, contests, and the local scene. It was a voice and vision and a larger understanding of skateboarding and its people.

So, in the early '80s, under the mantra "skate and destroy," *Thrasher* was birthed by Fausto Vitello and original editor-in-chief Kevin "KT" Thatcher. The magazine was a DIY outsider homegrown effort, based in San Francisco, not Venice or Hollywood. It rallied people back to skateboarding after the sport's near death due to shifts in tastes and culture and the natural descent that followed the rocket-ride pop-culture rise of the Z-Boys era.

Skaters from the '80s and '90s will remember that no matter where you lived, *Thrasher* magazine guided your actions and identity. It helped you build your crew, and inspired you to grab a lo-fi-type camera: Instamatic, Polaroid, black-and-white film loaded in a Nikon N90 or whatever Canon you could get your hands on. Sure, the formats changed but the good times skating remained the same.

After KT left the role of editor-in-chief and passed it along to Jake Phelps, the magazine continued to grow and kept to its full-speed-ahead "skate and destroy" motto.

Burnett's story also places something else in context, often not discussed in skateboarding: education. Attending college in Boulder, he made the hot switch from history class to photography. In the process he would find what would become the most important facet of his life, documenting skateboarding.

As Burnett tells it, school is where they hide what skaters need—resources. He used the school's to build out his resume and his practice with those zines. (That is partly why he's been such a great advocate for the College Skateboarding Educational Foundation.) His experience at school helped him

reach out to the illustrious editor of *Thrasher*, Jake Phelps, and pitch an article about his local scene in Colorado with writing and photos—the combo that is music to any editor's ears.

In the mid-'90s, Burnett got his big break—an offer to join *Thrasher* as a photojournalist. He would be assuming the position vacated by the incomparable photog Chris Ortiz (see page 170). Burnett's mellow demeanor made skateboarding's greatest comfortable shooting with him, which generated spectacular cover photos and challenged the perception of *Thrasher* as a bit out of step with the hottest skaters. While it was the monster magazine in the '80s, it had lost a little of its sparkle in the '90s, with many more skaters turning toward the glossy layouts and photography in *Thrasher*'s main rival, *TransWorld SKATEboarding*. *TWS* was the first love for many skaters because of the photos and the level of expertise behind the lens. The paper stock alone was heavyweight, never mind the team and its litany of powerhouses: J. Grant Brittain, Dave Swift, Bryan Ridgeway, Daniel Sturt, and Miki Vuckovich, to name a few. It's where Spike Jonze's

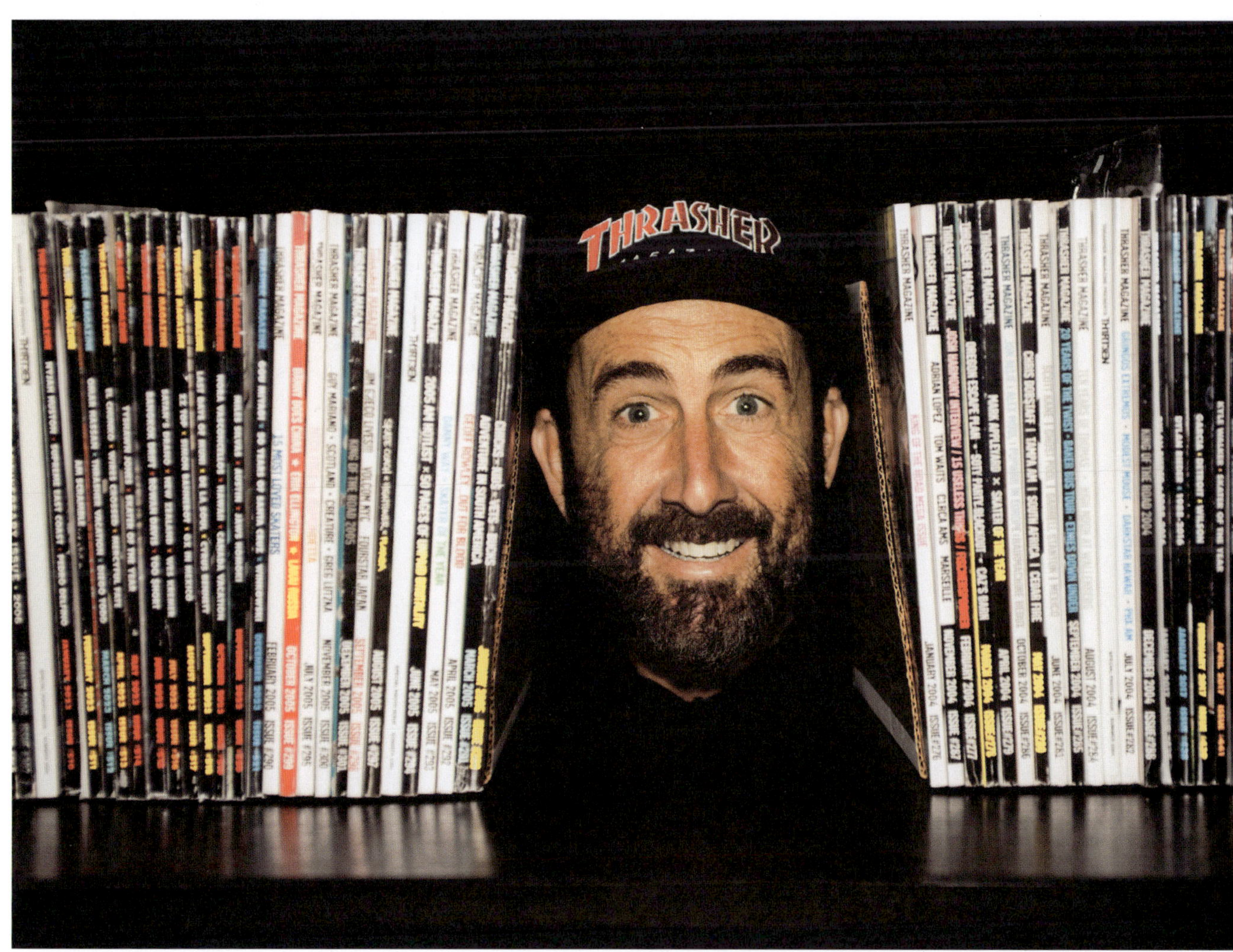

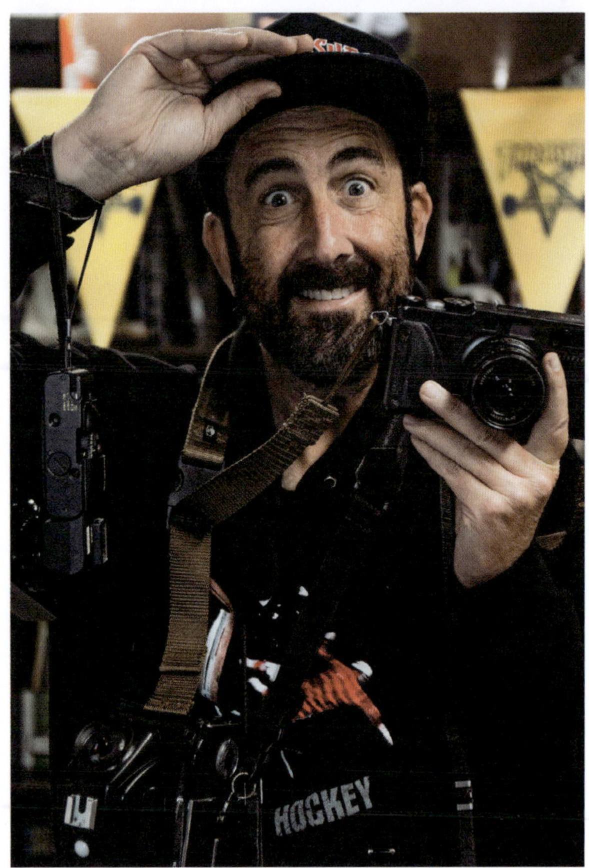

in his issues that make them a lifeblood for skaters from all walks.

The stuff that Burnett loves? The fun material—the "in-between" days, the gossip, the cheeky recipes, the interviews, the pleasure, the pain—came to life in *Thrasher*. Burnett had those celebrated chunks of content in mind when he took his place as the magazine's SoCal liaison in 1997. He knew skaters still loved the magazine; they just needed to reconnect to it. To rebuild, his SoCal post positioned him right next to a new gen of skaters hungry for the limelight. The right messenger for *Thrasher*'s "skate and destroy" attitude, yet also full of humility, Burnett reminded skaters that there would always be room for them in the magazine as long as they were willing to put their lives on the line and give blood to skateboarding. Raw skateboarding always has a place in *Thrasher*. In line with Jake Phelps, Burnett wanted the magazine to remain gnarly and inspirational yet improve in photos and vibe. The approach worked and the *Thrasher* cover photo became synonymous with the *gnarliest* trick.

Over time, *Thrasher* amassed new staff members foaming at the mouth to get the work done in photos and editorials. From photographers and videographers Eric "Rodent" Cheslak, Chris "Rhino" Rooney, and Preston "P-Stone" Maigetter (RIP) to writer Ted Barrow, the magazine was pulling it together and putting out nets to capture new talent and cover more of the national and global scene.

Now, after more than 20 years as editor, Burnett has succeeded in building a bridge between NorCal and SoCal. He's been a man on a mission to make the mag open to everyone and to be *the* source for every aspect of skating. From news and rumor mill sections—always read first—to skater interviews to recipes and musical spotlights, *Thrasher* makes skaters around the world feel like they're in the know and part of the scenes in New York, Los Angeles, San Francisco, San Diego, and beyond.

Under Burnett's watch, *Thrasher* has matured along with its readership, touching on topics once taboo with skaters, such as rehab and the hardest tricks they've done. Often the former is the latter. A confident Burnett also helped the publication represent the human element of skateboarding in every aspect of skate life. With time, *Thrasher* has evolved to remind people—male, female, nonbinary, whatever their identity—that regardless of where they came from or what body they inhabit, the feeling of stoke is the same in every skater.

star began to rise and where Atiba Jefferson, Tod Swank, and Seu Trinh started their careers.

It might seem difficult to compete with those icons but Burnett was patient and spent quality time building relationships that paid off when it came to who he was able to recruit. The next generation of up-and-comers on now-seminal brands like Toy Machine, Zero, Baker, and Flip were down to roll with *Thrasher* and get on board again. Burnett's low-key disposition and ability to talk less and shoot more also allowed him to develop his signature documentary style. Of course, he also got all the amazing pics that made you love skateboarding, like Arto Saari's fakie backside lipslide at Point Loma for his 2001 *Thrasher* Skater of the Year cover. Or that heater 2003 cover of Bastien Salabanzi and his fakie flip down the brick stairs in L.A., or his fakie flip in the shallow end of an abandoned pool, but who's counting. There are more than 20 years of fire that Burnett's committed to the magazine's legacy, but what makes his signature style is his obsession with capturing the highlights and hijinks of skate life off board. The moments when the crowd is going wild as a free board is tossed to the masses, to skaters slapping each other, painting each other, or creating music on the road with cheap gas-station banjos and the like. Those are the things that Burnett includes

L.A.'S CONFIDENTIAL CAPTURER

SEU TRINH

Humble, soulful lensman who makes ethereal art

Former staff photographer for _TransWorld SKATEboarding_

**Former head photographer for the Almost Skateboards
and Diamond Supply Co. teams**

Since the mid-'90s, Vietnamese American lensman extraordinaire Seu Trinh has delivered photos that feel like an intimate dialogue between his subject, himself, and their skateboards. Seu's photos can bring the rapid heartbeat of a city as populous as Los Angeles to a slow pulse—then with a snap freeze time so that it can be observed and explored from multiple angles. His images often hint at a world passed over, one he brings us into with a dreamlike focus.

Born in Saigon, Vietnam, Seu immigrated to Boston when he was two. After a five-year stint in Celtics country, his family headed to L.A. Their voyage was skateboarding's gain and Seu has long since offered a multitude of skaters the chance to team up and produce editorials and covers for some of the best in the culture.

Over time, Seu has become a titan, earning a place as staff photographer for _TransWorld SKATEboarding_ (_TWS_) during its heyday from the aughts to the late 2010s. He became the go-to guy in L.A. County, bringing the San Diego–based publication the premier players and gritty bits of skateboarding from that bigger city's finest.

Skate photographers have regularly used similar vocabulary and equipment: the long (telephoto) lens; short lenses, or 50mm and the like (for street documentary photos); wide-angle and the most often used ultra-wide or fish-eye lens, which helps make the skater or the gap become the most prominent, or epic, object in the frame. What sets a photographer's work apart is how the vision and technology deliver the outcome. Seu's photos exude an ethereal quality that conveys the weight and

breathlessness of each moment. He captures these junctures, where he bathes an iconic figure or the newest amateur in light and darkness and grants us access to the dance between skater, skateboard, and city. This rare ability to evoke a sense of stillness amid the chaos of the city is a testament to his ability to internalize, then project, how skaters see the world. We can all recognize a Seu when we see one: an extraordinary photo of Rodney Mullen (see page 54) launching a primo slide, sliding along on the axles, shot from below, which earned Seu the cover of the August 2004 issue of _TWS_, or a delicate portrayal of pro skater Jason Dill's switch backside smith grind, properly dipped, locked in, and loaded, across the decades.

This all tracks considering how Seu began his career as a skateboarding photographer. He learned to skate by using his brother's homemade board. His own first board was a Tony Hawk Bonite. He learned to shoot starting in seventh grade, with old-school film, in his hometown of Azusa, California, taking pics of friends. Some of them in turn introduced him to professional skaters.

Seu's first foray into the pro world came at age 18 thanks to a chance meetup with pro skater Julio De La Cruz at Utility Board Shop (now defunct), where Seu's images adorned the walls. The two started talking, and Julio mentioned that his new company, Neighborhood, was going on tour and needed a photographer. That could have been it, just words.

Then out of the blue soon after, Julio showed up at Seu's door and told him it was time to go. Instead of asking questions, Seu applied the most valuable principle any skater can in their formative years: GET IN THE VAN.

The tour not only offered a new environment for Seu to hone his photography techniques in, it was also his first entry into an inclusive skateboarding family. They all bonded over being from lower-income households. "We all just loved skateboarding," Seu told me. Collectively, the motley Neighbors crew pulled Seu out of his shell, and he inspired them to be more reflective—well, as reflective as 18-to-21-year-olds can be. They brought down their barriers together, updated their craft, and found the joy and subtlety in skateboarding, and in each other. These elements continue to be instrumental to Seu's work.

His images since then have never been about just the tricks, but rather what stories they tell. For a billboard for Diamond Footwear with Torey Pudwill prominently displayed on L.A.'s Fairfax Avenue, Seu captures the delicate feel of the city during golden hour in a way that few can. He takes a stock scenario of Torey skating a handrail and somehow removes the cacophony of L.A. and instead caresses Torey in a mixture of light and shadow that moves the photo into another plane. Seu quietly has given you the sole ownership of this particular moment in time. It's present in all his work, but particularly in his photos of skate luminary Mike Carroll doing a throwback ollie airwalk (an ollie where you grab the front of your board and stretch your legs into the splits) across a back-alley gap. The shot distills skating to its essence—board, shoes, skater—we're barely able to perceive Mike, but that's the point. It quiets the clutter and presents the world according to Seu.

When I guest-edited an issue of *Skateism* in December 2020, Seu was the first person I called to photograph one of the other most wavy skaters of the decade, U.S. Olympic team member Samarria Brevard (see page 273). My hope was that the two brightest hearts in skateboarding would produce epic images, and they did.

Seu also delivered his signature visuals of the subtle beauty of the vibrant greens of the foliage and the red-orange of the rusty fence while recognizing that skaters are also excited by Samarria's perfectly executed backside smith grind and backside disaster on a stone-cold gray jersey barrier DIY spot. Each image featured a canary yellow sign above the barrier labeling the area a dead end, a fitting representation of the way many outside of skateboarding look at the sport, even though it's our passion and livelihood. Skaters get the irony of the image. That's Seu Trinh, stringing together soliloquies of beauty, with a lil' hint of fun in every frame.

Daewon Song, frontside ollie, captured by Seu Trinh

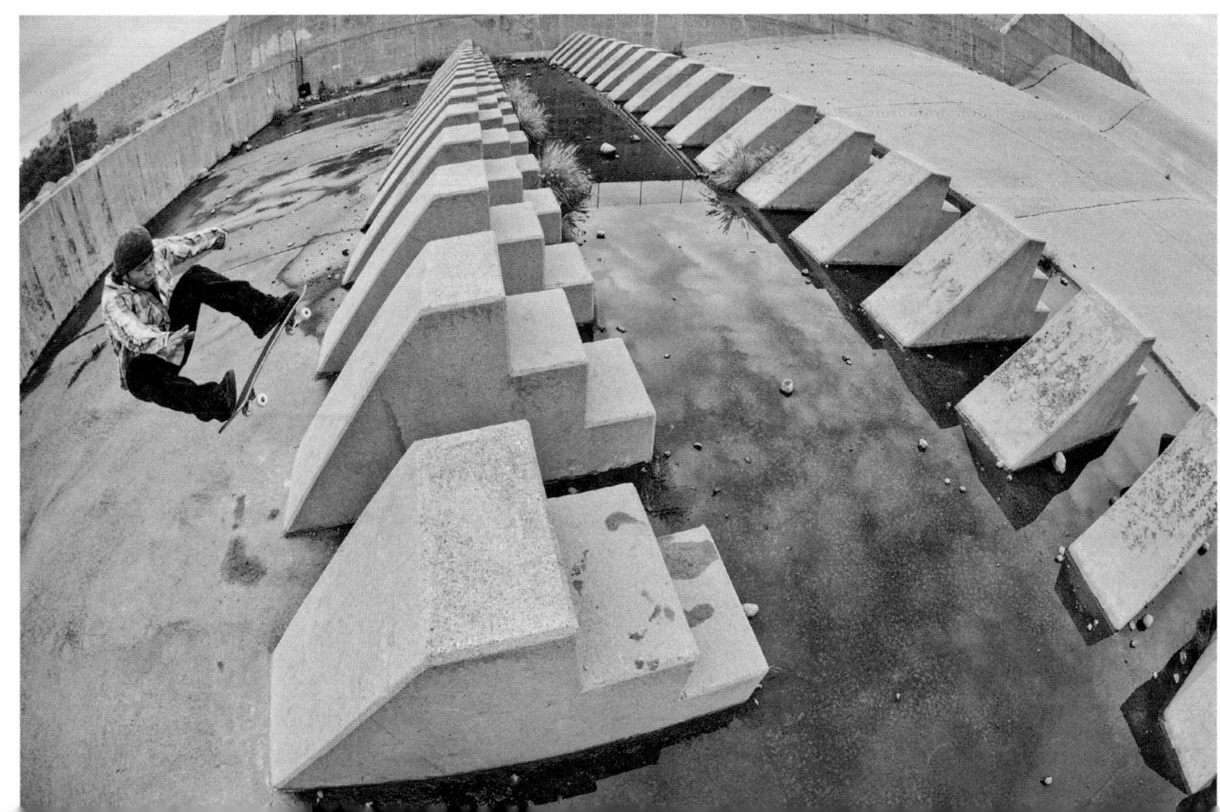

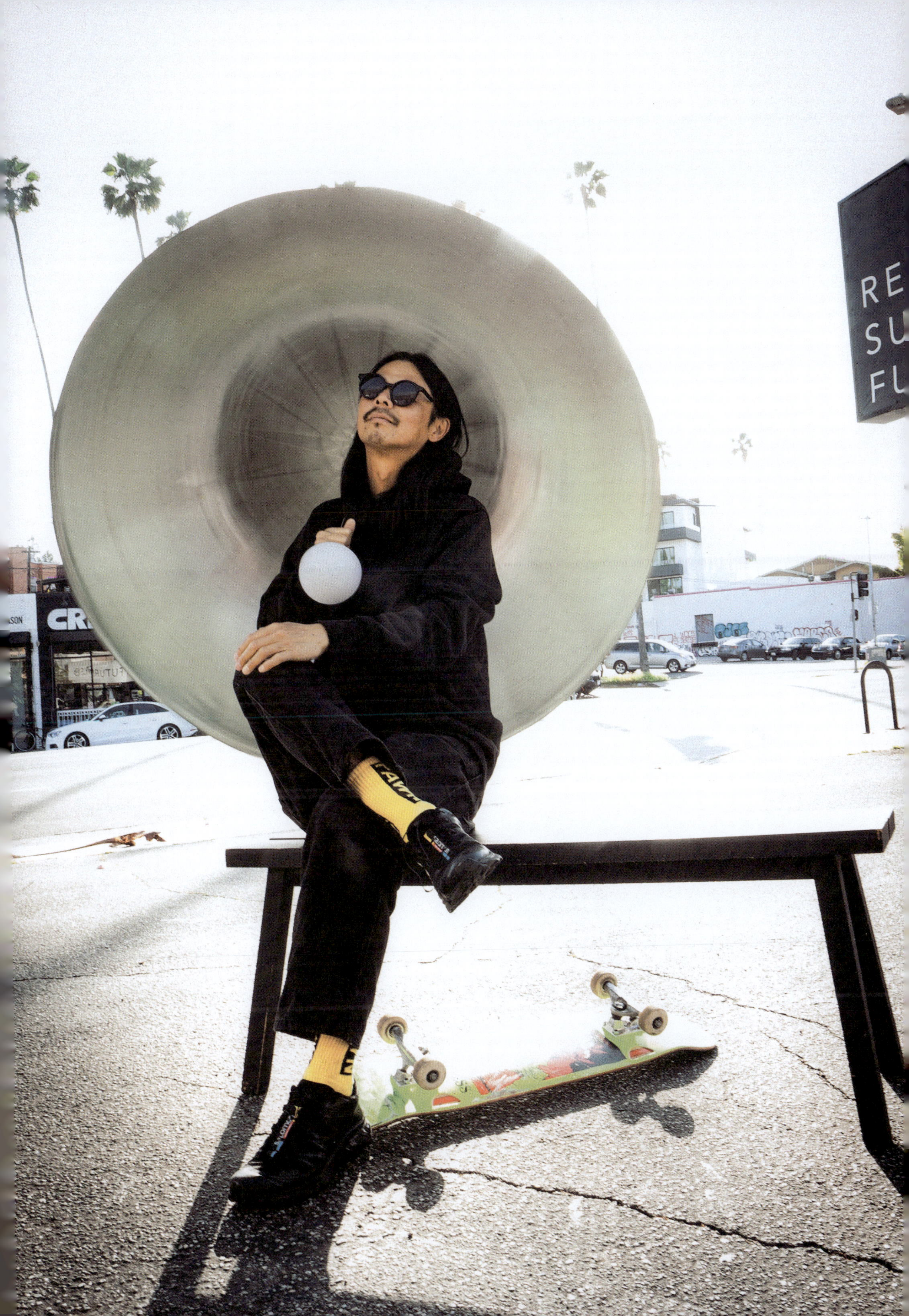

RE
SU
FU
CR
FUTUR

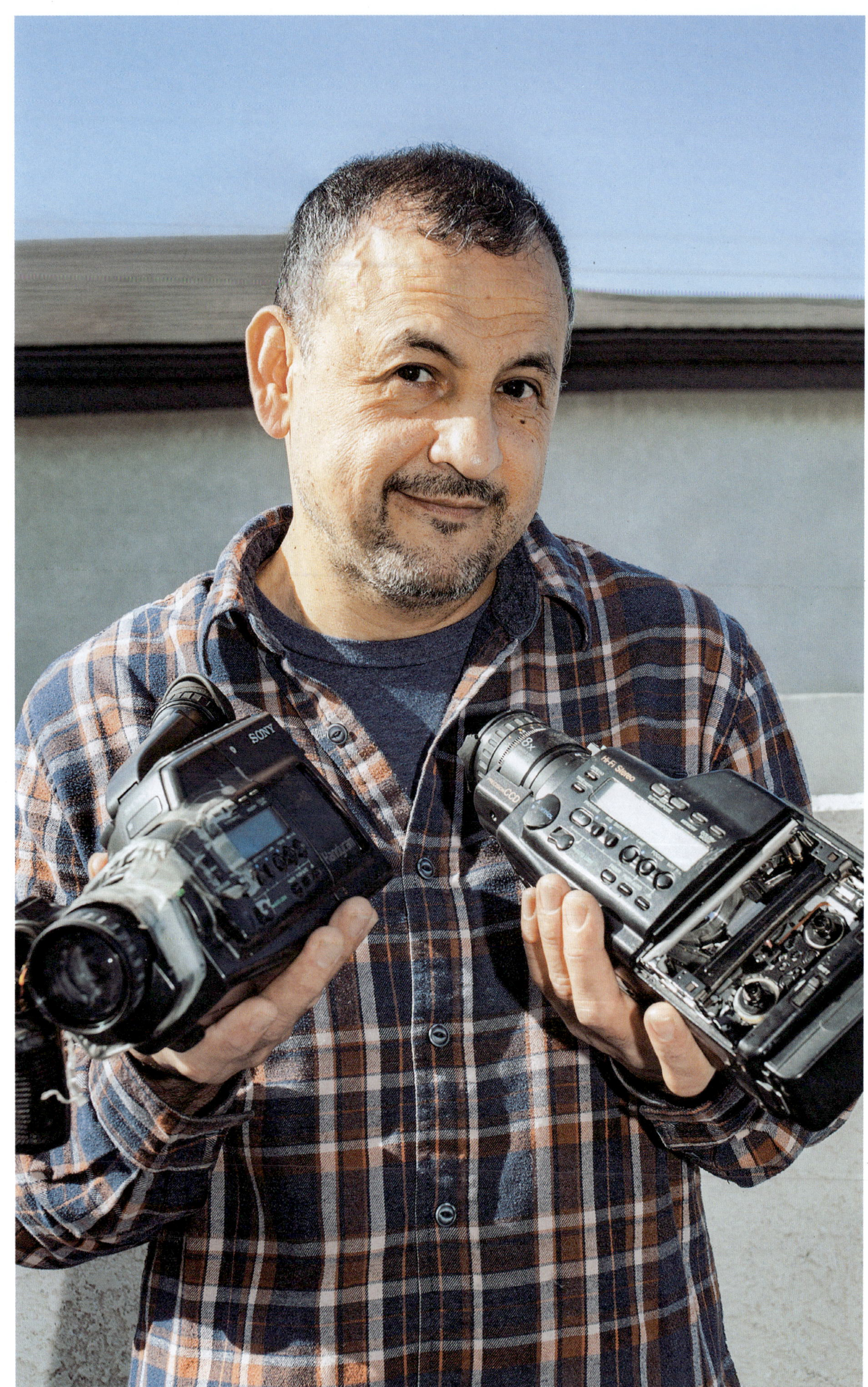

THE UNSUNG ACE OF SKATEBOARDING VIDEOGRAPHY
SOCRATES LEAL

Storied videographer of Rodney Mullen and World Industries

Unsung historian of 1990s skateboarding

Architect of the posse shot

Responsible for the elements that inspired the Berrics

Cinematographer and editor Socrates Leal is hands down responsible for the largest collection of moving images from the golden era of skateboarding across teams, brands, and continents, from the 1990s to the mid-2010s. The fits, the kicks, the tricks—Socrates captured it all. If Soc didn't film, it probably didn't happen, or, it simply *wasn't that happening.* Just the names on his dailies bring tears to the eyes of any skate nerd: Gino Iannucci, Kareem Campbell, Jason Dill, Adam McNatt, the McBrides, Rodney Mullen . . . the list is endless. Daniel Castillo, Daewon Song, Keenan Milton (RIP)—a litany of phenomenal skaters at the beginning of their careers. Soc was there to record all the highs and "content warning" hijinks that would make them household names, at least in skateboarding households.

The names on the marquee changed, but Soc—as he's known throughout the diaspora—has forever been the most trusted videographer in the game. Soc stealthily snapped some of the greatest moments of #skateboardingeverydamnday, long before the hashtag. Soc's documentation of powerhouses allows skate historians and everyone else with even a passing interest to see, for example, the wonder that is the World Industries camp in all its flourishes and incarnations, offering a plethora of insight into the generations of riders situated within the World, Blind, 101, CityStars, Plan B, and Axion Footwear factions, and nearly all of the riders from Girl and from Chocolate. Plus, he's responsible for capturing some of the most memorable antics and skits in skateboarding video history—the true legal tender in skate culture.

The master lensman grew up with his brother and mother, Mexican immigrants to Southern California living in hyper-tight formation. Soc's mother eventually remarried and, according to Soc, never spoke at length about the family's departure from Mexico or their father and kin who remained behind, other than to exclaim that life below the border was "dangerous."

For our purposes, Soc's skate life begins in Lawndale, California, a small city situated roughly three miles away from the Pacific Ocean. Surprisingly, that sliver of distance between the beach and inland L.A. equated to a world full of difference. "If you don't live like right along the ocean, in the beach cities . . . as soon as you go east anywhere closer to the 110, you might as well just be living in L.A. proper," Soc told me. He listed some landlocked local burgs: "Gardena, Hawthorne, all those . . . Lawndale is kind of smack in between and Gardena is *very* urban culture."

Socrates's nod to his home city and the urban aesthetic belies the informal class and culture wars of this swath of L.A. life. Coastal Redondo Beach and Hermosa Beach represented the laid-back lifestyle of hippie-beach living, with Lawndale and its sister cities acting as a dividing line between them and pretty much everyone else. Sandwiched amid the urban and suburban clash of Gardena, those streets and his pursuit of skateboarding documentation would birth Soc's relationship with lifelong skateboarding companions, pro skater Daniel Castillo, and Skater of the Year and Hall of Famer Daewon Song (see page 28).

The socioeconomic and cultural differences between the beach and the streets showed up early in Soc's teens, when he was one of the sole skaters in his sophomore year of 1986–87. Skateboarding was not in vogue, and even worse, to those clowning him at Leuzinger High School, all action sports seemed interchangeable. "'Hey surfer boy,' or, 'Gnarly waves!' when I'm carrying a skateboard," Soc told me, laughing at the memory. "Not a surfboard. Idiots!" He continued: "It was all the same blond-haired, blue-eyed white dudes with surfboards to them. I was supposed to fit their idea of what was Mexican. That imagery didn't include skateboarding or lean in a positive direction. When I was growing up, if you didn't join a gang, you were nobody. That's what you had to do." Soon, though, Socrates would establish a new, indelible representation of the Mexican American as a leader in skateboarding videography.

While Soc's fame came from rolling tape, his original aspirations began with the still image. Socrates learned a bit of photography at school, but building a career as a photographer can require deeper pockets. Lighting and cameras are expensive, and back then there were also film and processing costs to consider. In the '80s and '90s, before every phone had a camera, only magazine-supported staff photographers had access to free film and developing. A photographer might burn through a mountain of film capturing one trick. You didn't know if you had the trick until the slides came back from the lab. I shot skateboarding on slide film for years, and always waited anxiously for the results. What's worse is that you didn't know you'd missed the shot until—well, you didn't have the shot. Trust me, word gets around about photogs who miss the shot and need a do-over. "Skaters don't want to do a trick again" was a gem Soc dropped on me early on. "Filming came easier. They could see the footage immediately. If it looks good, you earn their trust." The Socrates Leal name became synonymous with dependability.

The videographer role also won out because it required less of the most crucial resource: time. Photography is a trial and error and error and error process. It's difficult to keep people patient when their careers are on the line and the learning curve

is steep. The more pro tips you pick up, the faster you can get ahead. Unfortunately for Soc, those tips and mentors were few and far between. "No one wanted to help, man. Nobody," he said. "But I get it—it's their job and they weren't trying to lose it." The lack of support made the switch to videography a much more promising option. "I had a kid on the way, and I needed steady income," he said. "It made the most sense."

Though he didn't crack the code with photography, Socrates excelled with moving images and became the go-to videographer for empresario Rodney Mullen (see page 54) and the entire World Industries team, with a hand in creating scores of momentous skateboarding videos. Soc's lens would be the first to introduce the world to an adolescent Daewon Song in the World video *Love Child* (1992), backed by the Supremes song of the same name. He introduced some of the greats with *New World Order* (1993), and *20 Shot Sequence* (1995) featuring a rough and raw '90s hip-hop soundtrack; and again, with the crème de la crème of that run, 1996's World Industries video *Trilogy*. That video was everything: an open letter to those skaters who had exited the brand (the Girl/Chocolate skateboards camp), proclaiming that it was still all love—but that their team remained unstoppable. Soc played a critical role in filming and editing every aspect of these celluloid gems, in collaboration with the World team, all growing into their roles as cultural icons. The work he did created generational classics such as *Rodney Mullen vs. Daewon Song Round 1, 2*, and *3* (commonly referred to as the Almost Skateboards video). He did the same for the wonder that was *Cheese & Crackers* (2006), which caused an explosion of what was literally a dead discipline, mini-ramp (small-scale half-pipe) skating.

Before their transformation into trendsetters, however, many now-famous skaters were just adolescents excited to be sponsored. Part of what made those videos landmarks involved Socrates's ability to chronicle the antithesis of professionalism—skateboarding's straight-up *fun*. Soc's philosophy of "Don't look through your eyes; look through the lens" created a raw record of moments in time, and we all owe him a debt for that approach. His head on a swivel, filming incessantly, Soc captured not only the trick, but the response and communal context. He originated the '90s posse shot—filling his frame with the skaters en masse behind the key skaters, kickin' it, stretchin', or waiting their turn, opening us all to the silly waves, dances, and the ballyhoo of hype and group adoration usually conducted off camera during every trick. Soc provided a visual history of skateboarding biased only by the belief that every second of skateboarding was invaluable. This was cinema verité for our scene, and similar to Warhol's interpretation, Soc absorbed the minuscule and the mega and delivered it all, unflinchingly, to tape.

More than anyone else during that '90s golden age, Socrates presented the *lifestyle* of skateboarding, which effectively offered everyday skaters like me a glimpse of the BIPOC crews moving through the city. Watching those videos at home back east, damn, we were part of those L.A. crews! They looked like us. We wanted to be like them: skating in the streets, riding blank boards, issuing beatdowns at Lockwood school, sliding

"DON'T LOOK THROUGH YOUR EYES; LOOK THROUGH THE LENS."

down a carpeted flight of stairs on bare skate decks, fleeing from police, and (sorry, Mom) taking part in those international debauchery tours. From the shreddin' to the Armageddon of the Bong Olympics (*Big Brother* magazine's pot-smoking competition for skaters)—in L.A. and Amsterdam—Soc showed us an unfettered skateboarding lifestyle, as skaters lived and breathed and created it.

Socrates's approach aligned with the advent of video magazines in the mid-'90s to the aughts. This gave him the unique opportunity to contribute multiple videos on global skate through outlets such as *411 Video Magazine*, *Digital Skateboarding* video magazine, and *Puzzle* in Europe, along with many others. Ironically, Socrates's transition to video also meant that his work wound up in print magazines. During the mid- to late '90s, skateboarding tricks had reached such a degree of technical prowess that their performances were too fast for film cameras to adequately capture, driving up the relevance of video with its the slo-mo button. World Industries was also at odds with *TransWorld SKATEboarding* and *Thrasher*, and decided to publish their own magazine, *Big Brother*. Soc's videos would appear as "screen grabbed" or paused video sequences as part of full-page ads and editorial. *Big Brother* went on

to release its own videos, which became the catalyst for what is now known as the *Jackass* franchise. Yep, Socrates operated on the ground floor of the same place that would bring about the rise of Johnny Knoxville, Jeff Tremaine, and Steve-O during their first forays into MTV and Hollywood.

In the entertainment industry sector of L.A., grandiose visions are a dime a dozen, but day-to-day execution? That is rare and priceless. That's where Socrates lives, operating with a blue-collar aesthetic that allows everyone around him to execute their wildest or dreamiest ideas.

Auteur directors in skateboarding videos with grand ideas tend to come and go, but Soc's work is timeless. It is labor-intensive, no-nonsense, and delivered on deadline. Throughout his career, he has captured footage that exists as the embodiment of perfectly executed skateboarding, so that an external narrative could occur *through* it. The good, the bad, the benign, he made all the rawness look fresh. Capturing footage like that is remarkable—just like Soc himself. It's the reason for the recent trend in purchasing outdated video tech. Skaters don't want 8K resolution—they want that old thang back. That '90s thang of slightly grainy vids and what is now lo-fi gritty production that Soc helped pioneer.

When it's time to dole out accolades, Socrates Leal's dyed-in-the-wool ability to do the damn thing is often forgotten, but we ain't forgetting around here. Socrates has always been a true and living master of the craft walking among us. He'll forever be out with legends and the new gods, always searching for better angles to give us a glimpse of the magic in front of and behind the curtain. You can bet on that #everydamnday.

CHRIS ORTIZ & BRYCE KANIGHTS

OG California photographers who have seen and shot it all

Apprenticed and worked together at *Thrasher*

Helped define skateboarding media with *411* (Ortiz)

Created legendary photo of Mark "Gonz" Gonzales at Alcatraz (BK)

Chris Ortiz and Bryce Kanights, or "Ortiz" and "BK" as we all know them, are two of the early dons and made men of skateboarding photography. Beginning their career ascent in the 1980s, they each offered perspective on their communities with L.A. and the Inland Empire (IE) for Ortiz and San Francisco Bay and NorCal for BK. They offered their blood, sweat, and film rolls to skateboarding long before most of us knew how to set up a flash. In my own career, it's an honor to have accidentally stumbled into their shots during my first photo gig for the Maloof Money Cup skate competition and eventually earn their friendship.

While they lived in different parts of California, Ortiz and BK both came up under the *Thrasher* OG banner, under Mörizen Föche, also known as Mofo or Richard Knoll, and Kevin Thatcher. During that era, Mofo was a hell of a photo editor and sage to photographers like Ortiz and BK. A cantankerous sage, but a sage nonetheless. As Ortiz describes it, Mofo would be the type to offer a young photog a friendly critique that equated to: If you bought a fish-eye lens to get right into the action, why the hell are you shooting from so far away! Classic Mofo and classic training in an era when photographers sent in slides via snail mail and waited to hear back upon receipt.

Even though it took time for the answers to arrive, the great advantage for Ortiz back then was that he was still a kid in school; the concept of a career in skateboarding was not totally on the horizon yet. Cutting his teeth growing up in Inglewood, Buena Park, and the IE in Southern California, he was in the right place at the right time. During the '70s and early '80s, the IE was a breeding ground for future legends like Steve and Micke Alba and others who were high school kids making a name for themselves in contests and backyard pools and full pipes (exactly what it sounds like: a full pipe instead of a half-pipe). The holy grail of full pipes then was the famous 20-foot-high drainage pipe known as Mount Baldy, hidden in the depths of the IE.

Access is one of the key elements of photography, and over time Ortiz became known for always having a camera with him. With support from his high school teacher, he gained the ability to process film and learn the fundamentals, while also getting to shoot some of the best in the game.

Just ask skate Hall of Famer Kareem Campbell (see page 46), and he will tell you Ortiz gets down like Bone Crusher—he ain't never skerred. "Ortiz is a day one," 'Reem said. "He will show up in the hoodest of hoods at any time to get the shot and was never afraid to jump a fence to get it done."

It's that attitude that propelled him first to be a major player in the *Thrasher* organization, then to become a staff photographer for *TransWorld SKATEboarding*. He also became a mainstay at Giant Skateboard Distribution, which housed skateboarding brands Element and New Deal, and then at the highly influential *411 Video Magazine*. Film or photography, Ortiz was on it and the hardest-working man in skateboarding media. It's only fitting that he became a key figure in the revamped Dew Tour and remains a go-to photographer working everywhere from the X Games to the Skateboarding Hall of Fame. An icon in the industry, he continues to inspire the next generations of photographers and skateboarders.

The same holds true for his compatriot, Bryce Kanights. BK got his start at age six, shooting photos on mediocre equipment in the late '70s, until his father recognized his affinity. Kanights Sr. was an exceptional photographer and gifted his son a used Canon camera. BK learned by trial and error and gained insights into what he should be looking for when composing shots. That speaks volumes about how informal support and environment can have a positive impact on a young photog's career.

BK became smitten with the shutter, shooting his friends and studying the pages of magazines like *Skateboarder*, which was the bible for skaters in the mid- to late '1970s. Those photos of legends like Tony Alva and Stacy Peralta, Peggy Oki and Laura Thornhill, Marty Grimes and Lonny Hiramoto showed that skateboarding could be a space for everyone, and BK became hungry to capture them all. However, unlike Ortiz, who mailed in his photos to take a haranguing from Mofo, San Francisco–born and raised BK could take it in person.

He nabbed an internship at newly created *Thrasher* and learned the operation from soup to nuts, earning a role as a darkroom tech and making sure the place was cleaned and ready to go. His access also increased because he himself became a professional skater—a flag few photographers get to fly. During the late '80s, he rode for Schmitt Stix skateboards, created by skateboard constructor extraordinaire Paul Schmitt (see page 209) under Vision Skateboards before Schmitt left to form PS Stix and cofound New Deal. BK was skating

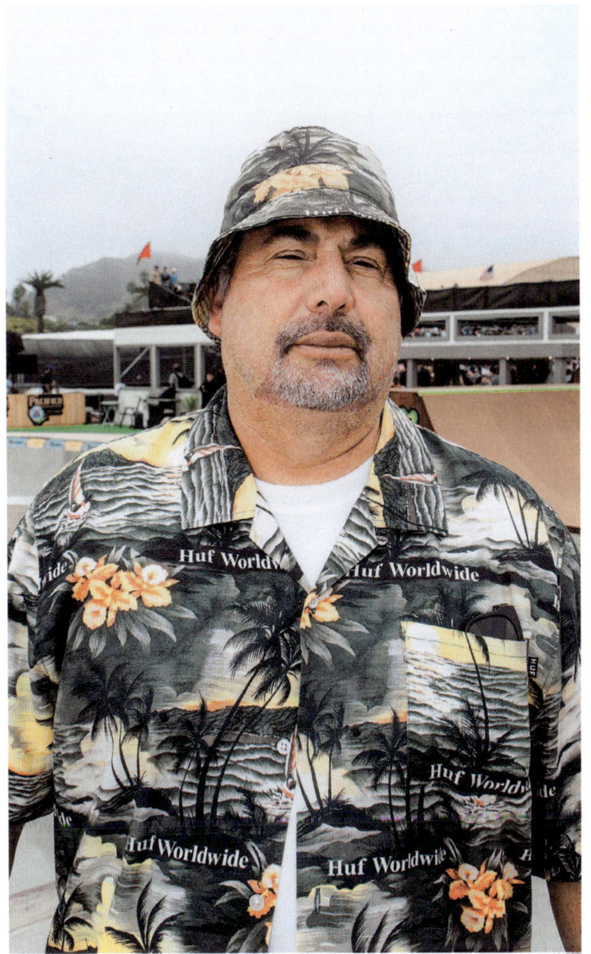

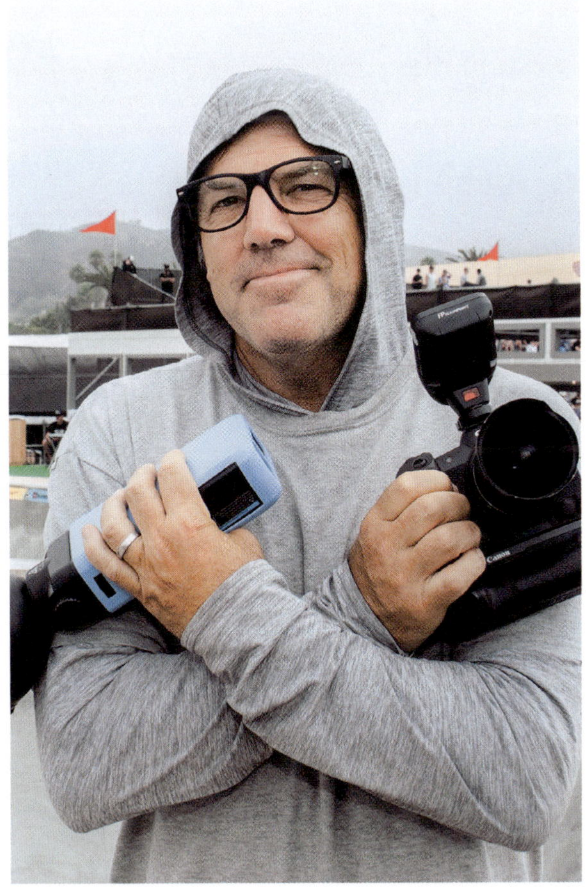

the streets and in contests and backyard pools, making a name for himself. The Bryce Kanights board featured a gargoyle and was very popular in several of its incarnations—I owned one. Even with royalty checks in place, BK never stopped working at *Thrasher* and being part of the magazine's growth. He would become the photo editor and Ortiz's boss for a few years, creating a deep bond between them based on mutual respect.

His contributions to *Thrasher* and the S.F. scene also extended to his creating Studio 43, the skate mecca of indoor ramp skating in S.F. in the early to mid-'90s. Studio 43 began as a dream to have a warehouse skate space with 24-hour access, and eventually became a wonderful folkloric home to

the S.F. scene as home to one of the only vert ramps in the Bay. It housed many a famous session with locals like Max Schaaf, John Cardiel, Chris Pastras, Jim Thiebaud, and Tommy Guerrero regularly burning the studio down with their wizardry.

All the while BK was still shooting in the streets, including one of the most celebrated sessions of all time, Mark "Gonz" Gonzales (see page 92) skating in Alcatraz.

BK would eventually aid in building a team around Gonz: the Adidas Skate Team. BK would ultimately leave his role at Adidas, moving into bigger territory, creating his own brand, Lifeblood Skateboards, and shooting for every brand under the sun. From Vans to Nike, Red Bull to Monster

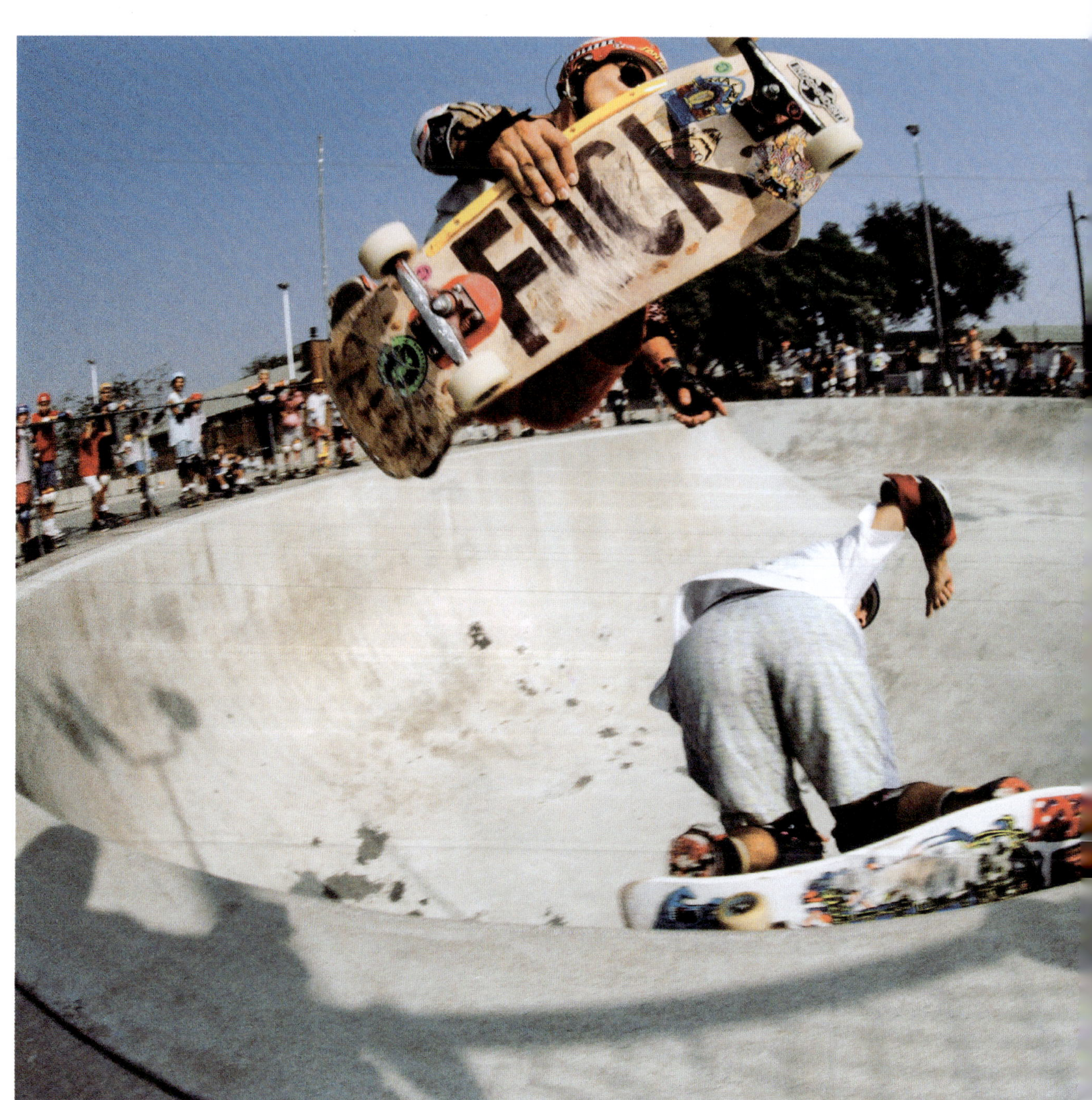

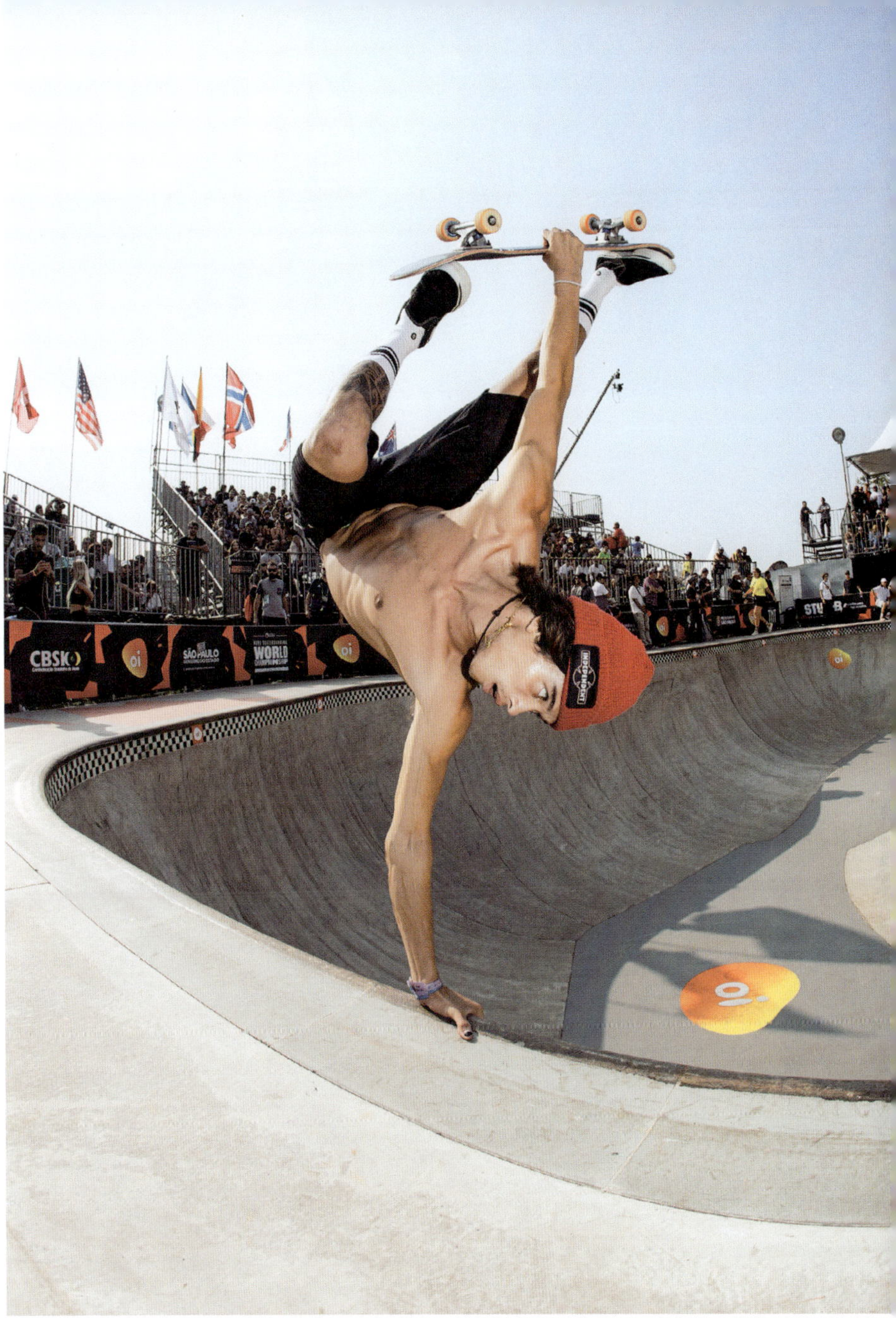

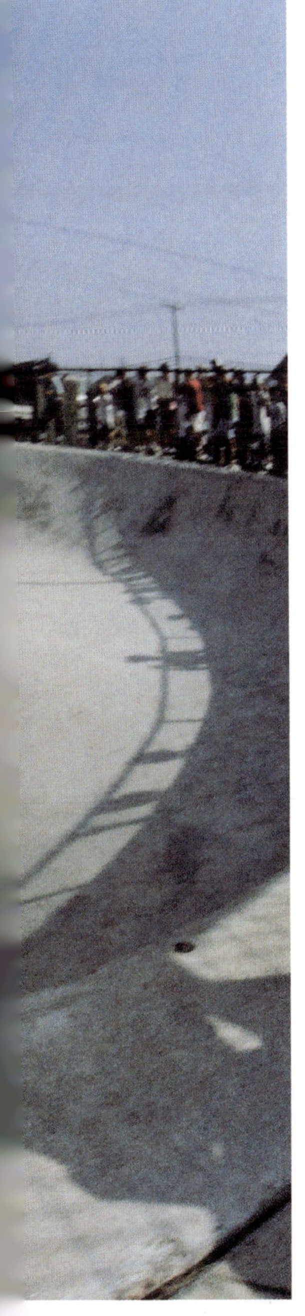

Energy, Oakley to Skullcandy, the Maloof Money
Cup (where he was my boss) to official shooter at the
Olympics, his time in the game is nothing if not a
testament to the notion that if you do what you love
well, what you love will do well by you.

Both Ortiz and BK have put their lives on the
line for skateboarding. Each lives life on his back,
looking through the lens. From lying in the gutter
and hopping fences to compose the perfect shot
to building actual homes away from home where
skaters could practice their crafts, they are made
men not just because they carry a camera but
because of the decades of care they have shown
their subjects.

THE
ACTIV
ISTS

We live together. We love together. We roll together.

The Activists move the needle and encourage skateboarding to be a place for everyone. Truth be told, some days, that ish ain't easy. People can act totally out of pocket sometimes—but these folks and the rest of our fam carry the light and fight for positive change. They uplift our ranks by making sure anyone who cares about skateboarding can become part of the community. Give them your tired, your weary, your needy, your heel-bruised new set, or achy kneed—the Activists will extend a hand and a proper training of legs and feet to help new people find joy and experience this thing we love.

These folks lead by example and make skateboarding a home and a family. They represent every community under the sun and strengthen our resolve as we skate through the days of our lives.

WHEN YOU SEE SOMETHING, DO SOMETHING ABOUT IT

AMELIA BRODKA

Founded Exposure Skate, the world's largest contest for women and nonbinary skaters

Former Olympic skateboarder for Poland

Created the award-winning documentary *Underexposed*

Women's rights activist

Athlete. Documentarian. Activist. Announcer and all-around ripper. The first of her name in skateboarding—Amelia Brodka.

My USC Trojan sister-in-arms has dedicated her life to ensuring women and nonbinary people can see skateboarding as their own. She noticed that women were not getting a fair shake in the skateboarding industry and had no problem poking the bear to ask why or what the actual.

Once she got the answers, she did what any self-respecting skater would do when feeling lost and alone on an island—she built a damn ship herself and set sail, leaving the BS behind and picking up her girls along the way. That ship was a boatload of opportunity aptly titled *Exposure*, for reasons I'll reveal below.

But first, how does one go from being an aspiring X Games competitor to founding and running the largest women's and nonbinary skate competition in the world? By giving an ish and, when the doors close, hacksawing a window through the patriarchy to make her lane.

That tenacity comes from her earliest days, growing up in Nowa Sarzyna, Poland, then emigrating to New Jersey with her parents at eight years old. Rolling into a new country without knowing the language at that age is already hard enough. Imagine having to learn a new tongue *and* to skateboard in the Northeast. That's asking a lot, but that's just what happened. After she stumbled into watching a contest at an X Games in Philly that featured one of the first ladies of skateboarding, the great Cara-Beth Burnside (see page 12), the skate angels aimed at Amelia's heart and hit a bull's-eye.

Now, Amelia and I share several things in common, and one of those is growing up skating the East Coast, a different beast from skating in the sunshine of San Diego, L.A.'s Dogtown, and the like. Back east, *all* the weather hits, and during the winter, the icy ground hits back hard. That's not counting the fact that when it comes to the non-skating public, well, the vibes can be hella harsh toward skateboarding. However, Amelia had support from her parents, which eventually landed her deep in New England at a Maine boarding school with a little makeshift ramp for her to skate. With her parents' focus on education, as is often the case with immigrant families, finding the middle ground between studying and skateboarding became the best way for Amelia to think about the future.

While there weren't many women skaters around in Maine, that did not keep her from making professional skateboarding her goal. A true skate rat, she hit the Amtrak, the Greyhound, the school bus caravan, the hitchhike, and the couch-crash just to get to better skate spots and improve the outlook of her skate life.

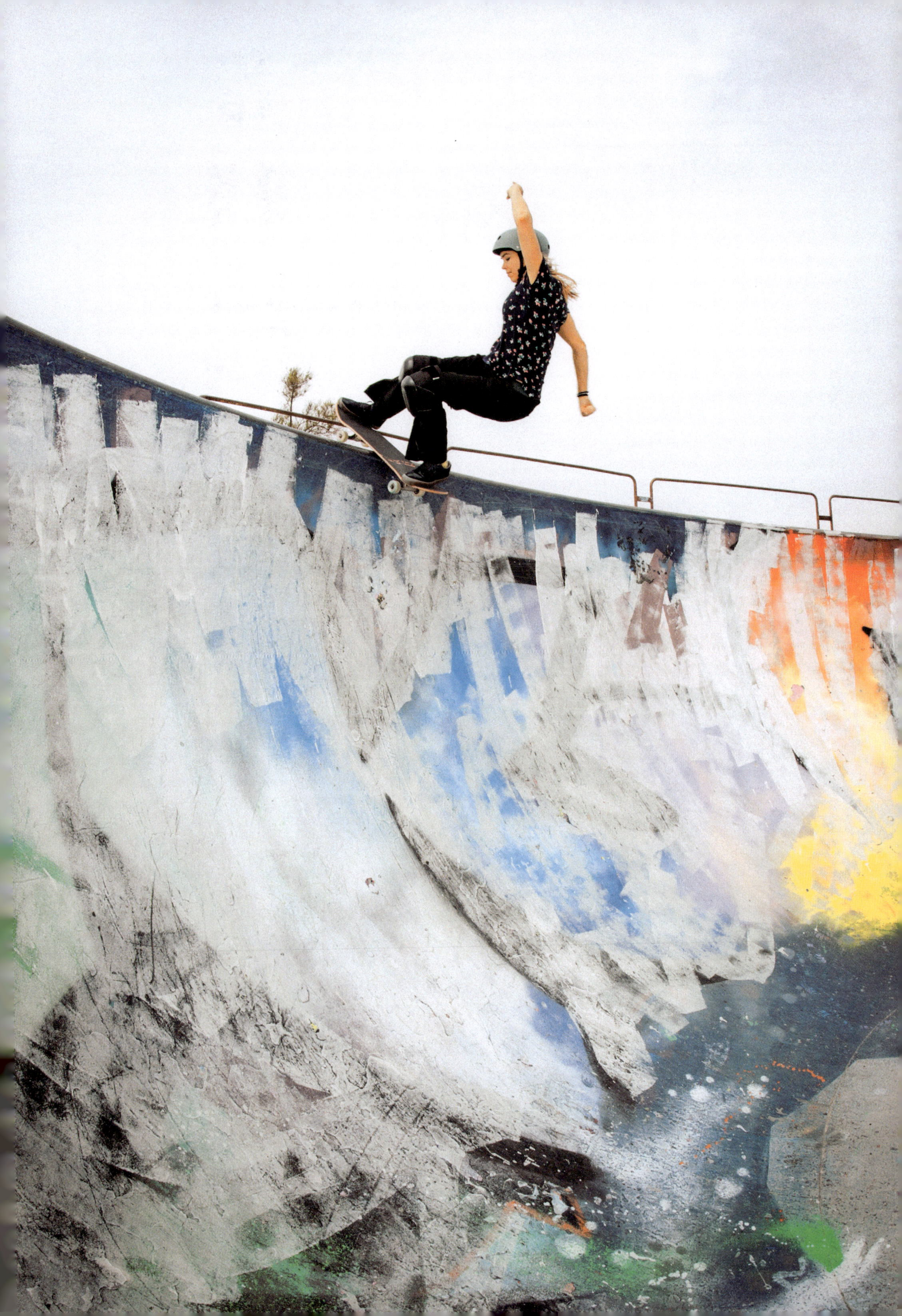

Those first endeavors and that love of skateboarding paid off when she set out a plan to make her life revolve around skating. She crafted a painstakingly detailed pitch to her parents about the caliber of the schools in California and also kept in mind her goal of applying only to schools within 60 miles of a vert ramp. She landed in L.A. for school and San Diego for home. I've been lucky enough to be close to Amelia for a chunk of that journey. We were at USC simultaneously, two skate rats on campus working on separate projects—me on the framework for skate diplomacy and education, and Amelia shooting her groundbreaking documentary *Underexposed* (2014) about the lack of women's representation in skate media. The award-winning film would go on to change the skate world by providing a deep dive into how the industry either tacitly or passively excluded women from the sponsored and pro ranks.

Besides her activism behind the camera, Amelia was also a best-in-decades talent. She had the skate game on lock, and not just street skating—Amelia's accolades came from skating vert. Yep, of all the skating she could be doing, this boss of all bosses skates vert, the most challenging terrain to skate. I've seen grown men drop to their knees and then stomachs to peer over the edge of a ramp with one to two feet vert.

That's exactly what became the impetus for the documentary. Where were the contests and the opportunities for women and girls like Amelia to show their skills? They were nowhere to be found. Within that context, the documentary asked crucial questions, and Amelia provided the answers. Rather than waiting for things to change, she did the damn thing herself.

After releasing *Underexposed*, she developed Exposure, a women-only skate event that became the most prominent women's and nonbinary skateboarding event in the world. From Vanessa to Bryce, Sky to Leticia, and Coco to Arisa, the greatest women skateboarders passed through her San Diego event.

That level of participation and growth came from ignoring the skateboarding adage that she had to be "core" and only have sponsors endemic to skateboarding, like a sneaker or skateboarding brand, as had been the case for a majority of skateboarding's history. Instead, she took sponsors that had relevance for women in particular—from women's health and wellness to beauty and beyond. She eventually placed the (gasp) women-centric brands alongside the previously mostly male-centric skateboarding brands now clamoring to get in on the action. The same brands who claimed they didn't have the money to invest in women's skateboarding eventually came around with pay and support.

This has been one of the great successes of Exposure: Amelia provided the best crop of talent of women and young girls anywhere. In turn, *everyone* realized they had been ignoring a growing demographic of women rippers. She used to feel trepidation when she called core skate brands and media, but now they reach out to shoot photos of her and be directed to new people in the women's and nonbinary movement. The irony is that Amelia grew a home for all women and for the LGBTQ+ community in her *adopted* home—the skateboarding industry's backyard.

Amelia also added a level of service that had never been present in the skate world prior. Rather than focusing on herself and her mission, she thought about others less fortunate. For the past 13 years, Exposure has also given back to victims of domestic violence by doing supply drives for the Community Resource Center, a shelter and transitional housing organization located in North County San Diego.

Watching her now, you would never know that Amelia had ever experienced any trepidation when working with major skate brands. She is the go-to person when it comes to women's events for every brand from Vans to Etnies, from the Boardr to the IOC, and a leader in the field. Even my students line up to volunteer for her and Exposure, with two former students becoming staff at her organization.

Amelia's efforts have also earned her a place as the voice of a generation as an announcer for the Olympics and the X Games. She has her own pro model with Arbor Skateboards, and is not only the sight but also the sound of skateboarding in SoCal, where she hosts "The Skate Report" on 91XFM in San Diego and Mexico. She also realized her dream of being in *Thrasher* years ago. Now her dreams are bigger and continue to come true. One of them included finding a lifelong partner, and in true #skatelife fashion, her husband, Alec Beck, is not only a ripping skater but a fellow activist as well. And as all fairy tales go, the beginning of their union started off as authentic to skate life as could be, when after years together Alec proposed to her after performing an air and then sliding to one knee on the deck of the Vans Combi Pool—a replica of one of the most significant skate spots in history—while she was announcing a skate contest live on air. She of course answered yes and delivered a storybook ending for the ages.

BRIANA KING

Founder of Girl and Queer Skate Sesh

BIPOC skateboarding activist and community organizer

Pro skater for There Skateboards, one of the first LGBTQ+–led skateboarding companies

Quintessential It Girl for our times

Skater. Friend. Model. Actress. Activist. Manifester of dreams—these are a few names of crowd favorite . . . B.King.

Yep, go ahead and sing her praises. A beacon to women and queer skaters and anyone who loves skateboarding culture, the late-20s / early-30s (Black people don't tell on each other like that) Briana King has put skateboarding on the map in new arenas, all while keeping BIPOC and LGBTQ+ skaters and would-be skaters (coz really isn't everyone) in the limelight. Rarely has someone exploded on the scene and been so many things to so many people in so short a time. You need her for a skate meetup so that BIPOC folx feel seen? She there. Need her for the Jordan ad? (Yep, she's Jordan certified.) She ready. Need her to put that extra swag in your Dior ad? Done. Need her for a study about skateboarding's effect on mental health (our team's work)? Yep, she turns up in spades.

Besides being the most in-demand queen of all trades for skateboarding and the fashion industry, if you ask anyone in her crew, she is the also glue for her skate community and the dreamer of a bigger, broader world of skateboarding where everyone is included. Unlike skaters who find their place in skateboarding by what tricks they can do, Briana helps others see that tricks are only one part of skateboarding.

While she attempted to skate early in her teens, the L.A. native didn't find her skateboarding self until a bit later in life. Part of that stemmed from an early injury that would take a decade to repair.

Heading west to California has been the historical route to reinvention in the U.S. Who *docsn't* want to forget their past and bask in powder-pink-hued

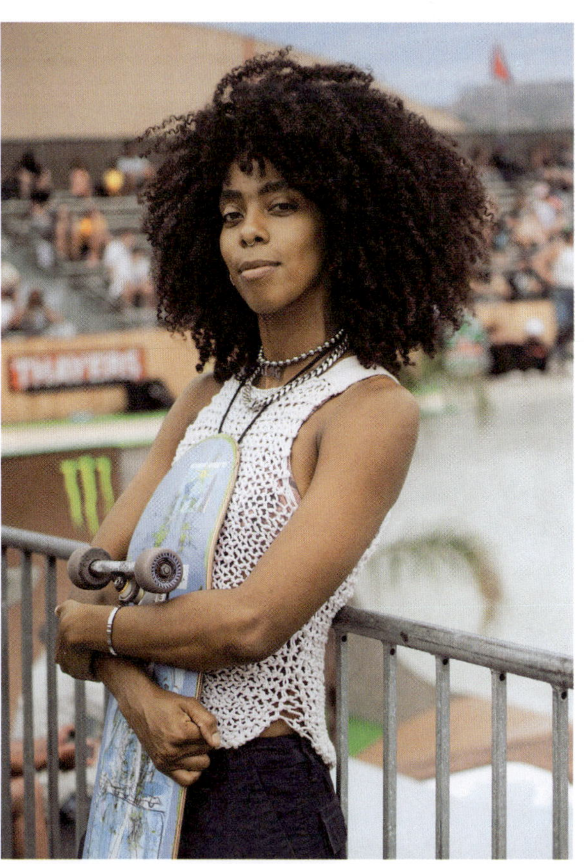

sunsets off the Pacific, then change clothes—and go? That is just the path Briana took when she told me she bounced from LAX to Oz to chase a bit of a dream. She found her voice, style, and swag in Australia, where she began to model and was reminded that skateboarding looks lit everywhere—always. Living across from a skatepark and the ocean, as she would recall, she didn't skate or surf, yet both would become integral to her life later.

Once she returned to the States in 2017 and began modeling in New York City, the thirst for skateboarding from her youth called her back. She went from watching it to thinking incessantly about skating. And this time, fear wouldn't get in the way. She answered the call regardless of what anyone may have thought about this Black woman stepping on board and creating space for herself. In a short time she found a crew of women and queer folk to skate with and began to realize that she wasn't the only one unsure about whether she belonged at the skatepark. Corralling space with kinfolk in New York City, she would return to L.A. and bring that spirit of creating belonging. She became what she didn't see at first—a Black woman leading the pack at the park. She manifested her dream and not only led some of the most attended skate meetups, she became the quintessential It Girl, using her platform as an activist, model, and influencer to help others stand with her and find their own light. It's no wonder that everyone is seeking her out for any and every campaign. Even Virgil Abloh (RIP) found her and brought her into his collective. With the world vying for her attention, Briana still chose to give back, even if that meant working with other skaters on Zoom to help build out the first USC-TSP (The Skatepark Project) skate study and add the element that had been missing from most skate academic work at the time—the voices of women and LGBTQ+ folks.

Skaters from every background saw that she was the real deal. She loved and shed blood for skateboarding. Moving fast and breaking norms and stereotypes—that makes anyone a 100 percent skateboarder every time. Once, Briana embodied that ethos so much that when trying to satisfy someone else's artistic concept around skateboarding, she put herself in peril so they could get the look they wanted for an ad. She broke her leg during the shoot, and still tried to go on and please the director.

Briana came to see me at USC one of the times she was hurt. Injuries can take an existential toll. What will happen when you're no longer It? Will people really be there for you? This young, strong, and independent woman who had been able to take the world by storm, build her own brand, and become a team member for There Skateboards was now faced with a slowed pace and a sudden need for help.

Briana was not afraid to come to the table with us and talk about how difficult those times were, and most important, to seek professional help. What came from the study was also her revelation of how much she loved her friends and how they cared for her even when there was no skateboarding, and during a time when she wasn't the It Girl. She was their lit girl and they were rolling with her no matter what. Since then, she has become an even greater advocate for mental and physical health and built sharing that with more people into her practice.

Now she is a pro skater for There Skateboards, and her women- and queer-led skate meetups intersect with her identity as a skater, a Black woman, and an ambassador for Jordan and Givenchy.

I saw her at a contest recently, with adoring fans and fams, and it was as it was meant to be. A bright light on this Black woman reinventing skateboarding for those who didn't know they had a space. Afterward people asked me, *You know her?* Hmm, I believe I do.

BRIANA KING HAS PUT SKATEBOARDING ON THE MAP IN NEW ARENAS, ALL WHILE KEEPING BIPOC AND LGBTQ+ SKATERS AND WOULD-BE SKATERS (COZ REALLY ISN'T EVERYONE) IN THE LIMELIGHT.

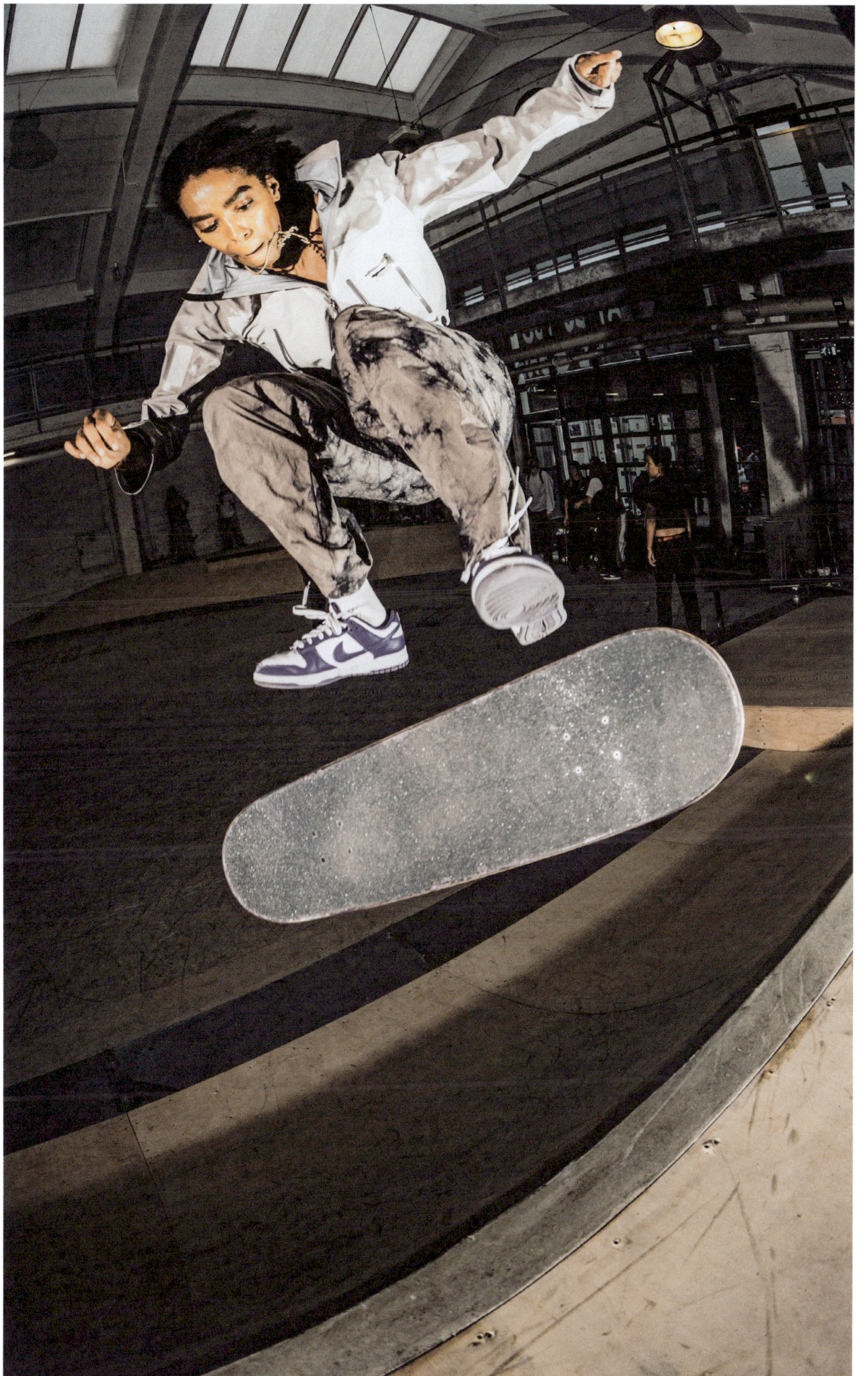

MILES JACKSON & LAUREN BRADLEY OF CUBA SKATE

Cofounders of groundbreaking international skateboarding NGO Cuba Skate

Building skateparks and delivering skate supplies

A decade and counting of building bridges between the U.S. and Cuba

With 10 years under their belt, many nonprofits and NGOs can say that they have put in good work toward their causes, but for Miles Jackson, founder and executive director of the nonprofit Cuba Skate, there is no time for resting. "It's just a drop in the bucket compared to the amount of time the embargo or 'blockade' has existed between the U.S. and Cuba," he says. Enough said. As a duo on a mission, Miles and cofounder Lauren Bradley have been working to steadily defuse eight decades of tensions between the two countries by engaging in humanitarian efforts centered on the exploration of where skateboarding could sit in the Cuban sport and cultural pantheon.

During my time with Miles, he has often discussed how Cuba exists in the minds of Americans. "People think Cuba is just a magical land with cigars and old-school cars and exotic locales," he says. "They don't realize how the fight with the U.S. causes so many hardships for the Cuban people. The lack of access to basic resources is devastating." For skaters in Cuba, this of course means there are no skate shops, no skateboards, no skate shoes to outfit the pool of talented skaters that is growing seemingly against all odds, but unable to regularly pursue skateboarding.

Cuban skaters steeped in skateboarding culture are painfully aware of how that lack of access affects their individual and collective identities as skaters. I've seen firsthand how connected they are to U.S. and global skate culture, through the dog-eared issues of *Thrasher* and *TransWorld SKATEboarding* magazines, smuggled in like contraband.

In 2010, Miles Jackson and Lauren Bradley, both in their early 20s, plotted a path toward a better future after an educational exchange in Cuba through their alma mater, University of Michigan. Miles was not even a full-fledged street skater at the time, yet in his earliest pushes around the island he saw the difficulty in operating in Cuba. The lack of a proper skate shop to center the community and provide boards and shoes instantly stifled progression. As any new skater knows, nothing is worse than going hard, avoiding security, and shedding blood, sweat, and tears skating a perfect spot, only to break your board. Then what?

A board break like that in Cuba means you are out a lot more than just your transportation home. A broken board might put you out of commission for weeks or months. Why you ask? While sports are the lifeblood of Cuba, the informal nature of skateboarding, and its use of the cityscape, makes it unruly and contested there. Equal parts aggression and reflection, it pushes back on traditional sports power norms with its lack of hierarchy. Which is just what young Cuban skaters are after—a sense of freedom and agency. Yet it also holds to Cuban goals of collectivism and shared learning. A win-win for both the U.S. and Cuba. Beyond that, it offers Cuban skaters a new way to process their identity through the beauty of urban exploration.

With status as a U.S. NGO and a 501(c)(3) nonprofit based in D.C., L.A., and Havana, Cuba Skate follows the protocols necessary to operate in compliance with the American and Cuban governments, and is authorized by the U.S. State Department to run programs in Cuba.

When Miles and Lauren arrived, they saw the community there and the ingenuity and undeniable spirit of the Cuban skaters who would later become part of the original crew of Cuba Skate's team, 23yG. That's the name of the intersection of streets and a small park in Havana, which equates to one of the original spaces where skaters in Cuba cut their teeth. That intersection is corralled by the mashup of cement and green space that runs down the middle of a major boulevard. Equipped with ledges, stairs, and a slight downhill runup, it's one of the most skateable spots in the city.

Truthfully, while there are some spots that are skateable in Cuba, in general it is difficult to move forward figuratively and literally as a skater. It is a harsh environment and that's both from the attitudes toward skaters as vagrants and trespassers and the actual lived environment. A pair of skate shoes might last you a few months in the U.S. but in Cuba, there's a serious half-life to everything. The unpaved roads, the rough concrete, the tropical weather pushing sweat through your socks and shoes, and the humidity that prompts tropical downpours all contribute to turning your flash into trash.

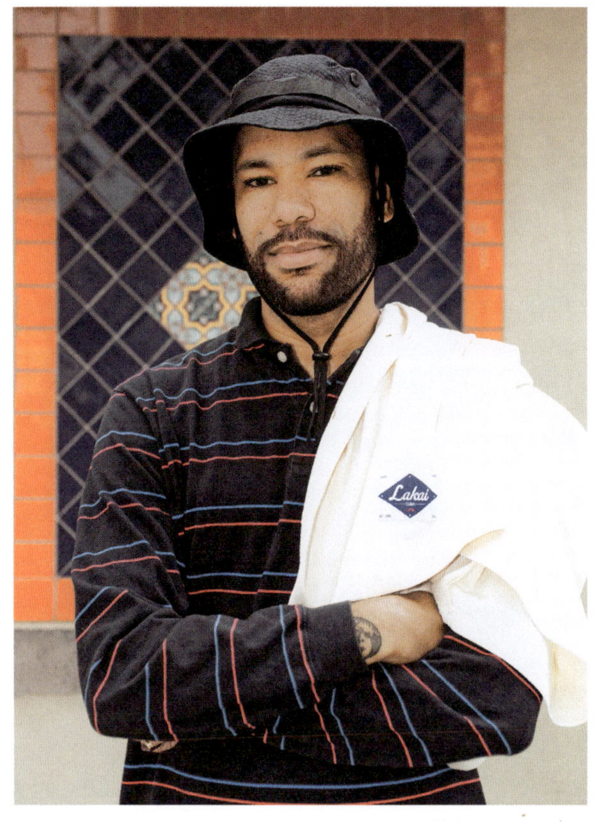

The same goes for your boards, which start to go "soggy"—they lose their stiffness from humidity's moisture getting into the glue and the wood and warping them. If the boards do last through that, they also become razor tails (when the back of a board constantly makes contact with the ground) super quickly, because the ground is rough asphalt, pudding stone, and porous concrete. That means a board that might last a few months in nearby Miami is gone in a few days.

Facts is facts, Cuba is not for the faint of heart. That's why only the lionhearted skated, prompting Miles and Lauren to think how special skateboarding was to Cubans who participated; for them it was a way to find individual expression and build community as *patinadores*—as

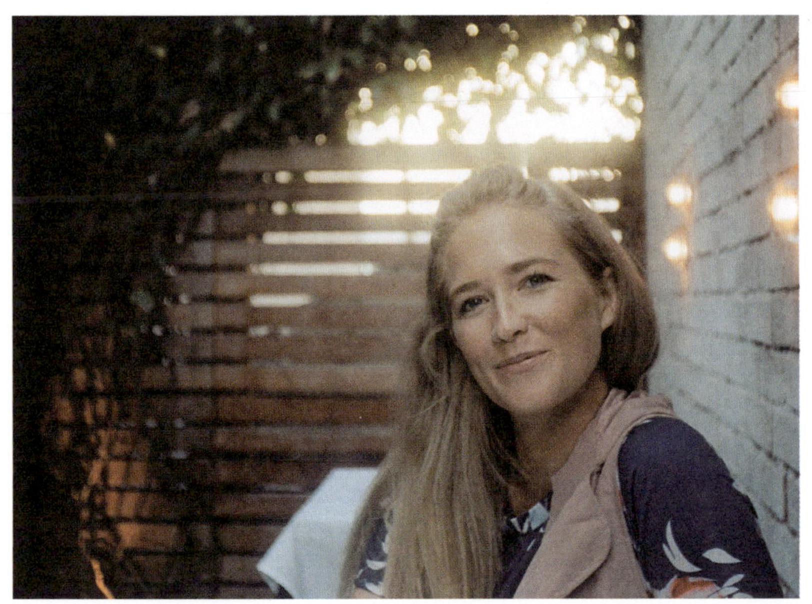

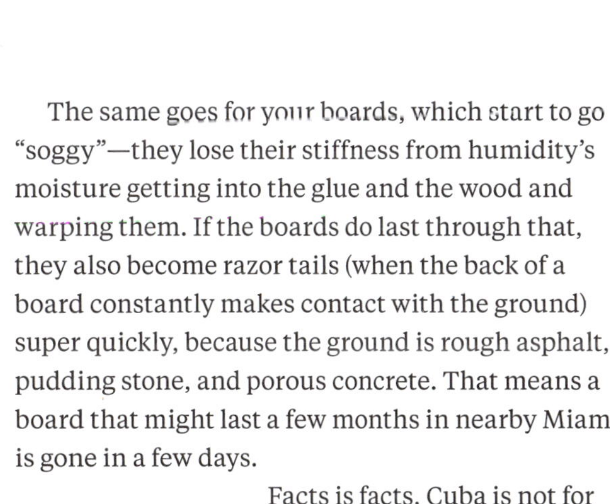

Cofounders of Cuba Skate:
Miles Jackson (top),
Lauren Bradley (bottom)

skaters. Miles saw the promise in the skaters in Cuba and set the wheels in motion to bring Cuba Skate to life. They would return to the U.S. and bring skateboards to the country as part of a larger humanitarian and educational agenda and put the word out to the global skate community that these skaters were worth the attention.

From that extemporaneous idea, flash forward more than 10 years. The work accomplished by Cuba Skate has created a network dedicated to bringing money, time, and people power together so that U.S. skaters and Cuban skaters can grow together. Whether it's building DIY skateparks in the midst of abandoned buildings outside Havana or scouring the world to deliver low-fi, transportable tech so that skaters can press their own boards, Cuba Skate's goal is to furnish whatever is necessary to build love, compassion, and understanding between the U.S. and Cuba.

While there has been plenty of positive press on Cuba Skate in the U.S. and internationally, those glowing reviews didn't happen overnight. The U.S. government questioned how their work aligned with American values of freedom in a communist space. Was Cuba Skate simply a new form of U.S.-led collegiate communist sympathizers? The Cuban government, for its part, questioned where skateboarding and its projected antiestablishment streaks fit into a society focused on collectivism. Who were these young American apostles attempting to develop the near "anti-sport" of skateboarding and what right did they have to engage with Cuban youth? Those types of questions led to stoppages on both sides of the border—yet Miles and Lauren rolled on tirelessly, bringing boards back and forth across the border to do the humanitarian work of providing resources to skaters and sharing the message that skaters across the world and across the U.S. borders have love for the skaters of Cuba.

Those donations came directly from skaters in the U.S. who gave their old and new boards to their local skate shop so they could be collected, shipped, and distributed to skaters on the island. The difficulty in coordinating all of this is astounding. Skaters throughout the U.S., sending UPS packages to Miles and Lauren every day? At any given moment, their home resembled a war room, with pushpinned diagrams, maps, and a fire-hazard level of sticky notes lining the walls, halls, and flooring. Skaters visiting, checking visas and passports, and dropping in to be assigned tasks: Who is going on the trip? Who is running logistics, counting products, answering phone calls and emails? It was

a 24-hour operation—difficult for any organization, but particularly one run by twentysomethings still earning their degrees in international relations and public diplomacy when not working day jobs at the local skate shop and veterinary firms. It wasn't easy, but their drive created space for a dialogue between this next generation of skaters and those in the continental U.S.

During the second Obama administration, relations thawed between the two countries. Cuba Skate caught fire and the org began to gain support and visibility. Global media from PBS to NBC, CBS to the BBC all came knocking, excited to see how the org navigated the dance of diplomacy. They weren't the first skaters to work on the island.

Recognition also came in from the skateboarding community. Miles went from skating on his own with his Cuban friends to leading exploratory trips with some of skateboarding's finest.

Miles told me, "In Cuba, there is a phrase that means you help someone and don't expect anything in return. That's the Cuban way. I try to never forget it."

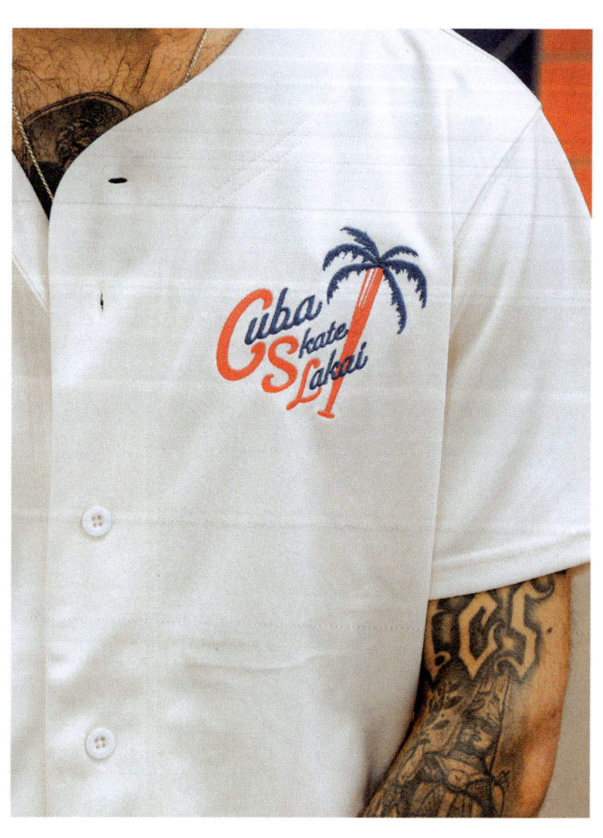

LIVING THEIR TRUTH

LEO BAKER

X Games gold medalist

Epitomizes inclusivity

Subject of the documentary *Stay On Board*

Celebrated pro skater L. Baker was a leading voice in the world of women's skateboarding and heading toward the Olympics with the U.S. team. All that changed when they decided to live out loud and reintroduce themselves to the world as the now much-lauded changemaker, activist, and celebrated male pro skater Leo Baker.

That was perhaps the most daring maneuver anyone had ever accomplished in skateboarding, choosing to move undeterred in a world as harsh as ours. One that bans books on inclusion and dares anyone to suggest any notion of inequality.

After years of personal reflection, and despite these pressures and with a promising career arc then on the cusp of taking them to the Tokyo Olympics, Leo altered their path and embodied a skateboarding mantra: Do what matters to you.

Some things are worth everything, and this was one of them. Their story resonated at the right frequency for the world to notice. They became a staunch advocate for LGBTQ+ rights and have been seen in everything from magazine covers to Nike ads. Their ability to talk about the process of transitioning and the obstacles they faced offers a new generation a way to see skateboarding as a place where diverse voices might contribute to a deeper discussion and understanding of what it means to be inclusive.

I knew Leo during their younger days as part of the Element family, at the time when Johnny Schillereff (see page 231) ran the company and was trying to ensure space for women in his skateboarding team. That crew was a one-of-a-kind group. It was Leo, Vanessa Torres, and Amy Caron, a group put together by the famed Lisa Whitaker, founder of Meow. In those days, they were running a tight clique, and they were killing it skating in contests, filming videos, and making a name for themselves in productions like the Villa Villa Cola *Getting Nowhere Faster* video and a slew of others.

Leo put in the work, skating a good mix of everything and excelling on street, on their way to possibly turning pro. That is until the bottom fell out of the skateboarding industry in the mid-aughts. The 2008 financial crisis caused most skate companies to cut their rosters to meet budget deficits, and Element didn't re-up our protagonist's new contract. In that instance, Leo lost their love for the industry, which had always given women the last-hired-first-fired treatment, even when times were good.

Despite the lack of support, the skills in their repertoire remained. Their game was so tight that they were able to leave skateboarding professionally to earn an art degree, get a job in L.A., and then roll up into contests and podium without a sponsor. That is a *hard* flex, *chéri*.

Leo consistently placed in every street skating contest and could put a real hurt on the competition. The X Games records bring it all to light: bronze in street at the 2006 games, then a banging gold in 2014; back-to-back wins in 2016, 2017, and 2018. As discussions about who should represent Team USA in the 2020 Olympics came around, they were the premier person in women's skateboarding and broadly considered a likely contender for a medal. I remember the Baker fervor hitting globally. I was in Norway during the

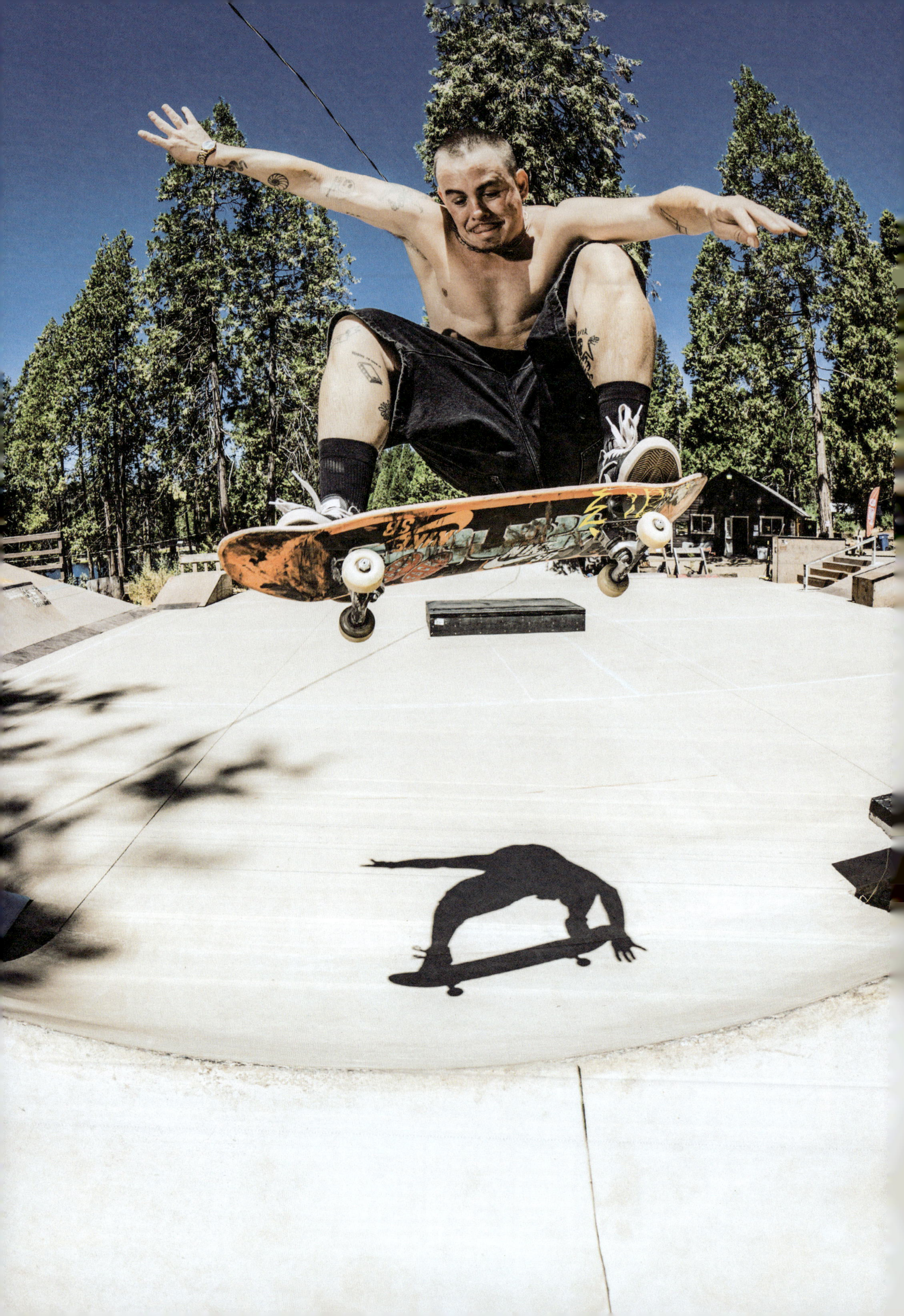

X Games in the summer of 2018, and my phone was blowing up from the Norwegian homies taking photos of Leo Baker and Ryan Sheckler, skateboarding royalty.

Perhaps all of this could bring Leo joy. Instead, as Leo told *Time* magazine, they weren't happy within their skin. It was time for a drastic change. That was the beginning of the transition to Leo. Lots of support came from skaters like superstar Brian Anderson, who had recently come out publicly in a video for Vice Sports directed by legendary photographer Giovanni Reda, and the skateboarding community and the world at large took notice. The vid helped provide perspective on Brian's relationship with his husband and how keeping his sexuality under lock and key had continually diminished his mental health. He feared losing his comrades and sponsors but could no longer lead a double life. Coming out offered his true friends the opportunity to support him and provided him with the peace of mind to move forward as unburdened as life might allow.

Leo embarked on a similar path. They were in an even more precarious situation than Brian. Since the early 1990s, men's skateboarding has relied on filming video parts and limited the need for contests to gain a following. Not so for women's skateboarding. When sponsors' checks were drying up, those contests provided money and exposure for women skaters. Those winnings gave Leo the credibility to be a substantial part of the discussion of what women's skateboarding might look like in the future.

With their transition under way, there was no place for them at the Tokyo Olympics. The points Leo had accrued through contests were for the women's events. The Olympics did not have a space for nonbinary folks in every sport, though hopefully that is on the horizon.

Missing out on the Olympics is part of what came to light when Leo began working with Reda on the documentary *Stay On Board: The Leo Baker Story* (2022). Leo had requested that if they were to participate in a documentary based on their experience, Reda—one of the most storied photographers and now videographers—would be the person hitting record and representing skateboarding in a manner authentic to the culture. Reda, who is a cisgender Italian American man, wanted to apply a holistic approach to honoring Leo and their legacy, so he partnered with a LGBTQ+ principal videographer and team, who were best equipped to represent the LGBTQ+ community accurately. It was a daunting task, but together, they attempted to cover the complexity of the life before them, forever changed by a decision to be their authentic self.

There would be no first time at the Olympics, no Wheaties box, and no Toyota deals. There would only be Leo. The film was universally lauded and provided a growth moment for all of skateboarding because of Leo's bravery. With a renewed sense of self, Leo departed Meow Skateboards—a brand that had been home for them since its inception. Wind at their back, Leo took the initiative to launch Glue skateboards with another set of genre-defining friends: Cher Strauberry and Stephen Ostrowski. Under Glue, skateboarding continues to progress with more queer and transgender skaters finding mentors, heroes, and people who look like them and reflect their experiences. Leo Baker has created a new lane: one where skateboarding is for everyone and can be precisely what you make of it.

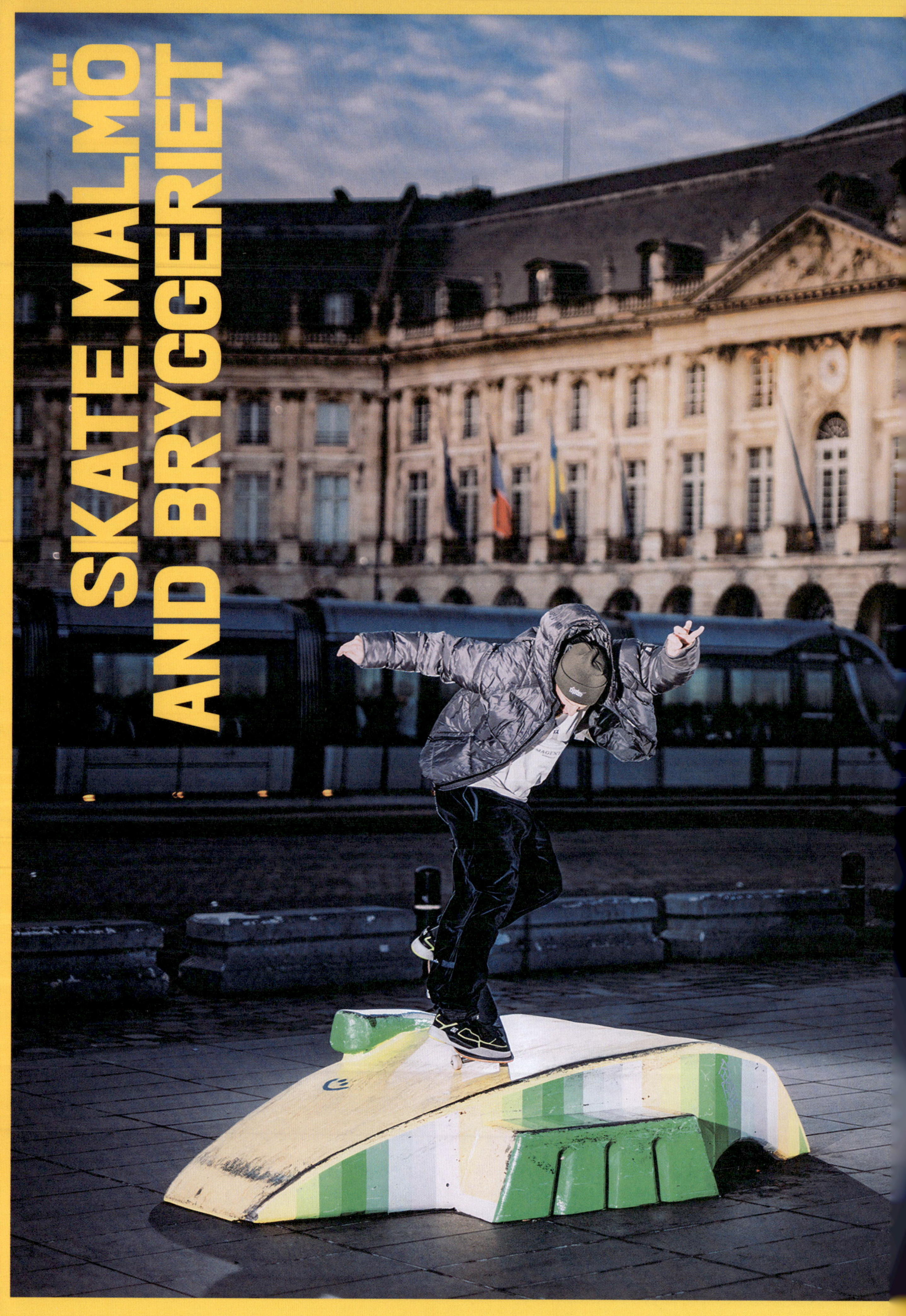
SKATE MALMÖ
AND BRYGGERIET

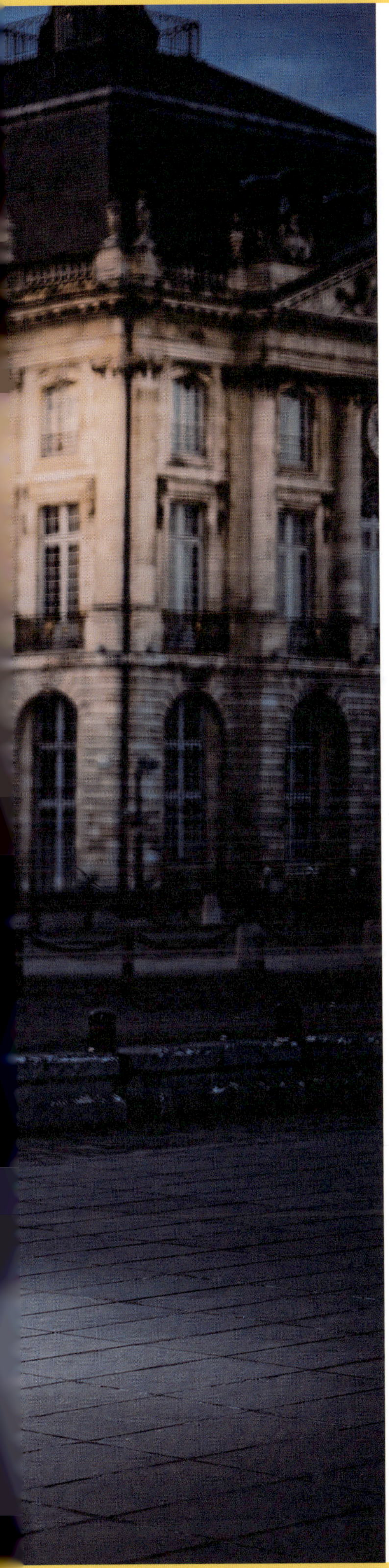

The City of Skate: Malmö, Sweden. Located in the country's south and the third-largest city in the land, Malmö offers hope for a bright skate-centric future and is leading the way in making cities more skateable, which, it turns out, makes them more livable for everyone.

Want to activate that underused area? Place a skate sculpture there and see how quickly it becomes a hot spot for young people. Then that will give birth to a hip coffee shop. Slowly but surely a vegan place will move in, and a skate shop. Then a café/bar will open to serve drinks to the skaters, who of course are also involved in the creative economy. Those same skaters are getting married, eventually buying their first homes and having their first children—all near those same first skate spots in the cities that supported their skate life. Build it and they will stay—and thrive. In fact, they will raise a new generation that will also enjoy the fruits of the city's labor.

Malmö even has Bryggeriet's Gymnasium, a high school with skateboarding as its focus. How's that for a city being responsive to its citizens!

Bryggeriet is a marvel, and stands as a testament to the skaters and young students who created an academic group to advocate within Malmö for a scholastic institution centered on their passion. Today, not only can the school teach you the skills you need to land a job in the real world, it can also prepare you for a career as a pro skater thanks to the professional-quality indoor park on campus. For those in the arts, there is a full multimedia lab where skaters can work toward a career behind the lens within the action sports industry, while still earning the credits needed for a high school diploma. They can learn from some of the best photographers in the world, such as Marcel Veldman, founder of the Netherlands' *Fluff* magazine, or learn what it takes to compete in the X Games and the Olympics from Malmö pro skater Oskar "Oski" Rozenberg Hallberg (himself a graduate of the school). The vice principal, John Dahlquist, a lifelong skater, is now writing a book that highlights his philosophy of skateboarding and running the school. He has also served as team manager and head coach in charge of training other countries' athletes for skateboarding's Olympic debut in 2021, and offers his expertise to international skateboarding nonprofits. Hopefully other countries will begin to adopt the skateboarding high school model and be able to inspire more young students the world over to excel in academics while centering their love of skateboarding.

Bryggeriet makes perfect sense here. Skate Malmö, an effort led by Malmö's official skateboarding coordinator, Gustav Svanborg Edén, has created a city that welcomes skaters as citizens who bring value to the community. Edén's was the world's first city-sponsored role in charge of skateboarding. Since 2014, he's done yeoman's placemaking work as well as welcoming global skate tourism to the city. Thanks to this and more, the municipality and the nonskating residents have built an enviable rapport with skaters.

The city has embraced skateboarding as a legitimate form of transportation, a sporting activity, and a lifestyle. In turn, skaters the world over have visited Malmö and sung its praises as the city of the

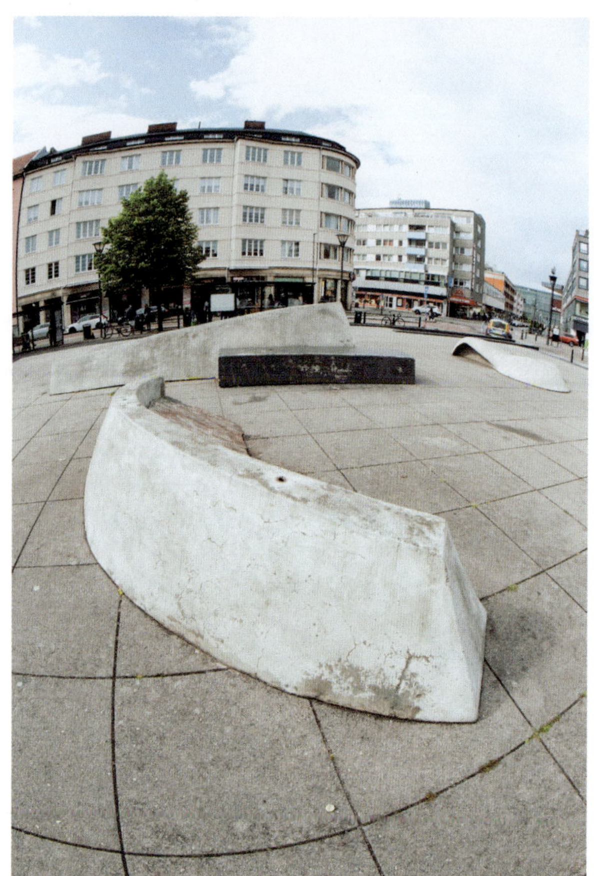

inform the city that as citizens, they deserved to have their needs met.

While they were marching on city hall, they had already been successful in reclaiming areas around the city that were in disuse. One of the originals was the Pig Barrier, a collection of yellow-painted transitions located near an unused warehouse area that helped give skaters the feel of a backyard pool in compact form and provided a place to hone their transition or mini-ramp skating skills. There is a remarkable level of dedication to the OG spot that continues to this day, and there are always changes and new obstacles being introduced here. It is home to skateboarding and summer barbecues and is a place where all skaters feel the wild elements, sloshing and pouring concrete, shaping it and sipping a brew during the 17 to 18 hours of daylight that come with being this far north.

Maybe it's that extra time in the sun that helps them be so productive. Not only is there the Pig Barrier, but there is the DIY near an industrial train line along an obsolete bike path. Malmö is an extremely bike-friendly city (near Netherlands levels), and when a path of smooth ground near the train station *and* behind a factory was no longer being used by the municipality, well, leave it to the skaters to create a series of amazing small quarter-pipes, wedges, ledges, and a smorgasbord of unnameable but fully skateable concrete objects up and down the path. You need to see it to believe it.

While the skaters created those and other wonderful spots across the city, like the wedge ledge built into the brick banks of an overpass originally built to escape those rainy fall and winter months that also come early up north, their relationship with the city blossomed as well. This led to the not-at-all DIY installation of skateable sculptures designed by Olympian Alexis Sablone (see page 254). Malmö has also taken top honors in the city diplomacy space, partnering with artists to create skateable sculptures that are either re-created or shipped between the cities of Malmö, Toronto, and Bordeaux. (Bordeaux's movement is gaining traction so quickly that it has moved beyond installations into developing an academic conference spearheaded by Magenta Skateboards pro skater Leo Valls, pictured in this section.)

At the time of this writing, the latest and greatest activities within the skateable sculpture sphere involve a collaboration with the City of Philadelphia's Parks & Recreation department and the celebrated Love Park benches and ledges. Thanks to Gustav's efforts and Skate Malmö, these ledges have been shipped to Sweden, restored, and used to create a deep cultural connection.

future. Gustav has also worked with Dr. Karin Book, a professor at Malmö University, to discuss the phenomenon that is Malmö and how its approach can be incorporated into other cities.

Malmö has been home to multiday events like Oski Blast, a series of family-friendly skateboarding sessions in the streets and in parks. (The name comes from Malmö's own pro skater Oskar "Oski" Rozenberg Hallberg.)

Now, before you get teary-eyed (trust me, I wept the first time I visited), it was not always that way. As Gustav tells it, in the mid-'90s there had been a more adversarial relationship between the city and its skaters, the classic us versus them. If you know, you know: if a city doesn't give skaters a place to skate, we will simply find it and make it our own—and watch out for the cops. This is the model for street skating in almost every other municipality in the world.

While skateboarding is now accepted and encouraged in Malmö, Gustav tells us that this is only because of the do-it-yourself ethic of the city's skaters, which manifested in two forms: first the skaters built what they could across the city, then they came together as a voting constituency to

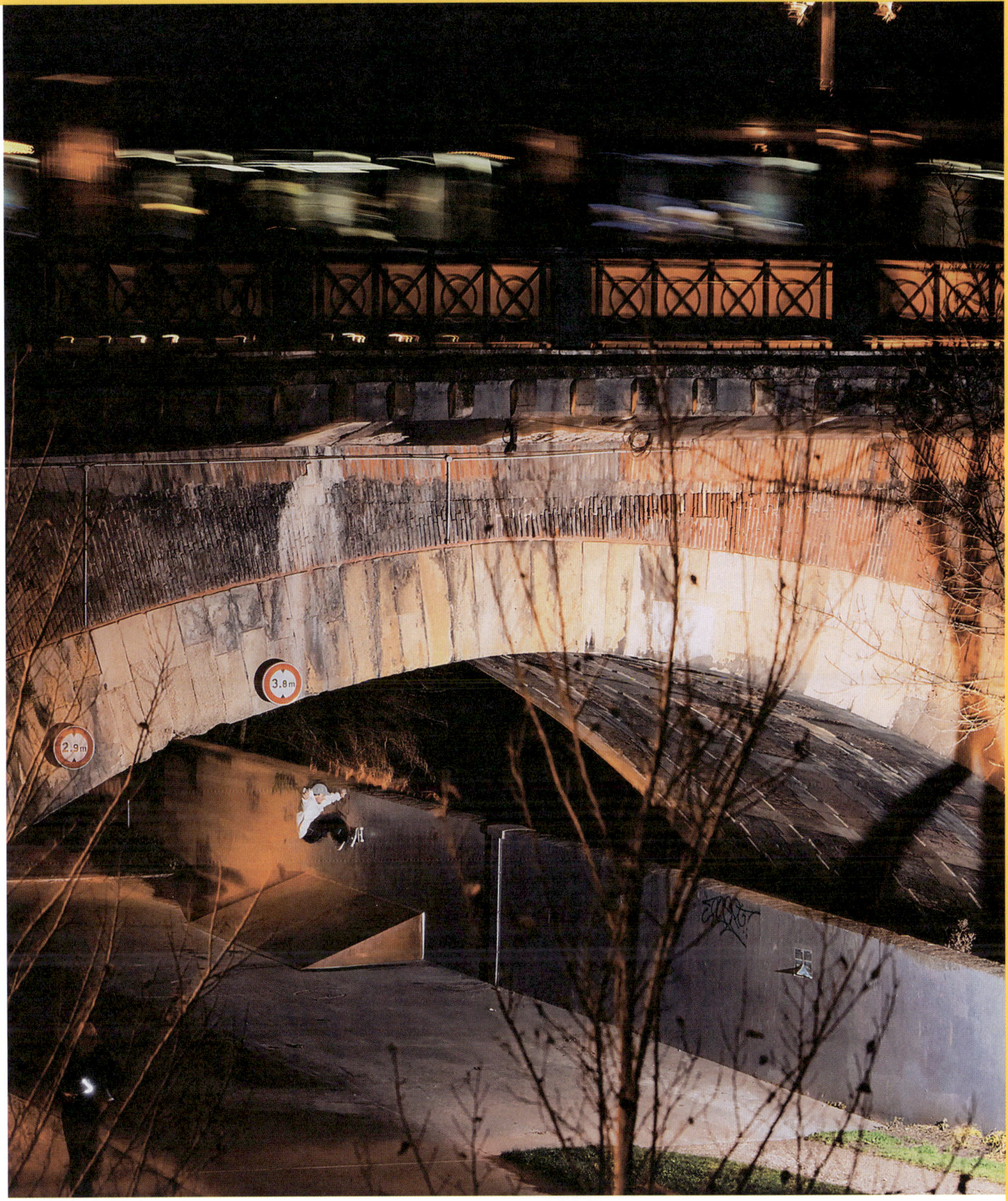

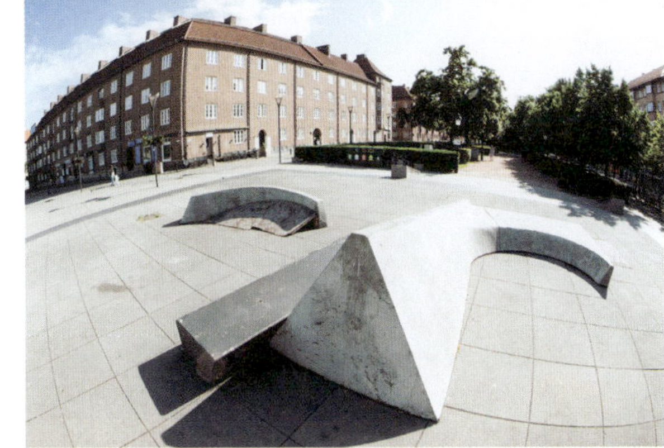

Opposite: A section of the
Alexis Slabone–designed
skateable sculpture, Malmö,
Sweden

Above: Leo Valls, frontside
wallride at Pointe de Pierre
in Bordeaux

Right: Close-up of the
Lady in the Square skate
sculpture in the public square,
Värnhemstorget, Malmö, Sweden

THE KEEPER OF THE FLAME IN WOMEN'S SKATEBOARDING
MIMI KNOOP

Women's high-performance director and coach for USA Skateboarding

Founder of the Women's Skateboarding Alliance

Cofounder of Hoopla Skateboards

Organized X Games boycott over pay equity

It was all a dream, I used to read Thrasher *magazine, Jen O'Brien, Cara-Beth blastin' airs over limousines. Hangin' pictures on my wall, every Saturday Gap Attack, Elissa Steamer, Vanessa T., and Jaime Reyes is on the call . . .*

By the time you read this, the dream of women's skateboarding as a fixture in the Olympics will have been in place for several Games. Sky Brown will have grown a foot taller and have another medal under her belt, Vanessa Torres will be a regular fixture on national TV preaching the gospel about action sports, culture, and the LGBTQ+ community. Samarria Brevard (see page 273) will have 360-flipped the Hollywood High stair set for a new *Thrasher* cover, and Bryce Wettstein (see page 252) and Rayssa Leal (see page 258) will have continued winning medals in park and street. Okay, so maybe that is my dream, but IRL, Bryce already won a bronze, Samarria nabbed a cover for a different trick, Vanessa announced at the Games, and Sky won Tokyo bronze. The accolades are sure to keep rolling in and these ladies are going to continue to live an Olympic-size dream life.

The actualization of the current and coming dreams of that group, and those of so many other talented girl and women skateboarders, owes a debt to the concerted efforts of the person aiding and supporting their dreams and truths: Mimi Knoop. Mimi gave voice to the need for greater equity in skateboarding, informed by slangin' more than a few boards for bread to make ends meet. Through it all, she pictured a momentous dream for all of women's skateboarding, for the Olympics and beyond, and while still in motion, the women's movement has continued to propel skateboarding in a better, more accessible direction, with no chance of it being returned to the old status quo.

Mimi's work with major brands like Nike, Sony, and Visa sees to that. As cofounder of the Women's Skateboarding Alliance, in 2005, and as USA Skateboarding's women's high-performance director, managing the national team programming for the 2020 Tokyo Olympics, Mimi ensured that all athletes were able to point their boards toward the sky. While the Olympics are in the limelight every four years, Knoop was the first to hold that job title in Tokyo, where she stood in the spotlight of the first U.S. skateboarding Olympic coaching movement. Sure, her title was a mouthful, but it's one worth savoring. It's a position decades in the making, and no less than what she deserves for her patience and perseverance and decades of women's representation.

Originally from Chesapeake, Virginia, a half-hour drive from Virginia Beach, Mimi embraced the skate life earlier and a tad differently than others. Beginning at age seven or eight is unique on its own, but the fact that she began skating during her father's stint on base in Cuba as a military physician puts a geographical spike in the punch. (One time,

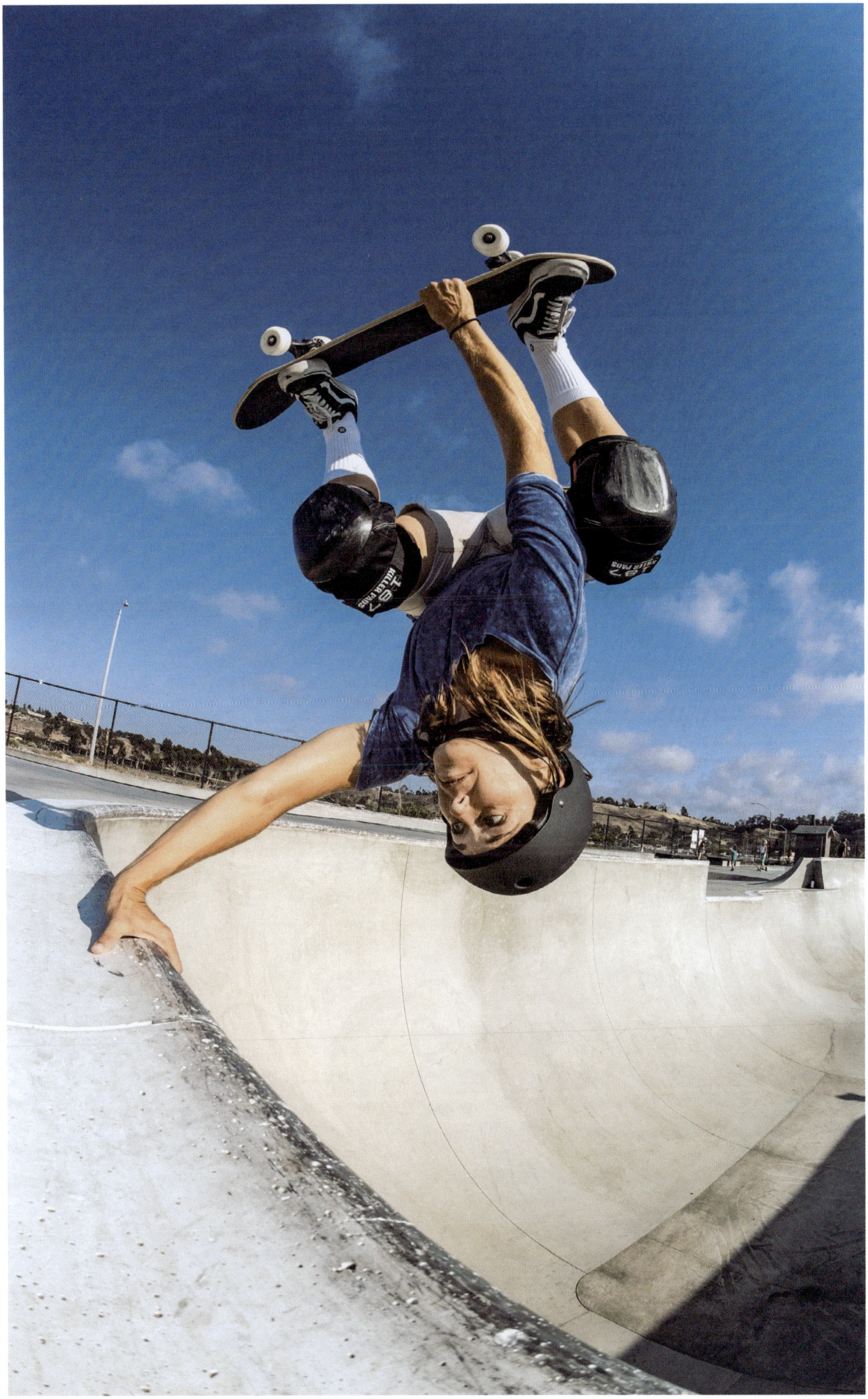

we bonded during our discussion of my work with the Cuba Skate NGO.) Where Mimi's parents saw skateboarding as child's play—which back then was only logical—she found a lifelong love affair.

Returning to Virginia after her father's residency in Cincinnati, Mimi found herself the only girl surrounded by multiple bands of brothers, but nevertheless felt supported during those early steps. Though she wouldn't meet another female skater

in person until she reached adulthood, she did see Cara-Beth Burnside on the cover of *Thrasher*. CB was one of the rare women to grace *Thrasher*'s pages in the early decades, and Mimi still cherishes that cover. Like many from that era, Mimi found that skateboarding became her lifeblood, but she never considered it a serious endeavor. A source of joy, sure, but payment for something you loved to do? Highly suspect—especially when coming from an East Coast state of mind. I felt those same sentiments skateboarding in and around Boston.

Rather than chase a dream, Mimi chased a degree, earning her B.A. in graphic design and fine arts at Radford University in Virginia. The possibility of a career in the skate life wouldn't manifest until she finally headed westward to San Diego County after several months of soaking up the sun in the Virgin Islands, working as a bartender and enjoying the good life. Initially searching for more waves, instead she found a rekindling with skateboarding. As a bonus, landing in skateboarding's ancestral home brought Mimi closer to more—although not tons more quite yet—sisters in skate. Once posted up in Encinitas, California, Mimi sought out bigger and better terrain, pools, ramps, and mega ramps—even though it's common knowledge that she is afraid of heights. Not one to let a little thing like fear stop her, Knoop dove headfirst into the literal deep end, and earned her first payday from skateboarding. That modest $100 prize purse lit a fire in her that has never burned out.

Reimagining a life where a paycheck and skateboarding might coexist, Mimi focused on competition. Digging deep, she honed her craft against and alongside the best in the business, regardless of gender, including heroes like Cara-Beth Burnside, Jen O'Brien, and Steve Caballero.

Turning pro in 2003, Mimi established herself as a fierce competitor, blasting big, smooth backside ollies out of the deep end of any pools daring to stand in her way. I'd advise you not to stand too close to the lip either because besides those face-high backside ollies, Mimi's aggressive "slash it and take no prisoners" approach is definitely gonna cost you a foot if you spend too much time gawking. As my class would attest, "Professor, she's super mellow and speaks softly—then turns the f#$k up at a contest!" You can thank them for the expletives. Knoop's "let it all hang out" approach served her well and landed her five medals during her X Games years.

As it happens, Mimi's "turnup" and power don't only apply to contests, as the X Games leadership found out. Unafraid to kick the hornet's nest, Mimi put her name on the line in pursuit of better pay for women in skateboarding, and organized a potential boycott of the 2005 women's X Games skateboarding contest. "It was just the right thing to do and for better or for worse, I didn't care about the consequences," she revealed to my class. Years later, the same X Games director who had pushed against her during the potential boycott praised her for sticking to her principles. It is those guiding principles of fairness and equity that led Mimi to continue to pursue change via the Women's Skateboarding Alliance.

Partnered with luminary women's skateboarding advocate Lisa Whitaker (see page 158) and others, Knoop guided multiple generations of women and nonbinary folx into the fold. The list of mentees reads like a roll call to skateboarding Valhalla—Torres, Brevard, Wettstein, Brodka, Caron, Sablone, just to name a few. While those names are sacrosanct now, back then many were neophytes, and the WSA offered much needed support across the board, literally and figuratively. The WSA acted as a linchpin, providing philanthropy for those in need of skate supplies, holding skate events, and providing athlete representation and consulting services for those interested in participating in learning, or supporting the WSA agenda.

While shepherding the future, Knoop remained a bastion for the sport, dominating the coveted Pro-Tec Pool Party Combi Bowl competition in back-to-back wins in 2013 and 2014. *Who else does that?* Those wins only added to Mimi's legitimacy among comrades and competitors. Though the Combi Pool would eventually dole out some retribution for her "skate and destroy" attitude (a wicked yearlong ankle injury), Knoop simply then hit the gas on her executive role at the Women's Skate Alliance, and on supporting other athletes' pursuit of medal counts.

An incredible moment of mentorship occurred during the Tokyo 2021 Olympic Games, when skater Alana Smith chose to write "they/them" as their pronouns on their grip tape. Shown during the broadcast of skateboarding's Olympic debut, it caused just as much of an international ruckus as you might expect. Other coaches and countries might have scoffed at personal politics taking center stage, breaking the Olympics' cardinal rule, yet Mimi was *there* offering unwavering support.

That is the key element of her success. Mimi has rolled through the streets, skated giant vert ramps, and taken an aversion to heights and turned it into triumphs. Everyone has fears, but the best turn it into fuel—that's quintessentially skateboarding, and Mimi is about that life and brings it out in others.

Running women's contests with WSA since 2005, she's had a hand in mentoring women skateboarders in the U.S. and across the globe. Let us not forget that while many were boycotting the Olympics and questioning its relevance, Knoop quietly seized the moment to create a cultural exchange between countries. Occurring before the Games, the trip allowed women and nonbinary folx from the U.S. to engage with women and young girls in Japan during a goodwill tour. Crossing boards and borders, Mimi brought everyone together.

We also can't forget how she wove her art and design degree into an influential skateboarding brand, Hoopla, created with business partner and skate icon Cara-Beth Burnside. The duo launched an industry tour de force—skateboarding focused on women and young girls in both marketing and graphics. Supported by Michael Furukawa and George Powell from legendary company Powell/Skate One, Hoopla created a passion that I saw firsthand when covering the annual Supergirl Skate Pro contest. Every young female skater had a Hoopla board or would be near faint or whispering, "There she is," or "That's her!" when Mimi passed by. While a superstar in their eyes, and mine as well, Mimi has remained connected to the community, whether signing autographs, judging a contest, or competing; she consistently projects a quiet, undeniable power that encourages women's and young girls' participation.

Selling countless boards over time, Hoopla became the brand home to many of today's greatest skaters, like Alana Smith and Samarria Brevard. Formed in the early aughts in a much less receptive space for women's skateboarding, Hoopla brought a unique sense of art and design sensibility to the market with graphics and imagery that appealed to a younger and vastly underserved female and female-identifying demographic.

Through Hoopla, Knoop and Burnside et al. designed a system to support women and young girls with the space to build their career on their own terms. While now shuttered, the brand was a crucial part of the current women's movement and its closure is bittersweet to all involved. "Building and letting go of the business was hard," Mimi told my class. "Hoopla was meant to be a stepping stone and support women when no one else would." She added this, too: "Now women are on all the major teams. Like, Nora [Vasconcellos] is on Adidas, Samarria is on Enjoi, there is just less need for it. It wasn't meant to last forever." Even though sponsors may change, the sentiment remains the same. Women were making headway.

While the brand allowed people to buy into skateboarding, it is the *van* that allowed them to live it. You see, the first stage to a pro career is to throw caution to the wind and "get in the van." Earning entrance into the tour van at Hoopla or WSA, or any team, signifies that other skaters want to get to know you and feel out your presence on the road, as an informal way of gleaning if your vibe works well with them. Mimi Knoop offered hundreds of girls a seat in the van, never seeking praise or fanfare, and set the tone for those same women to offer seats to others later in their careers. This is table-setting, my friends. She did the work. Logging thousands of miles, contests, and demonstrations with the WSA, she and Lisa Whitaker offered a safe place where parents could support their kids and allow them to experience the fun and freedom of the road and spark their futures. What Mimi and the WSA offered was not an impenetrable boys' club, but a safe place for women to be and feel like themselves.

Without Mimi Knoop creating a path of fun and frolic and ferocity, skateboarding would not be where it is today. Her quiet but firm guidance showed all of us that the sky was truly the limit.

SKATEISTAN:
GETTING THE WORLD ON BOARD

OLIVER PERCOVICH

Launched skate diplomacy NGO in Kabul, Afghanistan

Advocate for women's rights and girls' rise in skateboarding

Featured in the Oscar-winning documentary
Learning to Skateboard in a Warzone: If You're a Girl

Silence. Anticipation. And, the golden moment. The 2019 Academy Award for Best Documentary Short goes to . . .

Cue the tears of joy by Australia-born skater Oliver Percovich and the excitement of the global team at Skateistan. Carol Dysinger and Elena Andreicheva's award-winning film followed the Afghanistan-based NGO, highlighting how skateboarding positively affected a group of young girls in Kabul and allowed them to find freedom, and themselves, through skateboarding.

Oliver—call him Ollie, like the original act of skateboarding levitation—founded Skateistan in 2009. He told me, "Skateboarding was the hook to get kids in Afghanistan interested in education, and they stayed to learn from each other and build with one another and to gain an education not allowed under previous Taliban rule. Now the world can see the power of skateboarding." It was a public recognition of 10 years of efforts to make Skateistan a reality—the combined work of hundreds of Afghan youths and families, and of countless donations from those across the globe.

Skateistan's win propelled both the nonprofit and skateboarding documentary itself into a new epoch—one where the world of film and the broader public acknowledged skateboarding's ability to create change. More important than the accolades in the West, however, is what the Skateistan Afghanistan outpost came to stand for—a team, a crew, a family who dared to cut through the dogma of the Taliban and bring new joy to children, women, and families in a place where skateboarding represented a respite from such harsh rule, if only for a time.

But who is this Oliver Percovich? As Bryan Ridgeway, cofounder of *TransWorld SKATEboarding* magazine, joked, "Oliver is the guy who used to sleep on my floor trying to figure out how to get skateboards and funding to take care of the kids in Kabul. Now he's working with heads of state and changing the world." That ain't hyperbole—the man works with heads of state in Germany, Belgium, and the U.S. However, Oliver is the first to say, "I'm just a skater who came into an opportunity to help at the right time." The call to action requires a huge heart and tenacious spirit that coalesced around a single mission—if you can give the gift of skateboarding, then you should—even under the thumb and threat of the Taliban.

Oliver's origin story starts in Melbourne, Australia, where he grew up and was a street skater. Oz has always been a home for action sports culture, nurturing global greats like pro skaters Jake Brown and Shane O'Neill and current rising superstar Chloe Covell. As with so many of us indoctrinated into skateboarding, the urge to explore new places and spaces can cause wanderlust. In Oliver's case, it would bring him to parts formerly unknown to most of us—Kabul, Afghanistan.

Oliver joined a friend and a tight crew in media studies who were documenting life in Kabul, but since they also were college students, boards in tow, they made a little time to skate. Unbeknownst to him at the time, that board and group of friends would spark a lifelong curiosity that would affect relations between the Western world and Kabul in magnificent ways.

Once they touched down in the Afghan capital, Oliver and his cohorts began exploring the land and sparking their curiosity and that of the local community through their skateboarding. A few Kabul youths became fascinated by the fun, surprise, and autonomy of getting their roll on with the never-before-seen skateboard. Oliver told me, "The kids' eyes would light up, and they were excited about the newness of the skateboard and skateboarding." Oliver would eventually leave Afghanistan, but he was encouraged by the progress and changed by these young people so eager to skate.

He would return in 2008 to put down roots, attempt to find a safe space to skate, and facilitate more young people learning skateboarding. This desire would eventually shape what we now know as the internationally acclaimed skateboarding and educational outreach program Skateistan. First setting up shop in an empty, drained water fountain, where he and his skateboard sparked the interest of those original few, he soon found a new group excited to take lessons. According to Oliver, it was love at first sight, and his legions grew from three to five kids to 10 to 25—with word spreading fast. Operating as a foreigner within Kabul, Oliver needed to earn the trust of both the young people and their parents.

While Oliver did not carry the same baggage as an American, it did not lessen his proximity to danger. In 2010 and throughout the operation of Skateistan, there was an active war in Afghanistan with U.S. and NATO forces in constant engagement with the Taliban and later Al Qaeda. These young skaters weren't living in a vacuum, and faced the same constant threats as others residing there. The Taliban wanted to keep women from participating in sports and gaining an education and any person engaged in "Western ways" was considered an

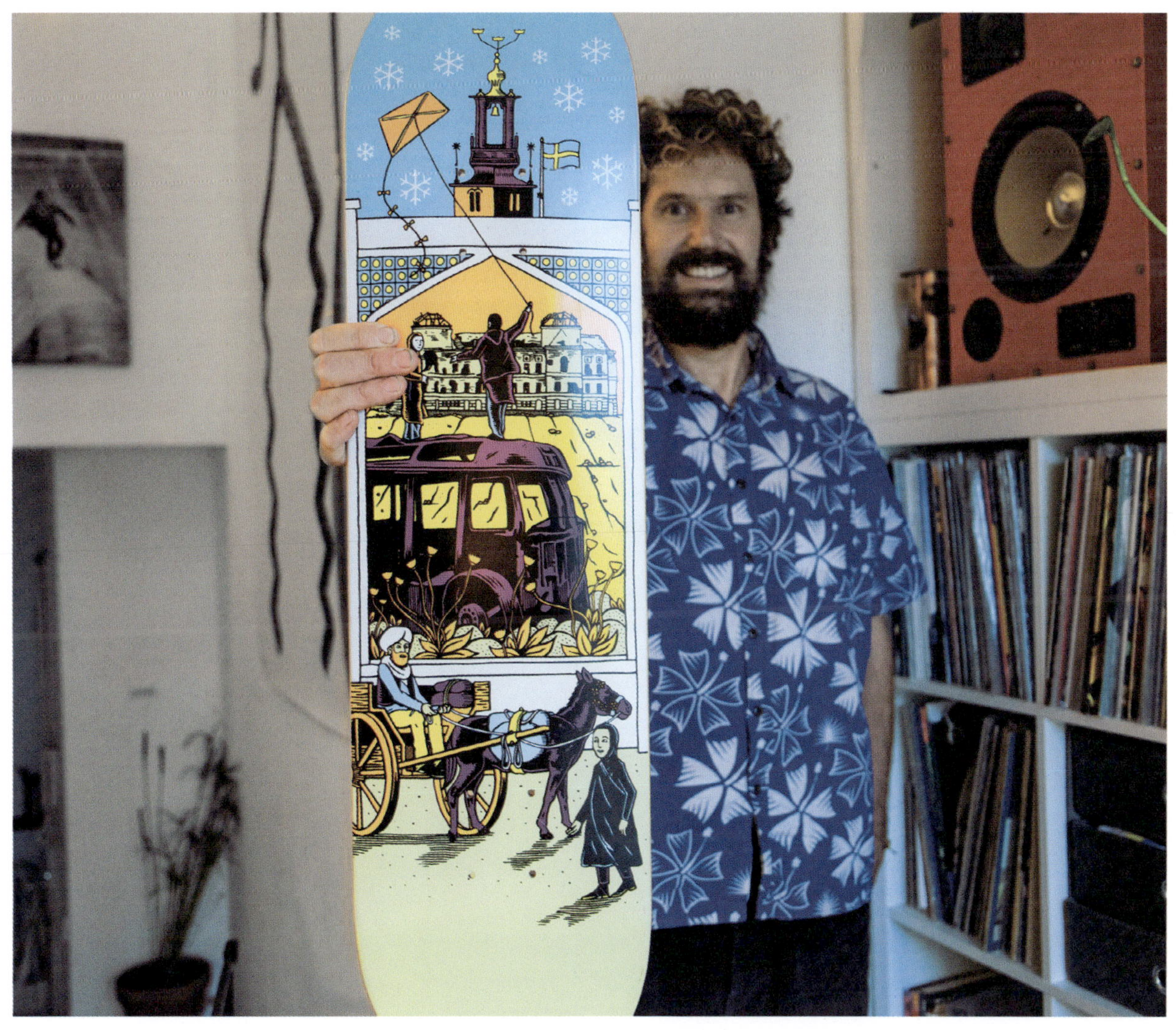

enemy. Despite this, Oliver became dedicated to helping skaters find their place and their voice through skateboarding. He made progress but also grieved losing skaters to radicalization, militant forces, and errant artillery strikes in the fog of war. Any of those tragic outcomes means that a young person never returns home to their makeshift school, their parents, or their community. Heartbreaking losses and fear were part of operating Skateistan in the early days, and even now, Oliver can be overwhelmed with emotion when he talks about it.

Yet, despite the severe losses and strained day-to-day, Oliver continued to push toward a brighter future for his students.

What made Skateistan inspirational and operational under the government in Kabul was its newness; without a specific skateboarding history in Kabul, it was difficult for it to be differentiated from play. In turn, it's hard to hate what you can't define, and in any place in the world, there is a hope that children can play.

Taking out the "American aspects" was crucial to Skateistan's success. While the soundtrack of skateboarding is part of what makes skateboarding unique, Oliver distilled it down to its core—fun, movement, and friends. Clothing or music of the West in any style—punk, hip-hop, or otherwise—would instantly bring the ire of the Taliban. And what's more, girls were not allowed to play sports or seek an education.

Of course, all of this seems contradictory to the conditions in Afghanistan. But in this limited sphere, skateboarding began to thrive. Oliver would slowly tell the larger skateboarding community about the work being done in Kabul, through word of mouth and little video clips, eventually inviting those brave enough to take the voyage—enlisting the help of Europe's first female professional skater, Dutch-Algerian Louisa Menke, and U.S. pro skater and now coach of the Thai Olympic team Kenny "The Traveler" Reed.

Skateistan's focus was on women and young girls, and it grew with a grant from the Swedish government, which meant no more empty pools and makeshift spots for lessons. Instead, a safe skating space was built in a former hangar. Skateistan would become a hallmark for women's rights and the rise of young girls in the sport. Gradually, the boundaries in learning would blur and move beyond skating at skate school to real academic learning and instruction. For Oliver, it was a case of building the plane as they were flying it. He said, "Skateboarding [w]as the carrot to learning. Once kids were excited about learning to skate, they were open to finding fun learning anything else we had to offer." In this case it offered a gateway to a formal education.

A level of stability in Kabul helped Oliver first establish Skateistan's offices in Berlin, Germany, in 2012, and place the organization closer to many EU policymakers and diplomats. Oliver would also develop Skateistan in Johannesburg, South Africa, in 2016, and Phnom Penh, Cambodia, in 2018. He also gained a new advocate—the then eight-year-old fastest-rising skateboarding superstar Sky Brown (see page 263). Sky became an instant, generational connector.

Cambodian students would learn about elite skateboarding from Sky. She was in awe of the students' love of skateboarding, in the face of poverty and distress. It would move her to work with Skateistan and her sponsor, Almost Skateboards, in 2017 to create a skateboard whose proceeds benefited

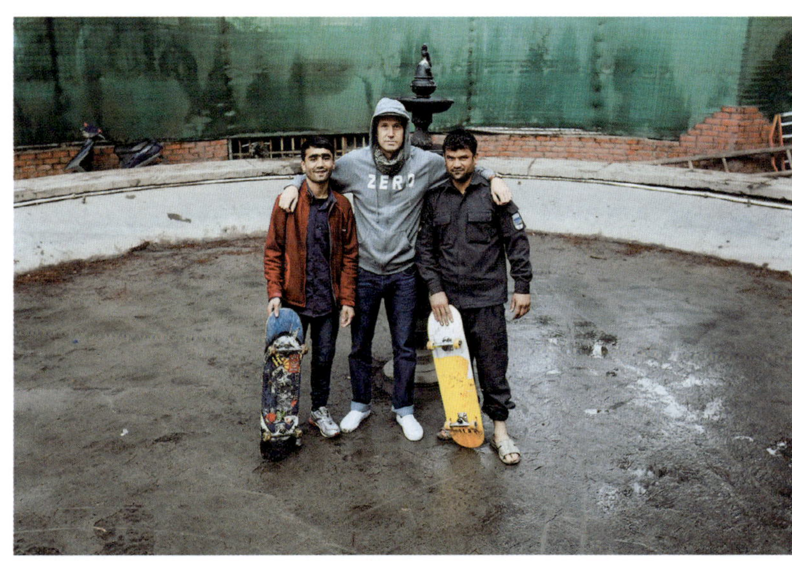

Back where it all started with the Skateistan crew, Kabul, 2018

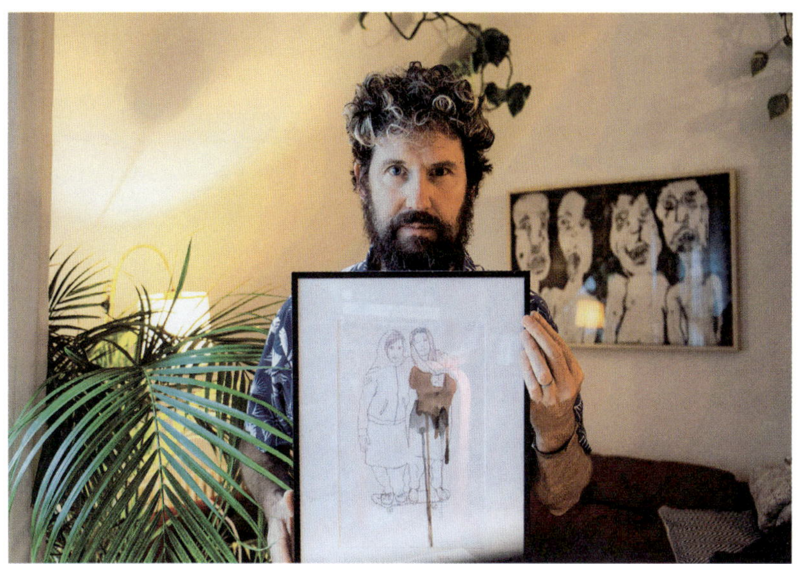

the Cambodian skate school. This attracted new donors and audiences to Skateistan.

Shortly after that, knowledge of the NGO crossed over to the general public, thanks in part to articles in the *New York Times* and *Los Angeles Times*. We were at a critical turn as Western nations recognized the effects of America's longest war. During this time, the skateboarding girls of Afghanistan went viral. Their skating, their resilience, and their love of learning all counterbalanced the standard stories of suffering.

But all this was happening as a mysterious virus began to affect China; while plans were underway for significant distribution, and an increase in donations and programming, the victory lap would fall apart under the world shutdown brought about by COVID-19. Then, amid that standstill, the Black Lives Matter movement and the murder of George Floyd became an integral part of the public discourse around creating social change.

The Black Lives Matter movement would also profoundly affect Oliver, who had already begun to internally critique the traditional Western development model, where white Europeans were often in charge of NGOs located in the Global South while the people directly affected by the conditions around them were rarely in charge. He knew he needed to make a change and evolve Skateistan into something else. "I was now part of the problem," he told me. "We were feeding the narrative of helping the poor Black and Brown people in other countries while living or having development offices run out of the U.S., Berlin, and Western Europe."

Oliver would change the Skateistan model, where power and funding sat at the top of the

Western pyramid before being doled out to the unrepresented people of color. When we spoke, he had begun his commitment to a horizontal power structure.

However, before that change was announced, Skateistan in Afghanistan would enter an existential phase prompted by the 2021 U.S. withdrawal from Afghanistan. The pullout meant that none of the citizens of Skateistan Kabul were safe.

All the good they did would now potentially be undone. There was only one thing to do: help evacuate the Skateistan staff, students, and their families.

Through tireless nights and exhausting days, a quiet force led behind the scenes to move Afghan families who would have been targeted for their involvement with U.S. skateboarding and U.S. operatives. Slowly but surely, those young people and their families were pulled out and resettled around the globe.

With everyone safe, Oliver got back to the people's business. He is creating change in Skateistan by flattening the power structure and pushing for greater transparency and empowerment within the org, implementing a horizontal, shared power structure, and ensuring that women make up at least 50 percent of the organization's decision-making board. He now shares the executive director position with Hala Khalaf, the former deputy executive director.

He also dove straight into the collaboration known as the Goodpush. Documenting and offering support and expertise to over 500 skateboarding NGOs, Goodpush helps amass best practices to keep all skate NGOs moving in the right direction.

SANDY ALIBO

Afro–Caribbean native of Martinique who helped put Ghana on the action sports map

Built Freedom Skatepark in Accra, Ghana

Entrepreneur, activist, and leader in the skate and surf tourism sector

Developed key partnership with designer Virgil Abloh and Facebook

Sandy Alibo is a global surf and skate aficionado, and an entrepreneur turned founder of Surf Ghana. She and Josh Odamtten, founder of Skate Nation Ghana's first skate meetup group, have put Ghanaian skateboarding on the global map while still keeping their roots with the people of Ghana to create social change and upward mobility through skate culture. Everyone from French President Emmanuel Macron to rapper Kendrick Lamar has shown love and support to the efforts of skate NGO Surf Ghana and the tour de force that is its leader, Sandy Alibo.

Few women around the world have led an entire skate and surf scene without ever being a top contender in a contest. But that's Sandy. An Afro-Caribbean native of Martinique, Sandy did the work to help grow here. Like anyone who has visited Ghana, Sandy fell in love with its streets, the shores, the drip, and the youth culture. From her initial visit in 2016, she saw right away the prospects for a thriving skate and surf culture and the efforts of Josh from Skate Nation Ghana to build a skate scene. After Sandy's initial visit and return to Martinique—well, home just didn't seem the same. Sandy hopped on a plane to return to Ghana with a plan to help everyone live long and prosper through skateboarding and surfing. Sandy brought with her substantial experience in marketing and operations in action sports and music from her career in France and throughout Europe.

However, while she earned her stripes in Europe, the environment wasn't always welcoming; even

with her experience, it was a constant challenge to break into the skate scene as a woman and person of color in the late aughts. The microaggressions she experienced fueled her passion to find a place and power of her own. Instead of working to make brands more popular, she reframed it for herself— how could she make *her* dreams possible and create space for Black Africans and the diaspora via surfing and skateboarding? Through Surf Ghana.

When Sandy first returned to Ghana, she set out to tap into the exploratory and familial relationships in skateboarding and surfing and merge them into one core mission: "emphasizing tourism with a pro-Black experience." Rather than exploiting the spaces, places, and cultures of BIPOC cultures who live in exoticized locales that can drive the wanderlust of skate and surf tourism, she hoped to instead integrate knowledge of the land and the needs of the people into a new tourism model. Instead of just skating and surfing tours, they would offer service tours with the opportunity to support community-centered work that would contribute to anti-colonialism. This was revolutionary. Once she joined up with Josh from Skate Nation, the merged endeavor transformed into the umbrella org Surf Ghana, the one-stop shop and agency for all your action sports needs.

What began as a loose-knit group of roughly 40 skaters gained traction when legendary designer Virgil Abloh (RIP) became aware of Surf Ghana first through social media and then by meeting the crew in person while visiting the country several times in the late aughts. Virgil passed away far too young, but he lived out loud. He was a kindred spirit who loved action sports. As the first African American designer of Louis Vuitton, he rocketed to the stratosphere, but instead of leaving the planet, he helped others take off. In the skateboarding world, he not only worked with skaters like Lucien Clarke to create Lucien's first pro model shoe for LV but also supported skaters in the Surf Ghana collective.

In a short time, Surf Ghana team members gained exposure in major publications such as *Vogue* and in media outlets like the BBC. Skate Nation and Surf Ghana's crews were also featured in a commercial that ran during the Tokyo Olympics' skateboarding debut. Of all the skateboarders in the world, the crew most visible during the Olympic commercials was the team from Ghana. Amazing. While Tony Hawk (see page 63) is the most celebrated skater to visit the White House, Sandy and the Surf Ghana crew looked "very presidential" when they received a visit from Vice President Kamala Harris. That's without counting the visits with Macron while working with the French Sport for Development program to discuss skateboarding's role in sport and reconciliation to combat colonialism. For a small skate crew, they give everyone a run for their money on the heads-of-state-visit political bingo card.

The accolades don't stop there. Through partnerships with Vans and with global donations growing, in 2019 Surf Ghana generated the money to build Accra's first skatepark. Freedom Skatepark became the jewel of the city and part of a multipronged approach to bring more tourism to Accra through action sports. All of the support and exposure helped them put into place their dreams of a surf house, a skate house, and guided service tours of the city. What couldn't they do?

With their reputation increasing across the globe, they were able to get Dashawn Jordan (see page 256), 2019 U.S. Olympic team member and Street League Skateboarding champion, to be one of the first skaters to bless the Accra skatepark, in 2022, and demonstrate just how "radical" skateboarding could be in the hands of Black people. Dashawn put on the

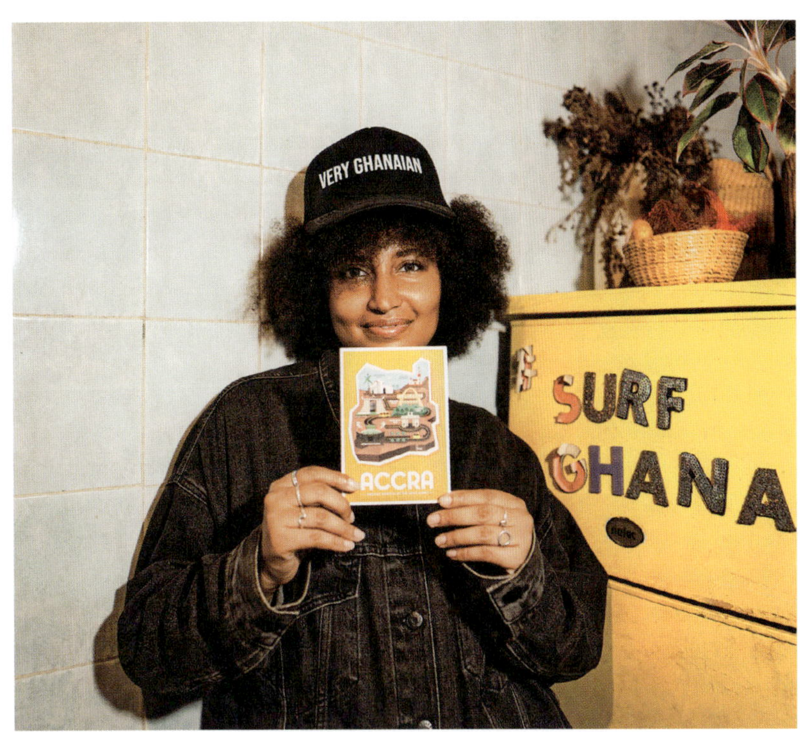

demo of a lifetime during his stay and only paused the skate onslaught long enough to pay tribute and snap selfies under the "Virgil was here" canary-yellow mural. That day brought dreams of Black skate life full circle. As it stood, the park itself was already a manifestation of dreams by the locals. Adding Dashawn and the spirit of Virgil—the chef's kiss.

Advocated for by Sandy and the Surf Ghana team, who had been using makeshift spaces and mini ramps throughout Accra to give lessons, the Freedom Skatepark is a thing of beauty. Surrounded by palm trees and more than 500 square meters in size, it offers an oasis in the midst of the country's bustle. The language of the people is also literally part of the design. The Asante people's "Fawohodie," the *adinkra*—or symbol—of independence, freedom, and emancipation with its double "U"-shape form, found its way into a modern interpretation as a concrete fixture in the new skateable space.

Freedom's design features everything a skater needs in order to learn. Street obstacles like handrails and flat rails prepare you for the urban environment. It also has some of the smoothest of transitions, crafted lovingly with help from Wonders Around the World (an NGO dedicated to international skatepark construction). Funding for the park came from collaborations with Daily Paper—a collective of Ghanaian friends Jefferson Osei, Abderrahmane Trabsini, and Hussein Suleiman—and Virgil Abloh's Off-White brand. Vans also committed to supporting the project by providing money, apparel, surfboards, and skateboards.

Each obstacle, trimmed in yellow paint, is a focal point of the skate energy and excitement that lives within the Freedom Skatepark, and that energy is infectious. Ask Kendrick Lamar, who pulled up to the park in 2022 after hearing about it on social media and from Virgil. It looked so good that he told the Surf Ghana family he needed to check if he still knew how to ollie and could get his thang straight on a board. Another mind-melting event occurred when Vice President Harris dropped by on a trip to Ghana—although she didn't drop in—at the compound. These milestones are the stuff of dreams for a crew that had only been together for a few years. VPs, MCs, and the President of France on the cellie constitute the high life.

By late summer 2023, the collective spanned not only the skatepark but also music and video production, art shows, and organic public diplomacy—Sandy and the crew were accomplishing more than anyone could ask for. Then, tragedy struck. They came under attack from the very officials and populace they were helping grow on the international stage. According to Sandy, the team showed up one day to unlock the park only to find that there were private workers poised to take it apart brick by brick. Surf Ghana had grown too large over the previous two years and now, instead of being viewed as the jewel of Accra, it had somehow been declared public enemy number one. Their work had made the land valuable as a home for the future of Accra, which upset the old guard. The park's leases were called into question, the land

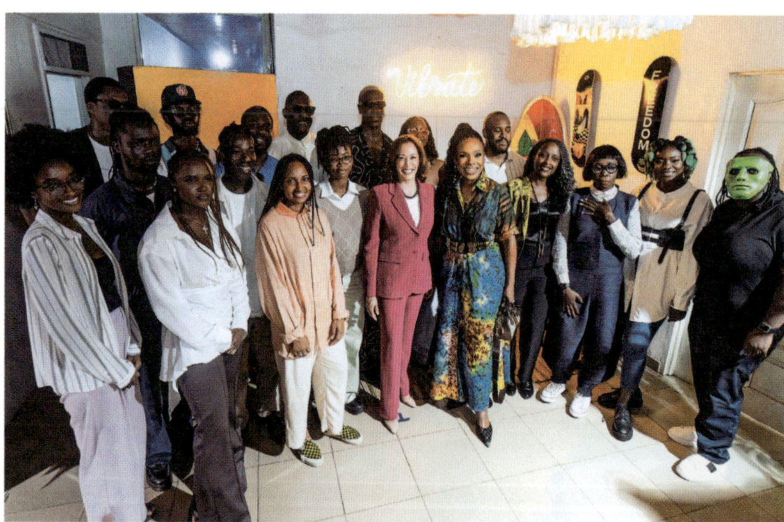

Left: Sandy Alibo and the Surf Ghana Crew with former U.S. vice president Kamala Harris (foreground, center)

Bottom: The Freedom Skatepark in Accra

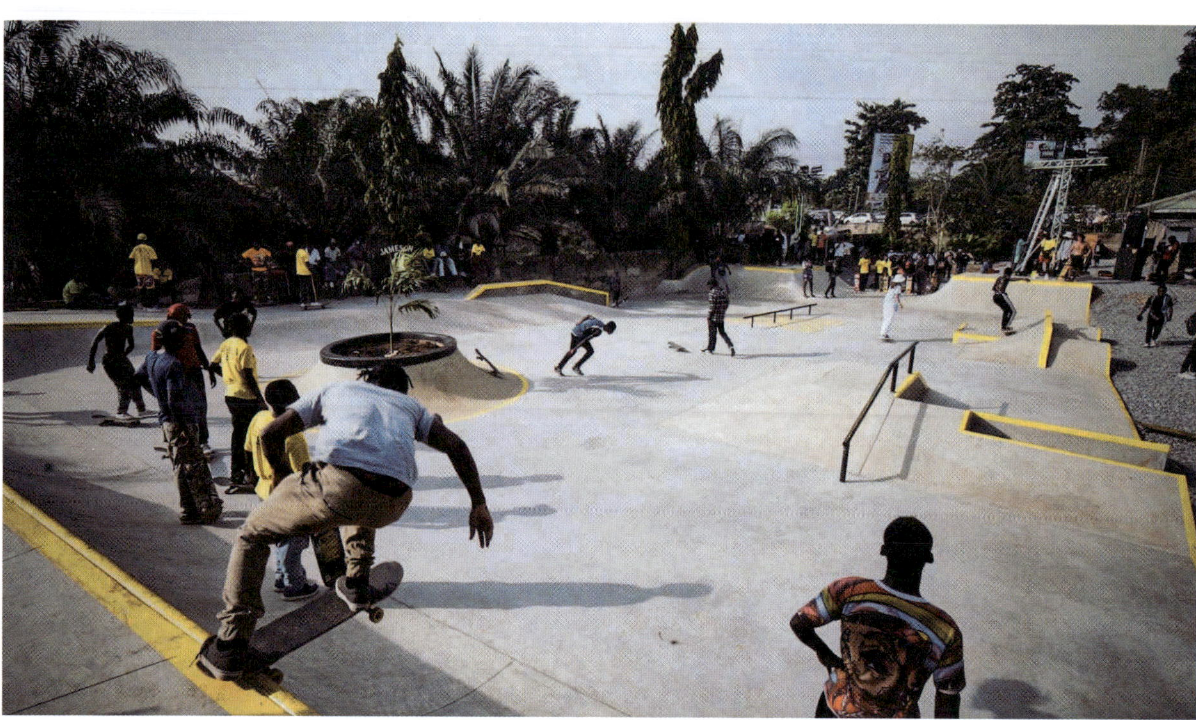

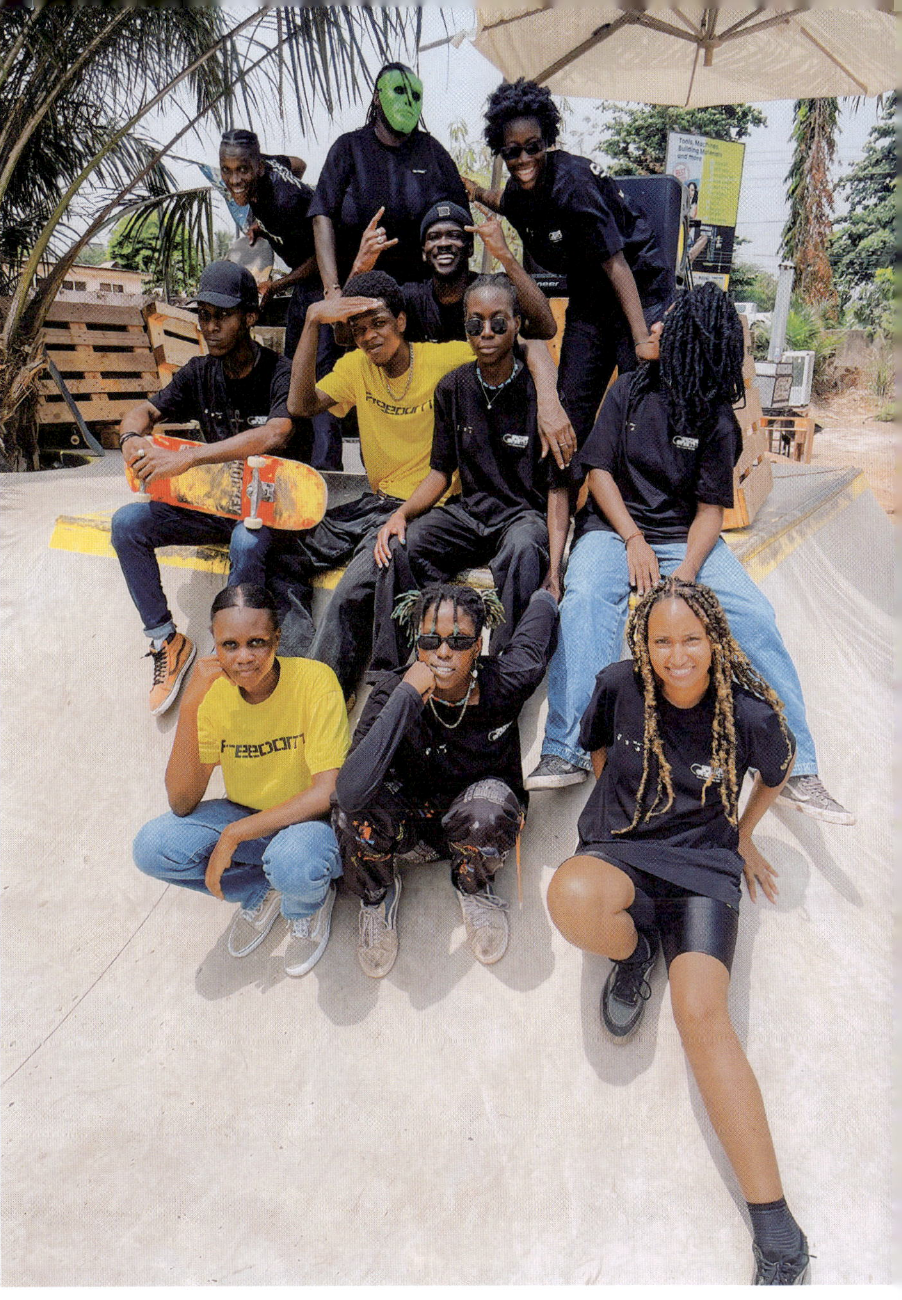

The Skate Ghana crew ready to roll at the Freedom Skatepark in Accra, Ghana

somehow turned out not to be owned by the person they'd signed with, and now the "real" owner was telling the city that it was his land, and he wanted it back—immediately. Hired hands were not hard to come by to dismantle this disruption to the system. Sandy told me there were tensions with the old guard because of her Martinique roots, with its French connection. It was a reminder that although she had built a skateboarding and surfing family in the country, those officials and townspeople continued to see her as an outsider, "doin' too much"—too much shining, too much building, too much good to go unpunished.

That's the thing about skateboarding, though. We have been hopping fences and dodging gatekeepers for decades. We have faced adversity since we were in the "two roller skates and some plywood" zone.

This setback is not stopping Surf Ghana. Just as quickly as the op moved in to shut them down, the crew moved to another spot in the city, still giving lessons and activating the youth. The dreams cannot be diminished, and while the land is tied up in bureaucracy, freedom and the spirit of Freedom Park remain where they always have—under their feet.

THE TECHNOLOGISTS

Like all true visionaries, the technologists answer the question of "What if . . . ?" by telling you . . . *What it do*. Whether it's giving you grip, fixin' your flat feet, time-telling, or rebelling against board constructions, park development, and all points in between, these innovators and iconoclasts shatter the status quo. Somehow, they always know what's missing long before the rest of us know we even have needs. They forage through mechanical and mental outer rims, imagining how to harness the day's catch and the assemblages needed to keep you performing however you choose.

These mavericks and makers in skateboarding tear out the pages of the rulebooks and burn them. They turn the knobs, set the dials. Run the risk of losing fingers, funds, and friends in their relentless pursuit of perfection. It always begins with them tinkering around the edges and gradually builds to seismic shifts in our skate life. They disappear for days on end and then rematerialize, goggles up, covered in liquids, solids, sawdust, and green gunk, with new and better equipment and ideas for us. Their quests ensure our skate family goes faster and farther and lasts longer than ever before.

GET ON THE GOOD FOOT
JASON GUADALAJARA

Creator of Footprint Insoles and Footprint Footwear

Creator of Colours Collectiv Skateboards and Crupiê Wheels

What do you get when you cross Newtonian technology, bowling balls, Axion Footwear, and a torn ACL? The sage of innovation and a constantly evolving technologist: entrepreneur Jason Guadalajara.

Lacking a silver spoon or a connected family network, Jason was undeterred; he put his nose to the grindstone and let his power rip. Selling his coveted collection of Axion Footwear shoes to fund his startup, he began what is now a revolution in skateboarding products: Footprint Insoles.

Let's rewind a bit. An avid Latinx, sponsored skater from Los Angeles, Jason was beginning to make his mark in the mid-1990s through his video parts. At the time, he was doing a superb mix of technical skating on ledges and down stairs that became progressively bigger as he improved. The problem was, the more intense the skating, the more intense the stress to his feet and ultimately to his knees. As bad luck would have it, he tore his ACL while skating. The doctor told him that the injury had come about because of his flat feet: jumping down stairs was, in essence, sending shocks directly to his knees, and he would need surgery. "That surgery sucked," he told my class. "Then I did the rehab that I needed to do to get back on my board." That should have been the end of it, but lightning struck twice. "I tore it [his ACL] again," he said. "The doctor said that because I had flat feet, I was just more prone and there was nothing anyone could do about it—except explore podiatrist-prescribed custom orthotic insoles."

As a skater with flat feet myself, having faced down two skate-related MCL tears, I understand that pain. No cushion when out pushin' and facing down big drops and gaps unprotected sends the impact straight to the knees. Sadly, this injury remains common among skaters, and during the mid-'90s and early aughts it took out skateboarding professionals. Many skaters didn't have health insurance, and the price of custom orthotics was wallet draining and the cost of rehab often a career-ender.

Jason wanted to offer skaters a chance to protect their careers and their relationship to skateboarding. Following a "God bless the child that's got his own" notion, Jason entered the skate business market to ensure no one else would go through this type of agony. "I just decided there had to be something better than just blaming flat feet," he said. "I had to do something to support other skaters. That's why I created Footprint."

In the early aughts, Jason sold his collection of vintage Axion footwear—Kareem Campbell, Gino Iannucci, and Guy Mariano's signature shoes—to fund his first trip to China, where he stayed for months visiting shoe factories, learning about the production and technology that go into making insoles. He eventually merged two processes: developing an open cell foam, and injecting it with a heated recurable urethane, so the foam could take on the shape of anyone's foot. Genius.

Jason's proprietary technology stood above the rest because it could actually lessen the impact of skateboarding on skaters. Instead of just adding a layer of shock protection, he created a product that dissipates 98 percent of the energy you throw at it. Put simply, your dogs wouldn't burn after kickflipping down a 14-stair while wearing Footprint—or "FP"—insoles. That's a product every skater needs in their arsenal.

Jason also wanted to create technology that worked for any shoe. One that considered that every person's foot is shaped differently and needs a custom product, but would still be affordable for everyone. Jason's final step of genius lay in creating a custom insole dubbed the Gamechanger, which went through a heat-activated process. You bring the Gamechangers up to 225 degrees in the oven, then pull them out and, after an eight-minute walk-around, the orthotics mold to your feet. In a short time, he made insoles that got everyone moving on the good foot—flat feet, high arches, bruised heels, you name it.

While the product was revolutionary, it still took time to get it into shops. It launched near the time of the 2008 financial crisis, when it was difficult for skate shops to stock new products, especially because many had invested in other insole brands that didn't sell. Footprint battled the uphill climb first by showing skaters that the product worked, then by slowly building a team of pro skaters like Joey Brezinski, Kevin Romar, and Brandon Biebel, who endorsed the product because of its merits. While it would take nearly three years for skate shops to build Footprint into their offering, skaters purchased them on their own through the website based on word of mouth and personal experiences.

With skaters adopting the technology and the brand gaining market share, skate media began to take notice, including *Skateboard Mag* and *Thrasher*. *Thrasher* featured FP when Aaron "Jaws" Homoki wore their insoles and launched into the history books with the largest ollie in history, the legendary city of Lyon's 25-stair set. Real in the streets, so even the sheets of the other magazines looked at what FP had to offer. The GOAT Tony Hawk (see page 63) listed FP Insoles as among his favorite gear in a 2015 interview in the *Wall Street Journal*. That kind of ringing endorsement also elevated the FP profile beyond skateboarding. Within the action sports family, snowboarders also adopted the product to save them from sky-high impact, leading Footprint to stomp out the competition for six straight years in *The Good Ride* (a snowboard products guide) readers' poll. And even NASA has tapped them to make custom insoles for training astronauts headed to the International Space Station. There are also police officers running

around in FP insoles—but I believe they send a full notice that says, "If you buy these skate insoles, you cannot chase skateboarders." I'm pretty sure that's in a contract somewhere. Or at least should be.

While the Hawk endorsement brought about a wave of support for Footprint, its greatest marketing is the one built on the ground. People don't believe the hype. They want the proof. Jason created a simple visual explanation that went viral on social media. He and pro skater and team rider Brezinski placed product from four other brands in a line. Then they took a 10-pound bowling ball and dropped it on the competition. Each time they did, that bowling ball launched to the stars. Impact in and impact straight back at you—your feet, your knees, your spine. When they dropped it on the Footprint insoles—*thwap*. Nothing but a dull thud: the bowling ball stopped and calmly rolled off the insole. Skaters got it and got on it themselves, creating a flurry of vids of their own to show that they had become believers. In the videos, they place a piece of glass or a concrete block under the insoles, and proceed to drop the bowling ball and see what is crushed and what remains the same. Footprint wins every time.

Today, FP is available globally under the banner Concrete Visionary and has set up a new factory and storefronts on four continents. Jason has even added Crupiê Wheels and Colours Collectiv skateboards to the FP portfolio.

Nothing signifies FP's arrival more than other competing shoemakers now trying to engage Jason to see if they can incorporate FP insoles into their production line. The future is bright for FP and Jason Guadalajara, the man who knew that all skaters' dogs bark, and found the safest way to let them off the leash.

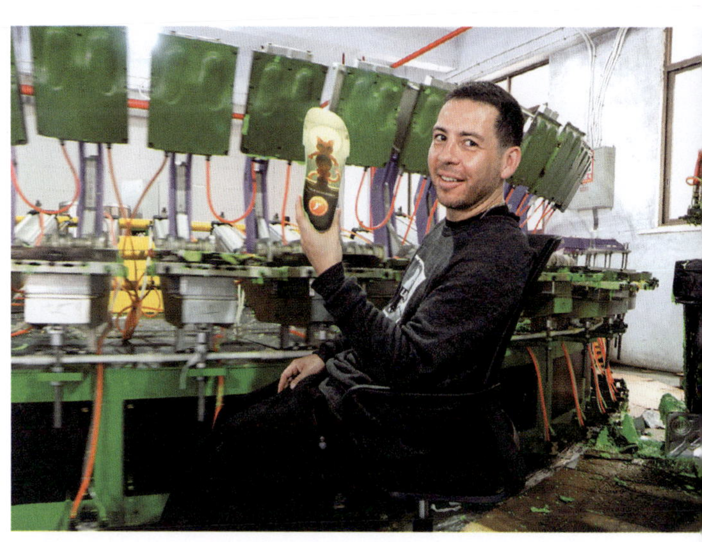

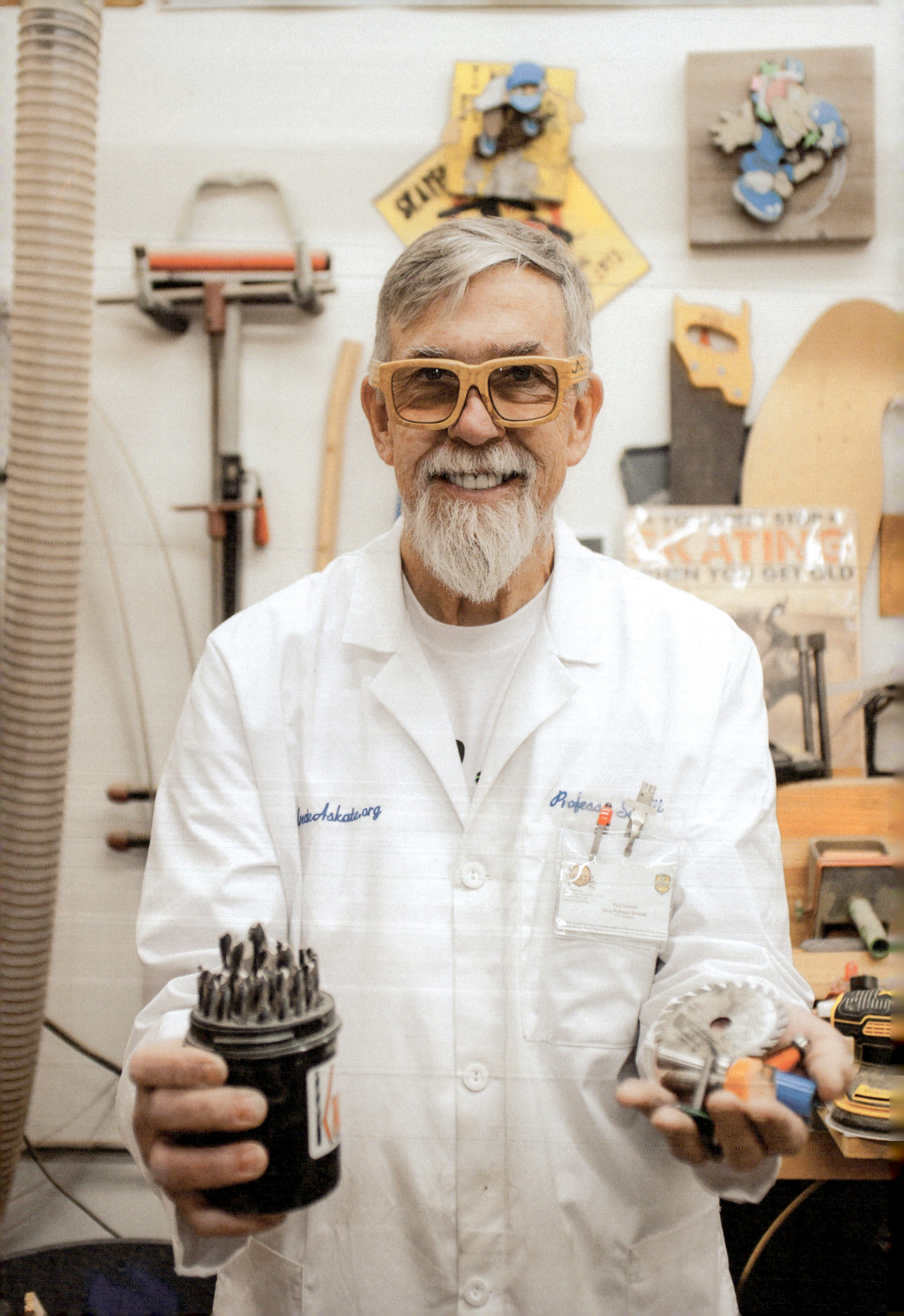

TINKERER EXTRAORDINAIRE

PAUL "THE PROFESSOR" SCHMITT

Designer of some of the world's best skateboards

Owner and founder of PS Stix Skateboard manufacturing

Cofounder of New Deal Skateboards

Put the soul in skateboarding science

Founder of CreateAskate

Paul "The Professor" Schmitt is a nerd, and thank God for that. Without his dedication to experimentation and his obsession with the most mundane of details, he never would have designed and created some of the best skateboards on the market since the early 1980s.

Today, everyone who meets The Professor knows that version of him, the graybeard in the lab coat who gave himself the industry's most perfect nickname. He's probably explaining his term #skativity to you. In short: he's grown into almost the archetype of an inventor, an innovator, indeed, a professor.

Long before the lab coat, however, young Paul was what we all were—a kid enthralled with skateboarding and having fun with his friends. Wisconsin-born and Florida-bred, he helped design ramps and early technology with anything he could get his hands on.

This was during those dismal times in the early '80s when skateboarding was kept alive with Scotch tape, X-Acto knives, and glue sticks. Paul's dad was

a woodworker who built theater sets, and his son inherited that love of building, soon crafting rails out of fiberglass in the family garage. He worked on board designs with epoxy, polymers, wood, and urethane, and learned quickly to care about innovative design and building a better skateboard. And talk about DIY: he was making skateboard molds and pressing wood by backing his mother's car onto the press and letting the cured wood sit under the vehicle.

In time, The Professor moved from boards to ramps and became inundated with requests for assistance in creating them. He would pass those asks on to the great ramp builder Tim Payne, a Florida local who would go on to build the legendary company Team Pain Skateparks.

In the early stages of his career, Paul came up with the right mix of compounds to give skaters an edge by producing rails that made it easier for skaters to slide and hold on when doing airs. Those pieces of plastic affixed to the edges of our boards became a standard in the '80s and early '90s, and he was the best designer of that product. While they are less popular now, at the time they were an important part of skateboarding, and people sang his rails' praises from coast to coast. It wasn't long before 16-year-old Paul traded the quaint spot of his bedroom and garage for new digs in California under Vision Skateboards, one of the giants of the '80s.

Moving at light speed, he tweaked processes to fit in new routing and painting and efficiency practices that improved the quality of product for Vision. With all the space and experimentation, plus making things run like clockwork, the prodigy was granted his own imprint, the iconic Schmitt Stix.

Schmitt Stix became the home of progressive board shapes and early innovations. First, Paul discovered how to make a full concave the length of the board. This meant we could have more control of our boards, regardless of where our feet were placed, and could attempt more radical tricks. From that point, it was onward and upward: the Ripsaw board, with jagged cutouts along the edge because, well, it was fun; the Yard Stick, an extra-long deck and a precursor to what would become a modern cruiser board shape; the Double Kick (with the nose and tail having the same kicktail and concave, which supports street skating) made first for Vision Skateboards and dubbed the Double Vision (though under the New Deal banner it would become the Siamese Dream different boards. The Professor introduced the conical wheel, which was designed with an aluminum hub to make it go faster. He also taught a generation about the importance and meaning of wheelbase, the distance between trucks and the effect it would have on our collective skateboarding.

By the late '80s, Schmitt Stix was working with some of the biggest names in skateboarding: the U.K.-born ex-pat Steve Douglas, the *Thrasher* magazine photographer and pro skater Bryce Kanights, Oz's Andrew Morrison, and East Coast beacon Andy Howell. The secret was out that Schmitt Stix boards were the best ride.

In his spare time, The Professor developed a partnership with John Lucero and produced boards for John's brand Lucero Skateboards (now called Black Label Skateboards), which at the time was home to one of the highest-ranked amateur of the late '80s, Jeff Grosso. Lucero's collaboration with Schmitt continues to this day, a testament to the quality of the product.

The Professor got his proverbial PhD when he finally made the decision to depart Vision (encouraged to leave the nest by Schmitt Stix pros Steve Douglas and Andy Howell) and quietly set up his own woodshop, PS Stix. In the early '90s, he teamed up with Steve and Andy to create New Deal, a new skater-led company. That yellow sun graphic, created by Andy, would become the symbol of this new company. The concept for New Deal bounded out of their minds, onto the pages of magazines, and into skateboarding history.

New Deal was the perfect antidote to the staleness of the skateboarding industry, an industry still largely focused on vertical skateboarding when street skating was the future. New Deal was poised for success with their contest-winning and highly influential pro street skater Andy Howell. With him on the team, New Deal and Schmitt were able to sell boards even though they were a new brand. Coupled with their singular board graphics, ranging from Alice in Wonderland to Iceberg Slim–type illustrations, the brand took off. Equal parts lunacy and advocacy, the quirky artwork offered everyone something for their tastes. All those incredible graphics were affixed to Schmitt's indomitable and soulfully developed board construction. Armed with the best products and graphics, the team would grow as well. In time New Deal would become home to some of the heaviest of hitters in '90s skateboarding, and would feature a huge East Coast presence and people of color, like legends Armando Barajas and Julio De La Cruz. They would also launch another double kick deck, when PS Stix created the Siamese Doublekick.

Paul and the brands would continue beyond New Deal and sprout into other brands, including Mad Circle, Popwar, and *411 Video Magazine*, which became one of the most influential skateboarding video series of all time. They also became home to the bestselling skateboarding brand of all time, Element Skateboards.

Paul's dedication to skateboard manufacturing has remained a constant. PS Stix still discreetly makes boards for many brands—some are in the public sphere, others aren't—but all that matters is that a PS Stix lives and breathes right under your feet. Take Cordano Russell, for example. Cordano is an amazing Black skater living in San Diego who rides street for Team Canada. He is six feet, four inches, 215 pounds, and eats handrails from North County to Tijuana for breakfast. He also breaks boards consistently with that frame. Every few weeks, Professor Schmitt meets with him and helps him create a custom board. The raw data and broken boards go to the PS Stix factory, and the new experimental boards go to Cordano so that he can light up the land with his giant-size, genre-defining skateboarding. The fruits of that collaboration were on display during the Paris Olympics, where Cordano and his PS Stix–manufactured board defied the odds of both placement and board-breaking. Landing in the top eight, Cordano held his own against some of the world's greatest, including Nyjah Huston (see page 32) and Olympic gold medalist Yuto Horigome (see page 279).

A life well lived now seeds the future through Paul's educational endeavor, Create A Skate, codirected by Jim Fitzpatrick. The duo works with schools so that young people can make their own boards and gain a greater interest in STEM by learning how to design and innovate in the world around them.

Throughout the decades, Paul has poured his heart and soul into innovative design that keeps the best in skateboarding rolling onward.

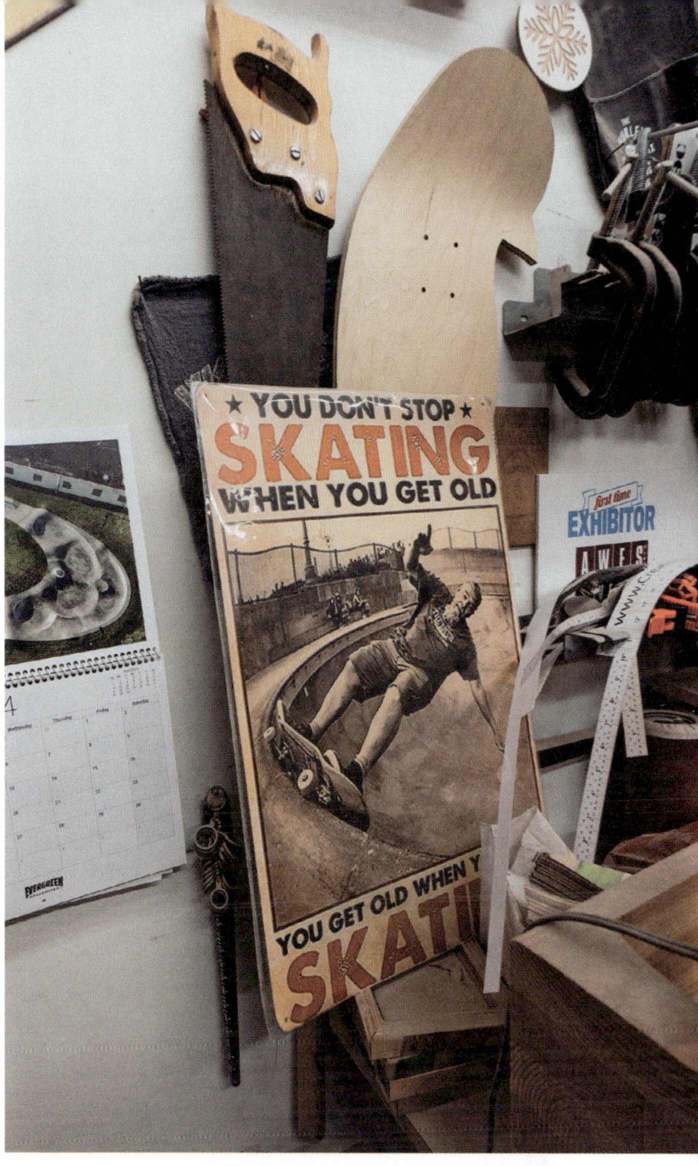

Right: Paul "The Professor" Schmitt's words to live by: "You don't stop skating when you get old, you get old when you stop skating."

Bottom: Wood veneers for creating skateboards in The Professor's warehouse, Orange County, California

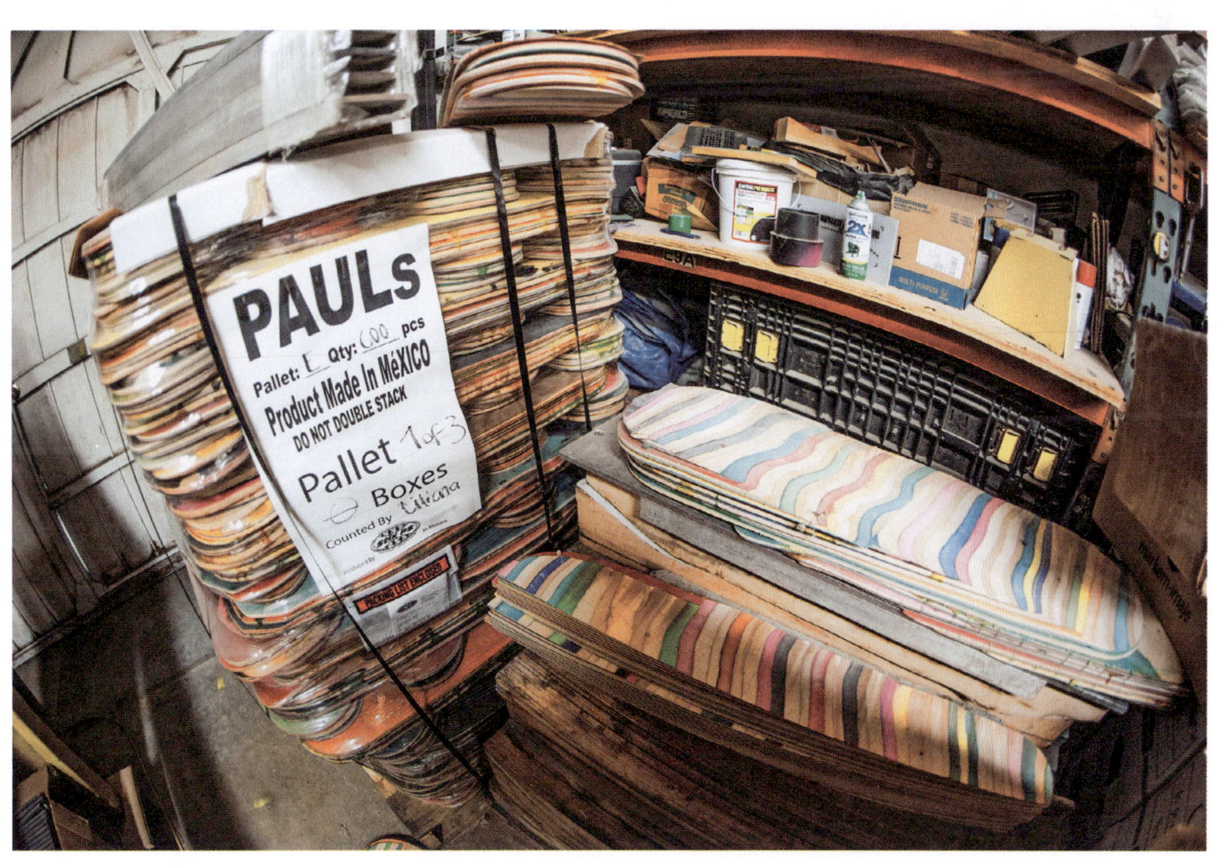

CHAD DINENNA & ANDY LAATS

Launched Nixon watches

Action sports' top name in timepieces

Sponsored the dream team of action sports legends

I see a future when skaters and snowboarders and surfers will all be on time. *Said no one ever.*

For anyone working within or around anyone with a love for action sports, when that group is seeking the stoke, time stands still for them and not for you. That means, if you aren't in the streets, on the mountain, or in the water with them when the magic is happening, well, they are gonna be late.

However, Chad DiNenna and his partner Andy Laats were the visionaries who imagined a day when surfers would know the depth of the water they were in and how long they'd been in it. Skaters would be able to land or slam and still look good (even if being cuffed by the police) and snowboarders could track how much time was left on their run without getting out of their gear.

Enter Nixon watches. Launched in 1997, Nixon put that icy glow on your wrist before you knew you needed it. They are the unabashed Rolls-Royces of action sports timepieces, an uncharted category before DiNenna and Laats entered the game. For more than 25 years, DiNenna and Laats have been helping skaters get to school, make it to the skate spots, and catch flights on time via the classiest watches in the sector. Sure, there were other watches, but Nixons were designed for us by us in the action sports world. Snowboarding with huge gloves on? Covered. Duck diving in the surf and free diving? Covered. Taking a slam down the 16-stair handrail at Hollywood High? Covered, with the nigh-invulnerable Nixon.

Before Nixon debuted, the assumption was that skate, surf, and snow aficionados who regularly tossed their carcasses into the fray wouldn't want a valuable timepiece. The stereotype of the action sports athlete was that they were ruled by the stoke and the sun, not the sundial. Skate shops across the country also felt they knew their customer base and couldn't imagine them paying a premium price for product when most skateboarding paraphernalia is disposable by design.

It turns out they were all dead wrong and, in fact, many skaters and action sports enthusiasts *wanted* something of their own that held some status beyond skateboarding. Nixons became *the* gift for skaters.

Nixon wanted to make products that were inspirational and aspirational. Such was the case when they created the Player watch, the first skateboarding watch to feature a diamond in the face. When Nixon dropped that piece, it hit like Dilla and Slum Village on the industry—raw and on the edge but still shining.

Nixon's developers were an unlikely duo. Laats, who held a bachelor's degree in mechanical engineering from Cornell University, worked for Burton Snowboards in product design before heading westward to nab an MBA from Stanford. DiNenna was immersed in the action sports lifestyle in Southern California—surfing, skating, and snowboarding—and attended California State University, Long Beach, working sales at the famous

TransWorld SKATEboarding offices. A chance meeting at a Stanford party was where DiNenna shared with Laats his secret idea to develop a high-end watch for the most untouched category in timepieces—action sports.

The duo debated the proposition, determining its feasibility. Laats approached it analytically and saw several logistical problems to solve. DiNenna had a more optimistic view, and had the access to the professional and insider world of the action sports industry. Eventually they saw eye to eye and founded Nixon in 1997.

Nixon also launched the brand with the best team in action sports, which only grew over time. Tony Hawk, Paul Rodriguez, Chad Muska, Danny Way, Bruce Irons, Colin McKay, and Bob Burnquist. True icons. Now with the addition of surfer Caity Simmers, transition demigoddess Nora Vasconcellos, and Olympian Zion Wright, they round out the best class of this decade. Being part of the Nixon team was special. You weren't just an acquisition by the corporate stiffs.

Today, Nixon has expanded beyond action sports, collaborating with bands like Metallica and the Rolling Stones, and George Lucas and the *Star Wars* franchise.

Nixon's other special sauce was that its ads were shot by visionary action sports photographers like J. Grant Brittain (see page 150) and Atiba Jefferson (see page 143).

DiNenna and Laats produced their first watches in the back of DiNenna's garage, delivering them out of the back of his truck in Encinitas, California. Thanks to DiNenna's marketing and ability to add star power to the team, and Laats's ability to create a quality product, they expanded from Southern California into seven different countries after their first year in business. As action sports became more in demand and a greater part of popular culture, Nixon was initially acquired by the surf brand Billabong International for over $100 million in 2006. DiNenna and Laats would retake control of their company, which had grown in value to around $465 million, in 2012. This new level of control allows them to spearhead the brand and innovate in the same way they did when it began.

With renewed vigor and an eye on the future, Chad DiNenna and Andy Laats now focus on making Nixon sustainable and creating partnerships that repurpose plastic ocean debris and recycle it into new plastic material to create top-of-the-line Nixon products. With this and other processes in place, Nixon wants to demonstrate that sound products can be produced in an equally sound and eco-friendly way. These efforts are just one reason Nixon remains number one on our wrists and in our hearts.

Chad DiNenna, always on time with vision and values

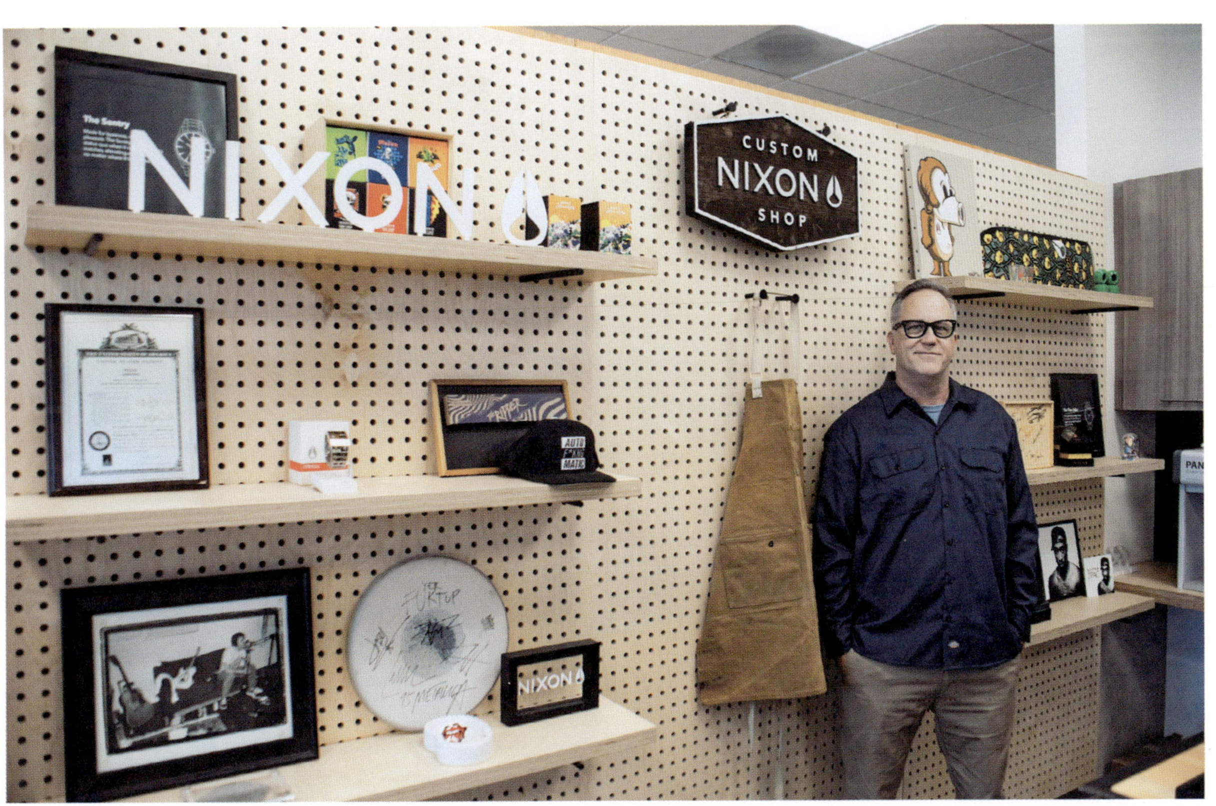

"IF YOU BUILD IT, THEY WILL COME"

TYLER LARGE

The Fannie Mae and Freddie Mac of skateboarding

Founder of OC Ramps

Over a quarter-million mini-ramp kits sold since 2005

You get a mini ramp, and you *get a mini ramp! You get a butter bench, and* you *get a butter bench!* That is the philosophy behind the work of OC Ramps and its owner, Tyler Large—skate obstacles for everyone.

Whether you are SpaceX, Google, a weekend warrior, or a parent getting your kids started in skateboarding, Tyler is the plug. Tyler's company has mastered the art of affordable delivery, production, and manufacturing of quality skate ramps and street obstacles, providing portable benches, ledges, rails, and mini ramps to the masses and democratizing skateboarding for a new generation.

Thanks to Tyler's work, if you want a mini ramp (a scaled-down half-pipe) in your backyard, it can happen. At the church BBQ and fish fry? Done. You call and it's there. He even provides pro skater demos if you need them. Tyler's OC Ramps is a one-stop shop for skateboarding. He's compared the business he does with the IKEA model, selling more than 250,000 skate ramp kits since the company launched in 2005. I think of him more as the Fannie Mae and Freddie Mac of skateboarding—Tyler Large brings the wonders of home-ramp ownership to the people. Through OC Ramps, he has the choose-your-own-adventure skatepark market on lock.

With roughly 84 million skaters worldwide, you would think ramp building would be a robust industry, but in reality, it's a lost art, and most skaters spent decades cobbling together makeshift ramps and obstacles at home for personal use. Plus, in order to build a ramp, or have a ramp at home, you have to have the space to make it happen, and the know-how to build something solid and safe.

You want to scare the parentals? Ask them to build you a new mini ramp with a deck capable of holding the eight neighborhood kids you plan on inviting over. Crickets. The mini ramps constructed will be few and far between.

In the 1980s, there was a real separation between skaters who had ramps and private spaces in which to practice and get good, and those who didn't. Not everyone has a family member who knows how to build a ramp or has access to those resources. OC Ramps closed this gap and gave everyone access.

Today, OC Ramps designs and delivers skate demos for some of the biggest companies in the business: Google, Spotify, Amazon, you name it. When people need that "spectacular-spectacular," they call Tyler and the team to bring it to life.

But it wasn't always so. Growing up in Huntington Beach, California, Tyler and his brother began skating with their friends in their early teens. Tyler's work ethic and penchant for ply come from his father, who saw skateboarding as a healthy activity and wanted to make sure that his sons and the neighborhood kids had safe, sturdy places to skate. He built directly from *Thrasher* magazine's OG ramp plans (a set of blueprints are available for a fee directly from the mag's headquarters), some of the only readily accessible designs in the world. Tyler, his dad, and his brother started constructing skateboarding obstacles for themselves and their friends.

My talks with Tyler revealed that those initial ramps brought about the most important parts of skateboarding for him: having fun with family and building a community. Providing the blueprint and

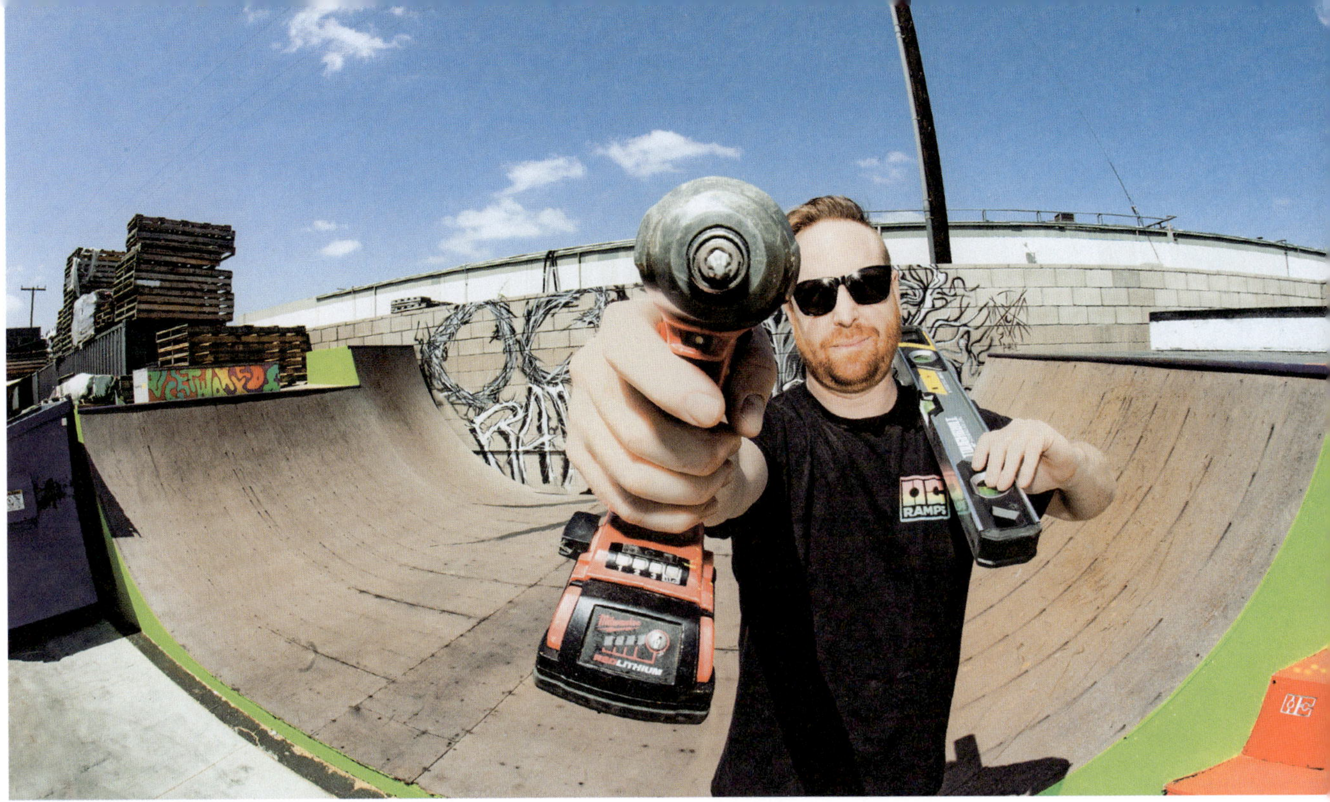

the components to a new generation also serves as an homage to his late father's legacy of service to skateboarding and the community.

OC Ramps quenches your thirst for skate products with more than 79 products for sale, including eight different mini ramps, "butter" benches (meaning they slide well), funboxes, ledges, and rails in a host of dimensions to meet all needs. They also do custom builds, but it's the care and dedication to the craft, evident in all that they produce, that has made them the Johnny Appleseeds of half-pipes.

I've been lucky to see it firsthand. In L.A., Tyler's team provided the mini ramps for our event, The Nation Skate: Diplomacy, Diversity, and Global Engagement through Skateboarding, at the University of Southern California. Watching the mini-ramp creation from scratch assuaged any fear of shoddy construction. The school's head of safety even acknowledged that their work well exceeded his expectations. Proof of stability and design really came to light when the crowd, faculty, and community, witnessed the ramp be put through the paces by none other than superstar and future Olympian Sky Brown (see page 263). The combination of Sky's transition skills and Tyler's design helped dispel any previously held beliefs that skateboarding couldn't exist on campus in a safe and controlled environment.

OC Ramps' work also provided the canvas for the Nation Skate and Finding a Line jazz and skateboarding experience at the Ford theater in L.A. Under the lights of the L.A. stars, Tyler's mini ramp became the springboard of ideas and the final instrument in a mashup with piano, bass, drums, sax, and lyrical MCs. Together they delivered a new remix of "Beats, Rhymes & (Skate) Life" with the mini ramp and Tyler's opus as the central performer.

Bilingual in Spanish and English, a licensed general contractor, and an engineer with a business economics degree, Tyler takes time to speak to students and any organization serving young people. He hopes to inspire others to find what it is that they love and to build a business around that passion. OC Ramps also proudly declares that it is the "only ramp company that has a fully sponsored skate team." With pro skaters like Greg Lutzka and Cody McEntire providing demonstrations, the team helps new audiences envision how Tyler's products can best be used.

Tyler lives by the humble mantra "If you build it, they will come." However, more accurately, Tyler builds *good* ish, and that's why they come—and keep coming back. He has guided students and skaters alike to the drawing board and beyond. His efforts to innovate and put skate spots within the reach and imagination of everyone are a marvel that will long have a place in skate history. Let us toast Mr. Large, the tech innovator slangin' the golden hammer.

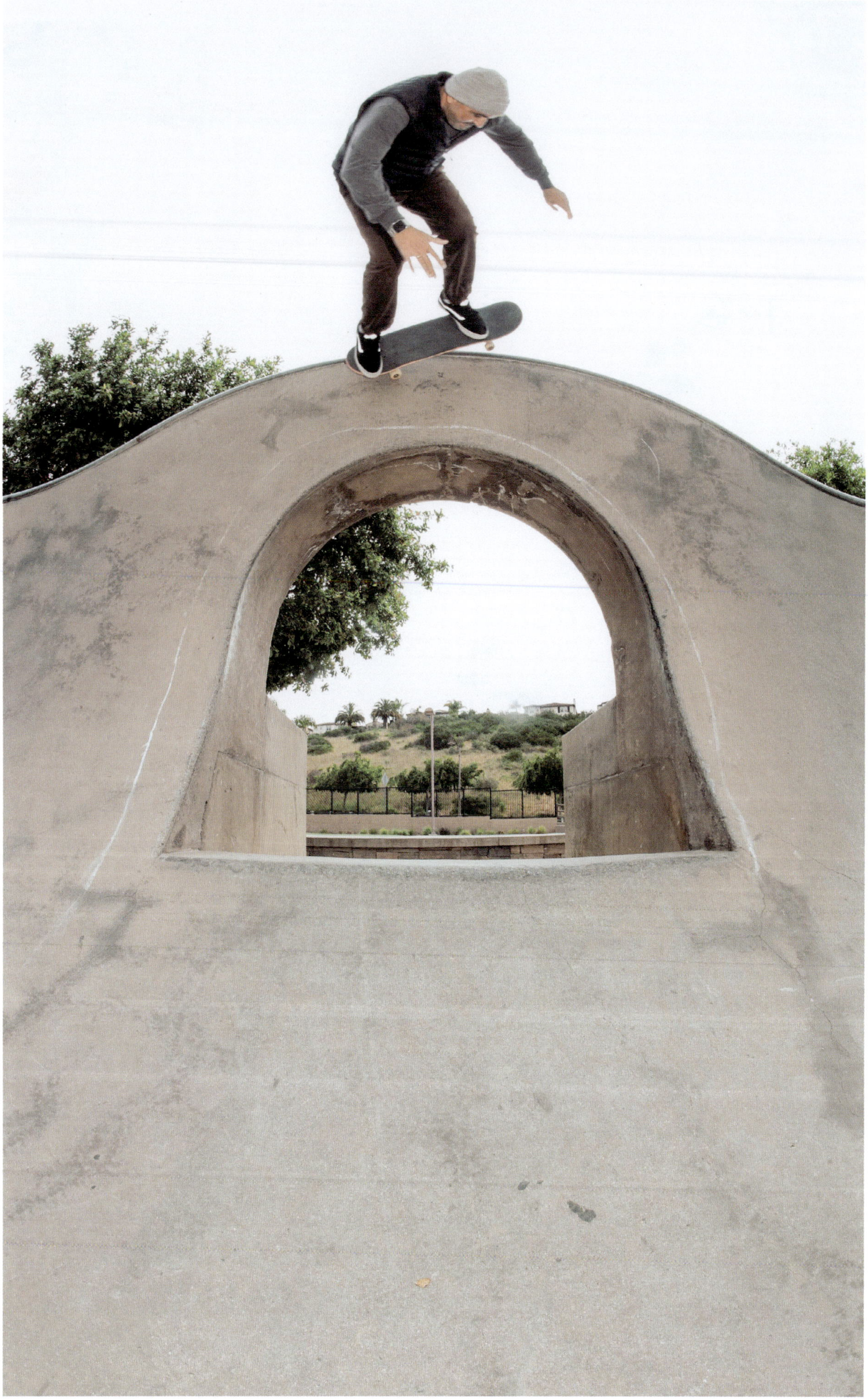

SKATIN' AND CREATIN'

KANTEN RUSSELL

A leader of the historic San Diego skate scene

Supported a community of Black skateboarders

Director of design for New Line Skateparks

Big Skating and Big Love and Big Ideas. These are the first things that come to mind when thinking about San Diego's legendary African American pro skater and lead skatepark designer Kanten Russell.

Kanten is a certified S.D. golden child, a six-foot, three-inch titan who showed that a Big Man skatin' could rock with swagger, style, and finesse—which is no easy act. Bigger bodies, bigger weight, and bigger feet usually equal broken boards and sometimes a slight disconnect between mind, limbs, and actions. As a taller skater, I know what it looks like; sometimes you try walking like a panther and end up stomping like an elephant. But not Kanten. That brother had the juice. He crushed huge stair sets (and innumerable boards) and could throw up tech tricks with the best of them. In S.D. he was the playground legend that all skaters compared themselves to. There is a laundry list of spots from coast to coast, S.D. to N.Y., and beyond. His name rang bells across the globe, with the spots he conquered, including two of the most famous: an ollie over a massive cement 20-stair set in France, one of the biggest sets ever attempted during the early aughts, and was one of the first to launch an ollie down the mighty MACBA's giant four-stair set in Barcelona.

Then there's the epic *TransWorld SKATEboarding* 1993 cover featuring his backside 180 down a 14-stair set, and then his sequence photo featuring a Caballerial (360-degree ollie going in reverse) down the famous San Diego City College 12-stair set. Kanten even did handrails and stair sets the "wrong" way, meaning instead of just skating down them—from the top stair to the bottom—he skated *across* them, launching huge backside 180 ollies off the top step and over the handrail and the remaining stairs and landing backward.

He lived for hurling himself into space and loved that hang time between the ollie and the landing, pushing himself and his skateboard to make those fleeting moments of weightlessness last as long as possible. That was true whether he was firing himself from the back of a loading dock and heelflipping over dumpsters or doing a giant backside 180 heelflip across a 10-foot gap between the edges of one parking lot and another. He powered through nonstop in the aughts, in even more precarious instances, like the time he soared from the top of a pile of iron highway beams on an uncompleted freeway extension across gritty jersey barriers to the gravel-covered earth. Gnarly.

It was during the late '90s and early aughts that Kanten showcased his fearlessness and excess—tackling excessive numbers of stairs and excessive gaps—at any skate spot. You might have been resting and catching your breath at the San Diego Sports Arena double set (a dual set of stairs with a fat section between them), half paying attention, and then, *bam*, Kanten would just float a huge backside heelflip down the set, and fakie half Cab (a fakie backside 180 ollie) the second set while you were catching your breath.

Let me put it this way: Kanten had the cover of *Big Brother* at a time when the last thing an L.A. magazine wanted to do was push S.D. riders. That cover of him skating the massive Long Beach set? That was an impossible spot that skaters had drooled over and dreamed of landing.

Kanten was and remains a businessman, too. During his early professional career, he and another S.D. legend, Oscar "OJ" Jordan, created Shaft Skateboards, a Black-centric board brand through skater Mike McGill's company. They recognized that they had their *own voice* (also the name of a previous incarnation of the brand) and they wanted it to be heard.

Admittedly, putting the Black perspective in skateboarding in the mix of S.D. from the late '80s through the '90s was no easy feat. While skateboarding was more diverse in Los Angeles and San Francisco, in that era, S.D.'s population of African Americans simply wasn't high. This isn't to say that they felt alone in skateboarding, but this was prior to skateboarding being as openly embraced as a space for Black people by the non-skate populace. Kanten and OJ endured years of grumbling about skateboarding's lack of value to the Black community, all while they simultaneously kept their Black identity front and center as they built their name.

Luckily for them, there were a few other Black skaters in S.D., such as OG Tyrone "T-Bone" Olson. However, what made Kanten special is that his family was a nucleus for Black skateboarding in S.D. Kanten's parents recognized that many of the Black skaters coming up in the late '80s and early '90s came from homes that could be considered dysfunctional or at the least latchkey. The Russells offered a space where everyone could see the model of a Black family surviving in America. The realization that he was blessed to have strong family figures helped Kanten to see all Black skaters as part of his extended family, and to take on the responsibility to integrate compassion and empathy into all of his endeavors.

When he came up, they all came up, and he ensured that other Black skaters also got product and access to the boards, wheels, shoes—whatever he could do to keep everyone skating. This in turn built a communal practice of care carried forward by skaters on the receiving end, like then–child prodigy pro skater Brandon Turner. Turner now gives back as a pro skater and as the director of West Side Recovery, which uses skateboarding to support the physical and mental health of those in addiction recovery.

The same would hold true when Kanten later landed a spot on the lauded Planet Earth Skateboards team, created by Skateboarding Hall of Famer Chris Miller. There, Kanten would mentor skaters, offer his unique perspective to the team, and contribute design ideas. His voice and vision also transferred over into his work with other sponsors, like when he designed a signature pro model for Osiris Shoes while filming for the team video *The Storm* (1999). The Osiris team won the *TransWorld SKATEboarding* readers' poll for the best team skate video, and Kanten stood out for conquering big sets of stairs and handrail skating, perfectly blending a new mix of technical ledge and bench skating. He remained true to himself while incorporating the new technical trends and skating with a star-studded cast that included his new Osiris teammates Peter Smolik and Jerry Hsu.

Throughout his pro career, Kanten contributed greatly to every aspect of the San Diego scene, skating big, thinking big, and setting the standard for the city. What makes him truly exceptional is his ability to show that there is a professional career path beyond having technical skills on a board. How so? Kanten Russell is now the first African American pro skater and designer at New Line Skateparks. The audacity of this Black man in America, thwarting the odds by taking his career and hard-earned time in skateboarding and finding a new way to flame on, instead of out.

After riding for S.D. giants like Expedition and creating a pro model shoe with Osiris, he went back to school with a focus on art and design. He wanted to develop new skateboarding spaces, ensuring that skaters of every level could enjoy the pleasure of the push.

Being a pro street skater offers a unique voice at the design table. Kanten knows from his own experience and perspective as a skater the difference between materials and layout that makes one ledge design buttery and the other bollocks. He also knows the sad truth that most municipalities would rather listen to anyone other than the young people they are trying to serve. There is still a bias against these young people, as if they lack the ability to articulate why they love skateboarding. That leads to Rec and Parks departments being swindled by bad designs, overpaying, and ending up with a facility skaters don't actually want to use.

Kanten's design process creates a balanced mix of street and transition skating. (For those pooh-poohing transition in favor of more street, you never know when a transition skater like the Birdman might roll by your local park and put on a demo. I have seen it live, and it's phenomenal.) However, before street skaters yell treason, note that each park needs the element street skaters are searching for, while also providing for other types of skaters, so they don't keep searching for pools and finding themselves at odds with local law enforcement,

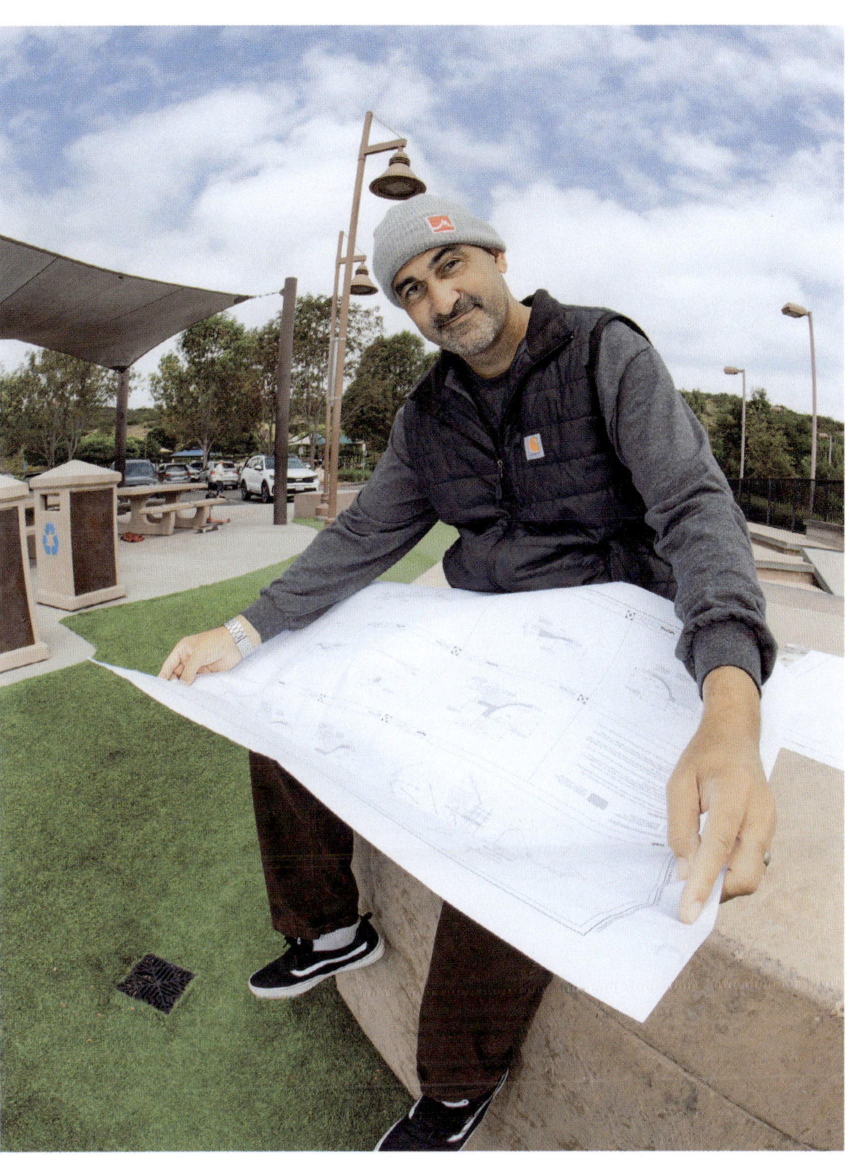

homeowners, and shopkeepers. Kanten brings this authenticity to the design phase—he's been in the streets.

Now, as a designer, he takes that same ability to navigate trends and transitions to create a more inclusive space through skatepark design. While he's opened Poplar Bluff Skate Plaza in Missouri and several parks throughout California, the design of the LaGrange skatepark in Georgia is a standout for access for its compliance with the Americans with Disabilities Act. As Kanten told me, "We want everyone to enjoy the skatepark, so we are removing walls and changing the transitions around the park so it can be wheelchair accessible and support multiple wheeled use." That turn toward accessibility even supports those who are visually impaired like pro skater Dan Mancina— legally blind, he was on hand to skate and support the opening of LaGrange and has begun preparing other visually impaired skaters with the necessary techniques to skate safely.

What has always been the case with Kanten Russell is that he cares and continues to move forward. He does the same when dealing with the NIMBY ("not in my backyard") people who are unsupportive of skatepark construction. It takes a big heart, big patience, and a big man to deal with the quagmire of municipal bureaucracy. Even greater is Kanten's perseverance and ingenuity to move naysayers and bring together diverse groups in order to carry those projects across the finish line and continue launching skateboarding into new arenas.

CHRIS ROBERTS & JERON WILSON

Founders of the *Nine Club* podcast

Professional skaters for Girl and Chocolate Skateboards

Ahh, one of the best plays on words in skateboarding.

Seriously, the only thing more ironic than a podcast with the motto "the show that has skaters talking" (as opposed to skating or acting typically noncommunicative) could be to name your podcast after the highest marks a skater can earn in a Street League Skateboarding (SLS) contest, 9 or above. A skater who accomplishes it has "joined the Nine Club."

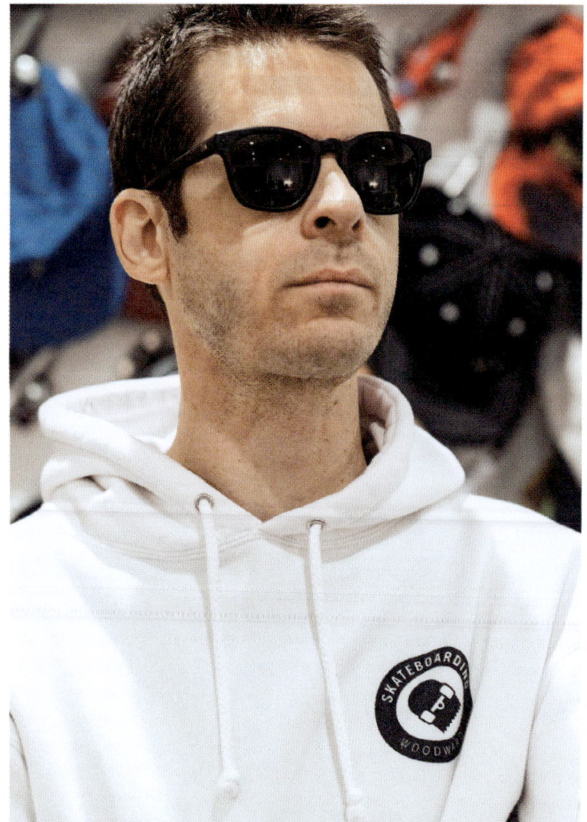

Chris Roberts at Crailtap HQ

Chris Roberts and his cofounder Roger Bagley began the pod in 2016. It was one of the first skate-centered podcasts and immediately gained a large following. Roberts is a pro skater for Chocolate Skateboards, the other half of the Girl/Chocolate coalition of skateboarding companies, and has a decades-deep career with the Crailtap family.

Born in Malibu and raised skating the streets of Los Angeles and Venice, he got his start loving the original World and Blind skate teams, like all of us, and became a fan of Girl and Chocolate. However, unlike the rest of us, he was able to join the illustrious team.

First skating in Venice, meeting skaters like Daniel Castillo and filming with Tim Dowling in the *L.A. County* video, over time he earned his place in the Chocolate crew. Through skating and producing seminal parts for Chocolate's videos, like *Hot Chocolate* (2004), and filming with the team and Spike Jonze (see page 154), Chris Roberts became a household name in the skate community.

He also saw that there were more stories and discussions to be had in skateboarding than traditional skate media had space for. Taking his fervor to connect with skaters and favorite pros, he began working with the seminal Northeast videographer and jack-of-all-trades Roger Bagley. They created a small empire: *The Nine Club*.

Bagley eventually moved behind the scenes, and the most recent incarnation of the cohosting team consists of Roberts and "brother from another mother" Crailtap Distribution and Girl Skateboards pro Jeron Wilson. They operate alongside Expedition One pro skater Kelly Hart with a roundtable of guests ranging from Glen E. Friedman to Paul "P-Rod" Rodriguez; Samarria Brevard to Nora Vasconcellos; and truthfully any skater who has been culturally relevant in the past or present. Their loose format allows skaters to expound for hours about multiple topics and has created one of the largest oral archives in all of skateboarding.

Shot in a studio adorned with skate memorabilia near the Venice Beach Skate Park, the show offers something for every type of skater and discipline, including conversations with artists, videographers, and those skate-adjacent folks who help move the skate zeitgeist. Along with the interviews, there are also "drop-ins," where guests can express what is happening at that moment in their lives or offer a quick take on current events in the industry. The show keeps skaters informed, inspires their skating, and encourages the chatter.

A key component of the program, Jeron Wilson is a long-serving pro skater and company owner who has seen it all. Carrying the torch for Girl Skateboards, Jeron—or "J-Dubs," as he is known to his friends—has also been involved in multiple aspects of the skateboarding business, as a longtime athlete and leading figure in the highly influential skate/streetwear brand Diamond Supply Co. Hardware. With pro model shoes for brands like DVS and later Diamond and video parts in some of the greatest releases in skateboarding, such as the DVS *Skate More* (2005) video and Girl videos from *Goldfish* (1994) to *Pretty Sweet* (2012), he is a mainstay and one of the most continually progressing and inspiring skaters, able to move and shift with his skating and attitude from decade to decade.

With so much time in the skate game, Jeron has had a seat at the table during some of skateboarding's greatest junctures. He was a member of the Real Skateboards team in his early teens and came up under the tutelage of '93 *Thrasher* Skater of the Year and Skateboarding Hall of Fame member Salman Agah. He was a part of the illustrious (and sometimes infamous) World Industries camp, riding for Blind Skateboards during its second renaissance after Mark "Gonz" Gonzales (see page 92) had left and it was largely the charge of Steve Rocco. That Blind team featured a new generation of late-teens and early-twenties sensations like pros Tim Gavin and Henry Sanchez.

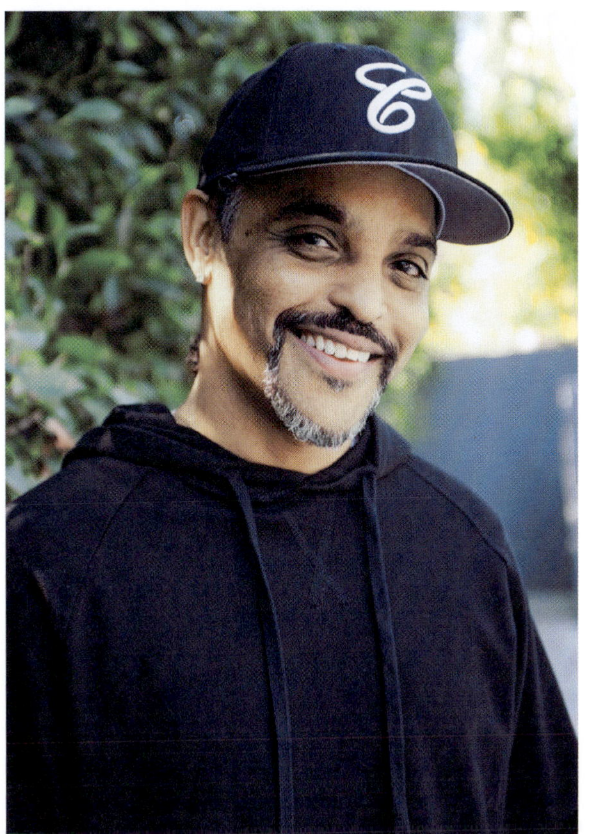

Jeron Wilson at home

While an amateur there, Jeron filmed two of the most memorable parts in early '90s skateboarding. One was the FTC skate shop video called *Finally . . . an FTC Video*, where he skated into our brains under the overtures of Mary J. Blige's version of the Chaka Khan hit song "Sweet Thing." Blige's modern version fit this young African American skater to a T. It was mellow and smooth but still street with the backing beat, and it felt tailor-made for the young phenom tackling S.F.'s and L.A.'s most famed skate spots. Jeron was the envy of every viewer. Barely in his teens, he was turning out tech maneuvers well ahead of his time, like switch manual to switch heel out in that video way before most people even had a switch ollie.

Jeron punctuated his presence on the Blind team with footage in the beloved "Our Friends" section of the Plan B *Virtual Reality* video in 1993, skating to the Beatles' "With a Little Help from My Friends." In just over a minute's worth of footage, he showed us the technical tricks of our dreams, launching nonchalantly over the cement hips of L.A. schoolyards and down cement ledges right alongside the best pros of the '90s.

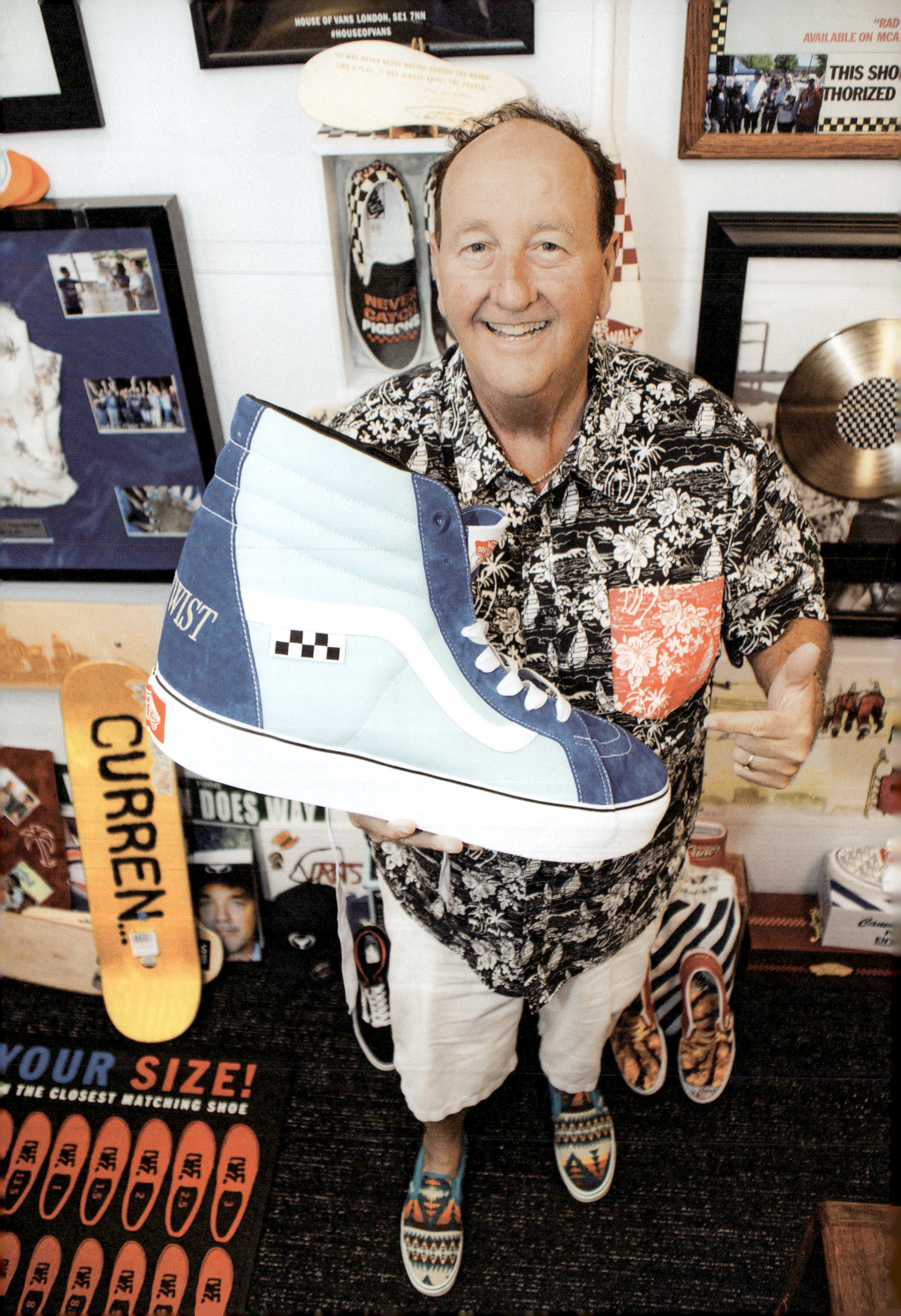

HOUSE OF VANS LONDON, SE1 7NN
#HOUSEOFVANS
NEVER CATCH PIGEONS
CURREN...
YOUR SIZE!
THE CLOSEST MATCHING SHOE
VANS
DOES WAY
"RAD"
AVAILABLE ON MCA
THIS SHO
THORIZED
TWIST

THE SULTAN OF STOKE
STEVE VAN DOREN

Heir to the Vans sneaker dynasty

Premier sponsor of the Vans Warped Tour

Title sponsor of the U.S. Open of Surfing

A man of the people

Few people have done more to exhibit a "make no person a stranger" mantra than Mr. Steve Van Doren, as in Van of Vans sneakers. Steve is arguably the best-known member of the family-named business and is the longtime VP of events and promotions. Skaters the world over love Steve for delivering miles of smiles, flipping enough burgers and dogs to partially stave off world hunger, and, during the free food BBQs Vans hosted, attempting to save the planet by planting each and every foot in a pair of Vans.

Both Steve and Vans are ubiquitous on the skateboarding scene and in action sports as a whole. The checkerboard, the waffle sole—untouchable. From skate, surf, and snowboarding to moto and BMX to stage, screen, and song, Vans earned their moniker, The Original.

What other company is cited in interviews with Samuel L. Jackson? Had the party rockin' with that hyphy "they got their Vans on" (shout-out to The Pack) and got served in looks by A$AP Rocky and Kendrick Lamar? That's without the host of other stars and runway models that consistently slip in and out of those classic old-school styles. And without counting the quintessential silver-screen Vans moment: Sean Penn as stoner surfer Jeff Spicoli in *Fast Times at Ridgemont High*.

You can't put a price on that kind of cool. Well, *actually* you can, and it's to the tune of about 486 million *doo-llars*, as RuPaul would say. That's what it cost conglomerate VF Corporation to acquire Vans in 2010. But decades before the big offer, Vans began in a place where "cool" most often referred to a drop in temperature—Boston, Massachusetts. The Van Doren family started their enterprise as an early forerunner in the footwear market, called the Van Doren Rubber Company. Paul Van Doren and his brothers then moved the business and family to Anaheim, California, in 1966, set up shop, and built a factory that featured two revolutionary items: the custom shoe and the vulcanized sole.

As Steve told me, "My dad and uncles built the business caring about the customer. You bring the material and you will get *your* shoe. Custom-made with what was important to you." Genius. That approach helped Vans hold a special place in customers' hearts. You gave them a piece of yourself, and they gave you a way to wear your heart on your feet.

That connection between heart and sole was true even in the earliest days, when Vans first established their action sports connection. Their ability to make shoes from custom materials created a legacy in surfing when, in 1966, they used the now iconic Aloha print from a shirt belonging to legendary surfer and Olympian Duke Kahanamoku to make a pair of custom Aloha Vans. Worn by the Native Hawai'ian progenitor of surfing, this shirt-and-shoe combo helped set in motion an enduring synergy with surfing, and then with the emerging action sport, skateboarding.

Steve is quick to reveal that the Van Doren Rubber Company didn't set out to create the "original" skateboarding shoe, they just wanted to make a quality product. The outcome of developing the vulcanized waffle sole, with double the rubber used by the competition, perfectly aligned with the needs of the customer. "The best people in skateboarding adopted Vans early on," Steve said. "Tony Alva spoke, and we listened to what he and others said." That communication is what drove business and earned Vans a place within the skateboarding community.

Beginning with Alva in the '70s, those associated with Vans, like Steve Caballero in the '80s, Salman Agah, Cara-Beth Burnside, and Geoff Rowley in the '90s to the aughts, all continued Vans's relationship with skateboarding. Newer innovators such as Beatrice Domond, the first African American woman with a Vans pro model shoe, and Lizzie Armanto, who designed a unisex shoe, are part of the faithful crew, and regularly are in conversation with Steve and the team about how to improve upon the product and support the community.

Steve's legacy includes Vans's commitment to support every facet of skateboarding and action sports, including the music. It was Steve and the team who supported the wonder of all wonders, the Vans Warped Tour, which put skateboarding front and center, whether the world was ready for it or not.

It seems passé now, but there was a time when no one wanted to believe that skateboarding, kids under 18, and the action sport's soundtrack had value—all of which was the impetus for the Warped Tour. They created a show for all ages, with 20 different bands performing and 20 different skaters crisscrossing coast to coast from Long Beach to Amherst, Massachusetts, with spots in the heartland and breadbasket of America. It was a traveling community, bonding lovers of the sight, sound, and spectacle of skate culture. The tour came to my neck of the woods in Northampton, Massachusetts, in the late '90s, and it called out to kids across New England, who clamored to see the singers and skaters whose posters lined their bedroom walls. None of that would have been possible without Steve's insight and understanding that while everyone loved Cali culture, not everyone lived in California. Hats off.

Steve and the Vans team also delivered the Vans Park Series, a precursor to park as an Olympic sport. The Vans Triple Crown, the Vans U.S. Open

of Surfing, the Maloof Money Cup, and the epic Downtown Showdown, where the skate contest took place on the Hollywood Paramount Studio lot. Imagine skating where some of the most popular films of all time were produced: *Star Trek, Mission: Impossible, Citizen Kane* and even *King Kong*? Epic! Skateboarding never looked so spectacular, or was steeped in so much rich history. Steve Van Doren and his former director of marketing, Justin Regan, as always, took skateboarding to the next level. The Downtown Showdown has now been to Paris, Amsterdam, and London. Vans is ubiquitous—

where there are action sports, or really, any sport, the waffle sole is present. The brand even made a custom cleat for SoCal native and Major League Baseballer Michael Lorenzen.

Steve perpetuates Vans's omnipresence in the culture as the spirit of the company. He reminds us not to take ourselves too seriously and to love what we do.

But there were some hurdles that the brand had to overcome. It wasn't always smooth sailing. Take for example when Steve's Uncle Jimmy took over as director. He wanted to steer the company away from its original skateboarding clientele in favor of the hard-core athletic market. They soon found out that being a specialty brand with a niche market didn't translate to the consumers they hoped to draw in. Traditional sports brands like Asics, Adidas, Nike, New Balance, and their ilk spent billions trying to make anyone in the athletic or athleisure market their converts. In contrast, in skateboarding and action sports, Vans has been the sneaker of choice. That's a sizable framework and positive wind to have at your back. It would take almost losing the company in bankruptcy court for Vans to remember that. Steve's father, Paul, then returned to the fold and attempted to save the company from being sold off. The judge asked the elder Van Doren to describe what the Vans company was. The answer he went with was a skateboarding shoe manufacturer:

he brought it back to the roots of the company. Turned out, that answer saved them. Rather than liquidating Vans during a financial downturn, the judge presiding over the case let them work to repay their debt. Which they did—fully. Few companies have the integrity, grit, and wherewithal to know who they are and where their strengths lie.

The original motto for Vans is "Off The Wall," a throwback to the type of righteous skating being done in backyard pools during contemporary skateboarding's raucous origins. "Off The Wall" has come to mean so many things, but above all it stands for those unafraid to push boundaries or go beyond the line. Steve Van Doren and Vans sneakers have gone far beyond their earliest intent in Boston. They created shoes that people liked that delivered good value. They now give a great return to their corporate owners, VF (owners of Timberland, Dickies, Eastpak, and JanSport, among others). Vans offers VF the opportunity to keep its finger on the pulse of youth culture, and VF offers Vans the internal funding to create rich experiences and world-class events for its customers.

And Vans is as current as ever in skate culture. Look at its takeover of fashion week during the run-up to the 2024 Paris Olympics. Vans began its launch at Place de la Bastille with a skateboarding art show and demonstration that celebrated the work of Atiba Jefferson (see page 143) and Virgil Abloh (RIP). It closed out in spectacular fashion with a skateable bowl/sculpture laid at the feet of the Basilica of the Sacré-Cœur in Montmartre, with renowned electronic music duo Justice DJing. Creating these types of events with an owner who understands the business allows Vans to stay at the top of the game. It ensures they are in the limelight, whether in the pages of *Vogue* or *Vanity Fair*, and that their drops are a staple for wearers from the Hypebeast to your hyped bae.

Vans is the primordial home for the rule breakers and tastemakers who needed something a little extra to release their radness . . . a pair of Vans. Steve Van Doren and Vans supported the stoke for decades with only bigger and better things on the horizon. And why not? They were there with the first ones in the pool, and they damn sure deserve to be the last ones out.

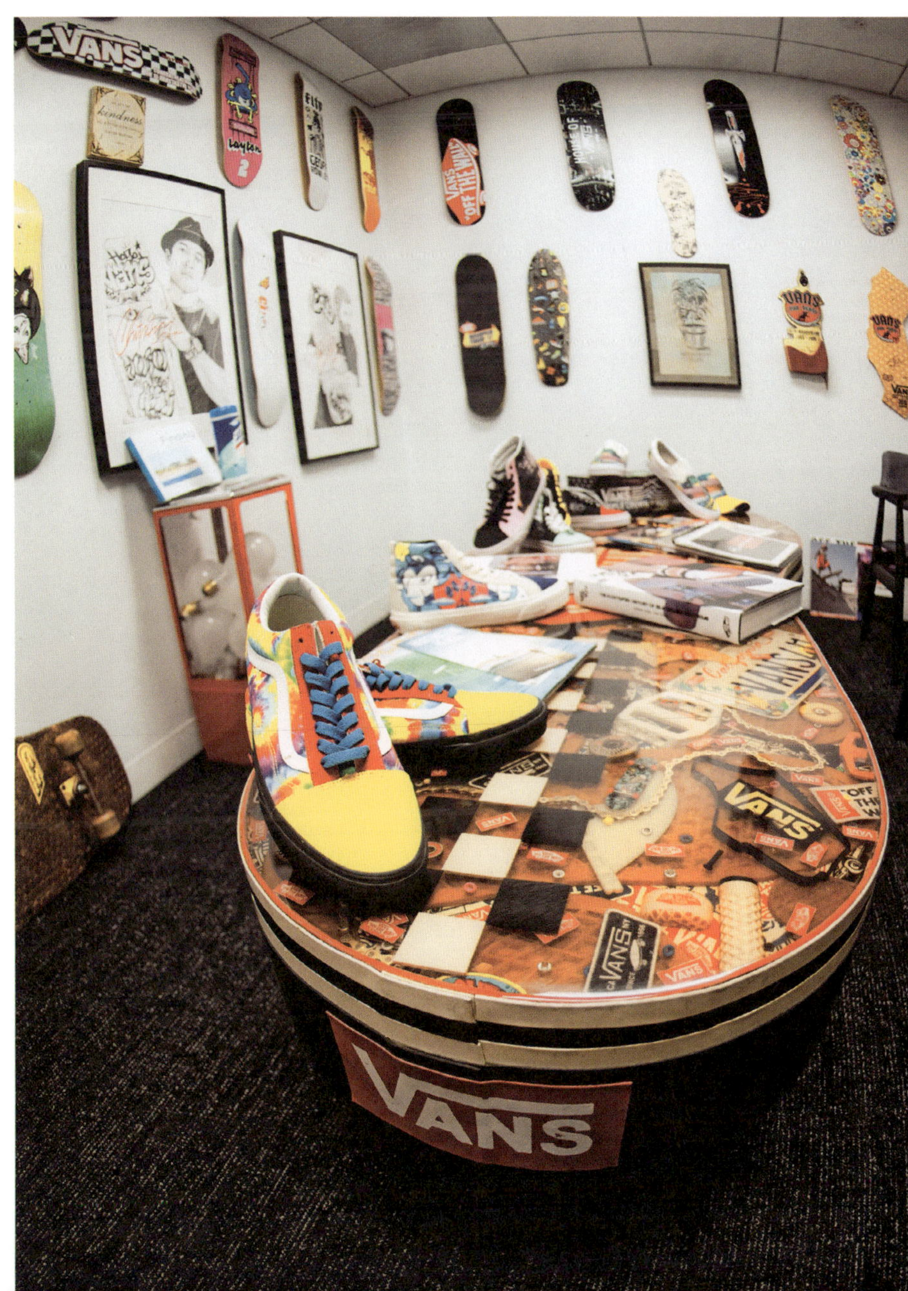

Inside a Vans HQ memorabilia room featuring a giant waffle-sole coffee table and Vans artifacts

THE FUTURISTS

Fasten your seatbelt; it's time for a change.

Looking for help getting your paper right? Your wheelbase locked and loaded? Yourself into the best "Damn Am" contests in the world? Or the best board under your feet? Well, you came to the right place. Everyone on these pages represents a greater whole responsible for making skateboarding that goes . . .

Individually, these folks help float the ark of our culture through countless storms. They remain ten toes down whether skaters are showered with love or muddied with insults, and for decades, they have kept the hugs and high-fives happening. They envision a future where all skaters are loved and respected, and they create opportunities for this to come to fruition. Whether the sentiment around skateboarding is hot and smooth or cold and callous, they demand that skaters get what they deserve.

Paving the way for new tomorrows is complex, and these vanguards march through growing pains to manage mindsets, mega-events, monumental teams, and territory. They deliver perspectives that shift the culture, and their efforts represent a change in attitudes and alliances, solidifying a new standard in skateboarding.

THE PRINCE OF PARIS
STÉPHANE LARANCE

Sport manager of skateboard and freestyle BMX at the 2024 Paris Olympics

Leader of Black Parisian skateboarding in the mid–'90s to early aughts

Former team manager for DC Shoes Europe

Icon of Lordz skateboard video

First Black French pro street skater with a signature model

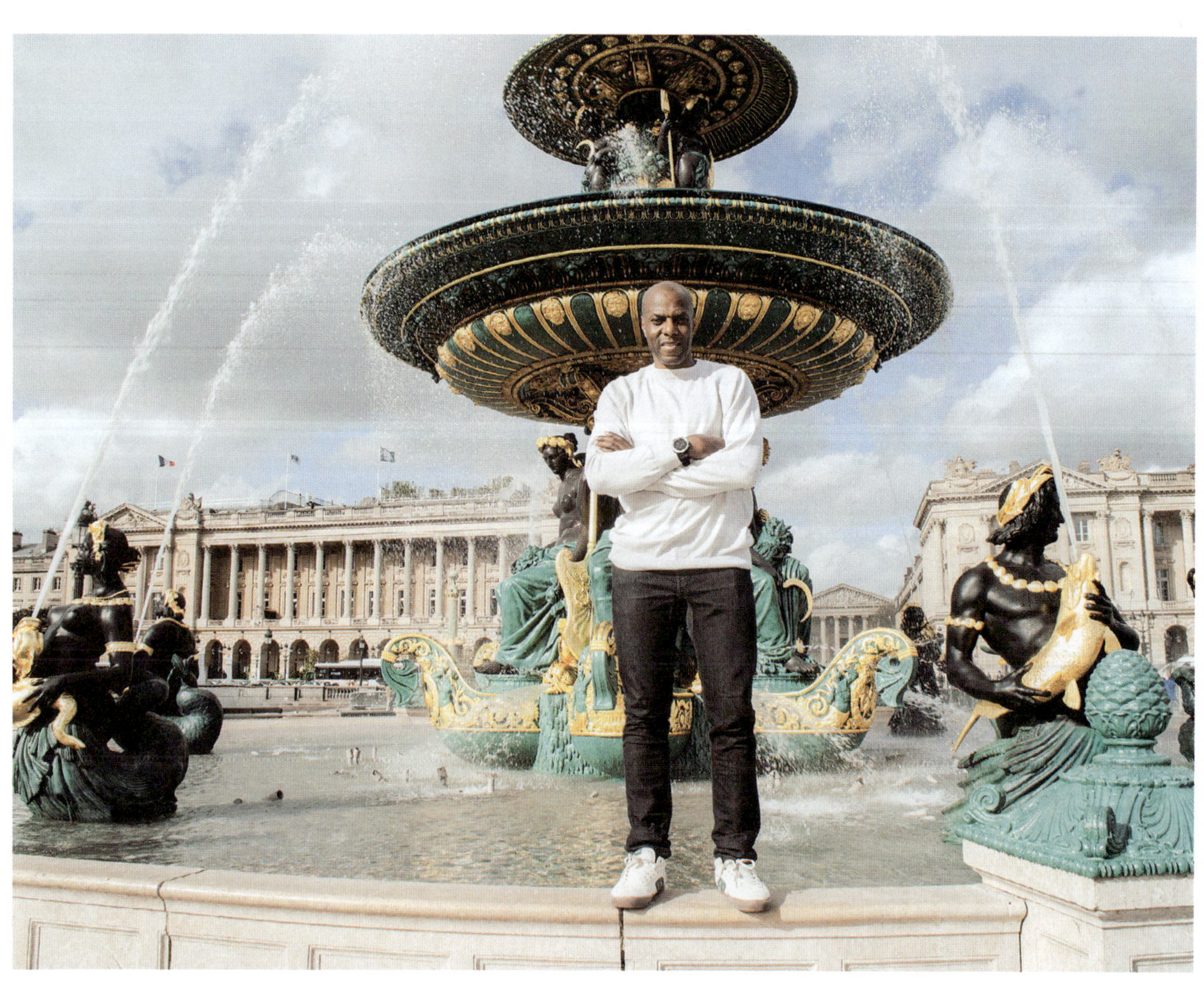

Stéphane Larance is a member of the French Olympic Federation, the sport manager of skateboard and freestyle BMX, and perhaps France's most decorated skateboarding vet. In our conversations leading up to the 2024 Olympics, he talked about what it meant to have the Olympics in Paris—his city. Paris is one of the best spots for skating: The architecture is beautiful. There are places like the Palais de Tokyo, which have become skate havens. The pools beneath the Eiffel Tower are a dream to skate and have only been attempted by a select few.

A year before the Olympics, Stéphane told me every intimate detail being put into making Paris the best skateboarding contest ever—from the height of the rails, to the materials for the ledges, the colors to be used, you name it—there was a lot of pressure to make it perfect. Partly, he cared about the city, of course, but he was also the first Black Parisian in charge of the skateboarding exhibition for the Olympics. As the soon-to-be head judge and the coordinator for the city, he lived and breathed the 2024 Paris skateboarding Olympics so the rest of us could enjoy the games, the city, the love.

It turns out that everyone of all ages was a fan—from kids to parents, aunties and uncles to grandparents. The crowds of skateboarding spectators were massive, and that is a testament to the work of Stéphane and his team.

When the course was unveiled, it was majestic in all its purple and pink and gold handrails, perfectly mimicking the authentic spots in the streets. The same held true for the park section, which was a dreamy spot to "send it," put every bit of effort into your skating. You knew this through the explosive runs that were churned out by Sky Brown, Tom Schaar, and others. When the course is right, the pros put on a show.

Stéphane and the team worked tirelessly, pouring his 20 years of experience into every inch of that course. If a skater thought a spot was too slick? Bam! They appeared from the ether to sand it down. If a line was not straight or level, it got corrected. Whatever the request, Stéphane made the course majestic.

Throughout the city, French team skaters like Aurélien Giraud, Vincent Milou, and Charlotte Hym were getting their shine on and promoting skateboard along with French NGOs, all basking in the limelight of the games.

This was Stéphane's love letter to the city that helped him build a career and his opportunity to return the favor. Stéphane's parents immigrated to France from continental Africa, but as he's told me many times, he *is* French, a point of pride that his mom instilled in him early on and that he wears on his sleeve. It is an important armor to have, especially when waves of rising anti-immigrant rhetoric rear their ugly heads in the E.U. and beyond.

He put his French finesse on display when he first burst onto the scene in a 1997 issue of *411* and in 2000 in the *Conspiracy* video from wheel maker Lordz. And Stéphane gave the world its first taste of Black Parisian skateboarding in the late '90s, bringing in 360 flips and nollie flips that were as smooth as silk—a buttery style, as we say. He could skate big gaps and throw tech tricks down

anywhere, and even with a large frame, he hit the crown with a je ne sais quoi that made his tricks always look perfect. No matter the environment, he ain't breaking a sweat.

At that time, in the U.S., we knew there were skaters in France, but not that *we* was in France, not like *that*. Black people in Paris—and they ain't visitin'. Imagine that. Stéphane brought that notion to the table. It made us all feel more connected to global skateboarding. Sure, we knew about our Black key figures in blues and jazz and Black intellectuals who had taken refuge in Paris to ease the pain of the thrashing monster of racism and its need to feed on Black and Brown bodies. Paris—it is where Miles fell in love, Dizzy hit with the Double Six, and Hazel Scott, Josephine Baker, and Baldwin set up home. But to see one of *us* is there, open and living what it means to be Black and of the African diaspora in the city of lights, was something else altogether.

I learned that when Stéphane was a teenager in Paris, most kids assigned each other nicknames. Stinky, or Timely (for those who were always late); you get the gist. Blackie was Stéphane's moniker, until one day he had enough. As his friends recalled to me, Stéphane said: "My name is Stéphane Larance. You can call me Stéphane, even Steph—but you cannot call me Blackie." There he was, aware of the world and the implications of his Blackness.

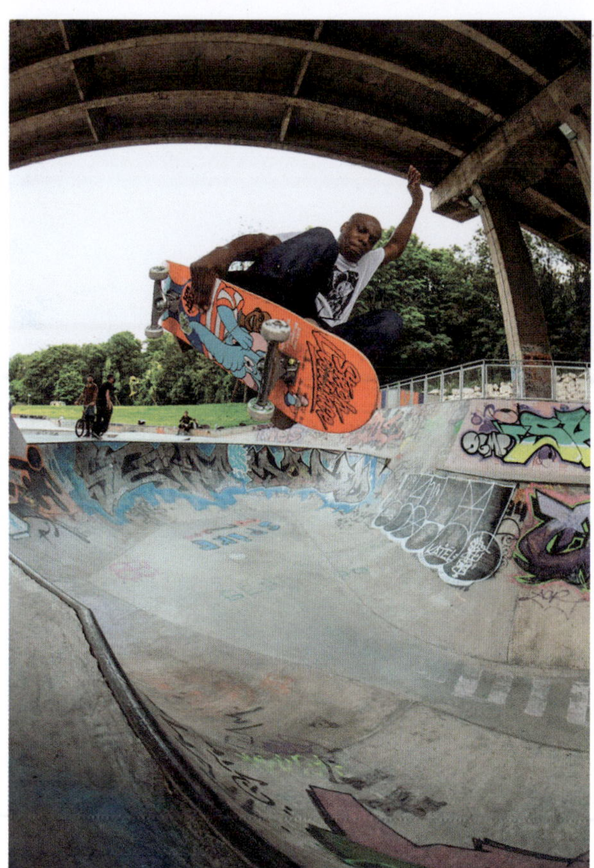

Some were annoyed, but ultimately everyone changed.

During this time, he also tried to build a real career in skateboarding, which meant making the trip across the pond. He became well-known in L.A. and San Diego, and eventually settled in S.D. (A little-known fact is that his first sponsor was the preeminent African American skateboarder Sal Barbier's [see page 87] 23 Skateboard Co., a testament to Stéphane's skills and to Sal's ability to spot talent.) By the time the world saw Stéphane, he was blowing doors and quickly earned a pro model board from San Diego–based brand Expedition One. On Expedition, he rose to fame appearing in ads and filming parts in team vids, proving he had the skills to join skateboarding's elite ranks. However, while he cherished those times deeply, he returned home often over the years. Most skaters eventually settle in to the land of America's milk and honey—yet for Stéphane it was never fully sweet.

"The French lifestyle and U.S. lifestyle of skating are very different. In France we enjoy the whole process. We skate or train to the [skate] spots. We decide what spots best suit our style and work with the photographers there. It's very personal. It's very French," he noted with a laugh. "In the U.S. you drive everywhere. You are in the car or the van with a spot the photographer picked out—then you all pile out and see what trick you can get. Then back in the van to the next spot. It's not as free and skater-centric as in France."

His moves between the two countries inspired some of his teammates on Expedition One and DC Shoes as well. Several made the biannual crossing of the Atlantic to experience the inspiring sentiment themselves. Yet in the U.S., for better or worse, we like our skaters close by, which eventually created tensions. Stéphane needed his freedom. And in the mid-aughts, he made his last official trip as a U.S.-sponsored pro skater. Once home, he felt rejuvenated—he was on his soil, the returning hero. He had made France and Black Parisians a mainstay in U.S. skateboarding. Satisfied, he fell right back into the business side of skating with roles as team manager for multiple brands, including DC Shoes, and organizer of skateboarding events and championships. He hosted visiting pros and he still skated amazingly well, tapping into every aspect of European skateboarding. From the magazines, to tours, to photographers and videographers—he remained plugged in and a seminal figure in French skateboarding.

In the same way that the 2018 French World Cup Team showed the world that French men of color could be the great hope of France when they won the world's biggest soccer championship with a team majority of Black players, Stéphane has offered a perspective on race and ethnicity for decades. For those of us in the U.S., who were less informed about not only the African diaspora but also the effect of Black people on the global skate diaspora, we could not have imagined finding or being more inspired by a kindred spirit in France. Stéphane will always be known around the world as the Parisian forever standin' on business and keeping the lights of his city alive.

FROM THE HOODS TO THE WOODS

JOHNNY SCHILLEREFF

CEO and president of USA Skateboarding

Founder of pop culture crossover Element Skateboards

Cofounder of the Heart Supply and its Xala, Mexico, eco-friendly skatepark

Original scout and home for skate phenoms Nyjah Huston and Bam Margera

Every athlete and artist dreams of moving the needle in their chosen field, and every so often someone drops the needle and moves both worlds like a DJ running the ones and twos to their whim. The mix master in this case is the great Johnny "Schill" Schillereff. Has his name escaped you? You're not alone. Schill is one of the few entrepreneurs and company owners within skateboarding culture to be a seminal force without making the gnarliest flick on board, but doing it instead with the flick of a wrist (and the dash of a pen).

His artistic vision was informed by a mash-up of East Coast aesthetics. Raised in urban Atlanta in the late 1970s and early '80s but with jaunts to the serenity of Maine and the Northeast, Schill used his art to present skateboarding as a positive force for everyone "from the hoods to the woods" and back again. That mantra became the driving force behind creating one of the most successful and continuously running skateboarding companies of all time: Element Skateboards. Its iconic logo, which depicts wind, water, fire, and earth, and the Element name are as synonymous with skateboarding as Billabong is with surf and Patagonia is with the great outdoors. While you may not know Johnny's name, you are still privy to the world he built over his 30-year career. From

Element's logo stickers adhered to every surface across the globe to the black T-shirts that read "Listen to Bob Marley," everyone has seen his handiwork. Bam Margera of the Element team was one of the first skaters to have crossover success in film and on MTV. And let's not forget that Element was the original home to the illustrious contest-winning machine, Olympian Nyjah Huston (see page 32).

Of course, gaining that level of exposure and omnipresence evolved through an ungodly mix of timing and toil, debacle and design. The critical seeds to Element's growth began with a thought: "Why can't a skateboarding company be as big as a surfing company?" Next came the idea that the brand name matters more than the individual members of the company team. In other team sports, this concept is referred to as "front of jersey" (city name) and "back of jersey" (player's last name).

A big wave has to start somewhere, and this one began with the founding of New Deal Skateboards. New Deal was started by U.K.-born former pro skater Steve Douglas, and then artist and pro upstart Andy Howell, and one of the greatest skateboarding manufacturers of all time, Paul Schmitt (see page 209). Additional art duties were handled by Gorm Boberg and day-to-day administration by editor of the legendary video

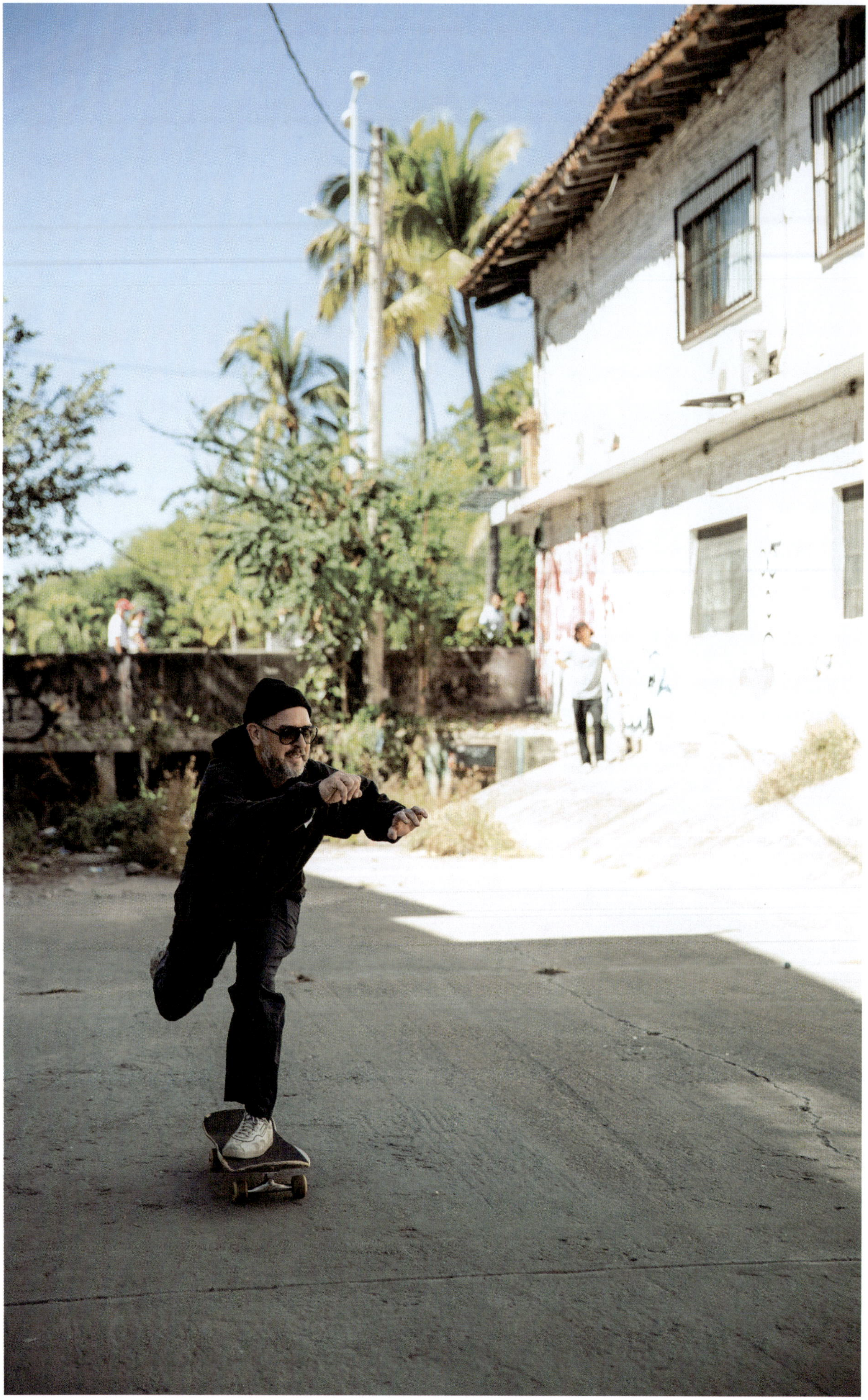

magazine *411* Josh Friedberg. New Deal (and its later subsidiaries, which would eventually lead to the creation of umbrella company Giant Skateboard Distribution) formed the precursor to Element, Underworld Element. Underworld Element existed as an offshoot of the New Deal brand led by one of the greatest artists and most influential skaters, and an East Coast icon, Atlanta's own Andy Howell. They featured a team and iconography fitting of the time, and gave us a hefty dose of street and urban life, including the best of what both the East Coast and San Francisco had to offer in those early days. Rick Ibaseta, Bill Pepper, Jeff Pang, Julien Stranger, Chris Hall, Andy Stone, and the like would all be part of the OG Underworld Element lineup, which later added icons Harold Hunter (RIP), Stevie Williams, and so many more.

Underworld's original ads, art, and aesthetics, circa 1992, documented the fact that a multiracial cadre of skaters were in the streets igniting the imagination of skaters worldwide. Their art and iconography represented a cast of characters in street life I saw myself; the urban representations aligned with my views and visions of the city.

The first Schillereff and Howell promo video released for Underworld Element, aptly named *Fine Artists*, and its subsequent release, *Skypager*, showcased East Coast skating at its core—a change from most films that spotlighted California skating. Philadelphia's Love Park and D.C.'s Freedom Plaza (better known to skaters as Pulaski Park because of the statue of Casimir Pulaski at the end of the grounds), a stone's throw away from the White House, were feasts for the eyes that centered those locations as hubs for modern technical street skating. Brand Nubian and other seminal hip-hop groups that sounded a little more "gangsta-gangsta" provided the soundtrack, subtly overtaking the rock element of previous skate videos. It was new life and new energy, and we all felt it.

One of the standout skaters in the films was Pepe Martinez (RIP). Pepe, along with Chris Hall and others, showed everyone that switch-stance skating (skating with the nondominant foot) was as at home in D.C. as it was in L.A. Furthermore, Pepe proved skateboarding in Timberland boots *was* a thing, and if you didn't know, "you better ax somebody."

Andy Howell and then-partner Schill kept skating's "scrappy but steady" (and slightly scandalous) vibe front and center.

Schill started finding his voice in the '80s through graffiti, cyphers, skating contests, and membership in a hip-hop group with the incomparable Lil Jon. Yet, the young Jewish skater also had a meditative side, and a bond with nature. Deeply personal, it was compartmentalized in a sometimes rebellious relationship to what his military father had taught him about outdoor life in their cabin in Wolfeboro, New Hampshire. In our discussions, Schill recalled attempts to invite friends to see some majesty beyond the density of the city. But the pull of the big and imperfect city and its culture was strong. The skateboarding graphics and ads that he and Howell propagated through Underworld Element began to reflect real-world altercations with the police in New York and Atlanta. Losing a close friend and skaters too early due to street violence (and a host of other ills) prompted Schill to withdraw from that world, split from Howell, and reposition the brand as simply Element. Howell would eventually take over the "underworld" portion and incorporate it into his Zero Sophisto brand. Element would be an idea larger than the skaters themselves, thus making skateboarding unconsciously attached to something bigger—a play at skateboarding as essential as the elements.

Now, all of this would not have worked without a key element that backed up the new direction: the team. Schill recruited heavyweights into a small tight unit—killers in every idiom. Street, park, you name it. Kenny Hughes, Bill Pepper, Tim O'Connor, Jake Rupp, and the list goes on. It didn't hurt that Element made the strongest boards on the market at the time, executive-produced by Paul Schmitt, whose skateboard construction is so good he's in the Skateboarding Hall of Fame.

Element also featured the first legitimate women's skate clothing line, partly in homage to his sister, who gave Schill his first skateboards. Element had more women on the team than any other company during their early-aughts run. This included Vanessa Torres, Alexis Sablone, and they ran and supported women skateboarding. While

Element did not always have enough power to be as transformational as it would have liked to be, the ground was laid. From the women-led Villa Villa Cola video *Getting Nowhere Faster*, produced by Lisa Whitaker (see page 158) and featuring Amy Caron and the godmothers of the modern era of skateboarding, to the first women's skate clothing line or the women's weeks at the Visalia skate camp, the ladies built it under the Element banner. The list goes on and on. Hard to fight with a brand that delivered under Schill's vision.

Element even ran the table with skateboarding art. Schill's vision for board graphics called for a consistent theme across a series of boards, rather than individual themes or narratives for each pro model, as had been the case for decades. Each pro model graphic would reinforce the overall motif. In his mind, Element should be akin to the Dodgers, a brand bigger than the sum of its parts. He carried that into the selection of the brand's aesthetic. At a time when skateboarding art was so individualized, Element was consistent and straightforward, and it paid off. Across the globe, skate shop owners would do the unheard of—purchase *all* the boards in a series rather than just picking out one popular signature model. If art direction was good, the whole line sold and appealed to anyone visiting a shop.

Therein lies the rub, however. When things are hot, they often get co-opted by those who are not. Element was so successful that the big corps that

Schill envisioned competing with now attempted to buy the brand rather than challenge him. Skateboarding was exploding and major brands like Billabong and Quiksilver wanted a piece of it. Those companies invested in Element and let Schill continue to grow the brand. Pushing forward has always been a part of the brand's ethos.

But the best intentions can still cause issues. While his singular vision of Element having meaning beyond the team's individual members made sense at the time, it also crowded out the voices of folks within the team who wanted to express their individuality. Take Vanessa Torres (see page 112) and her influential thrift store goddess/vintage rock and roll take on functional skateboarding attire. Her keen eye for fashion caused tension at Element, where she was in direct breach of contract for not wearing Element from head to toe. While my sisters at Element were treated better than women at other skate brands, there was still a gap between the amount of power and agency women received there and the amount men did. In a twist of fate, Schill would connect Vanessa with his wife, Kori, to finally develop a women's line, starting with a stretch denim jean. Element pro skater Bam Margera wore them on MTV as part of his rocker look, and began a trend of ultra-tight jeans for men. Eventually Element Women's blossomed into a moneymaker for the brand and became one of the most successful women's clothing companies in action sports—after Vanessa

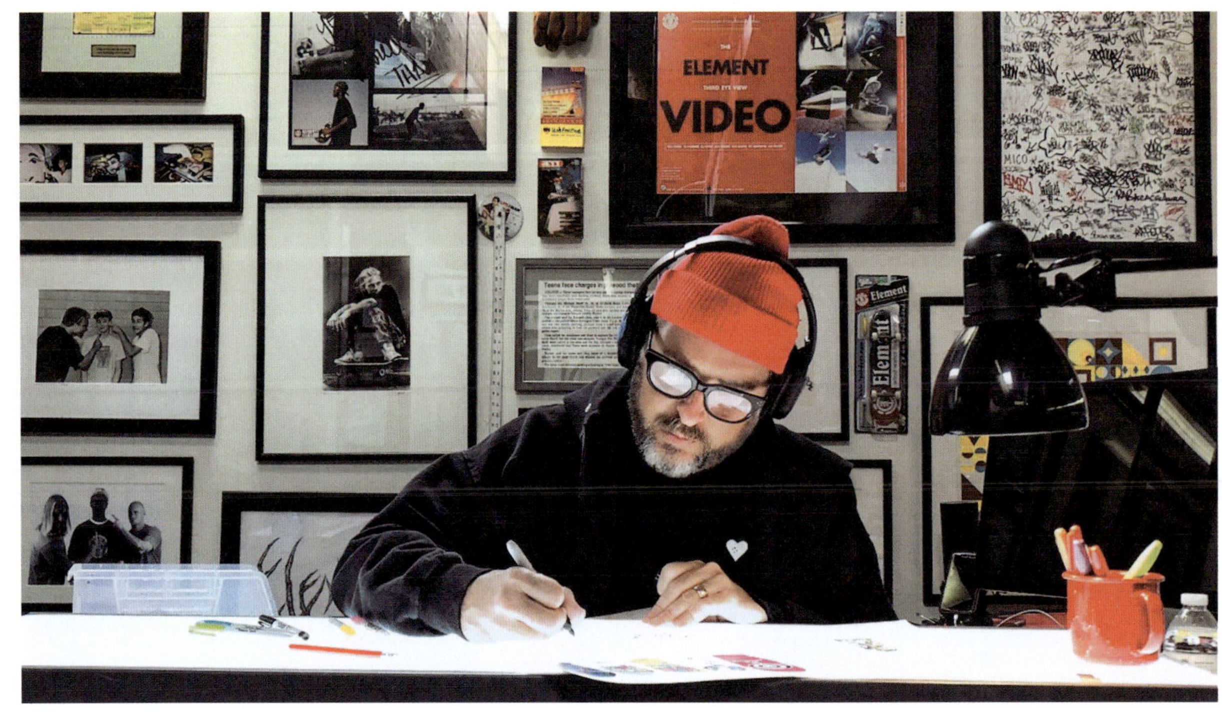

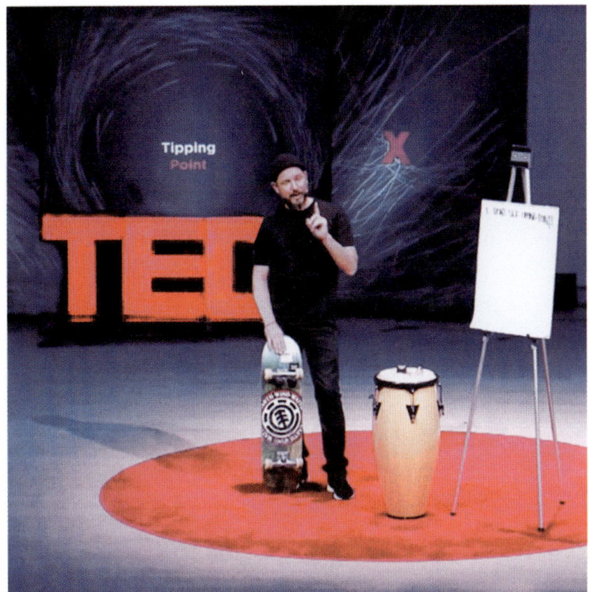

left Element. A tragedy that they both admit didn't end the way it should have.

In retrospect, Johnny Schillereff feels that he should have been more open and understanding, but things were getting big and real money meant real contracts and more opportunities for freethinking skaters to be caught up in the crosshairs of lawyers and opportunists. Plus, there was mounting pressure to share the abundance as the brand became a behemoth in the industry. When other brands got requests from NGOs and grassroots organizations, they now had an easy scapegoat for denying support. "Oh, its environmental, send it to Johnny, that's what they do." "Oh, they want to change the world, send it to Johnny. Education, Johnny. Positivity around skateboarding—send it to Johnny." The influx of pitches and ideas came by the truckload, and it was hard to determine what to do.

Schill has talked many times about the joy of building a global company contrasted with the frustration of having to report to a non-skating overseer or board of directors. This can be debilitating for anyone. In this case, the brand was sold three different times, and as he informed me, continually marching to the board to tell them projections and the cost-saving measures he was undertaking just to support their bottom line began to be too much. What Schill saw after so many buyouts was that for the corporate overlords, it all seemed transactional. Tensions rose and he began to be known as crazy hippie Johnny with wild ideas to create change in the world instead of dollars. To be fair, he did move a portion of the corporate

headquarters to Boise, Idaho, when they bought the SoCal based Element—so that was a bit of a stretch. He had good reasons, but they want good dividends. A corporate board likes a steady ship.

Eventually the levee would break . . . and so would Schill from Element. No disrespect, of course, the brand is still the biggest and remains influential. For Schill, however, the skateboarding he loved still needed a home in the market. He left the game, took all his marbles, and thought of a new plan.

Taping up his broken heart, he and his family formed the Heart Supply, where a portion of the proceeds from board sales goes to giving free skateboards to kids in need.

Thinking about the future, he has created a skatepark in Xala, a restorative stretch of Mexican regenerative ecotourism, as a way for skaters to connect with nature and themselves. An extension of what began with Schill's original Element skate camp and his connection to the outdoors, Xala lives as the ultimate expression of his dedication to skateboarding leading toward greater sustainability.

He and the Heart Supply are also continually thinking about kids' first encounters with skateboarding: they reach parents at everyday retail. This is how the majority of kids receive their first board, so why not make it a quality product? In 2024, you can get a certified deck, including Olympic medalist Jagger Eaton's (see page 277) and Olympic team member Heimana Reynolds's (see page 260) models, from Target. This will surely impact a new generation of skaters and hopefully help newcomers learn to love and progress with skateboarding.

For his final act, Schill has dedicated himself to helping young skaters' dreams come true by taking over the nonprofit U.S. Olympic organization USA Skateboarding, where he serves as CEO and president. His effort paid dividends when Heart Supply pro skater Jagger Eaton earned a bronze medal at the 2020 Tokyo Olympics and a silver medal at the 2024 Paris Olympics. Big ideas and big heart are what Johnny Schillereff offers the world in his attempt to support skateboarding from the hoods to the woods.

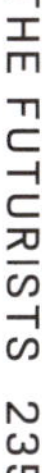

PALAIS DE TOKYO

Skateboarding and modern art go together like café au lait and croissants. Leave it to the French to have their own version of the MACBA (see page 40): Le Dôme—better known by its government name, Palais de Tokyo—which has hosted street skaters and tourists for decades.

Located on the north side of the Seine, parallel to avenue de New-York, which under previous French administrations was known as avenue de Tokio (hence the name), the museum is one of the largest and most famous in Paris and focuses on modern art.

On the same grounds that hold some of the finest interpretations of contemporary art movements (inside), videographers and photographers have captured skaters' energetic movement against a cement canvas (outside). This landscape has provided multiple generations with the chance to add their touch to the tapestry, which is a bit larger than a soccer pitch.

Now, if you come at the Palais from the back, where most people are dropped off to visit the museum, you wouldn't know that there's anything to skate. If your intent is to learn to ollie rather than to see a Dalí, you might be put off by the long lines of tourists heading into the museum and think you are at the wrong place. However, once you've dodged those lines, you will look out onto an oasis, as skaters have since the 1990s.

Immediately beyond the throngs are the fabled hubba ledges (cement ledges going down stairs) that will leave you humbled. They are more than waist high and not for everyone's appetite. But if you're looking to pay homage to the skate dukes of Paris who put it on display for us all, this is the place to go. If you film a trick here, it will be for the record books.

One of the first to bring the spot to global light was skater Marc Haziza, a French national treasure who skated for seminal brands like Etnies beginning in the '90s. (Marc was honored by the Paris Skateboarding Olympic committee, opening the 2024 Games' skateboarding park event with the ceremonial banging of the staff.) Other skaters—including Stéphane Larance (see page 228) and Florentin Marfaing, one of the greatest skaters to come out of Europe—also showed that at the Palais no ledge should go unslayed. Mix in the efforts of Eniz Fazliov also eating it for breakfast, and it's easy to see it as a place skaters consistently return to.

What else makes it a perennial favorite? Well, part of the answer lies in the construction and layout beyond the hubbas. It's well known that smooth ground—granite, well-laid concrete, and marble—is a siren song for any skater in a hundred-mile radius. The Palais's smooth surface gives skaters the ability to push cleanly and gain speed. You can learn anything if the ground is smooth enough, and that unobstructed space allows skaters of every age to find their footing.

Below the smooth footpath is a shallow square pool that the most skillful can launch tricks into. That area even played host to an amazing Paralympics launch event for adaptive skateboarding in 2024.

Now mix in the fact that there are also two sets of stairs at the ends of flat sections above the pool. One features a perfect black wooden

Top right: Local skater lipslide with the best view of the Eiffel Tower

Bottom right: Local skaters gettin' busy at the steps of greatness

ledge that allows skaters to do tricks right in front of the statues at the lower entrance to the museum. The other set includes a 3 flat 4 (a set of three stairs with a flat gap between them to the next set of four stairs) that allows skaters with enough chutzpah to launch their tricks across the divide into the area below. The landing itself adds a learning curve because while you *will* land on a sidewalk, you have a scant second to prepare yourself for rolling onto the long driveway in front of the Palais, in full view of the alabaster sculptures.

With skaters from some of the local shops (there's always a crew from Nozbone and the other famous French shops there) cheering their peers on, the good vibes and good times are ever present. Even if you don't stick your landing, you will be looking across the river right at the Eiffel Tower and be reminded that you could have fallen anywhere in the world—but you fell here in Paris.

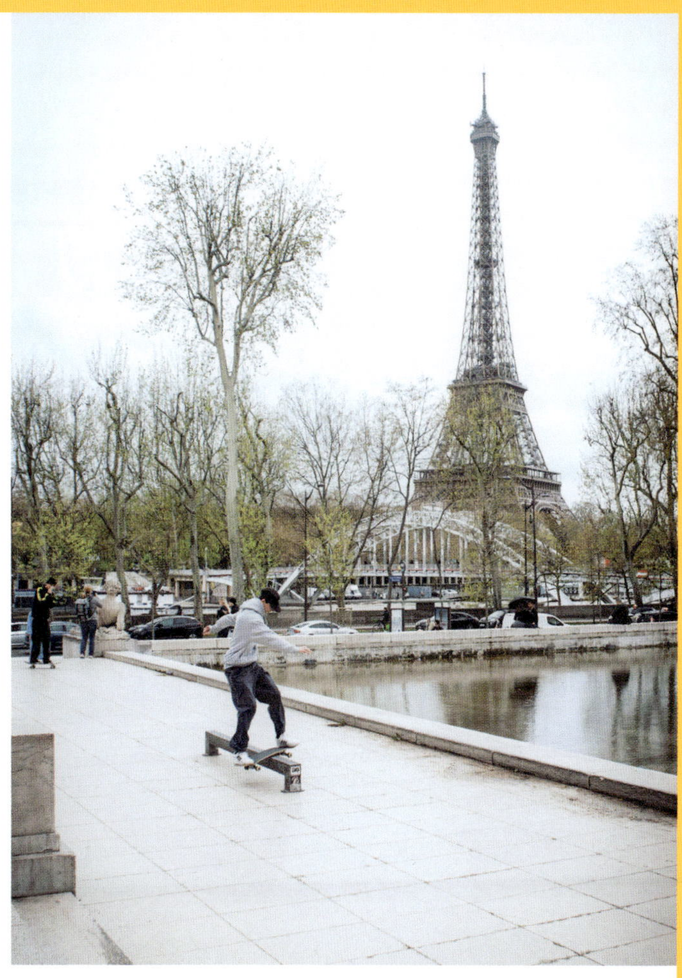

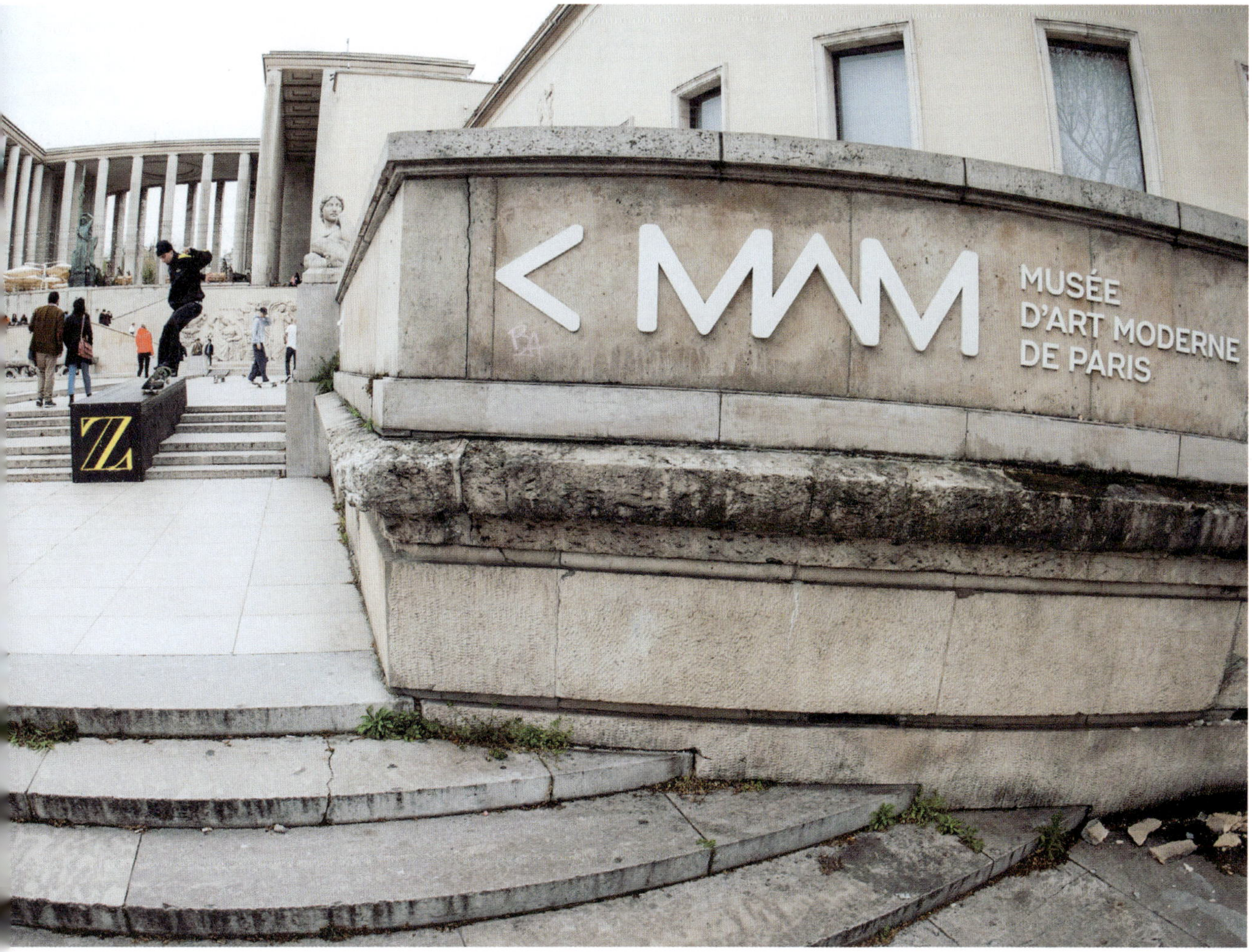

SKATEBOARDING AND ACTION SPORTS OG "GOOD TROUBLE" MAKER

CIRCE WALLACE

First female agent in action sports

Negotiated the first Nike skateboarding million-dollar deal

Former pro snowboarder with RIDE

Designed pro model snowboard boot for Vans

The nymph Circe is a strong female archetype in literature and comic book lore. Historically, she's spun as the original troublemaker to the patriarchy, but really, she's a *boss*. She tormented Ulysses, and leered at, loved, and "learned-you somethin'" to more than a few men, gods, and Eternals, if you count the silver screen. However, my favorite tales of Circe are those of Circe Wallace, skateboarding and action sports athlete.

To fully appreciate Circe's role in the evolution of action sports requires a step back in time. As a young teen in mid-'80s Oregon, Circe found a passion for skateboarding. Street skating can be hard on the body, and the weight on the mind was heavy sans many female role models. With representations at minimum and haters at maximum, Circe did not graduate beyond the casual-but-committed skateboarding ranks.

While a career flinging herself down stairs escaped her, the benefits of an independent nature did not. That rebellious spirit, stoked by a rough parental divorce, was always questioning authority—and damn near anybody else— which placed Circe ideologically in line with the skateboarding of the day. However, unlike most of us, Circe would move from skateboarding as an icebreaker into a newly emerging member of the action sports trinity: snowboarding.

This alternative to skiing's staleness provided just the habitat in which the teenager could shine.

Open to the elements, Circe found freedom, traversing mountain after mountain as the sport was being formed. More at home in the backcountry than on the half-pipe, Circe found a fundamental pursuit in the snowboarding of the '90s: personal expression. She earned membership on the distinguished RIDE Snowboards team and in 1997 competed in the first Winter X Games, which pushed women's snowboarding into millions of households. Meanwhile, more important than medals, Circe increased equity, access, and representation for women by designing Vans's first-ever women's snowboard boot.

Circe painted us in a light usually reserved for traditional sports. She was first an essential figure in women's snowboarding history, and solidified her position as an inspiration for women across the globe—until an accident changed her career trajectory. Sidelined by a second ACL reconstruction, she was unceremoniously retired by her sponsor. Suing her former brand for wrongful termination launched Circe into a crash course with the legal system. Although she found a lawyer, counsel required her to build the case herself, from scratch, which she had no experience doing. Drawing strength from the gods of DIY, Circe prevailed—and without a college degree.

Inspired by the outcome, Circe hoped to create a greater change in the action sports industry and drew on her experience as someone who deeply understood how vulnerable and disposable action sports athletes could be—especially skaters, who were grossly undervalued. They generated millions for brands, but were paid pennies on the dollar. Skaters competed without health care and our history is littered with riders facing career-ending injuries that could have easily been fixed through rehab. The pain was more than physical; some even filed Chapter 11 when the medical bills came in.

Circe set out to build a more financially secure space for skaters, prompting her to become a sports agent and athlete advocate. Her transition from athlete to mega sports agent offered action sports its first corporate seer. If you were a '90s pro skateboarder, some of your biggest dreams involved owning a lowered Honda Civic with 20-inch rims and splitting a rented apartment with the homies. After Circe, clients like Paul "P-Rod" Rodriguez (see page 36) owned multiple homes, businesses, bodegas, and breweries—transforming the dream to *making payroll* with the homies. Athletes were able to set their own agendas and sifted through bids from brands jockeying for their time and energy.

When Circe landed *Thrasher*'s 1996 Skater of the Year Eric Koston as a client, it really put the action sports industry on notice. As one of the most respected skaters in the world, Eric deciding to have representation encouraged others to seek out the same. In fact, Eric's role as a mentor to P-Rod helped Circe sign P-Rod to her roster. Under her management, there are skaters whose income grew 250 percent.

Big picture, Circe raised the price on corporate America by signing those first multimillion-dollar deals with Nike. Those coveted P-Rod "Tiffany" Dunks from Nike SB? You can thank Circe for that reimagining of the OG Nicky "Diamond" × Nike collaboration. Circe set goals high with her client, a young P-Rod, reaching beyond his wildest dreams to create a partnership with Nike, the home of his hero, Michael Jordan. Now 10 signature sneaker models deep, the fruits of Circe's labor stand the test of time. Managing Olympic bronze medalist Jagger Eaton (see page 277) and park champ Heimana Reynolds (see page 260), Circe reps riders who have an unparalleled level of exposure. Their boards are available in every Target in America, thanks to the partnership deal with the Heart Supply skateboards she negotiated. That's just the tip of her action sports athlete empire at Wasserman, a prominent sports agency, where she also steers the careers of snowboarders Torah Bright and Travis Rice.

Circe's efforts have earned her the title of executive vice president, action sports and Olympics, at Wasserman. She has also been a fashion designer and business owner, and remains a mother and wife, and a multihyphenate ceiling-smasher. As hard as she has fought for her corner office, Circe also brought other women into the Wasserman ranks, including action sports agent rising star Yulin Olliver. In our conversation about the state of the action sports industry, Circe said, "This job is not glamorous. I fight tooth and nail for every inch, for my clients every day. No one gives you anything." Commenting on current glass ceilings, she said: "Some days it's literally the '90s again. You wouldn't believe the crap I hear in meetings about brands wanting 'diversity' and a photo op but unwilling to truly support athletes." To combat this and move in league with her ideals, she is part of the Collective, an initiative focused on research and equity around BIPOC and LGBTQ+ women in sports.

Circe is our "good trouble" maker, and no less powerful than the OG deity of sorcery. As an agent (literally) for change in action sports, Circe Wallace cuts through institutional BS with the magic and mastery of her namesake.

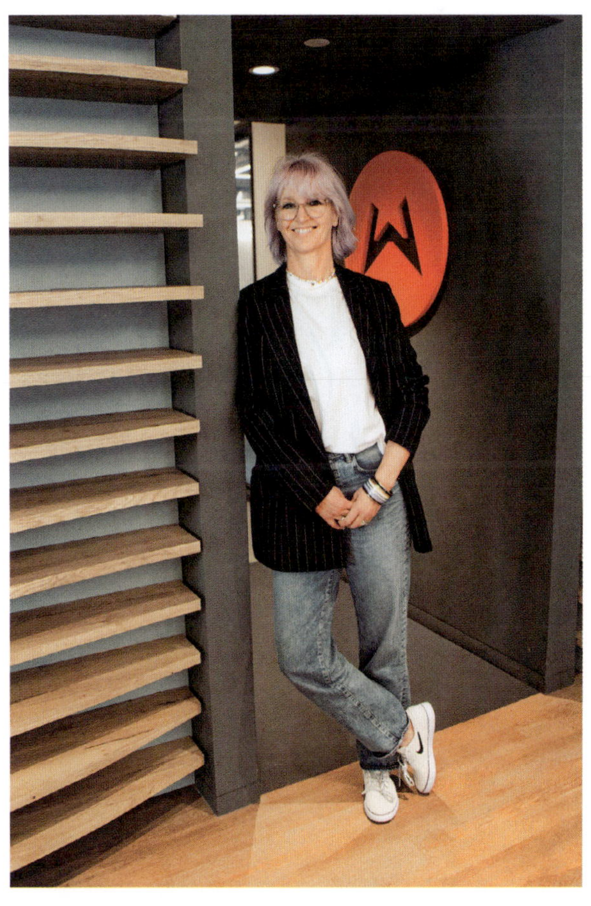

THE MOST INFLUENTIAL WOMAN IN THE SKATEBOARDING BUSINESS
MEGAN BALTIMORE

CEO of Girl Skateboards and Chocolate Skateboards

CEO of Crailtap skateboarding distribution company

Megan Baltimore. Megan Baltimore?! Who dat? This is the response I hear all too often when I ask skaters and students about one of the most important figures in the skateboarding industry. Ask them about Rayssa Leal, Yuto Horigome, Sky Brown, Briana King, or Breana Geering and watch their faces light up! Megan, though, not so much—*What's the deets, professor? School me!* Let the schooling begin.

Megan Baltimore, born and raised in Torrance, California, is the CEO of Girl and Chocolate, two of the most storied skateboarding franchises in skate history, and the glue that holds together the entire Crailtap distribution company, which includes Royal Skateboard Trucks.

Let's keep singing her praises so Megan ain't unsung. She is one of the most historically significant women in skateboarding. As the sole woman leading a skateboarding enterprise that included *Thrasher*'s 1994 Skater of the Year Mike Carroll, pro skater Rick Howard, and auteur filmmaker and artist Spike Jonze (see page 154), Megan provided support, guidance, and providence as they launched a mass exodus from World Industries in 1992 to form their own home and hub of skateboarding culture.

Megan came into skateboarding through the simplest of avenues—the clerical department. As unassuming as it may sound, that office lay within the magical editorial home of a founding publication in action sports, *BMX Plus!* Within those confines, Megan shared space with what would become one of the most respected creative teams in skateboarding, the talent merger of Spike and artiste extraordinaire Andy Jenkins (see page 121),

and later Evan Hecox, which would ultimately turn into Girl's now-legendary creative department, the Art Dump.

Becoming friends and later roommates with Spike placed Megan at the center of a new wave of skateboarding independence, specifically when Spike was recruited by Steve Rocco for the then-fledgling SMA (Santa Monica Airlines) which later became World Industries.

There, she became a key confidante to everyone within the organization. As the company grew in stature with the iconic World team, including Mike Vallely, Mark "Gonz" Gonzales, and Jesse Martinez, and the best amateur skaters like Jason Lee, Rocco created space for more women in the company. Megan was a mainstay and, for a time, the ranks of women improved within the brand. In her recollection, at one point circa '88 or '89, there were 10 to 12 women at World. It was smooth sailing—until World ran aground.

One fateful day in '89, Rocco confided in Megan that they had to cut a large portion of the World Industries staff. He wanted a reset. Rocco told Megan that she, along with Rodney Mullen (see page 54), Spike, and a few others, would now steer the ship. She rose to the occasion and settled in, driving more of the business. Under this management, the marquee brand and its subsidiaries thrived for a number of years, and World became the most powerful and influential force in skateboarding. As the brand's influence expanded, Rocco began to set more professional guidelines than were traditional for the brands. Gone were the days of raiding the warehouse and filling up shopping carts with free product whenever team members visited. Rocco began to establish more rules, and cracks began to show. Disagreements with Rocco continued, and Megan, Spike, Rick, and Mike left to found Girl Skateboards. One year later, a second group from World also exited the fold and came to Girl to form Chocolate Skateboards.

Spike, Rick, and Mike took care of the design part of the business, and there was still a large amount of fun in the approach to everything. Fitting, since Mike Carroll was only 17 years old at the time, and the others were between 16 and 25. Megan was only in her mid-20s, yet she and Spike served as senior leadership, and even in that role she was looked at as the only adult in the room. Spike was the genre-bending artist, and the rest of the collective were naïve about business and most anything beyond being a professional skateboarder. Someone needed to be the voice of reason and take the reins if the endeavor were to succeed. Thankfully, Megan accepted the proposition of becoming the queen of the joyful calamity.

For 25 years, Megan has been at the helm, developing and supporting the good decisions, vetoing the bad ones, and inspiring the squad on a daily basis. Megan is the one who introduced the most altruistic element of their company, their yearly collaboration with RED, U2 frontman Bono's organization for combating AIDS in Africa. On a trip back from meeting with Girl's European arm, Megan read about RED's work and was inspired to do something more to help the world through skateboarding. The relationship between Spike and Bono was called upon, and while Girl/Chocolate couldn't contribute the vast sums of money that others could, it was able to deliver something powerful and youth-centric through skateboarding and creating decks in partnership with RED.

As a full partner in the Girl and Chocolate enterprise, Megan has been partially responsible for all of Crailtap, yet her name is often not mentioned because she is the rare person from that era who is not a skateboarder shredding in the streets. She is in-house nearly every day, okaying decisions and building the brand in the boardroom. She makes the calls with the team, and her place in history is secured as co-owner of one of the greatest units ever, including Rick, Mike, Eric Koston, Jeron Wilson, and Rick McCrank, and many other skaters who remain influential to this day.

None of that would have been possible in the same way without Megan—even though she's usually behind the scenes. Her absence from the public eye is by choice. According to Megan, "When Girl started, social skateboarding events with a lot of women weren't common. Later Rick, Mike, and Spike thought it was cool that I didn't go to the awards and the industry events. They liked that I wasn't using it as an excuse to party hard the way many skaters were at the time. That wasn't me, and I still rarely do appearances at major skate events."

That separation of church and state is part of the magic that drives the company. Megan manages the business as the CEO, and the operation is steadily steered under her hand, but as she told me, "None of this would be a success if it wasn't for working with three people that are my equals. I have three amazing men for partners—they are fun, creative, and bright and they are compassionate; they have empathy and are open-minded. They have been the same, whether it was the first day, or now 20-plus years later."

Megan and her partners know each other's sensibilities well and trust each other to take care of what needs to get done. In skateboarding, there has never quite been a collective so cohesive for so long, especially one that has been led by a woman.

Megan Baltimore shows us the best of what the present and future of skateboarding can look like when you have one of skateboarding's greatest in charge.

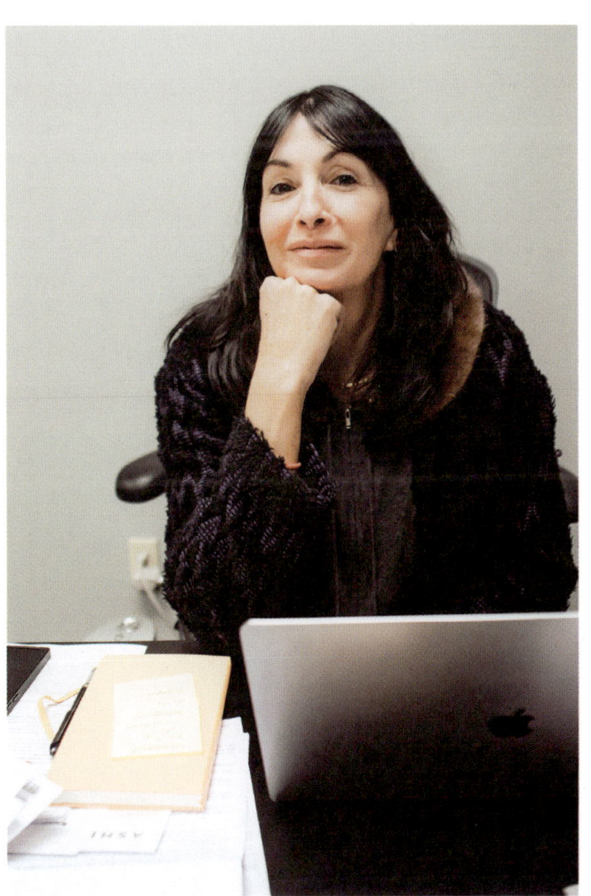

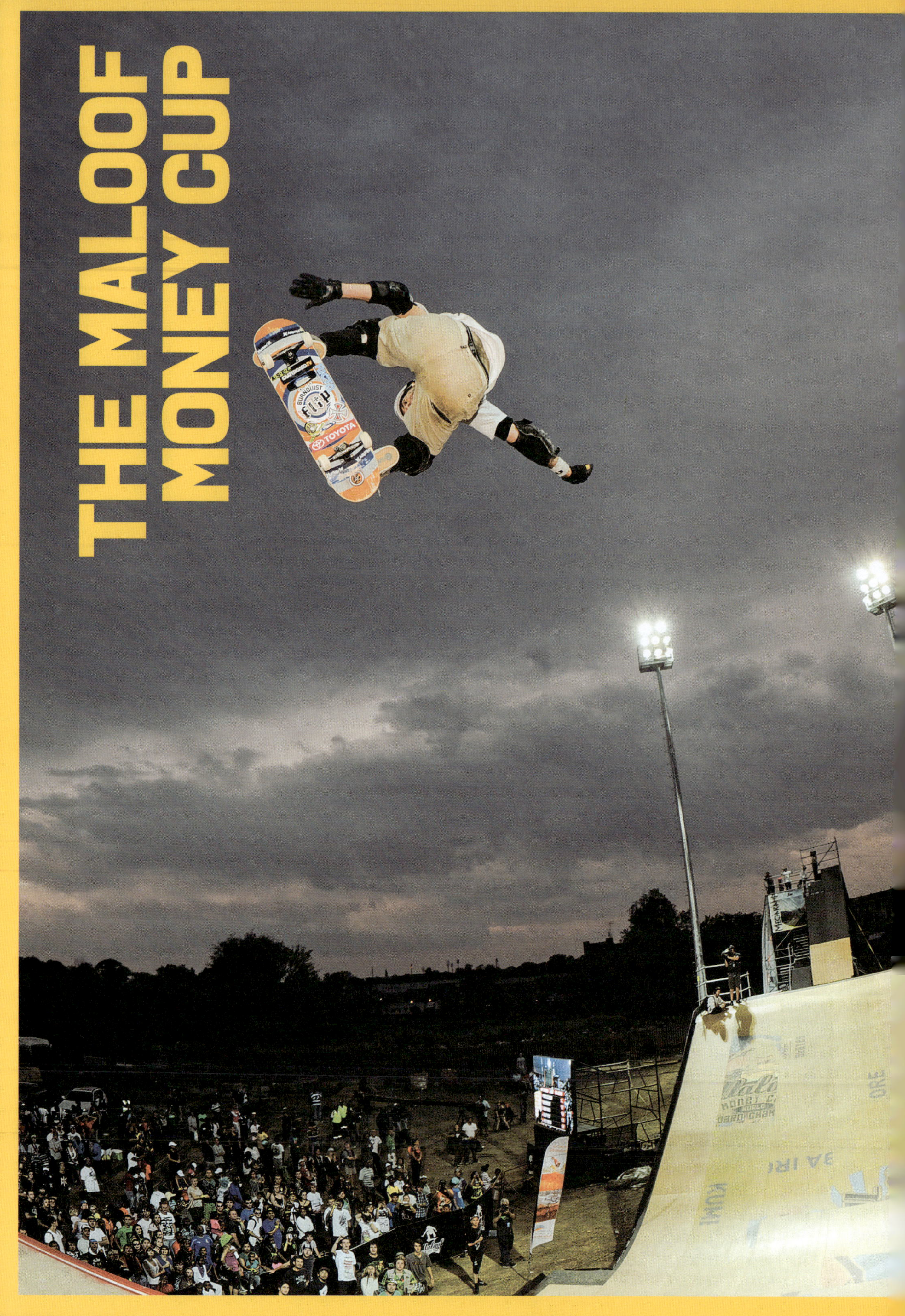
THE MALOOF
MONEY CUP

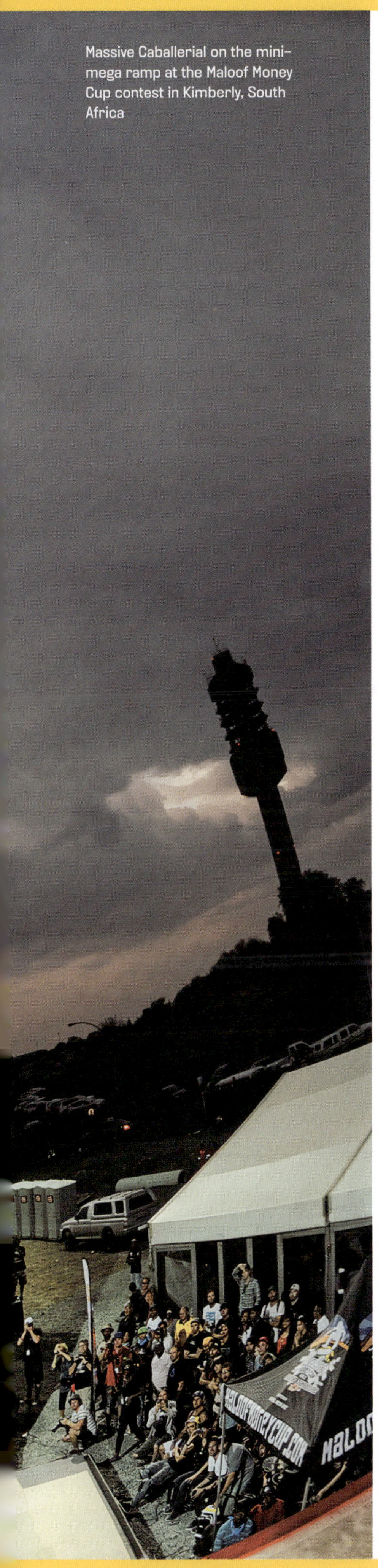
Massive Caballerial on the mini-mega ramp at the Maloof Money Cup contest in Kimberly, South Africa

One hundred thousand dollars for first place? For *skateboarding*?! That's what the entire skateboarding industry said when Joe and Gavin Maloof put that money on the line in 2008 in Orange County, California, setting skateboarding at center stage on a whole other level.

"What do you mean, you know Dennis Rodman, professor?" Students usually ask this question with wide eyes. "Oh, that's from my other life," I respond. "That comes from when I was a student myself, working with the Maloofs and the Maloof Money Cup contest."

In my mind, there is my skate life before the skate contest and my skate life post. And I'm far from alone—the Maloofs changed many skaters' lives for the better, and they helped pave the way for the Olympics and for skaters to earn the money they deserved.

Before the Maloof Cup, there was no major prize money in skateboarding. After, skaters were buying houses with the winnings. How? Well, the Maloofs did something that had never previously been done in skateboarding. They put that 100K in the hands of the winners of the men's street contest, when the high end in other leading contests was maybe three-tenths of that. Plus the Maloof Cup awarded $30,000 for the women's contest—today that wouldn't play as equitable, but at the time, it was an unheard-of lofty amount, far outpacing the likes of the Dew Tour and X Games.

The Maloofs' contests were fantastic, even for the pro skaters and their peers. They brought out skaters who never skated contests. At the first-ever event, at the Orange County Fair, people like Daewon Song (see page 28) and Rick Howard and Mike Carroll showed up to skate and see how this format that re-created legendary skate spots like San Diego's Arco Rail could be incorporated into a contest. Additionally, people wanted to see if the money and support were real. Who was this family? Why would these trad sport owners want to roll with us?

Joe and Gavin Maloof owned the Palms Casino Resort in Las Vegas and the Sacramento Kings basketball team. Their confidant and advisor Pasqual Ross told them that skateboarding was growing. And then attendees to their star-studded basketball camp started showing up on skateboards and talking just as much about skateboarding legends like Tony Hawk (see page 63) and Paul "P-Rod" Rodriguez (see page 36) as they were about LeBron James and the late Kobe Bryant. Even their family members were skating and saying how much they loved it. All this sent Joe and Gavin to find out how skateboarding was attracting so many people.

They found their answer—skateboarding was rebellious and incredible. There were no rules, no coaches—instead it was *100 percent get down.*

Just like that the Maloof siblings—Joe and Gavin as well as brothers George and Phillip and sister Adrienne, at times—were in it. You might think it odd that this powerful family, coming from other sectors, was able to navigate the insular world of skateboarding. Especially when wealthy outsiders such as ESPN had faced boycotts from skaters for their practices.

Well, the Maloofs had a secret weapon. They were working with pro skater and celebrity Rob Dyrdek when they began the contest series in 2008. Rolling with Rob, they were able to gain firsthand knowledge and expertise from a skater who knew the ins and outs and was respected for his business sense. With the Maloofs' money and business know-how matched with Rob's street credibility, they set out to do something that had never been done before: pay skaters what they were worth.

The Maloof Cup's arrival jolted an industry that had grown complacent. It made skaters rethink their own value, and reset just how much money some of the larger corporate interests might have to offer up. And not only did the Maloofs change the game in their approach, but they also had something else to offer skateboarding that no other brand had at the time . . . *Vegas, baby, Vegas.*

The Maloofs rolled out the red carpet. Then the kid gloves were off. From the moment the Maloofs opened their doors, skaters were more than welcome; in fact, the doors were essentially kicked in from that point on.

Skaters like myself began having a love affair with Vegas that for some continues to this day. Thanks to the Maloofs, we were treated like royalty, and the pros were able to enjoy all the benefits of being part of a multibillion-dollar franchise.

In addition to the purse and the strip, the Maloofs set a new standard for sustainability practices in the design and building of skateparks. For the Maloof Cup, they partnered with California Skateparks, one of the best designers in the business, to build the parks to emulate real skate spots in each host city. Most important, they left the parks open and skateable for the cities' inhabitants to use until the Maloof Cup returned a year later for the next round.

Let's make it plain: a celebration of your local spots, a brand-new skatepark in your city, and the best pros in the world coming through to skate it once a year—what municipality doesn't want that? Queens, New York, opted in, and the Maloof Skate Park in Flushing Meadows, emulating the best spots in the city, is still being sessioned now. Washington, D.C., requested the Maloof touch as well, and the team built a skatepark by RFK Stadium, reproducing some of the most famous spots in D.C. They brought the same energy when creating a skatepark and hosting a contest in Kimberley, South Africa, when few in the sport were thinking deeply about Africa or the Global South at that time.

Partnering with the tourism board for South Africa, the Maloofs took skaters to the motherland, many for the first time, and build a deep connection with the people of Kimberley, who were looking at skateboarding as a cost-effective way to engage their youth in sport. Conducting the contest there brought global attention to the largely rural area and expanded the minds of U.S. and European skaters. The visiting pro skaters went out on safaris and cultural tours, explored the mines, and with assistance from the locals attempted to embed themselves in the culture of the host city and explore the joy present in South Africa. The local scene also received greater visibility, along with funding from the Maloofs, to help support the efforts of the land's endemic skaters.

Thinking back to the original contest in the O.C., the Maloofs delivered on proof of concept—would people want to watch a brand-new contest series not led by the familiar faces of the X Games and ESPN or NBC? The answer was undoubtedly yes. When there is real thought put into the contest format, the architecture, and the purse, the public will arrive en masse, and the skaters will enjoy the new opportunity. Chris Cole won the first contest, and a young Nyjah Huston (see page 32) placed second; from there it was apparent that something new was afoot and appreciated. The only issue that soured the skate community was that after the O.C. event, the skatepark was destroyed. The Maloofs vowed to make their next effort more sustainable, and they made good on that oath in the creation of subsequent contests. Greg Lutzka, the winner of two Maloof Cups, would say it was one of the greatest contests of all time.

They even did spin-off events like the *Guinness Book of World Records'* high ollie contest, where Aldrin Garcia set a world record against some of the best of the time. The Maloofs opened the door for so many things. Through initial partnerships with Etnies, Sole Tech, and Vans, they put money up and, most important, offered skateboarding a serious chance, a level of credibility within the traditional sports space. It was exciting to have our skaters alongside icons in attendance and performing, like Lil Jon, Ron Artest (aka Metta World Peace), or Dennis Rodman. I was there in each of those moments, from watching the first 900 spun by Elliot Sloan on South African soil in Kimberley, to Bob Burnquist skating the mini-mega ramp, to feeding cheetahs on mini-safari, and the late nights in D.C. and NYC with Jaime Reyes and the crew at Max Fish.

What the Maloofs did was offer a new perspective for everyone to build from. I even learned key elements of shooting from Joe himself. He helped me think through not only delivering for skaters but for the grandeur—as Joe would say, "That's the Maloof way." It was about making the event look majestic and focusing less on the individual skater, which was the antithesis of my skateboarding photography up to that point. He didn't want me

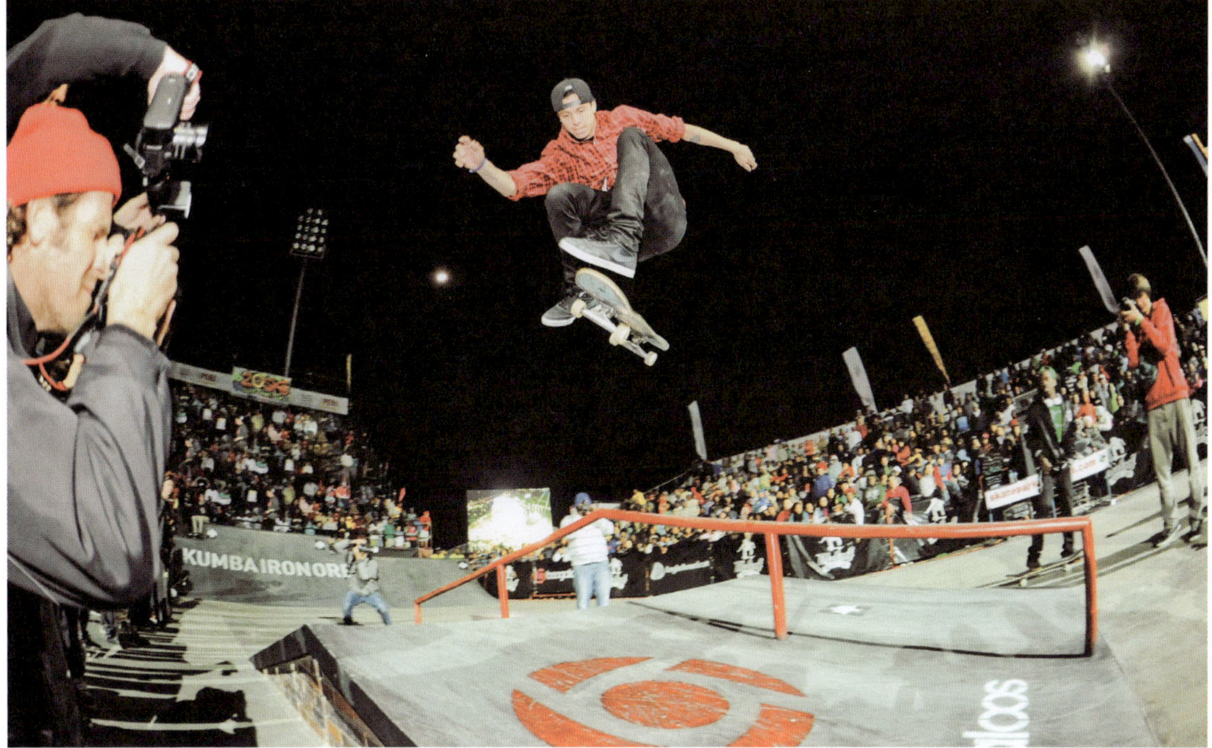

Top: Impeccable hardflip over the A-frame in Kimberly, South Africa

Right: Tory Pudwill and P. Rod (left) battle it out during the finals at the Maloof Money Cup in Queens, New York

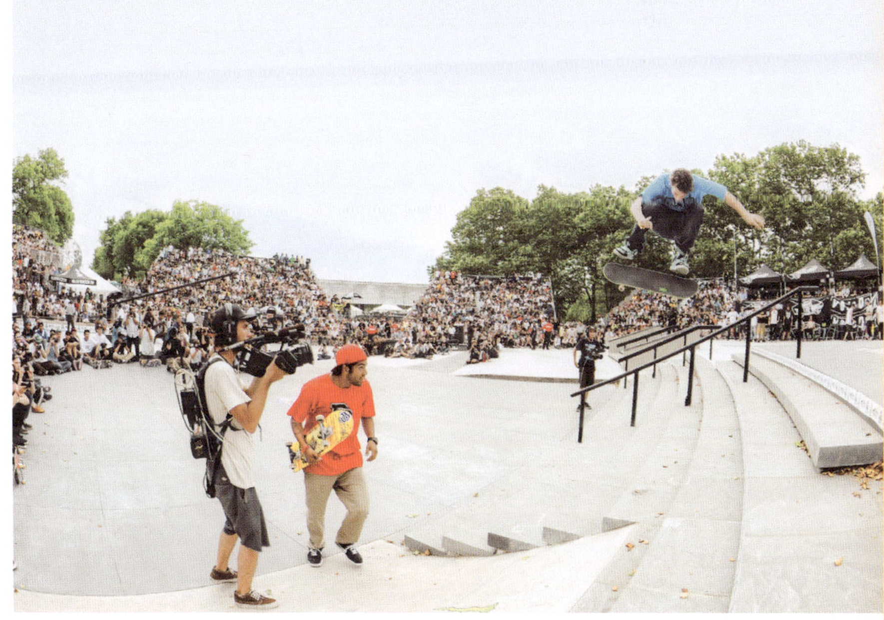

to shoot those pics where 15 photographers were fighting at the bottom of the rail. He wanted the perspective of the viewer amid all the skaters. Joe wanted me to capture images that spoke to everyone, not just skaters. It was one of the most important bits of advice I ever received in my career.

During my talks with Joe, he said his reason for creating space for skateboarding was simple: Skateboarding was fun. He loved our style, our personalities, and our love for the sport even though we were treated like outlaws. While we exhibited the same strength and athleticism as other athletes, we did it while being chased by the police and making space for ourselves, even if it was unsanctioned. We lived skateboarding regardless of the environment and public perception and Joe and the rest of the family were drawn to this love of action.

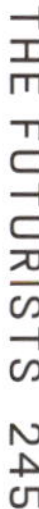

SKATEPARK OF TAMPA & THE BOARDR

Built by Brian Schaefer, Ryan Clements, Scotty Conley, Rob Meronek, and Barak Wiser

Created skateboarding's "field of dreams"

Home to the best skate contests—the Tampa Pro, the Tampa Am, and the Damn Am

Home to the best athlete management agency

Family. That is at the center of skateboarding, and of the work of the Boardr and the Skatepark of Tampa. These two Florida-built businesses are shining lights of the American dream, where people with ideas, talent, and effort can transform their personal love of skateboarding into careers that positively impact the skate community.

The Boardr is three operations launched in 2013 by Ryan Clements, Scotty Conley, and Rob Meronek out of their passion to build a business in skateboarding event management, skatepark design and construction, and personal management for skateboarders.

The Skatepark of Tampa was created by Brian Schaefer in '93 and is one of the greatest and most well-respected skateparks on earth, as well as being home to some of the most respected skate contests: the Tampa Pro, the Tampa Am, and the Damn Am series.

While they are both their own entities now, I was lucky enough to work with them as staff when we were all under one roof at the Skatepark of Tampa, or as it is affectionately known to the world, SPoT. When we were a unified force, we were made up of Brian, Ryan, Scotty, Rob, and Barak Wiser.

Brian is an excellent vert skater and ramp builder from Florida and a friend of Paul Zitzer, a Florida vert skating legend. Paul was the owner of a vert ramp that was being ousted from its original location due to trouble with the locals, who wrongly believed that skaters were accomplices to a death in the area.

Rather than simply finding an adequate spot for the ramp, Brian added a twist to the equation by finding a warehouse location capable of housing the ramp as well as his hide. Why leave the ramp when it can serve double duty as your new home? Genius. For nearly a year the ramp stayed a private facility, a place where friends could meet and crash. However, with the lull in construction of vert ramps in the '90s, people came from everywhere to skate the newly assembled ramp.

It's hard to imagine now, but the concept of having a vert ramp with clean running water and a bathroom and a hot plate and microwave? It was just the kind of paradise that skaters needed. A place to lay your head, then get up and shred? That's music to the ears of any skater—especially those desperate to find a vert ramp to skate. There were so few vert ramps back then that even Tony Hawk (see page 63) came out to bless SPoT's and complete an NBD (never-been-done) kickflip 540 on it.

Once situated, the ramp park became a hub that embodied the Floridan ethos: fun and filming with friends. While the vert lovers finally had a home, it turns out that there was surely enough room in the industrial warehouse they rented for some additions. First, Schaefer created a small skate shop simply to facilitate the needs of the visiting skaters who spent months at a time living on the floors and sleeping in the empty office spaces. During the '90s, many pro skaters earned small salaries but received an abundance of skateboarding products from their sponsors that they could sell off to pay their bills. Skaters unable to help Brian make rent on the warehouse could turn some of that product over to him to sell at the makeshift shop. There was also a need for access to skateboarding staples like grip tape (the grippy stuff on the top of skateboards),

mounting hardware (which keeps the trucks and wheels attached to the board), and bearings. Those are all components that need to be replaced often and are generally the hardest to find when you need them. Those two conditions helped birth the Skatepark of Tampa Skate Shop.

Skaters began to bring in other street-style obstacles (like rails, banks, and quarter-pipes) that they had built at home but that needed a little love they could no longer provide, or at a minimum required a roof overhead in the face of the brutally hot, humid, and often stormy Florida climate. Donating them to Brian's warehouse created a new trajectory for the warehouse and living space; it began to shift into a refuge for both vert skaters and street skaters.

As street skaters visited the warehouse more often, word spread quickly that the donated obstacles had been improved and that Brian and other local skaters had added more obstacles worth skating, in fact worth paying for—and money was something Brian desperately needed. In response to that need, SPoT officially opened to the public.

Rather than simply constructing obstacles and leaving them to be skated until they became dilapidated, Brian would often reevaluate, redesign, and change the layout of the park. This creative cycle kept skaters interested in what was next and inspired more skaters to visit and pay admission, which helped drive sales in the shop, which paid the rent and kept the lights on.

The hallowed halls of the Skatepark of Tampa

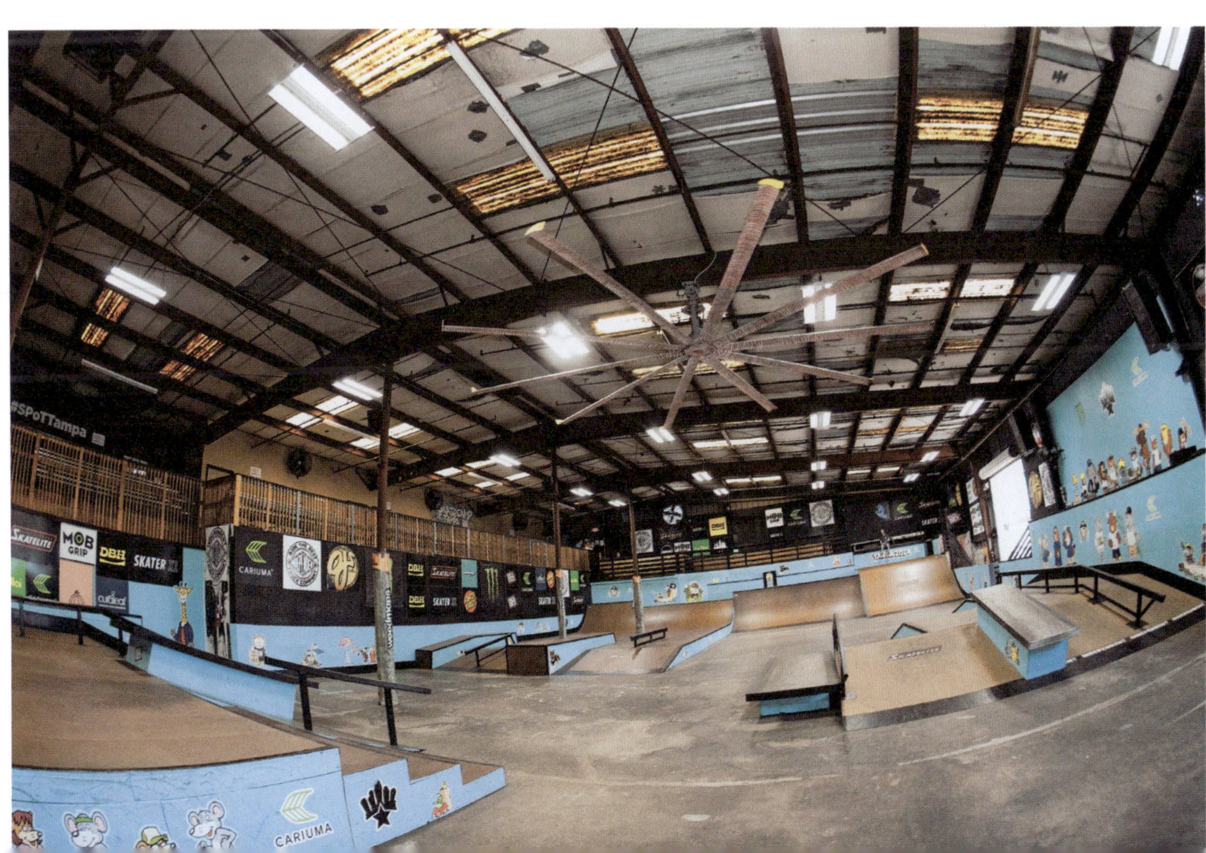

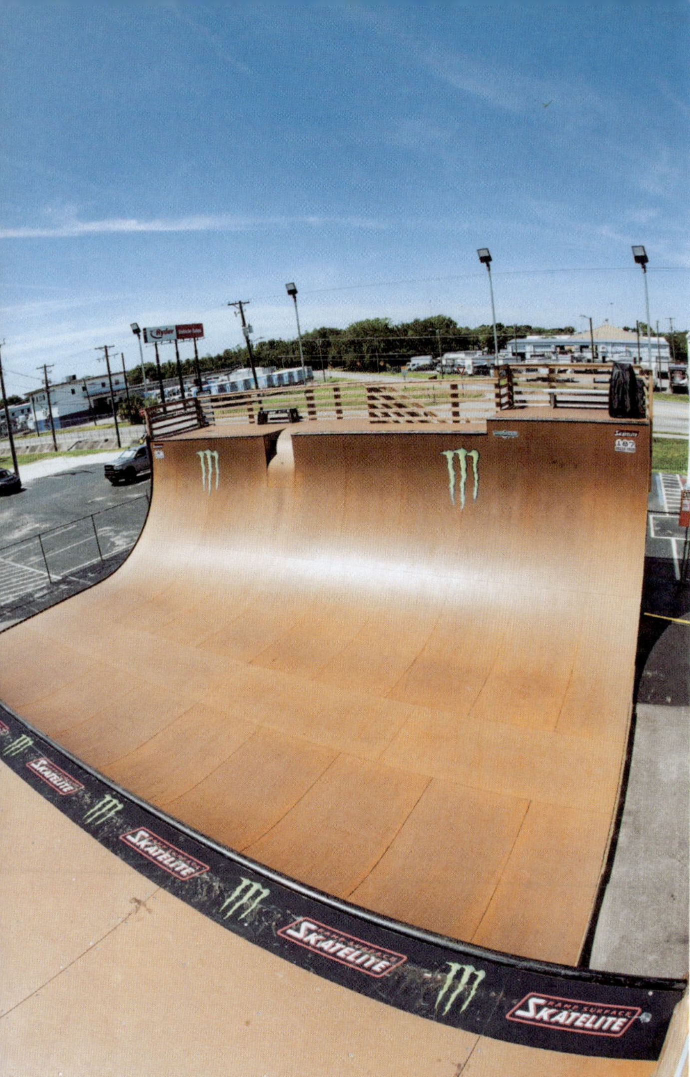

Gaining a real reputation as a home away from home for skaters, SPoT would really come into its own in 1995, when Brian and company invited the skateboarding industry to the first-ever Tampa Pro contest. Brian and the SPoT team dreamed it up as way to build community during the mid-'90s, when skating was largely insular and less mainstream. The initial idea became a sensation that still flourishes to this day as the most popular and respected skate contest in history.

The factors that made it perfect were simple: the SPoT contest was a down-home chilled event developed, designed, and judged in a skate space created by your peers. What's not to like? If you were in the Northeast skate scene in Boston, NYC, Philly, etc., you know those pros were all incredible in the mid-'90s but often plagued by inclement weather. If you were a West Coast pro skater, Tampa offered a change of pace. This was an event created for the fun of it for skaters and by skaters—plus all of the skate industry had been hearing about the beautiful

beaches and the Tampa nightlife as well. A real skate vacation.

That first contest was won by pro skater Mike Vallely and enjoyed by every pro, every spectator, and every fan of skateboarding in attendance, solidifying SPoT's role as having the greatest contest vibes on earth.

Unlike made-for-TV gigs and skate contests such as the Dew Tour and the X Games during the late '90s/early aughts, where skateboarding is made more digestible and explained to the masses, at SPoT, there is no explanation needed. The judges know just how hard the tricks are and have all been lifelong skaters. You are home, that's why a trophy at SPoT is the sincerest contest accolade you can earn from the skateboarding community. I've watched Paul "P-Rod" Rodriguez (see page 36) battle it out with Nyjah Huston (see page 32), up close, witnessed Boston's own Jereme Rogers nab a podium spot. Seen Greg Lutzka demolish the course to take home top honors, and kids with no name in the game beyond their own holler, like Mike Peterson, rise to fame.

To this day, the stories of those who head to SPoT on a Tampa-or-bust mission permeate the space like the dusty air circulated through the metal blades of the giant fan projecting from the ceiling. If you want the crown bad enough, you can come from anywhere and be added to the list of those who came to Tampa and conquered, like when African American skater Gershon Mosley simply rolled up in '99 and put a hurt on the course in a way no one expected and won the contest that year.

Tampa provides that level of esteem even for amateurs, who skate in the now illustrious Tampa Am (amateur contest). Take Felipe Gustavo from Brasília, whose dad sold the family car to purchase two flights to Tampa although Felipe had no sponsors and spoke no English, on a half-hearted promise made by Ryan that if somehow they did make it to Florida, Felipe could enter the Tampa Am contest, which he won. That is the Cinderella story of Tampa. Hell, even if you don't win, it's still righteous, like in the case of Alexis Sablone (see page 254). She competed against men during the contest and sent many packing, as did Elissa Steamer (see page 21). Those events helped shape their rise to pro status, reminded male skaters that skateboarding is open to everyone, and set the stage for the influx of amazing women and girls in skateboarding now.

At the height of its powers, SPoT generated so much *everything* (commerce, contests, products, videos, etc.) that every business clamoring for the 16-to-30 male demographic came knocking. SPoT also excelled in other ways in the late 2010s: Rob invented arguably the best judging system to date, with automatic updates, making it easier for skaters to know what they needed to score in order to win. This patented system was the first of its kind in skateboarding.

Ryan, meanwhile, realized that many of the pro and amateur skaters SPoT issued first-place checks and trophies to lacked a comprehensive financial plan for the future, and many needed help navigating and understanding endorsement deals and potential earnings. To combat this, Ryan and Meronek developed a management company to support pro skaters and help them stay fiscally sound. This new endeavor moved SPoT from its austere origins to guiding the most talented skaters toward a bright future. With so much cultural cachet and increasing revenue streams, SPoT became the premiere name in skateboarding events and management.

With time, things started getting a little tense inside the organization. Even after gaining accolades as the supergroup the Skatepark of Tampa, skateboarding's version of the Beatles suffered an internal struggle that led staff members Ryan Clemonts, Rob Meronek, Scotty Conoley, Jorge "Porpe" Angel, filmer Joe "HiDefJoe" Pelman, and Bob Freeman to leave to form the new venture the Boardr. That divorce launched new programs that supported everyone's talents. Ryan now heads the management, while also putting on events and running skate contests with Porpe as a lead agent with the best tech designed by Rob. Scotty began to take announcing seriously and recognized that he had much to offer through his voice; he blossomed on the mic and stepped into his power. Brian had the other half of the business in SPoTlight Productions, full-throttle SPoT webshows on YouTube, and other media outlets. Barak, the maven of the front-of-house business operations and king of creating SPoT collabs, set sail for broader pastures in New York with JanSport and its subsidiaries. He had masterminded all the early skate collaborations; over time, he helped brands come up with and design marketing; over time he went on to do it for himself.

Collectively, the group developed the future for all skate shops in branding, partnerships, and collabs.

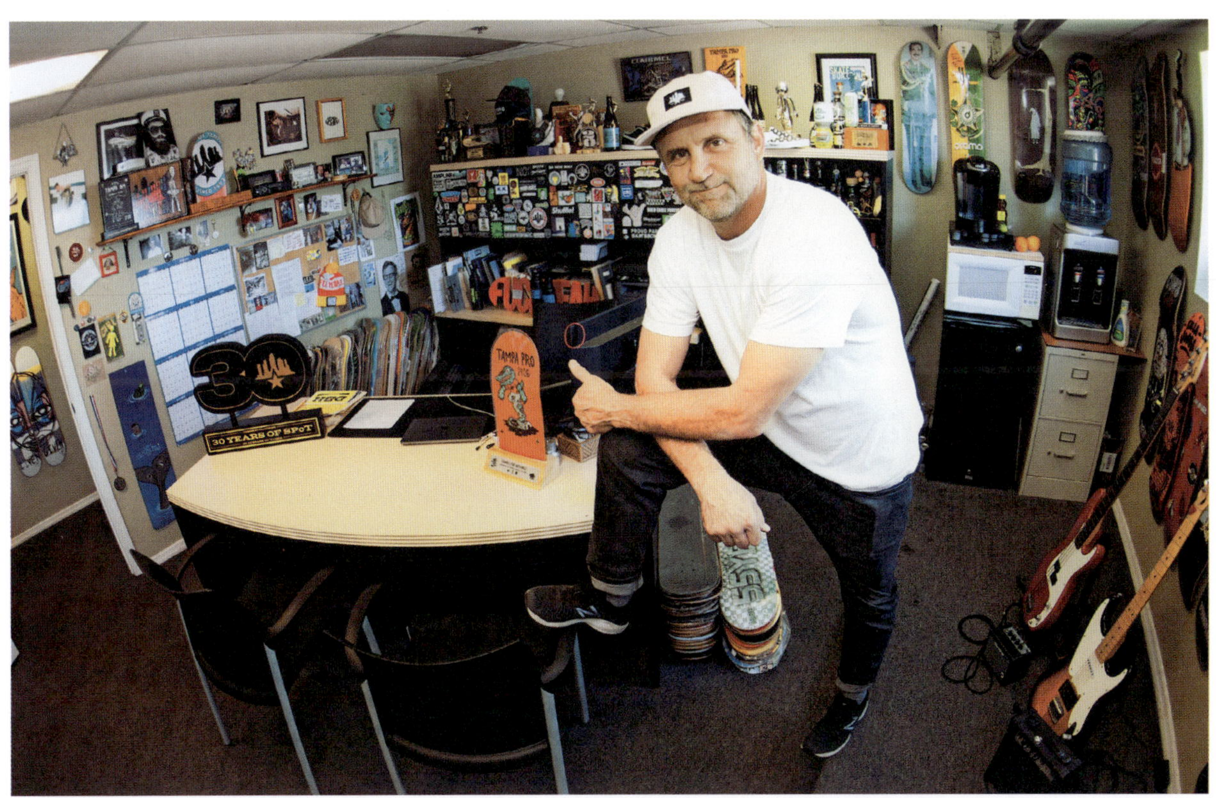

THE OLYMPISTS

These history makers in the ever-changing landscape of skateboarding have moved into the final frontier: the Olympics. While our passion has been a global phenomenon since the 1970s, it is this new realm that placed the sport directly in the purview of the masses and brought it all the pomp and circumstance associated with its new recognition as a legitimate athletic culture—whether spectators were prepared or not. For many skaters the focus is not solely on obtaining medals; they're there for the experience. Some featured here made the Olympic team but didn't go to the Games. Some made the team, then went and staged protests. That's what you get when you cross skateboarding with any institution—fireworks.

Skaters will use the course, the platform, and the moment to be who they are and remind you why the same group of individuals can boycott, bolster, and beguile the Olympic stage.

UKULELE-ING INTO HISTORY
BRYCE WETTSTEIN

Effervescent free spirit

San Diego's Olympian in Park skateboarding (Tokyo 2020)

National champion in women's park

Bubbles. Music. Poetry. Art. The rainbow socks and overalls that make up her classic fits. These words characterize the skateboarding and lifestyle of Olympian Bryce Wettstein. Even in the most serious of training sessions for the U.S. Olympic team, Bryce breaks into impromptu sessions of "follow the leader" around the park, or ukulele jam sessions that break any tension and remind everyone that skateboarding is about friendship, family, and fun. Bryce brings a level of elasticity to skateboarding that is electrifying and inspiring. Take her frontside and backslide ollies. These two tricks are simple yet denote a mastery of skateboarding and act as a skater's signature. How much is their front leg tweaked out? How does their rear leg trail? Where are their hands? Do they unconsciously point to the spot where they are going to land in the ramp? Bryce's ollies are floaters, meaning she can launch into the air, catch her ollie at the peak, but hold it just that extra second that makes you draw in a breath . . . Is she gonna bail it or hold on? And hold on she does—a wild ride every time. The same with her Caballerials, fakie 360 ollies.

Every contest, Bryce offers a piece of herself, dropping into major competitions like the X Games with the same level of free-spiritedness she has skating her backyard "iguana ramp"—named after her deceased reptilian friend. Take a past contest at the Santa Barbara bowl at the Orchid Skatepark—a flower farm with an amazing bowl and street course at a working nursery. The sun was high overhead, and the session had gotten heavy. You could feel that skaters were going bossed-out and looking to bring home some of the green for podium wins.

In the right-hand corner of the kidney-shaped section of the bowl sat Bryce, cross-legged, with a few other female skaters. Sporting a soap bubble necklace with a blower tool, she took the time to sign autographs, hug young female skaters, dispense knowledge to young upstarts, and blow bubbles. When it was time for her run, she donned her signature blue helmet and found a spot on the crowded deck to drop in from.

What transpired next was like watching poetry in motion. She carved floaty frontside ollies in the ramp and went into those speedy Caballerials (360-degree ollies going backward), then launched herself on the deck into an elegant 360 boneless one where she plants her forward foot and turns around in a 360 before diving back into the ramp.

Born in 2004 in Encinitas, California, Bryce began skating at seven years old, placing herself in a trial by fire at the legendary Combi Pool, a notoriously difficult chunk of skateboarding architecture from the 1970s.

She also grew up skating the famed Encinitas skatepark, home to skaters like Tony Hawk (see page 63) and Amelia Brodka (see page 176), where she cultivated a skateboarding style that breathes easily. That type of skating is truly transcendent and no less powerful than a more aggressive run. Bryce has the bangers, like the noseblunts frontside and backside, which she spreads across the deck of any skatepark at will. She's always in motion. Even mid-conversation, she might drop into a skateboarding handstand then continue talking like nothing happened. Her skateboarding is an expression of her motion and emotion. It's a celebration of the self, not unlike the great Mark "Gonz" Gonzales's (see page 92).

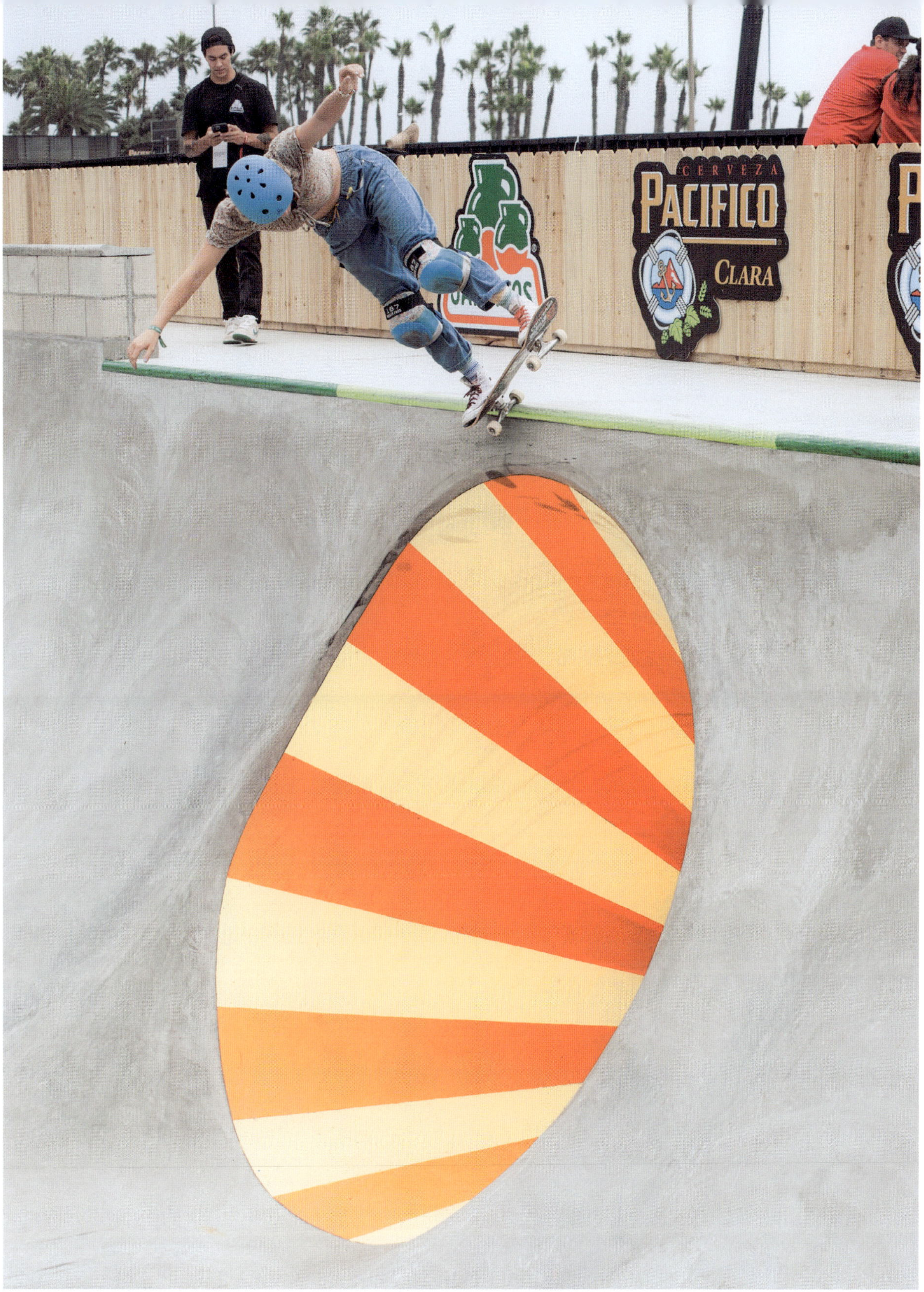

She's sponsored by Stereo Skateboards (see page 97), a natural fit for her. The brand's visual and auditory repertoire—heavily steeped in jazz and Americana—uniting with a ukulele-wielding, poetry-reading skater feels like a heavenly combination of spirits.

Even at the Olympics, when nerves were sky-high, Bryce soothed contest jitters by performing a ukulele-supported serenade for the team, adding levity to the greatest sporting spectacle on earth.

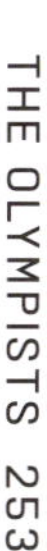

WORKING-CLASS HERO, ARCHITECT OF DREAMS

ALEXIS SABLONE

One of the most influential female skaters in history

Seven-time X Games medalist and Team USA member

The quintessential New England skater

Queer woman and cultural icon

Alexis Sablone is 100 percent certified. LGBTQ+ action sports icon. Ivy Leaguer. Architect. Converse brand ambassador. Small-business owner. And Olympian—in 2021, at age 35, she earned fourth place at skateboarding's Olympic debut in Tokyo. Alexis is an iconic face in skateboarding. Her accomplishments deliver like a throaty rendition of Percy Bysshe Shelley's, offering an "Ode to Doin' the Damn Thang—E'ry Day."

Sablone's accolades carry extra weight because she came up in the Boston skate scene, a blue-collar collective (spanning Maine, New Hampshire, Connecticut, Vermont, and Rhode Island, along with Massachusetts) filled with working-class heroes and heroines building community amid rough-and-tumble trails and tongues, winter-pocked pavement, and parades of pedestrians.

Alexis is the quintessential New England skater. To the uninitiated, that means skating by yourself in empty garages, searching for asphalt skate spots, and laying lit cardboard and lighter fluid mixtures on the blacktop to dry off a potential spot to skate. Driving hours through blizzards and black ice to get to the one open skatepark. Falling on ground so cold that a single slam threatens to shatter your growth plate. Yep, that type of New England skateboarding, and Alexis had been doing it since she was a teen. Her debut in the famous Coliseum video *PJ Ladd's Wonderful, Horrible, Life* (2002) only solidified what locals already knew: she had all the tenacity, chops,

and heart to represent professional skateboarding on the world stage. And keeping it completely real, she remained sponsored by an East Coast company, Alltimers skateboards, until they recently shuttered their doors.

Back in the day, if you stopped the average person on the street and told them that professional skateboarder was an actual job title, they would scoff. Well, that was until Alexis appeared in *GQ* in May 2023 and did an interview with the *New York Times* as a cultural icon, particularly for the LGBTQ+ community. As a queer woman, she has been outspoken about pay disparity and making improvements in skateboarding and in realizing her own self-worth. Her vision manifests in her multiple designs for Converse, in her pride in being part of the Olympic team, and in inspiring the next generation of skaters by co-owning a new skate shop in Connecticut, instead of the sun-drenched and precipitation-light epicenter of U.S. skateboarding, Southern California.

She's always been her own person. In her school days, between bouts of studying she peppered in skate contests from the X Games to the Dew Tour to make ends meet. She's Alexis, it's just what she does. She rolls up her sleeves and manifests. She's in the winter beanie, vest, and the baggy fits not for fashion shoots but to shoot the streets.

Among the collective in Boston proper were producers Matt Roman and Arty Vagianos and filmer Dave Kordan, who made Coliseum's GOAT-ish and New England–centric skate shop video, *P. J. Ladd's Wonderful, Horrible, Life*, which broke the internet before the internet was up and running and set the stage for an explosion of skateboarding in Boston. Luminaries in the video included PJ Ladd (whose trick combinations were otherworldly), Ryan Gallant, Jereme Rogers, and representing Old Saybrook, Connecticut, Alexis Sablone, the sole female skater in the video. Sablone's representation marked a new phase of East Coast skating where young rippers could be of any gender. Alexis and PJ were inseparable at that time. Who else was he going to call and skate with at 4 a.m.? That is blue-collar skateboarding. Putting all the time and effort into the craft. Working on tricks in the basement, making a love a life.

What Alexis delivered were real, undeniable skills, always the truest hallmark of skateboarding. She demonstrated that women were not the future, but the present—you just needed to look and support them. Operating alongside PJ, arguably one of the greatest skaters at the time, Alexis emanated presence and her perfect nollie flips and signature kickflip 50-50 still send skaters back to the woodshed to work on fundamentals.

But more than any degree of action performed on board, the most resonant trick Alexis brings to skateboarding are her actual degrees. While most skaters focused solely on skateboarding, Alexis earned her bachelor's degree from Columbia's Barnard College, then a master's in design from MIT. Alexis is also part of the global skateable sculpture movement. Her work is exhibited in Malmö, Sweden, and she is now one of the first calls people make in mixed-use design.

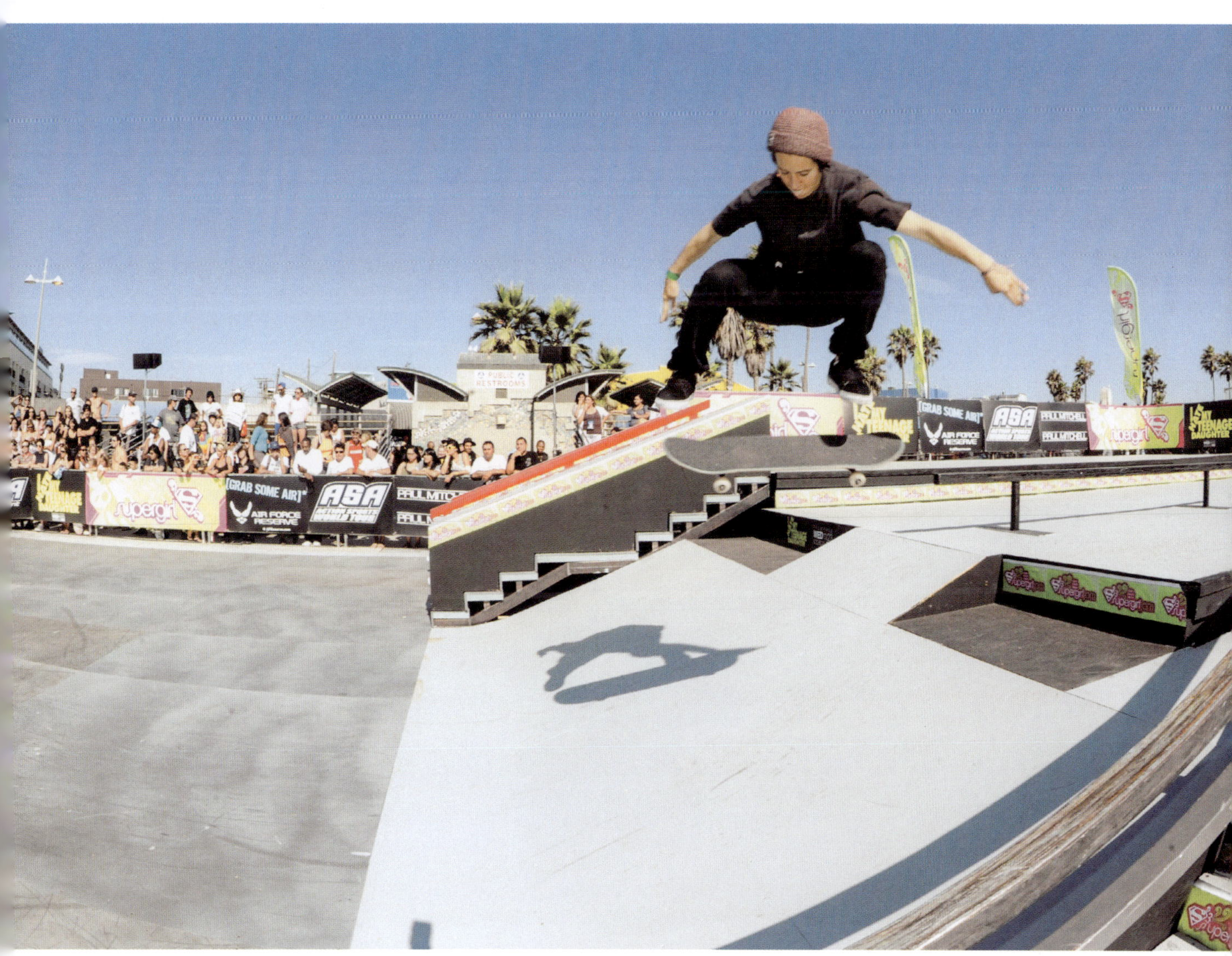

DASHAWN JORDAN

Winner of the coveted Tampa Am contest

Winner of Street League Skateboarding Chicago

2020 USA Olympics Skateboarding team member

"One got away." That's what I think every time I see Dashawn Jordan putting in work. Somewhere out there is a team missing a championship-winning touchdown, a buzzer-beating three-pointer, or a match-defining *gooooooalll*—all because a young Black skater shook the shackles of traditional sports and instead found a home in skateboarding. Dashawn has all the makings of a traditional athlete—broad shoulders and the sinewy musculature that demands a dunk or rushing for a hundred yards on a punt return—and in high school he played on sports teams and had a promising future. Yet he left all that behind because skateboarding pulled him in, allowing him to be his

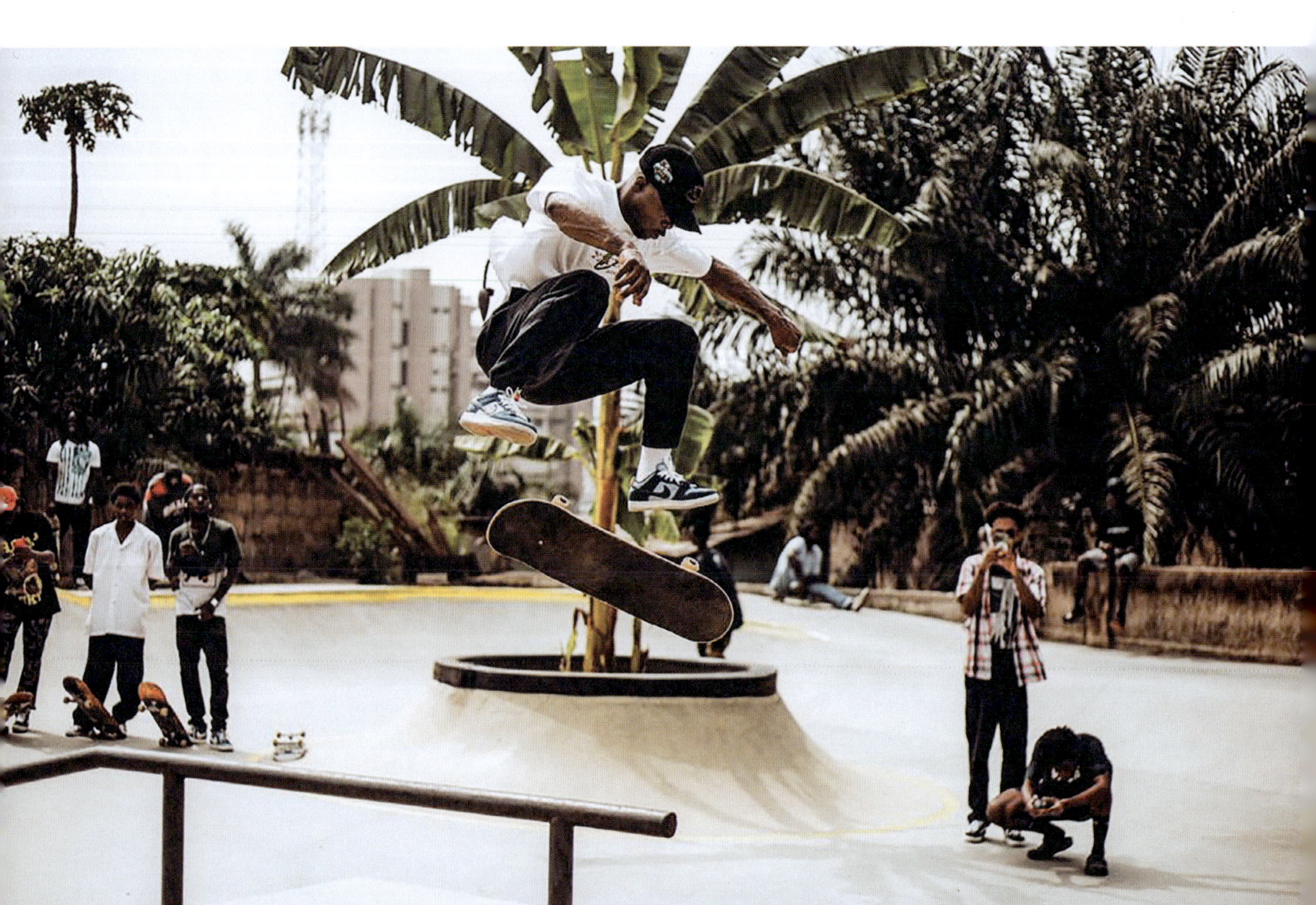

ultimate uninhibited self. Tech skating with mind-blowing combos, big rails, stairs, ledges, hubbas—one of the few Black skaters from Arizona, Dashawn can skate everything.

Now, you may be thinking, AZ is really getting down like that? Ahh, yes. While we often think of California and New York as central figures in skateboarding, spots like Arizona have always had a healthy scene thanks to mainstays like Cowtown skate shop and others creating contests and events for skaters to enliven a skate scene that faces summers that hit 100 degrees in the shade. There is a style of skating there that respects the hard times: rough sun-cracked cement, scorching-hot rails, and gaps lying in wait to dish you out a side salad à la road rash. Few outsiders are ready to face those conditions. Dashawn battled his way up through the ranks in AZ by putting skateboarding first and the flash second. It's different when you come up without the spotlight of the California or the New York scene. Places like Arizona (Texas, I see you, too) come up by simply showing the goods and not needing the limelight—but when they get it, they get down.

As an amateur in 2016, Dashawn competed in the prestigious Tampa Am contest, which has launched the careers of hundreds of pro skaters. Tampa is one of the few skateboarding contests that was designed by for skaters by skaters, making it the skateboarding contest equivalent of FUBU (for us by us). When you win Tampa, it is a crowning achievement that certifies that you have the skills to be a professional skateboarder. For Dashawn, this particular win earned him a place in the Rob Dyrdek–founded Street League Skateboarding (SLS) pro contest circuit, where he became the first non-pro to win.

When he bounced out of AZ to put his stamp on the spots that made California kings and queens, he did so humbly, but with a mission to let people know he was in the building. In Los Angeles, choosing the notorious set of stairs known as the Hollywood High 16, Dashawn stomped out not one but two NBDs (never-been-dones). First, he slapped the rail with a frontside 270 ollie to lipslide. Second, he launched a perfectly caught frontside laser flip down the 16—with enough swagger to join the great Rakim in a quintessential *"I slam it when I'm done and make sure it's broke."*

Born in 1997, Dashawn starting skating at age eight. He is part of a new generation of skateboarders like Yuto Horigome (see page 278) and Rayssa Leal (see page 258) who can easily transition from the streets to the Olympic movement. Winning in the streets and in contests, Dashawn uses each outlet to express his thoughts on skateboarding as easily as most of us catch a cold. Putting it all on the line for the thrill with no fear for the spill. During a contest, he can toss aside a safe skateboarding run in favor of wildin' out and literally going the wrong way at an obstacle, just to let the judges and the audience know that he is deadly serious about reducing anything you throw at him to rubble—and still skating away clean. It's that unique approach that landed him a spot on the Nike SB footwear team and eventually Team USA Skateboarding.

Growing up among few Black skaters in Arizona, for Dashawn, contests are a visible exercise in expanding possibilities and perceptions. As a Black skater, he sees contests as an opportunity to be something greater than himself, a wink and a nudge that might inspire the next generation and keep their eyes filled with wonder. Not every skater of color feels that way and wants to shoulder that responsibility, but Dashawn is different. Dashawn wants all kids to find the voice that drives them *inside.*

Following his own internal voice led Dashawn to take a risk when he chose a small startup for his pro debut. Business & Company, spearheaded by Marc Johnson, one of the most innovative skateboarding technicians in skate history. Though the brand would be short-lived, even Dashawn's pro model made an immediate impact. The Dashawn Jordan Prince/Aladdin Rain/Bowie deck, a mashup of Prince's *Under the Cherry Moon* graphic and Bowie's Ziggy Stardust lightning bolt face paint, was an instant classic.

Beyond his skating, Dashawn Jordan uses the mic as an MC in his other device to show just how nice he truly is. He is aware of his influence as a role model and revels in doing things that celebrate life and separate him from the pack.

THE *FADINHA DO SKATE*
RAYSSA LEAL

Youngest to win SLS World Tour

Silver Olympic medalist at 13 years old (Tokyo 2020)

2022 X Games medalist

2024 Olympic Bronze medalist in street skateboarding

Before we doomscrolled and social media overwhelmed our feeds with paid content and divisiveness, on occasion it brought us something new and interesting. Like the rest of the world on September 7, 2015, I watched footage of a seven-year-old Brazilian girl in a fairy costume working hard at her heelflips. Once Tony Hawk (see page 63) shared the clip, it went viral. This was just the opening stanza of the Rayssa Leal experience. Her drive and determination have become hallmarks of her career: she is the first woman to dominate Street League Skateboarding, and at 13, was the only Brazilian skater to stand at the podium at the Tokyo Olympics, earning silver in street.

One of her favorite showstopping tricks is called a hurricane. Picture contorting yourself into a pretzel and unraveling at the last second. Or, to go deeper here: you backside 180 over the rail and lay your back truck in a grind going backward until the last moment when you pop forward, back out to regular, and ride away smooth. As you can see, it's a mouthful to describe and incredibly difficult to accomplish. Think of it like the Kid 'n Play dance of skateboarding. You're holding your right leg up in a figure 4 leglock and jumping over the other leg. Now imagine doing it down a flight of stairs. Now picture that pretzel configuration being unleashed on a skinny-az round handrail. There's less surface area and more opportunity for it all to go wrong. It is one of the most difficult tricks in skateboarding and it's now a Rayssa signature. What a difference a few years made.

While she may have more wins now than when she began, Rayssa remains the young fairy who loved skateboarding so much she neglected to change out of her children's parade outfit because it would have cut into her skate time. Whether she's skating at a contest or in the streets, she's still as excited about every skate session as if it were the first one. I see her chattering with Leticia Bufoni, and Pâmela Rosa, and Gabriela Mazetto, thinking about angles and approaches to hitting the rails, laughing, and supporting each other, with her demonstrating poise beyond her years.

Rayssa's movement from grammar school to becoming one of the most important female skaters from South America speaks to the ferocity of Brazilian skateboarding today. I can tell you firsthand from visiting São Paulo and Rio and points in between that skateboarding is the *business* in Brazil. It's not all about soccer as you might think. As pro skater Felipe Gustavo told me, "Every time you go back to Brazil, there is another unknown amazing skater who could be pro in the U.S." Rayssa has risen to the *nata da colheita*, or cream of the crop, there.

Though it might seem that she entered the competitive ranks easily, it took real effort to arrive on the scene. She was born in Imperatriz, in northeast Brazil, and her parents came from humble backgrounds. They pinched every penny they had to keep Rayssa skating, and to travel to contests in other parts of Brazil so that skaters already making waves could see her potential.

Once Rayssa left her hometown with its literal rough ground, rougher streets, and difficult-to-utilize skateparks and had the chance to skate on high-caliber skateparks, she began to shine. People started to see Rayssa as more than just a cute kid skateboarding. She was getting taller, adding power, and attempting more difficult skateboarding, spurred on by rolling with more advanced skaters.

During that time, the media also started to notice her. She was naturally media-savvy and learned how to work the camera from her biggest inspiration, Leticia Bufoni (see page 287). Rayssa also became Brazil's darling when Globo, the leading producer of media in Brazil, dedicated a specific section of a television program to her. The producers, with support from pro skaters Bob Burnquist and Sandro Dias, arranged for Leticia to walk on during an interview with Rayssa.

According to pro skater and Brazilian skateboarding agent Tulio De Oliveira, "That show was a turning point. Everyone in Brazil knew who she [Rayssa] was after the episode. The whole country was behind her."

From there, Rayssa had a solid spot on the Nike team in Brazil's highly competitive skateboarding market. With that level of support, Rayssa exploded, making a solid line of wins at contests, and later landing a spot with the highly influential skateboarding brand April, where she gained her own signature pro model.

Rayssa has spoken about mental health, employing a sports psychologist and encouraging other young people to seek professional help when they need it. She's also taken a page from Leticia and is now entering the fashion world, attending couture shows and leaning into the paparazzi.

Rayssa Leal, a Brazilian powerhouse by the age of 14, leads the change in a country that is creating the greatest skaters on the planet.

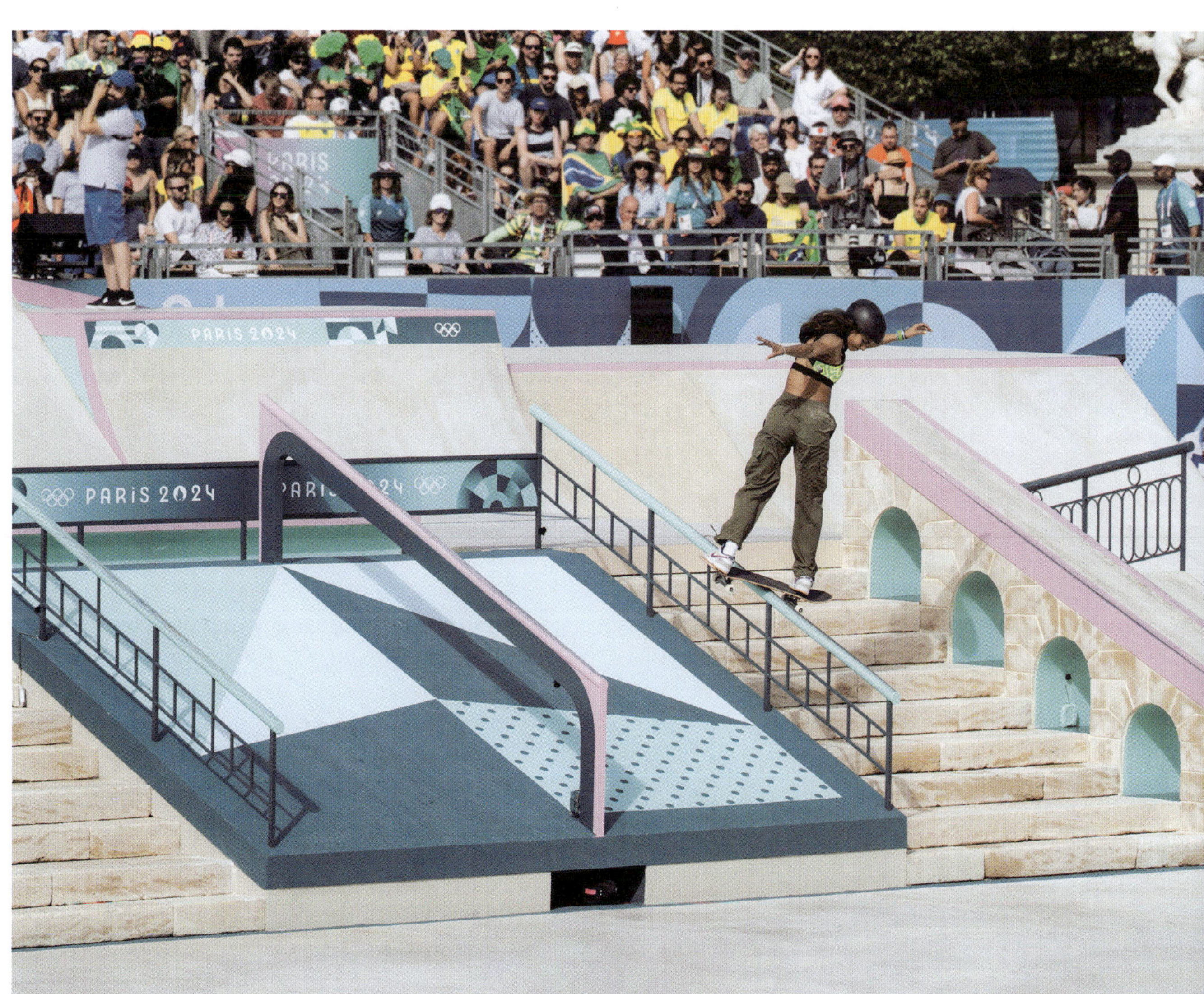

Fearless backside lipslide during the
Paris 2024 Street Finals

THE HIGH-FLYING HAWAIʻIAN

HEIMANA REYNOLDS

Hawaiʻian hero

Carries on a tradition of AAPI excellence

2019 world park champion

2020 USA Olympic team member

Heimana was the number-one seeded park skater going into Tokyo 2020. He is a 2019 world park champ (São Paulo) who also has multiple X Games under his belt. Heimana carries on a legacy of tight carving and high-flying skateboarding that evokes decades of the expressive "surf-skate" style that has been a part of Hawaiʻian skateboarding since the 1970s.

Born in 1998 in Honolulu to parents both Pacific Islander and Asian American (his father is Hawaiʻian and Tahitian, his mother Filipino and white), Heimana had surfing and skating as part of his family heritage. Whether carving the banks in town or skating homemade plywood "jump" and "junk ramps" (sometimes the same thing), his father and uncles instilled in him that adventure was normal. Skating and surfing were par for the course on islands.

But Heimana's family didn't push him into skateboarding; he explored sports that interested him, including football, baseball, and basketball, yet nothing took. But at age seven, when he stepped on a skateboard, Heimana found his first love and it has endured. Seeing the spark in his son and his natural affinity, Mark, his father, quickly became Heimana's "s-coach" (skate coach). After his son's

success, the Reynoldses went on to open their own skate shop, Proper Rideshop on Oʻahu.

Growing up near the constant ebb and flow of the ocean, chasing the waves, charging into the swell, pumping, pulsing, and feeling the waves, holding his breath and rock training in undersea caves, all made Heimana's surf skate approach on a board as sick as they come. That's what happens when you come up skating in the tawdry imperfections of the Hawaiʻian landscape. Straight fire. Heimana's ability to unlock the cheat code to big air and great style instantly drew comparisons to other iconic skaters, including Asian American and Pacific Islander skaters like Christian Hosoi (see page 17).

Heimana pushes the park to the edge, and it pushes back: Can he contain his skating to the park, and does the park have enough surface to contain his antics? There are no in-betweens in that no-guts-no-glory approach. He either launches farther and higher than the competition or ends up in a pile at the bottom of the park. He wouldn't want it any other way.

He is also proud to carry on a tradition of Asian American Pacific Islander (AAPI) excellence in

HEIMANA PUSHES THE PARK TO THE EDGE, AND IT PUSHES BACK.

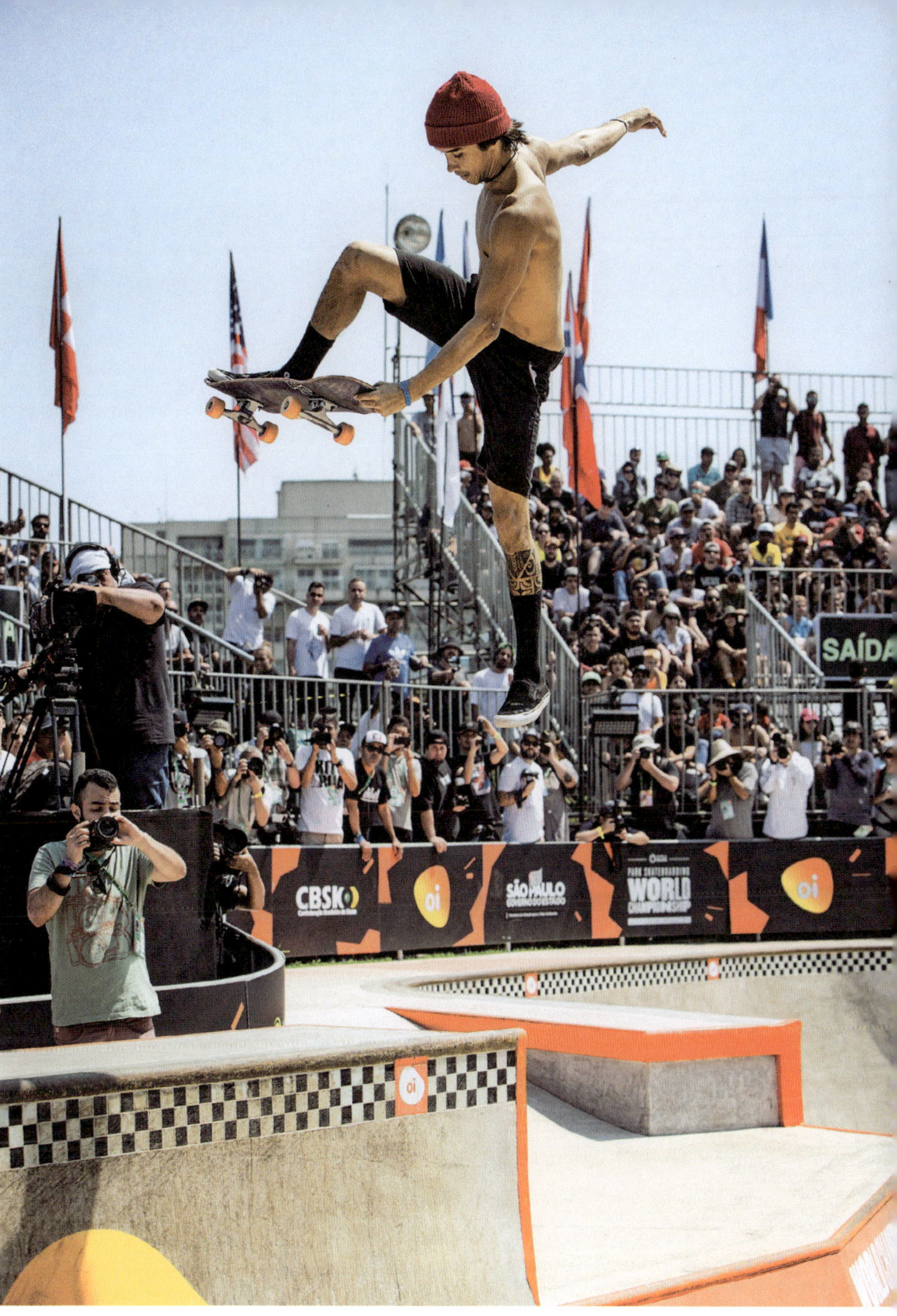

Heimana Reynolds, hella-lofted
Madonna air

skateboarding, and wears his surf skate style as a badge of honor. To grow up in a family with skating and surfing at its core is a rarity, and it's even rarer to be a person of color with that pedigree. Before joining the Olympic stage for skateboarding's debut in 2021, Heimana said his skating represents the blood of Hawai'i. His and his teammates' boards are the first of their kind to be made available for purchase through a major skateboard brand and retailer, the Heart Supply, at the same quality level as the ones they rode during their Olympic debut.

Heimana knows he is part of a living legacy of excellence from the 50th state. One of the first inspirations for the Z-Boys' aggressive skate style extends from their attempts to emulate Hawai'i's early son, Black surfer Montgomery "Buttons" Kaluhiokalani (RIP). Other '90s pros like Rene Matthyssen made the OG skatepark 'A'ala Park their home and designated Hawai'i as a hotbed of talent. Monumental skateboarder Jaime Reyes called that park home and went on to influence all of skateboarding as the first female Pacific Islander and street skater to grace the cover of *Thrasher* magazine. That vibe of exceptional skateboarders continues to this day with other female skaters such as Hawai'i-born Olympic women's team skater Jordyn Barratt.

In Heimana's mind, every push honors his family, state, and nation. He says if he can inspire young people to skate and adults to see skateboarding not as a "rebel sport" but as a sport that's an extension of the soul, then he's done his job.

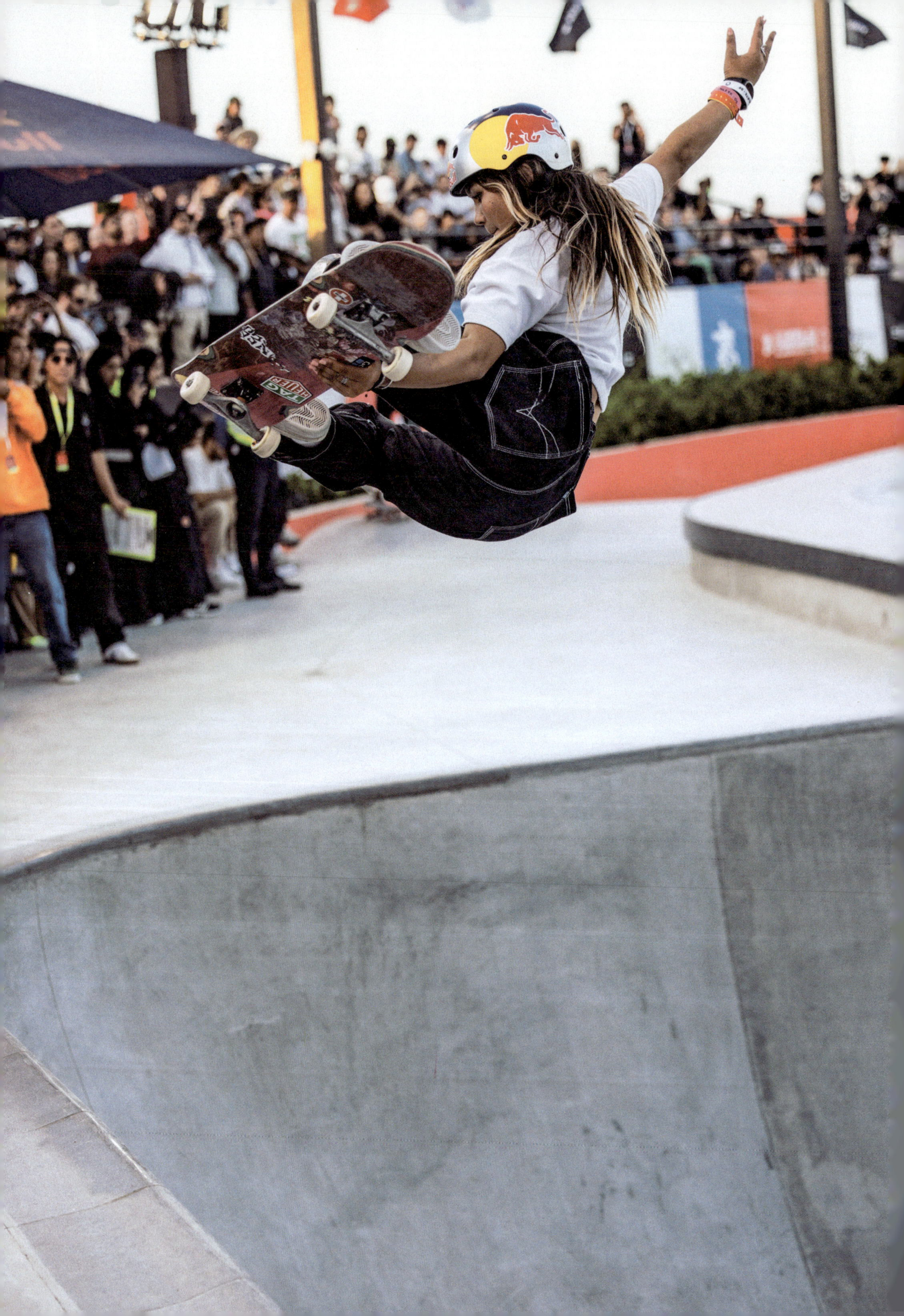

THE PRODIGY

SKY BROWN

World Champion at age 14

Youngest Olympian ever to compete for Great Britain

Dubbed one of the best skateboarders ever by Tony Hawk

Pop culture crossover star

Sky Brown bounded into my life as a seven-year-old with a "soul skater" hat, rainbow high socks, and a smile that melted my USC classroom, where I used to teach and had guest speakers galore from the game. She was accompanied by Skateboarding Hall of Famer Cindy Whitehead, an innovator in women's skateboarding during the turbulent 1970s and an advocate and supporter of women's skating since. Cindy told me that Sky would be the one to spark a new wave of women and young girls in skating. Facts.

Sky's presence changed the way we think about the skateboarding culture and how it might become more inclusive. Sky has kicked the doors wide open with what might have been a size-three shoe, and only a fool would not be looking out for the next amazing young women and girls to innovate and keep driving the sport in the future.

Sky is—and embodies—a global phenomenon. She divides her time between Miyazaki, Japan, where she was born and her mother is from, and Southern California, where the family lives. (Her father is British, and Sky chose to compete for Great Britain in the Olympics.)

Sky came into skateboarding with a heart filled with love for the sport and arms wrapped around her little brother, her family, and her board. In 2015, there were significantly fewer women and young girls in skateboarding and her position as a wunderkind was exceptional. With few skaters her own age to serve as role models, Sky set out to show that young girls could be ripping skaters.

Thinking back, the 2015 class was the first of its kind and Sky was one of the first contemporary young female prodigies leading the women's and girls' movement. However, now she's sponsored by Nike, heading a top women's brand in skateboarding alongside fellow superstar Leticia Bufoni (see page 267). Sky also had an entire section dedicated to her skateboarding exploits in the Young V&A museum in the U.K. She is the youngest ever Summer Olympian to compete for Great Britain. She picked up a bronze medal in park skating at the 2020 Games, and earned a world championship in 2023 in park skating. There was also her full-length documentary, *Reaching the Sky* (2021), featuring Tony Hawk's (see page 63) comments marking her as the future of skateboarding.

Beyond all that is the fact that Sky's attitude remains positive. As half of the Instagram handle @AWSMKids, she and her even younger brother, Ocean, set the stage for the world to embrace a new skilled set of youthful skaters breaking the confines of gender and age. The AWSM kids' vids caught fire, earning the siblings spots on *Steve Harvey*, *Ellen*, and a host of other talk shows, which quickly escalated into Sky becoming a household name. In a short time, she showed the world she could skate street and park, and surf with the best of them.

I can attest to watching the world become enthralled with the personality, skills, and spark of Sky across international borders. While working in 2018 on a skate diplomacy trip for the U.S. Department of State, I had the honor of seeing

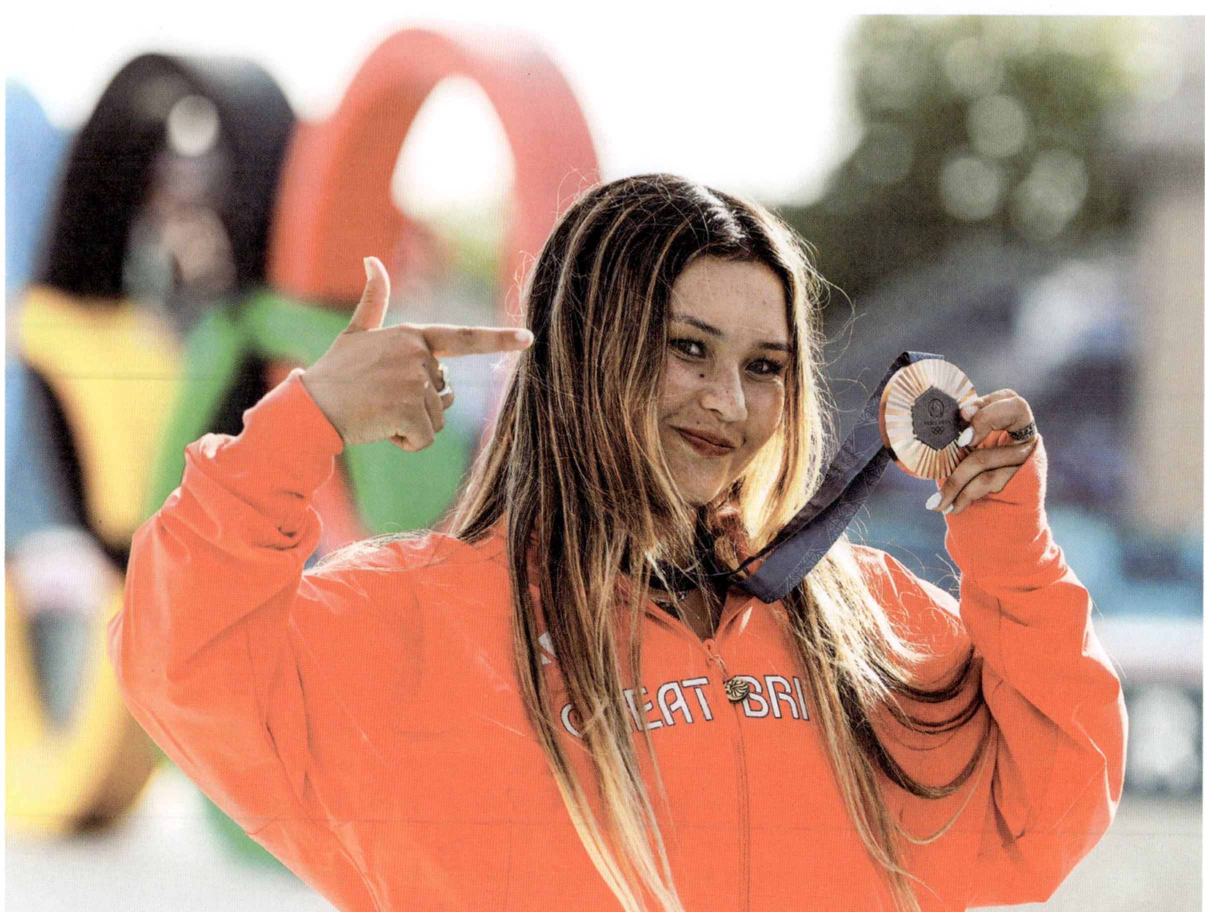

Sky's star shine on a hot, humid day in Cambodia. Sky's love for skateboarding and the kids who were there learning and practicing was so infectious it still makes me smile, a reminder of the fun that skateboarding is.

At the front doors of the Skateistan NGO's headquarters in Phnom Penh, Cambodia, Sky showed up holding on to the back of her dad Stu's rented moped, with TV camera crews in tow that had been filming the two zipping down the impossibly crowded streets. The energy that Sky brought to that day's skate session was incredible. Skateistan was abuzz. She worked on tricks with skaters, teaching some to kickflip, then began a 30-minute deep dive into a mini-ramp clinic. Make no mistake, though, Sky makes for some lit-ass skateboarding. She had just learned noseblunts and locked them right in on the first try on the mini ramp so I could get a photo. She did several so I could have a choice. That's how dialed in her skating was even at nine years old. She's giving me pics to choose from. Me! I was just trying to learn noseblunts last week. No wonder she's an Olympian.

The other thing that stayed with me from that excursion with Sky is that beyond the skills, she has the heart to be a champion. I remember overhearing

Stu and Sky talk about the state of the world and her understanding that she was living a privileged life.

After visiting Cambodia and seeing the level of support that young people there need to obtain an education, Sky became Skateistan's youngest ambassador. She still advocates for people to support its work so that young girls in Cambodia and Afghanistan might be able to pursue an education—and skateboarding—in Skateistan's schools. Partnered with Almost Skateboards, she released a limited-edition deck dedicated to the children of Skateistan, with proceeds supporting the programming in Cambodia. She wasn't even a pro skater then. Just a young girl who saw some of the conditions of her fellow children in Cambodia and wanted to do something about it.

Let's move back to the States. You might be one of the lucky ones to catch Sky in a hot session skating the Venice skatepark and surfing the California coasts on her vacation time, split between L.A. and Orange County. Outside of contest season and school breaks, at last check she still attended school in Japan and lives a relatively normal life in a small fishing village, albeit interspersed with the pro contest circuit.

From backyard minis to appearing on the packaging of Clif Bars to making commercials for

Samsung, Sky has shown the world that she is an inspirational tour de force.

Sky may never fully know the monumental impact she's had on the entire skateboarding industry but she was an unstoppable light. In the early 2010s, companies were in uncharted territory with an eight-year-old girl as a cultural and sporting focal point. Professional skateboarding was largely represented by young men and older teens. Going on tour traditionally meant a bunch of them laying their lives on the line filming and finding themselves through time with the homies. How would team managers manage a young child on tour when most of their experience had revolved around managing skaters ages 16 to 25? Some opted for the safe road: Avoid the kids, and especially a young girl. Avoid the potential for controversy.

All of that changed when the *Los Angeles Times* ran an article that went viral, with video of Sky slaying the cement in Venice. Sky had more followers in a week than most skateboarding brands with 20-year legacies. (She's at 1.4 million on Instagram as I type this.) Sky appeared in every media outlet. As hip-hop super group Goodie Mob would put it, her earned media stats were "Sky High." All at a time when the world had begun to quantify social media's reach and construct the language for influencers. Most important, Sky was becoming famous for shredding.

Beyond everyone clamoring for Sky to join their team, when the pendulum swung in her favor, it didn't just affect Sky's life, it affected all of skateboarding. It moved companies and brands past watching out only for their current rosters to thinking deeply about how white and male those rosters were, and to an idea of what their trajectory *could* look like if they were to include the other 51 percent of the populace. In particular, Sky sent everyone off to the woodshed about how they could support the next generation of women in skateboarding.

Sky's ascent also caused a shift in other areas of the sport. As her skating became more powerful, and she began landing tricks like 540s and rodeo flips that were well beyond her years, this inadvertently created a subtle, but real, growing pain for her competition. Everyone had to consider that she was skating for fun, and they were skating for rent.

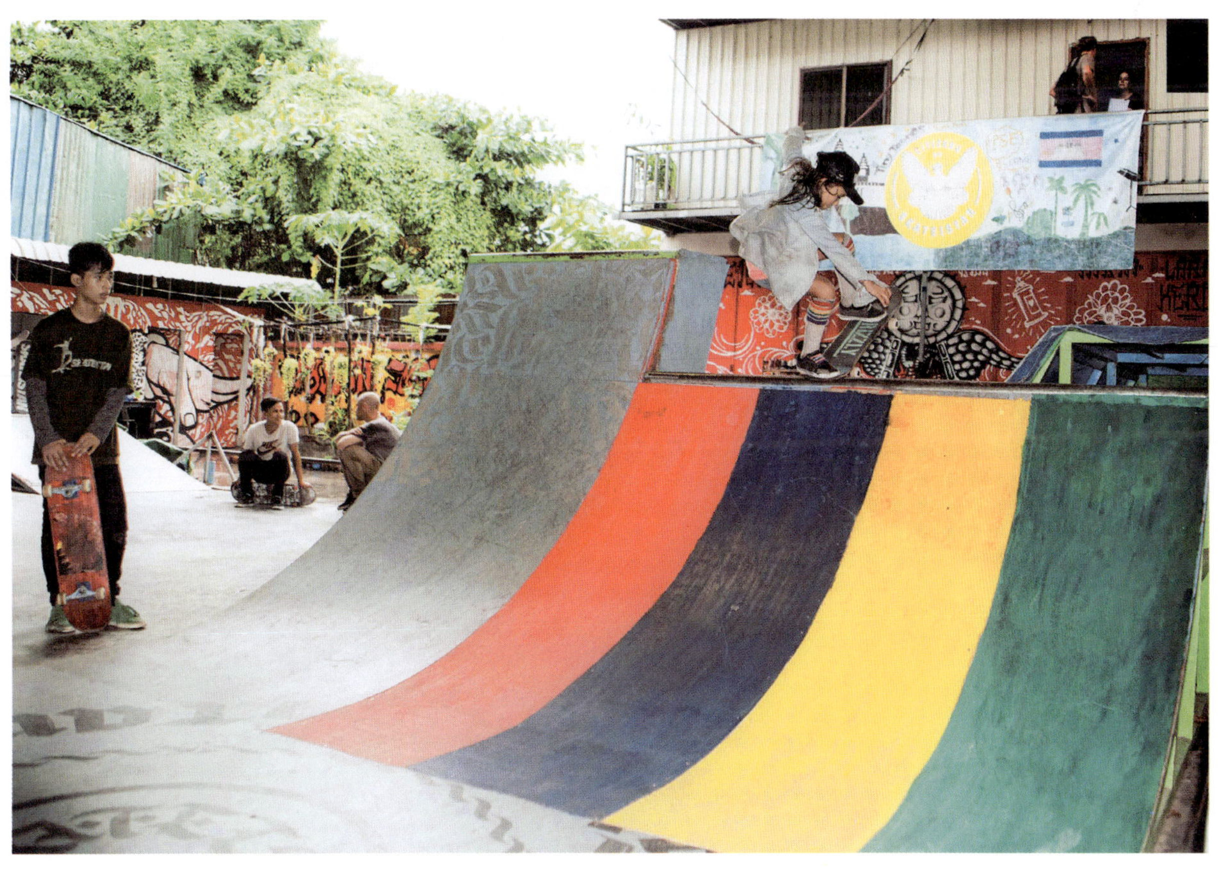

Despite the change in attitude from some of her competition, Sky's skating helped her secure her position on team Great Britian. At the Olympics, spectators witnessed skateboarders operating on two levels—first as competitive athletes but also as a supportive community who rallied behind their own. When Sky fell during her early two runs, competitors from several countries, including the United States and Japan, rallied behind her to offer support. They gave her the strength to link all her tricks on her last run and earn a bronze medal. That's nearly unheard of in other sports. What's more, when it came time to shoot photos of the medalists, the girls all stood together rather than posing in their respective podium positions. This was a collection of powerful young women

skateboarders and they set a new standard for Olympic etiquette. It was one of the best lessons from the Games, and one that writers and viewers around the world picked up on. Nike used to run an ad that said, "What if we treated all athletes like skateboarders?" In that moment the zeitgeist shifted to, "What if all athletes treated sports like skateboarders do?" Indeed.

Case in point, the greatest young skater of our time decided to do *Dancing with the Stars: Juniors*. Beginning her time there with a kickflip on the very board that was created after her visit to Skateistan, Sky hopped right into choreographed line with her partner, JT, and let the world know that besides kickflips, she could also do backflips, the Charleston, the tango, and every style under the sun.

Tony Hawk has said she is one of the most naturally gifted skaters he has ever seen. Those are big words coming from the Big Birdman. He invited Sky to skate his giant vert ramp on more than one occasion. During one session, Sky fell. Very hard.

Enough to fracture her face and put her in the hospital. She had attempted a new trick over the gap between the ramps, didn't quite have the power to make it over, and fell through the open channel. A 15-foot drop and a 10-year-old falling on her face.

There was a lot of backlash on social media. The discussion quickly turned to gendered protection of a little girl in a man's sport. Everyone's biggest fears came out. I spoke with many skaters and scholars attempting to sort this out in their own heads and figuring out how they would react to the same situation with their own kids.

But that's just it. Sky is a phenomenon, and we all need to wrestle with our biases to push back against a narrative that says she and other girls can't be as great or as aggressive as they want to be.

While we fussed and stressed, Sky *healed*. The vids came quick of her doing what she always does: dancing, singing, and having fun. She reminded us that she was strong, she was young, and she was resilient. And in 2023, she won the world championship in the UAE.

Sky Brown, the dancer, the surfer, the skater, the leader, the bridge between the U.K., the U.S., and Japan, the link between generations. Sky Brown, the one who continues to lead by example and demonstrate to us what it looks like to walk a fearless path.

THE MOST DECORATED WOMAN IN BRAZILIAN SKATEBOARDING
LETICIA BUFONI

Ranked number-one women's street skateboarder by World Cup Skate from 2010 to 2013

Most medals—12—of any female Summer X Games athlete (as of this writing)

Trailblazing athlete ambassador for Brazil

SLS Super Crown champion, media sensation, and global fan favorite who transcends sport

Athlete ambassador for Brazil, emissary for women's skateboarding, skateboarding company founder, race car driver, parachuter, skateboarder while parachuting, wakeboarder, snowboarder, X Games medalist, Guinness World Record holder for most women's summer X Games medals, *ESPN The Magazine* Body Issue fan favorite. It's impossible to think about women's skateboarding without Leticia Bufoni. She has shattered records and has empowered a new generation of female athletes to demand the respect they deserve of skateboarding and non-skateboarding audiences alike. She has helped elevate women's skateboarding into the mainstream consciousness through her countless commercials, interviews, and ads with endemic and non-endemic brands like Toyota and Beats by Dre. She has done it all and continues to find new ways to dominate skateboarding and action sports.

My students at USC had learned about Leticia in class, but in 2016, Street League Skateboarding came to USC's Galen Center. Part of a sold-out crowd, my class was able to see in person Leticia's ability to push the limits of women's skating. She always tries to set herself apart from the competition, not only in technical trick selection but in brawn. She chose to skate a gap-to-rail and land in a lipslide, meaning she would have to ollie a huge gap just to try to connect with a section of the rail much farther away and hope to safely slide across it horizontally. This was also a section of the course that the men used. Her attempts put all the other women on notice. Hitting those big rails set off a chain of events, resulting in more women now making those obstacles part of their winning arsenal.

At age 14, Leticia left São Paolo in 2008, without her family or friends, to come to the U.S. to compete as an alternate at the X Games in Los Angeles. She bit right into that event and never let go. As Leticia needed a stable place to live in L.A., skateboarder Liza Araujo took Leticia under her wing—she mentored her, enrolled her at Hollywood High, and helped her focus on her skateboarding.

Leticia, with Liza's help, convinced her father that she could make it here. Assisted by Ana Paula Negrao, a skater and also one of the top female skate photographers of all time, they formed a powerful crew. They handily kicked down companies' doors from L.A. to the O.C. to help Leticia earn her first sponsors. At the time, lots of brands did not see the value of having women on their teams. Even those that did still had a hard time figuring out how to market a "women's line" for their brands. In those days, it was difficult for talented women to find a home at a "core" skateboarding company.

Nevertheless, Leticia crushed it. As of this writing, she is a six-time X Games gold medalist, the most medaled woman in skateboarding history. The sum of those experiences was part of the impetus for Leticia to eventually cofound her own brand, Monarch Project, with Sky Brown in 2021. She was on the *Forbes* Brazil "Under 30" list and is one of the most marketable women athletes in the world. She's now transitioning into other roles as the athlete ambassador for Brazilian skateboarding.

Leticia represents a light for all the female skateboarders of Brazil, and has found ways to show everyone that you can be a true skateboarder but also be about your business as an athlete. While men have the luxury of not needing to skate in contests to prove their worth, that has not been the case for women. For decades the only way for women to sustain a professional career was through contests, and Leticia made the best of it. She used the camera and the podium to gain accolades on live TV. She set up a new generation of women to see themselves excelling on the small screen. Eventually, brands and advertisers flocked to her, too.

Their interest showed that Leticia's hard work could deliver conniptions for the competition. She was featured on the cover of *GQ*, but not everyone commended her for it. Brazilian pro skater and agent Tulio De Oliveira noted that Leticia received a lot of hate for handling the spotlight so well, with comments about her running the gamut: "She's too pretty, she's too sexy, she's too strong, she's too good." What's worse is that those snide comments came from both male and female voices. But Leticia understood that skateboarding could be great for everything. Why shouldn't she have been on the cover of *GQ Brazil* at the time? Or skating in *Maxim* or doing ads for Secret board-sliding a handrail in a dress? She is capable of bridging a gap between mainstream sports and the skate world, and she wears the mantle well. She's one of the most relatable figures in action sports, and offers an international level of panache that appeals to multiple audiences and across generations. The Nickelodeon Kids' Choice Awards, the Teen Choice Awards, *Sports Illustrated*, the ESPYs, Ferrari, Victoria's Secret, the Chair of World Skate's International Skateboarding Technical Commission . . . and Leticia the cultural dynamo at the center of it all.

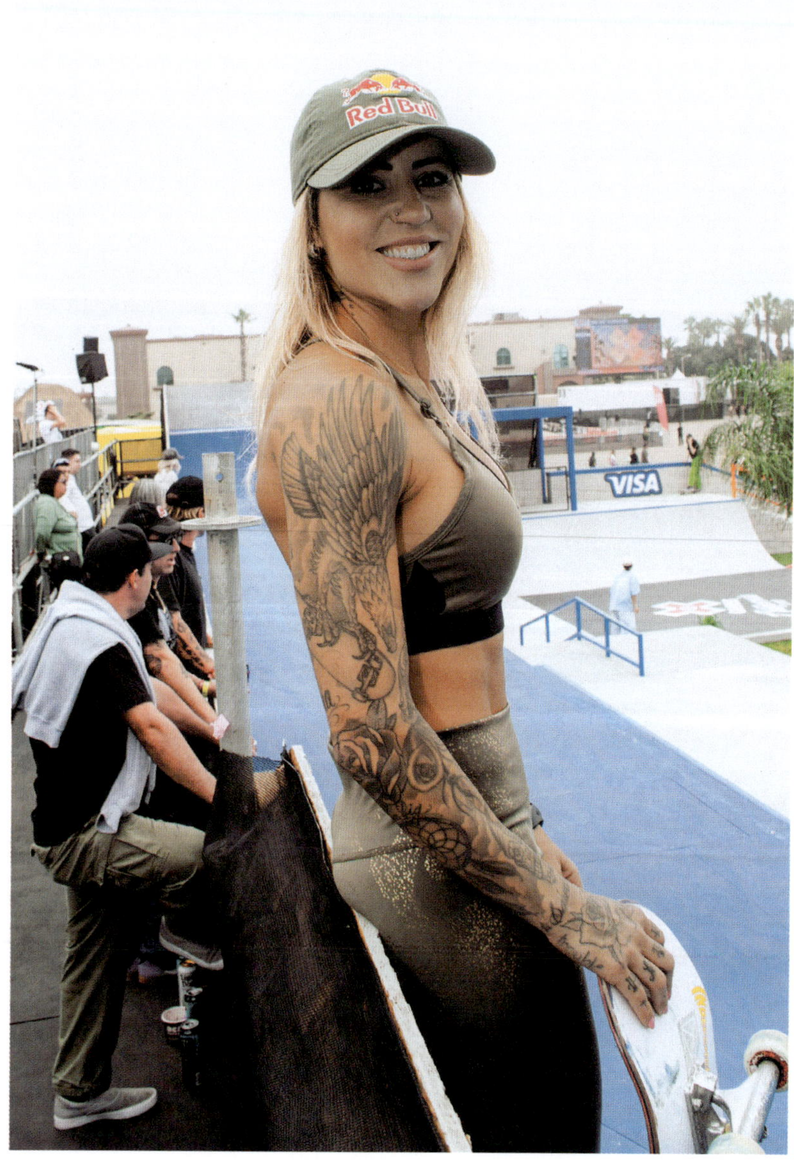

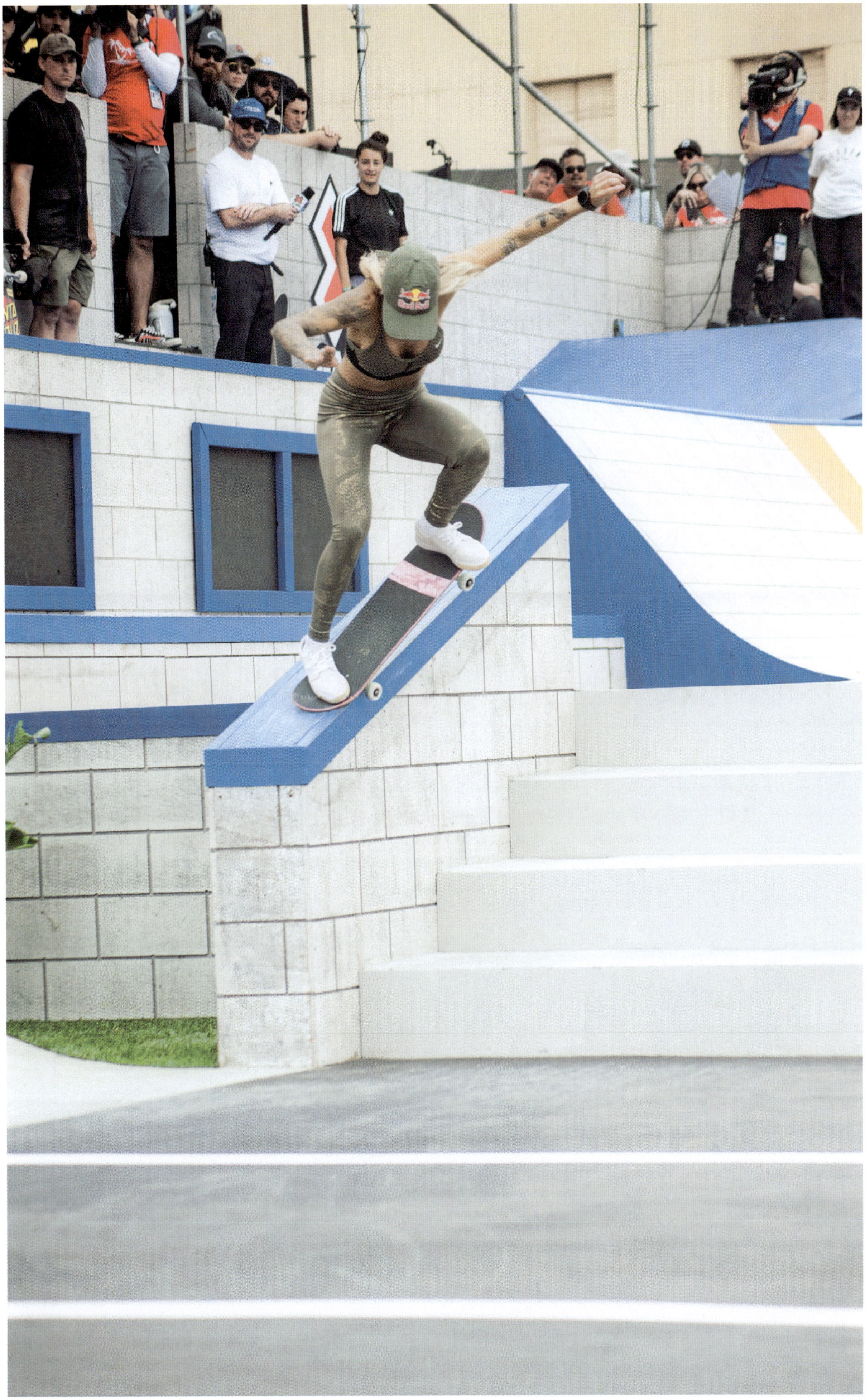

THE OLYMPICS: THE GREAT DEBATE

Top right: Brazil's Rayssa Leal and Holland's Keet Oldenbeuving sharing a moment between runs at the 2024 Paris Olympics.

Bottom right: The 2024 Paris Olympics Podium for Men's Street Skateboarding, (center) Yuto Horigome (gold), (left) Jagger Eaton (silver), (right) Nyjah Huston (bronze)

To be or not to be an Olympian. That is the question.

Actually, it's no longer the question because it has already been answered. Whether you take a position of blissful enthusiasm or one of wistful distress when questioning the necessity or validity of the Olympic experience as it connects to skateboarding culture, for better or for worse, Olympic skateboarding is here to stay.

As a sports scholar and a skateboarder, I'm constantly asked by others why anyone wouldn't want to be involved in the world's largest sports spectacle. "It's good for your industry" and "It makes skateboarding a legitimate sport" are also lobbed.

However, just as many sports historians, scholars, journalists, and everyday skaters equate any alliance with the five rings as "selling out" skateboarding and joining the masses. At minimum, for some skateboarders it represents a push away from the anti-sports origins they embraced and which helped them find their voices through skateboarding.

Deeper still are the accusations stating that anything special about skateboarding and its countercultural roots floated away like embers from a bonfire escaping into the night the moment the ink dried upon the alliance between traditional sports institutions and skateboarding.

My personal favorite is the academic and elitist argument that skateboarding doesn't *deserve* to be in the Olympics. This nonsense goes something like this, "It's the place of athletes; your people don't train and don't even want to be there." The Games, they state, should be reserved for those who live every waking moment dedicated to the pursuit of the ultimate trophy—a gold medal in their discipline.

Those folks would like to see skateboarding marginalized for as long as possible. As long as we are the ones chased by police and maligned in media as the dregs of society, the sports they love will face less competition and greater access to resources, despite skateboarding growing exponentially across the globe—unlike other traditional sports on the decline.

As with all things, it is what one does with a platform that matters. If we hold any truth as self-evident, it is that skateboarders take a platform and express themselves through it. It's literally the origin of skateboarding, so it's kind of our thing. It is as appalling to hear that we aren't worthy of carrying the Olympic moniker or don't *belong* in the Olympics as it is to hear from skaters that we are incapable of *delivering* something new to the Olympics because what we love is *beyond* sharing. Nothing worth loving is beyond sharing; that's why we skate alone and then together when we recognize other members of our family. The need to move from a monologue to a dialogue is inherent in the DNA. The eventual move to a chorus of voices is integral to skateboarding's diversity, and whether it is on your block or on the blocks of the podium, the call and response between skaters and those with whom skating resonates will continue to grow. We might as well send the beacon out to bring our family in.

Nevertheless, the concept of going for gold has never sat well with every member of the skateboarding community, never mind outsiders.

It is relentlessly mired in personal feelings, positionality, pomp and power, pride, and prejudice.

Part of the argument some skaters have has always been why participate in an endeavor that is as widely criticized as it is supported, and often seen by many as problematic. To paraphrase the Birdman himself, Tony Hawk (see page 63), "the Olympics needs skateboarding more than skateboarding needs the Olympics." This need for skateboarding and newer sports comes directly from the International Olympic Committee itself, whose investment derives from a hope that these newer sports will invigorate a flagging audience. Or, more optimistically, that recognition from sport's ultimate arena means that "competitive sport" can exist in multiple forms and skateboarding represents a new perspective on the boundaries of sport. It doesn't hurt that it is a no-brainer. Skateboarding continues to grow organically and it makes sense to have such a globally practiced sport be recognized by the largest spectacle of sport in the world. Win–win. Well, not so fast.

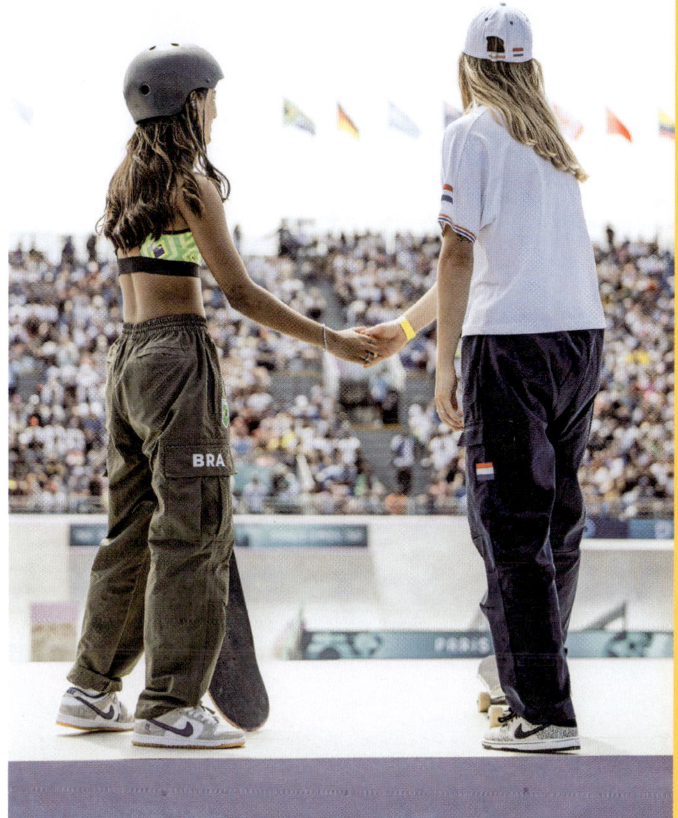

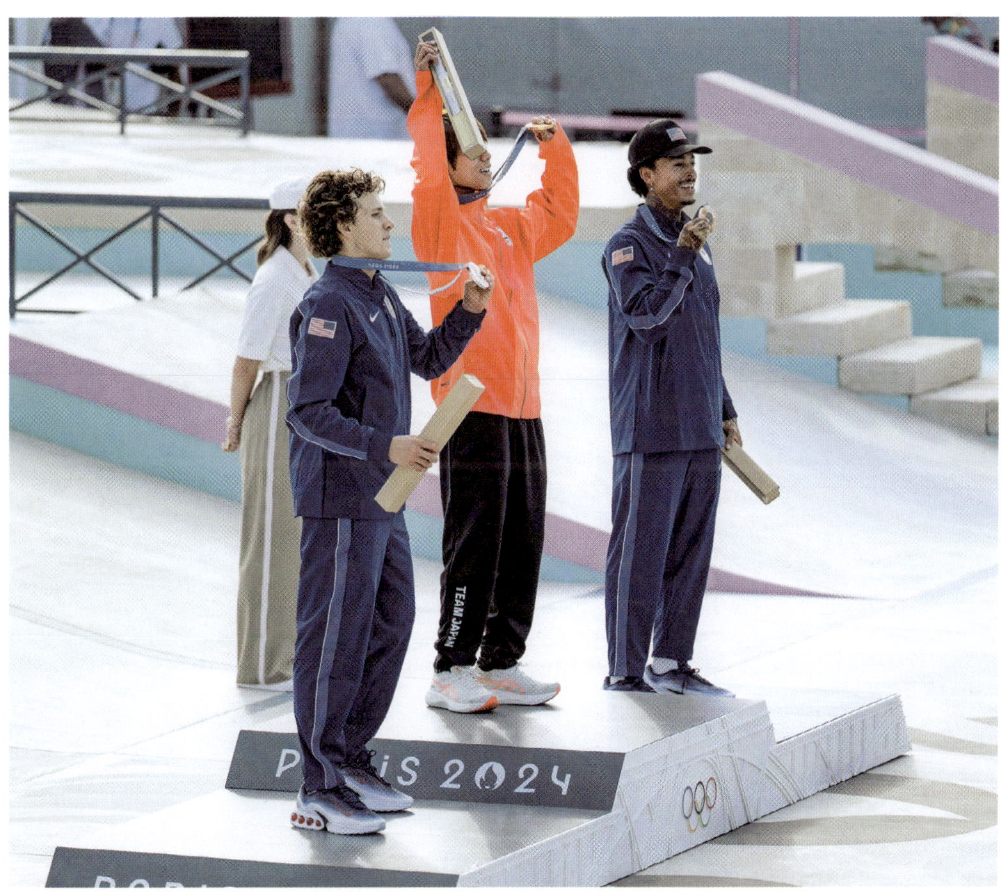

When skateboarding was first proposed for the Olympics, the petitions against it began, including those from more than 3,000 everyday skateboarders who signed asking for skateboarding not to be added. Even at the time of this writing, some skaters and academics push back on the need for skateboarding in the Olympics.

What I offer to that conversation is the belief that skateboarding the verb can continue to exist even as skateboarding the noun comes into play on larger stages. Since the days of OG crews from Dogtown, the Sadlands, the Badlands, London Skates Dominates, Florida to Florianópolis, there have always been skaters who felt skateboarding should be appreciated at the highest level. Performing for the fam or converting a congregation never compromised their skateboarding, and this conversation began at the moment the first contests occurred.

My conversation with the legendary Kareem Campbell (see page 46) summed it up well. He told me simply, "We *are* athletes, and we can compete with anyone. Skateboarding is beautiful. Everyone should see how hard it is and how dope our sh*% is—period." Well, there you have it. The Olympics owns the market on visibility and some people ain't skirred to be seen.

Skaters willing to participate should have the option to hit the stage and do what they love in the same manner as I skate to a store. Let them feel the spirit any way they want. Contests aren't for everyone, and they were never meant to be. They are conversations between participants, obstacles, spectators, and the ethereal energy between them. It ain't gonna change my push to the store, but it might change the storeowner's perception of my transportation choice.

And therein lies the key. There is the possibility that visibility might affect *everyone's* perception. Most important, if you have the mic and the podium, no need to shy away. If we use that ish to declare that skateboarding in any contest is a temporary moment regardless of the monetary stakes, then skateboarding—the noun, the verb, the culture—will survive.

For proof, just look at skateboarding's Olympic debut. It was a multigenerational, multiracial, multigendered coalition who showed skateboarding as the united family it can be and often is. We did it our way and I have faith it will remain so. Pushing in the streets, at the parks, at the contests, at the Olympics, and beyond, we will find a way to move forward under bright lights in any big city.

Chandler Burton's backside flip from deck to ramp on the skateable sculpture by Raphaël Zarka and Jean-Benoît Vétillard at Centre Pompidou in Paris

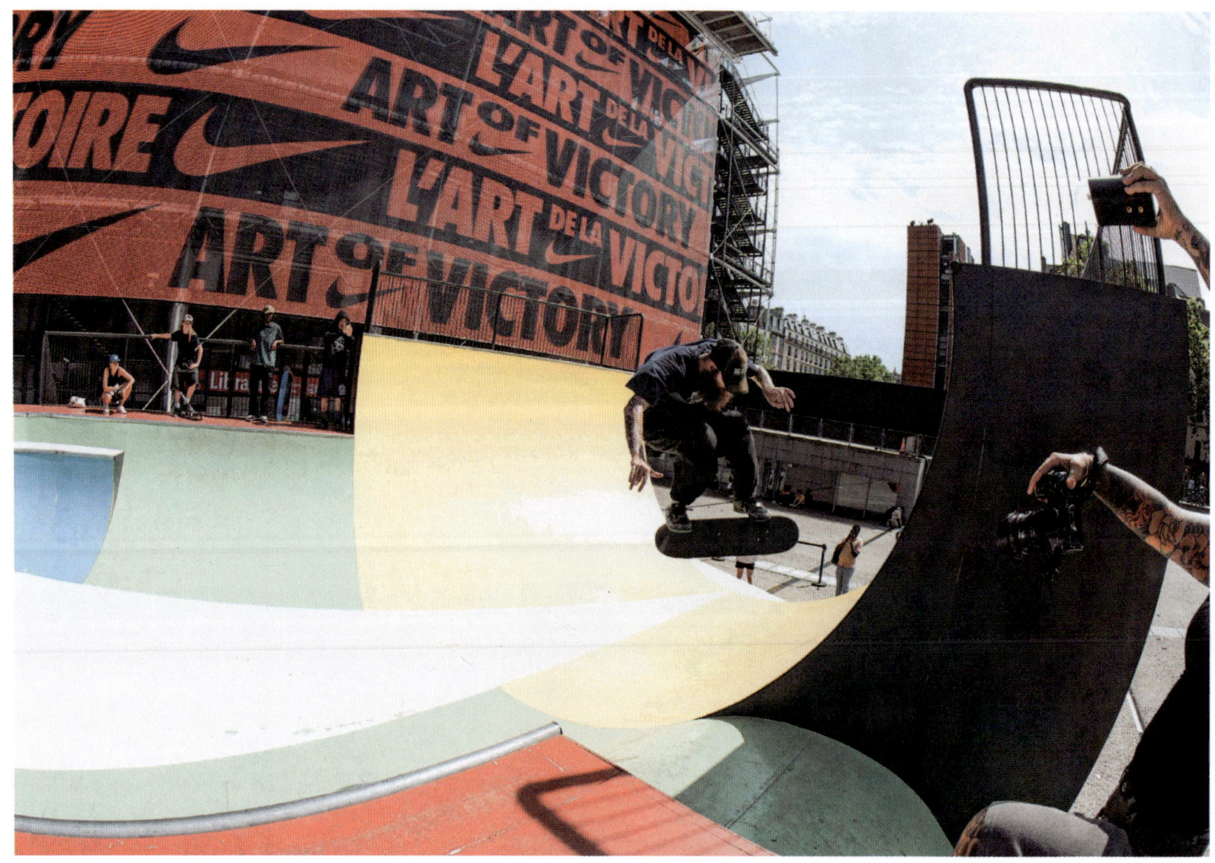

THE SERENA WILLIAMS OF SKATEBOARDING

SAMARRIA BREVARD

A manifestation of Black Joy told through skateboarding

First African American woman on the USA Skateboarding team

First African American female X Games medalist

First African American pro street skater for Enjoi skateboards

First African American woman featured on the cover of *Thrasher*

Few skaters radiate Black Joy like my sister Samarria Brevard. She gives 100 percent of her being to her skateboarding, whether in the streets or in the contests. Armed with an electrifying smile, she watches the competition, then lets her skateboarding do the talking. She is often referred to as the "Serena Williams of skateboarding" because of her groundbreaking role as one of the few African American female street skaters competing at the highest level, like the X Games and Street League Skateboarding. Most important, like the Williams sisters, Samarria unabashedly identifies with and supports the Black community and experience, as demonstrated by one of her signature models for Enjoi skateboards, which features a graphic of a raised Black fist. Though now defunct, the brand was a seminal part of skateboarding in the mid- to late aughts, their *Bag of Suck* (2006) video winning the *TransWorld SKATEboarding* Video of the Year award. With the

"I'M JUST TRYING TO LIVE MY BEST LIFE AND BRING IT EVERY DAY."

addition of Samarria to its roster, Enjoi won the *Thrasher* King of the Road Tour in 2016.

Prior to her emergence, there were decidedly fewer Black women in skateboarding, especially in the elite ranks, with the last visible ambassador being vertical skateboarding pro Stephanie Person (see page 104) in the 1980s. Samarria brings a new energy and vibe, and immediately created a new legacy for African American women in skateboarding not only as casual skaters but also as competitors. She's equally at home in the streets and on the covers of *Thrasher* magazine and *Skateism* as in contests, and her comfort and skill at both is one of the reasons she is a member of the USA Olympic skateboarding team.

I've been lucky enough to watch Samarria and her exceptional skating for nearly a decade, though it began as a bit of a fluke. I was hired in 2011 to shoot the Warner Bros. Supergirl Jam contest in Venice Beach, California, a trifecta of surf, skate, and snowboarding competitions. At the time, the women's contest scene ran lean (primarily due to a lack of male support), and I was excited to chronicle my sisters.

While waiting for the women's pro contest to start, Samarria was skating in the amateurs. I didn't know who she was at the time, but the moment she entered the arena, I was *in*. She greeted the other female skaters with support, and also skated like she owned the place, throwing down tricks in three ways that all skaters love: big, solid, and smooth. Samarria floated down the manufactured stairs with ease, executing huge 180 ollies and on-demand kickflips with power and poise. However, it was her 360 flips that did it for me. A proper 360 flip, or "tre flip," is often the gold standard for measuring a skater's board control. Samarria's tre is one for the decades, delivered effortlessly from snap to pop to catch. Watching her flow like water across the course, it never looked like the contest caused her a drop of worry. Capturing her first-place image on the podium, I realized that I had witnessed a phenomenon—the future of Black female excellence in street skateboarding.

Samarria grew up in Riverside, California, a city that somehow seems to produce smooth, unbothered athletes like African American MLB players Dusty Baker and Bobby Bonds and basketball great Cheryl Miller, so it is only fitting that she could make light work of skateboarding. Originally, she excelled at basketball and chased hoop dreams until the day she saw her brother and other family members skateboarding. Their brilliance was contagious. "They just looked like they were having so much fun," she told me. "I knew then it was for me." Her innate athleticism and coordination quickly earned her a place within the local crew.

Imagine it. Samarria grew up in a changing era and narrative around skateboarding. One where skateboarding was a symbol of Black athletics and pride. Her skateboarding developed organically within a Black family and a Black community, and she radiates the spirit of Black Joy in every outing. This hits differently than previous generations of skaters who were often forced to navigate other people's perceptions of their participation in a "white" sport. Samarria recognized that for just

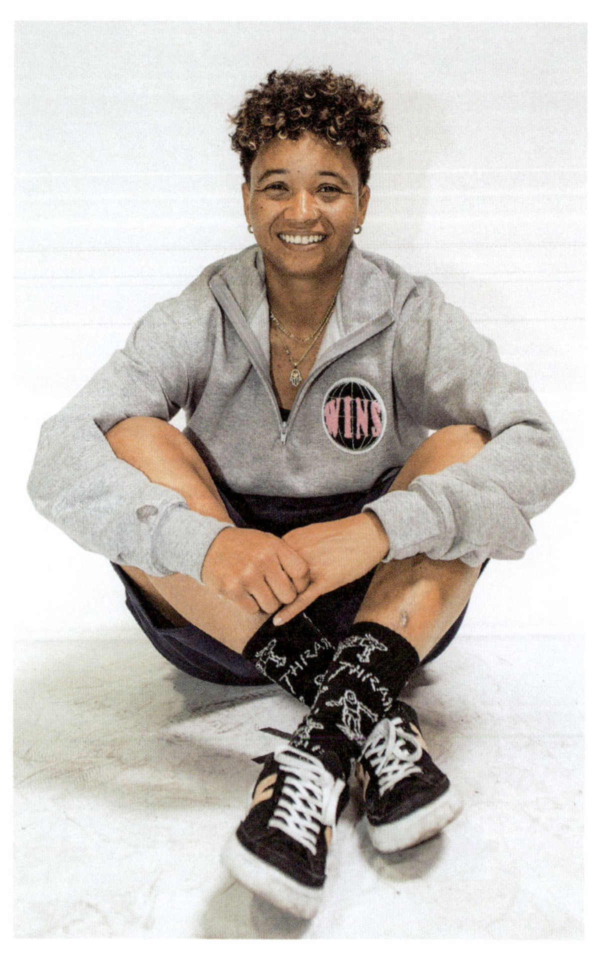

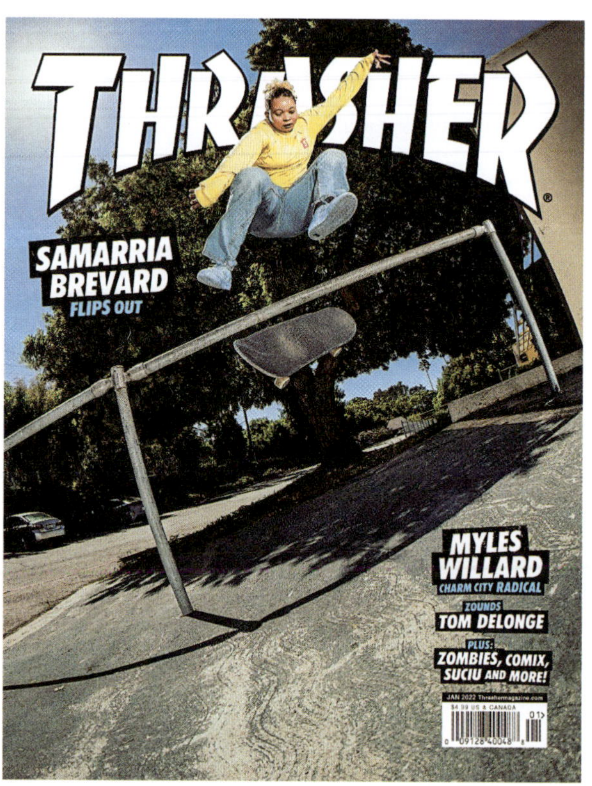

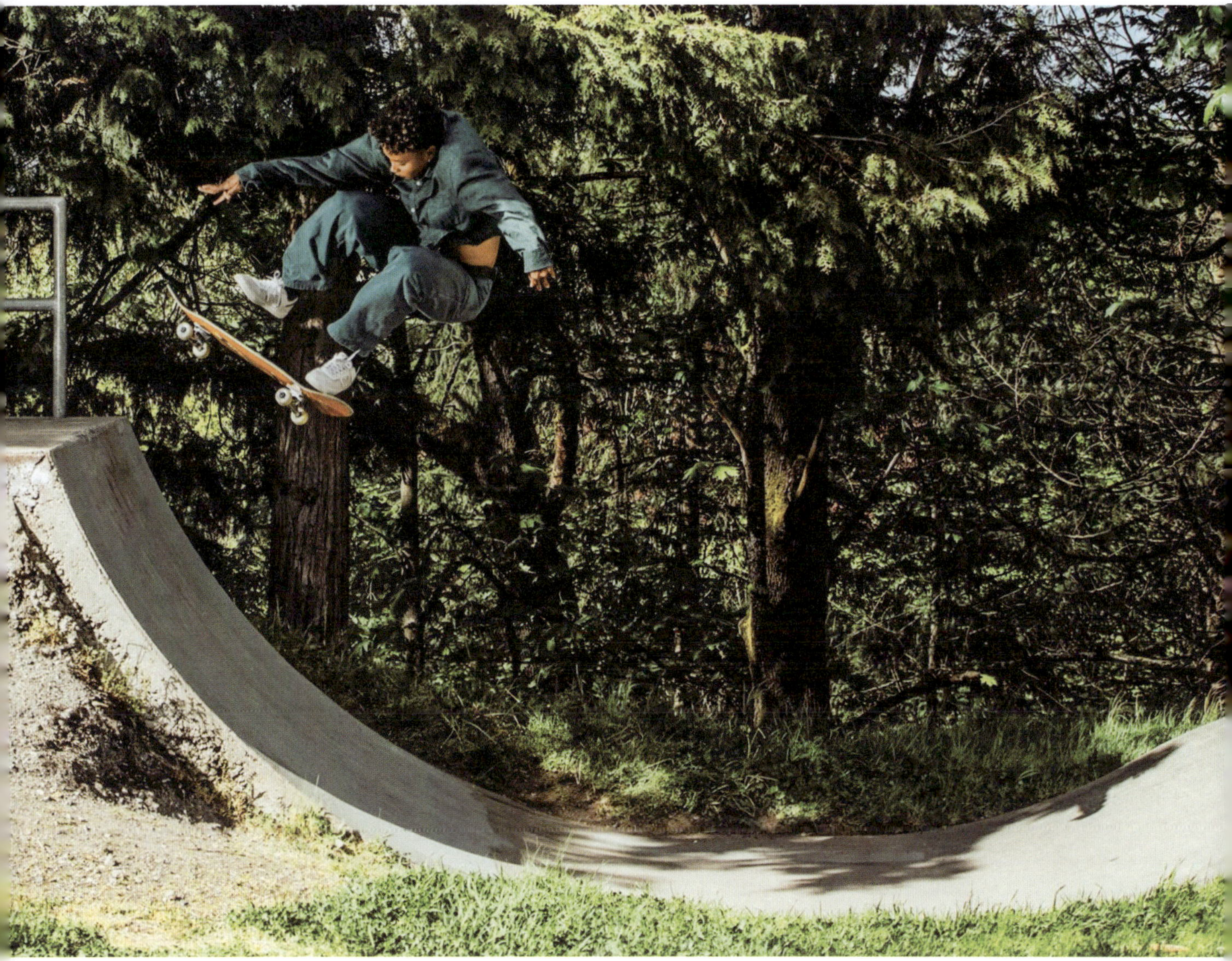

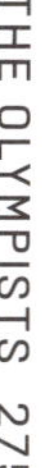

Top: Samarria Brevard, kickflip to fakie

Opposite, from left: Samarria Brevard;
kickflip through the bar with hippie jump
over, timeless innovation by Samarria
Brevard

a little bit, she wasn't pushing against a swell of skateboarding stereotypes at home. Instead, there were helping hands bringing her into the fold. Samarria, along with a handful of others, is part of a new generation of skaters born into a world where skateboarding is "Black" to them because they were introduced to it by Black people. There is something magnificent in that for generations of skaters of color.

Samarria's quiet power is incredibly exciting for the future of competitive skateboarding. She is humble about herself and her skating, and yet even with all the pressure of having been a star on the Olympic team, she is just doing the damn thing on her terms. While it could be a burden to be known as the Serena Williams of skateboarding, Samarria takes the accolades and responsibility in stride. She told me that the contests are never her ultimate goal, and that the "real wins" to her are taking care of her mental and physical health. That's the key to longevity and progression in skateboarding. Regardless of rankings or contests, her presence as a gifted Black woman skateboarder has made an indelible impact on skateboarding culture.

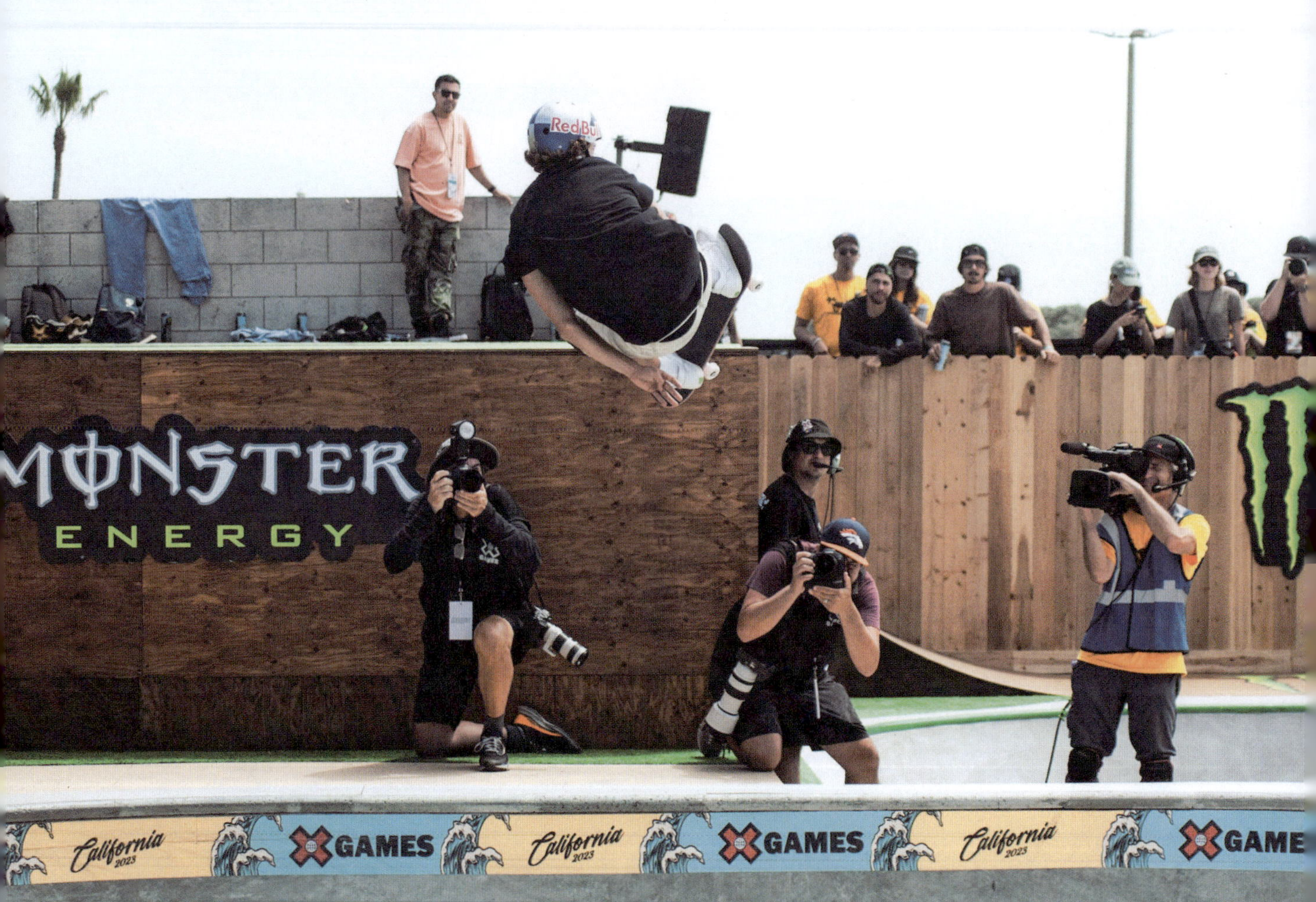

MEDALS ON HIS MIND
JAGGER EATON

First skater to win both street *and* park at the World Championships

Second-generation Olympian

Bronze medalist at the Tokyo Olympics

Silver medalist at the Paris Olympics

2014 Tampa Am Contest champion at 13 years old

2018 Tampa Pro Contest winner

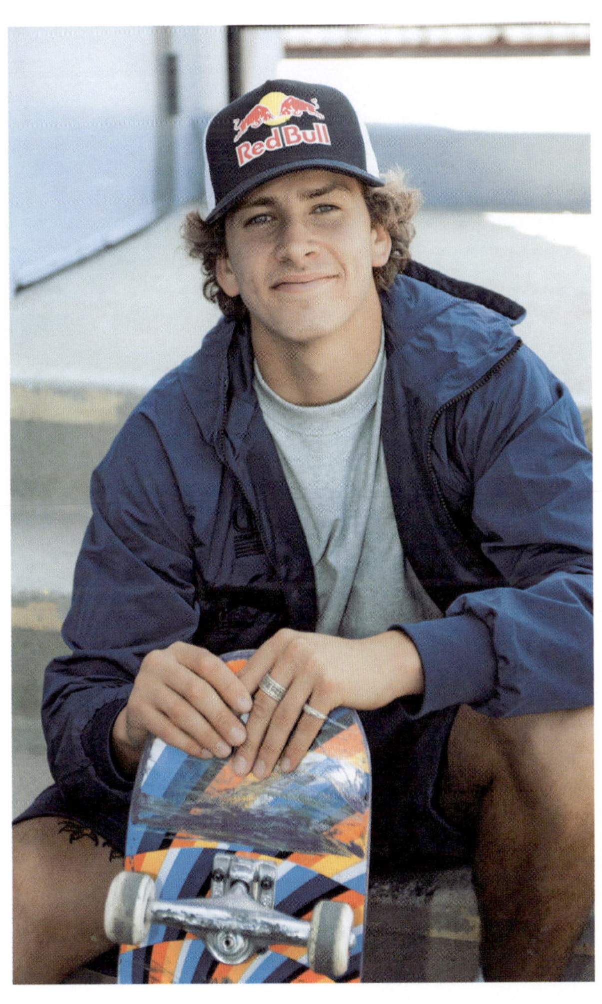

What makes Jagger Eaton, Olympic bronze medalist in street skateboarding, tick? Putting a whupping on the competition. That right there—that's a different kind of skateboarder. Jagger does not shy away from doing it all for the love, but he also relishes being in competition and seeing how an event stacked with talent can push an athlete to rise to the top. Disciplines? Park or street? Nah, Jagger is a skater who envisions himself ending up on the podium no matter what course he faces. Why so serious? Simple. Jagger wants to be the first Olympic skater to win gold medals in park *and* street. The ultimate NBD (never-been-done). Now, let's acknowledge that in the '70s, most skaters competed in everything— slalom, freestyle, pool, limbo, ballet, underwater basket weaving. However, the caveat is that back then modern skateboarding was still being invented. Of course you skated everything! Who knew if that ish would even be there tomorrow? Who wouldn't try to get a win?

The skills and styles required to be the best in park and the best in street are usually distinct. Street requires command and technique; park requires power and finesse. There are a few skaters who rip in both fields, but what sets Jagger apart is that he wants to win *gold* in both. He pulled off this first-of-its-kind win at the World Skateboarding championships in the UAE. When it came time for the big stage in Tokyo, he brought home the bronze medal for the U.S. And he experienced a new degree of fame, appearing on *The Tonight Show*, *Jimmy Kimmel Live!*, and morning shows; in features in *Forbes* and other media outlets; and even on the catwalk at the Tom Ford show in 2021. Fire.

What it takes to win in both disciplines is unfathomable. Sure, you can be an amazing street skater and win street contests like Paul "P-Rod" Rodriguez (see page 36) and Nyjah Huston (see page 32) do. They brought their street skating technique to the X Games and Dew Tour street contests and showed that they could perform in any context. However, that is not the same as performing across contexts and disciplines. Imagine you love basketball and baseball. They both use a ball and require hand-eye coordination, but they require different skills and different strategies. Street skating is basketball—you're coming up with multiple ways to make points manifest. Skating the park is baseball—it's you against the pitcher, trying to understand what the designer laid out, then translating in your language what can be accomplished within said space.

In 2023, Jagger won street and park at the World Skateboarding competition in the UAE, a startling feat. As impressive as his young career has been, it hasn't been without controversy. The haters run a little wild with Jagger. At age 11, he was one of the youngest competitors in X Games history. Adding to his mystique, in 2014 he won the Tampa Am at age 12. In 2018, he entered the Tampa Pro as an amateur to see where he might place in such a heavy competition. As the contest whittled down from quarters to semis, it became apparent that Jagger was a contender. He signed a sponsorship deal with Plan B Skateboards between heats. The newly contracted Jagger not only officially turned pro at the Tampa contest, he won it. Champion Sound.

Jagger comes from a pedigree of athletes. His parents are Olympic gymnasts, and his grandfather trained Olympic gymnasts. His father also operated an exclusive facility in Arizona known as Kids That Rip. At four years old, Jagger began putting the world on notice. Skating big air early on with a docuseries, *Jagger Eaton's Mega Life* (2016) on Nickelodeon, he set the stage for a type of skateboarding different from that of other skaters, who often found the sport in their teens. Jagger makes it all look easy.

One of his signature tricks is the backside 180 kickflip to fakie nosegrind. Even with all the stress of the Olympics, he still managed to put it down on the square rail at the Tokyo games. That trick requires two key steps. First, lock in a backside 180 kickflip, then land in a backside nosegrind and stand up tall in your grind while coming out backward or "fakie." Hella hazardous. You might over-rotate the flip and end up sliding on the rail upside down and sacking yourself on the rail or spinning your body wildly out of control. Not a good look. Jagger also did the whole thing "gapping out"—meaning he had to ollie away from the stairs to a half-rail midway down the set of stairs. Precarious. Yet there he went, making it look like he was born for this.

As for business and brand: as part of Heart Supply, Jagger's board is available at Target stores, making him one of the most accessible Olympic winners of all time. Imagine picking up his full Olympic pro model kit for under $100 at the same place your parents pick up soap and mouthwash.

Winning an Olympic medal is the crowning achievement in every sport and Jagger Eaton had that under his belt at age 21. Now that he's beginning to win across disciplines, who knows what we'll see from him in the years to come. It's a question that is probably making other skaters lose sleep—Jagger wouldn't want it any other way.

> **JAGGER IS A SKATER WHO ENVISIONS HIMSELF ENDING UP ON THE PODIUM NO MATTER WHAT COURSE HE FACES.**

YUTO HORIGOME

The king of the NBDs (never-been-dones)

Won Olympic Gold in his Tokyo hometown and in Paris

First at X Games in 20-plus years to win both street *and* street best trick

Helping to destigmatize skateboarding in Japan

Yuto Horigome's place is solidified in the history books of skateboarding. Never before has a skater embodied such a flawless combination of power, grace, and fundamental inventiveness. I was lucky enough to get my first glimpse of this phenomenon early, while checking in with Blind team manager Bill Weiss and skate videographer extraordinaire Socrates Leal (see page 167). What I witnessed had my jaw on the floor. His video part wasn't a collection of tricks done *on* and *down* ledges and rails. It was something more. He rolled *through* the obstacles as if they weren't actually there. He danced through tricks weightlessly, mystically shadowboxing above, into, and beyond obstacles that couldn't stop him from performing any trick he wanted. Falling seemed like it was actually beneath him. That footage shook me to my core. I knew I was witnessing an unstoppable force. When I told Weiss I thought he had found Blind's secret weapon, he responded, "Yep, I've never seen anything like it." Neither had I.

Most skaters battle tricks on obstacles, looking to power or thrash their way into and out of moves. But Yuto, he skates like he's embracing each object as an old friend. He uses the marble benches' weight and density against them, defying gravity by flipping into and out of tricks using only the slightest touch and most minimal effort. Not only is he an amazing street skater but he also skates vert with a style usually reserved for veterans—blasting head-high airs out of the ramps in Tokyo. Who was this kid and what did he have to do to make the skate gods bless him with such skills? Whatever it was, please sign me up. Yes, I know you might think that great skateboarding is great skateboarding, but

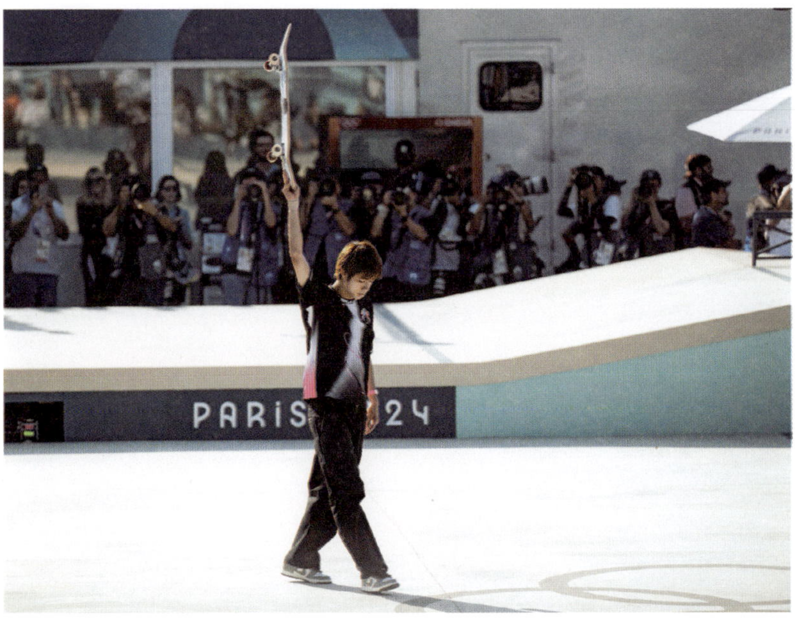

allow me to introduce you to Yuto, who is truly otherworldly.

Yuto has what I define as the "the spins," and it is pushing his game to another level. That's what makes his skateboarding operate on a higher plane: he is spinning on an imaginary axis that very few skaters can access. It's not that other skaters can't turn out of a trick with a 180. It's something we work on. It's that it is painfully obvious that Yuto can spin in and out and in any direction—ollie 180–360, nollie 180–nollie 360, switch 180–switch 360; he can pivot into whatever the hell he might want to—and invent tricks in front of our eyes because this MF's not fazed. Want an example? He nollie 180 to fakie 5-0'd down the ledge in a contest as easily as if he were rolling.

In layperson's terms: Yuto spins into things he can't even see, and has made it his signature. I'm sorry, folks, but you simply cannot imitate that. You also can't take him out in a contest with tricks that people have done before because . . . well, they have been done before. Even if they are difficult to do, you know they can be done. There is a precedent. Yuto—all NBDs (never-been-dones). All the time. Hard to match. Nearly impossible to beat.

We saw it at the 2023 X Games, where he became the first competitor in more than 20 years to win both street and street best trick. We saw it at the 2020 Tokyo Olympics, where he won street gold—in his hometown. We all lost our minds when we saw it happen again at Paris 2024 when he launched into a backside nollie 270 bluntside down the 10-stair contest handrail. I was seated with legendary pro skater Kareem Campbell (see page 46) when we witnessed history in the making. Yuto simply invented that trick during the contest—and failed to land it twice. Yet during his last attempt, under the eyes of the world and the pressure of his previous gold medal win in Japan, Yuto delivered.

Yuto is simply working to outdo himself every time. The rest of us? Well . . . you do you.

For anyone who has been watching, Yuto represents a new standard of excellence that has emerged out of Japan. It's called *mastery* and they are handing out doses like it's extra helpings at Grandma's. Yuto and the Japan's women's team are a movement that is proving skateboarding doesn't belong to the U.S., taking names in a way that makes it look like they invented the sport. In case you're wondering, I'm here for it.

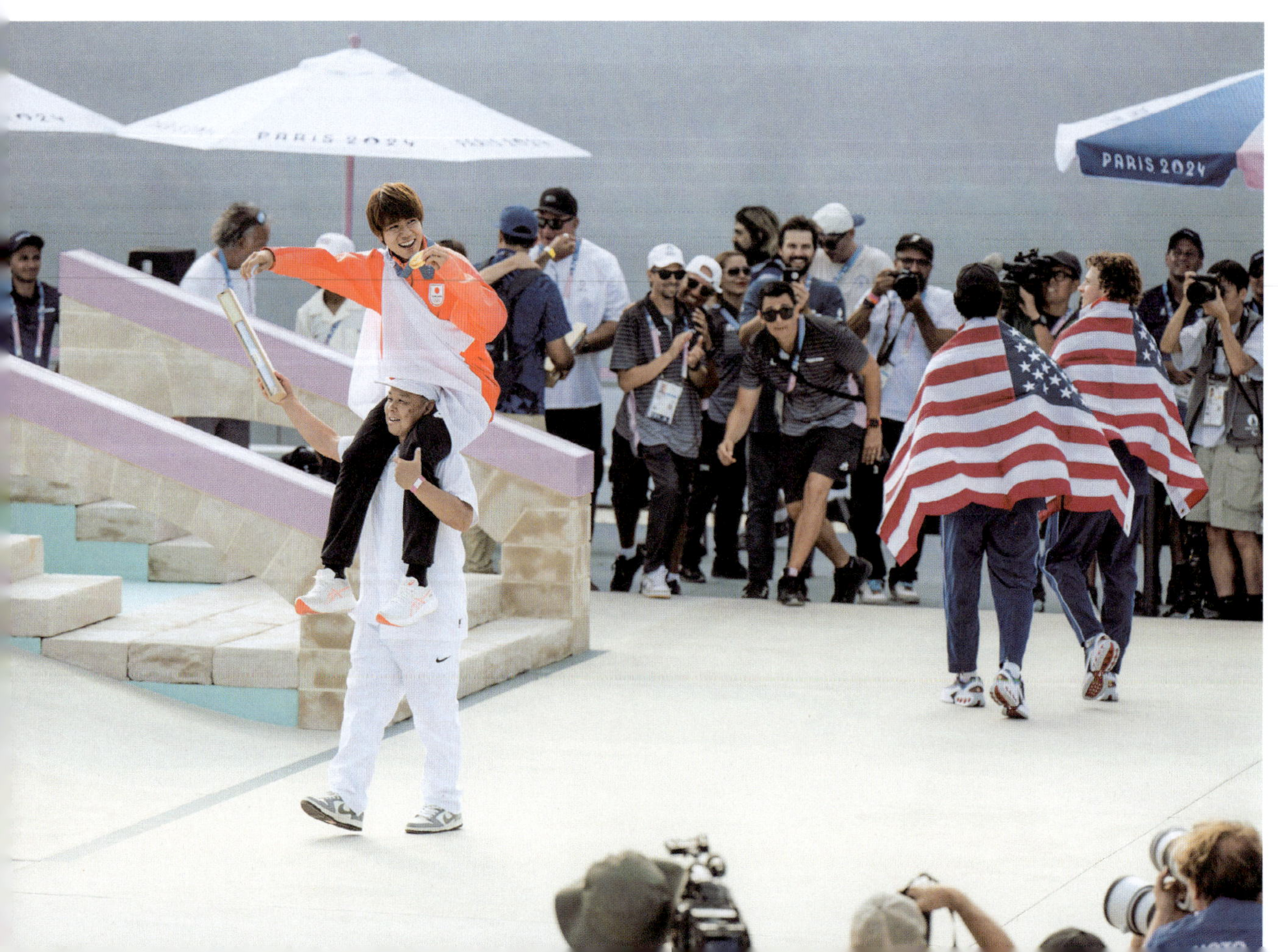

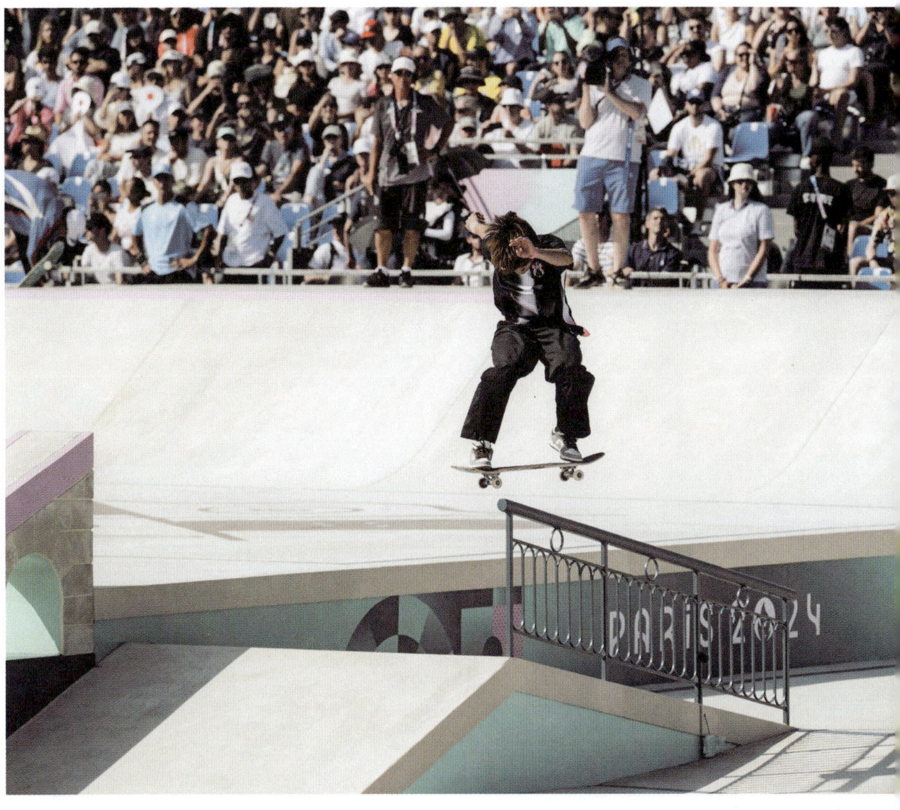

Opposite: Yuto Horigome atop his father's shoulders after his gold medal win in men's street at the 2024 Paris Olympics.

Right: Yuto Horigome, nollie 270–flipside

Yuto started skating when he was six years old, as a second-generation skater. His father felt all of the pain of being a skater in Japan, where it was frowned upon—and still is, even with Yuto's Olympic win. But success has at least created an opening. Sometimes skateboarding has to speak to the powers that be in the language they understand. For Japan, that is winning, and the cultural aspects are secondary and hard-fought. Skateboarding is still an outlaw activity there, so Yuto not only has the world on his back by showcasing skateboarding in the Olympics, but he took on the stigma and showed that Japan was just as capable of delivering world-class skateboarding as the U.S.

Yuto changed the way people see skaters, with his signature *no smile, here's the best skateboarding, but I was actually on my way to a movie so no stress, can I go now?* steeze. Gary Rogers from the hottest spot on the interwebs, *Skateline*, said it best when we talked at the X Games: "What did we do to Yuto that he has to just show up and whup everybody's ass in skateboarding so bad? Did someone tease him, did they bully him? Whatever it was, man, watch out."

That, my friend, is a Culturalist and an Olympist. If all continues in the same direction, Yuto will be an Uberist, having wrestled skateboarding to the ground and showed it who's boss without ever looking like he lifted a finger. Winning competitions nonstop. Being a favorite of big-time, non-skate, brands. That's Yuto. That's skateboarding. That's the changing of the guard.

Lest anyone think that his mastery reflects a lack of connection to skate culture, let's set the record all the way straight. Yuto's coup de grâce is something immensely personal that speaks to the culture of skateboarding always being at the forefront of his art.

First, Yuto filmed an entire video part in Tokyo, something that most skaters believed couldn't be done. There were too many factors at play. It is a security-heavy city. Skateboarding was too new and too stigmatized and difficult to make fly in such a populous locale. Better to film it somewhere else. But Yuto's access to the arcane knows no bounds. He shot footage at 2 a.m., when there were moments of quiet. He danced with the dawn at 5 a.m., or just bogarted spots during rush hour—whatever he could to make his video come to light. He is the son of his city and he put it down in his city, in his hometown, among his people.

Second, he put us all on notice that we were gonna respect him and where he comes from in his signature shoe for Nike, a literal cultural artifact of his identity. The colorway comes from the park he grew up skating—Ōjima Komatsugawa Park in Tokyo—and the subdued tones of the paths that bring you to the gate of the park: gray for the marble and a hint of pink for the cherry blossoms.

Finally, he made you put some respect on his name by placing the two feathers of his family crest, designed by Japanese artist Verdy, on and inside the shoe. All of that and the sterling video part sings loud as *Dreamgirls'* "You're gonna love me." You right, Yuto, we do. All hail the new normal. Yuto putting in the work to place skateboarding on the map, and making all of our heads . . . spin.

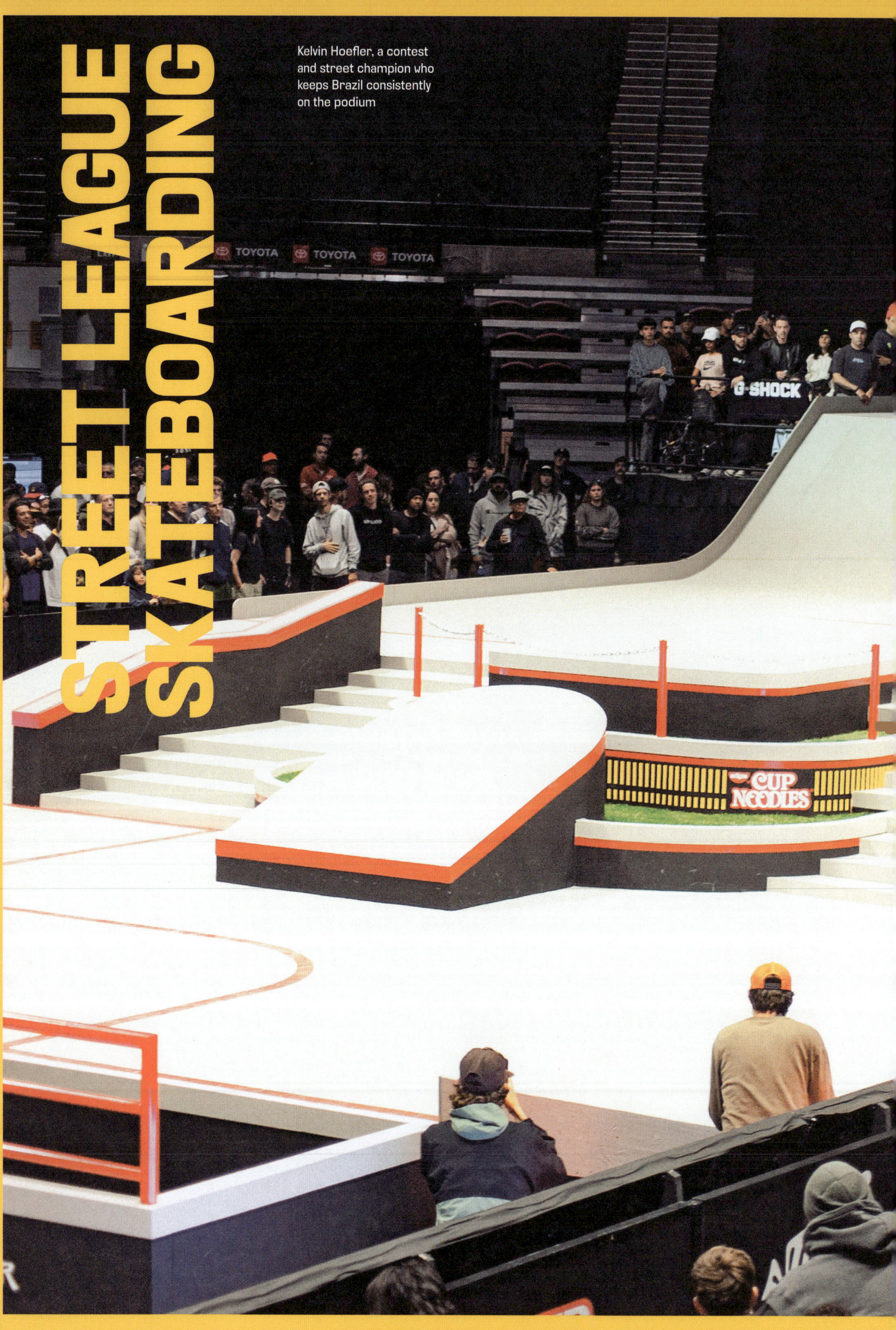

STREET LEAGUE SKATEBOARDING

Kelvin Hoefler, a contest and street champion who keeps Brazil consistently on the podium

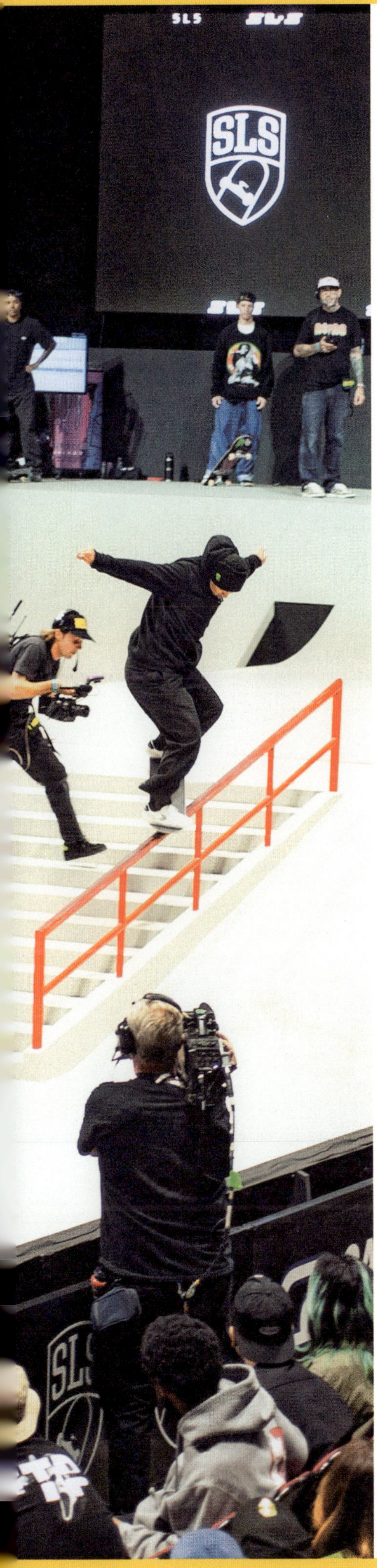

The Street League Skateboarding contest series was pro skater, entrepreneur, and MTV host Rob Dyrdek's first outing after leaving the Maloof Money Cup contest, which he co-created with the Maloof family. Launched in 2010 and offering a new format, Street League Skateboarding (SLS) was different in a number of ways. First, it focused on a limited amount of invite-only skaters, offering them maximum exposure over a yearlong nationwide tour. Historically, skate contests were constructed in an open format, which allowed anyone to compete. The philosophical change meant money could be spent promoting those willing to dedicate the year to the contest rather than dipping in and out to attend other contests or endeavors. This allowed SLS to offer consistency in branding and the ability to depend on skaters, and to market them to potential sponsors with accuracy.

For skaters, this also generated a reliable income and a guarantee they would receive a certain amount of coverage as contestants in this exclusive space. While this approach was unique, it also had its detractors, who felt that the contests' exclusivity and marriage between the skater and the contest locked skaters out of other potential opportunities. SLS responded over time with changes that expanded to a more open call for participants, and larger invites and wild cards, which allowed for more flexibility and permitted a greater range of skaters to participate.

As part of the SLS vision to broaden the traditional sports feel of the tours, the contests boasted an arena format that allowed a larger number of attendees and placed skateboarding in a more professional, crowd-controlled environment. This could also support the fan experience and deliver a spectacle. Some of the sold-out arenas SLS has played throughout the years include the 10,000-seat Galen Center at USC in Los Angeles, the Adidas Arena in Porte de la Chapelle, just north of Paris, and Arena Carioca 1 in Rio de Janeiro, Brazil.

SLS also focused on offering near-instantaneous judging. For years, scores didn't show up until the end of a contest. Now, numbers posted after each run for all the skaters and the audience to see. This adds to the hype of each trick, and allows for strategy, letting skaters know what to do to win. SLS also brought instant replays to the big screens and jumbotrons at venues, offering a fantastic fan service that helps make the contest feel similar to a traditional sporting event experience.

In the fervor surrounding the scoring and instant replays, SLS inadvertently created the space for a new phrase in the skate vernacular: "joining the Nine Club." The phrase meant scoring a 9 out of 10 in the SLS scoring system, which required completing a trick or run with a high degree of difficulty. It became a badge of honor on the SLS circuit and something skaters and fans celebrate.

Admirably, at each stop of the contest, SLS tries to incorporate local skate landmarks within the course. In San Diego, at SDSU's Viejas Arena, organizers fabricated the city's famous Rincon "gap to rail" and the "chain fence to bank" that was dominated (and largely shut down) by a mellow afternoon session with British pro skater Tom Penny. Also

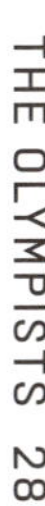

at the San Diego stop, African American pro skater Brandon Turner proceeded to bless the replica with an impromptu switch hardflip over the rail—while wearing a backpack—like it wasn't going to be the best trick we saw on the obstacle! He wasn't even in the contest or on the tour. The audacity.

That's the beauty of skateboarding. Even with rules in place, skateboarding remains a family, and there is respect for the OGs. SLS opened the door to the S.D. legends who helped build skateboarding and came out to watch the event and the practice sessions, like Brandon.

While Street League has now greatly opened their qualifying event, SLS also hosts private events, called "resurrections." These events are sponsored by SLS and its partners such as Monster Energy, Nissin Foods' Cup Noodles, Nikon, and GoPro. One paid homage to a famous ledge dubbed the "Hubba Hideout" in San Francisco, built entirely to spec of the legendary spot by California Skateparks. While some skaters bemoan the copies as not truly authentic, they do offer a chance for skaters of a new generation to experience the kinds of spots that are unskateable now due to policing, skate stoppers (tiny strips bisecting outdoor rails or benches in order to discourage skaters from attempting tricks), and changes in the path toward the obstacles. For fans of the contest and the original spots, Street League adds an element of the unknown, and allows one to imagine what could have happened if skaters were left unfettered.

Rob Dyrdek sold his majority stake in SLS to action sports group Nitro Circus at the tail end of 2019, and since then SLS has expanded again, creating a more open format and new opportunities for new skaters to join the tour and in their locations. Contests in Brazil, the Netherlands, France, and other countries have allowed whole new sets of fans to follow the tour with a sense of hometown pride.

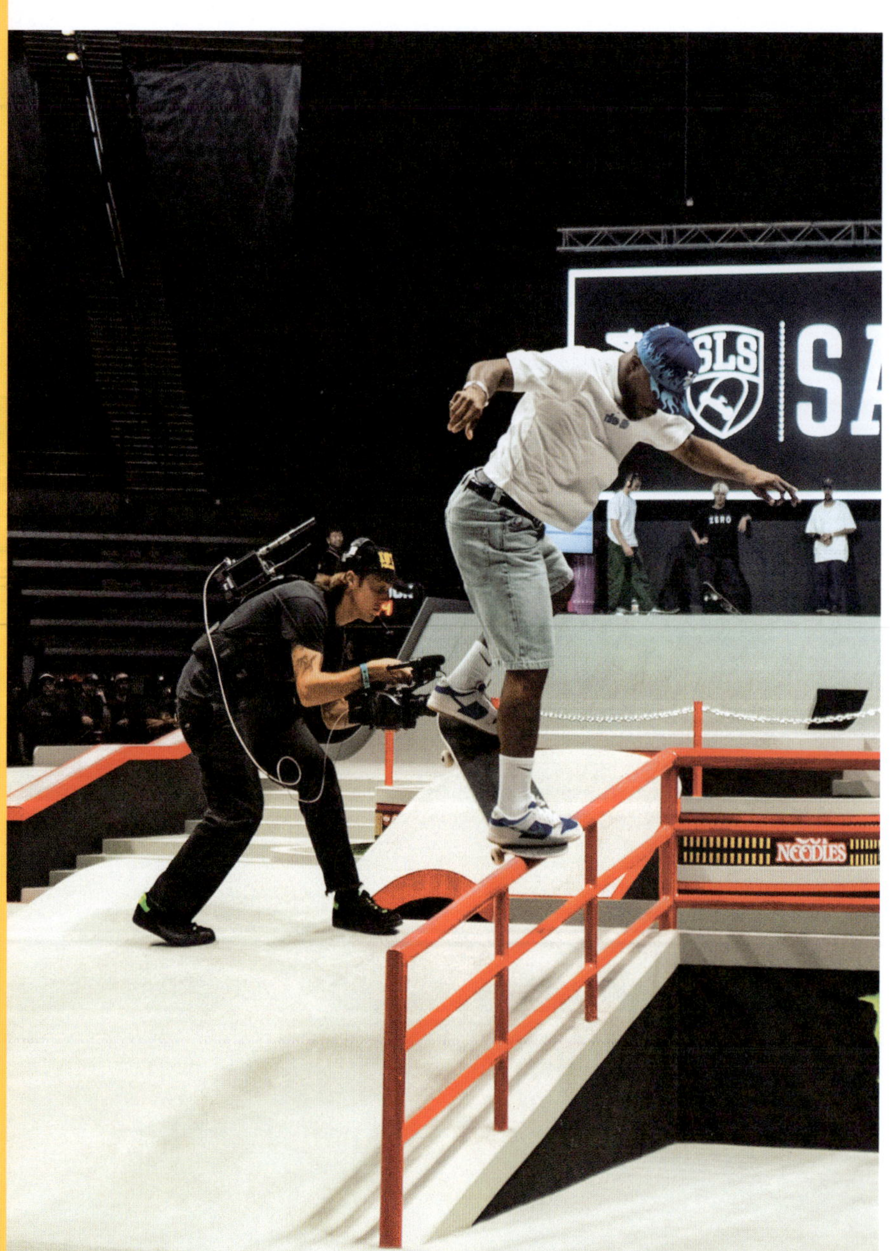

Dashawn Jordan, gap-out to frontside crooked grind for the cameras and the fans

Right: Chloe "The Flow" Covell, kickflip over the chain gap

Bottom: Nyjah Huston, backside noseblunt slide for a capacity crowd at USC's Galen Center

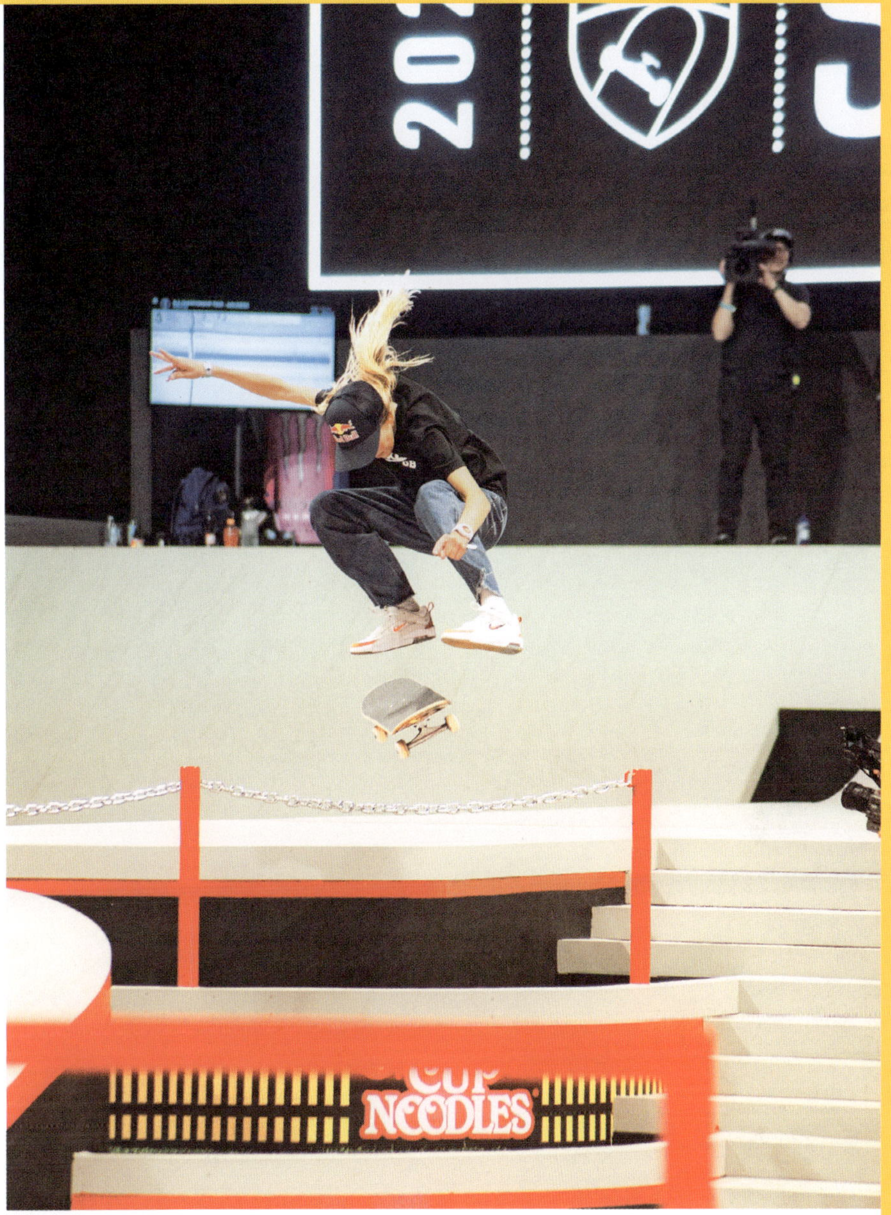

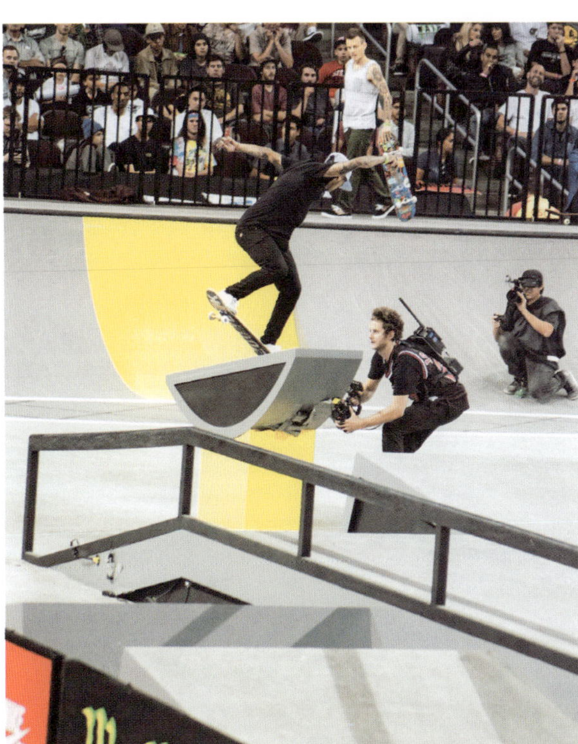

Attending SLS as a professor with my students, I found the energy immeasurable. My classes have seen private warm-ups and have met pros such as Rayssa Leal, Yuto Horigome, and Manny Santiago. Alongside the athletes, they've connected with architects of modern skateboarding from Paul "The Professor" Schmitt to Steve James from Tech Deck, and met hosts of the illustrious skateboarding podcast *The Nine Club*. Bearing witness to those kinds of victories and excellent skateboarding up close is the gift of Street League Skateboarding, which offers some of the best and most exciting skateboarding on the planet. No cap.

ACKNOWLEDGMENTS

First, I thank my wonderful supportive wife, Rachele Williams, and my newborn baby, Wren Williams, for the sacrifices they both endured to get this book done. Thank you for your love and patience and guidance. Rachele, thank you for the long days and nights you have given me to work and working with me and loving me despite the weight of this publication. Thanks to you for supporting me in all my efforts during moments that could be spent relaxing but more often than not are spent planning the next project. You are the most incredible partner, and I am blessed and honored to stand by your side. Wren, being your father is the greatest joy, and Mommy and Daddy love you more than you can know.

Thank you to our wonderful families, the Williams family, the Honchariks, and the LaCocos, for enduring the process when we are on the road working during weddings, vacations, parties, and general family-relaxing festivities.

Thanks to our AWE family for always supporting me since before we knew we would be doing any work—Reed, Mike, Ryan, and Will. Thank you to the two people who are not here to see this come to fruition, my uncle Luke Williams and Anthony Labasco, both of whom were with me during skateboarding's inception in my life. We will continue to move forward, never forgetting any of the lessons you provided.

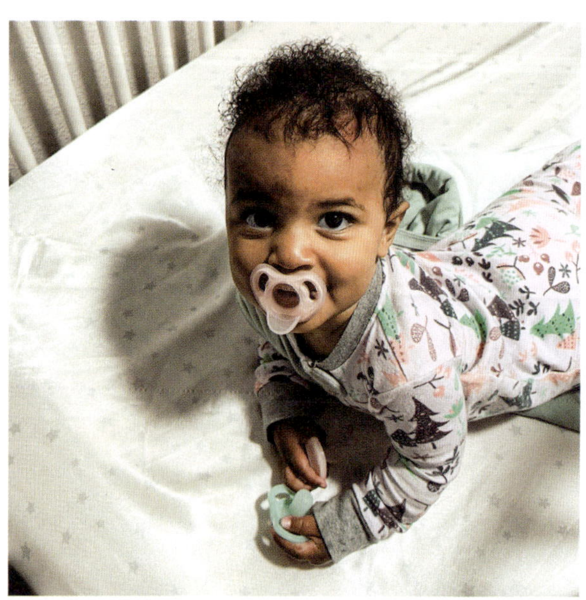

Thanks to Eryn Kalavsky and the Salky team for believing that I could tell the story of our community. Thanks to Shoshana Gutmajer and Abby Knudsen and the entire Artisan team, especially Nina Simoneaux and Donna Brown, and the Workman and Hachette literary families for their tireless efforts to help me bring this book to you. Jeremy Rosenberg, thank you for being the soundboard, glue, and distiller of every aspect of this book. It would not have come together without you fighting for my vision of the text even when my wellspring of ideas went dry. You would give me a good chat and remind me that I could not only do this but needed to always do it to the best of my ability. Thanks for having my back. Also gratitude to Garth Ross and James at the SkateFolk crew in D.C. for all their support.

Thanks to my students and the SDSU College of Arts and Letters and our sociology department for being the home of our Center for Skateboarding, Action Sports, and Social Change. Thanks to Paige Dawson and David Kamper for being the foundation of our team. Thanks to Tony Hawk and The Skatepark Project for their unwavering support of all of my work in skateboarding and actions sports and for creating the conditions for skateboarding to reach so many hearts. Thanks to all my USC skate scholar family, especially Zoe Corwin, Stefani Relles and Gordon Stables, Alan Green, Rafael C. Angulo, Robert Scheer, and Diana O'Leary.

Thanks to the U.S. Department of State for providing me the opportunities to design and implement strategies for skate diplomacy. Lastly, thanks to Joe Maloof, Burton and the Carpenter family, Selema Masekela, Nyla Hassel, Zeb Powell, and all my skate, surf, and snow families for helping me stay on board at all times.

This book would need to be triple the size to come close to including everyone—but then, well, it would be too heavy for you to skate to class with, or read on the plane, or hold when you're reading these stories to your children.

While all of the family is not showcased within the confines of these pages, they are within the pages in spirit. Some of that family appears as classic photos reprinted here, and others are the connective tissue between the people on these